Black Sea

THRACE
• Abdera

ASIA

MINOR

an Sea

• Pergamum

• Clazomenae

Rhamnus    • Colophon    • Hieropolis

SAMOS    • Ephesus

• Miletus

36

CRETE

CYPRUS    • Citium

Sea

Jerusalem •

4

3 2

Alexandria •

28

I C A    EGYPT

*second edition*

# PHILOSOPHIC CLASSICS

## Volume I: Thales to Ockham

*basic texts selected and edited with prefaces by*

WALTER KAUFMANN

Prentice-Hall, Inc., *Englewood Cliffs, New Jersey*

Acknowledgment is gratefully made to the following: **Cambridge University Press,** for selections from *The Pre-Socratic Philosophers: A Critical History with a Selection of Texts* by G. S. Kirk and J. E. Raven, 1957. For selections from *Plato's Phaedo,* trans. with Introduction and Commentary by R. Hackforth, 1955. For complete text of the dialogue in *Plato's Phaedrus,* trans. with Introduction and Commentary by R. Hackforth, 1952. For "The Hymn of Cleanthes" from *The Vitality of Platonism* by James Adam, 1911. **The Clarendon Press,** for selections from *The Oxford Translation of Aristotle,* Vol. VIII, trans. and ed. W. D. Ross, 1908. For selections from *Aristotle's Categories and De Interpretatione,* trans. J. L. Ackrill, 1963. **Harvard University Press,** for selections from *Ancilla to the Pre-Socratic Philosophers* by Kathleen Freeman, 1947. **The Loeb Classical Library,** for selections from *Sextus Empiricus: Outlines of Pyrrhonism,* Vol. I, trans. The Rev. R. G. Bury, 1933, rev. 1939. For selections from *Plato's Seventh Letter,* Vol. VII, trans. The Rev. R. G. Bury, 1929, rev. 1942. For selections from Aristotle's *The Nicomachean Ethics,* trans. H. Rackham, 1926, rev. 1934. For selections from Aristotle's *On the Heavens,* trans. W. K. C. Guthrie, 1939. For selections from Aristotle's *On the Soul,* trans. W. S. Hett, 1936, rev. 1957. For selections from both volumes of Aristotle's *Physics,* trans. Philip H. Wicksteed and Francis M. Cornford, 1929, 1934, rev. 1935, 1957. For selections from *Diogenes Laertius,* Vol. II, trans. R. D. Hicks, 1925. For selections from *Epictetus,* Vol. II, trans. W. A. Oldfather, 1928. **Oxford University Press, Inc.,** for selections from Aristotle's *Analytica Posteriora,* trans. G. R. G. Mure in *The Works of Aristotle Translated into English,* ed. W. D. Ross. **Penguin Books, Ltd.,** for selections from *Protagoras and Meno,* trans. W. K. C. Guthrie, 1956. **Random House, Inc.,** for selections from *Basic Writings of Saint Thomas Aquinas,* Vols. I and II, ed. Anton C. Pegis, 1945. **Routledge & Kegan Paul, Ltd.,** for selections from *Plato's Theory of Knowledge,* 1935, *Plato's Cosmology,* 1937, and *Plato and Parmenides,* 1939, trans. F. M. Cornford. **Thomas Nelson & Sons, Ltd.,** for selections from *Ockham: Philosophical Writings,* trans. and ed. Philotheus Boehner, O.P.M., 1957. **Washington Square Press, Inc.,** for selections from the book *The Pocket Aquinas* by Vernon J. Bourke. Copyright, ©, 1960 by Washington Square Press, Inc. Reprinted by permission of the publisher.

PRENTICE-HALL INTERNATIONAL, INC., *London*
PRENTICE-HALL OF AUSTRALIA, PTY. LTD., *Sydney*
PRENTICE-HALL OF CANADA, LTD., *Toronto*
PRENTICE-HALL OF INDIA PRIVATE LTD., *New Delhi*
PRENTICE-HALL OF JAPAN, INC., *Tokyo*

Library of Congress Catalog Card Number: 68-15350

Printed in the United States of America

Current printing (last number):

10  9  8  7  6  5  4  3  2  1

*This volume is dedicated to*

**JOHN WILLIAM MILLER**

*Mark Hopkins Professor Emeritus of Intellectual and Moral Philosophy
Williams College*

# BOOKS BY WALTER KAUFMANN

*Nietzsche: Philosopher, Psychologist, Antichrist*
*Critique of Religion and Philosophy*
*From Shakespeare to Existentialism*
*The Faith of a Heretic*
*Cain and Other Poems*
*Hegel: A Reinterpretation*

## Nietzsche Translations

*The Portable Nietzsche*
*Thus Spoke Zarathustra*
*Beyond Good and Evil*
*The Birth of Tragedy & The Case of Wagner*
*The Will to Power*
*On the Genealogy of Morals & Ecce Homo*

## Other Translations

*Judaism and Christianity: Essays by Leo Baeck*
*Goethe's Faust*
*Twenty German Poets*
*Hegel: Texts and Commentary*

## Edited by

*Existentialism from Dostoevsky to Sartre*
*Philosophic Classics: 2 volumes*
*Religion from Tolstoy to Camus*

# PREFACE

I

There is no better introduction to philosophy, whether you read for yourself or take a course, than to read some of the great philosophers. But few books are more difficult than Aristotle's *Metaphysics* or Spinoza's *Ethics* or Kant's *Critique of Pure Reason*. And even works that are less puzzling are sometimes like snippets of a conversation that you overhear on entering a room: what is said is clear, only you can't be sure you have got the point because you do not know just what has gone before. A slight point may be crucial to refute some earlier suggestion, and a seemingly pointless remark may contain a barbed allusion. Too often nonphilosophers despair: It does not occur to them that whenever they choose to begin, they can still get in at the start of the conversation. They need only begin with Thales and the other pre-Socratics. Nobody should fear that going back so far will expose him to a tedious excursion. On the contrary, in quick succession you encounter some of the most fascinating thinkers of all time and find yourself regretting that so little of their writings has survived.

Soon you come to Socrates and Plato and become involved in philosophical discussions that continue to this day. In the early dialogues of Plato, the most brilliant literary power is employed to introduce you to philosophy; but you gain ever so much more from your reading if you know the pre-Socratics.

The later dialogues are much more difficult, and so is much of Aristotle, but no serious student will be satisfied to remain completely innocent of all these classics, and most teachers will want to read at least some of this material with their students.

Altogether, it is not the point of either this book or its companion volume to avoid all difficulties. On the contrary, philosophy begins in perplexity, as both Plato and Aristotle noted; and those who spurn perplexity and want unquestioned answers have not begun to understand philosophy. One of the first things you discover in the study of philosophy is that intelligent and even brilliant men are frequently in disagreement, and that some of the most interesting problems seem to have no ready-made solutions. It might be argued that anyone who has not found this out still needs an education.

It is an uncomfortable discovery, however, and many people try to dodge it. Instead of being challenged by one great philosopher after another to reconsider preconceived opinions and to become more careful, thoughtful, and conscientious, many a student would like to learn, once and for all, the "central doctrines" of the great philosophers: that way he has something definite that he can memorize, and he does not have to think, himself.

Alas, the "central doctrines" of a great philosopher often turn out to be very problematic in the context of the whole work in which they are said to be presented; and matters become yet less reassuring as we compare the first edition of some classics with the second, or one book with another by the same philosopher. Often, there are passages in which the "central doctrine" seems to be presented; but the philosopher did not always oblige us by ceasing to think after formulating his position in this manner: typically, he continued to reflect on the same topic and on other problems that have some relation to it; and in the end his position turns out to be hotly disputed by scholars. The greatest Plato scholars still argue not only about Plato's meaning in specific sentences but also about "central doctrines"; and the situation is no better in the case of Aristotle. No one who loves philosophy is seriously dismayed by that: what Plato and Aristotle teach us is not a body of assured results but rather a way of thinking—the delights of thinking.

The most damning comment on a course I ever heard came from a student who, after a semester's freshman course which he had taken with one of my colleagues, said that now he knew all about modern philosophy —adding only, as he noted my surprise, "at least since Descartes."

Carving up great books to excerpt "essential doctrines" is one of the sins against the spirit of philosophy. If the reading of a whole Platonic dialogue leaves a man more doubtful and less sure of himself than the perusal of a brief epitome, that is all to the good, as Plato himself noted many times, for example, at the end of the *Theaetetus*. It is part of the point of philosophy to make men a little less sure about things. And Socrates, who converted Plato to philosophy, insisted that what distinguished him from other men was not that he knew all, or even most, answers but rather that he realized his ignorance.

Nobody can be introduced to philosophy without being exposed to wonder and perplexity, without being made aware of his ignorance, and without discovering that the great philosophers, far from settling all our doubts, present us with a host of puzzles. Not the least of these is often what precisely the philosopher's position was. Those who have never read a complete book by a philosopher are very often sure about his doctrines, whereas those who have studied the man thoroughly are usually much less sure—and those who do feel sure often disagree with each other.

No reader of this book or its companion volume should feel that he now knows all about Plato or Kant, Aristotle or Spinoza. He will find many complete and unabridged works, supplemented with selections; but these, far from being tailored to some one interpretation of the man, should give some impression of the range of his thought and of the problems that confront interpreters. The reader should not emerge with a spurious sense that he knows what in fact he does not know; rather he should come, if possible, to love philosophy. The *Apology* may communicate the philosophic spirit, and the *Symposium* and the *Phaedrus,* also uncut, might convince the reader that here are works of great beauty which may well require many a delightful reading before they yield up even most of their treasures. It is thus that one is won for philosophy.

II

There is much continuity in these selections: those from the pre-Socratics are relevant for an understanding of Plato, Aristotle, Epicurus, and many later writers, and the previously suggested metaphor of the conversation should be taken seriously. Hobbes' objections to Descartes have been included with Descartes' replies before Thomas Hobbes is introduced in his own right; but even where the dialogue is not quite so explicit it is well to ask oneself to what ideas of his predecessors a philosopher is probably responding.

Where translations had to be used, versions in the public domain that could be reprinted without permissions and fees were usually available, but a great deal of effort was devoted to obtain some of the fine translations done in recent years by the best scholars. Professionals will appreciate instantly what it means (to give but a very few examples) that Kirk and Raven's work on *The Presocratic Philosophers* (1957) could be used along with Cornford's and Hackforth's excellent translations of some of Plato's more difficult dialogues; that Aquinas is offered in the translation edited by Pegis; and that Philip Wiener's revised versions of his fine Leibniz translations are presented.

A single case may be discussed in just a little more detail. Old translations, in the public domain but not respected by the scholars in the field, of much material by and about the pre-Socratics are available. The versions reprinted in two of the most popular texts come from Arthur Fairbanks' *The First Philosophers of Greece* (1898), of which R. D. Hicks showed in *The Classical Review* (1899, pp. 450 ff.) that "a pupil who followed the translation . . . would be liable to serious misconceptions at almost every step"—a verdict seconded by Gregory Vlastos in *The Philo-*

*sophical Review* (October 1959). The student who wants versions based on the latest scholarship can turn to Kathleen Freeman's *Ancilla to the Pre-Socratic Philosophers* (1947) and find their fragments but none of the often equally important paraphrases or reports about their doctrines —though much of their thought is known to us only indirectly in this manner. For additional material he can consult Freeman's *The Pre-Socratic Philosophers: A Companion to Diels, Fragmente der Vorsokratiker* (1946). Or he can turn to Kirk and Raven and find many of the testimonies and those fragments—often all too few—that the authors cite in the course of their scholarly discussions. But to give only two examples, those who consult Kirk and Raven will miss out on many of Heraclitus' most striking sayings and on almost all the abundant sayings of Democritus on ethics. In Freeman's *Ancilla,* on the other hand, they will miss the atomistic world view of Democritus, which is known almost exclusively from testimonies. What is offered in the following pages, then, is—quite apart from some emendations of the translations presented—no mere reprint but, at least in places, material never previously presented in anything like the present form.

Zeno represents an especially dramatic case. Few, if any, pre-Socratic fragments have elicited as much interest and discussion as his famous paradoxes; but in recent years some of the foremost scholars have repudiated earlier translations of this material and proposed new readings. No English version hitherto in print is really up to date. The section on Zeno, therefore, was contributed by Gregory Vlastos and constitutes an important contribution to pre-Socratic scholarship.

III

Nothing has been offered of Chinese and Indian philosophy. The little that might have been put into these two volumes could not have done justice to India or China and would only have taken away valuable space from Western thinkers. To do justice to Oriental thought, another volume as large as one of the present volumes would be necessary. The same reasoning applies to Western philosophy since Kant. Not enough could have been included along with the men from Bacon to Kant to be satisfactory for students of nineteenth- or twentieth-century philosophy. It therefore seemed best to devote as much space as possible to philosophers of the seventeenth and eighteenth centuries.

The treatment of medieval thought also requires comment. In line with the points just made, it could be argued that the Middle Ages should have been left out entirely; but for two reasons a few samples of medieval philosophy have been presented. Unlike Oriental philosophy— which stands entirely apart from the development recorded in these volumes—and unlike philosophy since Kant, which comes afterwards as the sequel, medieval philosophy must be conceded to have been either a link or an interruption, and probably both, in the story that is here presented. Our understanding of Bacon, Descartes, and Spinoza is enhanced by even a slight knowledge of Augustine, Anselm, Aquinas, and Ockham. Moreover, interest in St. Thomas Aquinas is widespread, and his thought is as much discussed in the twentieth century as ever before. It is therefore customary in many colleges to bring in just a little of medieval philosophy at the end of a course on Greek philosophy, and this makes good sense. But any great expansion of this section, either by offering more of the writings of the four men represented here or by introducing others, such as Erigena, Scotus, and Eckhart, was not feasible for the same reasons that led to the exclusion of Oriental and recent philosophy: not enough could have been offered for the serious student or for a semester's course, and the value of the remaining part of the volume would have been impaired too seriously by the required cuts. Everything considered, it seemed best to concentrate chiefly on one medieval philosopher—and to select St. Thomas Aquinas for this purpose.

Those who use one of these volumes as the basis of a one-term course need hardly be told that there is more material here than can easily fit into one semester. But the editor does not apologize for offering some choice or for giving teachers who offer the same course year after year an easy opportunity for varying their fare.

IV

In this second edition I have made many small revisions as well as the following *major* changes:

Plato's *Meno* is now offered in W. K. C. Guthrie's translation, which takes its place alongside Cornford's and Hackforth's versions as the best we have.

The selections from Aristotle's *Categories* are now offered in John Ackrill's superior translation, which had not yet appeared when the first edition of *Philosophic Classics* was published.

The very substantial selections from Aristotle's *Metaphysics* have been strengthened in two ways: they are now presented in W. D. Ross's superb translation, and Book VII has also been included.

In the chapter on Hellenistic Philosophy I have added a good deal of material about early Greek Stoicism, including part of the account Diogenes Laertius gives of Stoic ethics and all of his report of Stoic "physics."

Finally, Volume I has been extended beyond Thomas Aquinas to Ockham; a complete essay by Aquinas has been added; and Part V has been given a new title: "Medieval Philosophy."

In Volume II I have added selections from Descartes' correspondence with Princess Elizabeth; further selections from Spinoza's *Ethics*, Locke's *Essay*, and Berkeley's *Principles*; and a short essay by Leibniz translated especially for this volume by Professor Montgomery Furth.

The last quotation from Xenophanes may serve as a motto for both volumes: "Not from the beginning have the gods revealed all things to mortals, but by long seeking, men find what is better."

NOTE: In many instances, the page numbers of a standard edition have been retained—in the running heads at the top of the page in the selections from Aristotle; in brackets at the end of the line in the selections from Plato and (in the second volume) from Hobbes and Kant. This should facilitate the checking of scholarly citations as well as comparison with the original or with other editions. Moreover, where omissions are indicated, this device shows at a glance approximately how much has been omitted.

In making my selections for these two volumes, I have had the invaluable advantage of discussions with and advice from many colleagues: Richard Cartwright, Irving Copi, Willis Doney, Dennis O'Brien, George Pitcher, and Gregory Vlastos. Having taught a variety of courses in the history of philosophy, they gave me the benefit of their considerable experience, and I am glad to have this opportunity to express my gratitude.

In preparing the second edition, I have again profited from the advice of many colleagues, but I am most profoundly indebted to Professor Montgomery Furth, whose detailed and expert comments were exceedingly helpful. Besides suggesting many of the changes enumerated above, he also made a new translation of an essay by Leibniz especially for Volume II.

Professor Vlastos has also contributed the section on Zeno—both the translations and the editorial matter. For this, too, I am deeply indebted to him.

Everybody with whom I have dealt at Prentice-Hall has been most cooperative and helpful.

W. K.

# CONTENTS

### part one

# BEFORE SOCRATES

I

Almost all histories of philosophy and all philosophers agree that the so-called pre-Socratics were the first philosophers, at least in the Western world. Unlike most of the early thinkers of India and China, the pre-Socratics did not think exegetically: they did not read their ideas into, or out of, ancient scriptures or poems. On the contrary, they spoke as disrespectfully of the greatest poets as they did of each other. They made bold to speak out on their own behalf, each for himself, claiming neither the authority of divine inspiration nor the sanction of tradition. They come before us as thinking men who challenge us to think for ourselves as they did.

There are excellent reasons for beginning a study of philosophy with these men and then proceeding to Socrates and Plato. This, after all, is how Western philosophy did begin, and we can still recapture the movement from the bald statements of Thales to the all-embracing questioning of Socrates, and hence to Plato's efforts to fuse criticism with construction.

If a deep dissatisfaction with all facile answers is the starting point of philosophic thought, the fragments of the pre-Socratics are doubly appropriate for a beginning. Not one of their works has survived complete: all we have are quotations and reports in later writers. As a result, pre-Socratic thought has a mysterious quality that makes flat statements highly questionable. Cryptic passages and forceful aphorisms whose original context is lost give us food for thought and stimulate our imagination. Instead of looking for "the" answer, one is fascinated by reflecting on a wealth of possibilities. And in the effort to show why some suggested interpretations are untenable, one can also develop one's critical faculties.

Some of these fragments may remind the reader of archaic statues, heads with broken noses, torsos without heads or arms—pieces so perfect in the form in which they have survived that one has no regrets and even feels that the freshly completed work could not have been so fascinating.

For all that, most interest in the pre-Socratics is motivated by the fact that they furnish the backdrop for the thought of Socrates, Plato, and Aristotle: that is why one lumps them together as "the pre-Socratics." But the magnificent succession of thinker upon thinker was anything but luck. The Chinese *Tao-Teh-Ching* is also wonderful and enigmatic, but one understands why the book was never followed by a philosophic crescendo. Though they are often enigmatic and at times somewhat oracular, the pre-Socratics are distinguished by their appeal to reason. In this way each one makes it possible for his successors to subject his thought to criticisms, to amend it, to develop an alternative, to go beyond it.

In the pre-Socratics, wisdom ceases to soliloquize and becomes dialogue. Sage speaks to sage, often acidly, but not with the finality of monologue or revelation. In the Upanishads of ancient India we are invited to ponder infinite wisdom that claims to be derived from still more ancient poems, and any failure to assent is charged to lack of understanding. There is no room for argument and disagreement. The pre-Socratics confront us with constant disagreement. They are not mystagogues but heretics.

To picture them either as positivistic scientists, as John Burnet came close to doing in his *Early Greek Philosophy*, or as theologians, as Werner Jaeger did in *The Theology of the Early Greek Philosophers*, is to miss something of their very essence. Theology suggests the exegetic mode of thought, a loyalty to a traditional religion, and an effort to provide a systematic statement of, and rational foundation for, traditional beliefs and rites. In all three respects, the pre-Socratics stand opposed to all theology. None of them condoned traditional religion or any popular beliefs or cults. Some were scientists, but their world was not devoid of mystery—on the contrary. They neither denied mystery nor did they try to expound it to the point where it might cease to be mysterious. They were exuberant in their reliance on reason, and they wrote poetry about it, or superbly fashioned aphorisms. They delighted in the light of sane thought but always retained a profound sense of the outer darkness, the unexpected, and the uncanny.

II

Their influence on Plato was so great that a study of their thought is essential to an understanding of many passages in his dialogues, of his intentions—many problems were suggested to him by Heraclitus, the Eleatics, and the Pythagoreans—and, of course, his originality. Aristotle studied the pre-Socratics closely and discussed them at length in the first book of his *Metaphysics*, which is reprinted in its entirety below, under Aristotle. Of the later Greek philosophers it has often been remarked that the Stoics were particularly influenced by Heraclitus, the Epicureans by Democritus. Elements of Orphism, an early Greek religious movement, also found their way into the pre-Socratics—most obviously, but by no means only, into Pythagoreanism—and hence into Plato and, later, into Christianity. In fact, a few of the fragments survived as quotations in the works of early Christian writers.

Most scholars would probably agree that the most important work on the pre-Socratics has been done by an international cast of philologists. Even so, there is still a great deal of discussion about the meaning of many fragments and the views of some of these early philosophers; and not only classical philologists have taken an interest in this literature.

Among modern philosophers, Hegel was the first to deal with pre-Socratic thought at loving length, in his posthumously published lectures on the history of philosophy. As a professor of classical philology at the University of Basel, Switzerland, Friedrich Nietzsche dealt in great detail with "The Pre-Platonic Philosophers" or, as he put it in the title of another posthumously published manuscript, with "Philosophy in the Tragic Era of the Greeks." In the books he himself published, too, there are occasional suggestions that in some respects these early thinkers may have been superior to their successors and that in some ways Plato may represent a decline, with his bifurcation of the world and of man and with his pre-Christian depreciation of *this* world and the senses.

In his first philosophic book, "The Psychology of World Views" (1919), Karl Jaspers based his discussion of "Types of Philosophic Thinking" on "the pre-Socratics, on account of their relative simplicity, on account of their greatness, and above all on account of Nietzsche's example" (p. 204). Jaspers' comments were admittedly based mainly on Nietzsche's essay on "Philosophy in the Tragic Era of the Greeks." The other great protagonist of German existentialism, Martin Heidegger—actually, both Jaspers and Heidegger repudiate the label of existentialism—has published a large body of interpretations of pre-Socratic fragments and has suggested again and again that the whole of Western philosophy from Plato to Nietzsche represents a tragic fall from the sensibility, the world feeling, the insights of the pre-Socratics to which our generation must somehow recover an approach. Philologists do not take Heidegger's laborious exegeses seriously, and it is worth pointing out that he quite misses their most distinctive break with the past: their refusal to think exegetically. Even so, it is interesting that the so-called existentialists, at least in Germany, have done their utmost to redirect attention to the pre-Socratics. Some feeling for at least a few of these early thinkers might be expected among a generation that has rediscovered archaic Greek art and has come to prefer the best of it to the (until recently) more celebrated classical and postclassical works.

III

The surviving quotations from the works of the pre-Socratics were collected by a nineteenth-century German scholar, Hermann Diels, in *Die Fragmente der Vorsokratiker*. Diels assembled the original Greek texts and furnished German translations of all the fragments. He also collected and printed, but did not translate, reports of ancient authors about the lives, works, and ideas of the pre-Socratics. His work went through several editions and has been periodically revised and kept up to date since his death. No other work has ever replaced the latest edition of Diels.

In English there are primarily, though certainly not only, three works that offer pre-Socratic fragments in English. First, John Burnet translated and discussed many of the fragments in his *Early Greek Philosophy* (1st ed., 1892; 4th ed., 1930, reprinted as a paperback by Meridian Books; for some brief comments on his work, see section I, preceding). Then Kathleen Freeman published *An Ancilla to The Pre-Socratic Philosophers: A complete translation of the Fragments in Diels, Fragmente der Vorsokratiker* (Harvard University Press, 1947). Like Diels, she translated only the fragments, not the ancient paraphrases and reports about the philosophers' lives and works. Finally, there is *The Presocratic Philosophers: A Critical History with a Selection of Texts* by G. S. Kirk and J. E. Raven (Cambridge University Press, 1957). Here the emphasis falls on a careful, critical discussion of some of the texts against the background of recent scholarly books and articles; and in the course of the discussion many, but not most, of the fragments, paraphrases, and reports are both cited in Greek and, at the bottom of the page on which the original is cited, rendered into English. For the serious students of the pre-Socratics, the book is a delight and a constant help; for the less serious reader, and especially for those with no knowledge of Greek, Freeman's book is likely to be more satisfactory, if only because it offers all the fragments.

Almost all the translations that follow are either those of Kirk or Raven (marked accordingly with a *K* or *R*, followed by the number that the passage bears in their book) or those of Freeman (marked with an *F*). An asterisk (*) indicates that the translation has been revised slightly—often, but not always, very slightly indeed, for purely stylistic reasons. In a very few cases the translation is my own and marked *WK*. After direct quotations, these symbols (*K*, *R*, *F*, and *WK*) are preceded by the number that the fragment bears in the fifth edition of Diels's standard work. Freeman's numbering is the same as Diels's. After paraphrases, the ancient works in which they occur are cited briefly, using the standard abbreviations. Those interested in an evaluation of these paraphrases, which are by no means always completely reliable, will find illuminating, if occasionally controversial, discussions in Kirk and Raven.

The reason for often using Kirk's and Raven's versions is that they embody the latest scholarship; the reason for not relying solely on them is that there is so much material that they have not translated. Moreover, their wording— and Miss Freeman's, too—is now and then excessively academic. Miss Freeman also uses capital letters very profusely—to the point of distraction—and I have departed from this practice.

The reader should not forget that some of the pre-Socratics were very great writers, but that both here and throughout these readings every effort has been made to take into account the work of the best scholars in the field. Nowhere has accuracy been knowingly sacrificed to beauty; but one need not give the impression, in the name of accuracy, that the pre-Socratics wrote like classical philologists.

What follows is a selection. There is no such thing as a complete roster of the pre-Socratics. The so-called Sophists were Socrates' contemporaries, but Protagoras and Gorgias were older than he and acquired great reputations before he came along and challenged them; and they are included here. After all, it was partly in response to their teaching that his thought was developed. Among the older writers, it is arguable who was, and who was not, a philosopher. Various poets, for example, are occasionally included among the pre-Socratics. Not counting the Sophists, the present selection concentrates on the twelve major figures. They might conveniently be arranged in four groups of three: the Milesians (Thales, Anaximander, and Anaximenes); then three men who came from different places and stood each by himself (Pythagoras, Xenophanes, and Heraclitus); then the so-called Eleatics (Parmenides, Zeno, and Melissus); and finally the pluralists (Empedocles, Anaxagoras, and Democritus). The only major name that is missing in this list is that of Leucippus, the founder of the atomistic philosophy, who is presented together with his great follower, Democritus.

Offering all the fragments of the twelve main figures, one would have to include such items as the following, each of which I now proceed to cite in its entirety: "The joint connects two things"; "as when fig juice binds white milk"; and "having kneaded together barley-meal with water" (Empedocles, fragments 32, 33, 34).

The selections that follow are generally very inclusive. They are meant to give an idea not only of each man's major teachings, as far as possible in his own words, but also of his way of thinking and feeling, his style—in short, of the man who still confronts the student across roughly 2,500 years. Where a striking sentence has given rise to widely different translations, this is noted.

# THE MILESIANS

## THALES

Thales is generally considered the first Western philosopher—not so much by virtue of some one thing he said as because an unbroken line leads from him to Socrates, Plato, and Aristotle. He lived in Miletus in Asia Minor and is said to have predicted an eclipse of the sun that occurred in 585 B.C. He was thus a contemporary of the Hebrew prophet, Jeremiah, who predicted the fall of Jerusalem, which, to his regret, he lived to see in 586 B.C.

According to both Herodotus, the great fifth-century historian who has been called "the father of history," and Diogenes Laertius, who, in the third century A.D., composed the fascinating, anecdotal, but by no means always reliable *Lives of Famous Philosophers*, Thales was of Phoenician descent. But not all scholars are convinced that he was a pure Semite. In any case, the Greek-speaking population of Miletus was racially very mixed, and Greek philosophy originated in a melting pot of many cultures. The ancients were agreed that Thales had learned a great deal from the Egyptians, Babylonians, and Phoenicians.

Like many other pre-Socratics, Thales was by no means a philosopher only. Among other things, he was also a statesman, an astronomer, a geometer, and a renowned sage. He probably did not write any book, but ancient literature contains many statements about him, a few of which follow.

• • •

A witty and attractive Thracian serv-
ant-girl is said to have mocked Thales
for falling into a well while he was observing the stars and gazing upwards;

6

declaring that he was eager to know the things in the sky, but that what was behind him and just by his feet escaped his notice. [Plato, *Theaetetus* 174A; K 74.]

When they reproached him because of his poverty, as though philosophy were no use, it is said that, having observed through his study of the heavenly bodies that there would be a large olive-crop, he raised a little capital while it was still winter, and paid deposits on all the olive presses in Miletus and Chios, hiring them cheaply because no one bid against him. When the appropriate time came there was a sudden rush of requests for the presses; he then hired them out on his own terms and so made a large profit, thus demonstrating that it is easy for philosophers to be rich, if they wish, but that it is not in this that they are interested. [Aristotle, *Politics* A11, 1259a; K 75.]

When he came to the Halys river, Croesus then, as I say, put his army across by the existing bridges; but, according to the common account of the Greeks, Thales the Milesian transferred the army for him. For it is said that Croesus was at a loss how his army should cross the river, since these bridges did not yet exist at this period; and that Thales, who was present in the army, made the river, which flowed on the left hand of the army, flow on the right hand also. He did so in this way; beginning upstream of the army he dug a deep channel, giving it a crescent shape, so that it should flow round the back of

where the army was encamped, being diverted in this way from its old course by the channel, and passing the camp should flow into its old course once more. The result was that as soon as the river was divided it became fordable in both of its parts. [Herodotus I, 75; K 67.]

· · ·

Moist natural substance, since it is easily formed into each different thing, is accustomed to undergo very various changes: that part of it which is exhaled is made into air, and the finest part is kindled from air into aether, while when water is compacted and changes into slime it becomes earth. Therefore Thales declared that water, of the four elements, was the most active, as it were, as cause. [Heraclitus Homericus, *Quaest. Hom.* 22; K 89. These may not really have been Thales' reasons.]

He [Thales] said that the world is held up by water and rides like a ship, and when it is said to "quake" it is actually rocking because of the water's movement. [Seneca, *Qu. Nat.* III, 14; K 90.]

Thales, too, seems, from what they relate, to have supposed that the soul was something kinetic, if he said that the [Magnesian] stone possesses soul because it moves iron. [Aristotle, *De Anima* A2, 405a; K 91.]

Some say that it [soul] is intermingled in the universe, for which reason, perhaps, Thales also thought that all things are full of gods. [Aristotle, *De Anima* A5, 411a; K 93.]

# ANAXIMANDER

The second Milesian philosopher hazarded a number of interesting guesses about nature. He may also have been the first among the Greeks to compose a book of prose. But what has fascinated his successors, down to the present, far more than anything else about him is the one sentence, or half-sentence, from that book, which has survived because Simplicius quoted it. In these few words one may detect an echo of ancient Orphic notions of original sin, although this interpretation is by no means certain. It was Anaximander at any rate who introduced the notion of the *apeiron*, the unlimited, boundless, infinite, or indefinite, which he considered the fundamental principle of the world, thus replacing Thales' conception of water.

. . .

Anaximander son of Praxiades, of Miletus, philosopher, was a kinsman, pupil and successor of Thales. He first discovered the equinox and solstices and hour-indicators, and that the earth lies in the center. He introduced the gnomon [a vertical rod whose shadow indicates the sun's direction and height] and in general made known an outline of geometry. He wrote *On Nature, Circuit of the Earth, and On the Fixed Stars,* and *Celestial Globe,* and some other works. [Suda s.v.; K 97. Some of this has been disputed.]

[Anaximander] was the first of the Greeks whom we know who ventured to produce a written account on nature. [Themistius *Or.* 26; K 98.]

. . .

Of those who say that it is one, moving, and infinite, Anaximander son of Praxiades, a Milesian, the successor and pupil of Thales, said that the principle and element of existing things was the *apeiron* [indefinite, *or* infinite], being the first to introduce this name of the material principle. He says that it is neither water nor any other of the so-called elements, but some other *apeiron* nature, from which come into being all the heavens and the worlds in them. And the source of coming-to-be for existing things is that into which destruction, too, happens "according to necessity; for they pay penalty and retribution to each other for their injustice according to the assessment of time," as he describes it in these rather poetical terms. It is clear

that he, seeing the changing of the four elements into each other, thought it right to make none of these the substratum, but something else besides these; and he produces coming-to-be not through the alteration of the element, but by the separation off of the opposites through the eternal motion. [Simplicius, *Phys.* 24; K 103A and 121. The phrase quoted from Anaximander's work has elicited a large literature, including a 48-page essay by Martin Heideggger. Some scholars believe that the quotation begins earlier and comprises the whole sentence.]

He says that that which is productive from the eternal of hot and cold was separated off at the coming-to-be of this world, and that a kind of sphere of flame from this was formed round the air surrounding the earth, like bark around a tree. When this was broken off and shut off in certain circles, the sun and moon and stars were formed. [Ps.-Plutarch, *Strom.* 2; K 123.]

He says that the earth is cylindrical in shape, and that its depth is a third of its width. [*Ibid.*; K 124A.]

Its shape is curved, round, similar to the drum of a column; of its flat surfaces we walk on one, and the other is on the opposite side. [Hippolytus, *Ref.* I, 6, 3; K 124B.]

Anaximander says the sun is a circle 28 times the size of the earth, like a chariot wheel, with its rim hollow and full of fire, and showing the fire at a certain point through an aperture as though through the nozzle of a bellows. [Aetius II, 20; K 128*.]

Anaximander said that the first living creatures were born in moisture, enclosed in thorny barks; and that as their age increased they came forth on to the drier part and, when the bark had broken off, they lived a different kind of life for a short time. [Aetius V, 19; K 136.]

Further he says that in the beginning man was born from creatures of a different kind; because other creatures are soon self-supporting, but man alone needs prolonged nursing. For this reason he would not have survived if this had been his original form. [Ps.-Plutarch, *Strom.* 2; K 137.]

Therefore they [the Syrians] actually revere the fish as being of similar race and nurturing. In this they philosophize more suitably than Anaximander; for he declares, not that fishes and men came into being in the same parents, but that originally men came into being inside fishes, and that, having been nurtured there—like sharks—and having become adequate to look after themselves, they then came forth and took to the land. [Plutarch, *Symp.* VIII, 730E; K 140.]

# ANAXIMENES

The third and last of the Milesian philosophers proposed air as the basic principle of the world. Perhaps this suggestion can be understood as an attempted synthesis of the ideas of his predecessors: air, more than water, seems to partake of the nature of the boundless, the unlimited, the infinite, the indefinite—the *apeiron* of Anaximander.

. . .

Anaximenes son of Eurystratus, of Miletus, was a pupil of Anaximander ... He said that the material principle was air and the infinite; and that the stars move, not under the earth, but round it. He used simple and unsuperfluous Ionic speech. He was active, according to what Apollodorus says, around the time of the capture of Sardis [by Cyrus in 546/5 B.C.?], and died in the 63rd Olympiad. [Diogenes Laertius II, 3; K 141.]

He [Anaximander] left Anaximenes as his disciple and successor, who attributed all the causes of things to infinite air, and did not deny that there were gods, or pass them over in silence; yet he believed not the air was made by them, but that they arose from air. [Augustine, *City of God*, VIII, 2; K 149.]

And all things are produced by a kind of condensation, and again rarefaction, of this [air]. Motion, indeed, exists from everlasting; he says that when the air felts, there first of all comes into being the earth, quite flat—therefore it accordingly rides on the air; and sun and moon and the remaining heavenly bodies have their source of generation from earth. At least, he declares the sun to be earth, but that through the rapid motion it obtains heat in great sufficiency. [Ps.-Plutarch, *Strom.* 3; K 151.]

# THREE SOLITARY FIGURES

## PYTHAGORAS

Born on the island of Samos, just off the coast of Asia Minor and very close to Miletus, Pythagoras moved to southern Italy, where the Greeks had colonies, and settled at Croton, on the bay of Tarentum. He founded a quasi-religious sect that still existed in Plato's time, 150 years later. It exerted a decisive influence on Plato's thought, second only to the impact of his revered teacher, Socrates.

Pythagoras was soon associated with so many legends that few scholars would dare to say much about his life and personality, or even about his teachings, without adding that we cannot really be sure whether our information is accurate. That there really was a man named Pythagoras who founded the sect, we need not doubt: among the witnesses to that was his younger contemporary, Heraclitus, who thought ill of him (see below under Heraclitus, section D). The big question is this: what did Pythagoras himself do and say, and what did others later ascribe to him?

Today he is best known for the so-called Pythagorean theorem in geometry (cited below). His interest in mathematics is as well attested to as his concern with religion and philosophy, and we may safely surmise that, like Plato after him, he considered the study of mathematics essential for the conversion of the soul from the world of the senses to the contemplation of the eternal.

The following ideas evidently influenced Plato especially: the dualistic juxtaposition of body and soul and the conception of the body (*soma* in Greek) as the tomb (*sema* in Greek) of the soul; the belief in the immortality of the soul; the doctrine of the transmigration of souls; the idea that knowledge and a philosophic life are required for the salvation of the soul; the notion that one might design a society that would be an instrument of salvation for its members; the admission of women to this society; the suggestion that all members should hold their property in common; and, finally, the division of mankind into three basic types—tradesmen being the lowest class; those in whom the competitive spirit and ambition are highly developed, a little higher; and those who prefer contemplation, the most excellent.

The whole development of Plato's thought from his early works to his last ones may be understood as a gradual departure from the heritage of Socrates and a sustained effort to absorb Pythagoreanism. And it was the Pythagorean Plato rather than the Socratic one who decisively influenced the subsequent development of Christian thought.

· · ·

According to my information from the Greeks who live beside the Hellespont and Pontus, this Salmoxis, a real man, was a slave in Samos to Pythagoras son of Mnesarchus ... but I believe that this Salmoxis lived many years before Pythagoras. [Herodotus IV, 95; R 255.]

Aristoxenus says that at the age of forty, seeing that the tyranny of Polycrates had grown more intense, ... he eventually migrated to Italy. [Porphyry V.P. 9; R 256.]

He emigrated to Croton in Italy and there, by legislating for the Italians, won renown together with his pupils. They numbered nearly 300, and they administered the affairs of state so well that the constitution was virtually an aristocracy. [Diogenes Laertius VIII, 3; R 257.]

Pythagoras wrote nothing, nor did Socrates. ... [Plutarch, *Alex. fort.* 1, 4, 328; R 267.]

· · ·

Ten is the very nature of number. All Greeks and all barbarians alike count up to ten, and having reached ten revert again to the unit. And again, Pythagoras maintains, the power of the number ten lies in the number four, the tetrad. This is the reason: if one starts at the unit and adds the successive numbers up to four, one will make up the number ten; and if one exceeds the tetrad, one will exceed ten, too. If, that is, one takes the unit, adds two, then three, and then four, one will make up the number ten. ... So the Pythagoreans used to invoke the tetrad as their most binding oath: "Nay, by him that gave to our generation the tetractys, which contains the fount and root of eternal nature." [Aetius I, 3, 8; R 280.]

The square of the hypotenuse of a right-angled triangle is equal to the sum of the squares on the sides enclosing the right angle. [The text of the next sentence is corrupt, but the sense is:] If we pay any attention to those who like to recount ancient history, we may find some of them referring this theorem to Pythagoras, and saying that he sacrificed an ox in honor of his discovery. [Proclus, *In Eucl.*, p. 426 Friedl.; R 281.]

· · ·

On the subject of reincarnation, Xenophanes bears witness in an elegy which begins: "Now I will turn to another tale and show the way." What he says about Pythagoras runs thus: "Once they say that he was passing by when a puppy was being whipped, and he took pity and said: Stop, do not beat it; for it is the soul of a friend that I recognized when I heard it giving tongue." [Diogenes Laertius VIII, 36; Xenophanes, fragment 7; R 268.]

Moreover, the Egyptians are the first to have maintained the doctrine that the soul of man is immortal and that, when the body perishes, it enters into another animal that is being born at the time, and when it has been the complete round of the creatures of the dry land and of the sea and of the air it enters again into the body of a man at birth; and its cycle is completed in 3000 years. There are some Greeks who have adopted this doctrine, some in former times and some in later, as if it were their own invention; their names I know but refrain from writing down. [Herodotus II, 123; R 270.]

None the less the following became universally known: first that he maintains that the soul is immortal; next, that it changes into other kinds of living things; also that events recur in certain cycles, and that nothing is ever absolutely new; and finally, that all living things should be regarded as akin. Pythagoras seems to have been the first to bring these beliefs into Greece. [Porphyry, *Vita Pythagorae* 19; R 271.]

If one were to believe the Pythagoreans that events recur in an arithmetical cycle, and that I shall be talking to you again sitting as you are now, with this pointer in my hand, and that everything else will be just as it is now, then it is plausible to suppose that the time, too, will be the same as now. [Eudemus *ap.* Simplic. *Phys.*, 732, 30; R 272. The doctrine of the eternal recurrence of the same events at gigantic intervals was revived in modern times by Friedrich Nietzsche; cf. Walter Kaufmann's *Nietzsche*, Princeton 1950, Meridian Books 1956, Chapter 11, "Overman and Eternal Recurrence."]

•   •   •

Let the rules to be pondered be these:

1. When you are going out to a temple, worship first, and on your way neither say nor do anything else connected with your daily life.

2. On a journey neither enter a temple nor worship at all, not even if you are passing the very doors.

3. Sacrifice and worship without shoes on.

4. Turn aside from highways and walk by footpaths. . . .

6. Follow the gods and restrain your tongue above all else. . . .

8. Stir not the fire with iron. . . .

10. Help a man who is loading freight, but not one who is unloading.

11. Putting on your shoes, start with the right foot; washing your feet, with the left.

12 Speak not of Pythagorean matters without light.

13. Never step over a cross-bar.

14. When you are out from home, look not back, for the furies come after you. . . .

22. Do not wear a ring. . . .

23. Do not look in a mirror beside a lamp. . . .

30. Eat not the heart. . . .

32. Spit upon the trimmings of your hair and finger-nails. . . .

37. Abstain from beans. . . .

39. Abstain from living things. [Iamblichus, *Protr.* 21; R 275. These were some of the rules of the sect founded by Pythagoras.]

Phythagoras turned geometrical philosophy into a form of liberal education by seeking its first principles in a higher realm of reality. [Procl., *In Eucl.*, p. 65 Friedl.; R 277.]

Life, he said, is like a festival; just as some come to the festival to compete, some to ply their trade, but the best people come as spectators, so in life the slavish men go hunting for fame or gain, the philosophers for the truth. [Diogenes Laertius VIII, 8; R 278.]

# XENOPHANES

A contemporary of Pythagoras, Xenophanes came from Colophon on the mainland of Asia Minor, a few miles inland and approximately fifty miles north of Miletus and less than fifteen miles north of Ephesus. He traveled a great deal and recited his poetry of which only a few fragments survive. At one time he was supposed to have been Parmenides' teacher and the founder of the Eleatic school, no doubt on account of his conception of one sole, unmoving god—a notion readily associated with Parmenides' idea of being. But this supposition is now generally rejected, and Xenophanes is seen as an essentially solitary figure. Little of his work has come down to us, but what little there is is unforgettable.

.   .   .

Xenophanes son of Dexios or, according to Apollodorus, of Orthomenes, of Colophon . . . being expelled from his native land, passed his time in Zancle in Sicily and in Catana. . . . He wrote in epic metre, also elegiacs and iambics, against Hesiod and Homer, reproving them for what they said about the gods. But he himself also recited his own original poems. He is said to have held contrary opinions to Thales and Pythagoras, and to have rebuked Epimenides, too. He had an extremely long life, as he himself somewhere says: "Already there are seven and sixty years tossing my thought up and down the land of Greece; and from my birth there were another twenty-five to add to these, if I know how to speak truly about these things." [Diogenes Laertius IX, 18; K 164.]

Homer and Hesiod ascribed to the gods whatever is infamy and reproach among men: theft and adultery and deceiving each other. [II; WK.]

Mortals suppose that the gods are born and have clothes and voices and shapes like their own [14; WK.]

But if oxen, horses, and lions had hands or could paint with their hands and fashion works as men do, horses would paint horselike images of gods and oxen oxlike ones, and each would fashion bodies like their own. [15; WK.]

The Ethiopians consider the gods flat-nosed and black; the Thracians blue-eyed and red-haired. [16; WK.]

There is one god, among gods and men the greatest, not at all like mortals in body or mind. [23; F*.]

He sees as a whole, thinks as a whole, and hears as a whole. [24; F.]

But without toil he moves everything by the thought of his mind. [25; F*.]

He always remains in the same place, not moving at all, nor is it fitting for him to change his position at different times. [26; F.]

Everything comes from earth and returns to earth in the end. [27; F*.]

No man knows or ever will know the truth about the gods and about everything I speak of: for even if one chanced to say the complete truth, yet oneself knows it not; but seeming is wrought over all things. [34; K 189.]

Not from the beginning have the gods revealed all things to mortals, but by long seeking men find what is better. [18; WK.]

## HERACLITUS

Heraclitus of Ephesus flourished around 500 B.C. The ancients already called him "the dark philosopher," but there is nothing obscure about his cutting strictures of Xenophanes and Pythagoras, Homer and Hesiod, or about his contempt for common sense and common men. He was clearly a man of very great literary genius, and his epigrams, though often paradoxical and elusive, are immensely suggestive, invite frequent rereading, and haunt the mind. In his sayings, as in those of no previous philosopher, one feels that one encounters the personality of the thinker. After almost twenty-five centuries, he still evokes instant antipathy in some readers and the highest admiration in others. Among those who have paid lavish tribute to him are Hegel and Nietzsche.

Because so many of his sayings have survived and are worth quoting here, it seemed advisable to arrange them under a few topical headings. Regarding the two items in the first section (A), it may be noted that the claim about the three parts of his book has been questioned; indeed, some have doubted that he wrote any book at all—but this doubt strikes me as unreasonable.

The term *Logos*, left untranslated in section B, is sometimes rendered as reason, sometimes as word (as in the first sentence of the fourth Gospel: "In the beginning was the Word"); and it may also denote a rational principle in the world. The so-called river fragments are included in section C. In the following section, the role assigned to fire is striking. Thales had considered water the basic principle; Anaximenes, air; now Heraclitus introduces fire. It would seem that fire was associated in his mind with both change, which it represents even much more strikingly than water, and with strife and war; but the last two fragments in that section also raise the question whether he may not possibly have been influenced by the religion of the Persians, who had conquered the Babylonian empire during Heraclitus' lifetime. It was the Persians who put an end to the Babylonian exile of the Jews, and it was probably from the Persians that the conception of a fiery judgment day entered first Jewish speculation and later the Christian religion. The Persians, following their great prophet Zarathustra, or Zoroaster, also believed that there were two great gods, one of the good and of light, the other of evil and darkness, and that man must assist the former, Ormuzd, against the latter, Ahriman. This idea, which the Jews emphatically rejected, was not accepted by Heraclitus either (cf., e.g., fragments 57 and 102 in section D). That Heraclitus knew something of the religion of the Persians is by no means established. It seems probable to me, but some eminent scholars doubt it. It has also been suggested that Heraclitus associated fire not only with change but also with permanence.

Plato frequently referred to Heraclitus and named one of his dialogues after Heraclitus' follower, Cratylus. In the *Cratylus* he speaks of "the opinion of Heraclitus that all things flow," and this phrase, "all things flow" (*panta rhei*) has often been cited as the quintessence of Heracliteanism. With some slight oversimplification, one might say that Plato was convinced by Heraclitus that in this world all things are in flux; that he also believed that if everything were in flux no rational discourse would be possible; and that he concluded that there must be another world beyond the world of sense experience—a realm utterly free from change, motion, and time. At that point he was probably influenced not only by the Pythagoreans but also by Parmenides, the next great pre-Socratic after Heraclitus.

•   •   •

## A.   The Man

Antisthenes, in his *Successions*, quotes as a sign of his [Heraclitus'] arrogance that he resigned the hereditary kingship to his brother. [Diogenes Laertius IX, 6; K 194.]

The book said to be his is called *On Nature*, from its chief content, and is divided into three discourses: On the Universe, Politics, Theology. He dedicated it and placed it in the temple of Artemis, as some say, having purposely written it rather obscurely so that only those of rank and influence should have access to it, and it should not be easily despised by the populace. . . . The work had so great a reputation that from it arose disciples, those call Heracliteans. [*Ibid.*, IX, 5; 195.]

## B.   Logos and Senses

Those awake have one ordered universe in common, but in sleep every man turns away to one of his own. [89; WK.]

The thinking faculty is common to all. [113; F.]

Of the Logos, which is as I describe it, men always prove to be uncomprehending, both before they have heard it and when once they have heard it. For although all things happen according to this Logos men are like people of no experience, even when they experience such words and deeds as I explain, when I distinguish each thing according to its constitution and declare how it is; but the rest of men fail to notice what they do after they wake up just as they forget what they do when asleep. [1; K 197.]

Therefore it is necessary to follow the common; but although the Logos is common the many live as though they had a private understanding. [2; K 198.]

Listening not to me but to the Logos it is wise to agree that all things are one. [50; K 199.]

The things of which there is seeing and hearing and perception, these I prefer. [55; K 200.]

The eyes are more exact witnesses than the ears. [101a; F.]

If all existing things turned to smoke, the nose would be the discriminating organ. [7; F.]

Evil witnesses are eyes and ears for men if they have souls that do not understand their language. [107; K 201.]

## C.   Cosmos

The path up and down are one and the same. [60; K 203*.]

The sun is new each day. [6; F.]

Sun will not overstep his measures; else the Erinyes, Justice's ministers, will find him out. [94; K 299*.]

In the same river we both step and do not step, we are and are not. [49a; F*.]

It is not possible to step twice into the same river. [91; F.]

Upon those that step into the same rivers different and different waters flow. [12; K 217.]

Sea is the most pure and polluted water: for fishes it is drinkable and salutary, but for men undrinkable and perilous. [61; K 202*.]

Disease makes health pleasant and good, hunger satiety, weariness rest. [111; K 204.]

What is in opposition is in concert, and from what differs comes the most beautiful harmony. [8; F*.]

War is the father of all, the king of all; and some he shows as gods, some as men; some he makes slaves, some free. [53; K 215*.]

One must know that war is common and justice is strife, and that all things happen by strife and necessity. [80; K 214.*]

For souls it is death to become water, for water death to become earth; from earth water comes-to-be, and from water, soul. [36; K 232*.]

Immortals are mortal, mortals immortal, living each other's death, dying each other's life. [62; WK.]

After death things await men which they do not expect or imagine. [27; F*.]

Time is a child playing a game of draughts; the kingship is in the hands of a child. [52; F.]

## D.   Religion and Fire

Being a polymath does not teach understanding: else Hesiod would have had it and Pythagoras; also Xenophanes and Hekataeus. [40; WK.]

Homer deserves to be thrown out of the contests and whipped, and Archilochus, too. [42; WK.]

The most popular teacher is Hesiod. Of him people think he knew most—he who did not even know day and night: they are one. [57; WK.]

They purify themselves by staining themselves with other blood, as if one stepped into mud to wash off mud. But a man would be thought mad if one of his fellowmen saw him do that. Also, they talk to statues as one might talk with houses, in ignorance of the nature of gods and heroes. [5; F*.]

The consecrations of the mysteries, as practised among men, are unholy. [14; WK.]

Corpses should be thrown away more than dung. [96; WK. To appreciate the full measure of this heresy, one should recall Sophocles' *Antigone* and Homer's *Iliad*.]

To god all things are beautiful and good and just, but men have supposed some things to be unjust, some just. [102; K 209*.]

Man is called childish compared with divinity, just as a boy compared with a man. [79; F.]

Fire lives the death of earth, and air the death of fire; water lives the death of air, earth that of water. [76; F*.]

Fire, having come upon them, will judge and seize upon [condemn] all things. [66; F.]

This cosmos [the same of all] none of gods or men made, but it always was and is and shall be: an everlasting fire, kindling in measures and going out in measures. [30; K 220*.]

## E.   Men and Morals

Asses prefer chaff to gold. [9; F*.]

Dogs bark at those whom they do not recognize. [97; F.]

If happiness lay in bodily pleasures, we should call oxen happy when they find vetch to eat. [4; F*.]

It is not good for men to obtain all they wish. [110; F*.]

Sane thinking is the greatest virtue, and wisdom is speaking the truth and acting according to nature, paying heed. [112; F*.]

All men are granted what is needed for knowing oneself and sane thinking. [116; WK.]

A dry soul is wisest and best. [118; K 233.]

A man when he is drunk is led by an unfledged boy, stumbling and not knowing where he goes, having his soul moist. [117; K 234.]

The best choose one above all else: everlasting fame above mortals. The majority are contented like well-fed cattle. [29; WK.]

The people must fight on behalf of the law as though for the city wall. [44; K 252.]

One man to me is ten thousand if he is the best. [49; F*.]

The Ephesians would do well to hang themselves, every adult man, and leave their city to adolescents, since they expelled Hermodorus, the worthiest man among them, saying: Let us not have even one worthy man; but if we do, let him go elsewhere and live among others! [121; F*.]

## F.   Epilogue

I sought myself. [101; WK.]

If one does not expect the unexpected one will not find it, for it is not reached by search or trail. [18; WK.]

Character is man's fate. [119; WK.]

Nature loves hiding. [123; WK.]

The Sybil, uttering her unlaughing, unadorned, unincensed words with raving mouth, reaches out over a thousand years with her voice, through the god. [92; F*.]

The lord whose oracle is in Delphi neither speaks out nor conceals, but gives a sign. [93; K 247.]

# THE ELEATICS

## PARMENIDES

Parmenides, a younger contemporary of Heraclitus and an older contemporary of Socrates, lived in Elea in southern Italy, on the west coast, a few miles south of the ancient Posidonia (now Paestum) where a magnificent temple of Poseidon stands to this day along with two other fine temples that also belong to the time of Parmenides. He may have been born about 510 B.C., something like thirty years after Heraclitus. Plato gave free expression to his reverence for Parmenides and introduced him into one of his dialogues, named after him (part of it is reprinted in this volume). According to that dialogue, Parmenides visited Athens when he was about sixty-five, accompanied by his chief pupil, Zeno, then nearly forty, and conversed with Socrates who was still "quite young." Whether the visit to Athens really took place, we do not know; that Socrates met Parmenides is not especially likely; but that they did not have the conversation reported in the dialogue is absolutely clear: for that discussion presupposes Plato's own earlier work and explores difficulties in the theory of forms expounded in the *Phaedo* and the *Republic*—difficulties that Plato evidently had not noticed when he wrote those dialogues long after the death of Socrates.

That Plato raised Parmenides to such heights, allowing him to instruct the young Socrates (generally, Socrates bests or teaches those with whom he converses in Plato's dialogues), confirms the impression one gets in any case, that there were few men to whom Plato felt a greater debt. Specifically, his dichotomy of knowledge and belief and of an unchanging, eternal, timeless reality and ever changing, temporal appearance was derived from

Parmenides. The Eleatic idea that reality is one, devoid of any plurality, Plato did not accept: he peopled the "real" world with a number of unchanging, eternal forms. But when he realized later that this theory was open to serious objections, he put the criticisms that occurred to him into the mouth of the great Parmenides. And in a still later dialogue, the *Sophist* (also reprinted in large part in this volume), Plato occupied himself with another Parmenidean dichotomy: that of being and nonbeing.

Parmenides' distinction between the one, undifferentiated, timeless, changeless reality and the merely apparent world of sense experience invites comparison with the slightly older philosophy of the Indian Upanishads; and Pythagoras' belief in the transmigration of souls points in the same direction. No Indian influence on the pre-Socratics has ever been demonstrated, but this, of course, does not prove that there was no such influence.

Parmenides, as the philosopher of changeless being, has often been contrasted with Heraclitus, as the philosopher of change and becoming. But it should not be overlooked that both are at one in repudiating the wisdom of tradition as well as common sense. One is as radical as the other.

The fragments that follow are parts of a poem in which, after an imposing prologue, the ways of knowledge and belief, of being and nonbeing, are distinguished.

. . .

The steeds that bear me took me as far as my heart's desire after they brought me to the renowned way of the goddess that leads the man who knows through every town. On that way I was borne, for there the wise chariot-steeds bore me, and the maidens led the way. [Lines 1-5.]

The axle, glowing in the socket, urged round by the whirling wheels at each end, made the naves sing, as the daughters of the sun, hastening to convey me to the light, left the abode of night and threw back the veils from their faces. [Lines 6-10.]

There are the gates of the ways of night and day, with a lintel above and a threshold of stone below. They themselves, lofty, are filled with huge doors, and avenging Justice wields the changing bolts. [Lines 11-14.]

Her the maidens entreated with gentle words, persuading her cleverly to unfasten the bolted bar quickly from the gates. Flung open, they revealed a wide,

gaping space, as the brazen posts with their rivets and nails swung in turn on their hinges. There, straight through the gates, on that road the maidens guided the chariot and steeds. [Lines 15-21.]

Then the goddess greeted me kindly, took my right hand in hers, and spoke to me, addressing me thus: [Lines 22-23.]

O youth, companion of immortal charioteers and steeds that brought you to our abode: welcome! No evil fate, but right and justice, sent you on this way, far from the beaten track of men. You must needs learn all: both the unshaken heart of well-rounded[1] truth and the opinions of mortals in which there is no true belief. Nevertheless, you shall learn these things also, how, passing right through all things, one should judge the things that seem to be. [Lines 24-32; fragment 1 comprises lines 1-32. Raven's translation is based on Burnet's;

---

[1] Cf. Fragment 5, following.

the above version was arrived at after also consulting Diels's and Freeman's.]

Come, I will tell you; hear my word and carry it away. These are the only ways of inquiry that can be thought of [literally: that exist for thinking (Raven)]: one way, that it is and cannot not-be, is the path of persuasion, for it attends upon truth; the other, that it is-not and needs must not-be, that, I tell you, is a path altogether unthinkable. For you could not know that which is-not (that is impossible), nor utter it. [2; R 344*.]

For the same thing can be thought as can be. [3; R 344. Raven construes the literal meaning as: the same thing exists for thinking and for being; Burnet: for it is the same thing that can be thought as can be. Freeman's "For it is the same thing to think and to be" is based on Diels's *Denn (das Seiende) denken und sein ist dasselbe*. This much-discussed sentence seems to be continuous with the preceding two fragments.]

Look steadfastly at things which, though far off, are yet present to your mind; for you shall not cut off what is from clinging to what is, neither scattering itself everywhere in order nor crowding together. [4; R 349.]

It is all one to me where I begin; for I shall come back there again in time. [5; R 343.]

That which can be spoken and thought needs must be; for it is possible for it, but not for nothing, to be; that is what I bid you ponder. This is the first way of inquiry from which I hold you back, and then also from that way on which mortals wander, knowing nothing, two-minded; for helplessness guides the wandering thoughts in their breasts: they are carried along, deaf and blind at once, dazed altogether, hordes without judgment, persuaded that to be and to be-not are the same, yet not the same, and that the path of all things

turns back. [6; R 345*. Freeman renders the final words: in everything there is a way of opposing stress. Either way, many interpreters believe that Parmenides here alludes to Heraclitus.]

For never shall this be proved, that things that are not are. Hold back your thought from this way of inquiry, nor let custom, born of much experience, force you to let roam along this road your eye, sightless, your ear, noise-filled, or your tongue. But by means of the logos judge the much-debated proof that I utter. [7; R 346*.]

Only one way remains; that it is. To this way there are very many sign-posts: that being has no coming-into-being and no destruction, for it is whole of limb, without motion, and without end. And it never was, nor will be, because it is now, a whole all together, one, continuous; for what creation of it will you look? How, whence sprung? Nor shall I allow you to speak or think of it as springing from not-being; for it is neither expressible nor thinkable that what-is-not is. Also, what necessity impelled it, if it did spring from nothing, to be produced later or earlier? Thus it must be absolutely, or not at all. Nor will the force of credibility ever admit that anything should come into being, beside being itself, out of not-being. So far as that is concerned, justice has never released (*being*) from its fetters and set it free either to come into being or to perish, but holds it fast. The decision on these matters depends on the following: it is, or it is not. It is therefore decided, as is inevitable: ignore the one way as unthinkable and inexpressible (for it is no true way) and take the other as the way of being and reality. How could being perish? How could it come into being? If it came into being, it is not; and so too if it is about-to-be at some future time. Thus coming-into-being is quenched, and destruction also into the unseen.

Nor is being divisible, since it is all alike. Nor is there anything there which could prevent it from holding together, nor any lesser thing, but all is full of being. Therefore it is altogether continuous; for being is close to being.

But it is motionless in the limits of mighty bonds, without beginning, without cease, since becoming and destruction have been driven very far away, and true conviction has rejected them. And remaining the same in the same place, it rests by itself and thus remains there fixed; for powerful necessity holds it in the bonds of a limit, which constrains it round about, because it is decreed by divine law that being shall not be without boundary. For it is not lacking; but if it were (spatially infinite), it would be lacking everything.[2]

To think is the same as the thought that it is; for you will not find thinking without being to which it refers. For nothing else either is or shall be except being, since fate has tied it down to be a whole and motionless; therefore all things that mortals have established, believing in their truth, are just a name: becoming and perishing, being and not-being, and change of position, and alteration of bright colour.

But since there is a (spatial) limit, it is complete on every side, like the mass of a well-rounded sphere, equally balanced from its centre in every direction; for it is not bound to be at all either greater or less in this direction or that; nor is there not-being which could check it from reaching to the same point, nor is it possible for being to be more in this direction, less in that, than being, because it is an inviolate whole. For, in all directions equal to itself, it reaches its limits uniformly.

At this point I cease my reliable theory (Logos) and thought, concerning Truth;

from here onwards you must learn the opinions of mortals, listening to the deceptive order of my words.

They have established (the custom of) naming two forms, one of which ought not to be (mentioned): that is where they have gone astray. They have distinguished them as opposite in form, and have marked them off from another by giving them different signs: on one side the flaming fire in the heavens, mild, very light (in weight), the same as itself in every direction, and not the same as the other. This (other) also is by itself and opposite: dark night, a dense and heavy body. This world-order I describe to you throughout as it appears with all its phenomena, in order that no intellect of mortal men may outstrip you. [8; F*.]

But since all things are named light and night, and names have been given to each class of things according to the power of one or the other, everything is full equally of light and invisible night, as both are equal, because to neither of them belongs any share (of the other). [9. Kranz takes ἐπεί with the previous line, and translates: "For nothing is possible which does not come under either of the two" (i.e. everything belongs to one or other of the two categories light and night); F*.]

You shall know the nature of the heavens, and all the signs in the heavens, and the destructive works of the pure bright torch of the sun, and whence they came into being. And you shall learn of the wandering works of the round-faced moon, and its nature; and you shall know also the surrounding heaven, whence it sprang and how necessity brought and constrained it to hold the limits of the stars. [10; F.]

(I will describe) how earth and sun and moon, and the aether common to all, and the milky way in the heavens, and outermost Olympus, and the hot power of the stars, hastened to come into being. [11; F.]

---

[2] Reading and meaning doubtful. Diels-Kranz: "if it lacked Limit, it would fall short of being a Whole," but without any certainty. [F]

For the narrower rings were filled with unmixed fire, and those next to them with night, but between (*these*) rushes the portion of flame. And in the centre of these is the goddess who guides everything; for throughout she rules over cruel birth and mating, sending the female to mate with the male, and conversely again the male with the female. [12; F.]

First of all the gods she devised Love. [13; F.]

(*The moon*): Shining by night with a light not her own, wandering round the earth. [14; F.]

# ZENO[1]

According to Plato's Parmenides, Zeno was "close to forty" when Parmenides was sixty-five and Socrates (born 469 B.C.) was a very young man (127b); while still young (128d) he wrote a book (128a)[2] whose purpose was "a defence of Parmenides' argument against those who try to ridicule it by arguing that ludicrous and self-contradictory consequences follow from the hypothesis that [only] One exists. This book talks to those who affirm the Many [i.e., that many things exist.] It pays them back in the same coin, and with something to spare. What it aims to make clear is that if the case is properly made, their own hypothesis, that there are many, has still more ridiculous consequences than the hypothesis that there is [only] One [128cd]." In other words, the purpose of Zeno's book was not to expound his own doctrine, or that of his master, but to counter-attack Parmenides' critics. Elsewhere (*Phaedrus* 261d) Plato speaks of Zeno as

---

[1] This section on Zeno has been contributed by Gregory Vlastos. When I prepared the original edition of 1961, Professor Vlastos very generously agreed to contribute not only translations but a detailed discussion of Zeno's arguments. In a note he explained: "I consented only because I know, from my own experience in teaching Zeno to undergraduates, how hard it is for the nonspecialist to get from currently available textbooks an even approximately adequate idea of what the historical Zeno is likely to have thought and written ... I should add that everything in this chapter represents purely *provisional* results of work-in-progress that will be published elsewhere in due course; that I try to avoid, as far as possible, controversial questions; and that when I find it necessary to take sides (as I do in almost every paragraph), I do not burden the text by explaining, or even naming, respectable scholarly alternatives to the views I expound, nor do I attempt to marshal *all* the evidence that can be cited for my own positions."

In 1966, Professor Vlastos published his results on "Zeno's Race Course, with Appendix on the Achilles," in *Journal of the History of Philosophy*, 4, 95–108, and "A Note on Zeno's Arrow" in *Phronesis* 11, 3–18. These articles supersede his earlier treatment of Zeno's arguments against motion, and this part of the discussion has therefore been omitted in the present edition, although the texts themselves are, of course, still offered in this volume. Vlastos' recent results are also embodied in his article on Zeno in the *Encyclopedia of Philosophy* (1967), vol. 8, 369–79. W.K.

[2] Or books? Several titles are mentioned by Suidas, *Vorsokratiker* 29 A 2. Plato speaks of "writings" at 127c, but this is inconclusive.

"that Eleatic Palamedes[3] who by his art makes the same things appear to his listeners both like and unlike, both one and many, both at rest and in motion."

Zeno's puzzles have fascinated philosophers, logicians, and mathematicians ever since, and never more than in our own time: probably more has been written on his paradoxes in the last hundred years than in all the preceding two thousand.[4] Much of this work is cheerfully unconcerned with the connection, if any, between its "Zeno" and Zeno. Reading it one might form extravagant notions of the reasoning powers of this remote Greek. One might come to think of him as a logical superman who enjoyed a charmed infallibility and an uncanny insight into difficulties that baffled all others for more than two millennia after his time. Anyone who has swallowed this legend will get a shock when he comes face to face with what Zeno wrote and sees how, on the best available evidence, this man must have thought and reasoned.[5] But if one persists in seeking facts, instead of wish-fulfilments, and is not totally lacking in historical imagination, one may still come to feel in the end that, for all his crudities and blunders, this pioneer in the art of argument deserves an honored place in the history of thought.

## A.   Arguments Against Plurality

Hermann Diels identified four fragments as verbatim citations from Zeno's original book (or books), and numbered them as B1, B2, B3, and B4.[6] The authenticity of the first three has never been called into question. The third of these, B3, is a beautifully self-contained logical argument that speaks for itself; it will be cited as such without much commentary as "The Second Argument Against Plurality." The first two fragments, B1 and B2, are almost certainly pieces from a much longer piece of argumentation, which

---

3 "($\Pi\alpha\lambda\alpha\mu\eta\delta\eta s$, "the handy or contriving one"), a proverbially (cf. Aristophanes *Frogs* 1451) clever hero ... His chief distinctions are the invention of letters and his cunning while serving with Agamemnon. ..." H. J. Rose, *s.v.*, *Oxford Classical Dictionary*, Oxford, 1941.

4 For some idea of the vast literature on Zeno see F. Cajori, "The History of Zeno's Arguments on Motion," *American Mathematical Monthly* 22 (1915), pp. 1 ff., 39 ff., 77 ff., 109 ff., 143 ff., 179 ff., 253 ff., 292 ff.; the bibliography in H. D. P. Lee, *Zeno of Elea*, Cambridge, 1936, pp. 124-5. Interesting samples of the more recent literature: The nine papers in *Analysis* 12-15 (1951-5), most of them listed in Max Black, *Problems of Analysis*, Ithaca, 1954, p. 109, n. 1; the whole of the section on Zeno's Paradoxes in this book by Max Black; the chapter on "Achilles and the Tortoise" in *Dilemmas* (Cambridge, 1954) by Gilbert Ryle; and A. Gruenbaum, "Modern Science and the Refutation of the Paradoxes of Zeno," *Scientific Monthly* 81 (1955), pp. 234 ff.; D. S. Schwayder, "Achilles Unbound," *Journal of Philosophy* 52 (1955), pp. 449 ff.

5 The most important paper by a philologist that established the right perspective for understanding the historical Zeno is H. Fraenkel, "Zeno of Elea's Attacks on Plurality," *American Journal of Philology* 63 (1942), pp. 1 ff. and 193 ff.

6 This number has been preserved in current editions of *Vorsokratiker*, in spite of the fact that it is now generally recognized that B2 preceded B1 in Zeno's text.

preceded B3 in Zeno's text,[7] and may for that reason be called Zeno's "First Argument Against Plurality."[8] To figure out the structure of this whole argument and tell just where B1 and B2 fit and what part they play in it is a difficult problem of historical scholarship. But I think it is fair to say that it has been solved in principle by Hermann Fraenkel.[9] The main lines of his reconstruction, but with important modifications of my own,[10] are incorporated in the following version:

### First Argument Against Plurality

This began with a section that has been lost to us, although this sentence from Simplicius (*Physics* 139, 18-19), gives some idea of what it tried to prove and how: "He showed earlier [i.e., prior to the parts of the argument constituting B1 and B2] that nothing has size because each of the many is self-identical and one."

It so happens that Zeno's contemporary and fellow-disciple of the great Parmenides, Melissus, has an argument that runs as follows (in verbatim citation):

If it existed, it would have to be one; but if it were one, it could not have body; for if it had thickness, it would have parts; and then it would not be one.[11]

This gives us a fair idea of the logical bridge a disciple of Parmenides would build from 'x is one' (or, more fully, from 'x is one and self-identical') to 'x has no size.' If it is one, he would argue, it can have no parts, and hence, can have no size. The latter inference would be drawn on the assumption that anything that does have size is at least *logically* divisible and has at least logically discriminable parts;[12] the former, on the assumption that anything that has parts in any sense whatever cannot be strictly or absolutely "one."[13] Thus the whole of this argument might have gone somewhat as follows:

If anything is one and self-identical, it would not have parts, and then it would not have size. But if anything exists, it must be one and self-identical.

---

[7] Simplicius, *Physics* 140, 34.

[8] It may, or may not, have been preceded by other arguments against plurality in Zeno's original text.

[9] In the paper cited above, n. 5.

[10] Some of these are defended in my review of H. Fraenkel, *Wege und Formen fruehgriechischen Denkens* (Munich, 1955), in *Gnomon* 31 (1959), pp. 193 ff.; and in a paper entitled, "A Zenonian Argument Against Plurality," which I presented to the Society for Ancient Greek Philosophy at Harvard on December 27, 1957: this paper has not been published, but copies of it were distributed to the members of the Society and to some other scholars.

[11] *Vorsokratiker* 30 B 9.

[12] Zeno (or Mellissus) would not, of course, have used such language. Words for what *we* express by "logical" and "physical" did not exist at that time.

[13] For various versions of arguments, attributed to Zeno by later writers, which ring the changes on this theme, see items 1, 3, 5 in Lee, *op. cit.*

Hence if the Many exist (or, if there are many), then each of the Many would have to be one and self-identical, and hence none of them would have size.

Zeno's next move was to turn around and argue that, on the contrary, if the many exist, they *must* have size, on the grounds that something without size would not even exist. This part of the argument (B2 in Diels) survives intact in a verbatim citation by Simplicius:

For [a] if it [something having no size] were added to another, it would make it [the latter] no larger. For [b] having no size, it could not contribute anything by way of size when added. And thus [c] the thing added would be nothing. [d] If indeed when [something is] subtracted from another, the latter is not reduced, nor again increased when [something is] added [to it], it is clear that what is added or subtracted is nothing.

This is not a smooth translation—which is all to the good, for the original is just as rough; and this is not surprising, for the use of written prose for this kind of abstract argumentation was something new under the sun: it had never been done before, so far as we know, except in geometry. What may seem a bit more disturbing than the clumsy formulation is the peculiar inverted order, which is best seen if we compare the text above with a modernized version of it (simplified by using symbols to cut out unnecessary verbiage), exhibiting the true logical order of the intended argument:

1. If $x$ did not increase $y$, when added to it, nor decrease $y$, when subtracted from it, then $x$ would be nothing.
2. If $x$ had no size, then $x$ would not increase $y$, when added to it, nor decrease $y$, when subtracted from it. Therefore,
3. If $x$ had no size, it would be nothing.

A comparison with the above text will show that the last proposition there, (d), is in fact (1) here, the first premise of the argument; and the conclusion here, (3), appears at (c) above, *before* (d). This is odd, but commits no logical fault; it is no rule of logic that the premise *has* to be written (or spoken) ahead of the conclusion (and sometimes it is not in live arguments; e.g., 'A and B are both right angles, so they must be equal—all right angles are equal.') What does look like a logical fault is not that the premise (1) should be stuck at the end of the argument, but that it should be used as a premise at all.

A modern reader might object: 'How can Zeno ask me to agree to (1), when he professes to have proved to me a moment ago that no existent has size; that would entail that all existents are incorporeal, and hence that (1) is false, since it could only be true if all existents were corporeal.' But this objection would misconceive the purpose of Zeno's argument, which is purely dialectical. Addressed to *his* contemporaries—not ours, or even Plato's—its aim was to show them that their thinking was crisscrossed with contradiction. And since the notion of incorporeal existence cannot be claimed for anyone at this time outside of Eleatic circles, Zeno's own readers would have been assuming the truth of (1) all along. Hence Zeno, given his purpose to convince them they had been holding inconsistent beliefs, could claim the right to use the premises he did in the first section *and* (1) in this section, since prior to this argument they would have agreed immediately to all of them. It was clumsy of him to do it in just this way; but it committed no fault of logic.

We are now ready for the climax of the whole argument:

So if [the many] exist, each one [of them] must have some size and thickness and one part [of each] must extend beyond the other [part of the same existent]. And the same reasoning holds of the projecting [part]. For this too will have size and some part of *it* will project. Now to say this once is as good as saying it for ever. For no such [part, i.e., no part resulting by subdivision, no matter how far this process is carried out] will be the last or without one [part similarly] related to another [part].

Thus, if there are many, they must be both small and great: on one hand, so small as to have no size; on the other, so large as to be infinite.

The reasoning in this lap of the argument (on the above translation) is perfectly straightforward: If there are many existents, each of them must have some size; this is just a carry-over from the preceding section, B2. But if something has size, it must be spread out in space, so you can distinguish in it a "here" from a "there"; having such nonoverlapping parts, Zeno might have explained, is part of what we mean by having size. These parts are clearly not intended to be physically separate; they don't arise by splitting an object, or cutting it up, but a purely logical process of discriminating different regions within it. And this process can go on *ad infinitum*; we can distinguish parts *b* and *c* within *a*, parts *d* and *e* within *c*, and so forth, as in the accompanying diagram:

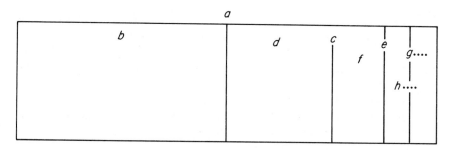

The series—*a, c, e, g,* . . . —has no last member.

So far so good. But how could Zeno expect us to go from this point to the extraordinary conclusion he wants to reach and which he evidently thinks *can* be reached by moving along this road: that *a* (which stands for any existent) is infinitely large? He must have assumed, as too obvious for mention, some such additional intervening steps as these:

4. *a* is the sum of an infinite number of terms, each of which has a finite size ($a = b + d + f + \ldots$). This follows correctly from the preceding.

5. The sum of an infinite number of terms, each of which has a finite size, is infinitely large. Therefore,

6. *a* is infinitely large. This follows from (4) and (5).[14]

That something has gone wrong here is evident, and it is not hard to see just where: (5) is clearly false. To show this it is sufficient to call attention to any convergent series, e.g., to the series, $\frac{1}{2}$, $\frac{1}{4}$, $\frac{1}{8}$, $\frac{1}{16}$, such as the *b*, *d*, *f*, . . . series might well have been by the terms of the construction. It is false to say that the sum of this series is infinitely large, and Zeno himself might have satisfied himself that this is false by the arithmetic at his disposal. He could have reasoned: when there are two terms in this series, $\frac{1}{2} + \frac{1}{4}$, their sum is $\frac{3}{4}$; when there are three, $\frac{1}{2} + \frac{1}{4} + \frac{1}{8}$, the sum is $\frac{7}{8}$; in both cases it is less than 1; and this will always be true, no matter how many terms are put into the series, since the last term added will never be the whole of the difference between 1 and the sum of the preceding terms, but always half of that difference. So the sum could never be more than 1. Or, if Zeno were averse to arithmetic, he might have seen the error of (5) by just reasoning from a diagram, like the one in the text above: since *all* the magnitudes included in the *b*, *d*, *f*, . . . series are nonoverlapping *parts* of *a*, their sum will always fall short of *a*, so long as a finite number of terms have been put into the series; and if the whole infinite lot of them could be put in, they would *exhaust a* (no part of *a* would be left unincluded), and hence the sum of the series would be precisely equal to *a*; and since *a* is finite, how could that sum be infinite? So there is no getting around the point that here, at (5), our clever Zeno walked into a booby trap, which, one would think, he could have avoided with the materials at his disposal. What is it then that could have made him go wrong?

Consider the following proposition, (5a), and compare it carefully with (5) above:

5a. The sum of an infinite number of terms, the *smallest* of which has a finite size, is infinitely large.

---

14 Many modern readers will find it impossible to believe that such a vital part of the chain of argument was left purely tacit in the original text. Before he makes up his mind on this point, he would do well to study other arguments in Greek philosophical texts and note how elliptical they sometimes are, even in authors like Plato and Aristotle, who have the benefit of enormous intervening progress in the art of argument. Only long and bitter experience teaches philosophers that every argument must be made as fully explicit as possible, even at the risk of saying the obvious at tedious length, for it is in just those stretches of it that look most obvious that mistakes are likely to occur. As for the present case, it is, of course, not *certain* that the gap in the reasoning was also present in Zeno's original text; it is possible that something dropped out of the text at this point. But since it would be just this portion of the argument that would have had the greatest interest for Zeno's own contemporaries and successors all the way down to the faithful Simplicius, the chance that such a portion as this was lost in the transmission is so small that no historian can reasonably bank on it.

The only difference between (5a) and (5) is that "the smallest" at (5a) replaces "each" at (5). But what a difference that makes: (5a) refers only to a collection that does have a smallest term (or, smallest terms), while (5) refers to any collection whatever, *including* series that have no smallest term. The result of the difference is that (5a) is true, as one can see by noting (i), that given an infinite number of things such that the smallest of them has any size at all, their sum would be infinitely large, since if that smallest term were added to itself an infinite number of times the sum would be infinitely large, and hence *a fortiori* if added to an infinite number of terms larger than itself the sum would certainly be infinitely large; and (ii), that the convergent series that falsified (5) would not falsify (5a), for it would be irrelevant to (5a): having no last term, it would have no smallest term. But after seeing all this, note finally how easily even a very clever man *could* have confused (5a) with (5). Since at (5) he is thinking of an infinite number of parts *all of which have size*, it would be easy for him to say, 'Well, if they *all* have size, it must be the case that even the smallest of them has size,' failing to see that, in saying this, he is making the fatal assumption that "smallest" does apply to this infinitely decreasing series. This failure would be a symptom of the tendency to extrapolate from what remains true of the series so long as it has a finite number of terms to what would be the case if *all* its terms were present in it. Zeno's best hope of checking this tendency lay in making the assumption as explicit as possible. Had he actually *said*, 'the series $b$, $d$, $f$, ... must have a smallest member,' his chances of noticing the contradiction with the fact that, as he himself says, it has no last, would have immeasurably improved. He threw this chance away when he treated the steps intervening between the argument that makes up the first paragraph of B1 above and the conclusion to '$a$ is infinitely large' as too obvious to deserve a place in his text.

We can now look back over the whole argument, and see how, on the present reconstruction of it, Zeno thought he could prove the conclusion at B1: If there are many existents, then each of them must be both (I) so small as to have no size and (II) so large as to be infinite. (I) he would infer from the first section of the argument: if no existent has *any* size, then it is indeed "so small as to have no size." (II) he would infer by the long drawn-out process that begins by propping up again, at B2, the common-sense belief knocked down in the first section, that existents have size, and deducing therefrom by the explicit reasoning at B1 and its tacit sequel—(4), (5), (6), above—that every one of them must be "so large as to be infinite."[15]

## Second Argument Against Plurality

B3. [Simplicius, *Phys.* 140, 30.] If there are many, they must be just so many as they are, neither more nor fewer. But if they are just so many as

---

15 For a new interpretation of the last sentence of B1, which puts an entirely different face on the logical structure of the whole of this First Argument Against Plurality, see now F. Solmsen, *Aristotle's Physical World*, Ithaca, 1960, p. 172 and n. 56. Though I find this an extremely interesting and attractive suggestion, I do not waver in my adherence to the interpretation I have set out here.

they are, they must be finite [in number]. If there are many, the existents are infinite [in number]: for there are always other [existents] between existents, and again others between these. And thus the existents are infinite [in number].

The first horn of the dilemma is proved by arguing that if there are many things, they must be just so many, i.e., they have a number; and then inferring that this must be a *finite* number. This is a very respectable inference. It could not have been known to be false prior to the discovery of transfinite cardinal numbers by Georg Cantor, more than 2,300 years after this time.

The second horn is proved by arguing that given any two distinct existents, there must be other existents between them. The existents Zeno is thinking of here must be physically separate objects, and he must be assuming that to be separate, any two objects, *a* and *b*, must be separated by at least one separate object *c*; hence he infers correctly that *a* must be separated from *c* by *d*, so too *a* from *d* by *e*, and so forth.

## B.   Arguments Against Motion

**The Race Course**

Aristotle has four references to this argument:

[*Topics*, 160b 7.] For we have many arguments contrary to (common) beliefs, whose solution is yet difficult, like Zeno's that it is impossible to move or to traverse the race course.[16]

[*Phys.* 233a 21.] For this reason Zeno's argument too assumes falsely that it is impossible to traverse or to come in contact with each one of an infinite number [of things] in a finite time.

[*Phys.* 239b 11.] The first [of Zeno's arguments against motion "which cause difficulty to those who try to solve the problems they raise"] says that there is no motion, because the moving [body] must reach the midpoint before it gets to the end.

[*Phys.* 263a 5.] In the same way one should reply to those who pose [literally, "ask"] Zeno's argument, claiming that it is always necessary to traverse the half [i.e., to traverse any given distance we must first traverse its first half], and these [*sc.* half-distances] are infinitely numerous, while it is impossible to traverse an infinity....

We get a somewhat different version of the argument in the late commentators.[17] The following, from Simplicius (Phys. 1013, 4ff.), is typical:

If there is motion, the moving object must traverse an infinity in a finite [time]: and this is impossible. Hence motion does not exist. He demonstrates his hypothesis thus: The moving object must move a certain stretch. And since

---

16 Evidently the stage setting of the argument is a race course. On this ground it is better to call the argument by this name, instead of "The Dichotomy," as is often done in the literature, keeping "The Stadium" as the generally accepted name of the fourth argument.

17 They are all in Lee, *op. cit.*, pp. 44 ff.

every stretch is infinitely divisible, the
moving object must first traverse half
the stretch it is moving, and then the
whole; but before the whole of the half,
half of that and, again, the half of that.
If then these halves are infinite, since,
whatever may be the given [stretch] it
is possible to halve it, and [if, further,]
it is impossible to traverse the infinity
[of these stretches] in a finite time ... it
follows that it is impossible to traverse
any given length in a finite time.

### The Achilles

[Aristotle, *Phys.* 239b 14.] The second [of Zeno's arguments against mo-
tion] is the so-called "Achilles." This is
that the slowest will never be overtaken
by the swiftest; for the pursuer must first
reach [the point] whence the pursued
started, so that the slower must always
be some distance ahead.

### The Arrow

[Aristotle's account of this argument
will be found below, in Book VI, Chapter IX of *Physics:* "Against Zeno,"
p. 393. WK.]

### The Stadium

Aristotle's account of this argument
may be consulted at *Phys.* 239b 33. [See
*ibid.* WK.]

### C.   Against Space

[Aristotle, *Phys.* 210b 23.] Zeno's
puzzle—"if place exists, in what does it
exist?"—is not hard to solve. [*Ibid.* 209a
23.] Further, if it [place] is itself an
existent, where will it exist? For Zeno's
puzzle demands some explanation. For
if every existent is in a place, clearly
there will have to be a place of a place,
and so on *ad infinitum*.

'Why think that such a thing as place exists?' asks Zeno. If his contemporaries reply, as they doubtless would, 'Because whatever exists must be
somewhere—in some place,' they are caught in his trap, unless they can then
go on to explain what sort of "existent" place (or, space) is, how different
from the things we ordinarily think of as existents which do 'exist in space.'
To do this would be to launch an inquiry into the different senses of the
word *to be* (there is no separate word for *to exist* in Greek), anticipating
Aristotle by a century. No wonder Zeno's question went begging for a
hundred years.

### D.   The Paradox of
### the Millet Seed

[Simplicius, *Phys.* 1108, 18 ff.] By this
means he [Aristotle at *Phys.* 250a 19]
solves the puzzle which Zeno the Eleatic
put to Protagoras the Sophist. 'Tell me,
Protagoras,' he said, 'does a single millet
seed, or the ten thousandth part of a
seed, make a noise when they fall?'
When Protagoras said they did not, he
said: 'does the bushel then make a noise
when it falls or not?' When Protagoras

said this did, Zeno said: 'Is there not
then some ratio of the bushel to one
seed and to a ten thousandth of a seed?'
When Protagoras said there was, Zeno
said: 'But then must not the respective
noises stand to one another in the same
ratios? For as the sounding bodies are
to one another, so must be the sounds
they make. This being so, if the bushel
of millet makes a noise, then the single
millet seed must also make a noise, and
so must the ten thousandth of a millet
seed.'

The dialogue form in which this argument appears is not Zeno's, and Simplicius does not pretend that it is. But neither is there any reason to doubt that the gist of the argument did go back to Zeno. (Cf. H. D. P. Lee, *Zeno of Elea*, Cambridge, 1936, p. 110).

The argument speaks for itself. Along similar lines Leibniz argued that because we hear the roar of the sea we must have a "small perception" of "the little sounds" that come from each wave. *New Essays of Human Understanding, Introduction* (R. Latta, Leibniz, *The Monadology etc.*, Oxford, 1898, p. 371). If Leibniz were trying to show, not that we have "small perceptions," but that sense perception as such is delusive, he would not have stopped at the sounds made by each wave but would have gone on, like Zeno, to the vastly smaller ones made by each of the minute particles that compose each wave.

# MELISSUS

Melissus is said to have come from Samos, like Pythagoras, and to have flourished about 440 B.C. He wrote a book "About Nature or Reality," probably some time after the completion of Zeno's more celebrated work. Melissus, too, was concerned to defend Parmenides, and it is therefore convenient to have a single label for the philosophy of these three men. They are traditionally called Eleatics, after the small town in southern Italy where Parmenides made his home, Elea.

• • •

Melissus son of Ithagenes, a Samian. He was a pupil of Parmenides. . . . He was a statesman, and was held in great honor by the citizens; and later, when he was elected admiral, he won even greater fame for his personal courage. . . . [Diogenes Laertius, IX, 24; R 379.]

When Pericles had set sail, Melissus son of Ithagenes, a philosopher who was then in command of Samos, was so contemptuous of the small number of the Athenian ships or of their com-mander's inexperience that he persuaded the Samians to attack. A battle took place which the Samians won. They took so many prisoners and destroyed so many ships that they had command of the sea, and they devoted to the prosecution of the war certain supplies which they did not till then possess. Pericles himself, according to Aristotle, had also been defeated by Melissus in an earlier naval battle. [Plutarch, *Pericles* 26; R 380. The great battle referred to took place in 441/40 B.C.]

• • •

All his genuine fragments follow, in Freeman's translation:

1. That which was, always and always will be. For if it had come into being, it necessarily follows that before it came into being, nothing existed. If however nothing existed, in no way could anything come into being out of nothing.

2. Since therefore it did not come into being, it is and always was and always

will be, and has no beginning or end, but it is eternal. For if it had come into being, it would have a beginning (for it would have come into being at some time, and so begun), and an end (for since it had come into being, it would have ended [for it would at some time have stopped coming into being: Raven]). But since it has neither begun nor ended, it always was and always will be and has no beginning nor end. For it is impossible for anything to be [exist forever: Raven] unless it is completely.

3. But as it is always, so also its size must always be infinite.

4. Nothing that has a beginning and an end is either everlasting or infinite.

5. If it were not one, it would form a boundary in relation to something else.

6. If it were infinite, it would be one; for if it were two, (these) could not be (spatially) infinite, but each would have boundaries in relation to each other.

7. (1) Thus therefore it is everlasting and unlimited and one and like throughout (homogeneous).

(2) And neither could it perish or become larger or change its (inner) arrangement, nor does it feel pain or grief. For if it suffered any of these things, it would no longer be one. For if being alters, it follows that it is not the same, but that that which previously was is destroyed, and that not-being has come into being. Hence if it were to become different by a single hair in ten thousand years, so it must be utterly destroyed in the whole of time.

(3) But it is not possible for it to be rearranged either, for the previous arrangement is not destroyed, nor does a nonexistent arrangement come into being. And since it is neither increased by any addition, nor destroyed, nor changed, how could it have undergone a rearrangement of what exists? For if it were different in any respect, then there would at once be a rearrangement.

(4) Nor does it feel pain; for it could not be completely if it were in pain; for a thing which is in pain could not always be. Nor has it equal power with what is healthy. Nor would it be the same if it were in pain; for it would feel pain through the subtraction or addition of something, and could no longer be the same.

(5) Nor could that which is healthy feel pain, for the healthy—that which is —would perish, and that which is not would come into being.

(6) And with regard to grief, the same reasoning applies as to pain.

(7) Nor is there any emptiness; for the empty is nothing; and so that which is nothing cannot be. Nor does it move; for it cannot withdraw in any direction, but (all) is full. For if there were any empty, it would have withdrawn into the empty; but as the empty does not exist, there is nowhere for it (being) to withdraw.

(8) And there can be no dense and rare. For the rare cannot possibly be as full as the dense, but the rare must at once become more empty than the dense.

(9) The following distinction must be made between the full and the not-full: if a thing has room for or admits something, it is not full; if it neither has room for nor admits anything, it is full.

(10) It (being) must necessarily be full, therefore, if there is no empty. If therefore it is full, it does not move.

8. (1) This argument is the greatest proof that it (being) is one only; but there are also the following proofs:

(2) If things were many, they would have to be of the same kind as I say the one is. For if there is earth and water and air and fire and iron and gold, and that which is living and that which is dead, and black and white and all the rest of the things which men say are real: if these things exist, and we see and hear correctly, each thing must be of such a kind as it seemed to us to be in the first place, and it cannot change or become different, but each thing must

always be what it is. But now, we say we see and hear and understand correctly,

(3) and it seems to us that the hot becomes cold and the cold hot, and the hard soft and the soft hard, and that the living thing dies and comes into being from what is not living, and that all things change, and that what was and what now is are not at all the same, but iron which is hard is worn away by contact with the finger, and gold and stone and whatever seems to be entirely strong (*is worn away*); and that from water, earth and stone come into being. So that it comes about that we neither see nor know existing things.

(4) So these statements are not consistent with one another. For although we say that there are many things, everlasting(?), having forms and strength, it seems to us that they all alter and change from what is seen on each occasion.

(5) It is clear therefore that we have not been seeing correctly, and that those things do not correctly seem to us to be many; for they would not change if they were real, but each would be as it seemed to be. For nothing is stronger than that which is real.

(6) And if it changed, being would have been destroyed, and not-being would have come into being. Thus, therefore, if things are many, they must be such as the one is.

9. If therefore being is, it must be one; and if it is one, it is bound not to have body. But if it had bulk, it would have parts, and would no longer be. [Cf. Vlastos's translation on page 24 above.]

10. If being is divided, it moves; and if it moved, it could not be.

. . .

# THE PLURALISTS

## EMPEDOCLES

The philosophers who came after the Eleatics, down to Plato and Aristotle, were concerned to show how change *was* possible. The first three philosophers to make this attempt are sometimes lumped together as "the Pluralists," for each of them tried to explain change by invoking several ultimate principles.

The first of these was Empedocles of Agrigentum, in Sicily, where an excellently preserved Greek temple of his time still stands, along with the ruins of several others. Like the more legendary Pythagoras, he fused scientific thought with religious concerns and left other people with the definite impression that he had performed miracles. He is said to have ended his life by leaping into the crater of Mount Etna. Friedrich Hölderlin, one of the greatest German poets, who was also a close friend of Hegel's, left several drafts, one almost finished, for a drama on "The Death of Empedocles," in five acts.

Empedocles wrote two poems, "On Nature" and "Purifications." The former is said to have been divided into two books, totalling 2,000 lines, of which less than 400 have survived. According to Diogenes Laertius, the two poems together came to 5,000 lines; if so, even less than one-fifth of the "Purifications" has come down to us.

As a person, Empedocles comes to life for us more than any other pre-Socratic, save only Heraclitus. Of an aristocratic family, he opposed tyranny and reputedly refused the crown of his native town. Like Pythagoras, he believed in the transmigration of souls; also like Pythagoras, he spoke of himself as a god. E. R. Dodds, in his splendidly illuminating and suggestive book *on The Greeks and Irrational* (published as a paperback by the University of California Press), speaks of Empedocles as a shaman.

Empedocles was the first great synthesizer of the history of philosophy. Around 450 B.C., a full century before Aristotle, he tried to find a place in his thought for all the major contributions of his predecessors. By explaining generation and destruction, if not all change, in terms of mixture and separation, Empedocles tried to reconcile Heraclitus' insistence on the reality of change with the Eleatic claim that generation and destruction are unthinkable. Going back to the Greeks' traditional belief in four elements, he found a place for Thales' water, Anaximenes' air, and Heraclitus' fire, adding to them earth. In addition to these four, which Aristotle might have called "material causes," Empedocles postulated two "efficient causes": strife (Heraclitus' great principle) and love. He envisaged four successive ages: an age of love or perfect mixture in the beginning; then gradual separation as strife enters; then complete separation as strife rules; finally, as love enters again, a gradual mixture.

The fragments are given in Freeman's translations.

. . .

Empedocles of Agrigentum was born not long after Anaxagoras, and was an admirer and associate of Parmenides, and even more of the Pythagoreans. [Simplicius, *Phys.* 25, 19; R 411.]

Anaxagoras of Clazomenae, though older than Empedocles, was later in his philosophical activity. [Aristotle, *Metaphysics* A 3, 984 a; see below under Aristotle.]

. . .

2. For limited are the means of grasping (*i.e. the organs of sense-perception*) which are scattered throughout their limbs, and many are the miseries that press in and blunt the thoughts. And having looked at (*only*) a small part of existence during their lives, doomed to perish swiftly like smoke they are carried aloft and wafted away, believing only that upon which as individuals they chance to hit as they wander in all directions; but every man preens himself on having found the Whole: so little are these things to be seen by men or to be heard, or to be comprehended by the mind! But you, since you have come

here into retirement, shall learn—not more than mortal intellect can attain.

. . .

8. I shall tell you another thing: there is no creation of substance in any one of mortal existences, nor any end in execrable death, but only mixing and exchange of what has been mixed; and the name "substance" (*Physis, "nature"*) is applied to them by mankind.

. . .

9. But men, when these (*the Elements*) have been mixed in the form of a man and come into the light, or in the form of a species of wild animals, or plants, or birds, then say that this has "come into being"; and when they separate, this men call sad fate (*death*). The terms that right demands they do not use; but through custom I myself also apply these names.

. . .

12. From what in no wise exists, it is impossible for anything to come into being; and for being to perish completely is incapable of fulfilment and unthinkable; for it will always be there, wher-

ever anyone may place it on any occasion.

13. Nor is there any part of the whole that is empty or overfull.

14. No part of the whole is empty; so whence could anything additional come?

• • •

17. I shall tell of a double (*process*): at one time it increased so as to be a single one out of many; at another time again it grew apart so as to be many out of one. There is a double creation of mortals and a double decline: the union of all things causes the birth and destruction of the one (*race of mortals*), the other is reared as the elements grow apart, and then flies asunder. And these (*elements*) never cease their continuous exchange, sometimes uniting under the influence of love, so that all become one, at other times again each moving apart through the hostile force of hate. Thus in so far as they have the power to grow into one out of many, and again, when the one grows apart and many are formed, in this sense they come into being and have no stable life; but in so far as they never cease their continuous exchange, in this sense they remain always unmoved (*unaltered*) as they follow the cyclic process.

But come, listen to my discourse! For be assured, learning will increase your understanding. As I said before, revealing the aims of my discourse, I shall tell you of a double process. At one time it increased so as to be a single one out of many; at another time it grew apart so as to be many out of one—fire and water and earth and the boundless height of air, and also execrable hate apart from these, of equal weight in all directions, and love in their midst, their equal in length and breadth. Observe her with your mind, and do not sit with wondering eyes! She it is who is believed to be implanted in mortal limbs also; through her they think friendly thoughts and perform harmonious actions, calling her joy

and Aphrodite. No mortal man has perceived her as she moves in and out among them. But *you* must listen to the undeceitful progress of my argument.

All these (*elements*) are equal and of the same age in their creation; but each presides over its own office, and each has its own character, and they prevail in turn in the course of time. And besides these, nothing else comes into being, nor does anything cease. For if they had been perishing continuously, they would be no more; and what could increase the whole? And whence could it have come? In what direction could it perish, since nothing is empty of these things? No, but these things alone exist, and running through one another they become different things at different times, and are ever continuously the same.

• • •

20. This process is clearly to be seen throughout the mass of mortal limbs: sometimes through love all the limbs which the body has as its lot come together into one, in the prime of flourishing life; at another time again, sundered by evil feuds, they wander severally by the breakers of the shore of life. Likewise too with shrub-plants and fish in their watery dwelling, and beasts with mountain lairs and diver-birds that travel on wings.

21. But come, observe the following witness to my previous discourse, lest in my former statements there was any substance of which the form was missing. Observe the sun, bright to see and hot everywhere, and all the immortal things (*heavenly bodies*) drenched with its heat and brilliant light; and the rain, dark and chill over everything; and from the earth issue forth things based on the soil and solid. But in (*the reign of*) wrath they are all different in form and separate, while in (*the reign of*) love they come together and long for one another. For from these (*elements*) come all things that were and are and

will be; and trees spring up, and men and women, and beasts and birds and water-nurtured fish, and even the long-lived gods who are highest in honour. For these (*elements*) alone exist, but by running through one another they become different; to such a degree does mixing change them.

22. For all these things—beaming sun and earth and heaven and sea—are connected in harmony with their own parts: all those (*parts*) which have been sundered from them and exist in mortal limbs. Similarly all those things which are suitable for mixture are made like one another and united in affection by Aphrodite. But those things which differ most from one another in origin and mixture and the forms in which they are moulded are completely unaccustomed to combine, and are very baneful because of the commands of hate, in that hate has wrought their origin.

. . .

24. ... Touching on summit after summit, not to follow a single path of discourse to the end.

25. For what is right can well be uttered even twice.

26. In turn they get the upper hand in the revolving cycle, and perish into one another and increase in the turn appointed by fate. For they alone exist, but running through one another they become men and the tribes of other animals, sometimes uniting under the influence of love into one ordered whole, at other times again each moving apart through the hostile force of hate, until growing together into the whole which is one, they are quelled. Thus in so far as they have the power to grow into one out of many, and again, when the one grows apart and many are formed, in this sense they come into being and have no stable life; but in so far as they never cease their continuous exchange, in this sense they remain always unmoved (*unaltered*) as they follow the cyclic process.

27. (*The sphere under the dominion of love*): Therein are articulated neither the swift limbs of the sun, nor the shaggy might of earth, nor the sea: so firmly is it (*the whole*) fixed in a close-set secrecy, a rounded Sphere enjoying a circular solitude.

. . .

28. But he (*god*) is equal in all directions to himself and altogether eternal, a rounded sphere enjoying a circular solitude.

29. For there do not start two branches from his back; (*he has*) no feet, no swift knees, no organs of reproduction; but he was a sphere, and in all directions equal to himself.

. . .

35. But I will go back to the path of song which I formerly laid down, drawing one argument from another: that (*path which shows how*) when hate has reached the bottommost abyss of the eddy, and when love reaches the middle of the whirl, then in it (*the whirl*) all these things come together so as to be one—not all at once, but voluntarily uniting, some from one quarter, others from another. And as they mixed, there poured forth countless races of mortals. But many things stand unmixed side by side with the things mixing—all those which hate (*still*) aloft checked, since it had not yet faultlessly withdrawn from the whole to the outermost limits of the circle, but was remaining in some places, and in other places departing from the limbs (*of the sphere*). But in so far as it went on quietly streaming out, to the same extent there was entering a benevolent immortal inrush of faultless love. And swiftly those things became mortal which previously had experienced immortality, and things formerly unmixed became mixed, changing their paths. And as they mixed, there poured forth countless races of mortals, equipped with forms of every sort, a marvel to behold.

36. As they came together, hate returned to the outermost.

.   .   .

45. There whirls round the earth a circular borrowed light.

.   .   .

48. It is the earth that makes night by coming in the way of the (*sun's*) rays.

.   .   .

55. Sea, the sweat of earth.

.   .   .

58. Limbs wandered alone.

.   .   .

60. Creatures with rolling gait and innumerable hands.

.   .   .

100. The way everything breathes in and out is as follows: all have tubes of flesh, empty of blood, which extend over the surface of the body; and at the mouths of these tubes the outermost surface of the skin is perforated with frequent pores, so as to keep in the blood while a free way is cut for the passage of the air. Thus, when the thin blood flows back from here, the air, bubbling, rushes in in a mighty wave; and when the blood leaps up (*to the surface*), there is an expiration of air. As when a girl, playing with a water-catcher of shining brass—when, having placed the mouth of the pipe on her well-shaped hand she dips the vessel into the yielding substance of silvery water, still the volume of air pressing from inside on the many holes keeps out the water, until she uncovers the condensed stream (*of air*). Then at once when the air flows out, the water flows in in an equal quantity. Similarly, when water occupies the depths of the brazen vessel, and the opening or passage is stopped by the human flesh (*hand*), and the air out-side, striving to get in, checks the water, by controlling the surface at the entrance of the noisy strainer until she lets go with her hand: then again, in exactly the opposite way from what happened before, as the air rushes in, the water flows out in equal volume. Similarly when the thin blood, rushing through the limbs. flows back into the interior, straightway a stream of air flows in with a rush; and when the blood flows up again, again there is a breathing-out in equal volume.

.   .   .

110. If you press them deep into your firm mind, and contemplate them with good will and a studious care that is pure, these things will all assuredly remain with you throughout your life; and you will obtain many other things from them; for these things of themselves cause each (*element*) to increase in the character, according to the way of each man's nature. But if you intend to grasp after different things such as dwell among men in countless numbers and blunt their thoughts, miserable (*trifles*), certainly these things will quickly desert you in the course of time, longing to return to their own original kind. For all things, be assured, have intelligence and a portion of thought.

111. You shall learn all the drugs that exist as a defence against illness and old age; for you alone will I accomplish all this. You shall check the force of the unwearying winds which rush upon the earth with their blasts and lay waste the cultivated fields. And again, if you wish, you shall conduct the breezes back again. You shall create a seasonable dryness after the dark rain for mankind, and again you shall create after summer drought the streams that nourish the trees and [which will flow in the sky].[1] And you shall bring out of Hades a dead man restored to strength.

---

1 Reading corrupt.

## Katharmoi *(Purifications)*

112. Friends, who dwell in the great town on the city's heights, looking down on yellow Agrigentum, you who are occupied with good deeds, who are harbours treating foreigners with respect, and who are unacquainted with wickedness: greeting! I go about among you as an immortal god, no longer a mortal, held in honour by all, as I seem (*to them to deserve*), crowned with fillets and flowing garlands. When I come to them in their flourishing towns, to men and women, I am honoured; and they follow me in thousands, to inquire where is the path of advantage, some desiring oracles, while others ask to hear a word of healing for their manifold diseases, since they have long been pierced with cruel pains.

113. But why do I lay stress on these things, as if I were achieving something great in that I surpass mortal men who are liable to many forms of destruction?

114. Friends, I know that truth is present in the story that I shall tell; but it is actually very difficult for men, and the impact of conviction on their minds is unwelcome.

115. There is an oracle of necessity, an ancient decree of the gods, eternal, sealed fast with broad oaths, that when one of the divine spirits whose portion is long life sinfully stains his own limbs with bloodshed, and following hate has sworn a false oath—these must wander for thrice ten thousand seasons far from the company of the blessed, being born throughout the period into all kinds of mortal shapes, which exchange one hard way of life for another. For the mighty air chases them into the sea, and the sea spews them forth on to the dry land, and the earth (*drives them*) towards the rays of the blazing sun; and the Sun hurls them into the eddies of the Aether. One (*Element*) receives them from the other, and all loathe them. Of this number am I too now, a fugitive from heaven and a wanderer, because I trusted in raging Hate.

. . .

117. For by now I have been born as boy, girl, plant, bird, and dumb sea-fish.

118. I wept and wailed when I saw the unfamiliar land (*at birth*).

119. How great the honour, how deep the happiness from which (*I am exiled*)!

136. Will ye not cease from this harsh-sounding slaughter? Do you not see that you are devouring one another in the thoughtlessness of your minds?

. . .

# ANAXAGORAS

Anaxagoras came from Clazomenae on the coast of Asia Minor, not far northwest of Colophon (Xenophanes' home) and Ephesus (Heraclitus' home). He was the first of the Greek philosophers to move to Athens, where he became a good friend of Pericles, the greatest statesman of the time, who gave his name to the whole epoch. The dates are uncertain, but he may have been born about 500 B.C. and come to Athens around 480. He lived in Athens during the time of her greatest glory, a contemporary of Aeschylus, Sophocles, and Euripides.

He taught that everything consists of an infinite number of particles or seeds, and that in all things there is a portion of everything. Hair could not come from what is not hair, nor could flesh come from what is not flesh. The names we apply to things are determined by the preponderance of certain kinds of seeds in them, e.g., hair seeds or flesh seeds. Like Empedocles, he added to such "material causes" an "efficient cause" to account for the motion and direction of things—however, he added only one "efficient cause," which was mind, *nous* in Greek. The introduction of mind led Aristotle to hail Anaxagoras as the only sober man among the pre-Socratics; but Aristotle found fault with Anaxagoras for not making more use of this new principle to explain natural events. The modern reader is more likely to commend Anaxagoras on that score, having wearied of centuries of purposive explanations.

Anaxagoras was the first philosopher to be tried formally on a charge of heresy or impiety. He went into exile at Lampsacus on the Hellespont, where he died about 428/7, a year after Pericles. His sole book was still on sale in Athens at the end of the century, for one drachma.

The fragments are given in Freeman's translations, for once with her profuse capitals.

· · ·

He is said to have been twenty years old at the time of Xerxes' crossing, and to have lived to seventy-two. . . . He began to be a philosopher at Athens in the archonship of Callias, at the age of twenty, as Demetrius Phalereus tells us in his *Register of Archons,* and is said to have spent thirty years there. . . . Of his trial different accounts are given. Sotion, in his *Succession of Philosophers,* says that he was prosecuted for impiety by Cleon, because he claimed that the sun was a red-hot mass of metal, and that after Pericles, his pupil, had made a speech in his defense, he was fined five talents and exiled. Satyrus, in his *Lives,* on the other hand, says that the charge was brought by Thucydides in his political campaign against Pericles; and he adds that the charge was not only for impiety but for Medism ["treasonable correspondence with Persia," as another translator puts it] as well; and he was condemned to death in absence. . . . Finally he withdrew to Lampsacus, and there died. It is said that when the rulers of the city asked him what privilege he wished to be granted, he replied that the children should be given a holiday every year in the month in which he died. The custom is preserved to the present day. When he died, the Lampsacenes buried him with full honors. [Diogenes Laertius II, 7-15; R 487.]

Anaxagoras, the natural philosopher, was a distinguished Clazomenion . . . and his own pupils included . . . Euripides, the poet. [Strabo 14, p. 645 Cas.; R 490.]

Those who wrote only one book include Melissus, Parmenides, and Anaxagoras. [Diogenes Laertius I, 16; R 494.]

· · ·

1. (*Opening sentences from his book "On Natural Science"*) All Things were together, infinite in number and in smallness. For the Small also was infinite. And since all were together, nothing was distinguishable because of its smallness. For Air and Aether dominated all things, both of them being infinite. For these are the most important (*Elements*) in the total mixture, both in number and in size.

2. Air and Aether are separated off from the surrounding multiplicity, and that which surrounds is infinite in number.

3. For in Small there is no Least, but only a Lesser: for it is impossible that Being should Not-Be [that what is should cease to be: Raven], and in Great there is always a Greater. And it is equal in number to the small, but each thing is [in relation: Raven] to itself both great and small.

4. Conditions being thus, one must believe that there are many things of all sorts in all composite products, and the seeds of all Things, which contain all kinds of shapes and colours and pleasant savours. And men too were fitted together, and all other creatures which have life. And the men possessed both inhabited cities and artificial works [cultivated fields: Raven] just like ourselves, and they had sun and moon and the rest, just as we have, and the earth produced for them many and diverse things, of which they collected the most useful, and now use them for [or, "in"] their dwellings. This I say concerning Separation, that it must have taken place not only with us, but elsewhere.

Before these things were separated off, all things were together, nor was any colour distinguishable, for the mixing of all Things prevented this, *(namely)* the mixing of moist and dry and hot and cold and bright and dark, and there was a great quantity of earth in the mixture, and seeds infinite in number, not at all like one another. For none of the other things either is like any other. And as this was so, one must believe that all Things were present in the Whole.

5. These things being thus separated off, one must understand that all things are in no wise less or more (for it is not possible for them to be more than All), but all things are forever equal *(in quantity)*.

6. And since there are equal *(quantitative)* parts of Great and Small, so too similarly in everything there must be everything. It is not possible *(for them)* to exist apart, but all things contain a portion of everything. Since it is not possible for the Least to exist, it cannot be isolated, nor come into being by itself; but as it was in the beginning, so now, all things are together. In all things there are many things, and of the things separated off, there are equal numbers in *(the categories)* Great and Small.

7. So that the number of the things separated off cannot be known either in thought or in fact.

8. The things in the one Cosmos are not separated off from one another with an axe, neither the Hot from the Cold, nor the Cold from the Hot.

9. Thus these things circulate and are separated off by force and speed. The speed makes the force. Their speed is not like the speed of any of the Things now existing among mankind, but altogether many times as fast.

10. How can hair come from not-hair, and flesh from not-flesh?

11. In everything there is a portion of everything except Mind; and some things contain Mind also.

12. Other things all contain a part of everything, but Mind is infinite and self-ruling, and is mixed with no Thing, but is alone by itself. If it were not by itself, but were mixed with anything else, it would have had a share of all Things, if it were mixed with anything; for in everything there is a portion of everything, as I have said before. And the things mixed *(with Mind)* would have prevented it, so that it could not rule over any Thing in the same way as it can being alone by itself. For it is the finest of all Things, and the purest, and has complete understanding of everything, and has the greatest power. All things which have life, both the greater and the less, are ruled by Mind. Mind took command of the universal revolution, so as to make *(things)* re-

volve at the outset. And at first things began to revolve from some small point, but now the revolution extends over a greater area, and will spread even further. And the things which were mixed together, and separated off, and divided, were all understood by Mind. And whatever they were going to be, and whatever things were then in existence that are not now, and all things that now exist and whatever shall exist—all were arranged by Mind, as also the revolution now followed by the stars, the sun and moon, and the Air and Aether which were separated off. It was this revolution which caused the separation off. And dense separates from rare, and hot from cold, and bright from dark, and dry from wet. There are many portions of many things. And nothing is absolutely separated off or divided the one from the other except Mind. Mind is all alike, both the greater and the less. But nothing else is like anything else, but each individual thing is and was most obviously that of which it contains the most.

13. And when Mind began the motion, there was a separating-off from all that was being moved; and all that Mind set in motion was separated (internally); and as things were moving and separating off (internally), the revolution greatly increased this (internal) separation.

14. Mind, which ever Is, certainly still exists also where all other things are, (namely) in the multiple surrounding (mass) and in the things which were separated off before, and in the things already separated off [things that have been either aggregated or separated: Raven].

15. The dense and moist and cold and dark (Elements) collected here, where now is Earth, and the rare and hot and dry went outwards to the furthest part of the Aether.

16. From these, while they are separating off, Earth solidifies; for from the clouds, water is separated off, and from the water, earth, and from the earth, stones are solidified by the cold; and these rush outward rather than the water.

17. The Greeks have an incorrect belief on Coming into Being and Passing Away. No Thing comes into being or passes away, but it is mixed together or separated from existing Things. Thus they would be correct if they called coming into being "mixing," and passing away "separation-off."

18. It is the sun that endows the moon with its brilliance.

19. We give the name Iris to the reflection of the sun on the clouds. It is therefore the sign of a storm, for the water which flows round the cloud produces wind or forces out rain.

. . .

21. Through the weakness of the sense-perceptions, we cannot judge truth.

. . .

# DEMOCRITUS (and LEUCIPPUS)

Democritus of Abdera, on the coast of Thrace, was probably born in 460 B.C. Together with Leucippus, his teacher, he was the prime exponent of the philosophy known as atomism. Leucippus' work has perished, but we have many reports about the atomistic philosophy, especially in its Democritean form; a few of Democritus' remarks on knowledge and reality have survived; a collection of Democritus' ethical maxims—the so-called Gnomae—has come down to us; and finally we also have a large number of fragments from his other writings, dealing with ethics. This material is offered in four sections here: first, the reports (in Raven's translations); then the metaphysical and epistemological fragments; next, the *Gnomae;* and eventually the fragments on ethics—all in Freeman's versions.

There are three reasons for allotting so much space to Democritus. First, we have much more material on him than on any of his predecessors. Second, although atomism represents another pluralistic answer to Parmenides, along with the philosophies of Empedocles and Anaxagoras, and although Leucippus was a pre-Socratic, Democritus was actually a slightly younger contemporary of Socrates and an older contemporary of Plato. His philosophy may be viewed as an important alternative to Platonism— as one follows the development of pre-Socratic thought, the road forks in the end, one path leading to Democritus, the other to Plato. Third, Democritus does not by any means represent a dead end; his thought was taken up first by Epicurus and then, in Roman times, by Lucretius. Epicurus is represented later in the present volume, but Lucretius is not. Because we are here dispensing with Roman copies, we are in a position to give more space to the Greek originals.

That so much of Democritus' thought on ethics has come down to us is our good fortune: atomism has often been contrasted with Platonism as materialism versus idealism. It is worth noting, then, that Democritus' ethic was no less lofty than Plato's.

• • •

## A. Ancient Reports on Atomism

Leucippus of Elea or Miletus (both accounts are current) had associated with Parmenides in philosophy, but in his view of reality he did not follow the same path as Parmenides and Xenophanes but rather, it seems, the opposite path. For while they regarded the whole as one, motionless, uncreated, and limited, and forbade even the search for what is not, he posited innumerable elements in perpetual motion—namely the atoms—and held that the number of their shapes was infinite, on the ground that there was no reason why any atom should be of one shape rather than another; for he observed too that coming-into-being and change are incessant in the world. Further he held that not-being exists as well as being, and the two are equally the causes of things coming-into-being. The nature of

atoms he supposed to be compact and full; that, he said, was being, and it moved in the void, which he called not-being and held to exist no less than being. In the same way his associate, Democritus of Abdera, posited as principles the full and the void. [Simplicius, *Phys.* 28, 4; R 546.]

Apollodorus in the *Chronicles* says that Epicurus was instructed by Nausiphanes and Praxiphanes; but Epicurus himself denies this, saying in the letter to Eurylochus that he instructed himself. He and Hemarchus both maintain that there never was a philosopher Leucippus, who, some (including Apollodorus the Epicurean) say, was the teacher of Democritus. [Diogenes Laertius X, 13; R 547.]

Leucippus postulated atoms and void, and in this Democritus resembled him though in other respects he was more productive. [Cicero, *Academica pr.* II, 37, 118; R 548.]

Later he [Democritus] met Leucippus and, according to some, Anaxagoras also, whose junior he was by forty years. . . . As he himself says in the *Little World-System,* he was a young man in the old age of Anaxagoras, being forty years younger. [Diogenes Laertius IX, 34; R 549.]

Demetrius in his *Homonyms* and Antisthenes in his *Successions* say that he [Democritus] traveled to Egypt to visit the priests and learn geometry, and that he went also to Persia to visit the Chaldaeans, and to the Red Sea. Some say that he associated with the "naked philosophers" in India; also that he went to Ethiopia. [*Ibid.*, IX, 35; R 551.]

Leucippus thought he had a theory which, being consistent with sense-perception, would not do away with coming-into-being or perishing or motion or the multiplicity of things. So much he conceded to appearances, while to those who uphold the one [the Eleatics] he granted that motion is impossible without void, that the void is not-being, and that no part of being is not-being. For being in the proper sense is an absolute *plenum.* But such a *plenum* is not one, but there is an infinite number of them, and they are invisible owing to the smallness of their bulk. They move in the void (for the void exists), and by their coming together they effect coming-into-being, by their separation perishing. [Aristotle, *De Gen. et Corr.*, A 8, 325a; R 552.]

They [Leucippus, Democritus, and Epicurus] said that the first principles were infinite in number, and thought they were indivisible atoms and impassible owing to their compactness, and without any void in them; divisibility comes about because of the void in compound bodies. [Simplicius, *De Caelo* 242, 18; R 556.]

To this extent they differed, that one [Epicurus] supposed that all atoms were very small and on that account imperceptible; the other, Democritus, that there are some atoms that are very large. [Dionysius *ap.* Eusebium P.E. XIV, 23, 3; R 560.]

Democritus holds the same view as Leucippus about the elements, full and void . . . he spoke as if the things that are were in constant motion in the void; and there are innumerable worlds which differ in size. In some worlds there is no sun and moon, in others they are larger than in our world, and in others more numerous. The intervals between the worlds are unequal; in some parts there are more worlds, in others fewer; some are increasing, some at their height, some decreasing; in some parts they are arising, in other failing. They are destroyed by colliding with each other. There are some worlds without any living creatures, plants, or moisture. [Hyppolytus *Ref.* I, 13, 2; R 564*.]

Everything happens according to necessity; for the cause of the coming-into-being of all things is the whirl, which he calls necessity. [Diogenes Laertius IX, 45; R 565; cf. "the only extant saying of Leucippus himself, R 568, Fr. 2, Aetius I, 25, 4: Nothing occurs at random, but everything for a reason and by necessity."]

As they [the atoms] move, they collide and become entangled in such a way as to cling in close contact to one another, but not so as to form one substance of them in reality of any kind whatever; for it is very simple-minded to suppose that two or more could ever become one. The reason he gives for atoms staying together for a while is the intertwining and mutual hold of the primary bodies; for some of them are angular, some hooked, some concave, some convex, and indeed with countless other differences; so he thinks they cling to each other and stay together until such time as some stronger necessity comes from the surrounding and shakes and scatters them apart. [Aristotle *On Democritus ap.* Simplicium *De Caelo* 295, 11; R 581.]

Democritus says that the spherical is the most mobile of shapes; and such is mind and fire. [Aristotle, *De Anima*, A 2, 405a; R 583.]

Democritus and the majority of natural philosophers who discuss perception are guilty of a great absurdity, for they represent all perception as being by touch. [Aristotle, *De Sensu* 4, 442a; R 585.]

Leucippus, Democritus, and Epicurus say that perception and thought arise when images enter from outside; neither occurs to anybody without an image impinging. [Aetius IV, 8; R 586.]

Democritus explains sight by the visual image, which he describes in a peculiar way; the visual image does not arise directly in the pupil, but the air between the eye and the object of sight is contracted and stamped by the object seen and the seer; for from everything there is always a sort of effluence proceeding. So this air, which is solid and variously colored, appears in the eye, which is moist (?); the eye does not admit the dense part, but the moist passes through [Theophrastus, *De Sensu* 50; R 587.]

## B. Metaphysical and Epistemological Fragments

7. We know nothing about anything really, but opinion is for all individuals an inflowing (? *of the atoms*). (*From "On the Forms."*)

8. It will be obvious that it is impossible to understand how in reality each thing is. (*From "On the Forms."*)

9. Sweet exists by convention, bitter by convention, colour by convention; atoms and void (*alone*) exist in reality

... We know nothing accurately in reality, but (*only*) as it changes according to the bodily condition, and the constitution of those things that flow upon (*the body*) and impinge upon it.

10. It has often been demonstrated that we do not grasp how each thing is or is not.

11. There are two sorts of knowledge, one genuine, one bastard (*or "obscure"*). To the latter belong all the following: sight, hearing, smell, taste, touch. The real is separated from this. When the bastard can do no more—neither see more minutely, nor hear, nor smell, nor taste, nor perceive by touch—and a finer investigation is needed, then the genuine comes in as having a tool for distinguishing more finely. (*From "The Canon."*)

• • •

156. Naught exists just as much as Aught.

## C. The So-Called Gnomae (complete)

35. If any man listens to my opinions, here recorded, with intelligence, he will achieve many things worthy of a good man, and avoid doing many unworthy things.

36. It is right that men should value the soul rather than the body; for perfection of soul corrects the inferiority of the body, but physical strength without intelligence does nothing to improve the mind.

37. He who chooses the advantages of the soul chooses things more divine, but he who chooses those of the body, chooses things human.

38. It is noble to prevent the criminal; but if one cannot, one should not join him in crime.

39. One must either be good, or imitate a good man.

40. Men find happiness neither by

means of the body nor through posses-sions, but through uprightness and wis-dom.

41. Refrain from crimes not through fear but through duty.

42. It is a great thing, when one is in adversity, to think of duty.

43. Repentance for shameful deeds is salvation in life.

44. One should tell the truth, not speak at length.

45. The wrongdoer is more un-fortunate than the man wronged.

46. Magnanimity consists in endur-ing tactlessness with mildness.

47. Well-ordered behaviour consists in obedience to the law, the ruler, and the man wiser (*than oneself*).

48. When inferior men censure, the good man pays no heed.

49. It is hard to be governed by one's inferior.

50. The man completely enslaved to wealth can never be honest.

51. In power of persuasion, reasoning is far stronger than gold.

52. He who tries to give intelligent advice to one who thinks he has intel-ligence, is wasting his time.

53. Many who have not learnt reason, nevertheless live according to reason.

53a. Many whose actions are most disgraceful practise the best utterances.

54. The foolish learn sense through misfortune.

55. One should emulate the deeds and actions of virtue, not the words.

56. Noble deeds are recognised and emulated by those of natural good dis-position.

57. Good breeding in cattle depends on physical health, but in men on a well-formed character.

58. The hopes of right-thinking men are attainable, but those of the unintel-ligent are impossible.

59. Neither skill nor wisdom is at-tainable unless one learns.

60. It is better to examine one's own faults than those of others.

61. Those whose character is well-ordered have also a well-ordered life.

62. Virtue consists, not in avoiding wrong-doing, but in having no wish thereto.

63. To pronounce praise on noble deeds is noble; for to do so over base deeds is the work of a false deceiver.

64. Many much-learned men have no intelligence.

65. One should practise much-sense, not much-learning.

66. It is better to deliberate before action than to repent afterwards.

67. Believe not everything, but only what is approved: the former is foolish, the latter the act of a sensible man.

68. The worthy and the unworthy man (*are to be known*) not only by their actions, but also their wishes.

69. For all men, good and true are the same; but pleasant differs for dif-ferent men.

70. Immoderate desire is the mark of a child, not a man.

71. Untimely pleasures produce un-pleasantnesses.

72. Violent desire for one thing blinds the soul to all others.

73. Virtuous love consists in decorous desire for the beautiful.

74. Accept no pleasure unless it is beneficial.

75. It is better for fools to be ruled than to rule.

76. For the foolish, not reason but advantage is the teacher.

77. Fame and wealth without intel-ligence are dangerous possessions.

78. To make money is not without use, but if it comes from wrong-doing, nothing is worse.

79. It is a bad thing to imitate the bad, and not even to wish to imitate the good.

80. It is shameful to be so busy over the affairs of others that one knows nothing of one's own.

81. Constant delay means work undone.

82. The false and the seeming-good are those who do all in word, not in fact.

83. The cause of error is ignorance of the better.

84. The man who does shameful deeds must first feel shame in his own eyes.

85. He who contradicts and chatters much is ill-fitted for learning what he ought.

86. It is greed to do all the talking and not be willing to listen.

87. One must be on one's guard against the bad man, lest he seize his opportunity.

88. The envious man torments himself like an enemy.

89. An enemy is not he who injures, but he who wishes to do so.

90. The enmity of relatives is much worse than that of strangers.

91. Be not suspicious towards all, but be cautious and firm.

92. Accept favours in the foreknowledge that you will have to give a greater return for them.

93. When you do a favour, study the recipient first, lest he prove a scoundrel and repay evil for good.

94. Small favours at the right time are greatest to the recipients.

95. Marks of honour are greatly valued by right-thinking men, who understand why they are being honoured.

96. The generous man is he who does not look for a return, but who does good from choice.

97. Many who seem friendly are not so, and those who do not seem so, are.

98. The friendship of one intelligent man is better than that of all the unintelligent.

99. Life is not worth living for the man who has not even one good friend.

100. The man whose tested friends do not stay long with him is badtempered.

101. Many avoid their friends when they fall from wealth to poverty.

102. In all things, equality is fair, excess and deficiency not so, in my opinion.

103. The man who loves nobody is, I think, loved by no one.

104. In old age, a man is agreeable if his manner is pleasant and his speech serious.

105. Physical beauty is (*merely*) animal unless intelligence be present.

106. In prosperity it is easy to find a friend, in adversity nothing is so difficult.

107. Not all one's relatives are friends, but only those who agree with us about what is advantageous.

107a. It is proper, since we are human beings, not to laugh at the misfortunes of others, but to mourn.

108. Good things are obtained with difficulty if one seeks; but bad things come without our even seeking.

109. The censorious are not well-fitted for friendship.

110. A woman must not practise argument: this is dreadful.

111. To be ruled by a woman is the ultimate outrage for a man.

112. It is the mark of the divine intellect to be always calculating something noble.

113. Those who praise the unintelligent do (*them*) great harm.

114. It is better to be praised by another than by oneself.

115. If you do not recognise (*i.e. understand*) praise, believe that you are being flattered.

## D. Fragments on Ethics

3. The man who wishes to have serenity of spirit should not engage in many activities, either private or public, nor choose activities beyond his power and natural capacity. He must guard against this, so that when good fortune strikes him and leads him on to excess by means of (*false*) seeming, he must rate it low, and not attempt things beyond his powers. A reasonable fullness is better than overfullness.

4. Pleasure and absence of pleasure are the criteria of what is profitable and what is not.

• • •

31. Medicine heals diseases of the body, wisdom frees the soul from passions.

32. Coition is a slight attack of apoplexy. For man gushes forth from man, and is separated by being torn apart with a kind of blow.

33. Nature and instruction are similar; for instruction transforms the man, and in transforming, creates his nature.

34. Man is a universe in little (Microcosm).

．．．

118. (*I would*) rather discover one cause than gain the kingdom of Persia.

．．．

159. If the body brought a suit against the soul, for all the pains it had endured throughout life, and the illtreatment, and I were to be the judge of the suit, I would gladly condemn the soul, in that it had partly ruined the body by its neglect and dissolved it with bouts of drunkenness, and partly destroyed it and torn it in pieces with its passion for pleasure—as if, when a tool or a vessel were in a bad condition, I blamed the man who was using it carelessly.

160. (*To live badly is*) not to live badly, but to spend a long time dying.

．．．

169. Do not try to understand everything, lest you become ignorant of everything.

170. Happiness, like unhappiness, is a property of the soul.

171. Happiness does not dwell in cattle or gold. The soul is the dwelling-place of the (*good and evil*) genius.

．．．

174. The cheerful man, who is impelled towards works that are just and lawful, rejoices by day and by night, and is strong and free from care. But the man who neglects justice, and does not do what he ought, finds all such things disagreeable when he remembers any of them, and he is afraid and torments himself.

175. But the gods are the givers of all good things, both in the past and now. They are not, however, the givers of things which are bad, harmful or non-beneficial, either in the past or now, but men themselves fall into these through blindness of mind and lack of sense.

．．．

180. Education is an ornament for the prosperous, a refuge for the unfortunate.

181. The man who employs exhortation and persuasion will turn out to be a more effective guide to virtue than he who employs law and compulsion. For the man who is prevented by law from wrongdoing will probably do wrong in secret, whereas the man who is led towards duty by persuasion will probably not do anything untoward either secretly or openly. Therefore the man who acts rightly through understanding and knowledge becomes at the same time brave and upright.

182. Beautiful objects are wrought by study through effort, but ugly things are reaped automatically without toil. For even one who is unwilling is sometimes so wrought upon by learning . . . . (? *MMS. corrupt.*)

．．．

184. Continuous association with base men increases a disposition to crime.

．．．

186. Similarity of outlook creates friendship.

．．．

188. The criterion of the advantageous and disadvantageous is enjoyment and lack of enjoyment.

．．．

190. One must avoid even speaking of evil deeds.

191. Cheerfulness is created for men through moderation of enjoyment and harmoniousness of life. Things that are in excess or lacking are apt to change and cause great disturbance in the soul. Souls which are stirred by great divergences are neither stable nor cheerful. Therefore one must keep one's mind on what is attainable, and be content with what one has, paying little heed to things envied and admired, and not dwelling on them in one's mind. Rather must you consider the lives of those in distress, reflecting on their intense sufferings, in order that your own possessions and condition may seem great and enviable, and you may, by ceasing to desire more, cease to suffer in your soul. For he who admires those who have, and who are called happy by other mortals, and who dwells on them in his mind every hour, is constantly compelled to undertake something new and to run the risk, through his desire, of doing something irretrievable among those things which the laws prohibit. Hence one must not seek the latter, but must be content with the former, comparing one's own life with that of those in worse cases, and must consider oneself fortunate, reflecting on their sufferings, in being so much better off than they. If you keep to this way of thinking, you will live more serenely, and will expel those not-negligible curses in life, envy, jealousy and spite.

194. The great pleasures come from the contemplation of noble works.

•  •  •

198. The animal needing something knows how much it needs, the man does not.

199. People are fools who hate life and yet wish to live through fear of Hades.

200. People are fools who live without enjoyment of life.

201. People are fools who yearn for long life without pleasure in long life.

202. People are fools who yearn for what is absent, but neglect what they have even when it is more valuable than what has gone.

•  •  •

206. Fools want to live to be old because they fear death.

207. One should choose not every pleasure, but only that concerned with the beautiful.

208. The self-control of the father is the greatest example for the children.

•  •  •

210. A rich table is provided by luck, but a sufficient one by wisdom.

211. Moderation multiplies pleasures, and increases pleasure.

212. Sleep in the daytime signifies bodily trouble or aberration of mind or laziness or lack of training.

213. Courage minimises difficulties.

214. The brave man is not only he who overcomes the enemy, but he who is stronger than pleasures. Some men are masters of cities, but are enslaved to women.

215. The reward of justice is confidence of judgement and imperturbability, but the end of injustice is the fear of disaster.

216. Imperturbable wisdom is worth everything.

•  •  •

219. The passion for wealth, unless limited by satisfaction, is far more painful than extreme poverty; for greater passions create greater needs.

•  •  •

222. The excessive accumulation of wealth for one's children is an excuse for covetousness, which thus displays its peculiar nature.

223. The things needed by the body are available to all without toil and trouble. But the things which require

toil and trouble and which make life disagreeable are not desired by the body but by the ill-constitution of the mind.

. . .

226. Freedom of speech is the sign of freedom; but the danger lies in discerning the right occasion.

227. Misers have the fate of bees: they work as if they were going to live for ever.

. . .

231. The right-minded man is he who is not grieved by what he has not, but enjoys what he has.

. . .

234. Men ask in their prayers for health from the gods, but do not know that the power to attain this lies in themselves; and by doing the opposite through lack of control, they themselves become the betrayers of their own health to their desires.

. . .

236. It is hard to fight desire; but to control it is the sign of a reasonable man.

. . .

239. Bad men, when they escape, do not keep the oaths which they make in time of stress.

. . .

242. More men become good through practice than by nature.

243. All kinds of toil are pleasanter than rest, when men attain that for which they labour, or know that they will attain it. But whenever there is failure to attain, then labour is painful and hard.

244. Do not say or do what is base, even when you are alone. Learn to feel shame in your own eyes much more than before others.

. . .

247. To a wise man, the whole earth is open; for the native land of a good soul is the whole earth.

. . .

249. Civil war is harmful to both parties; for both to the conquerors and the conquered, the destruction is the same.

. . .

251. Poverty under democracy is as much to be preferred to so-called prosperity under an autocracy as freedom to slavery.

252. One must give the highest importance to affairs of the state, that it may be well run; one must not pursue quarrels contrary to right, nor acquire a power contrary to the common good. The well-run state is the greatest protection, and contains all in itself; when this is safe, all is safe; when this is destroyed, all is destroyed.

. . .

260. Anyone killing any brigand or pirate shall be exempt from penalty, whether he do it by his own hand, or by instigation, or by vote.

261. One must punish wrong-doers to the best of one's ability, and not neglect it. Such conduct is just and good, but the neglect of it is unjust and bad.

262. Those who do what is deserving of exile or imprisonment or other punishment must be condemned and not let off. Whoever contrary to the law acquits a man, judging according to profit or pleasure, does wrong, and this is bound to be on his conscience.

. . .

264. One must not respect the opinion of other men more than one's own; nor must one be more ready to do wrong if no one will know than if all will know. One must respect one's own opinion most, and this must stand as the law of one's soul, preventing one from doing anything improper.

265. Men remember one's mistakes rather than one's successes. This is just; for as those who return a deposit do not deserve praise, whereas those who do not do so deserve blame and punishment, so with the official: he was elected not to make mistakes but to do things well.

. . .

270. Use slaves as parts of the body: each to his own function.

. . .

272. The man who is fortunate in his choice of a son-in-law gains a son; the man unfortunate in his choice loses his daughter also.

273. A woman is far sharper than a man in malign thoughts.

274. An adornment for a woman is lack of garrulity. Paucity of adornment is also beautiful.

275. The rearing of children is full of pitfalls. Success is attended by strife and care, failure means grief beyond all others.

276. I do not think that one should have children. I observe in the acquisition of children many great risks and many griefs, whereas a harvest is rare, and even when it exists, it is thin and poor.

277. Whoever wants to have children should, in my opinion, choose them from the family of one of his friends. He will thus obtain a child such as he wishes, for he can select the kind he wants. And the one that seems fittest will be most likely to follow on his natural endowment. The difference is that in the latter way one can take one child out of many who is according to one's liking; but if one begets a child of one's own, the risks are many, for one is bound to accept him as he is.

. . .

284. If your desires are not great, a little will seem much to you; for small appetite makes poverty equivalent to wealth.

285. One should realise that human life is weak and brief and mixed with many cares and difficulties, in order that one may care only for moderate possessions, and that hardship may be measured by the standard of one's needs.

286. He is fortunate who is happy with moderate means, unfortunate who is unhappy with great possessions.

. . .

289. It is unreasonablenesss not to submit to the necessary conditions of life.

290. Cast forth uncontrollable grief from your benumbed soul by means of reason.

291. To bear poverty well is the sign of a sensible man.

292. The hopes of the unintelligent are senseless.

293. Those to whom their neighbours' misfortunes give pleasure do not understand that the blows of fate are common to all; and also they lack cause for personal joy.

294. The good things of youth are strength and beauty, but the flower of age is moderation.

# THREE SOPHISTS

## *PROTAGORAS*

Protagoras, like Democritus, came from Abdera, on the Thracian coast.
He was the first of those traveling teachers of philosophy and rhetoric
who became known as "Sophists." Plato considered it his task to oppose
these men, and since his dialogues survive while their writings do not, his
highly polemical pictures of the Sophists have been widely but unreasonably
accepted as fair and accurate portraits, and the very name "Sophist" has
become an opprobrium. Yet one should no more accept Plato's image of
the Sophists at face value than one should take the picture of the Pharisees
in the Gospels for the gospel truth.

The Sophists are the great representatives of the Greek enlightenment.
They come after the bold speculators and metaphysicians and ask what
we can really know. Their thought is critical, not constructive; and their
criticisms do not stop before all kinds of prejudices and traditions. Some
of them question the hallowed distinction between Greeks and barbarians
and that between masters and slaves: is not the supposition that barbarians
and slaves are more similar to the animals than to the Greeks based on
convention rather than on evidence? They do not only question prejudices
of this sort—which Plato and Aristotle sought to revive—but all knowledge
and all ethics: how much can be defended rationally, and how much is
merely a matter of convention?

Questioning of that sort is inseparable from honesty, at least at a certain
level of maturity. But the Sophists do not seem to have boasted of their
honesty; on the contrary, their manner tended to be somewhat playful and

occasionally somewhat cynical. They enjoyed debating, liked to construct skilful, craftsmanlike speeches, and offered to teach young men how to do likewise. For such instruction they accepted money, insisting quite reasonably that the skills they taught were likely to spell success, especially in politics.

This combination of qualities made it easy for Plato to picture the Sophists in the darkest colors. One as hostile to Plato as Plato was to the Sophists could easily portray him as a reactionary who sought some sanction in another world for convictions threatened by the Greek enlightenment. Plato makes skilful use of Socrates, contrasting his ironic modesty with the Sophists' pomp, his acid questioning with their big speeches, his concern with the moral fiber of a man with their admitted interest in success. Even if one agrees that Socrates was inimitably greater than any of the Sophists, this does not settle any of the crucial issues. After all, he was greater than almost any other man; he would have balked at the ideas which Plato in the dialogues put into his mouth quite as much as he had ever balked at any of the Sophists' views. The question of the limits of knowledge and the role played by convention, especially in ethics, cannot be answered by making capital of the less appealing traits of one or another Sophist.

In sum, the Sophists represent a milestone in the history of human thought. But exceedingly few fragments survive. The following selections concentrate on three representative figures.

Of Protagoras, born in Abdera about 480 B.C., an ancient story relates that he was at first a porter and that Democritus of Abdera saw him, admired his poise, and decided to instruct him; but this story is very doubtful. Protagoras reflected on language and developed a system of grammar. Having settled in Athens where he taught the youths, he won the respect of Pericles, who commissioned him to frame laws for the new colony of Thurii, in Italy. At the age of seventy, he was accused and convicted of atheism and is said to have left for Sicily and to have drowned at sea.

Plato introduces him in one of his dialogues, which is named after Protagoras. Some of Protagoras' ideas about truth are also considered at some length in one of Plato's later dialogues, the *Theaetetus;* and the relevant sections are reprinted below under Plato. The fragments are given in Freeman's translations.

• • •

1. (*From "Truth" or "Refutatory Arguments."*) Of all things the measure is Man, of the things that are, that they are, and of the things that are not, that they are not.

2. (*From "On Being."*) (PORPHYRY: 'Few of the writings of Plato's predecessors have survived, otherwise Plato perhaps would have been detected in further plagiarisms. At any rate, in the place where I happened to have been reading in Protagoras' book "On Being" the argument he uses against those who make Being One, I find that he uses the same refutatory terms. For I took the trouble to memorise the passage word for word.')

3. (*From a treatise entitled "Great*

*Logos."*) Teaching needs endowment and practice. Learning must begin in youth.

4. (*From "On the Gods."*) About the gods, I am not able to know whether they exist or do not exist, nor what they are like in form; for the factors preventing knowledge are many: the obscurity of the subject, and the shortness of human life.

• • •

6b. To make the weaker cause the stronger.

• • •

9. When his sons, who were fine young men, died within eight days, he (Pericles) bore it without mourning. For he held on to his serenity, from which every day he derived great benefit in happiness, freedom from suffering, and honour in the people's eyes—for all who saw him bearing his griefs valiantly thought him great-souled and brave and superior to themselves, well knowing their own helplessness in such a calamity.

10. Art without practice, and practice without art, are nothing.

11. Education does not take root in the soul unless one goes deep.

## GORGIAS

Next to Protagoras, Gorgias was probably the most renowned of all the Sophists. (Regarding the Sophists, see the preface to the selections from Protagoras.) Gorgias came from Leontini, in southern Sicily, a little to the east of Agrigentum. His dates are uncertain, but he is said to have died at the age of 108, possibly as late as 375 B.C. He first came to Athens on a mission from his countrymen, who had asked him to enlist Athenian help against Syracuse; in this he succeeded.

Like Protagoras, he is introduced as one of the two main figures (the other being Socrates) in one of Plato's dialogues, which is named after him. The following selections, all translated by Freeman, comprise the one philosophic fragment that has come down to us (as a long quotation in Sextus Empiricus), a sample speech (the encomium on Helen), and three very short bits that may help to round out the picture of Gorgias.

• • •

3. (SEXTUS, *from "On Not-Being" or "On Nature."*)
I.   Nothing exists.
   (*a*) Not-Being does not exist.
   (*b*) Being does not exist.
      i.   as everlasting.
      ii.  as created.
      iii. as both.
      iv.  as One.
      v.   as Many.
   (*c*) A mixture of Being and Not-Being does not exist.
II.  If anything exists, it is incomprehensible.

III. If it is comprehensible, it is incommunicable.
I.   Nothing exists.
   If anything exists, it must be either Being or Not-Being, or both Being and Not-Being.
   (*a*) It cannot be Not-Being, for Not-Being does not exist; if it did, it would be at the same time Being and Not-Being, which is impossible.
   (*b*) It cannot be Being, for Being does not exist. If Being exists, it must be either everlasting, or created, or both.

i. It cannot be everlasting; if it were, it would have no beginning, and therefore would be boundless; if it is boundless, then it has no position, for if it had position it would be contained in something, and so it would no longer be boundless; for that which contains is greater than that which is contained, and nothing is greater than the boundless. It cannot be contained by itself, for then the thing containing and the thing contained would be the same, and Being would become two things—both position and body—which is absurd. Hence if Being is everlasting, it is boundless; if boundless, it has no position ("is nowhere"); if without position, it does not exist.

ii. Similarly, Being cannot be created; if it were, it must come from something, either Being or Not-Being, both of which are impossible.

iii. Similarly, Being cannot be both everlasting and created, since they are opposite. Therefore Being does not exist.

iv. Being cannot be one, because if it exists it has size, and is therefore infinitely divisible; at least it is threefold, having length, breadth and depth.

v. It cannot be many, because the many is made up of an addition of ones, so that since the one does not exist, the many do not exist either.

(c) A mixture of Being and Not-Being is impossible. Therefore since Being does not exist, nothing exists.

II. If anything exists, it is incomprehensible.

If the concepts of the mind are not realities, reality cannot be thought if the thing thought is white, then white is thought about; if the thing thought is non-existent, then non-existence is thought about; this is equivalent to saying that "existence, reality, is not thought about, cannot be thought." Many things thought above are not realities: we can conceive of a chariot running on the sea, or a winged man. Also, since things seen are the objects of sight, and things heard are the objects of hearing, and we accept as real things seen without their being heard, and vice versa; so we would have to accept things thought without their being seen or heard; but this would mean believing in things like the chariot racing on the sea.

Therefore reality is not the object of thought, and cannot be comprehended by it. Pure mind, as opposed to sense-perception, or even as an equally valid criterion, is a myth.

III. If anything is comprehensible, it is incommunicable.

The things which exist are perceptibles; the objects of sight are apprehended by sight, the objects of hearing by hearing, and there is no interchange; so that these sense-perceptions cannot communicate with one another. Further, that with which we communicate is speech, and speech is not the same thing as the things that exist, the perceptibles; so that we communicate not the things which exist, but only speech; just as that which is seen cannot become that which is heard, so our speech cannot be equated with that which exists, since it is outside us. Further, speech is composed from the percepts which we receive from without, that is, from perceptibles; so that it is not speech which communicates perceptibles, but perceptibles which create speech. Further, speech can never exactly represent perceptibles, since it is different from them, and perceptibles are apprehended each by the one kind of organ, speech by another. Hence, since the objects of sight cannot be presented to any other organ but sight, and the different sense-organs cannot give their information to one another, similarly speech cannot give any information about perceptibles.

Therefore, if anything exists and is comprehended, it is incommunicable.

11. (*"Encomium on Helen"*: summary.)

(1) The glory (*cosmos*) of a city is courage, of a body, beauty, of a soul, wisdom, of action, virtue, of speech, truth; it is right in all circumstances to praise what is praiseworthy and blame what is blameworthy.

(2) It belongs to the same man both to speak the truth and to refute falsehood. Helen is universally condemned and regarded as the symbol of disasters; I wish to subject her story to critical examination, and so rescue her from ignorant calumny.

(3) She was of the highest parentage: her reputed father Tyndareus was the most powerful of men; her real father, Zeus, was king of all.

(4) From these origins she obtained her divine beauty, by the display of which she inspired love in countless men, and caused the assemblage of a great number of ambitious suitors, some endowed with wealth, others with ancestral fame, others with personal prowess, others with accumulated wisdom.

(5) I shall not relate the story of who won Helen or how: to tell an audience what it knows wins belief but gives no pleasure. I shall pass over this period and come to the beginning of my defence, setting out the probable reasons for her journey to Troy.

(6) She acted as she did either through Fate and the will of the gods and the decrees of Necessity, or because she was seized by force, or won over by persuasion (*or captivated by love*). If the first, it is her accuser who deserves blame; for no human foresight can hinder the will of God: the stronger cannot be hindered by the weaker, and God is stronger than man in every way. Therefore if the cause was Fate, Helen cannot be blamed.

(7) If she was carried off by force, clearly her abductor wronged her and she was unfortunate. He, a barbarian, committed an act of barbarism, and should receive blame, disgrace and punishment; she, being robbed of her country and friends, deserves pity rather than obloquy.

(8) If it was speech that persuaded her and deceived her soul, her defence remains easy. Speech is a great power, which achieves the most divine works by means of the smallest and least visible form; for it can even put a stop to fear, remove grief, create joy, and increase pity. This I shall now prove:

(9) All poetry can be called speech in metre. Its hearers shudder with terror, shed tears of pity, and yearn with sad longing; the soul, affected by the words, feels as its own an emotion aroused by the good and ill fortunes of other people's actions and lives.

(10) The inspired incantations of words can induce pleasure and avert grief; for the power of the incantations, uniting with the feeling in the soul, soothes and persuades and transports by means of its wizardry. Two types of wizardry and magic have been invented, which are errors in the soul and deceptions in the mind.

(11) Their persuasions by means of fictions are innumerable; for if everyone had recollection of the past, knowledge of the present, and foreknowledge of the future, the power of speech would not be so great. But as it is, when men can neither remember the past nor observe the present nor prophesy the future, deception is easy; so that most men offer opinion as advice to the soul. But opinion, being unreliable, involves those who accept it in equally uncertain fortunes.

(12) (*Text corrupt.*) Thus, persuasion by speech is equivalent to abduction by force, as she was compelled to agree to what was said, and consent to what was done. It was therefore the persuader, not Helen, who did wrong and should be blamed.

(13) That persuasion, when added to speech, can also make any impression it wishes on the soul, can be shown, firstly, from the arguments of the meteorologists, who by removing one opinion and implanting another, cause what is incredible and invisible to appear before the eyes of the mind; secondly, from legal contests, in which a speech can sway and persuade a crowd, by the skill of its composition, not by the truth of its statements; thirdly, from the philosophical debates, in which quickness of thought is shown easily altering opinion.

(14) The power of speech over the constitution of the soul can be compared with the effect of drugs on the bodily state: just as drugs by driving out different humours from the body can put an end either to the disease or to life, so with speech: different words can induce grief, pleasure or fear; or again, by means of a harmful kind of persuasion, words can drug and bewitch the soul.

(15) If Helen was persuaded by love, defence is equally easy. What we see has its own nature, not chosen by us; and the soul is impressed through sight.

(16) For instance, in war, the sight of enemy forms wearing hostile array is so disturbing to the soul that often men flee in terror as if the coming danger were already present. The powerful habit induced by custom is displaced by the fear aroused by sight, which causes oblivion of what custom judges honourable and of the advantage derived from victory.

(17) People who have seen a frightful sight have been driven out of their minds, so great is the power of fear; while many have fallen victims to use-less toils, dreadful diseases and incurable insanity, so vivid are the images of the things seen which vision engraves on the mind.

(18) Painters, however, when they create one shape from many colours, give pleasure to sight; and the pleasure afforded by sculpture to the eyes is divine; many objects engender in many people a love of many actions and forms.

(19) If therefore Helen's eye, delighted with Paris's form, engendered the passion of love in her soul, this is not remarkable; for if a god is at work with divine power, how can the weaker person resist him? And if the disease is human, due to the soul's ignorance, it must not be condemned as a crime but pitied as a misfortune, for it came about through the snares of Fate, not the choice of the will; by the compulsion of love, not by the plottings of art.

(20) Therefore, whichever of the four reasons caused Helen's action, she is innocent.

(21) I have expunged by my discourse this woman's ill fame, and have fulfilled the object set forth at the outset. I have tried to destroy the unjust blame and the ignorant opinion, and have chosen to write this speech as an Encomium on Helen and an amusement for myself.

&bull; &bull; &bull;

15. Beggarly toadying bards, who swear a false oath and swear it well.

&bull; &bull; &bull;

23. Tragedy, by means of legends and emotions, creates a deception in which the deceiver is more honest than the non-deceiver, and the deceived is wiser than the non-deceived.

&bull; &bull; &bull;

26. Being is unrecognisable unless it succeeds in seeming, and seeming is weak unless it succeeds in being.

&bull; &bull; &bull;

# *ANTIPHON*

Of the many ancient Greeks who bore this name, at least three were put to death. One, a poet of Attica who wrote tragedies, epics, and speeches, defied Dionysius the tyrant, answering the question, what brass is best, by saying, "that of which the statues of Harmodius and Aristogiton are made," they being the men who in 510 B.C. had delivered Athens from tyranny; and when this Antiphon also refused to praise the compositions of Dionysius, the tyrant had him executed. Another Antiphon, an orator, promised Philip of Macedonia, the father of Alexander the Great, that he would set fire to the citadel of Athens; for this promise he was put to death at the instigation of Demosthenes.

A third Antiphon, born at Rhamnus in Attica about 480 B.C., was one of the great orators of the fifth century. During the Peloponnesian War, he helped set up the oligarchy of the 400 in 411 B.C., and was condemned to death after the restoration of the democracy. Thucydides calls him "a man inferior in virtue to none of his contemporaries, and possessed of remarkable powers of thought and gifts of speech. He did not like to come forward in the assembly, or in any other public arena. To the multitude, who were suspicious of his great abilities, he was an object of dislike; but there was no man who could do more for any who consulted him, whether their business lay in the courts of justice or in the assembly. And when the government of the Four Hundred was overthrown and became exposed to the vengeance of the people, and he being accused of taking part in the plot had to speak in his own case, his defense was undoubtedly the best ever made by any man on a capital charge down to my time" (VIII. 68; Jowett's translation).

Most writers distinguish between Antiphon, the orator, and Antiphon, the Sophist, but it is by no means certain that the two were not identical. (Detailed arguments for identifying them may be found in Karl Joel's *Geschichte der antiken Philosophie*, 1921, p. 663, and A. E. Taylor leans the same way in his standard work on Plato, p. 102 of the Meridian paperback edition.) Among those who distinguish the orator and the Sophist, Karl Popper in *The Open Society and Its Enemies* (Princeton University Press) and R. B. Levinson in *In Defense of Plato* (Harvard University Press) arrive at opposite evaluations of Antiphon the Sophist: Popper sings his praises as a deeply humane thinker, while Levinson condemns him roundly as an enemy of civilization. It is generally admitted that at least some of his ideas are re-encountered in, and presumably greatly influenced, first the Cynic school of philosophy and later the Stoics. Some of the material cited below was discovered only in the twentieth century, on Egyptian papyri. The translations are Freeman's. (For the Sophists generally, see the preface to the selections from Protagoras.)

•  •  •

10. (*From "Truth"*) Hence he (*God*) needs nothing and receives no addition from anywhere, but is infinite and lacking nothing.

•  •  •

(*Oxyrhynchus papyrus. From "Truth."*)

44. Justice, then, is not to transgress that which is the law of the city in which one is a citizen. A man therefore can best conduct himself in harmony with justice, if when in the company of witnesses he upholds the laws, and when alone without witnesses he upholds the edicts of nature. For the edicts of the laws are imposed artificially, but those of nature are compulsory. And the edicts of the laws are arrived at by consent, not by natural growth, whereas those of nature are not a matter of consent.

So, if the man who transgresses the legal code evades those who have agreed to these edicts, he avoids both disgrace and penalty; otherwise not. But if a man violates against possibility any of the laws which are implanted in nature, even if he evades all men's detection, the ill is no less, and even if all see, it is no greater. For he is not hurt on account of an opinion, but because of truth. The examination of these things is in general for this reason, that the majority of just acts according to law are prescribed contrary to nature. For there is legislation about the eyes, what they must see and what not; and about the ears, what they must hear and what not; and about the tongue, what it must speak and what not; and about the hands, what they must do and what not; and about the feet, where they must go and where not. Now the law's prohibitions are in no way more agreeable to nature and more akin than the law's injunctions. But life belongs to nature, and death too, and life for them is derived from advantages, and death from disadvantages. And the advantages laid down by the laws are chains upon nature, but those laid down by nature are free. So that the things which hurt, according to true reasoning, do not benefit nature more than those which delight; and things which grieve are not more advantageous than those which please; for things truly advantageous must not really harm, but must benefit. The naturally advantageous things from among these...

(*According to law, they are justified*) who having suffered defend themselves and do not themselves begin action; and those who treat their parents well, even though their parents have treated them badly; and those who give the taking of an oath to others and do not themselves swear. Of these provisions, one could find many which are hostile to nature; and there is in them the possibility of suffering more when one could suffer less; and enjoying less when one could enjoy more; and faring ill when one need not. Now if the person who adapted himself to these provisions received support from the laws, and those who did not, but who opposed them, received damage, obedience to the laws would not be without benefit; but as things are, it is obvious that for those who adapt themselves to these things the justice proceeding from law is not strong enough to help, seeing that first of all it allows him who suffers to suffer, and him who does, to do, and does not prevent the sufferer from suffering or the doer from doing. And if the case is brought up for punishment, there is no advantage peculiar to the sufferer rather than to the doer. For the sufferer must convince those who are to inflict the punishment, that he has suffered; and he needs the ability to win his case. And it is open to the doer to deny, by the same means... and he can defend himself no less than the accuser can accuse, and persuasion is open to both parties, being a matter of technique. . . .

We revere and honour those born of noble fathers, but those who are not born of noble houses we neither revere nor honour. In this we are, in our relations with one another, like barbarians, since we are all by nature born the same in every way, both barbarians and Hellenes. And it is open to all men to observe the laws of nature, which are compulsory. Similarly all of these things can be acquired by all, and in none of these things is any of us distinguished as barbarian or Hellene. We all breathe into the air through mouth and nostrils, and we all eat with hands. . . .

* * *

49. Now let life proceed, and let him desire marriage and a wife. This day, this night begin a new destiny; for marriage is a great contest for mankind. If the woman turns out to be incompatible, what can one do about the disaster? Divorce is difficult: it means to make enemies of friends, who have the same thoughts, the same breath, and had been valued and had regarded one with esteem. And it is hard if one gets such a possession, that is, if when thinking to get pleasure, one brings home pain.

However, not to speak of malevolence: let us assume the utmost compatibility. What is pleasanter to a man than a wife after his own heart? What is sweeter, especially to a young man? But in the very pleasure lies near at hand the pain; pleasures do not come alone, but are attended by griefs and troubles. Olympic and Pythian victories and all pleasures are apt to be won by great pains. Honours, prizes, delights, which God has given to men, depend necessarily on great toils and exertions. For my part, if I had another body which was as much trouble to me as I am to myself, I could not live, so great is the trouble I give myself for the sake of health, the acquisition of a livelihood, and for fame, respectability, glory and a good reputation.

What then, if I acquired another body which was as much trouble? Is it not clear that a wife, if she is to his mind, gives her husband no less cause for love and pain than he does to himself, for the health of two bodies, the acquisition of two livelihoods, and for respectability and honour? Suppose children are born: then all is full of anxiety, and the youthful spring goes out of the mind, and the countenance is no longer the same.

* * *

51. The whole of life is wonderfully open to complaint, my friend; it has nothing remarkable, great or noble, but all is petty, feeble, brief-lasting, and mingled with sorrows.

* * *

53a. There are some who do not live the present life, but prepare with great diligence as if they were going to live another life, not the present one. Meanwhile time, being neglected, deserts them.

54. There is a story that a man seeing another man earning much money begged him to lend him a sum at interest. The other refused; and being of a mistrustful nature, unwilling to help anyone, he carried it off and hid it somewhere. Another man, observing him, filched it. Later, the man who had hidden it returning, could not find it; and being very grieved at the disaster—especially that he had not lent to the man who had asked him, because then it would have been safe and would have earned increment—he went to see the man who had asked for a loan, and bewailed his misfortune, saying that he had done wrong and was sorry not to have granted his request but to have refused it, as his money was completely lost. The other man told him to hide a stone in the same place, and think of his money as his and not lost: "For even when you had it you completely failed to use it; so that now too you can think you have lost nothing." For when a per-

son has not used and will not use anything, it makes no difference to him
either whether he has it or not. For
when God does not wish to give a man
complete good fortune—when he has
given him material wealth but made him
poor in right thinking—in taking away
one he has deprived him of both.

. . .

56. He is cowardly who is bold in
speech concerning absent and future
dangers, and hurries on in resolve, but
shrinks back when the fact is upon him.

. . .

58. Whoever, when going against his
neighbour with the intention of harming
him, is afraid lest by failing to achieve
his wishes he may get what he does not
wish, is wiser. For his fear means hesitation, and his hesitation means an interval
in which often his mind is deflected from
his purpose. There can be no reversal of
a thing that has happened: it is possible
only for what is in the future not to
happen. Whoever thinks he will illtreat
his neighbours and not suffer himself is
unwise. Hopes are not altogether a good
thing; such hopes have flung down many

into intolerable disaster, and what they
thought to inflict on their neighbours,
they have suffered themselves for all to
see. Prudence in another man can be
judged correctly by no one more than
him who fortifies his soul against immediate pleasures and can conquer himself. But whoever wishes to gratify his
soul immediately, wishes the worse instead of the better.

59. Whoever has not desired or
touched the base and the bad, is not
self-restrained; for there is nothing over
which he has gained the mastery and
proved himself well-behaved.

60. The first thing, I believe, for
mankind is education. For whenever
anyone does the beginning of anything
correctly, it is likely that the end also
will be right. As one sows, so can one
expect to reap. And if in a young body
one sows a noble education, this lives
and flourishes through the whole of his
life, and neither rain nor drought destroys it.

. . .

62. One's character must necessarily
grow like that with which one spends
the greater part of the day.

. . .

# EPILOGUE

## PERICLES (as reported by THUCYDIDES)

Neither Pericles, the great statesman, who succumbed to the pestilence
that struck Athens in 429 B.C., nor Thucydides, the great historian who died
about thirty years later, was a philosopher. The plain fact that they were
among the greatest minds produced by the fifth century would not ensure
their inclusion here; else, Aeschylus, Sophocles, and Euripides would have
to be introduced, too. For a number of reasons, however, it is eminently
worthwhile to bring in at this point the great speech that Pericles delivered
in 431 B.C. at the funeral of those who had been killed in the war.

First, it is important to recall that the Greek philosophers did not think
and write in ivory towers, but as men deeply involved in the public and
cultural life of their day. Therefore it is desirable, if only it were possible,
to bring to life, in a few pages, fifth century Athens. That is precisely
what Pericles succeeded in doing inimitably in his funeral speech.

Then one also wants something to which one might compare the *Apology*
of Socrates, as reported by Plato; and one wonders about Alcibiades' remark, near the end of the *Symposium*, that even Pericles' speeches had not
moved him the way Socrates' did, making him angry at the thought of his
own slavish state. There are other references to Pericles both in the preceding pages and in the selections that follow. Moreover—and this is decisive
—this speech, unlike anything in the great tragedies of the fifth century,
is a self-contained unit that does not suffer too greatly from being read out
of context. Some of Sophocles' great choruses, on the other hand, are seen
as pregnant with irony when they are considered in relation to the action
of the plays.

Finally, it is often said that Plato's critique of democracy, especially in Book VIII of the *Republic,* was entirely fitting in relation to Athenian democracy though, of course, not applicable to modern democracy. This is not the place to discuss the second point, but it is interesting to read the classical defense of Athenian democracy at its best, while keeping in mind that the democracy that put Socrates to death, thirty years after Pericles had died, was emphatically not democracy at its best, but rather an early and hideous example of what sometimes happens in democracies, especially after great wars. In this context, the first selection about Anaxagoras should be reread; also the end of the preface to the selections from Protagoras.

The first of our three selections from Thucydides' history of the Peloponnesian War comprises I. 22; the second runs from II. 34 through II. 46; the last comes from II. 65. All are offered in Benjamin Jowett's magnificent translation.

• • •

22. As to the speeches which were made either before or during the war, it was hard for me, and for others who reported them to me, to recollect the exact words. I have therefore put into the mouth of each speaker the sentiments proper to the occasion, expressed as I thought he would be likely to express them, while at the same time I endeavored, as nearly as I could, to give the general purport of what was actually said. Of the events of the war I have not ventured to speak from any chance information, nor according to any notion of my own; I have described nothing but what I either saw myself, or learned from others of whom I made the most careful and particular inquiry. The task was a laborious one, because eye-witnesses of the same occurrences gave different accounts of them, as they remembered or were interested in the actions of one side or the other. And very likely the strictly historical character of my narrative may be disappointing to the ear. But if he who desires to have before his eyes a true picture of the events which have happened, and of the like events which may be expected to happen

hereafter in the order of human things, shall pronounce what I have written to be useful, then I shall be satisfied. My history is an everlasting possession, not a prize composition which is heard and forgotten.

• • •

When the remains have been laid in the earth, some man of known ability and high reputation, chosen by the city, delivers a suitable oration over them; after which the people depart. Such is the manner of interment; and the ceremony was repeated from time to time throughout the war. Over those who were the first buried Pericles was chosen to speak. At the fitting moment he advanced from the sepulchre to a lofty stage, which had been erected in order that he might be heard as far as possible by the multitude, and spoke as follows: —

## [Funeral Oration]

35. "Most of those who have spoken here before me have commended the lawgiver who added this oration to our

other funeral customs; it seemed to them a worthy thing that such an honor should be given at their burial to the dead who have fallen on the field of battle. But I should have preferred that, when men's deeds have been brave, they should be honored in deed only, and with such an honor as this public funeral, which you are now witnessing. Then the reputation of many would not have been imperilled on the eloquence or want of eloquence of one, and their virtues believed or not as he spoke well or ill. For it is difficult to say neither too little nor too much; and even moderation is apt not to give the impression of truthfulness. The friend of the dead who knows the facts is likely to think that the words of the speaker fall short of his knowledge and of his wishes; another who is not so well informed, when he hears of anything which surpasses his own powers, will be envious and will suspect exaggeration. Mankind are tolerant of the praises of others so long as each hearer thinks that he can do as well or nearly as well himself, but, when the speaker rises above him, jealousy is aroused and he begins to be incredulous. However, since our ancestors have set the seal of their approval upon the practice, I must obey, and to the utmost of my power shall endeavor to satisfy the wishes and beliefs of all who hear me.

36. "I will speak first of our ancestors, for it is right and becoming that now, when we are lamenting the dead, a tribute should be paid to their memory. There has never been a time when they did not inhabit this land, which by their valor they have handed down from generation to generation, and we have received from them a free state. But if they were worthy of praise, still more were our fathers, who added to their inheritance, and after many a struggle transmitted to us their sons this great empire. And we ourselves assembled here to-day, who are still most of us in the vigor of life, have chiefly done the work of improvement, and have richly

endowed our city with all things, so that she is sufficient for herself both in peace and war. Of the military exploits by which our various possessions were acquired, or of the energy with which we or our fathers drove back the tide of war, Hellenic or Barbarian, I will not speak; for the tale would be long and is familiar to you. But before I praise the dead, I should like to point out by what principles of action we rose to power, and under what institutions and through what manner of life our empire became great. For I conceive that such thoughts are not unsuited to the occasion, and that this numerous assembly of citizens and strangers may profitably listen to them.

37. "Our form of government does not enter into rivalry with the institutions of others. We do not copy our neighbors, but are an example to them. It is true that we are called a democracy, for the administration is in the hands of the many and not of the few. But while the law secures equal justice to all alike in their private disputes, the claim of excellence is also recognized; and when a citizen is in any way distinguished, he is preferred to the public service, not as matter of privilege, but as the reward of merit. Neither is poverty a bar, but a man may benefit his country whatever be the obscurity of his condition. There is no exclusiveness in our private intercourse we are not suspicious of one another, nor angry with our neighbor if he does what he likes; we do not put on sour looks at him which, though harmless, are not pleasant. While we are thus unconstrained in our private intercourse, a spirit of reverence pervades our public acts; we are prevented from doing wrong by respect for authority and for the laws, having an especial regard to those which are ordained for the protection of the injured as well as to those unwritten laws which bring upon the transgressor of them the reprobation of the general sentiment.

38. "And we have not forgotten to provide for our weary spirits many re-

laxations from toil; we have regular games and sacrifices throughout the year; at home the style of our life is refined; and the delight which we daily feel in all these things helps to banish melancholy. Because of the greatness of our city the fruits of the whole earth flow in upon us; so that we enjoy the goods of other countries as freely as of our own.

39. "Then, again, our military training is in many respects superior to that of our adversaries. Our city is thrown open to the world, and we never expel a foreigner or prevent him from seeing or learning anything of which the secret if revealed to an enemy might profit him. We rely not upon management or trickery, but upon our own hearts and hands. And in the matter of education, whereas they from early youth are always undergoing laborious exercises which are to make them brave, we live at ease, and yet are equally ready to face the perils which they face. And here is the proof. The Lacedaemonians come into Attica not by themselves, but with their whole confederacy following; we go alone into a neighbor's country; and although our opponents are fighting for their homes and we on a foreign soil, we have seldom any difficulty in overcoming them. Our enemies have never yet felt our united strength; the care of a navy divides our attention, and on land we are obliged to send our own citizens everywhere. But they, if they meet and defeat a part of our army, are as proud as if they had routed us all, and when defeated they pretend to have been vanquished by us all.

"If then we prefer to meet danger with a light heart but without laborious training, and with a courage which is gained by habit and not enforced by law, are we not greatly the gainers? Since we do not anticipate the pain, although, when the hour comes, we can be as brave as those who never allow themselves to rest; and thus too [40] our city is equally admirable in peace and in war. For we are lovers of the beautiful, yet simple in our tastes, and we cultivate the mind without loss of manliness. Wealth we employ, not for talk and ostentation, but when there is a real use for it. To avow poverty with us is no disgrace: the true disgrace is in doing nothing to avoid it. An Athenian citizen does not neglect the state because he takes care of his own household; and even those of us who are engaged in business have a very fair idea of politics. We alone regard a man who takes no interest in public affairs, not as a harmless, but as a useless character; and if few of us are originators, we are all sound judges of a policy. The great impediment to action is, in our opinion, not discussion, but the want of that knowledge which is gained by discussion preparatory to action. For we have a peculiar power of thinking before we act and of acting too, whereas other men are courageous from ignorance but hesitate upon reflection. And they are surely to be esteemed the bravest spirits who, having the clearest sense both of the pains and pleasures of life, do not on that account shrink from danger. In doing good, again, we are unlike others; we make our friends by conferring, not by receiving favors. Now he who confers a favor is the firmer friend, because he would fain by kindness keep alive the memory of an obligation; but the recipient is colder in his feelings, because he knows that in requiting another's generosity he will not be winning gratitude, but only paying a debt. We alone do good to our neighbors not upon a calculation of interest, but in the confidence of freedom and in a frank and fearless spirit. To sum up: I say that Athens is the school of Hellas, and [41] that the individual Athenian in his own person seems to have the power of adapting himself to the most varied forms of action with the utmost versatility and grace. This is no passing and idle word, but truth and fact; and the assertion is verified by the position to which these qualities have raised the state. For in the hour of trial Athens alone among her contemporaries is superior to the report of her. No enemy who comes against her is indignant at the reverses which he sustains at the hands of such a city; no subject complains that his masters are unworthy of him. And we shall assuredly not be without witnesses; there are mighty monuments of our power which will make us the wonder of this and of succeeding ages; we shall not need the praises of Homer or of any other panegyrist whose poetry may please for the moment, although his representation of the facts will not bear the light of day. For we have compelled every land and every sea to open a path for our valor, and have everywhere planted eternal memorials of our friendship and of our enmity. Such is the city for whose sake these men nobly fought and died; they could not bear the thought that she might be taken from them; and every one of us who survive should gladly toil on her behalf.

42. "I have dwelt upon the greatness of Athens because I want to show you that we are contending for a higher prize than those who enjoy none of these privileges, and to establish by manifest proof the merit of these men whom I am now commemorating. Their loftiest praise has been already spoken. For in magnifying the city I have magnified them, and men like them whose virtues made her glorious. And of how few Hellenes can it be said as of them, that their deeds when weighed in the balance have been found equal to their fame! Methinks that a death such as theirs has been gives the true measure of a man's worth; it may be the first revelation of his virtues, but is at any rate their final seal. For even those who come short in other ways may justly plead the valor with which they have fought for their country; they have blotted out the evil with the good, and have benefited the state more by their public services than they have injured her by their private actions. None of

these men were enervated by wealth or hesitated to resign the pleasures of life; none of them put off the evil day in the hope, natural to poverty, that a man, though poor, may one day become rich. But, deeming that the punishment of their enemies was sweeter than any of these things, and that they could fall in no nobler cause, they determined at the hazard of their lives to be honorably avenged, and to leave the rest. They resigned to hope their unknown chance of happiness; but in the face of death they resolved to rely upon themselves alone. And when the moment came they were minded to resist and suffer, rather than to fly and save their lives; they ran away from the word of dishonor, but on the battle-field their feet stood fast, and in an instant, at the height of their fortune, they passed away from the scene, not of their fear, but of their glory.

43. "Such was the end of these men; they were worthy of Athens, and the living need not desire to have a more heroic spirit, although they may pray for a less fatal issue. The value of such a spirit is not to be expressed in words. Any one can discourse to you for ever about the advantages of a brave defence which you know already. But instead of listening to him I would have you day by day fix your eyes upon the greatness of Athens, until you become filled with the love of her; and when you are impressed by the spectacle of her glory, reflect that this empire has been acquired by men who knew their duty and had the courage to do it, who in the hour of conflict had the fear of dishonor always present to them, and who, if ever they failed in an enterprise, would not allow their virtues to be lost to their country, but freely gave their lives to her as the fairest offering which they could present at her feast. The sacrifice which they collectively made was individually repaid to them; for they received again each one for himself a praise which grows not old, and the noblest of all

sepulchres—I speak not of that in which their remains are laid, but of that in which their glory survives, and is proclaimed always and on every fitting occasion both in word and deed. For the whole earth is the sepulchre of famous men; not only are they commemorated by columns and inscriptions in their own country, but in foreign lands there dwells also an unwritten memorial of them, graven not on stone but in the hearts of men. Make them your examples, and, esteeming courage to be freedom and freedom to be happiness, do not weigh too nicely the perils of war. The unfortunate who has no hope of a change for the better has less reason to throw away his life than the prosperous who, if he survive, is always liable to a change for the worse, and to whom any accidental fall makes the most serious difference. To a man of spirit, cowardice and disaster coming together are far more bitter than death, striking him unperceived at a time when he is full of courage and animated by the general hope.

44. "Wherefore I do not now commiserate the parents of the dead who stand here; I would rather comfort them. You know that your life has been passed amid manifold vicissitudes; and that they may be deemed fortunate who have gained most honor, whether an honorable death like theirs, or an honorable sorrow like yours, and whose days have been so ordered that the term of their happiness is likewise the term of their life. I know how hard it is to make you feel this, when the good fortune of others will too often remind you of the gladness which once lightened your hearts. And sorrow is felt at the want of those blessings, not which a man never knew, but which were a part of his life before they were taken from him. Some of you are of an age at which they may hope to have other children, and they ought to bear their sorrow better; not only will the children who may hereafter be born make them forget their own lost ones, but the city will be doubly a gainer. She will not be left desolate, and she will be safer. For a man's counsel cannot have equal weight or worth, when he alone has no children to risk in the general danger. To those of you who have passed their prime, I say; 'Congratulate yourselves that you have been happy during the greater part of your days; remember that your life of sorrow will not last long, and be comforted by the glory of those who are gone. For the love of honor alone is ever young, and not riches, as some say, but honor is the delight of men when they are old and useless.'

45. "To you who are the sons and brothers of the departed, I see that the struggle to emulate them will be an arduous one. For all men praise the dead, and, however pre-eminent your virtue may be, hardly will you be thought, I do not say to equal, but even to approach them. The living have their rivals and detractors, but when a man is out of the way, the honor and good-will which he receives is unalloyed. And, if I am to speak of womanly virtues to those of you who will henceforth be widows, let me sum them up in one short admonition: To a woman not to show more weakness than is natural to her sex is a great glory, and not to be talked about for good or evil among men.

46. "I have paid the required tribute, in obedience to the law, making use of such fitting words as I had. The tribute of deeds has been paid in part; for the dead have been honorably interred, and it remains only that their children should be maintained at the public charge until they are grown up; this is the solid prize with which, as with a garland, Athens crowns her sons living and dead, after a struggle like theirs. For where the rewards of virtue are greatest, there the noblest citizens are enlisted in the service of the state. And now, when you have duly lamented,

every one his own dead, you may depart."

. . .

In private they felt their sufferings keenly; the common people had been deprived even of the little which they possessed, while the upper class had lost fair estates in the country with all their houses and rich furniture. Worst of all, instead of enjoying peace, they were now at war. The popular indignation was not pacified until they had fined Pericles; but, soon afterwards, with the usual fickleness of the multitude, they elected him general and committed all their affairs to his charge. Their private sorrows were beginning to be less acutely felt, and for a time of public need they thought that there was no man like him. During the peace while he was at the head of affairs he ruled with prudence; under his guidance Athens was safe, and reached the height of her greatness in his time. When the war began he showed that here too he had formed a true estimate of the Athenian power. He survived the commencement of hostilities two years and six months; and, after his death, his foresight was even better appreciated than during his life. For he had told the Athenians, that if they would be patient and would attend to their navy, and not seek to enlarge their dominion while the war was going on, nor imperil the existence of the city, they would be victorious; but they did all that he told them not to do, and in matters which seemingly had nothing to do with the war, from motives of private ambition and private interest they adopted a policy which had disastrous effects in respect both of themselves and of their allies; their measures, had they been successful, would only have brought honor and profit to individuals, and, when unsuccessful, crippled the city in the conduct of the war. The reason of the difference was that he, deriving authority from his capacity and acknowledged worth, being also a man of transparent integrity, was able to control the multitude in a free spirit; he led them rather than was led by them; for, not seeking power by dishonest arts, he had no need to say pleasant things, but, on the strength of his own high character, could venture to oppose and even to anger them. When he saw them unseasonably elated and arrogant, his words humbled and awed them; and when they were depressed by groundless fears, he sought to reanimate their confidence. Thus Athens, though still in name a democracy, was in fact ruled by her greatest citizen. But his successors were more on an equality with one another, and, each one struggling to be first himself, they were ready to sacrifice the whole conduct of affairs to the whims of the people. Such weakness in a great and imperial city led to many errors, of which the greatest was the Sicilian expedition; not that the Athenians miscalculated their enemy's power, but they themselves, instead of consulting for the interests of the expedition which they had sent out, were occupied in intriguing against one another for the leadership of the democracy, and not only grew remiss in the management of the army, but became embroiled, for the first time, in civil strife. And yet after they had lost in the Sicilian expedition the greater part of their fleet and army, and were distracted by revolution at home, still they held out three years not only against their former enemies, but against the Sicilians who had combined with them, and against most of their own allies who had risen in revolt. Even when Cyrus the son of the King joined in the war and supplied the Peloponnesian fleet with money, they continued to resist and were at last overthrown, not by their enemies, but by themselves and their own internal dissensions. So that at the time Pericles was more than justified in the conviction at which his foresight had arrived, that the Athenians would win an easy victory over the unaided forces of the Peloponnesians.

*part two*

# SOCRATES
# AND PLATO

I

Socrates is widely considered one of the greatest human beings of all time—largely on the basis of some of the texts that follow. He is known to us mainly through the works of Plato, his pupil; but we have some other sources of information about him, too.

Aristophanes (455–375 B.C.) made fun of Socrates in one of his comedies, *The Clouds*. First performed in 423, it received only the third prize, which is said to have galled the poet, who considered the play one of his best. He subsequently undertook, but did not complete, a revision. It is the revised version, never performed in the poet's lifetime, that has survived.

Xenophon, the general, known to elementary students of Greek as the author of *Anabasis*, recorded his memories of Socrates, his friend and master, in *Memorabilia*, in an *Apology of Socrates*, and in a *Symposium*. He wrote these works after the death of Socrates in an effort to defend him, and it is a commonplace that his Socrates is more innocuous and less exciting than Plato's.

Aristotle, Plato's great pupil, who was born fifteen years after the death of Socrates, makes many interesting statements about Socrates in his philosophic works, and there is no reason to believe that he relied solely on Plato's testimony.

Socrates was the son of Sophroniscus, a sculptor, and Phaenarete, a midwife. He is said to have done some sculpting in his youth and to have fashioned some impressively simple and elegant statues of the Graces. About his adult life and his death nothing could be said that has not been said better in the *Apology,* in the closing pages of the *Phaedo,* and in Alcibiades' great speech about him at the end of the *Symposium*. It is above all in these three works that Plato has borne witness of the man who first taught him philosophy. If Plato had never written anything else, his place would still be secure as one of the world's greatest writers; and if we knew nothing else about Socrates, his place, too, would be assured.

Plato's *Apology* is generally thought to be eminently faithful to what Socrates actually said when tried in 399 B.C., at the age of seventy, on charges of impiety and corruption of the youth. The speech was delivered in public and heard by a large audience; Plato has Socrates mention that Plato was present; and there is no need to doubt the historical veracity of the speech, at least in essentials.

In the *Crito*, not reprinted here, Plato has Crito visit Socrates in prison to assure him that his escape from Athens has been well prepared and to persuade him to consent to leave. That Socrates, in fact, refused to leave is certain; whether he used the arguments Plato ascribes to him is much less certain. In any case, anyone who has read the *Apology* will agree that, after delivering that speech, Socrates could not very well have escaped.

The *Meno* is one of several early Platonic dialogues that gives, at least in a general way, a very fine and faithful picture of the manner in which Socrates liked to practice the art of dialogue. The work has the added advantage of being both very brief and philosophically interesting.

That the account of Socrates' death at the very end of the *Phaedo* is historically accurate is a matter of common agreement. It is almost as widely agreed that in the preceding conversation, Plato has put his own views into the mouth of Socrates—views significantly different from those held by the real Socrates. A generation or more ago, John Burnet and A. E. Taylor, two scholars of repute, argued that the real Socrates did hold the views that Plato here ascribes to him. However, by the middle of the twentieth century, there was a virtual unanimity among scholars that the views the historic Socrates held about life after death are correctly represented at the end of the *Apology*, whereas the arguments for immortality that Plato introduces in the *Phaedo* owe a great deal to Pythagoreanism, which exerted an increasingly deep influence on Plato's thought. (See the preface to the Pythagorean selections, above.)

The *Symposium* certainly makes no claim to historic accuracy, except for the contents of Alcibiades' speech on Socrates: what is said there is no doubt true. As for the rest, we need not believe that Aristophanes, the comic poet, really told the moving myth ascribed to him, or that the others ever said what Plato makes them say. The *Symposium* is not history but a work of art, and it shows us Plato's literary powers at their peak. Even those not interested in philosophy can read and reread and enjoy it; and chances are that it may lead at least some to develop a strong feeling for, if not to fall in love with, philosophy. This dialogue represents the most perfect blend of philosophy and poetry ever achieved.

Only one other dialogue comes close to it in this respect—the *Phaedrus*. It too is reprinted without omission. One or another professional philosopher may wonder why two dialogues that deal with love had to be included. In the first place, a volume of this sort is not intended primarily for professional philosophers, but rather for those seeking an approach to philosophy; and from that point of view the *Apology, Meno, Symposium,* and *Phaedrus,* all of which are offered complete, can hardly be rivaled. Second, both the *Symposium* and the *Phaedrus* involve a great deal besides love and are of the utmost philosophic interest. Finally, these dialogues help to balance the selections from the later Plato, which are rather difficult and possibly discouraging for many beginners.

II

Plato was probably born in 428/7 B.C. He had two older brothers, Adimantus and Glaucon, who appear in Plato's *Republic,* and a sister, Potone. Plato was still a child when his father, Ariston, died, and his mother, Perictione remarried—her uncle, Pyrilampes, who is said to have been a close friend of Pericles. From a previous marriage, Plato's stepfather had a son, Demus, famous for his good looks; and from the second marriage, to Plato's mother, another boy was born, Antiphon, who appears in Plato's *Parmenides.*

Plato's mother had a brother, Charmides, and a cousin, Critias, who were prominent in politics in the days of the oligarchy that ruled Athens at the end of the Peloponnesian War. One of Plato's early dialogues bears the name *Charmides,* and from this dialogue it appears that Charmides knew Socrates quite well even before Plato was born. It is therefore possible that Plato knew Socrates from his childhood. But Plato may well have been close to twenty when he first came under the spell of Socrates, and as an ancient story has it, tore up the poetry he had written hitherto and resolved to devote his life to philosophy. Certainly, the death of Socrates made an enormous impression on Plato, who appears to have felt the call to bear witness for posterity of "the finest man"—to cite Plato's *Phaedo*—"of all whom we came to know in his generation; the wisest too, and the most righteous." Plato's early dialogues are as wonderful a monument as any man ever constructed for his teacher.

It was the restored democracy that put Socrates to death, and animosity against Socrates had certainly been nourished by his friendship with some of the oligarchs. Still, there is no need to suppose that this was the "real" reason, and that the charge of impiety and the corruption of the youth was a mere pretext for this political animus. The account Socrates gives of himself in the *Apology* fully accounts for the hatred that many must have felt against him. It also explains why Plato should have been almost as disillusioned with oligarchy (Socrates incriminates the oligarchs in no uncertain terms) as with democracy (seeing that the democracy put Socrates to death). Though Plato came from a most distinguished family and might have been fairly expected to follow the example of some of his relatives by going into politics, he decided definitely to abandon any such ambition in favor of philosophy.

His *Republic*, which contains lengthy criticisms of oligarchy and democracy and pictures only despotism as a still worse form of government, belongs to the same period of Plato's life as the *Phaedrus*, though the *Phaedrus* may have been written a little later. The *Republic* is entirely omitted here, because it would be a shame to excerpt it. Those who want to supplement the present volume with one further text could hardly do better than to turn to F. M. Cornford's translation, with commentary, of Plato's *Republic* (Oxford University Press, both in hard cover and in paperback). The English name of this dialogue is most unfortunate. Its Greek name is *politeia*, which means citizenship, civic life, politics, state, or commonwealth; and in Latin this was rendered as *res publica*. In German, it is called, with reasonable accuracy, *Der Staat*. The ideal city it describes is emphatically no republic. Rather, it is ruled by philosopher kings, and among its prominent features are censorship and a system of education that would probably make it impossible for any Socrates either to develop or to live there. Yet the arguments for this ideal are put into the mouth of Socrates. No irony appears to be intended. In the *Republic* and in those other late dialogues in which he appears, Socrates generally voices Plato's views, not those of the historic Socrates. And if occasionally Plato's own views are in doubt in some of the late dialogues, which are impassioned invitations to reflection rather than straightforward expositions of some doctrine, it is still agreed that what is said by Socrates is not to be ascribed to the historic Socrates.

Of Plato's late dialogues, five are here represented by long selections. The *Parmenides* marks a crisis in the development of Plato's thought. This is discussed briefly above, in the preface to the selections from Parmenides. The last part of the dialogue is omitted here because it is the most abstruse and difficult thing Plato ever wrote, and interpretations of it differ widely.

The *Theaetetus* deals with the problem of knowledge and contains an interesting discussion of some of the ideas of Protagoras, the Sophist. Besides much technical philosophy, it also offers some very charming digressions, and the conclusion of the dialogue, with its genuinely Socratic spirit, represents one of the highlights in Plato's works.

The selections from the *Sophist*, a fine example of Plato's later dialectic, is probably the most difficult material in this part of the book, but rewarding for the serious student.

The passages from the *Timaeus* and the *Laws* summarize some of Plato's theology, though they deal with other things as well. Although Socrates appears in the *Timaeus*, most of the talking is done not by him, but by the man whose name the dialogue bears. Timaeus tells how the world was created, and his account is heavily influenced by Pythagorean doctrines. In the early Middle Ages this was the only Platonic dialogue known, and it exerted an enormous influence.

The *Laws* was Plato's last work, written when he was eighty. Among his other dialogues, only the *Republic* equals it in length. The city described in the *Republic* is said in a famous passage to be an ideal—"a pattern set up in the heavens ... But whether it exists anywhere or ever will exist, is no matter" (592). This ideal city is governed by ideally wise men, without the benefit of laws. In the *Laws*, Plato outlines the best feasible city, and this is ruled by laws. For that reason, some interpreters consider it a significant step in the direction of democracy. But the selection offered here from the justly famous tenth book (there are twelve books in all) shows how far Plato was from the spirit of Jeffersonian, and by no means only Jeffersonian, democracy.

It was Plato who first introduced into Western thought—along with a great deal else—the twin notions of dogma and heresy. It was he who first tried to offer precise formulations of central and indispensable doctrines; and it was he, too, who first proposed a painstakingly graduated penal code for dealing with all those who might differ with one or another of these dogmas. Aquinas' ideas about the treatment of heretics are better understood against the background of Plato's. And Aquinas' theology as well as Aristotle's is also best considered against the background of Plato's.

In addition to the dialogues, we have a number of letters that are said to have been written by Plato. There has been a good deal of controversy about their authenticity, but the seventh letter, which is at least as interesting and significant as any, is generally conceded to be genuine. When Plato wrote it, he was about seventy-five.

The major events of his later life, alluded to in the seventh letter, revolve around two cities: Syracuse, in Sicily, and Athens. In 367 B.C., Dionysius I, tyrant of Syracuse, died and was succeeded by Dionysius II. Years before, Plato had gained the friendship and devotion of Dion, son-in-law of Dionysius I and brother-in-law of his successor. Dion called Plato to Syracuse to train Dionysius II, then thirty years old and unprepared for the tasks that suddenly confronted him. After a few months, however, the young tyrant sent away Dion as well as Plato, who returned to Athens. Plato's attempts to reconcile the brothers-in-law failed; but in 361/60, Plato made a second voyage to Syracuse. The tyrant had kept up a correspondence with him, and Plato thought it possible at this time to draft a constitution for a federation of Greek cities. At that time, Sicily was colonized not only by the Greeks but also by the Carthaginians, and the Greeks felt threatened by their rivals. Again there were intrigues, and Plato returned to Athens in 360. Three years later, Dion "liberated" Syracuse, but was later murdered. Plato still wrote two further letters to the remnants of Dion's party, and the "seventh letter" is one of these. It seems to have been written in 353 B.C.

In another great project, Plato succeeded. He founded a school in Athens, which came to be known as the Academy. One might call it the world's first university, and it endured as a center of higher learning for about 1,000 years, until a Christian emperor closed it in A.D. 529. In 367 B.C., young Aristotle entered the Academy and stayed on until after Plato died at eighty in 348/7 B.C.

III

The following translations have been used: for the *Apology, Symposium,* and *Laws,* those of Benjamin Jowett; for the *Meno,* that of W. K. C. Guthrie (Penguin Books); for the *Phaedo* and *Phaedrus,* those of R. Hackforth (Cambridge University Press); and for the *Parmenides, Theaetetus, Sophist,* and *Timaeus* those of F. M. Cornford (Routledge & Kegan Paul).

Jowett's translations are of the highest literary quality: they have some of the magnificence of the King James Bible without imposing any comparable difficulties on the modern reader. In fact, neither Cornford's versions nor Hackforth's are so immensely readable. In the earlier dialogues, where Plato's literary art is at its height, Jowett's beautiful translations appear most appropriate. But in most of the *Phaedo* and in the later dialogues, literary genius, though by no means altogether absent, tends to recede in importance; arguments become more and more central, the precise rendering of various concepts is frequently crucial, and it becomes essential to take into account the latest research. In this field, F. M. Cornford established himself as by far the most commanding figure. His translations, with commentary, of the *Parmenides,* (in *Plato and Parmenides,* 1939), of the *Theaetetus and Sophist* (in *Plato's Theory of Knowledge,* 1934), and of the *Timaeus* (in *Plato's Cosmology,* 1937) are models of graceful, lucid, and informative scholarship; it is a delight to be able to offer his translations here.

After Cornford's death, R. Hackforth undertook the task of dealing similarly with some of the other dialogues, and his versions of the *Phaedo* and *Phaedrus* have met with the same kind of acclaim. Permission to use them here greatly enhances the value of the present volume; and I am delighted that I have received permission to include Guthrie's version of the *Meno* in the second edition.

A few of Cornford's and Hackforth's footnotes have been retained, some because they are so very helpful, others to give at least some idea of the difficulties with which Plato scholars have to contend. Most of the footnotes and all of the commentary have been omitted. The marginal page numbers are the same in all scholarly editions, whether Greek, English, German, or French and are used in citing Plato in scholarly works. They are therefore indispensable for serious students.

Plato's letters are most conveniently consulted in the bilingual edition (Greek text and English translation on facing pages) in The Loeb Classical Library (Harvard University Press). All the translations in this series are very scholarly, and for the portions selected from the seventh letter, that of the Rev. R. G. Bury has been used.

Those seeking further help with the dialogues translated by Cornford and Hackforth could not do better than to turn to the original editions, which feature excellent commentaries. These commentaries are not written primarily for beginners, but rather for serious students and fellow scholars.

Books about Plato are, of course, legion. Those seeking a relatively simple, comprehensive, but high-level volume to assist them will find help aplenty in A. E. Taylor's *Plato* (Meridian Books, paperback), to which I am indebted for some of the material in Section II of this preface. Taylor's little book on *Socrates* is less good: the author tends to make an Anglican of Socrates.

IV

Any detailed commentary on the following selections is impossible in the confines of the present volume. The point here is to offer the texts.

But what of Plato's influence? At this point, a single sentence may suffice: Alfred North Whitehead, one of the outstanding philosophers of the twentieth century, said in one of his major works, *Process and Reality* (1929, p. 63): "The safest general characterization of the European philosophical tradition is that it consists of a series of footnotes to Plato."

# SOCRATES AND
# THE EARLIER PLATO

## APOLOGY (complete)

How you, O Athenians, have been affected by my accusers, I cannot tell; but I know that they almost made me forget who I was—so persuasively did they speak; and yet they have hardly uttered a word of truth. But of the many falsehoods told by them, there was one which quite amazed me;—I mean when they said that you should be upon your guard and not allow yourselves to be deceived by the force of my eloquence. To say this, when they were certain to be detected as soon as I opened my lips and proved myself to be anything but a great speaker, did indeed appear to me most shameless—unless by the force of eloquence they mean the force of truth; for if such is their meaning, I admit that I am eloquent. But in how different a way from theirs! Well, as I was saying, they have scarcely spoken the truth at all; but from me you shall hear the whole truth: not, however, delivered after their manner in a set oration duly ornamented with words and phrases. No, by heaven! but I shall use the words and arguments which occur to me at the moment; for I am confident in the justice of my cause:[1] at my time of life I ought not to be appearing before you, O men of Athens, in the character of a juvenile orator—let no one expect it of me. And I must beg of you to grant me a favour:—If I defend myself in my accustomed manner, and you hear me using the words which I have been in the habit of using in the agora, at the tables of the money-changers, or anywhere else, I would ask you not to be surprised, and not to interrupt me on this account. For I am more than seventy years of age, and appearing now for the first time in a court of law, I am quite a stranger to the language of the place; and therefore I would have you regard

_____

1 Or, I am certain that I am right in taking this course.

me as if I were really a stranger, whom you would excuse if he spoke in his native tongue, and after the fashion of his country:—Am I making an unfair [18] request of you? Never mind the manner, which may or may not be good; but think only of the truth of my words, and give heed to that: let the speaker speak truly and the judge decide justly.

And first, I have to reply to the older charges and to my first accusers, and then I will go on to the later ones. For of old I have had many accusers, who have accused me falsely to you during many years; and I am more afraid of them than of Anytus and his associates, who are dangerous, too, in their own way. But far more dangerous are the others, who began when you were children, and took possession of your minds with their falsehoods, telling of one Socrates, a wise man, who speculated about the heaven above, and searched into the earth beneath, and made the worse appear the better cause. The disseminators of this tale are the accusers whom I dread; for their hearers are apt to fancy that such enquirers do not believe in the existence of the gods. And they are many, and their charges against me are of ancient date, and they were made by them in the days when you were more impressible than you are now —in childhood, or it may have been in youth—and the cause when heard went by default, for there was none to answer. And hardest of all, I do not know and cannot tell the names of my accusers; unless in the chance case of a Comic poet. All who from envy and malice have persuaded you—some of them having first convinced themselves—all this class of men are most difficult to deal with, for I cannot have them up here, and cross-examine them, and therefore I must simply fight with shadows in my own defence, and argue when there is no one who answers. I will ask you then to assume with me, as I was saying,

that my opponents are of two kinds; one recent, the other ancient: and I hope that you will see the propriety of my answering the latter first, for these accusations you heard long before the others, and much oftener.

Well, then, I must make my defence, and endeavour to clear away in a [19] short time, a slander which has lasted a long time. May I succeed, if to succeed be for my good and yours, or likely to avail me in my cause! The task is not an easy one; I quite understand the nature of it. And so leaving the event with God, in obedience to the law I will now make my defence.

I will begin at the beginning, and ask what is the accusation which has given rise to the slander of me, and in fact has encouraged Meletus to prefer this charge against me. Well, what do the slanderers say? They shall be my prosecutors, and I will sum up their words in an affidavit: "Socrates is an evil-doer, and a curious person, who searches into things under the earth and in heaven, and he makes the worse appear the better cause; and he teaches the aforesaid doctrines to others." Such is the nature of the accusation: it is just what you have yourselves seen in the comedy of Aristophanes,[2] who has introduced a man whom he calls Socrates, going about and saying that he walks in air, and talking a deal of nonsense concerning matters of which I do not pretend to know either much or little— not that I mean to speak disparagingly of any one who is a student of natural philosophy. I should be very sorry if Meletus could bring so grave a charge against me. But the simple truth is, O Athenians, that I have nothing to do with physical speculations. Very many of those here present are witnesses to the truth of this, and to them I appeal. Speak then, you who have heard me,

---

[2] Aristoph., *Clouds*, 225 ff.

and tell your neighbours whether any of you have ever known me hold forth in few words or in many upon such matters. . . . You hear their answer. And from what they say of this part of the charge you will be able to judge of the truth of the rest.

As little foundation is there for the report that I am a teacher, and take money; this accusation has no more truth in it than the other. Although, if a man were really able to instruct mankind, to receive money for giving instruction would, in my opinion, be an honour to him. There is Gorgias of Leontium, and Prodicus of Ceos, and Hippias of Elis, who go the round of the cities, and are able to persuade the young men to leave their own citizens by whom they might be taught for nothing, and come to [20] them whom they not only pay, but are thankful if they may be allowed to pay them. There is at this time a Parian philosopher residing in Athens, of whom I have heard; and I came to hear of him in this way:—I came across a man who has spent a world of money on the Sophists, Callias, the son of Hipponicus, and knowing that he had sons, I asked him: "Callias," I said, "if your two sons were foals or calves, there would be no difficulty in finding some one to put over them; we should hire a trainer of horses, or a farmer probably, who would improve and perfect them in their own proper virtue and excellence; but as they are human beings, whom are you thinking of placing over them? Is there any one who understands human and political virtue? You must have thought about the matter, for you have sons; is there any one?" "There is," he said. "Who is he?" said I; "and of what country? and what does he charge?" "Evenus the Parian," he replied; "he is the man, and his charge is five minae." Happy is Evenus, I said to myself, if he really has this wisdom, and teaches at such a moderate charge. Had I the same, I should

have been very proud and conceited; but the truth is that I have no knowledge of the kind.

I dare say, Athenians, that some one among you will reply, "Yes, Socrates, but what is the origin of these accusations which are brought against you; there must have been something strange which you have been doing? All these rumours and this talk about you would never have arisen if you had been like other men: tell us, then, what is the cause of them, for we should be sorry to judge hastily of you." Now I regard this as a fair challenge, and I will endeavour to explain to you the reason why I am called wise and have such an evil fame. Please to attend then. And although some of you may think that I am joking, I declare that I will tell you the entire truth. Men of Athens, this reputation of mine has come of a certain sort of wisdom which I possess. If you ask me what kind of wisdom, I reply, wisdom such as may perhaps be attained by man, for to that extent I am inclined to believe that I am wise; whereas the persons of whom I was speaking have a superhuman wisdom, which I may fail to describe, because I have it not myself; and he who says that I have, speaks falsely, and is taking away my character. And here, O men of Athens, I must beg you not to interrupt me, even if I seem to say something extravagant. For the word which I will speak is not mine. I will refer you to a witness who is worthy of credit; that witness shall be the God of Delphi—he will tell you about my wisdom, if I have any, and of what sort it is. You must have known Chaerephon; he was early a friend of mine, and also a friend of yours, for he shared in the recent exile of the people, and re- [21] turned with you. Well, Chaerephon, as you know, was very impetuous in all his doings, and he went to Delphi and boldly asked the oracle to tell him whether—as I was saying, I must beg you not to interrupt—he asked the oracle to tell him whether any one was wiser than I was, and the Pythian prophetess answered, that there was no man wiser. Chaerephon is dead himself; but his brother, who is in court, will confirm the truth of what I am saying.

Why do I mention this? Because I am going to explain to you why I have such an evil name. When I heard the answer, I said to myself, What can the god mean? and what is the interpretation of his riddle? for I know that I have no wisdom, small or great. What then can he mean when he says that I am the wisest of men? And yet he is a god, and cannot lie; that would be against his nature. After long consideration, I thought of a method of trying the question. I reflected that if I could only find a man wiser than myself, then I might go to the god with a refutation in my hand. I should say to him, "Here is a man who is wiser than I am; but you said that I was the wisest." Accordingly I went to one who had the reputation of wisdom, and observed him—his name I need not mention; he was a politician whom I selected for examination—and the result was as follows: When I began to talk with him, I could not help thinking that he was not really wise, although he was thought wise by many, and still wiser by himself; and thereupon I tried to explain to him that he thought himself wise, but was not really wise; and the consequence was that he hated me, and his enmity was shared by several who were present and heard me. So I left him, saying to myself, as I went away: Well, although I do not suppose that either of us knows anything really beautiful and good, I am better off than he is,—for he knows nothing, and thinks that he knows; I neither know nor think that I know. In this latter particular, then, I seem to have slightly the advantage of him. Then I went to another who had still higher pretensions to wisdom,

and my conclusion was exactly the same. Whereupon I made another enemy of him, and of many others besides him.

Then I went to one man after another, being not unconsicous of the enmity which I provoked, and I lamented and feared this: but necessity was laid upon me,—the word of God, I thought, ought to be considered first. And I said to myself, Go I must to all who appear to know, and find out the meaning of the oracle. And I swear to you, Athenians, by the dog I swear!—for I must [22] tell you the truth—the result of my mission was just this: I found that the men most in repute were all but the most foolish; and that others less esteemed were really wiser and better. I will tell you the tale of my wanderings and of the "Herculean" labours, as I may call them, which I endured only to find at last the oracle irrefutable. After the politicians, I went to the poets; tragic, dithyrambic, and all sorts. And there, I said to myself, you will be instantly detected; now you will find out that you are more ignorant than they are. Accordingly, I took them some of the most elaborate passages in their own writings, and asked what was the meaning of them—thinking that they would teach me something. Will you believe me? I am almost ashamed to confess the truth, but I must say that there is hardly a person present who would not have talked better about their poetry than they did themselves. Then I knew that not by wisdom do poets write poetry, but by a sort of genius and inspiration; they are like diviners or soothsayers who also say many fine things, but do not understand the meaning of them. The poets appeared to me to be much in the same case; and I further observed that upon the strength of their poetry they believed themselves to be the wisest of men in other things in which they were not wise. So I departed, conceiving myself to be superior to them for the same reason that I was superior to the politicians.

At last I went to the artisans, for I was conscious that I knew nothing at all, as I may say, and I was sure that they knew many fine things; and here I was not mistaken, for they did know many things of which I was ignorant, and in this they certainly were wiser than I was. But I observed that even the good artisans fell into the same error as the poets;—because they were good workmen they thought that they also knew all sorts of high matters, and this defect in them overshadowed their wisdom; and therefore I asked myself on behalf of the oracle, whether I would like to be as I was, neither having their knowledge nor their ignorance, or like them in both; and I made answer to myself and to the oracle that I was better off as I was.

This inquisition has led to my having many enemies of the worst and most dangerous kind, and has given occasion also to many calumnies. And I am [23] called wise, for my hearers always imagine that I myself possess the wisdom which I find wanting in others: but the truth is, O men of Athens, that God only is wise; and by his answer he intends to show that the wisdom of men is worth little or nothing; he is not speaking of Socrates, he is only using my name by way of illustration, as if he said, He, O men, is the wisest, who, like Socrates, knows that his wisdom is in truth worth nothing. And so I go about the world, obedient to the god, and search and make enquiry into the wisdom of any one, whether citizen or stranger, who appears to be wise; and if he is not wise, then in vindication of the oracle I show him that he is not wise; and my occupation quite absorbs me, and I have no time to give either to any public matter of interest or to any concern of my own, but I am in utter poverty by reason of my devotion to the god.

There is another thing:—young men of the richer classes, who have not much

to do, come about me of their own accord; they like to hear the pretenders examined, and they often imitate me, and proceed to examine others; there are plenty of persons, as they quickly discover, who think that they know something, but really know little or nothing; and then those who are examined by them instead of being angry with themselves are angry with me: This confounded Socrates, they say; this villainous misleader of youth!—and then if somebody asks them, Why, what evil does he practise or teach? they do not know, and cannot tell; but in order that they may not appear to be at a loss, they repeat the ready-made charges which are used against all philosophers about teaching things up in the clouds and under the earth, and having no gods, and making the worse appear the better cause; for they do not like to confess that their pretence of knowledge has been detected —which is the truth; and as they are numerous and ambitious and energetic, and are drawn up in battle array and have persuasive tongues, they have filled your ears with their loud and inveterate calumnies. And this is the reason why my three accusers, Meletus and Anytus and Lycon, have set upon me; Meletus, who has a quarrel with me on behalf of the poets; Anytus, on behalf of the craftsmen and politicians; Lycon, on behalf of the rhetoricians: and as I [24] said at the beginning, I cannot expect to get rid of such a mass of calumny all in a moment. And this, O men of Athens, is the truth and the whole truth; I have concealed nothing, I have dissembled nothing. Any yet, I know that my plainness of speech makes them hate me, and what is their hatred but a proof that I am speaking the truth?—Hence has arisen the prejudice against me; and this is the reason of it, as you will find out either in this or in any future enquiry.

I have said enough in my defence against the first class of my accusers; I turn to the second class. They are headed by Meletus, that good man and true lover of his country, as he calls himself. Against these, too, I must try to make a defence. Let their affidavit be read; it contains something of this kind: It says that Socrates is a doer of evil, who corrupts the youth; and who does not believe in the gods of the state, but has other new divinities of his own. Such is the charge; and now let us examine the particular counts. He says that I am a doer of evil, and corrupt the youth; but I say, O men of Athens, that Meletus is a doer of evil, in that he pretends to be in earnest when he is only in jest, and is so eager to bring men to trial from a pretended zeal and interest about matters in which he really never had the smallest interest. And the truth of this I will endeavour to prove to you.

Come hither, Meletus, and let me ask a question of you. You think a great deal about the improvement of youth?

Yes, I do.

Tell the judges, then, who is their improver; for you must know, as you have taken the pains to discover their corrupter, and are citing and accusing me before them. Speak, then, and tell the judges who their improver is.—Observe, Meletus, that you are silent, and have nothing to say. But is not this rather disgraceful, and a very considerable proof of what I was saying, that you have no interest in the matter. Speak up, friend, and tell us who their improver is.

The laws.

But that, my good sir, is not my meaning. I want to know who the person is, who, in the first place, knows the laws.

The judges, Socrates, who are present in court.

What, do you mean to say, Meletus, that they are able to instruct and improve youth?

Certainly they are.

What, all of them, or some only and not others?

All of them.

By the goddess Here, that is good news! There are plenty of improvers,

then. And what do you say of the audience,—do they improve them?    [25]

Yes, they do.

And the senators?

Yes, the senators improve them.

But perhaps the members of the assembly corrupt them?—or do they too improve them?

They improve them.

Then every Athenian improves and elevates them; all with the exception of myself; and I alone am their corrupter? Is that what you affirm?

That is what I stoutly affirm.

I am very unfortunate if you are right. But suppose I ask you a question: How about horses? Does one man do them harm and all the world good? Is not the exact opposite the truth? One man is able to do them good, or at least not many;—the trainer of horses, that is to say, does them good, and others who have to do with them rather injure them? Is not that true, Meletus, of horses, or of any other animals? Most assuredly it is; whether you and Anytus say yes or no. Happy indeed would be the condition of youth if they had one corrupter only, and all the rest of the world were their improvers. But you, Meletus, have sufficiently shown that you never had a thought about the young: your carelessness is seen in your not caring about the very things which you bring against me.

And now, Meletus, I will ask you another question—by Zeus I will: Which is better, to live among bad citizens, or among good ones? Answer, friend, I say; the question is one which may be easily answered. Do not the good do their neighbours good, and the bad do them evil?

Certainly.

And is there any one who would rather be injured than benefited by those who live with him? Answer, my good friend, the law requires you to answer— does any one like to be injured?

Certainly not.

And when you accuse me of corrupting and deteriorating the youth, do you allege that I corrupt them intentionally or unintentionally?

Intentionally, I say.

But you have just admitted that the good do their neighbours good, and the evil do them evil. Now, is that a truth which your superior wisdom has recognized thus early in life, and am I, at my age, in such darkness and ignorance as not to know that if a man with whom I have to live is corrupted by me, I am very likely to be harmed by him; and yet I corrupt him, and intentionally, too—so you say, although neither I nor any other human being is ever likely to be convinced by you. But either I do [26] not corrupt them, or I corrupt them unintentionally; and on either view of the case you lie. If my offence is unintentional, the law has no cognizance of unintentional offences: you ought to have taken me privately, and warned and admonished me; for if I had been better advised, I should have left off doing what I only did unintentionally—no doubt I should; but you would have nothing to say to me and refused to teach me. And now you bring me up in this court, which is a place not of instruction, but of punishment.

It will be very clear to you, Athenians, as I was saying, that Meletus has no care at all, great or small, about the matter. But still I should like to know, Meletus, in what I am affirmed to corrupt the young. I suppose you mean, as I infer from your indictment, that I teach them not to acknowledge the gods which the state acknowledges, but some other new divinities or spiritual agencies in their stead. These are the lessons by which I corrupt the youth, as you say.

Yes, that I say emphatically.

Then, by the gods, Meletus, of whom we are speaking, tell me and the court, in somewhat plainer terms, what you mean! for I do not as yet understand whether you affirm that I teach other men to acknowledge some gods, and

therefore that I do believe in gods, and am not an entire atheist—this you do not lay to my charge,—but only you say that they are not the same gods which the city recognizes—the charge is that they are different gods. Or, do you mean that I am an atheist simply, and a teacher of atheism?

I mean the latter—that you are a complete atheist.

What an extraordinary statement! Why do you think so, Meletus? Do you mean that I do not believe in the godhead of the sun or moon, like other men?

I assure you, judges, that he does not: for he says that the sun is stone, and the moon earth.

Friend Meletus, you think that you are accusing Anaxagoras: and you have but a bad opinion of the judges, if you fancy them illiterate to such a degree as not to know that these doctrines are found in the books of Anaxagoras the Clazomenian, which are full of them. And so, forsooth, the youth are said to be taught them by Socrates, when there are not unfrequently exhibitions of them at the theatre[3] (price of admission one drachma at the most); and they might pay their money, and laugh at Socrates if he pretends to father these extraordinary views. And so, Meletus, you really think that I do not believe in any god?

I swear by Zeus that you believe absolutely in none at all.

Nobody will believe you, Meletus, and I am pretty sure that you do not believe yourself. I cannot help thinking, men of Athens, that Meletus is reckless and impudent, and that he has written this indictment in a spirit of mere wantonness and youthful bravado. Has he not [27] compounded a riddle, thinking to try me? He said to himself:—I shall see whether the wise Socrates will discover

---

[3] Probably in allusion to Aristophanes who caricatured, and to Euripides who borrowed the notions of Anaxagoras, as well as to other dramatic poets.

my facetious contradiction, or whether I shall be able to deceive him and the rest of them. For he certainly does appear to me to contradict himself in the indictment as much as if he said that Socrates is guilty of not believing in the gods, and yet of believing in them—but this is not like a person who is in earnest.

I should like you, O men of Athens, to join me in examining what I conceive to be his inconsistency; and do you, Meletus, answer. And I must remind the audience of my request that they would not make a disturbance if I speak in my accustomed manner:

Did ever man, Meletus, believe in the existence of human things, and not of human beings? ... I wish, men of Athens, that he would answer, and not be always trying to get up an interruption. Did ever any man believe in horsemanship, and not in horses? or in fluteplaying, and not in flute-players? No, my friend; I will answer to you and to the court, as you refuse to answer for yourself. There is no man who ever did. But now please to answer the next question: Can a man believe in spiritual and divine agencies, and not in spirits or demigods?

He cannot.

How lucky I am to have extracted that answer, by the assistance of the court! But then you swear in the indictment that I teach and believe in divine or spiritual agencies (new or old, no matter for that) ; at any rate, I believe in spiritual agencies,—so you say and swear in the affidavit; and yet if I believe in divine beings, how can I help believing in spirits or demigods;—must I not? To be sure I must; and therefore I may assume that your silence gives consent. Now what are spirits or demigods? are they not either gods or the sons of gods?

Certainly they are.

But this is what I call the facetious riddle invented by you: the demigods or spirits are gods, and you say first that I do not believe in gods, and then again

that I do believe in gods; that is, if I believe in demigods. For if the demigods are the illegitimate sons of gods, whether by the nymphs or by any other mothers, of whom they are said to be the sons— what human being will ever believe that there are no gods if they are the sons of gods? You might as well affirm the existence of mules, and deny that of horses and asses. Such nonsense, Meletus, could only have been intended by you to make trial of me. You have put this into the indictment because you had nothing real of which to accuse me. But no one who has a particle of understanding will ever be convinced by you that the same men can believe in divine and superhuman things, and yet not believe that there are gods and demigods and heroes.     [28]

I have said enough in answer to the charge of Meletus: any elaborate defence is unnecessary; but I know only too well how many are the enmities which I have incurred, and this is what will be my destruction if I am destroyed; —not Meletus, nor yet Anytus, but the envy and detraction of the world, which has been the death of many good men, and will probably be the death of many more; there is no danger of my being the last of them.

Some one will say: And are you not ashamed, Socrates, of a course of life which is likely to bring you to an untimely end? To him I may fairly answer: There you are mistaken: a man who is good for anything ought not to calculate the chance of living or dying; he ought only to consider whether in doing anything he is doing right or wrong—acting the part of a good man or of a bad. Whereas, upon your view, the heroes who fell at Troy were not good for much, and the son of Thetis above all, who altogether despised danger in comparison with disgrace; and when he was so eager to slay Hector, his goddess mother said to him, that if he avenged his companion Patroclus, and slew Hector, he would die himself—

"Fate," she said, in these or the like words, "waits for you next after Hector"; he, receiving this warning, utterly despised danger and death, and instead of fearing them, feared rather to live in dishonour, and not to avenge his friend. "Let me die forthwith," he replies, "and be avenged of my enemy, rather than abide here by the beaked ships, a laughing-stock and a burden of the earth." Had Achilles any thought of death and danger? For wherever a man's place is, whether the place which he has chosen or that in which he has been placed by a commander, there he ought to remain in the hour of danger; he should not think of death or of anything but of disgrace. And this, O men of Athens, is a true saying.

Strange, indeed, would be my conduct, O men of Athens, if I who, when I was ordered by the generals whom you chose to command me at Potidaea and Amphipolis and Delium, remained where they placed me, like any other man, facing death—if now, when, as I conceive and imagine, God orders me to fulfil the philosopher's mission of searching into myself and other men, I were to desert my post through fear of [29] death, or any other fear; that would indeed be strange, and I might justly be arraigned in court for denying the existence of the gods, if I disobeyed the oracle because I was afraid of death, fancying that I was wise when I was not wise. For the fear of death is indeed the pretence of wisdom, and not real wisdom, being a pretence of knowing the unknown; and no one knows whether death, which men in their fear apprehend to be the greatest evil, may not be the greatest good. Is not this ignorance of a disgraceful sort, the ignorance which is the conceit that a man knows what he does not know? And in this respect only I believe myself to differ from men in general, and may perhaps claim to be wiser than they are:—that whereas I know but little of the world below, I do not suppose that I know: but

I do know that injustice and disobedience to a better, whether God or man, is evil and dishonourable, and I will never fear or avoid a possible good rather than a certain evil. And therefore if you let me go now, and are not convinced by Anytus, who said that since I had been prosecuted I must be put to death: (or if not that I ought never to have been prosecuted at all); and that if I escape now, your sons will all be utterly ruined by listening to my words— if you say to me, Socrates, this time we will not mind Anytus, and you shall be let off, but upon one condition, that you are not to enquire and speculate in this way any more, and that if you are caught doing so again you shall die;—if this was the condition on which you let me go, I should reply: Men of Athens, I honour and love you; but I shall obey God rather than you, and while I have life and strength I shall never cease from the practice and teaching of philosophy, exhorting any one whom I meet and saying to him after my manner: You, my friend,—a citizen of the great and mighty and wise city of Athens,—are you not ashamed of heaping up the greatest amount of money and honour and reputation, and caring so little about wisdom and truth and the greatest improvement of the soul, which you never regard or heed at all? And if the person with whom I am arguing, says: Yes, but I do care; then I do not leave him or let him go at once; but I proceed to interrogate and examine and cross-examine him, and if I think that he has no virtue in him, but only says that he has, I reproach him with undervaluing the greater, and overvaluing the less. And I [30] shall repeat the same words to every one whom I meet, young and old, citizen and alien, but especially to the citizens inasmuch as they are my brethren. For know that this is the command of God; and I believe that no greater good has ever happened in the state than my service to the God. For I do nothing but go about persuading you all, old and young alike, not to take thought for your persons or your properties, but first and chiefly to care about the greatest improvement of the soul. I tell you that virtue is not given by money, but that from virtue comes money and every other good of man, public as well as private. This is my teaching, and if this is the doctrine which corrupts the youth, I am a mischievous person, if any one says that this is not my teaching, he is speaking an untruth. Wherefore, O men of Athens, I say to you, do as Anytus bids or not as Anytus bids, and either acquit me or not; but whichever you do, understand that I shall never alter my ways, not even if I have to die many times.

Men of Athens, do not interrupt, but hear me; there was an understanding between us that you should hear me to the end: I have something more to say, at which you may be inclined to cry out; but I believe that to hear me will be good for you, and therefore I beg that you will not cry out. I would have you know, that if you kill such an one as I am, you will injure yourselves more than you will injure me. Nothing will injure me, not Meletus nor yet Anytus—they cannot, for a bad man is not permitted to injure a better than himself. I do not deny that Anytus may, perhaps, kill him, or drive him into exile, or deprive him of civil rights; and he may imagine, and others may imagine, that he is inflicting a great injury upon him: but there I do not agree. For the evil of doing as he is doing—the evil of unjustly taking away the life of another—is greater far.

And now, Athenians, I am not going to argue for my own sake, as you may think, but for yours, that you may not sin against the God by condemning me, who am his gift to you. For if you kill me you will not easily find a successor to me, who, if I may use such a ludicrous figure of speech, am a sort of gadfly, given to the state by God; and the state is a great and noble steed who is tardy in his motions owing to his very size, and requires to be stirred into life. I am that gadfly which God [31] has attached to the state, and all day long and in all places am always fastening upon you, arousing and persuading and reproaching you. You will not easily find another like me, and therefore I would advise you to spare me. I dare say that you may feel out of temper (like a person who is suddenly awakened from sleep), and you think that you might easily strike me dead as Anytus advises, and then you would sleep on for the remainder of your lives unless God in his care of you sent you another gadfly. When I say that I am given to you by God, the proof of my mission is this:—if I had been like other men, I should not have neglected all my own concerns or patiently seen the neglect of them during all these years, and have been doing yours, coming to you individually like a father or elder brother, exhorting you to regard virtue; such conduct, I say, would be unlike human nature. If I had gained anything, or if my exhortations had been paid, there would have been some sense in my doing so, but now, as you will perceive, not even the impudence of my accusers dares to say that I have ever exacted or sought pay of any one; of that they have no witness. And I have a sufficient witness to the truth of what I say—my poverty.

Some one may wonder why I go about in private giving advice and busying myself with the concerns of others, but do not venture to come forward in public and advise the state. I will tell you why. You have heard me speak at sundry times and in divers places of an oracle or sign which comes to me, and is the divinity which Meletus ridicules in the indictment. This sign, which is a kind of voice, first began to come to me when I was a child; it always forbids but never commands me to do anything which I am going to do. This is what deters me from being a politician.

And rightly, as I think. For I am certain, O men of Athens, that if I had engaged in politics, I should have perished long ago, and done no good either to you or to myself. And do not be offended at my telling you the truth: for the truth is, that no man who goes to war with you or any other multitude, honestly striving against the many lawless and unrighteous deeds which are done in a state, will save [32] his life; he who will fight for the right, if he would live even for a brief space, must have a private station and not a public one.

I can give you convincing evidence of what I say, not words only, but what you value far more—actions. Let me relate to you a passage of my own life which will prove to you that I should never have yielded to injustice from any fear of death, and that "as I should have refused to yield" I must have died at once. I will tell you a tale of the courts, not very interesting perhaps, but nevertheless true. The only office of state which I ever held, O men of Athens, was that of senator: the tribe Antiochis, which is my tribe, had the presidency at the trial of the generals who had not taken up the bodies of the slain after the battle of Arginusae; and you proposed to try them in a body, contrary to law, as you all thought afterwards; but at the time I was the only one of the Prytanes who was opposed to the illegality, and I gave my vote against you; and when the orators threatened to impeach and arrest me, and you called and shouted, I made up my mind that I would run the risk, having law and justice with me, rather than take part in your injustice because I feared imprisonment and death. This happened in the days of the democracy. But when the oligarchy of the Thirty was in power, they sent for me and four others into the rotunda, and bade us bring Leon the Salaminian from Salamis, as they wanted to put him to death. This was a specimen of the sort of commands which they were always giving with the view of implicating as many as possible in their crimes; and then I showed, not in word only but in deed, that if I may be allowed to use such an expression, I cared not a straw for death, and that my great and only care was lest I should do an unrighteous or unholy thing. For the strong arm of that oppressive power did not frighten me into doing wrong; and when we came out of the rotunda the other four went to Salamis and fetched Leon, but I went quietly home. For which I might have lost my life, had not the power of the Thirty shortly afterwards come to an end. And many will witness to my words.

Now do you really imagine that I could have survived all these years, if I had led a public life, supposing that like a good man I had always maintained the right and had made justice, as I ought, the first thing? No indeed, men of Athens, neither I nor any other man. But I have been always the [33] same in all my actions, public as well as private, and never have I yielded any base compliance to those who are slanderously termed my disciples, or to any other. Not that I have any regular disciples. But if any one likes to come and hear me while I am pursuing my mission, whether he be young or old, he is not excluded. Nor do I converse only with those who pay; but any one, whether he be rich or poor, may ask and answer me and listen to my words; and whether he turns out to be a bad man or a good one, neither result can be justly imputed to me; for I never taught or professed to teach him anything. And if any one says that he has ever learned or heard anything from me in private which all the world has not heard, let me tell you that he is lying.

But I shall be asked, Why do people delight in continually conversing with you? I have told you already, Athenians, the whole truth about this matter: they like to hear the cross-examination of the pretenders to wisdom; there is amusement in it. Now this duty of cross-examining other men has been imposed upon me by God; and has been signified to me by oracles, visions, and in every way in which the will of divine power was ever intimated to any one. This is true, O Athenians; or, if not true, would be soon refuted. If I am or have been corrupting the youth, those of them who are now grown up and have become sensible that I gave them bad advice in the days of their youth should come forward as accusers, and take their revenge; or if they do not like to come themselves, some of their relatives, fathers, brothers, or other kinsmen, should say what evil their families have suffered at my hands. Now is their time. Many of them I see in the court. There is Crito, who is of the same age and of the same deme with myself, and there is Critobulus his son, whom I also see. Then again there is Lysanias of Sphettus, who is the father of Aeschines—he is present; and also there is Antiphon of Cephisus, who is the father of Epigenes; and there are the brothers of several who have associated with me. There is Nicostratus the son of Theosdotides, and the brother of Theodotus (now Theodotus himself is dead, and therefore he, at any rate, will not seek to stop him); and there is Paralus the son of Demodocus, who had a brother Theages; and Adeimantus the son [34] of Ariston, whose brother Plato is present; and Aeantodorus, who is the brother of Apollodorus, whom I also see. I might mention a great many others, some of whom Meletus should have produced as witnesses in the course of his speech; and let him still produce them, if he has forgotten—I will make way for him. And let him say, if he has any testimony of the sort which he can produce. Nay, Athenians, the very opposite is the truth. For all these are ready to witness on behalf of the corrupter, of the injurer of their kindred, as Meletus and Anytus call me; not the corrupted youth only—there might have been a motive for that—but their uncorrupted elder relatives. Why should they too support me with their testimony? Why, indeed, except for the sake of truth and justice, and because they know that I am speaking the truth, and that Meletus is a liar.

Well, Athenians, this and the like of this is all the defence which I have to offer. Yet a word more. Perhaps there may be some one who is offended at me, when he calls to mind how he himself on a similar, or even a less serious occasion, prayed and entreated the judges with many tears, and how he produced his children in court, which was a moving spectacle, together with a host of relations and friends; whereas I, who am probably in danger of my life, will do none of these things. The contrast may occur to his mind, and he may be set against me, and vote in anger because he is displeased at me on this account. Now if there be such a person among you,—mind, I do not say that there is,—to him I may fairly reply: My friend, I am a man, and like other men, a creature of flesh and blood, and not "of wood or stone," as Homer says; and I have a family, yes, and sons, O Athenians, three in number, one almost a man, and two others who are still young; and yet I will not bring any of them hither in order to petition you for an acquittal. And why not? Not from any self-assertion or want of respect for you. Whether I am or am not afraid of death is another question, of which I will not now speak. But, having regard to public opinion, I feel that such conduct would be discreditable to myself, and to you, and to the whole state. One who has reached my years, and who has a name for wisdom, ought not to demean himself. Whether this opinion of me be deserved or not, at any rate the world has decided that Socrates is in some way superior to other men. And [35] if those among you who are are said to be superior in wisdom and courage, and any other virtue, demean themselves in this way, how shameful is their conduct! I have seen men of reputation, when they have been condemned, behaving in the strangest manner: they seemed to fancy that they were going to suffer something dreadful if they died, and that they could be immortal if you only allowed them to live; and I think that such are a dishonour to the state, and that any stranger coming in would have said of them that the most eminent men of Athens, to whom the Athenians themselves give honour and command, are no better than women. And I say that these things ought not to be done by those of us who have a reputation; and if they are done, you ought not to permit them; you ought rather to show that you are far more disposed to condemn the man who gets up a doleful scene and makes the city ridiculous, than him who holds his peace.

But, setting aside the question of public opinion, there seems to be something wrong in asking a favour of a judge, and thus procuring an acquittal, instead of informing and convincing him. For his duty is, not to make a present of justice, but to give judgment; and he has sworn that he will judge according to the laws, and not according to his own good pleasure; and we ought not to encourage you, nor should you allow yourselves to be encouraged, in this habit of perjury—there can be no piety in that. Do not then require me to do what I consider dishonourable and impious and wrong, especially now, when I am being tried for impiety on the indictment of Meletus. For if, O men of Athens, by force of persuasion and entreaty I could overpower your oaths, then I should be teaching you to believe that there are no gods, and in defending should simply convict myself of the charge of not believing in them. But that is not so—far otherwise. For I do believe that there are gods, and in a sense higher than that in which any of my accusers believe in them. And to you and to God I commit my cause, to be determined by you as is best for you and me.

There are many reasons why I am not grieved, O men of Athens, [36] at the vote of condemnation. I expected it, and am only surprised that the votes are so nearly equal; for I had thought that the majority against me would have been far larger; but now, had thirty votes gone over to the other side, I should have been acquitted. And I may say, I think, that I have escaped Meletus. I may say more; for without the assistance of Anytus and Lycon, any one may see that he would not have had a fifth part of the votes, as the law requires, in which case he would have incurred a fine of a thousand drachmae.

And so he proposes death as the penalty. And what shall I propose on my part, O men of Athens? Clearly that which is my due. And what is my due? What return shall be made to the man who has never had the wit to be idle during his whole life; but has been careless of what the many care for—wealth, and family interests, and military offices, and speaking in the assembly, and magistracies, and plots, and parties. Reflecting that I was really too honest a man to be a politician and live, I did not go where I could do no good to you or to myself; but where I could do the greatest good privately to every one of you, thither I went, and sought to persuade every man among you that he must look to himself, and seek virtue and wisdom before he looks to his private interests, and look to the state before he looks to the interests of the state; and that this should be the order which he observes in all his actions. What shall be done to such an one? Doubtless some good thing, O men of Athens, if he has his reward; and the good should be of a kind suitable to him. What would be a reward suitable to a poor man who is your benefactor, and who desires leisure that he may instruct you? There can be no reward so fitting as maintenance in the Prytaneum, O men of Athens, a reward which he deserves far more than the citizen who has won the prize at Olympia in the horse or chariot race, whether the chariots were drawn by two horses or by many. For I am in want, and he has enough; and he only gives you the appearance of happiness, and I give you the reality. And if I am [37] to estimate the penalty fairly, I should say that maintenance in the Prytaneum is the just return.

Perhaps you think that I am braving you in what I am saying now, as in what I said before about the tears and prayers. But this is not so. I speak rather because I am convinced that I never intentionally wronged any one, although I cannot convince you—the time has been too short; if there were a law at Athens, as there is in other cities, that a capital cause should not be decided in one day, then I believe that I should have convinced you. But I cannot in a moment refute great slanders; and, as I am convinced that I never wronged another, I will assuredly not wrong myself. I will not say of myself that I deserve any evil, or propose any penalty. Why should I? Because I am afraid of the penalty of death which Meletus proposes? When I do not know whether death is a good or an evil, why should I propose a penalty which would certainly be an evil? Shall I say imprisonment? And why should I live in prison, and be the slave of the magistrates of the year—of the Eleven? Or shall the penalty be a fine, and imprisonment un-

til the fine is paid? There is the same objection. I should have to lie in prison, for money I have none, and cannot pay. And if I say exile (and this may possibly be the penalty which you will affix), I must indeed be blinded by the love of life, if I am so irrational as to expect that when you, who are my own citizens, cannot endure my discourses and words, and have found them so grievous and odious that you will have no more of them, others are likely to endure me. No indeed, men of Athens, that is not very likely. And what a life should I lead, at my age, wandering from city to city, ever changing my place of exile, and always being driven out! For I am quite sure that wherever I go, there, as here, the young men will flock to me; and if I drive them away, their elders will drive me out at their request; and if I let them come, their fathers and friends will drive me out for their sakes.

Some one will say: Yes, Socrates, but cannot you hold your tongue, and then you may go into a foreign city, and no one will interfere with you? Now I have great difficulty in making you understand my answer to this. For if I tell you that to do as you say would be a disobedience to the God, and therefore that I cannot hold my tongue, you will not believe that I am serious; and if I say again that daily to discourse about [38] virtue, and of those other things about which you hear me examining myself and others, is the greatest good of man, and that the unexamined life is not worth living, you are still less likely to believe me. Yet I say what is true, although a thing of which it is hard for me to persuade you. Also, I have never been accustomed to think that I deserve to suffer any harm. Had I money I might have estimated the offence at what I was able to pay, and not have been much the worse. But I have none, and therefore I must ask you to proportion the fine to my means. Well, perhaps I could afford a mina, and therefore I propose that penalty: Plato, Crito, Critobulus, and Apollodorus, my friends here, bid me say thirty minae, and they will be the sureties. Let thirty minae be the penalty; for which sum they will be ample security to you.

Not much time will be gained, O Athenians, in return for the evil name which you will get from the detractors of the city, who will say that you killed Socrates, a wise man; for they will call me wise, even although I am not wise, when they want to reproach you. If you had waited a little while, your desire would have been fulfilled in the course of nature. For I am far advanced in years, as you may perceive, and not far from death. I am speaking now not to all of you, but only to those who have condemned me to death. And I have another thing to say to them: You think that I was convicted because I had no words of the sort which would have procured my acquittal—I mean if I had throught fit to leave nothing undone or unsaid. Not so; the deficiency which led to my conviction was not of words—certainly not. But I had not the boldness or impudence or inclination to address you as you would have liked me to do, weeping and wailing and lamenting, and saying and doing many things which you have been accustomed to hear from others, and which, as I maintain, are unworthy of me. I thought at the time that I ought not to do anything common or mean when in danger: nor do I now repent of the style of my defence; I would rather die having spoken after my manner, than speak in your manner and live. For neither in war nor yet at law ought I or any man to use [39] every way of escaping death. Often in battle there can be no doubt that if a man will throw away his arms, and fall on his knees before his pursuers, he may escape death; and in other dangers there are other ways of escaping death, if a man is willing to say and do anything.

The difficulty, my friends, is not to avoid death, but to avoid unrighteousness; for that runs faster than death. I am old and move slowly, and the slower runner has overtaken me, and my accusers are keen and quick, and the faster runner, who is unrighteousness, has overtaken them. And now I depart hence condemned by you to suffer the penalty of death,—they too go their ways condemned by the truth to suffer the penalty of villainy and wrong; and I must abide by my reward—let them abide by theirs. I suppose that these things may be regarded as fated,—and I think that they are well.

And now, O men who have condemned me, I would fain prophesy to you; for I am about to die, and in the hour of death men are gifted with prophetic power. And I prophesy to you who are my murderers, that immediately after my departure punishment far heavier than you have inflicted on me will surely await you. Me you have killed because you wanted to escape the accuser, and not to give an account of your lives. But that will not be as you suppose: far otherwise. For I say that there will be more accusers of you than there are now; accusers whom hitherto I have restrained: and as they are younger they will be more inconsiderate with you, and you will be more offended at them. If you think that by killing men you can prevent some one from censuring your evil lives, you are mistaken; that is not a way of escape which is either possible or honourable; the easiest and the noblest way is not to be disabling others, but to be improving yourselves. This is the prophecy which I utter before my departure to the judges who have condemned me.

Friends, who would have acquitted me, I would like also to talk with you about the thing which has come to pass, while the magistrates are busy, and before I go to the place at which I must die. Stay then a little, for we may as well talk with one another while there is time. You are my friends, and I should like to show you the meaning of [40] this event which has happened to me. O my judges—for you I may truly call judges—I should like to tell you of a wonderful circumstance. Hitherto the divine faculty of which the internal oracle is the source has constantly been in the habit of opposing me even about trifles, if I was going to make a slip or error in any matter; and now as you see there has come upon me that which may be thought, and is generally believed to be, the last and worst evil. But the oracle made no sign of opposition, either when I was leaving my house in the morning, or when I was on my way to the court, or while I was speaking, at anything which I was going to say; and yet I have often been stopped in the middle of a speech, but now in nothing I either said or did touching the matter in hand has the oracle opposed me. What do I take to be the explanation of this silence? I will tell you. It is an intimation that what has happened to me is a good, and that those of us who think that death is an evil are in error. For the customary sign would surely have opposed me had I been going to evil and not to good.

Let us reflect in another way, and we shall see that there is great reason to hope that death is a good; for one of two things—either death is a state of nothingness and utter unconsciousness, or, as men say, there is a change and migration of the soul from this world to another. Now if you suppose that there is no consciousness, but a sleep like the sleep of him who is undisturbed even by dreams, death will be an unspeakable gain. For if a person were to select the night in which his sleep was undisturbed even by dreams, and were to compare with this the other days and nights of his life, and then were to tell us how many days and nights he had passed in the course of his life better and more pleasantly than this one, I think that any man, I will not say a private man,

but even the great king will not find many such days or nights, when compared with the others. Now if death be of such a nature, I say that to die is gain; for eternity is then only a single night. But if death is the journey to another place, and there, as men say, all the dead abide, what good, O my friends and judges, can be greater than this? If indeed when the pilgrim arrives in the world below, he is delivered from [41] the professors of justice in this world, and finds the true judges who are said to give judgment there, Minos and Rhadamanthus and Aeacus and Triptolemus, and other sons of God who were righteous in their own life, that pilgrimage will be worth making. What would not a man give if he might converse with Orpheus and Musaeus and Hesiod and Homer? Nay, if this be true, let me die again and again. I myself, too, shall have a wonderful interest in there meeting and conversing with Palamedes, and Ajax the son of Telamon, and any other ancient hero who has suffered death through an unjust judgment; and there will be no small pleasure, as I think, in comparing my own sufferings with theirs. Above all, I shall then be able to continue my search into true and false knowledge; as in this world, so also in the next; and I shall find out who is wise, and who pretends to be wise, and is not. What would not a man give, O judges, to be able to examine the leader of the great Trojan expedition; or Odysseus or Sisyphus, or numberless others, men and women too! What infinite delight would there be in conversing with them and asking them questions! In another world they do not put a man to death for asking questions: assuredly not. For besides being happier than we are, they will be immortal, if what is said is true.

Wherefore, O judges, be of good cheer about death, and know of a certainty, that no evil can happen to a good man, either in life or after death. He and his are not neglected by the gods; nor has my own approaching end happened by mere chance. But I see clearly that the time had arrived when it was better for me to die and be released from trouble; wherefore the oracle gave no sign. For which reason, also, I am not angry with my condemners, or with my accusers; they have done me no harm, although they did not mean to do me any good; and for this I may gently blame them.

Still I have a favour to ask of them. When my sons are grown up, I would ask you, O my friends, to punish them; and I would have you trouble them, as I have troubled you, if they seem to care about riches, or anything, more than about virtue; or if they pretend to be something when they are really nothing, —then reprove them, as I have reproved you, for not caring about that for which they ought to care, and thinking that they are something when they are really nothing. And if you do this, both [42] I and my sons will have received justice at your hands.

The hour of departure has arrived, and we go our ways—I to die, and you to live. Which is better God only knows.

# MENO (complete)

PERSONS OF THE DIALOGUE

MENO                 A SLAVE OF MENO
SOCRATES         ANYTUS

MENO. Can you tell me Socrates [70] —is virtue something that can be taught? Or does it come by practice? Or is it neither teaching nor practice that gives it to a man but natural aptitude or something else?

SOCRATES. Well Meno, in the old days the Thessalians had a great reputation among the Greeks for their wealth and their horsemanship. Now it seems they are philosophers as well—es- [B] pecially the men of Larissa, where your friend Aristippus comes from. It is Gorgias who has done it. He went to that city and captured the hearts of the foremost of the Aleuadae for his wisdom (among them your own admirer Aristippus), not to speak of other leading Thessalians. In particular he got you into the habit of answering any question you might be asked, with the confidence and dignity ap- [C] propriate to those who know the answers, just as he himself invites questions of every kind from anyone in the Greek world who wishes to ask, and never fails to answer them. But here at Athens, my dear Meno, it is just [71] the reverse. There is a dearth of wisdom, and it looks as if it had migrated from our part of the country to yours. At any rate if you put your question to any of our people, they will all alike laugh and say: "You must think I am singularly fortunate, to know whether virtue can be taught or how it is acquired. The fact is that far from knowing whether it can be taught, I have no idea what virtue itself is."

That is my own case. I share the [B] poverty of my fellow-countrymen in this respect, and confess to my shame that I have no knowledge about virtue at all. And how can I know a property of something when I don't even know what it is? Do you suppose that somebody entirely ignorant who Meno is could say whether he is handsome and rich and well-born or the reverse? Is that possible, do you think?

MENO. No. But is this true about yourself, Socrates, that you don't even [C] know what virtue is? Is this the report that we are to take home about you?

SOCR. Not only that; you may say also that, to the best of my belief, I have never yet met anyone who did know.

MENO. What! Didn't you meet Gorgias when he was here?

SOCR. Yes.

MENO. And you still didn't think he knew?

SOCR. I'm a forgetful sort of person, and I can't say just now what I thought at the time. Probably he did know, and I expect you know what he used to say about it. So remind me what it was, [D] or tell me yourself if you will. No doubt you agree with him.

MENO. Yes I do.

SOCR. Then let's leave him out of it, since after all he isn't here. What do you yourself say virtue is? I do ask you in all earnestness not to refuse me, but to speak out. I shall be only too happy to be proved wrong if you and Gorgias turn out to know this, although I said I had never met anyone who did.

MENO. But there is no difficulty [E] about it. First of all, if it is manly virtue you are after, it is easy to see that the virtue of a man consists in managing the city's affairs capably, and so that he will help his friends and injure his foes while taking care to come to no harm himself. Or if you want a woman's virtue, that is easily described. She must be a good housewife, careful with her stores and obedient to her husband. Then there is another virtue for a child, male or female, and another for an old man, free or slave as [72] you like; and a great many more kinds of virtue, so that no one need be at a loss to say what it is. For every act and every time of life, with reference to each separate function, there is a virtue for each one of us, and similarly, I should say, a vice.

SOCR. I seem to be in luck. I wanted one virtue and I find that you have a whole swarm of virtues to offer. But seriously, to carry on this metaphor of the swarm, suppose I asked you what a bee is, what is its essential nature, [B] and you replied that bees were of many different kinds, what would you say if I went on to ask: "And is it in being bees that they are many and various and different from one another? Or would you agree that it is not in this respect that they differ, but in something else, some other quality like size or beauty?"

MENO. I should say that in so far as they are bees, they don't differ from one another at all.

SOCR. Suppose I then continued: [C] "Well, this is just what I want you to tell me. What is that character in respect of which they don't differ at all, but are all the same?" I presume you would have something to say?

MENO. I should.

SOCR. Then do the same with the virtues. Even if they are many and various, yet at least they all have some common character which makes them virtues. That is what ought to be kept in view by anyone who answers the question: "What is virtue?" Do you [D] follow me?

MENO. I think I do, but I don't yet really grasp the question as I should wish.

SOCR. Well, does this apply in your mind only to virtue, that there is a different one for a man and a woman and the rest? Is it the same with health and size and strength, or has health the same character everywhere, if it is [E] health, whether it be in a man or any other creature?

MENO. I agree that health is the same in a man or in a woman.

SOCR. And what about size and strength? If a woman is strong, will it be the same thing, the same strength, that makes her strong? My meaning is that in its character as strength, it is no different, whether it be in a man or in a woman. Or do you think it is?

MENO. No.

SOCR. And will virtue differ, in its [73] character as virtue, whether it be in a child or an old man, a woman or a man?

MENO. I somehow feel that this is not on the same level as the other cases.

SOCR. Well then, didn't you say that a man's virtue lay in directing the city well, and a woman's in directing her household well?

MENO. Yes.

SOCR. And is it possible to direct anything well—city or household or anything else—if not temperately and justly?

MENO. Certainly not.                    [B]

SOCR. And that means with temperance and justice?

MENO. Of course.

SOCR. Then both man and woman need the same qualities, justice and temperance, if they are going to be good.

MENO. It looks like it.

SOCR. And what about your child and old man? Could they be good if they were incontinent and unjust?

MENO. Of course not.

SOCR. They must be temperate and just?

MENO. Yes.

SOCR. So everyone is good in the [c] same way, since they become good by possessing the same qualities.

MENO. So it seems.

SOCR. And if they did not share the same virtue, they would not be good in the same way.

MENO. No.

SOCR. Seeing then that they all have the same virtue, try to remember and tell me what Gorgias, and you who share his opinion, say it is.

MENO. It must be simply the capacity to govern men, if you are looking for one quality to cover all the instances. [D]

SOCR. Indeed I am. But does this virtue apply to a child or a slave? Should a slave be capable of governing his master, and if he does, is he still a slave?

MENO. I hardly think so.

SOCR. It certainly doesn't sound likely. And here is another point. You speak of "capacity to govern." Shall we not add "justly but not otherwise"?

MENO. I think we should, for justice is virtue.

SOCR. Virtue, do you say, or a vir- [E] tue?

MENO. What do you mean?

SOCR. Something quite general. Take roundness, for instance. I should say that it is a shape, not simply that it is shape, my reason being that there are other shapes as well.

MENO. I see your point, and I agree that there are other virtues besides justice.

SOCR. Tell me what they are. Just [74] as I could name other shapes if you told me to, in the same way mention some other virtues.

MENO. In my opinion then courage is a virtue and temperance and wisdom and dignity and many other things.

SOCR. This puts us back where we were. In a different way we have discovered a number of virtues when we were looking for one only. This single virtue, which permeates each of them, we cannot find.

MENO. No, I cannot yet grasp it [B] as you want, a single virtue covering them all, as I do in other instances.

SOCR. I'm not surprised, but I shall do my best to get us a bit further if I can. You understand, I expect, that the question applies to everything. If someone took the example I mentioned just now, and asked you: "What is shape?" and you replied that roundness is shape, and he then asked you as I did, "Do you mean it is shape or a shape?" you would reply of course that it is a shape.

MENO. Certainly.

SOCR. Your reason being that there [c] are other shapes as well.

MENO. Yes.

SOCR. And if he went on to ask you what they were, you would tell him.

MENO. Yes.

SOCR. And the same with colour—if he asked you what it is, and on your replying "White," took you up with: "Is white colour or *a* colour?" you would say that it is *a* colour, because there are other colours as well.

MENO. I should.

SOCR. And if he asked you to, you [D] would mention other colours which are just as much colours as white is.

MENO. Yes.

SOCR. Suppose then he pursued the question as I did, and objected: "We always arrive at a plurality, but that is not the kind of answer I want. Seeing that you call these many particulars by one and the same name, and say that every one of them is a shape, even though they are the contrary of each other, tell me what this is which embraces round as well as straight, and what you mean by shape when you [E] say that straightness is a shape as much as roundness. You do say that?"

MENO. Yes.

SOCR. "And in saying it, do you mean that roundness is no more round than straight, and straightness no more straight than round?"

MENO. Of course not.

SOCR. "Yet you do say that roundness is no more a shape than straightness, and the other way about."

MENO. Quite true.

SOCR. "Then what is this thing which is called 'shape'? Try to tell me." If when asked this question either about shape or colour you said: "But I [75] don't understand what you want, or what you mean," your questioner would perhaps be surprised and say: "Don't you see that I am looking for what is the same in all of them?" Would you even so be unable to reply, if the question was: "What is it that is common to roundness and straightness and the other things which you call shapes?"

Do your best to answer, as practice for the question about virtue.

MENO. No, you do it, Socrates. [B]

SOCR. Do you want me to give in to you?

MENO. Yes.

SOCR. And will you in your turn give me an answer about virtue?

MENO. I will.

SOCR. In that case I must do my best. It's in a good cause.

MENO. Certainly.

SOCR. Well now, let's try to tell you what shape is. See if you accept this definition. Let us define it as the only thing which always accompanies colour. Does that satisfy you, or do you want it in some other way? I should be content if your definition of virtue were on similar lines.

MENO. But that's a naive sort of [C] definition, Socrates.

SOCR. How?

MENO. Shape, if I understand what you say, is what always accompanies colour. Well and good—but if somebody says that he doesn't know what colour is, but is no better off with it than he is with shape, what sort of answer have you given him, do you think?

SOCR. A true one; and if my questioner were one of the clever, disputatious and quarrelsome kind, I should say to him: "You have heard my [D] answer. If it is wrong, it is for you to take up the argument and refute it." However, when friendly people, like you and me, want to converse with each other, one's reply must be milder and more conducive to discussion. By that I mean that it must not only be true, but must employ terms with which the questioner admits he is familiar. So I will try to answer you like that. Tell me therefore, whether you recognize the term "end"; I mean limit or boundary —all these words I use in the same [E] sense. Prodicus might perhaps quarrel with us, but I assume you speak of something being bounded or coming to an end. That is all I mean, nothing subtle.

MENO. I admit the notion, and believe I understand your meaning.

SOCR. And again, you recognize [76] "surface" and "solid," as they are used in geometry?

MENO. Yes.

SOCR. Then with these you should by this time understand my definition of shape. To cover all its instances, I say that shape is that in which a solid terminates, or more briefly, it is the limit of a solid.

MENO. And how do you define colour?

SOCR. What a shameless fellow you are, Meno. You keep bothering an old man to answer, but refuse to exercise your memory and tell me what was [B] Gorgias's definition of virtue.

MENO. I will, Socrates, as soon as you tell me this.

SOCR. Anyone talking to you could tell blindfold that you are a handsome man and still have your admirers.

MENO. Why so?

SOCR. Because you are for ever laying down the law as spoilt boys do, who act the tyrant as long as their youth lasts. No doubt you have discovered that I [C] can never resist good looks. Well, I will give in and let you have your answer.

MENO. Do by all means.

SOCR. Would you like an answer à la Gorgias, such as you would most readily follow?

MENO. Of course I should.

SOCR. You and he believe in Empedocles's theory of effluences, do you not?

MENO. Whole-heartedly.

SOCR. And passages to which and through which the effluences make their way?

MENO. Yes.

SOCR. Some of the effluences fit into some of the passages, whereas others [D] are too coarse or too fine.

MENO. That is right.

SOCR. Now you recognize the term "sight"?

MENO. Yes.

SOCR. From these notions, then, "grasp what I would tell," as Pindar says. Colour is an effluence from shapes commensurate with sight and perceptible by it.

MENO. That seems to me an excellent answer.

SOCR. No doubt it is the sort you are used to. And you probably see that it provides a way to define sound and smell and many similar things.

MENO. So it does.                            [E]

SOCR. Yes, it's a high-sounding answer, so you like it better than the one on shape.

MENO. I do.

SOCR. Nevertheless, son of Alexidemus, I am convinced that the other is better; and I believe you would agree with me if you had not, as you told me yesterday, to leave before the mysteries, but could stay and be initiated.[1]

MENO. I would stay, Socrates, if [77] you gave me more answers like this.

SOCR. You may be sure I shan't be lacking in keenness to do so, both for your sake and mine; but I'm afraid I may not be able to do it often. However, now it is your turn to do as you promised, and try to tell me the general nature of virtue. Stop making many out of one, as the humorists say when somebody breaks a plate. Just leave virtue whole and sound and tell me what it

_____

1 Evidently the Athenians are about to celebrate the famous rites of the Eleusinian Mysteries, but Meno has to return to Thessaly before they fall due. Plato frequently plays upon the analogy between religious initiation, which bestowed a revelation of divine secrets, and the insight which comes from initiation into the truths of philosophy.

is, as in the examples I have given [B] you.

MENO. It seems to me then, Socrates, that virtue is, in the words of the poet, "to rejoice in the fine and have power," and I define it as desiring fine things and being able to acquire them.

SOCR. When you speak of a man desiring fine things, do you mean it is good things he desires?

MENO. Certainly.

SOCR. Then do you think some [C] men desire evil and others good? Doesn't everyone, in your opinon, desire good things?

MENO. No.

SOCR. And would you say that the others suppose evils to be good, or do they still desire them although they recognize them as evil?

MENO. Both, I should say.

SOCR. What? Do you really think that anyone who recognizes evils for what they are, nevertheless desires them?

MENO. Yes.

SOCR. Desires in what way? To possess them?

MENO. Of course. [D]

SOCR. In the belief that evil things bring advantage to their possessor, or harm?

MENO. Some in the first belief, but some also in the second.

SOCR. And do you believe that those who suppose evil things bring advantage understand that they are evil?

MENO. No, that I can't really believe.

SOCR. Isn't it clear then that this class, who don't recognize evils for what they are, don't desire evil but what they [E] think is good, though in fact it is evil; those who through ignorance mistake bad things for good obviously desire the good.

MENO. For them I suppose that is true.

SOCR. Now as for those whom you speak of as desiring evils in the belief that they do harm to their possessor,

these presumably know that they will be injured by them?

MENO. They must.

SOCR. And don't they believe that [78] whoever is injured is, in so far as he is injured, unhappy?

MENO. That too they must believe.

SOCR. And unfortunate?

MENO. Yes.

SOCR. Well, does anybody want to be unhappy and unfortunate?

MENO. I suppose not.

SOCR. Then if not, nobody desires what is evil; for what else is unhappiness but desiring evil things and getting them?

MENO. It looks as if you are right, [B] Socrates, and nobody desires what is evil.

SOCR. Now you have just said that virtue consists in a wish for good things plus the power to acquire them. In this definition the wish is common to everyone, and in that respect no one is better than his neighbour.

MENO. So it appears.

SOCR. So if one man is better than another, it must evidently be in respect of the power, and virtue, according to your account, is the power of acquiring good things. [C]

MENO. Yes, my opinion is exactly as you now express it.

SOCR. Let us see whether you have hit the truth this time. You may well be right. The power of acquiring good things, you say, is virtue?

MENO. Yes.

SOCR. And by good do you mean such things as health and wealth?

MENO. I include the gaining both of gold and silver and of high and honourable office in the State.

SOCR. Are these the only classes of goods that you recognize?

MENO. Yes, I mean everything of that sort.

SOCR. Right. In the definition of [D] Meno, hereditary guest-friend of the

Great King, the acquisition of gold and silver is virtue. Do you add "just and righteous" to the word "acquisition," or doesn't it make any difference to you? Do you call it virtue all the same even if they are unjustly acquired?

MENO. Certainly not.

SOCR. Vice then?

MENO. Most certainly.

SOCR. So it seems that justice or temperance or piety, or some other part of virtue, must attach to the acquisition. Otherwise, although it is a means to good things, it will not be virtue.    [E]

MENO. No, how could you have virtue without these?

SOCR. In fact lack of gold and silver, if it results from failure to acquire it— either for oneself or another—in circumstances which would have made its acquisition unjust, is itself virtue.

MENO. It would seem so.

SOCR. Then to have such goods is no more virtue than to lack them. Rather we may say that whatever is accom- [79] panied by justice is virtue, whatever is without qualities of that sort is vice.

MENO. I agree that your conclusion seems inescapable.

SOCR. But a few minutes ago we called each of these—justice, temperance, and the rest—a part of virtue?

MENO. Yes, we did.

SOCR. So it seems you are making a fool of me.

MENO. How so, Socrates?

SOCR. I have just asked you not to break virtue up into fragments, and given you models of the type of answer I wanted, but taking no notice of this you tell me that virtue consists in [B] the acquisition of good things with justice; and justice, you agree, is a part of virtue.

MENO. True.

SOCR. So it follows from your own statements that to act with a part of virtue is virtue, if you call justice and all the rest parts of virtue. The point I want to make is that whereas I asked you to give me an account of virtue as a whole, far from telling me what it is itself you say that every action is virtue which exhibits a part of virtue, as if you had already told me what [C] the whole is, so that I should recognize it even if you chop it up into bits. It seems to me that we must put the same old question to you, my dear Meno— the question: "What is virtue?"—if every act becomes virtue when combined with a part of virtue. That is, after all, what it means to say that every act performed with justice is virtue. Don't you agree that the same question needs to be put? Does anyone know what a part of virtue is, without knowing the whole?

MENO. I suppose not.

SOCR. No, and if you remember, [D] when I replied to you about shape just now, I believe we rejected the type of answer that employs terms which are still in question and not yet agreed upon.

MENO. We did, and rightly.

SOCR. Then please do the same. While the nature of virtue as a whole is still under question, don't suppose that you can explain it to anyone in terms of its parts, or by any similar type of ex- [E] planation. Understand rather that the same question remains to be answered; you say this and that about virtue, but what is it? Does this seem nonsense to you?

MENO. No, to me it seems right enough.

SOCR. Then go back to the beginning and answer my question. What do and your friend say that virtue is?

MENO. Socrates, even before I met you they told me that in plain truth [80] you are a perplexed man yourself and reduce others to perplexity. At this moment I feel you are exercising magic and witchcraft upon me and positively laying me under your spell until I am just a mass of helplessness. If I may be flippant, I think that not only in outward appearance but in other respects as well you are exactly like the flat stingray that one meets in the sea. Whenever anyone comes into contact with it, it numbs him, and that is the sort of thing that you seem to be doing to me now. My mind and my lips are literally [B] numb, and I have nothing to reply to you. Yet I have spoken about virtue hundreds of times, held forth often on the subject in front of large audiences, and very well too, or so I thought. Now I can't even say what it is. In my opinon you are well advised not to leave Athens and live abroad. If you behaved like this as a foreigner in another country, you would most likely be arrested as a wizard.

SOCR. You're a real rascal, Meno. You nearly took me in.

MENO. Just what do you mean?

SOCR. I see why you used a simile [C] about me.

MENO. Why, do you think?

SOCR. To be compared to something in return. All good-looking people, I know perfectly well, enjoy a game of comparisons. They get the best of it, for naturally handsome folk provoke handsome similes. But I'm not going to oblige you. As for myself, if the stingray paralyses others only through being paralysed itself, then the comparison is just, but not otherwise. It isn't that, knowing the answers myself, I perplex other people. The truth is rather that I infect them also with the perplexity [D] I feel myself. So with virtue now. I don't know what it is. You may have known before you came into contact with me, but now you look as if you don't. Nevertheless I am ready to carry out, together with you, a joint investigation and inquiry into what it is.

MENO. But how will you look for something when you don't in the least know what it is? How on earth are you going to set up something you don't know as the object of your search? To put it another way, even if you come right up against it, how will you know that what you have found is the thing you didn't know?

SOCR. I know what you mean. Do you realize that what you are bringing [E] up is the trick argument that a man cannot try to discover either what he knows or what he does not know? He would not seek what he knows, for since he knows it there is no need of the inquiry, nor what he does not know, for in that case he does not even know what he is to look for.

MENO. Well, do you think it a [81] good argument?

SOCR. No.

MENO. Can you explain how it fails?

SOCR. I can. I have heard from men and women who understand the truths of religion—

[*Here he presumably pauses to emphasize the solemn change of tone which the dialogue undergoes at this point.*]

MENO. What did they say?

SOCR. Something true, I thought, and fine.

MENO. What was it, and who were they?

SOCR. Those who tell it are priests and priestesses of the sort who make it their business to be able to account for the functions which they perform. Pindar speaks of it too, and many another of the poets who are divinely [B] inspired. What they say is this—see whether you think they are speaking the truth. They say that the soul of man is immortal: at one time it comes to an end—that which is called death—and at another is born again, but is never finally exterminated. On these grounds a man must live all his days as righteously as possible. For those from whom

Persephone receives requital for ancient
    doom,

In the ninth year she restores again
Their souls to the sun above.
From whom rise noble kings                    [c]
And the swift in strength and greatest in
   wisdom;
And for the rest of time
They are called heroes and sanctified by
   men.[2]

Thus the soul, since it is immortal and has been born many times, and has seen all things both here and in the other world, has learned everything that is. So we need not be surprised if it can recall the knowledge of virtue or anything else which, as we see, it once possessed. All nature is akin, and the [D] soul has learned everything, so that when a man has recalled a single piece of knowledge—*learned* it, in ordinary language—there is no reason why he should not find out all the rest, if he keeps a stout heart and does not grow weary of the search; for seeking and learning are in fact nothing but recollection.

We ought not then to be led astray by the contentious argument you quoted. It would make us lazy, and is music in the ears of weaklings. The other doctrine produces energetic seekers after knowledge; and being convinced of its truth, I am ready, with your help, to in- [E] quire into the nature of virtue.

MENO. I see, Socrates. But what do you mean when you say that we don't learn anything, but that what we call learning is recollection? Can you teach me that it is so?

SOCR. I have just said that you're a rascal, and now you ask me if I can teach you, when I say there is no such thing as teaching, only recollection. [82] Evidently you want to catch me contradicting myself straight away.

MENO. No, honestly, Socrates, I wasn't thinking of that. It was just habit. If you can in any way make clear to me

_____
2 The quotation is from Pindar.

that what you say is true, please do.

SOCR. It isn't an easy thing, but still I should like to do what I can since you ask me. I see you have a large number of retainers here. Call one of them, anyone you like, and I will use him to demonstrate it to you.     [B]

MENO. Certainly. (*To a slave-boy.*) Come here.

SOCR. He is a Greek and speaks our language?

MENO. Indeed yes—born and bred in the house.

SOCR. Listen carefully then, and see whether it seems to you that he is learning from me or simply being reminded.

MENO. I will.

SOCR. Now boy, you know that a square is a figure like this?

(*Socrates begins to draw figures in the sand at his feet. He points to the square* ABCD.)

BOY. Yes.

SOCR. It has all these four sides [c] equal?

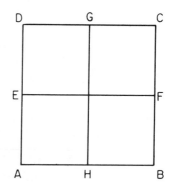

BOY. Yes.

SOCR. And these lines which go through the middle of it are also equal? (The lines EF, GH.)

BOY. Yes.

SOCR. Such a figure could be either larger or smaller, could it not?

BOY. Yes.

SOCR. Now if this side is two feet long, and this side the same, how many feet will the whole be? Put it this way. If it were two feet in this direction and only one in that, must not the area be two feet taken once?

BOY. Yes.

SOCR. But since it is two feet this [D] way also, does it not become twice two feet?

BOY. Yes.

SOCR. And how many feet is twice two? Work it out and tell me.

BOY. Four.

SOCR. Now could one draw another figure double the size of this, but similar, that is, with all its sides equal like this one?

BOY. Yes.

SOCR. How many feet will its area be?

BOY. Eight.

SOCR. Now then, try to tell me how long each of its sides will be. The [E] present figure has a side of two feet. What will be the side of the double-sized one?

BOY. It will be double, Socrates, obviously.

SOCR. You see, Meno, that I am not teaching him anything, only asking. Now he thinks he knows the length of the side of the eight-feet square.

MENO. Yes.

SOCR. But does he?

MENO. Certainly not.

SOCR. He thinks it is twice the length of the other.

MENO. Yes.

SOCR. Now watch how he recollects things in order—the proper way to rec-ollect.

You say that the side of double length produces the double-sized figure? Like this I mean, not long this way and [83] short that. It must be equal on all sides like the first figure, only twice its size, that is eight feet. Think a moment whether you still expect to get it from doubling the side.

BOY. Yes, I do.

SOCR. Well now, shall we have a line double the length of this (AB) if we add another the same length at this end (BJ)?

BOY. Yes.

SOCR. It is on this line then, ac- [B] cording to you, that we shall make the eight-feet square, by taking four of the same length?

BOY. Yes.

SOCR. Let us draw in four equal lines (*i.e. counting* AJ, *and adding* JK, KL, *and* LA *made complete by drawing in its second half* LD), using the first as a base. Does this not give us what you call the eight-feet figure?

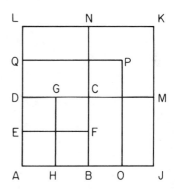

BOY. Certainly.

SOCR. But does it contain these four squares, each equal to the original four-feet one?

(*Socrates has drawn in the lines* CM, CN *to complete the squares that be wishes to point out.*)

BOY. Yes.

SOCR. How big is it then? Won't it be four times as big?

BOY. Of course.

SOCR. And is four times the same as twice?

BOY. Of course not.

SOCR. So doubling the side has [C] given us not a double but a fourfold figure?

BOY. True.

SOCR. And four times four are sixteen, are they not?

BOY. Yes.

SOCR. Then how big is the side of the eight-feet figure? This one has given us four times the original area, hasn't it?

BOY. Yes.

SOCR. And a side half the length gave us a square of four feet?

BOY. Yes.

SOCR. Good. And isn't a square of eight feet double this one and half that?

BOY. Yes.

SOCR. Will it not have a side [D] greater than this one but less than that?

BOY. I think it will.

SOCR. Right. Always answer what you think. Now tell me: was not this side two feet long, and this one four?

BOY. Yes.

SOCR. Then the side of the eight-feet figure must be longer than two feet but shorter than four?

BOY. It must.

SOCR. Try to say how long you [E] think it is.

BOY. Three feet.

SOCR. If so, shall we add half of this bit (BO, *half of* BJ) and make it three feet? Here are two, and this is one, and on this side similarly we have two plus one; and here is the figure you want.

(*Socrates completes the square* AOPQ.)

BOY. Yes.

SOCR. If it is three feet this way and three that, will the whole area be three times three feet?

BOY. It looks like it.

SOCR. And that is how many?

BOY. Nine.

SOCR. Whereas the square double our first square had to be how many?

BOY. Eight.

SOCR. But we haven't yet got the square of eight feet even from a three-feet side?

BOY. No.

SOCR. Then what length will give it? Try to tell us exactly. If you don't [84] want to count it up, just show us on the diagram.

BOY. It's no use, Socrates, I just don't know.

SOCR. Observe, Meno, the stage he has reached on the path of recollection. At the beginning he did not know the side of the square of eight feet. Nor indeed does he know it now, but then he thought he knew it and answered boldly, as was appropriate—he felt no perplexity. Now however he does feel perplexed. Not only does he not know the answer; he doesn't even think he knows.

MENO. Quite true.

SOCR. Isn't he in a better position now in relation to what he didn't know?

MENO. I admit that too.

SOCR. So in perplexing him and numbing him like the sting-ray, have we done him any harm?

MENO. I think not.

SOCR. In fact we have helped him to some extent towards finding out the right answer, for now not only is he ignorant of it but he will be quite glad to look for it. Up to now, he thought he could speak well and fluently, on many occasions and before large audiences, on the subject of a square double the size of a given square, maintaining that [C] it must have a side of double the length.

MENO. No doubt.

SOCR. Do you suppose then that he would have attempted to look for, or learn, what he thought he knew (though he did not), before he was thrown into perplexity, became aware of his ignorance, and felt a desire to know?

MENO. No.

SOCR. Then the numbing process was good for him?

MENO. I agree.

SOCR. Now notice what, starting from this state of perplexity, he will discover by seeking the truth in company with me, though I simply ask him ques- [D] tions without teaching him. Be ready to catch me if I give him any instruction or explanation instead of simply interrogating him on his own opinions.

*(Socrates here rubs out the previous figures and starts again.)*

Tell me, boy, is not this our square of four feet? (ABCD.) You understand?

BOY. Yes.

SOCR. Now we can add another equal to it like this? (BCEF.)

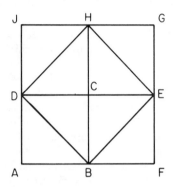

BOY. Yes.

SOCR. And a third here, equal to each of the others? (CEGH.)

BOY. Yes.

SOCR. And then we can fill in this one in the corner? (DCHJ.)

BOY. Yes. [E]

SOCR. Then here we have four equal squares?

BOY. Yes.

SOCR. And how many times the size of the first square is the whole?

BOY. Four times.

SOCR. And we want one double the size. You remember?

BOY. Yes.

SOCR. Now does this line going [85] from corner to corner cut each of these squares in half?

BOY. Yes.

SOCR. And these are four equal lines enclosing this area? (BEHD.)

BOY. They are.

SOCR. Now think. How big is this area?

BOY. I don't understand.

SOCR. Here are four squares. Has not each line cut off the inner half of each of them?

BOY. Yes.

SOCR. And how many such halves are there in this figure? (BEHD.)

BOY. Four.

SOCR. And how many in this one? (ABCD.)

BOY. Two.

SOCR. And what is the relation of four to two?

BOY. Double.

SOCR. How big is this figure then? [B]

BOY. Eight feet.

SOCR. On what base?

BOY. This one.

SOCR. The line which goes from cornor to corner of the square of four feet?

BOY. Yes.

SOCR. The technical name for it is "diagonal"; so if we use that name, it is your personal opinion that the square on the diagonal of the original square is double its area.

BOY. That is so, Socrates.

SOCR. What do you think, Meno? Has he answered with any opinions that were not his own?

MENO. No, they were all his. [C]

SOCR. Yet he did not know, as we agreed a few minutes ago.

MENO. True.

SOCR. But these opinions were somewhere in him, were they not?

MENO. Yes.

SOCR. So a man who does not know has in himself true opinions on a subject without having knowledge.

MENO. It would appear so.

SOCR. At present these opinions, being newly aroused, have a dream-like quality. But if the same questions are put to him on many occasions and in different ways, you can see that in the end he will have a knowledge on the subject [D] as accurate as anybody's.

MENO. Probably.

SOCR. This knowledge will not come from teaching but from questioning. He will recover it for himself.

MENO. Yes.

SOCR. And the spontaneous recovery of knowledge that is in him is recollection, isn't it?

MENO. Yes.

SOCR. Either then he has at some time acquired the knowledge which he now has, or he has always possessed it. If he always possessed it, he must always have known; if on the other hand he acquired it at some previous time, it cannot [E] have been in this life, unless somebody has taught him geometry. He will behave in the same way with all geometrical knowledge, and every other subject. Has anyone taught him all these? You ought to know, especially as he has been brought up in your household.

MENO. Yes, I know that no one ever taught him.

SOCR. And has he these opinions, or hasn't he?

MENO. It seems we can't deny it.

SOCR. Then if he did not acquire them in this life, isn't it immediately [86] clear that he possessed and had learned them during some other period?

MENO. It seems so.

SOCR. When he was not in human shape?

MENO. Yes.

SOCR. If then there are going to exist in him, both while he is and while he is not a man, true opinions which can be aroused by questioning and turned into knowledge, may we say that his soul has been for ever in a state of knowledge? Clearly he always either is or is not a man.

MENO. Clearly.

SOCR. And if the truth about reality is always in our soul, the soul must be [B] immortal, and one must take courage and try to discover—that is, to recollect —what one doesn't happen to know, or (more correctly) remember, at the moment.

MENO. Somehow or other I believe you are right.

SOCR. I think I am. I shouldn't like to take my oath on the whole story, but one thing I am ready to fight for as long as I can, in word and act: that is, that we shall be better, braver and more active men if we believe it right to look for what we don't know than if we [C] believe there is no point in looking because what we don't know we can never discover.

MENO. There too I am sure you are right.

SOCR. Then since we are agreed that it is right to inquire into something that one does not know, are you ready to face with me the question: what is virtue?

MENO. Quite ready. All the same, I would rather consider the question as I put it at the beginning, and hear your views on it; that is, are we to pursue virtue as something that can be taught, or do men have it as a gift of nature [D] or how?

SOCR. If I were your master as well as my own, Meno, we should not have inquired whether or not virtue can be taught until we had first asked the main question—what it is; but not only do you make no attempt to govern your own actions—you prize your freedom, I suppose—but you attempt to govern mine. And you succeed too, so I shall let you have your way. There's nothing else for it, and it seems we must inquire [E] into a single property of something about whose essential nature we are still in the dark. Just grant me one small relaxation of your sway, and allow me, in considering whether or not it can be taught, to make use of a hypothesis—the sort of thing, I mean, that geometers often use in their inquiries. When they are asked, for example, about a given area, whether it is possible for this area to be in- [87] scribed as a triangle in a given circle, they will probably reply: "I don't know yet whether it fulfils the conditions, but I think I have a hypothesis which will help us in the matter. It is this. If the area is such that, when one has applied it [sc. as a rectangle] to the given line [i.e. the diameter] of the circle, it is deficient by another rectangle similar to the one which is applied, then, I should say, one result follows; if not, the result is different. If you ask me, then, about [B] the inscription of the figure in the circle —whether it is possible or not—I am ready to answer you in this hypothetical way."[3]

Let us do the same about virtue. Since we don't know what it is or what it resembles, let us use a hypothesis in investigating whether it is teachable or not. We shall say: "What attribute of the soul must virtue be, if it is to be teachable or otherwise?" Well, in the first place, if it is anything else but knowledge, is there a possibility of anyone teaching it—or, in the language we used just now, reminding someone of it? We needn't worry about which name we are to give to the process, but simply ask: will it be teachable? Isn't it [C] plain to everyone that a man is not taught anything except knowledge?

MENO. That would be my view.

SOCR. If on the other hand virtue is some sort of knowledge, clearly it could be taught.

MENO. Certainly.

SOCR. So that question is easily settled; I mean, on what condition virtue would be teachable.

MENO. Yes.

SOCR. The next point then, I suppose, is to find out whether virtue is knowledge or something different.

MENO. That is the next question, I [D] agree.

SOCR. Well then, do we assert that virtue is something good? Is that assumption a firm one for us?

MENO. Undoubtedly.

---

[3] The geometrically illustration here adduced by Socrates is very loosely and obscurely expressed. Sir Thomas Heath in his *History of Greek Mathematics* (1921, vol. i, p. 298) says that C. Blass, writing in 1861, already know of thirty different interpretations, and that many more had appeared since then. Fortunately it is not necessary to understand the example in order to grasp the hypothetical method Socrates is expounding.

SOCR. That being so, if there exists any good thing different from, and not associated with, knowledge, virtue will not necessarily be any form of knowledge. If on the other hand knowledge embraces everything that is good, we shall be right to suspect that virtue is knowledge.

MENO. Agreed.

SOCR. First then, is it virtue which makes us good?

MENO. Yes.

SOCR. And if good, then advan- [E] tageous. All good things are advantageous, are they not?

MENO. Yes.

SOCR. So virtue itself must be something advantageous?

MENO. That follows also.

SOCR. Now suppose we consider what are the sort of things that profit us. Take them in a list. Health, we may say, and strength and good looks, and wealth— these and their like we call advantageous, you agree?

MENO. Yes.

SOCR. Yet we also speak of these [88] things as sometimes doing harm. Would you object to that statement?

MENO. No, it is so.

SOCR. Now look here: what is the controlling factor which determines whether each of these is advantageous or harmful? Isn't it right use which makes them advantageous, and lack of it, harmful?

MENO. Certainly.

SOCR. We must also take spiritual qualities into consideration. You recognize such things as temperance, justice, courage, quickness of mind, memory, nobility of character and others?

MENO. Yes of course I do. [B]

SOCR. Then take any such qualities which in your view are not knowledge but something different. Don't you think they may be harmful as well as advantageous? Courage for instance, if it is something thoughtless, is just a sort of confidence. Isn't it true that to be confident without reason does a man harm, whereas a reasoned confidence profits him?

MENO. Yes.

SOCR. Temperance and quickness of mind are no different. Learning and discipline are profitable in conjunction with wisdom, but without it harmful.

MENO. That is emphatically true. [c]

SOCR. In short, everything that the human spirit undertakes or suffers will lead to happiness when it is guided by wisdom, but to the opposite, when guided by folly.

MENO. A reasonable conclusion.

SOCR. If then virtue is an attribute of the spirit, and one which cannot fail to be beneficial, it must be wisdom; for all spiritual qualities in and by themselves are neither advantageous nor harmful, but become advantageous or harmful by the presence with them of wisdom or [D] folly. If we accept this argument, then virtue, to be something advantageous, must be a sort of wisdom.

MENO. I agree.

SOCR. To go back to the other class of things, wealth and the like, of which we said just now that they are sometimes good and sometimes harmful, isn't it the same with them? Just as wisdom when it governs our other psychological impulses turns them to advantage, and folly turns them to harm, so the mind by [E] its right use and control of these material assets makes them profitable, and by wrong use renders them harmful.

MENO. Certainly.

SOCR. And the right user is the mind of the wise man, the wrong user the mind of the foolish.

MENO. That is so.

SOCR. So we may say in general that the goodness of non-spiritual assets depends on our spiritual character, and the goodness of that on wisdom. This [89] argument shows that the advantageous element must be wisdom; and virtue, we agree, is advantageous, so that amounts to saying that virtue, either in whole or in part, is wisdom.

MENO. The argument seems to me fair enough.

SOCR. If so, good men cannot be good by nature.

MENO. I suppose not.

SOCR. There is another point. If [B] they were, there would probably be experts among us who could recognize the naturally good at an early stage. They would point them out to us and we should take them and shut them away safely in the Acropolis, sealing them up more carefully than bullion to protect them from corruption and ensure that when they came to maturity they would be of use to the State.

MENO. It would be likely enough.

SOCR. Since then goodness does not come by nature, is it got by learning? [c]

MENO. I don't see how we can escape the conclusion. Indeed it is obvious on our assumption that, if virtue is knowledge, it is teachable.

SOCR. I suppose so. But I wonder if we were right to bind ourselves to that.

MENO. Well, it seemed all right just now.

SOCR. Yes, but to be sound it has got to seem all right not only "just now" but at this moment and in the future.

MENO. Of course. But what has [D] occurred to you to make you turn against it and suspect that virtue may not be knowledge?

SOCR. I'll tell you. I don't withdraw from the position that if it is knowledge, it must be teachable; but as for its being knowledge, see whether you think my doubts on this point are well founded. If anything—not virtue only —is a possible subject of instruction, must there not be teachers and students of it?

MENO. Surely.                                    [E]

SOCR. And what of the converse, that if there are neither teachers nor students of a subject, we may safely infer that it cannot be taught?

MENO. That is true. But don't you think there are teachers of virtue?

SOCR. All I can say is that I have often looked to see if there are any, and in spite of all my efforts I cannot find them, though I have had plenty of fellow-searchers, the kind of men especially whom I believe to have most experience in such matters. But look, Meno, here's a piece of luck. Anytus has just sat [90] down beside us. We couldn't do better than make him a partner in our inquiry. In the first place he is the son of Anthemion, a man of property and good sense, who didn't get his money out of the blue or as a gift—like Ismenias of Thebes who has just come into the fortune of a Croesus—but earned it by his own brains and hard work. Besides this he shows himself a decent, modest citizen with no arrogance or bombast or offensiveness [B] about him. Also he brought up his son well and had him properly educated, as the Athenian people appreciate: look how they elect him into the highest offices in the State. This is certainly the right sort of man with whom to inquire whether there are any teachers of virtue, and if so who they are.

Please help us, Anytus—Meno, who is a friend of your family, and myself—to find out who may be the teachers of this subject. Look at it like this. If we wanted Meno to become a good doctor, [C] shouldn't we send him to the doctors to be taught?

ANYTUS. Of course.

SOCR. And if we wanted him to become a shoemaker, to the shoemakers?

ANYT. Yes.

SOCR. And so on with other trades?

ANYT. Yes.

SOCR. Now another relevant question. When we say that to make Meno a doctor we should be right in sending him to the doctors, have we in mind that the sensible thing is to send him [D] to those who profess the subject rather than to those who don't, men who charge a fee as professionals, having announced that they are prepared to teach whoever likes to come and learn?

ANYT. Yes.

SOCR. The same is surely true of flute-playing and other accomplishments. If you want to make someone a performer on the flute it would be very [E] foolish to refuse to send him to those who undertake to teach the art and are paid for it, but to go and bother other people instead and have him try to learn from them—people who don't set up to be teachers or take any pupils in the subject which we want our young man to learn. Doesn't that sound very unreasonable?

ANYT. Sheer stupidity I should say.

SOCR. I agree. And now we can both consult together about our visitor [91] Meno. He has been telling me all this while that the longs to acquire the kind of wisdom and virtue which fits men to manage an estate or govern a city, to look after their parents, and to entertain and send off guests in proper style, both their own countrymen and foreigners. With this in mind, to whom would [B] it be right to send him? What we have just said seems to show that the right people are those who profess to be teachers of virtue and offer their services freely to any Greek who wishes to learn, charging a fixed fee for their instruction.

ANYT. Whom do you mean by that, Socrates?

SOCR. Surely you know yourself that they are the men called Sophists.

ANYT. Good heavens, what a thing [C] to say! I hope no relative of mine or any of my friends, Athenian or foreign, would be so mad as to go and let himself be ruined by those people. That's what they are, the manifest ruin and corruption of anyone who comes into contact with them.

SOCR. What, Anytus? Can they be so different from other claimants to useful knowledge that they not only don't do good, like the rest, to the material that one puts in their charge, but on the [D] contrary spoil it—and have the effrontery to take money for doing so? I for one find it difficult to believe you. I know that one of them alone, Protagoras, earned more money from being a Sophist than an outstandingly fine craftsman like Phidias and ten other sculptors put together. A man who mends old shoes or restores coats couldn't get away with it for a month if he gave them back in [E] worse condition than he received them; he would soon find himself starving. Surely it is incredible that Protagoras took in the whole of Greece, corrupting his pupils and sending them away worse than when they came to him, for more than forty years. I believe he was nearly seventy when he died, and had been practising for forty years, and all that time—indeed to this very day—his reputation has been consistently high; and there are plenty of others besides [92] Protagoras, some before his time and others still alive. Are we to suppose from your remark that they consciously deceive and ruin young men, or are they unaware of it themselves? Can these remarkably clever men—as some regard them—be mad enough for that?

ANYT. Far from it, Socrates. It isn't they who are mad, but rather the young men who hand over their money, and those responsible for them, who let them get into the Sophists' hands, are even [B] worse. Worst of all are the cities who allow them in, or don't expel them, whether it be a foreigner or one of themselves who tries that sort of game.

SOCR. Has one of the Sophists done you a personal injury, or why are you so hard on them?

ANYT. Heavens, no! I've never in my life had anything to do with a single one of them, nor would I hear of any of my family doing so.

SOCR. So you've had no experience of them at all?

ANYT. And don't want any either. [C]

SOCR. You surprise me. How can you know what is good or bad in something when you have no experience of it?

ANYT. Quite easily. At any rate I know *their* kind, whether I've had experience or not.

SOCR. It must be second sight, I suppose; for how else you know about them, judging from what you tell me yourself, I can't imagine. However, we are not asking whose instruction it is that [D] would ruin Meno's character. Let us say that those are the Sophists if you like, and tell us instead about the ones we want. You can do a good turn to a friend of your father's house if you will let him know to whom in our great city he should apply for proficiency in the kind of virtue I have just described.

ANYT. Why not tell him yourself?

SOCR. Well, I did mention the men who in my opinion teach these things, but apparently I was talking nonsense. So you say, and you may well be right. [E] Now it is your turn to direct him; mention the name of any Athenian you like.

ANYT. But why mention a particular individual? Any decent Athenian gentleman whom he happens to meet, if he follows his advice, will make him a better man than the Sophists would.

SOCR. And did these gentlemen get their fine qualities spontaneously—self-taught, as it were, and yet able to teach this untaught virtue to others?     [93]

ANYT. I suppose they in their turn learned it from forebears who were gentlemen like themselves. Would you deny that there have been many good men in our city?

SOCR. On the contrary, there are plenty of good statesmen here in Athens and have been as good in the past. The question is, have they also been good teachers of their own virtue? That is the point we are discussing now—not whether or not there are good men in Athens or whether there have been in [B] past times, but whether virtue can be taught. It amounts to the question whether the good men of this and former times have known how to hand on to someone else the goodness that was in themselves, or whether on the contrary it is not something that can be handed over, or that one man can receive from another. That is what Meno and I have long been puzzling over. Look at it from your own point of view. You would [c] say that Themistocles was a good man?

ANYT. Yes, none better.

SOCR. And that he, if anyone, must have been a good teacher of his own virtue?

ANYT. I suppose so, if he wanted to be.

SOCR. But don't you think he must have wanted others to become worthy men—above all, surely, his own son? Do you suppose he grudged him this and purposely didn't pass on his own [D] virtue to him? You must have heard that he had his son Cleophantus so well trained in horsemanship that he could stand upright on horseback and throw a javelin from that position; and many other wonderful accomplishments the young man had, for his father had him taught and made expert in every skill that a good instructor could impart. You must have heard this from older people?

ANYT. Yes.

SOCR. No one, then, could say that there was anything wrong with the boy's natural powers?

ANYT. Perhaps not.                    [E]

SOCR. But have you ever heard anyone, young or old, say that Cleophantus the son of Themistocles was a good and wise man in the way that his father was?

ANYT. Certainly not.

SOCR. Must we conclude then that Themistocle's aim was to educate his son in other accomplishments, but not to make him any better than his neighbours in his own type of wisdom—that is, supposing that virtue could be taught?

ANYT. I hardly think we can.

SOCR. So much then for Themistocles as a teacher of virtue, whom you yourself agree to have been one of the best men of former times. Take another [94] example, Aristides son of Lysimachus. You accept him as a good man?

ANYT. Surely.

SOCR. He too gave his son Lysimachus the best education in Athens, in all subjects where a teacher could help; but did he make him a better man than his neighbour? You know him, I think, and can say what he is like. Or again there is Pericles, that great and wise man. [B] He brought up two sons, Paralus and Xanthippus, and had them taught riding, music, athletics, and all the other skilled pursuits till they were as good as any in Athens. Did he then not want to make them good men? Yes, he wanted that, no doubt, but I am afraid it is something that cannot be done by teaching. And in case you should think that only very few, and those the most [c] insignificant, lacked this power, consider that Thucydides also had two sons, Melesias and Stephanus, so whom he gave an excellent education. Among other things they were the best wrestlers in Athens, for he gave one to Xanthias to train and the other to Eudoxus—the two who, I understand, were considered the finest wrestlers of their time. You remember?

ANYT. I have heard of them.

SOCR. Surely then he would never have had his children taught these expensive pursuits and yet refused to teach them to be good men—which would have [D] cost nothing at all—if virtue could have been taught? You are not going to tell me that Thucydides was a man of no account, or that he had not plenty of friends both at Athens and among the allies? He came of an influential family and was a great power both here and in the rest of Greece. If virtue could have been taught, he would have found the man to make his sons good, either among our own citizens or abroad, supposing [E] his political duties left him no time to do it himself. No, my dear Anytus, it looks as if it cannot be taught.

ANYT. You seem to me, Socrates, to be too ready to run people down. My advice to you, if you will listen to it, is to be careful. I dare say that in all cities it is easier to do a man harm than good, and it is certainly so here, as I expect [95] you know yourself.

SOCR. Anytus seems angry, Meno, and I am not surprised. He thinks I am slandering our statesmen, and moreover he believes himself to be one of them. He doesn't know what slander really is: if he ever finds out he will forgive me.

However, tell me this yourself: are there not similar fine characters in your country?

MENO. Yes, certainly.

SOCR. Do they come forward of [B] their own accord to teach the young? Do they agree that they are teachers and that virtue can be taught?

MENO. No indeed, they don't agree on it at all. Sometimes you will hear them say that it can be taught, sometimes that it cannot.

SOCR. Ought we then to class as teachers of it men who are not even agreed that it can be taught?

MENO. Hardly, I think.

SOCR. And what about the Sophists, the only people who profess to teach [C] it? Do you think they do?

MENO. The thing I particularly admire about Gorgias, Socrates, is that you will never hear him make this claim; indeed he laughs at the others when he hears them do so. In his view his job is to make clever speakers.

SOCR. So you too don't think the Sophists are teachers?

MENO. I really can't say. Like most people I waver—sometimes I think they are and sometimes I think they are not.

SOCR. Has it ever occurred to you that you and our statesmen are not alone [D] in this? The poet Theognis likewise says in one place that virtue is teachable and in another that it is not.

MENO. Really? Where?

SOCR. In the elegiacs in which he writes:

Eat, drink, and sit with men of power and
   weight,

Nor scorn to gain the favour of the great.
For fine men's teaching to fine ways will
   win thee:                                       [E]
Low company destroys what wit is in thee.

There he speaks as if virtue can be taught, doesn't he?

MENO. Clearly.

SOCR. But elsewhere he changes his ground a little:

Were mind by art created and instilled
Immense rewards had soon the pockets
   filled

of the people who could do this. Moreover

No good man's son would ever worthless
   be,
Taught by wise counsel. But no teacher's
   skill                                           [96]
Can turn to good what is created ill.

Do you see how he contradicts himself?

MENO. Plainly.

SOCR. Can you name any other subject, in which the professed teachers are not only not recognized as teachers of others, but are thought to have no understanding of it themselves, and to [B] be no good at the very subject they profess to teach; whereas those who are acknowledged to be the best at it are in two minds whether it can be taught or not? When people are so confused about a subject, can you say that they are in a true sense teachers?

MENO. Certainly not.

SOCR. Well, if neither the Sophists nor those who display fine qualities themselves are teachers of virtue, I am sure no one else can be, and if there are [C] no teachers, there can be no students either.

MENO. I quite agree.

SOCR. And we have also agreed that a subject of which there were neither teachers nor students was not one which could be taught.

MENO. That is so.

SOCR. Now there turn out to be neither teachers nor students of virtue, so it would appear that virtue cannot be taught.

MENO. So it seems, if we have made [D] no mistake; and it makes me wonder, Socrates, whether there are in fact no good men at all, or how they are produced when they do appear.

SOCR. I have a suspicion, Meno, that you and I are not much good. Our masters Gorgias and Prodicus have not trained us properly. We must certainly take ourselves in hand, and try to find someone who will improve us by hook or by crook. I say this with our recent [E] discussion in mind, for absurdly enough we failed to perceive that it is not only under the guidance of knowledge that human action is well and rightly conducted. I believe that may be what prevents us from seeing how it is that men are made good.

MENO. What do you mean?

SOCR. This. We were correct, were we not, in agreeing that good men must be profitable or useful? It cannot be otherwise, can it?                              [97]

MENO. No.

SOCR. And again that they will be of some use if they conduct our affairs aright—that also was correct?

MENO. Yes.

SOCR. But in insisting that knowledge was a *sine qua non* for right leadership, we look like being mistaken.

MENO. How so?

SOCR. Let me explain. If someone knows the way to Larissa, or anywhere else you like, then when he goes there and takes others with him he will be a good and capable guide, you would agree?

MENO. Of course.

SOCR. But if a man judges correctly [B] which is the road, though he has never been there and doesn't know it, will he not also guide others aright?

MENO. Yes, he will.

SOCR. And as long as he has a correct opinion on the points about which the other has knowledge, he will be just as good a guide, believing the truth but not knowing it.

MENO. Just as good.

SOCR. Therefore true opinion is as good a guide as knowledge for the purpose of acting rightly. That is what we left out just now in our discussion of [C] the nature of virtue, when we said that knowledge is the only guide to right action. There was also, it seems, true opinion.

MENO. It seems so.

SOCR. So right opinion is something no less useful than knowledge.

MENO. Except that the man with knowledge will always be successful, and the man with right opinion only sometimes.

SOCR. What? Will he not always be successful so long as he has the right opinion?

MENO. That must be so, I suppose. [D] In that case, I wonder why knowledge should be so much more prized than right opinion, and indeed how there is any difference between them.

SOCR. Shall I tell you the reason for your surprise, or do you know it?

MENO. No, tell me.

SOCR. It is because you have not observed the statues of Daedalus. Perhaps you don't have them in your country.

MENO. What makes you say that?

SOCR. They too, if no one ties them down, run away and escape. If tied, they stay where they are put.

MENO. What of it?                              [E]

SOCR. If you have one of his works untethered, it is not worth much: it gives you the slip like a runaway slave. But a tethered specimen is very valuable, for they are magnificent creations. And that, I may say, has a bearing on the matter of true opinions. True opinions are a fine thing and do all sorts of good so long as they stay in their place; [98] but they will not stay long. They run away from a man's mind, so they are not worth much until you tether them by working out the reason. That process, my dear Meno, is recollection, as we agreed earlier. Once they are tied down, they become knowledge, and are stable. That is why knowledge is something more valuable than right opinion. What distinguishes one from the other is the tether.

MENO. It does seem something like that, certainly.

SOCR. Well of course, I have only [B] been using an analogy myself, not knowledge. But it is not, I am sure, a mere guess to say that right opinion and knowledge are different. There are few things that I should claim to know, but that at least is among them, whatever else is.

MENO. You are quite right.

SOCR. And is this right too, that true opinion when it governs any course of action produces as good a result as knowledge?

MENO. Yes, that too is right, I think.

SOCR. So that for practical purposes [C] right opinion is no less useful than knowledge, and the man who has it is no less useful than the one who knows.

MENO. That is so.

SOCR. Now we have agreed that the good man is useful.

MENO. Yes.

SOCR. To recapitulate then: assuming that there are men good and useful to the community, it is not only knowledge that makes them so, but also right [D] opinion, and neither of these comes by nature but both are acquired—or do you think either them *is* natural?

MENO. No.

SOCR. So if both are acquired, good men themselves are not good by nature.

MENO. No.

SOCR. That being so, the next thing we inquired was whether their goodness was a matter of teaching, and we decided that it would be, if virtue were knowledge, and conversely, that if it could be taught, it would be knowledge.

MENO. Yes.

SOCR. Next, that if there were teachers of it, it could be taught, but not if there were none.                                       [E]

MENO. That was so.

SOCR. But we have agreed that there are no teachers of it, and so that it cannot be taught and is not knowledge.

MENO. We did.

SOCR. At the same time we agreed that it is something good, and that to be useful and good consists in giving right guidance.

MENO. Yes.

SOCR. And that these two, true [99] opinion and knowledge, are the only things which direct us aright and the possession of which makes a man a true guide. We may except chance, because what turns out right by chance is not due to human direction, and say that where human control leads to right ends, these two principles are directive, true opinion and knowledge.

MENO. Yes, I agree.

SOCR. Now since virtue cannot be taught, we can no longer believe it to be knowledge, so that one of our two [B] good and useful principles is excluded, and knowledge is not the guide in public life.

MENO. No.

SOCR. It is not then by the possession of any wisdom that such men as Themistocles, and the others whom Anytus mentioned just now, became leaders in their cities. This fact, that they do not owe their eminence to knowledge, will explain why they are unable to make others like themselves.

MENO. No doubt it is as you say.

SOCR. That leaves us with the other alternative, that it is well-aimed con- [C] jecture which statesmen employ in upholding their countries' welfare. Their position in relation to knowledge is no different from that of prophets and tellers of oracles, who under divine inspiration utter many truths, but have no knowledge of what they are saying.

MENO. It must be something like that.

SOCR. And ought we not to reckon

those men divine who with no conscious thought are repeatedly and outstandingly successful in what they do or say?

MENO. Certainly.

SOCR. We are right therefore to give this title to the oracular priests and [D] the prophets that I mentioned, and to poets of every description. Statesmen too, when by their speeches they get great things done yet know nothing of what they are saying, are to be considered as acting no less under divine influence, inspired and possessed by the divinity.

MENO. Certainly.

SOCR. Women, you know, Meno, do call good men "divine," and the Spartans too, when they are singing a good man's praises, say "He is divine."

MENO. And it looks as if they are [E] right—though our friend Anytus may be annoyed with you for saying so.

SOCR. I can't help that. We will talk to him some other time. If all we have said in this discussion, and the questions we have asked, have been right, virtue will be acquired neither by nature nor by teaching. Whoever has it gets if by divine dispensation without taking [100] thought, unless he be the kind of statesman who can create another like himself. Should there be such a man, he would be among the living practically what Homer said Tiresias was among the dead, when he described him as the only one in the underworld who kept his wits —"the others are mere flitting shades." Where virtue is concerned such a man would be just like that, a solid reality among shadows.

MENO. That is finely put, Socrates. [B]

SOCR. On our present reasoning then, whoever has virtue gets it by divine dispensation. But we shall not understand the truth of the matter until, before asking how men get virtue, we try to discover what virtue is in and by itself. Now it is time for me to go; and my request to you is that you will allay the anger of your friend Anytus by convincing him that what you now believe is true. If you succeed, the Athenians may have cause to thank you.

## PHAEDO (in part : 72-82, 113-end)

### 72E-77A   A Complementary Argument. The Theory of Recollection

Cebes rejoined: "There is also [72E] another theory which, if true, points the same way, Socrates: the one that you are constantly asserting, namely that learning is really just recollection, from which it follows presumably that what we now call to mind we have learnt at some previous time; which would [73] not be possible unless our souls existed somewhere before being born in this human frame. Hence we seem to have another indication that the soul is something immortal."

Simmias now intervened to ask: "But how is that proved, Cebes? Please re-

mind me, as I can't quite remember at the moment."[1]

"First," replied Cebes, "by the excellent argument that when people are asked questions they can produce the right answers to anything of their own accord, provided that the questioning is done properly. Of course they wouldn't be able to do so unless they had knowledge and correct views within them. Secondly, if you confront people with anything in the nature of a diagram, you

---

1 Simmias' defective memory is doubtless no more than a device to make it more natural for Socrates to expound and defend a theory, which if it had in fact been his own, would presumably have been quite familiar to his present audience.

have the plainest proof of the point [B] in question."

"And if that doesn't convince you, Simmias," said Socrates, "I will suggest another consideration to which you may perhaps agree. You are evidently sceptical about the possibility of what is called learning being recollection."

"Not sceptical," said Simmias: "what I need is just what we are talking about, namely to recollect. In point of fact, thanks to Cebes's setting out of the arguments I do already almost remember, and am almost convinced; all the same, I should like now to hear how you yourself have set them out."

"I will tell you. We agree, I take [C] it, that to be reminded of something implies having at some previous time known it?"

"Certainly."

"And can we further agree that recollection may take the form of acquiring knowledge in a particular way, I mean like this: a man who has seen or heard or by some other sense perceived something may come to know something other than that, may think of something else besides that, something that is the object of a different knowledge. When this happens are we not justified in saying that he recollects or is reminded of the new object that he has thought of?"                                            [D]

"How do you mean?"

"To give an example, the knowledge of a man is different from that of a lyre."

"Of course."

"Well, you know how a lover feels when he sees a lyre or a cloak or some other object commonly used by his beloved: he apprehends the lyre, but he also conceives in his mind the form of the boy to whom it belongs; and that is reminder. Similarly one who sees Simmias is often reminded of Cebes, and we could think of any number of similar cases."

"Yes indeed, any number," agreed Simmias emphatically.

"Reminder then may take that [E] form: but it is most apt to occur in connexion with things that we have forgotten owing to the lapse of time and our not having thought about them. Isn't that so?"

"Yes, certainly."

"Another point: is it possible to see the picture of a horse or a lyre and be reminded of their owner: or again to see a picture of Simmias and be reminded of Cebes?"

"Certainly."

"Or alternatively to see a picture of Simmias and be reminded of Simmias?"

"Yes, that is possible."                    [74]

"And from all this it follows, doesn't it, that we may be reminded of things either by something like them or by something unlike them?"

"It does."

"Moreover, when it is by something like the other thing, are we not certain to find ourselves doing something else besides, namely asking ourselves whether the similarity between the object and the thing it reminds us of is defective or not?"

"Certainly we shall."

"Well now, see if you agree with my next point. We maintain, do we not, that there is such a thing as equality, not the equality of one log to another, or one stone to another, but something beyond all these cases, something different, equality itself. May we maintain that that exists, or may we not?"

"Most assuredly we may," answered Simmias: "not a doubt of it."      [B]

"And have we knowledge of it, in and by itself?"

"Certainly we have."

"Then where do we get that knowledge from? Mustn't it be from the objects we mentioned just now, the equal logs or stones or whatever they were that we saw? Didn't they lead us to conceive of that other something? You do regard it as something other than those things, don't you? Look at it like this: two stones or two logs equal in length sometimes seem equal to one man, but not to another, though they haven't changed."

"Yes certainly."

"But now, what about equals them- [c] selves? Have they ever appeared to you to be unequal, or equality to be inequality?"

"Never, Socrates."

"Then those equal objects are not the same as the equal itself."

"Far from it, I should say."

"And yet it is from those equal objects, different as they are from this equal, that you have conceived and acquired knowledge of the latter?"

"That is perfectly true."

"This latter being either like those others or unlike?"

"Just so."

"However, that point is immaterial; but so long as the sight of one thing leads you to conceive another, whether like it or unlike, a case of reminder [D] must have occurred."

"Yes, to be sure."

"And to continue: in the instance of those equal logs and other equal objects that we mentioned just now, is it our experience that they appear equal to the same degree as the equal itself? Is there some deficiency in respect of the likeness of the former to the latter, or is there none?"

"Yes, a considerable deficiency."

"Then when someone sees a certain object and says to himself 'The thing I am looking at wants to be like something else, but can resemble that other thing only defectively, as an inferior [E] copy,' may we agree that what he is saying necessarily implies a previous knowledge of that which he finds the object seen to resemble thus defectively?"

"That is necessarily implied."

"Well then, is our own experience of the equal objects and the equal itself that just described, or is it not?"

"Undoubtedly it is."

"So it necessarily follows that we knew the equal at a time previous to that first sight of equal objects which led us to conceive all these as striving to be [75] like *the* equal, but defectively succeeding."

"That is so."

"And we agree moreover on a further point, that the conception referred to has arisen only, and could have arisen only, from seeing or touching, or some other form of sense-perception: what I am saying applies to them all alike."

"And alike they are, Socrates, in respect of the point that our argument seeks to establish."

"But the fact is that these very sense-perceptions must lead us to conceive that all those objects of perception are [B] striving for that which *is* equal, but defectively attaining it. Is that right?"

"Yes."

"Hence before we ever began to see or hear or otherwise perceive things we must, it seems, have possessed knowledge of the equal itself, if we were going to refer the equal things of our sense-perceptions to that standard, that all such objects are doing their best to resemble it, yet are in fact inferior to it."

"That must follow from what we said before, Socrates."

"Well, we have been seeing and hearing things, and employing our other senses from the very moment we were born, have we not?"

"Certainly."

"And before doing so we must, so [C] we maintain, have possessed knowledge of the equal?"

"Yes."

"Then it seems that we must have possessed it before we were born."

"It does."

"Then if we were born with this knowledge,[2] having acquired it before birth, must we not have had knowledge,

---

[2] It is important to realise that both the introductory clause of this paragraph οὐκοῦν εἰ μέν ... τὰ τοιαῦτα and the second εἰ μέν clause at D7 put forward hypotheses which Socrates does *not* accept; that which he does accept comes at E2 with the εἰ δέ clause.

both before birth and immediately afterwards, not only of the equal, the greater
and the smaller, but of all things of that
sort? For our argument applies not merely to the equal, but with the same force
to the beautiful itself, the good itself,
the just, the holy, in fact, as I have just
said, to everything upon which we [D]
affix our seal and mark as being 'the
thing itself,' when we put our questions
and give our answers.[3] Of all these then
wc must have possessed the knowledge
before we were born."

"That is so."

"And if we do not each time forget
what we have acquired, we must be possessed of knowledge always, we must
have it throughout our whole life; for to
know means to have acquired knowledge
of something and not have lost it. The
losing of knowledge is what we mean by
forgetting, isn't it, Simmias?"

"Undoubtedly, Socrates."                [E]

"But if on the other hand we lost at
the moment of birth what we had acquired before birth, but afterwards by
directing our senses to the relevant object
recover that old knowledge, then, I take
it, what is called learning will consist in
recovering a knowledge which belongs
to us; and should we not be right in
calling this recollection?"

"Certainly."

"The reason being that we found [76]
that it was possible for a person who had
seen or heard or otherwise perceived an
object to go on to conceive another object which he had forgotten, something
with which the first object was connected, whether by resemblance or contrast.
Hence my two alternatives: either we
are all of us born knowing the things in
question, and retain the knowledge
throughout our life, or else those who
are said to learn are simply recollecting,
and learning will consist in recollection."

"I am quite sure you are right,
Socrates."

"Then which do you choose, Sim- [B]

───────────

[3] I.e. in philosophical dialogue or dialectic.

mias? Are we born with that knowledge,
or do we recollect a knowledge which
we once possessed?"

"At the moment, Socrates, I don't
know which to choose."

"Well, here is something about which
perhaps you can choose, and give me
your view. If a man knows certain things,
will he be able to give an account of
them, or will he not?"

"Unquestionably he will, Socrates."

"And do you think that everybody
could give an account of those objects
we were speaking of just now?"

"I only wish I did," replied Simmias;
"alas, on the contrary I fear that by this
time to-morrow there will be no man
left alive capable of doing so adequately."

"So you don't think that every- [C]
body knows those objects, Simmias."

"By no means."

"Can they then recollect what they
once learnt?"

"It must be so."

"But when did our souls acquire this
knowledge? Evidently not since our birth
as human beings."

"No indeed."

"Before that, then?"

"Yes."

"Then, Simmias, our souls did exist
before they were within this human
form, apart from our bodies and possessed of intelligence."

"Unless possibly it was at the actual
moment of birth that we acquired the
knowledge in question, Socrates; there is
that moment still left."

"Yes yes, my friend; but at what [D]
moment, may I ask, do we lose it? We
are not born with the knowledge: that
we agreed a moment ago: do we then
lose it at the very moment that we
acquire it, or is there some other moment that you can suggest?"

"No indeed, Socrates; I see now that
I was talking nonsense."

"Then may our position be put like
this, Simmias? If those objects exist
which are always on our lips, a beautiful

and a good and all reality of that sort, and if it is to that that we refer the content of our sense-perceptions, thereby recovering what was ours aforetime, and compare our percepts thereto, it must [E] follow that as surely as those objects exist so surely do our souls exist before we are born; but if the former do not exist, all our argument will have gone for nothing. Is that our position? Does the existence of our souls before birth stand or fall with the existence of those objects?"

"I am utterly convinced, Socrates," replied Simmias, "that it does so stand or fall: our argument is happily reduced to this, that it is equally certain that our souls exist before birth as that the [77] reality of which you now speak exists. I say happily, because there is nothing so plainly true to my mind as that all that sort of thing most assuredly does exist, a beautiful and a good and all those other things that you were speaking of just now. So I think we have had a satisfactory proof."[4]

### 77A-78B  Combined Results of The Two Preceding Arguments. Socrates as Charmer

"And what about Cebes?" asked Socrates; "we must convince him too." [77A]

"He is satisfied, I think," said Simmias, "though indeed he is the most obstinate sceptic in the world. I think he is fully persuaded that our souls existed before we were born; but will they [B] still exist after we die? That I myself don't think we have proved; we are still left with the ordinary man's misgiving which Cebes voiced a while ago, that when a man dies his soul is simultaneously dissipated and thus comes to the end of its existence. May it not be that, deriving its origin and construction from some external source, it exists before

entering into a human body, yet when it quits the body it has entered it too comes to an end and is destroyed?"

"You are right, Simmias," said [C] Cebes. "We seem to have proved half of what we want, namely that our souls existed before we were born; but we have yet to prove that they will equally exist after we die; only then will our proof be complete."

"But you have the complete proof already, my friends," said Socrates, "if you will combine the present argument with that which we agreed upon previously, that is to say the principle that everything that lives comes from what is dead. For if the soul exists before birth, and if its entry into life, its being born, must [D] necessarily have one and only one origin, namely death or the state of being dead, must it not follow, seeing that it is to be born again, that it still exists after it has died? So your point is indeed proved already. Nevertheless I fancy you and Simmias would like to have further discussion of this point too; you seem to have a childish fear that the wind [E] literally blows a soul to bits when it quits the body, and scatters it in all directions, more especially if one happens to die when it's blowing a full gale."

"Then, Socrates," replied Simmias with a smile, "see if you can argue us out of our fear. Or rather, not so much us as the child, maybe, within us that is given to such fears. See if you can persuade him to abandon his fear of this bogy called death."

"Well," said Socrates, "you will have to pronounce charms over him every day until you have charmed the bogy away."

"And where, Socrates," said Cebes, are we going to find an expert at [78] such charms, now that you are leaving us?"

"There is a wide field in Greece, Cebes, which must surely contain experts, and a wide field also in the world outside Greece, the whole of which you ought to explore in quest of your charmer; and you should spare neither money

---

[4] Sc. of the pre-natal existence of the soul; not, of course, of the existence of the Forms, which has been a premiss of the proof.

nor trouble, for you couldn't spend your money on a more pressing object. But you should search amongst yourselves too: I daresay you won't easily find anyone better at this task than you are."

"Very well," said Cebes, "we will see to that. But let us now, if it suits you, go back to the point at which we [B] broke off."

"Why, of course it suits me; what do you expect?"

"Excellent."

## 78B-80C Third Argument.
## The Kinship of Souls and Forms

Socrates then resumed: "Now [78B] the sort of question that we ought to put to ourselves is this: what kind of thing is in fact liable to undergo this dispersal that you speak of? For what kind of thing should we fear that it may be dispersed, and for what kind should we not? And next we should consider to which kind the soul belongs, and so find some ground for confidence or for apprehension about our own souls. Am I right?"

"Yes, you are."

"Well now, isn't anything that has [c] been compounded or has a composite nature liable to be split up into its component parts? Isn't it incomposite things alone that can possibly be exempt from that?"

"I agree that that is so," replied Cebes.

"And isn't it most probable that the incomposite things are those that are always constant and unchanging, while the composite ones are those that are different at different times and never constant?"

"I agree."

"Then let us revert to those objects which we spoke of earlier. What of that very reality of whose existence we give an account when we question and [D] answer each other?[5] Is that always unchanging and constant, or is it different

at different times? Can the equal itself, the beautiful itself, the being itself whatever it may be, ever admit any sort of change? Or does each of these real beings, uniform[6] and independent, remain unchanging and constant, never admitting any sort of alteration whatever?"

"They must be unchanging and constant," Cebes replied.

"But what about the many beautiful things, beautiful human beings, say, or horses or garments or anything else you like? What about the many equal [E] things? What about all the things that are called by the same name as those real beings? Are *they* constant, or in contrast to those is it too much to say that they are never identical with themselves nor identically related to one another?"

"You are right about them too," said Cebes," they are never constant."

"Then again, you can touch them and see them or otherwise perceive [79] them with your senses, whereas those unchanging objects cannot be apprehended save by the mind's reasoning. Things of that sort are invisible, are they not?"

"That is perfectly true."

"Then shall we say there are two kinds of thing, the visible and the invisible?"

"Very well."

"The invisible being always constant, the visible never?"

"We may agree to that too."

"To proceed: we ourselves are [B] partly body, partly soul, are we not?"

"Just so."

"Well, which kind of thing shall we say the body tends to resemble and be akin to?"

"The visible kind; anyone can see that."

"And the soul? It that visible or invisible?"

---

5 I.e. in philosophical discussions; cf. 75D2.

6 The term μονοειδές recurs at 80B in close conjunction with ἀδιάλυτον and it is used of the Form of beauty of Symp. 211B. It has the same force as πᾶν ὅμοιον which Parmenides asserts of his ἕν ὄν, viz. the denial of internal difference or distinction of unlike parts.

"Not visible to the human eye, at all events, Socrates."

"Oh well, we were speaking of what is or is not visible to mankind: or are you thinking of some other sort of being?"

"No: of a human being."

"Then what is our decision about the soul, that it can be seen, or cannot?"

"That it cannot."

"In fact it is invisible?"

"Yes."

"Hence soul rather than body is like the invisible, while body rather than soul is like the visible."

"Unquestionably, Socrates." [c]

"Now were we not saying some time ago that when the soul makes use of the body to investigate something through vision or hearing or some other sense—of course investigating by means of the body is the same as investigating by sense—it is dragged by the body towards objects that are never constant, and itself wanders in a sort of dizzy drunken confusion, inasmuch as it is apprehending confused objects?"

"Just so."

"But when it investigates by itself [d] alone, it passes to that other world of pure, everlasting, immortal, constant being, and by reason of its kinship thereto abides ever therewith, whensoever it has come to be by itself and is suffered to do so! and then it has rest from wandering and ever keeps close to that being, unchanged and constant, inasmuch as it is apprehending unchanging objects. And is not the experience which it then has called intelligence?"

"All you have said, Socrates, is true and admirably put."

"Once again, then, on the strength of our previous arguments as well as of this last, which of the two kinds of thing do you find that soul resembles and is more akin to?" [e]

"On the strength of our present line of inquiry, Socrates, I should think that the veriest dullard would agree that the soul has a far and away greater resem-blance to everlasting, unchanging being than to its opposite."

"And what does the body resemble?"

"The other kind."

"Now consider a further point. When soul and body are conjoined, Nature prescribes that the latter should be slave and subject, the former master and [80] ruler. Which of the two, in your judgment, does that suggest as being like the divine, and which like the mortal? Don't you think it naturally belongs to the divine to rule and lead, and to the mortal to be ruled and subjected?"

"Yes, I do."

"Then which is soul like?"

"Of course it is obvious, Socrates, that soul is like the divine, and body like the mortal."

"Would you say then, Cebes, that the result of our whole discussion amounts to this: on the one hand we have that which is divine, immortal, indestructi- [b] ble, of a single form, accessible to thought, ever constant and abiding true to itself; and the soul is very like it: on the other hand we have that which is human, mortal, destructible, of many forms, inaccessible to thought, never constant nor abiding true to itself; and the body is very like that. Is there anything to be said against that, dear Cebes?"

"Nothing."

"Well then, that being so, isn't it right and proper for the body to be quickly destroyed, but for the soul to be altogether indestructible, or nearly so?"

"Certainly." [c]

## 80C-82D  The After-Life of Unpurified Souls

"Now you are aware that when [80c] a man dies his body, the visible part of him which belongs to the visible world, the corpse as we call it, which in the natural course is destroyed, falling to pieces and scattered to the winds, does not undergo any part of this fate immediately, but survives for quite a considerable time, indeed for a very long

time if death finds the body in favourable condition and comes at a favourable
season: for that matter, a corpse that
has been shrunk and embalmed, in the
Egyptian fashion, will remain almost
entire for ages and ages; and some parts
of the body, such as bones, sinews and [D]
so forth, even when decomposition has
occurred, are virtually immortal. Isn't
that so?"

"Yes."

"What then of the soul, the invisible
thing which passes to an invisible region,
a region of splendour and purity, literally
the 'unseen' world of Hades,[7] into the
presence of the good and wise god,[8]
whither, if god will, my own soul must
shortly pass? Having found what its
nature is like, are we going to say that
when it quits the body it is immediately
blown to pieces and annihilated, as most
people maintain?[9] Far from it, my
friends: the truth of the matter is very
different. Let us suppose that a soul [E]
departs in a state of purity, trailing
nothing bodily after it inasmuch as dur-

ing life it has had as little connexion as
possible with the body, has shunned it
and gathered itself together to be by
itself—a state it has always been training for, training itself, in fact, to die
readily: which is precisely what true [81]
philosophy consists in, as I think you
would agree?"

"I agree entirely."

"Well, will not a soul in such condition depart into the world of the invisible which it resembles, where all is
divine, immortal and wise, and having
come thither attain happiness, released
from its wanderings and follies and fears,
its wild desires and all the other ills that
beset mankind? Will it not truly dwell,
as the initiated are alleged to dwell, in
the company of the gods for all time to
come?[10] May we say that, Cebes, or may
we not?"

"Yes, indeed we may," replied Cebes.

"But now let us suppose that an- [B]
other soul departs polluted uncleansed
of the body's taint, inasmuch as it
has always associated with the body
and tended it, filled with its lusts and
so bewitched by its passions and pleasures as to think nothing real save what
is bodily, what can be touched and seen
and eaten and made to serve sexual
enjoyment; while it has grown to hate
and shun with terror the things that are
invisible, obscure to the eyes but to
be seized by philosophic thought. Do you
believe that a soul in such condition as
that will depart unsullied, alone by it-
self?"                                              [c]

"That could never be so."

"No: it would be interspersed, I think,

---

7 Plato is ready to accept or reject popular
etymologies according as they do or do not
suit his momentary purpose. The etymology
of "Hades" here accepted is rejected at
*Cratylus* 404B.

8 I doubt whether any allusion is intended
to εὐβουλεύς as an epithet of Hades, as Burnet
suggests. Socrates has spoken earlier (63B)
of his going to join θεοὺς ἄλλους σοφούς τε καὶ
ἀγαθούς—in the plural, which he again uses at
81A9. Plato is notoriously indifferent about
speaking of "god" or "gods" (see Cornford,
*Plato's Cosmology*, p. 280), and Hades is
brought in here simply for the sake of the
etymology.

9 This is a noteworthy assertion, but perhaps
"most people" (οἱ πολλοὶ ἄνθρωποι) should
not be taken too literally; there was, no doubt,
much variety of belief or half-belief about the
soul's fate in the fourth century. "The Classical Age," writes Prof. Dodds (*op. cit.* p. 179),
"inherited a whole series of inconsistent pictures of the "soul" or "self"—the living corpse
in the grave, the shadowy image in Hades,
the perishable breath that is spilt in the air
or absorbed in the aether, the daemon that
is reborn in other bodies."

10 According to this passage the philosopher's soul can escape from the "wheel of
birth" after a single incarnation; herein our
dialogue differs from the *Phaedrus* (249A),
where it can only do so after three times
choosing the philosophic life: cf. Pindar, *Ol.*
II, 68 ff. ὅσοι δ' ἐτόλμασαν ἐστρὶς ἑκατέρωθι μείν-
αντες ἀπὸ πάμπαν ἀδίκων ἔχειν ψυτάν κ.τ.λ. The
discrepancy may be due to Plato's closer adherence in the later dialogue to the details
of Orphic eschatology.

with a bodily element which had been worked into its substance by unceasing commerce and association with the body, and by long training."

"Just so."

"Yes, my friend; and we must think of that element as a ponderous, heavy, earthy and visible substance; and the soul that carries it is weighed down and dragged back into the visible world; you know the stories about souls which, in their dread of the invisible that is called Hades, roam about tombs and burying-places, in the neighbourhood of [D] which, it is alleged, ghostly phantoms of souls have actually been seen—just the sort of wraiths that souls like that would produce, souls which are not pure when they are released but still retain some of that visible substance, which is just why they can be seen."

"It may well be so, Socrates."

"It may indeed, Cebes, and it is certainly not the souls of the righteous, but those of the wicked that are compelled to wander about such places, as the penalty for bad nurture in the past. And they must continue to wander until they are once more chained up in a body, by reason of the desires of that [E] bodily attendant which is ever at their side; and naturally they will be chained to the type of character that they have trained themselves to exhibit in their lifetime."

"What types have you in mind, Socrates?"

"I mean, for example, that those who have trained themselves in gluttony, unchastity and drunkenness, instead of carefully avoiding them, will naturally join the company of donkeys or [82] some such creatures, will they not?"

"Yes, very naturally."

"Whereas those who have set more value upon injuring and plundering and tyrannising over their fellows will join the wolves and hawks and kites. Or should we give such souls as these some other destination?"

"By no means," said Cebes; "leave them where you have put them."

"Then it is obvious, I take it, where all the other types will go conformably to the roles in which they have severally trained themselves."

"Quite obvious, I agree."

"Now if we may call any of these happy, the happiest, who pass to the most favoured region, are they that have practised the common virtues of social life, what are called temperance and [B] justice, virtues which spring from habit and training devoid of philosophic wisdom."

"Why are they the happiest?"

"Because they will naturally find themselves in another well-conducted society resembling their old one, a society of bees, perhaps, or wasps or ants; and later on they may rejoin the human race they have left, and turn into respectable men."

"Naturally enough."

"But the society of gods none shall join who has not sought wisdom and departed wholly pure; only the lover of knowledge may go thither. And that [C] is the reason, dear friends, why true philosophers abstain from the desires of the body, standing firm and never surrendering to them; they are not troubled about poverty and loss of estate like the common lover of riches, nor yet is their abstinence due to fear of the dishonour and disgrace that attach to an evil life, the fear felt by the lovers of power and position."

"No, that would be unworthy of them, Socrates," remarked Cebes.

"Most certainly it would," he re- [D] plied. "And that of course, Cebes, is why one who is concerned about his own soul, instead of spending his life getting his body into good shape, says good-bye to all that sort of thing; and while the rest follow a road which leads them they know not whither, he takes another one: holding that he must never act against philosophy and that deliverance and purification which philosophy achieves, he proceeds in the direction whither philosophy points him."

## 113D-115A    The Myth Concluded.
## Its Truth and Value

"Such then is the nature of the [D] earth's interior. Now when the dead are come to that place whither their several guardian spirits bring them, they that have lived well and righteously submit themselves to judgements, and likewise they that have not so lived. And such as are deemed to have lived indifferently well set off for Acheron, embarking on certain vessels appointed for them, which bring them to the lake; and while they dwell there they are purged and absolved from their evil deeds by making atonement therefor, and are rewarded for their good deeds, each according to his desert.

"But some there be who because [E] of the enormity of their sins are deemed incurable: such as have stolen much and often from the temples, or wrought wicked murder time and again, or committed other such crimes; these their due portion befalls, to be hurled into Tartarus, never to escape.

"Others there be whose sins are accounted curable, yet heinous: such as have been moved by anger to lay violent hands upon father or mother, yet [114] have lived thereafter a life of repentance; or such as have slaughtered a man in some similar condition, all these must be cast into Tartarus, but after abiding there for the space of a year the surging waters throw the parricides and matricides out by way of Pyriphlegethon, and the others by way of Cocytus. And when they have been swept along to a point near the Acherusian Lake, then do they cry aloud and call to those whom they have slain or despitefully used, begging and beseeching them that they would suffer them to come forth into the [B] lake and give them hearing. If they can prevail, they do come forth, and find an

end to their trouble; but if not, they are swept back into Tartarus, and thence into the rivers again; nor can they ever have respite from their woes until they prevail upon those whom they have injured; for such is the penalty appointed by their judges.

"But lastly there are those that are deemed to have made notable progress on the road to righteous living; and these are they that are freed and delivered from the prison-houses of this interior of the earth, and come to make [C] their habitation in the pure region above ground. And those of their number who have attained full purity through philosophy live for evermore without any bodies at all, and attain to habitations even fairer than those others; but the nature of these it would not be easy to reveal, even were time enough now left me.

"But now, Simmias, having regard to all these matters of our tale, we must endeavour ourselves to have part in goodness and intelligence while this life is ours; for the prize is glorious, and great is our hope thereof.

"Now to affirm confidently that [D] these things are as I have told them would not befit a man of good sense; yet seeing that the soul is found to be immortal, I think it is befitting to affirm that this or something like it is the truth about our souls and their habitations. I think too that we should do well in venturing—and a glorious venture it is —to believe it to be so. And we should treat such tales as spells to pronounce over ourselves, as in fact has been my own purpose all this while in telling my long story.

"And now surely, by reason of all this, no anxiety ought to be felt about his own soul by a man who all his lifetime has renounced the pleasures of the [E] body and its adornments as alien to him, and likely to do him more harm than good, and has pursued the pleasures of learning; who has adorned his soul with no alien adornment, but with its own, even with temperance and justice and courage and freedom and truth, [115] and thus adorned awaits that journey to Hades which he is ready to make whensoever destiny calls him.

"Well, Simmias, you and Cebes and the others will make the journey some day later on; but now ' 'tis I am called,' as a tragic hero might say, by destiny; and it is just about time[11] I made my way to the bath; I really think it is better to have a bath before drinking the poison rather than give the women the trouble of washing a dead body."

### 115B-118   Socrates' Death

To this Crito replied, "Very [115B] well, Socrates; but what instructions have you for our friends here or for me about the children, or about any other matter? We want to do just what would be of most service to you."

"Only what I am always telling you, Crito, nothing very new. Look after yourselves: then anything you do will be of service to me and mine, and to yourselves too, even if at this moment you make no promises to that effect, but if you neglect yourselves, and refuse to follow that path of life which has been traced out in this present conversation and in others that we have had before, then, plentiful and vehement though your present promises may be, all you do will be fruitless."                     [c]

"Then," said Crito, "we shall strive to do as you bid us. But how are we to bury you?"

"However you like," said Socrates, "provided you can catch me and prevent my escaping you." Then with a quiet laugh and a look in our direction he remarked, "You know, I can't persuade Crito that I am the Socrates here present, the person who is now talking to you and arranging the topics of our con-

versation; he imagines that I am the dead body which he will shortly be looking at, and so he asks how he is to [D] bury me. As for all I have been maintaining this long while, to wit that when I have drunk the poison I shall no longer be with you, but shall have taken my departure to some happy land of the blest, that, I suppose, he regards as idle talk, intended to console you all and myself as well. That being so, I want you to stand surety for me with Crito, but for the precise opposite of that for which he sought to stand surety with the court. His pledge then, offered under oath, was that I would stay where I was; but I want you to pledge yourselves under oath that I will not stay where I am after I have died, but will take my de- [E] parture; that will make it easier for Crito: when he sees my body being burnt or put under ground he won't have to distress himself on my behalf, as though I were being outraged, and won't have to say at the funeral that it is Socrates whom he is laying out or carrying to the grave or burying."

Then turning to Crito, "My best of friends," he continued, "I would assure you that misuse of language is not only distasteful in itself, but actually harmful to the soul. So you must be of good cheer, and say that you are burying my body; and do that in whatever [116] fashion you please and deem to be most conformable to custom."

With these words he rose and went into another room to take his bath. Crito went with him, and told us to stay where we were. This we did, discussing amongst ourselves and meditating upon all that had been said, or sometimes talking of the great sorrow that had come upon us; for truly we felt like children who had lost a father, condemned to live henceforth as orphans. However, when Socrates had had his bath his [B] children—two little boys and one bigger —were brought in to him, and those women relatives of his appeared; to these he addressed some words in the

---

[11] The abrupt way in which Socrates "comes down to earth" is perhaps intended to suggest his characteristic avoidance of pomposity and staginess.

presence of Crito, with certain directions as to his wishes. He then told the women and children to withdraw, and himself came over to us.

By this time it was near to sunset, for he had spent a long time in the inner room. So he came and sat with us after his bath, and did not talk much more. And now the agent of the prison [c] authorities had arrived, and stepping up to him said, "Socrates, I shan't have my usual ground for complaint in your case; many people get angry and abusive when I instruct them, at the behest of the authorities, to drink the poison; but I have always known you, while you have been here, for the most generous, the best tempered and the finest man of any that have entered this place; and in particular I feel sure now that you are not angry with me, but with those whom you know to be responsible for this. Well, you know what I have come to tell you: so now good-bye, and try to bear as [D] best you may what must be borne." As he said this, he burst into tears, and turned to leave us. Socrates looked up at him and said, "Good-bye to you: I will do as you say"; and then to us, "What a delightful person! All these weeks he has been coming to see me, and talking with me now and then, like the excellent fellow he is; and now see how generously he weeps for me! Well, come now, Crito, let us do his bidding. If the draught has been prepared, will someone please bring it me; if not, tell the man to prepare it."

"Oh, but I think, Socrates," said [E] Crito, "that the sun is still upon the mountains; it has not set yet. Besides, I know of people who have taken the draught long after they were told to do so, and had plenty to eat and drink, and even in some cases had intercourse with those whom they desired. Don't hurry: there is still plenty of time."

"It is quite natural, Crito," he replied, "that the people you speak of should do that: they think it brings them some advantage; and it is equally natural that I should not do so: I don't think I

should get any advantage out of taking the poison a little later on; I should [117] merely make myself ridiculous in my own eyes by clinging to life and eking out its last dregs. No, no: don't hamper me: do as I say."

At this Crito nodded to his slave who stood close by; whereupon the latter went out, and after a considerable time came back with the man who was to administer the poison, which he was carrying in a cup ready to drink. On seeing him Socrates exclaimed, "All right, good sir: you know about this business: what must I do?"

"Simply drink it," he replied, "and then walk about until you have a feeling of heaviness in your legs; then lie down, and it will act of itself." And as he [B] spoke he offered Socrates the cup. And I tell you, Echecrates, he took it quite calmly, without a tremor or any change of complexion or expression. He just fixed the man with his well-known glare and asked, "What do you say to using the drink for a libation? Or is that not allowed?" The man replied, "We only mix what we judge to be the right dose, Socrates."

"I see," he rejoined. "Well, at all [c] events it is allowed to pray to the gods, as indeed we must, for a happy journey to our new dwelling-place; and that is my prayer: so may it be." With these words he put the cup to his lips and drained it with no difficulty or distaste whatever.

So far most of us had more or less contrived to hold back our tears, but now, when we saw him drinking, and the cup emptied, it became impossible; for myself, despite my efforts the tears were pouring down my cheeks, so that I had to cover my face; but I was weeping not for him, no, but for myself and my own misfortune in losing such a [D] friend. Crito had got up and withdrawn already, finding that he could not restrain his tears; as for Apollodorus, he had even before this been weeping continuously, and at this last moment he burst into sobs, and his tears of distress were heart-breaking to all of us, except to Socrates himself, who exclaimed, "My dear good people, what a way to behave! Why, it was chiefly to avoid such a lapse that I sent the women away; for I [E] was always told that a man ought to die in peace and quiet. Come, calm yourselves and do not give way."

At that we felt ashamed, and ceased to weep. He walked round the room until, as he told us, his legs came to feel heavy, and then lay on his back, as he had been bidden. Thereupon the man who had brought the poison felt his body, and after a while examined his feet and legs, and then squeezed his foot tightly, asking if he felt anything. [118] Socrates said no; next he felt his legs again, and moving his hand gradually up he showed us that he was becoming cold and rigid. Touching him once more,

he told us that when the cold reached the heart all would be over.

By this time it had reached somewhere about the pit of the stomach, when he removed the covering which he had put over his face, and uttered his final words: "Crito, we owe a cock to Asklepios, pray do not forget to pay the debt." "It shall be done," said Crito. "Is there anything else you can think of?" There was no reply to this question; a moment afterwards he shuddered; the attendant uncovered his face again, and his gaze had become rigid; seeing which Crito closed his mouth and his eyes.

And that, Echecrates, was the end of our friend, the finest man—so we should say—of all whom we came to know in his generation; the wisest too, and the most righteous.

# SYMPOSIUM (complete)

### PERSONS OF THE DIALOGUE

APOLLODORUS, *who repeats to his companion the dialogue which he had heard from Aristodemus, and had already once narrated to Glaucon*

PHAEDRUS

PAUSANIAS

ERYXIMACHUS

ARISTOPHANES

AGATHON

SOCRATES

ALCIBIADES

A TROOP OF REVELLERS

SCENE:—*The House of Agathon*

Concerning the things about which you ask to be informed I believe that I am not ill-prepared with an answer. For the day before yesterday I was [172] coming from my own home at Phalerum to the city, and one of my acquaintance, who had caught a sight of me from behind, calling out playfully in the distance, said: Apollodorus, O thou Phalerian[1] man, halt! So I did as I was

bid; and then he said, I was looking for you, Apollodorus, only just now, that I might ask you about the speeches in praise of love, which were delivered by Socrates, Alcibiades, and others, at Agathon's supper. Phoenix, the son of Philip, told another person who told me of them; his narrative was very indistinct, but he said that you knew, and I wish that you would give me an account of them. Who, if not you, should be the reporter of the words of your

---

[1] Probably a play of words on φαλαρὸς, "bald-headed."

friend? And first tell me, he said, were you present at this meeting?

Your informant, Glaucon, I said, must have been very indistinct indeed, if you imagine that the occasion was recent; or that I could have been of the party.

Why, yes, he replied, I thought so.

Impossible: I said. Are you ignorant that for many years Agathon has not resided at Athens; and not three have elapsed since I became acquainted with Socrates, and have made it my daily business to know all that he says and does. There was a time when I was [173] running about the world, fancying myself to be well employed, but I was really a most wretched being, no better than you are now. I thought that I ought to do anything rather than be a philosopher.

Well, he said, jesting apart, tell me when the meeting occurred.

In our boyhood, I replied, when Agathon won the prize with his first tragedy, on the day after that on which he and his chorus offered the sacrifice of victory.

Then it must have been a long while ago, he said; and who told you—did Socrates?

No indeed, I replied, but the same person who told Phoenix;—he was a little fellow, who never wore any shoes, Aristodemus, of the deme of Cydathenaeum. He had been at Agathon's feast; and I think that in those days there was no one who was a more devoted admirer of Socrates. Moreover, I have asked Socrates about the truth of some parts of his narrative, and he confirmed them. Then, said Glaucon, let us have the tale over again; is not the road to Athens just made for conversation? And so we walked, and talked of the discourses on love; and therefore, as I said at first, I am not ill-prepared to comply with your request, and will have another rehearsal of them if you like. For to speak or to hear others speak of philosophy always gives me the greatest pleasure, to say nothing of the profit.

But when I hear another strain, especially that of you rich men and traders, such conversation displeases me; and I pity you who are my companions, because you think that you are doing something when in reality you are doing nothing. And I dare say that you pity me in return, whom you regard as an unhappy creature, and very probably you are right. But I certainly know of you what you only think of me—there is the difference.

COMPANION. I see, Apollodorus, that you are just the same—always speaking evil of yourself, and of others; and I do believe that you pity all mankind, with the exception of Socrates, yourself first of all, true in this to your old name, which, however deserved, I know not how you acquired, of Apollodorus the madman; for you are always raging against yourself and everybody but Socrates.

APOLLODORUS. Yes, friend, and the reason why I am said to be mad, and out of my wits, is just because I have these notions of myself and you; no other evidence is required.

COM. No more of that, Apollodorus; but let me renew my request that you would repeat the conversation.

APOLL. Well, the tale of love was [174] on this wise:—But perhaps I had better begin at the beginning, and endeavour to give you the exact words of Aristodemus:

He said that he met Socrates fresh from the bath and sandalled; and as the sight of the sandals was unusual, he asked him whither he was going that he had been converted into such a beau:—

To a banquet at Agathon's, he replied, whose invitation to his sacrifice of victory I refused yesterday, fearing a crowd, but promising that I would come to-day instead; and so I have put on my finery, because he is such a fine man. What say you to going with me unasked?

I will do as you bid me, I replied.

Follow then, he said, and let us demolish the proverb:—

"To the feasts of inferior men the good unbidden go";

instead of which our proverb will run:—

"To the feasts of the good the good unbidden go;"

and this alteration may be supported by the authority of Homer himself, who not only demolishes but literally outrages the proverb. For, after picturing Agamemnon as the most valiant of men, he makes Menelaus, who is but a faint-hearted warrior, come unbidden[2] to the banquet of Agamemnon, who is feasting and offering sacrifices, not the better to the worse, but the worse to the better.

I rather fear, Socrates, said Aristodemus, lest this may still be my case; and that, like Menelaus in Homer, I shall be the inferior person, who

"To the feasts of the wise unbidden goes."

But I shall say that I was bidden of you, and then you will have to make an excuse.

"Two going together,"

he replied, in Homeric fashion, one or other of them may invent an excuse by the way.[3]

This was the style of their conversation as they went along. Socrates dropped behind in a fit of abstraction, and desired Aristodemus, who was waiting, to go on before him. When he reached the house of Agathon he found the doors wide open, and a comical thing happened. A servant coming out met him, and led him at once into the banqueting-hall in which the guests were reclining, for the banquet was about to begin. Welcome, Aristodemus, said Agathon, as soon as he appeared—you are just in time to sup with us; if you come on any other matter put it off, and make one of us, as I was looking for you yesterday and meant to have

asked you, if I could have found you. But what have you done with Socrates?

I turned round, but Socrates was nowhere to be seen; and I had to explain that he had been with me a moment before, and that I came by his invitation to the supper.

You were quite right in coming, said Agathon; but where is he himself?

He was behind me just now, as I entered, he said, and I cannot [175] think what has become of him.

Go and look for him, boy, said Agathon, and bring him in; and do you, Aristodemus, meanwhile take the place by Eryximachus.

The servant then assisted him to wash, and he lay down, and presently another servant came in and reported that our friend Socrates had retired into the portico of the neighbouring house. "There he is fixed," said he, "and when I call to him he will not stir."

How strange, said Agathon; then you must call him again, and keep calling him.

Let him alone, said my informant; he has a way of stopping anywhere and losing himself without any reason. I believe that he will soon appear; do not therefore disturb him.

Well, if you think so, I will leave him, said Agathon. And then, turning to the servants, he added, "Let us have supper without waiting for him. Serve up whatever you please, for there is no one to give you orders; hitherto I have never left you to yourselves. But on this occasion imagine that you are our hosts, and that I and the company are your guests; treat us well, and then we shall commend you." After this, supper was served, but still no Socrates; and during the meal Agathon several times expressed a wish to send for him, but Aristodemus objected; and at last when the feast was about half over—for the fit, as usual, was not of long duration—Socrates entered. Agathon, who was reclining alone at the end of the table, begged that he would take the place next to

---

[2] *Iliad* ii. 408, and xvii. 588.
[3] *Iliad* x. 224.

him; that "I may touch you," he said, "and have the benefit of that wise thought which came into your mind in the portico, and is now in your possession; for I am certain that you would not have come away until you had found what you sought."

How I wish, said Socrates, taking his place as he was desired, that wisdom could be infused by touch, out of the fuller into the emptier man, as water runs through wool out of a fuller cup into an emptier one; if that were so, how greatly should I value the privilege of reclining at your side! For you would have filled me full with a stream of wisdom plenteous and fair; whereas my own is of a very mean and questionable sort, no better than a dream. But yours is bright and full of promise, and was manifested forth in all the splendour of youth the day before yesterday, in the presence of more than thirty thousand Hellenes.

You are mocking, Socrates, said Agathon, and ere long you and I will have to determine who bears off the palm of wisdom—of this Dionysus shall be the judge; but at present you are better occupied with supper.

Socrates took his place on the [176] couch, and supped with the rest; and then libations were offered, and after a hymn had been sung to the god, and there had been the usual ceremonies, they were about to commence drinking, when Pausanias said, And now, my friends, how can we drink with least injury to ourselves? I can assure you that I feel severely the effect of yesterday's potations, and must have time to recover; and I suspect that most of you are in the same predicament, for you were of the party yesterday. Consider then: How can the drinking be made easiest?

I entirely agree, said Aristophanes, that we should, by all means, avoid hard drinking, for I was myself one of those who were yesterday drowned in drink.

I think that you are right, said Eryximachus, the son of Acumenus; but I should still like to hear one other person speak: Is Agathon able to drink hard?

I am not equal to it, said Agathon.

Then, said Eryximachus, the weak heads like myself, Aristodemus, Phaedrus, and others who never can drink, are fortunate in finding that the stronger ones are not in a drinking mood. (I do not include Socrates, who is able either to drink or to abstain, and will not mind, whichever we do.) Well, as none of the company seem disposed to drink much, I may be forgiven for saying, as a physician, that drinking deep is a bad practice, which I never follow, if I can help, and certainly do not recommend to another, least of all to any one who still feels the effects of yesterday's carouse.

I always do what you advise, and especially what you prescribe as a physician, rejoined Phaedrus the Myrrhinusian, and the rest of the company, if they are wise, will do the same.

It was agreed that drinking was not to be the order of the day, but that they were all to drink only so much as they pleased.

Then, said Eryximachus, as you are all agreed that drinking is to be voluntary, and that there is to be no compulsion, I move, in the next place, that the flute-girl, who has just made her appearance, be told to go away and play to herself, or, if she likes, to the women who are within.[4] To-day let us have conversation instead; and, if you will allow me, I will tell you what sort of conversation. This proposal having been [177] accepted, Eryximachus proceeded as follows:—

I will begin, he said, after the manner of Melanippe in Euripides,

"Not mine the word"

which I am about to speak, but that of Phaedrus. For often he says to me in an

---

4 Cp. *Prot.* 347.

indignant tone:—"What a strange thing it is, Eryximachus, that, whereas other gods have poems and hymns made in their honour, the great and glorious god, Love, has no encomiast among all the poets who are so many. There are the worthy sophists too—the excellent Prodicus for example, who have descanted in prose on the virtues of Heracles and other heroes; and, what is still more extraordinary, I have met with a philosophical work in which the utility of salt has been made the theme of an eloquent discourse; and many other like things have had a like honour bestowed upon them. And only to think that there should have been an eager interest created about them, and yet that to this day no one has ever dared worthily to hymn Love's praises! So entirely has this great diety been neglected." Now in this Phaedrus seems to me to be quite right, and therefore I want to offer him a contribution; also I think that at the present moment we who are here assembled cannot do better than honour the god Love. If you agree with me, there will be no lack of conversation; for I mean to propose that each of us in turn, going from left to right, shall make a speech in honour of Love. Let him give us the best which he can; and Phaedrus, because he is sitting first on the left hand, and because he is the father of the thought, shall begin.

No one will vote against you, Eryximachus, said Socrates. How can I oppose your motion, who profess to understand nothing but matters of love; nor, I presume, will Agathon and Pausanias; and there can be no doubt of Aristophanes, whose whole concern is with Dionysus and Aphrodite; nor will any one disagree of those whom I see around me. The proposal, as I am aware, may seem rather hard upon us whose place is last; but we shall be contented if we hear some good speeches first. Let Phaedrus begin the praise of Love, and good luck to him. All the company expressed their assent, and desired him to do as Socrates bade him.                    [178]

Aristodemus did not recollect all that was said, nor do I recollect all that he related to me; but I will tell you what I thought most worthy of remembrance, and what the chief speakers said.

## The Speech of Phaedrus

Phaedrus began by affirming that Love is a mighty god, and wonderful among gods and men, but especially wonderful in his birth. For he is the eldest of the gods, which is an honour to him; and a proof of his claim to this honour is, that of his parents there is no memorial; neither poet nor prose-writer has ever affirmed that he had any. As Hesiod says:—

"First Chaos came, and then broad-
  bosomed Earth,
The everlasting seat of all that is,
And Love."

In other words, after Chaos, the Earth and Love, these two, came into being. Also Parmenides sings of Generation:

"First in the train of gods, he fashioned
  Love."

And Acusilaus agrees with Hesiod. Thus numerous are the witnesses who acknowledge Love to be the eldest of the gods. And not only is he the eldest, he is also the source of the greatest benefits to us. For I know not any greater blessing to a young man who is beginning life than a virtuous lover, or to the lover than a beloved youth. For the principle which ought to be the guide of men who would nobly live—that principle, I say, neither kindred, nor honour, nor wealth, nor any other motive is able to implant so well as love. Of what am I speaking? Of the sense of honour and dishonour, without which neither states nor individuals ever do any good or great work. And I say that a lover who is detected in doing any dishonourable act, or submitting through cowardice when any dishonour is done to him by another, will be more pained at being detected by his beloved than at being seen by his father, or by his companions, or by any one else. The beloved too, when he is found in any disgraceful situation, has the same feeling about his lover. And if there were only some way of contriving that a state or an army should be made up of lovers and their loves,[5] they would be the very best governors of their own city, abstaining from all dishonour, and emulating one another in honour; and when fighting at each other's side, [179] although a mere handful, they would overcome the world. For what lover would not choose rather to be seen by all mankind than by his beloved, either when abandoning his post or throwing away his arms? He would be ready to die a thousand deaths rather than endure this. Or who would desert his beloved or fail him in the hour of danger? The veriest coward would become an inspired hero, equal to the bravest, at such a time; Love would inspire him. That courage which, as Homer says, the god breathes into the souls of some heroes, Love of his own nature infuses into the lover.

Love will make men dare to die for their beloved—love alone; and women as well as men. Of this, Alcestis, the daughter of Pelias, is a monument to all Hellas; for she was willing to lay down her life on behalf of her husband, when no one else would, although he had a father and mother; but the tenderness of her love so far exceeded theirs, that she made them seem to be strangers in blood to their own son, and in name only related to him; and so noble did this action of hers appear to the gods, as well as to men, that among the many who have done virtuously she is one of the very few to whom, in admiration of her noble action, they have granted the privilege of returning alive to earth;

such exceeding honour is paid by the gods to the devotion and virtue of love. But Orpheus, the son of Oeagrus, the harper, they sent empty away, and presented to him an apparition only of her whom he sought, but herself they would not give up, because he showed no spirit; he was only a harp-player, and did not dare like Alcestis to die for love, but was contriving how he might enter Hades alive; moreover, they afterwards caused him to suffer death at the hands of women, as the punishment of his cowardliness. Very different was the reward of the true love of Achilles towards his lover Patroclus—his lover and not his love (the notion that Patroclus was the beloved one is a foolish error into which Aeschylus has fallen, for Achilles was surely the fairer of the two, fairer also than all the other heroes; and, as Homer informs us, he was still beardless, and younger far). And greatly as the gods honour the virtue of love still [180] the return of love on the part of the beloved to the lover is more admired and valued and rewarded by them, for the lover is more divine; because he is inspired by God. Now Achilles was quite aware, for he had been told by his mother, that he might avoid death and return home, and live to a good old age, if he abstained from slaying Hector. Nevertheless he gave his life to revenge his friend, and dared to die, not only in his defence, but after he was dead. Wherefore the gods honoured him even above Alcestis, and sent him to the Islands of the Blest. These are my reasons for affirming that Love is the eldest and noblest and mightiest of the gods, and the chiefest author and giver of virtue in life, and of happiness after death.

## The Speech of Pausanias

This, or something like this, was the speech of Phaedrus; and some other speeches followed which Aristodemus did not remember; the next which he re-

---

[5] Cp. *Rep.* v. 468 D.

peated was that of Pausanias. Phaedrus, he said, the argument has not been set before us, I think, quite in the right form;—we should not be called upon to praise Love in such an indiscriminate manner. If there were only one Love, then what you said would be well enough; but since there are more Loves than one, you should have begun by determining which of them was to be the theme of our praises. I will amend this defect; and first of all I will tell you which Love is deserving of praise, and then try to hymn the praiseworthy one in a manner worthy of him. For we all know that Love is inseparable from Aphrodite, and if there were only one Aphrodite there would be only one Love; but as there are two goddesses there must be two Loves. And am I not right in asserting that there are two goddesses? The elder one, having no mother, who is called the heavenly Aphrodite— she is the daughter of Uranus; the younger, who is the daughter of Zeus and Dione—her we call common; and the Love who is her fellow-worker is rightly named common, as the other love is called heavenly. All the gods ought to have praise given to them, but not without distinction of their natures; and therefore I must try to distinguish the characters of the two Loves. Now actions vary according to the manner of their performance. Take, for example, that which we are now doing, drinking, [181] singing and talking—these actions are not in themselves either good or evil, but they turn out in this or that way according to the mode of performing them; and when well done they are good, and when wrongly done they are evil; and in like manner not every love, but only that which has a noble purpose, is noble and worthy of praise. The Love who is the offspring of the common Aphrodite is essentially common, and has no discrimination, being such as the meaner sort of men feel, and is apt to be of women as well as of youths, and is of the body rather than of the

soul—the most foolish beings are the objects of this love which desires only to gain an end, but never thinks of accomplishing the end nobly, and therefore does good and evil quite indiscriminately. The goddess who is his mother is far younger than the other, and she was born of the union of the male and female, and partakes of both. But the offspring of the heavenly Aphrodite is derived from a mother in whose birth the female has no part,—she is from the male only; this is that love which is of youths, and the goddess being older, there is nothing of wantonness in her. Those who are inspired by this love turn to the male, and delight in him who is the more valiant and intelligent nature; any one may recognise the pure enthusiasts in the very character of their attachments. For they love not boys, but intelligent beings whose reason is beginning to be developed, much about the time at which their beards begin to grow. And in choosing young men to be their companions, they mean to be faithful to them, and pass their whole life in company with them, not to take them in their inexperience, and deceive them, and play the fool with them, or run away from one to another of them. But the love of young boys should be forbidden by law, because their future is uncertain; they may turn out good or bad, either in body or soul, and much noble enthusiasm may be thrown away upon them; in this matter the good are a law to themselves, and the coarser sort of lovers ought to be restrained by force, as we restrain or attempt to restrain them from fixing their affections on women of free birth. These are the [182] persons who bring a reproach on love; and some have been led to deny the lawfulness of such attachments because they see the impropriety and evil of them; for surely nothing that is decorously and lawfully done can justly be censured. Now here and in Lacedaemon the rules about love are perplexing, but in most cities they are simple and easily intelligible; in Elis and Boeotia, and in countries having no gifts of eloquence, they are very straightforward; the law is simply in favour of these connexions, and no one, whether young or old, has anything to say to their discredit; the reason being, as I suppose, that they are men of few words in those parts, and therefore the lovers do not like the trouble of pleading their suit. In Ionia and other places, and generally in countries which are subject to the barbarians, the custom is held to be dishonourable; loves of youths share the evil repute in which philosophy and gymnastics are held, because they are inimical to tyranny; for the interests of rulers require that their subjects should be poor in spirit[6] and that there should be no strong bond of friendship or society among them, which love, above all other motives, is likely to inspire, as our Athenian tyrants learned by experience; for the love of Aristogeiton and the constancy of Harmodius had a strength which undid their power. And, therefore, the ill-repute into which these attachements have fallen is to be ascribed to the evil condition of those who make them to be ill-reputed; that is to say, to the self-seeking of the governors and the cowardice of the governed; on the other hand, the indiscriminate honour which is given to them in some countries is attributable to the laziness of those who hold this opinion of them. In our own country a far better principle prevails, but, as I was saying, the explanation of it is rather perplexing For, observe that open loves are held to be more honourable than secret ones, and that the love of the noblest and highest, even if their persons are less beautiful than others, is especially honourable. Consider, too, how great is the encouragement which all the world gives to the lover; neither is he supposed to be doing anything dishonourable; but if

he succeeds he is praised, and if he fails he is blamed. And in the pursuit of his love the custom of mankind allows him to do many strange things, which philosophy would bitterly censure if [183] they were done from any motive of interest, or wish for office or power. He may pray, and entreat, and supplicate, and swear, and lie on a mat at the door, and endure slavery worse than that of any slave—in any other case friends and enemies would be equally ready to prevent him, but now there is no friend who will be ashamed of him and admonish him, and no enemy will charge him with meanness or flattery; the actions of a lover have a grace which ennobles them; and custom has decided that they are highly commendable and that there is no loss of character in them; and, what is strangest of all, he only may swear and forswear himself (so men say), and the gods will forgive his transgression, for there is no such thing as a lover's oath. Such is the entire liberty which gods and men have allowed the lover, according to the custom which prevails in our part of the world. From this point of view a man fairly argues that in Athens to love and to be loved is held to be a very honourable thing. But when parents forbid their sons to talk with their lovers, and place them under a tutor's care, who is appointed to see to these things, and their companions and equals cast in their teeth anything of the sort which they may observe, and their elders refuse to silence the reprovers and do not rebuke them —any one who reflects on all this will, on the contrary, think that we hold these practices to be most disgraceful. But, as I was saying at first, the truth as I imagine is, that whether such practices are honourable or whether they are dishonourable is not a simple question; they are honourable to him who follows them honourably, dishonourable to him who follows them dishonourably. There is dishonour in yielding to the evil, or in

---

6 Cp. Arist. *Politics*, v. II. §15.

an evil manner; but there is honour in yielding to the good, or in an honourable manner. Evil is the vulgar lover who loves the body rather than the soul, inasmuch as he is not even stable, because he loves a thing which is in itself unstable, and therefore when the bloom of youth which he was desiring is over, he takes wing and flies away, in spite of all his words and promises; whereas the love of the noble disposition is life-long, for it becomes one with the everlasting. The custom of our country would have both of them proven well and truly, [184] and would have us yield to the one sort of lover and avoid the other, and therefore encourages some to pursue, and others to fly; testing both the lover and beloved in contests and trials, until they show to which of the two classes they respectively belong. And this is the reason why, in the first place, a hasty attachment is held to be dishonourable, because time is the true test of this as of most other things; and secondly there is a dishonour in being overcome by the love of money, or of wealth, or of political power, whether a man is frightened into surrender by the loss of them, or, having experienced the benefits of money and political corruption, is unable to rise above the seductions of them. For none of these things are of a permanent or lasting nature; not to mention that no generous friendship ever sprang from them. There remains, then, only one way of honourable attachment which custom allows in the beloved, and this is the way of virtue; for as we admitted that any service which the lover does to him is not to be accounted flattery or a dishonour to himself, so the beloved has one way only of voluntary service which is not dishonourable, and this is virtuous service.

For we have a custom, and according to our custom any one who does service to another under the idea that he will be improved by him either in wisdom, or in some other particular of virtue—such a voluntary service, I say, is not to be regarded as a dishonour, and is not open to the charge of flattery. And these two customs, one the love of youth, and the other the practice of philosophy and virtue in general, ought to meet in one, and then the beloved may honourably indulge the lover. For when the lover and beloved come together, having each of them a law, and the lover thinks that he is right in doing any service which he can to his gracious loving one; and the other that he is right in showing any kindness which he can to him who is making him wise and good; the one capable of communicating wisdom and virtue, the other seeking to acquire them with a view to education and wisdom; when the two laws of love are fulfilled and meet in one—then, and then only, may the beloved yield with honour to the lover. Nor when love is of this disinterested sort is there any disgrace in being deceived, but in every other case there is equal disgrace in being or not being deceived. For he who is gracious to his lover under the impression that he is rich, and is [185] disappointed of his gains because he turns out to be poor, is disgraced all the same: for he has done his best to show that he would give himself up to any one's "uses base" for the sake of money; but this is not honourable. And on the same principle he who gives himself to a lover because he is a good man, and in the hope that he will be improved by him company, shows himself to be virtuous, even though the object of his affection turn out to be a villain, and to have no virtue; and if he is deceived he has committed a noble error. For he has proved that for his part he will do anything for anybody with a view to virtue and improvement, than which there can be nothing nobler. Thus noble in every case is the acceptance of another for the sake of virtue. This is that love which is the love of the heavenly goddess, and is heavenly, and of great price to individuals and cities, making the lover and the beloved alike eager in the work of their own improvement. But all other loves are the offspring of the other, who is the common goddess. To you, Phaedrus, I offer this my contribution in praise of love, which is as good as I could make extempore.

Pāusănĭās cāme tŏ a pāuse—this is the balanced way in which I have been taught by the wise to speak; and Aristodemus said that the turn of Aristophanes was next, but either he had eaten too much, or from some other cause he had the hiccough, and was obliged to change turns with Eryximachus the physician, who was reclining on the couch below him. Eryximachus, he said, you ought either to stop my hiccough, or to speak in my turn until I have left off.

I will do both, said Eryximachus: I will speak in your turn, and do you speak in mine; and while I am speaking let me recommend you to hold your breath, and if after you have done so for some time the hiccough is no better, then gargle with a little water; and if it still continues, tickle your nose with something and sneeze; and if you sneeze once or twice, even the most violent hiccough is sure to go. I will do as you prescribe, said Aristophanes, and now get on.

## The Speech of Eryximachus

*LOVE IS HARMONY*

Eryximachus spoke as follows: Seeing that Pausanias made a fair beginning, and but a lame ending, I must [186] endeavour to supply his deficiency. I think that he has rightly distinguished two kinds of love. But my art further informs me that the double love is not merely an affection of the soul of man towards the fair, or towards anything, but is to be found in the bodies of all animals and in productions of the earth, and I may say in all that is; such is the conclusion which I seem to have gathered from my own art of medicine, whence I learn how great and wonderful and universal is the deity of love, whose empire extends over all things, divine as well as human. And from medicine I will begin that I may do honour to my art. There are in the human body these two kinds of love, which are confessedly different and unlike, and being unlike, they have loves and desires which are unlike; and the desire of the healthy is one, and the desire of the diseased is another; and as Pausanias was just now saying that to indulge good men is honourable, and bad men dishonourable:—so too in the body the good and healthy elements are to be indulged, and the bad elements and the elements of disease are not to be indulged, but discouraged. And this is what the physician has to do, and in this the art of medicine consists: for medicine may be regarded generally as the knowledge of the loves and desires of the body, and how to satisfy them or not; and the best physician is he who is able to separate fair love for foul, or to convert one into the other; and he who knows how to eradicate and how to implant love, whichever is required, and can reconcile the most hostile elements in the constitution and make them loving friends, is a skilful practitioner. Now the most hostile are the most opposite, such as hot and cold, bitter and sweet, moist and dry, and the like. And my ancestor, Asclepius, knowing how to implant friendship and accord in these elements, was the creator of our art, as our friends the poets here tell us, and I believe them; and not only medicine in every branch, but the arts of gymnastic and husbandry are under his dominion. Any one who pays the least attention to [187] the subject will also perceive that in music there is the same reconciliation of opposites; and I suppose that this must have been the meaning of Heracleitus, although his words are not accurate; for he says that The One is united by disunion, like the harmony of the bow and the lyre. Now there is an absurdity in saying that harmony is discord or is composed of elements which are still in a state of discord. But what he probably meant was, that harmony is composed of differing notes of higher or lower pitch which disagreed once, but are now reconciled by the art of music; for if the higher and lower notes still disagreed, there could be no harmony,—clearly not. For harmony is a symphony, and symphony is an agreement; but an agreement of disagreements while they disagree there cannot be; you cannot harmonize that which disagrees. In like manner rhythm is compounded of elements short and long, once differing and now in accord; which accordance, as in the former instance, medicine, so in all these other cases, music implants, making love and unison to grow up among them; and thus music, too, is concerned with the principles of love in their application to harmony and rhythm. Again, in the essential nature of harmony and rhythm there is no difficulty in discerning love which has not yet become double. But when you want to use them in actual life, either in the composition of songs or in the correct performance of airs or metres composed already, which latter is called education, then the difficulty begins, and the good artist is needed. Then the old tale has to be repeated of fair and heavenly love—the love of Urania the fair and heavenly muse, and of the duty of accepting the temperate, and those who are as yet intemperate only that they may become temperate, and of preserving their love; and again, of the vulgar Polyhymnia, who must be used with circumspection that the pleasure be enjoyed, but may not generate licentiousness; just as in my own art it is a great matter so to regulate the desires of the epicure that he may gratify his tastes without the attendant evil of disease. Whence I infer that in music, in medicine, in all other things human as well as divine, both loves ought to be noted as far as may be, for they are both present.                    [188]

The course of the seasons is also full of both these principles; and when, as I was saying, the elements of hot and cold, moist and dry, attain the harmonious love of one another and blend in temperance and harmony, they bring to men, animals, and plants health and plenty, and do them no harm; whereas the wanton love, getting the upper hand and affecting the seasons of the year, is very destructive and injurious, being the source of pestilence, and bringing many other kinds of diseases on animals and plants; for hoar-frost and hail and blight spring from the excesses and disorders of these elements of love, which to know in relation to the revolutions of the heavenly bodies and the seasons of the year is termed astronomy. Furthermore all sacrifices and the whole province of divination, which is the art of communion between gods and men—these, I say, are concerned only with the preservation of the good and the cure of the evil love. For all manner of impiety is likely to ensue if, instead of accepting and honouring and reverencing the harmonious love in all his actions, a man honours the other love, whether in his feelings towards gods or parents, towards the living or the dead. Wherefore the business of divination is to see to these loves and to heal them, and divination is the peacemaker of gods and men, working by a knowledge of the religious or irreligious tendencies which exist in human loves. Such is the great and mighty, or rather omnipotent force of love in general. And the love, more especially, which is concerned with the good, and which is perfected in company with temperance and justice, whether among gods or men, has the greatest power, and is the source of all our happiness and harmony, and makes us friends with the gods who are above us, and with one another. I dare say that I too have omitted several things which might be said in praise of Love, but this was not intentional, and you, Aristophanes, may now supply the omission or take some other line of commendation; for I perceive that you are rid of the hiccough.

Yes, said Aristophanes, who followed, the hiccough is gone; not, however, [189] until I applied the sneezing; and I wonder whether the harmony of the body has a love of such noises and ticklings, for I no sooner applied the sneezing than I was cured.

Eryximachus said: Beware, friend Aristophanes, although you are going to speak, you are making fun of me; and I shall have to watch and see whether I cannot have a laugh at your expense, when you might speak in peace.

You are quite right, said Aristophanes, laughing. I will unsay my words; but do you please not to watch me, as I fear that in the speech which I am about to make, instead of others laughing with me, which is to the manner born of our muse and would be all the better, I shall only be laughed at by them.

Do you expect to shoot your bolt and escape, Aristophanes? Well, perhaps if you are very careful and bear in mind that you will be called to account, I may be induced to let you off.

## The Speech of Aristophanes

Aristophanes professed to open another vein of discourse; he had a mind to praise Love in another way, unlike that either of Pausanias or Eryximachus. Mankind, he said, judging by their neglect of him, have never, as I think, at all understood the power of Love. For if they had understood him they would surely have built noble temples and altars, and offered solemn sacrifices in his honour; but this is not done, and most certainly ought to be done: since of all the gods he is the best friend of men, the helper and the healer of the ills which are the great impediment to the happiness of the race. I will try to describe his power to you, and you shall teach the rest of the world what I am teaching you. In the first place, let me treat of the nature of man and what has happened to it; for the original human nature was not like the present, but different. The sexes were not two as they are now, but originally three in number; there was man, woman, and the union of the two, having a name corresponding to this double nature, which had once a real existence, but is now lost, and the word "Androgynous" is only preserved as a term of reproach. In the second place, the primeval man was round, his back and sides forming a circle; and he had four hands and four feet, one head with two faces, looking opposite ways, set on a round neck and precisely alike; also four ears, two privy members, and the re- [190] mainder to correspond. He could walk upright as men now do, backwards or forwards as he pleased, and he could also roll over and over at a great pace, turning on his four hands and four feet, eight in all, like tumblers going over and over with their legs in the air; this was when he wanted to run fast. Now the sexes were three, and such as I have described them; because the sun, moon, and earth are three; and the man was originally the child of the sun, the woman of the earth, and the man-woman of the moon, which is made up of sun and earth, and they were all round and moved round and round like their parents. Terrible was their might and strength, and the thoughts of their hearts were great, and they made an attack upon the gods; of them is told the tale of Otys and Ephialtes who, as Homer says, dared to scale heaven, and would have laid hands upon the gods. Doubt reigned in the celestial councils. Should they kill them and annihilate the race with thunderbolts, as they had done the giants, then there would be an end of the sacrifices and worship which men offered to them; but, on the other hand, the gods could not suffer their insolence to be unrestrained. At last, after a good deal of reflection, Zeus discovered a way. He said: "Methinks I have a plan which will humble their pride and improve their manners; men shall continue to exist, but I will cut them in two and then they will be diminished in strength and increased in numbers; this will have the advantage of making them more profitable to us. They shall walk upright on two legs, and if they continue insolent and will not be quiet, I will split them again and they shall hop about on a single leg" He spoke and cut men in two, like a sorb-apple which is halved for pickling, or as you might divide an egg with a hair; and as he cut them one after another, he bade Apollo give the face and the half of the neck a turn in order that the man might contemplate the section of himself: he would thus learn a lesson of humility. Apollo was also bidden to heal their wounds and compose their forms. So he gave a turn to the face and pulled the skin from the sides all over that which in our language is called the belly, like the purses which draw in, and he made one mouth at the centre, which he fastened in a knot (the same which is called the navel); he also moulded the breast and took out most of [191] the wrinkles, much as a shoemaker might smooth leather upon a last; he left a few, however, in the region of the belly and navel, as a memorial of the primeval state. After the division the two parts of man, each desiring his other half, came together, and throwing their arms about one another, entwined in mutual embraces, longing to grow into one, they were on the point of dying from hunger and self-neglect, because they did not like to do anything apart; and when one of the halves died and the other survived, the survivor sought another mate, man or woman as we call them, —being the sections of entire men or women,—and clung to that. They were being destroyed, when Zeus in pity of them invented a new plan: he turned the parts of generation round to the front, for this had not been always their position, and they sowed the seed no longer as hitherto like grasshoppers in the ground, but in one another; and after the transposition the male generated in the female in order that by the mutual embraces of man and woman they might breed, and the race might continue; or if man came to man they might be satisfied, and rest, and go their ways to the business of life: so ancient is the desire of one another which is implanted in us, reuniting our original nature, making one of two, and healing the state of man. Each of us when separated, having one side only, like a flat fish, is but the indenture of a man, and he is always looking for his other half. Men who are a section of that double nature which was once called Androgynous are lovers of women; adulterers are generally of this breed, and also adulterous women who lust after men: the women who are a section of the woman do not care for men, but have female attachments; the female companions are of this sort. But they who are a section of the male follow the male, and while they are young, being slices of the original man, they hang about men and embrace them, and they are themselves the best of [192] boys and youths, because they have the most manly nature. Some indeed assert that they are shameless, but this is not true; for they do not act thus from any want of shame, but because they are valiant and manly, and have a manly countenance, and they embrace that which is like them. And these when they grow up become our statesmen, and these only, which is a great proof of the truth of what I am saying. When they reach manhood they are lovers of youth, and are not naturally inclined to marry or beget children,—if at all, they do so only in obedience to the law; but they are satisfied if they may be allowed to live with one another unwedded; and such a nature is prone to love and ready to return love, always embracing that which is akin to him. And when one of them meets with his other half, the actual half of himself, whether he be a lover of youth or a lover of another sort, the pair are lost in an amazement of love and friendship and intimacy, and will not be out of the other's sight, as I may say, even for a moment: these are the people who pass their whole lives together; yet they could not explain what they desire of one another. For the intense yearning which each of them has towards the other does not appear to be the desire of lover's intercourse, but of something else which the soul of either evidently desires and cannot tell, and of which she has only a dark and doubtful presentiment. Suppose Hephaestus, with his instruments, to come to the pair who are lying side by side and to say to them, "What do you people want of one another?" they would be unable to explain. And suppose further, that when he saw their perplexity he said: "Do you desire to be wholly one; always and night to be in one another's company? for if this is what you desire, I am ready to melt you into one and let you grow together, so that

being two you shall become one, and while you live a common life as if you were a single man, and after your death in the world below still be one departed soul instead of two—I ask whether this is what you lovingly desire, and whether you are satisfied to attain this?"—there is not a man of them who when he heard the proposal would deny or would not acknowledge that this meeting and melting into one another, this becoming one instead of two, was the very expression of his ancient need.[7] And the reason is that human nature was originally one and we were a whole, and the desire and pursuit of the whole is called [193] love. There was a time, I say, when we were one, but now because of the wickedness of mankind God has dispersed us, as the Arcadians were dispersed into villages by the Lacedaemonians.[8] And if we are not obedient to the gods, there is a danger that we shall be split up again and go about in basso-relievo, like the profile figures having only half a nose which are sculptured on monuments, and that we shall be like tallies. Wherefore let us exhort all men to piety, that we may avoid evil, and obtain the good, of which Love is to us the lord and minister; and let no one oppose him—he is the enemy of the gods who oppose him. For if we are friends of the God and at peace with him we shall find our own true loves, which rarely happens in this world at present. I am serious, and therefore I must beg Eryximachus not to make fun or to find any allusion in which I am saying to Pausanias and Agathon, who, as I suspect, are both of the manly nature, and belong to the class which I have been describing. But my words have a wider application—they include men and women everywhere; and I

---

7 Cp. Arist. *Pol.* ii. 4, §6.
8 Cp. Arist. *Pol.* ii. 2, §3.

believe that if our loves were perfectly accomplished, and each one returning to his primeval nature had his original true love, then our race would be happy. And if this would be best of all, the best in the next degree and under present circumstances must be the nearest approach to such an union; and that will be the attainment of a congenial love. Wherefore, if we would praise him who has given to us the benefit, we must praise the god Love, who is our greatest benefactor, both leading us in this life back to our own nature, and giving us high hopes for the future, for he promises that if we are pious, he will restore us to our original state, and heal us and make us happy and blesssed. This, Eryximachus, is my discourse of love, which, although different to yours, I must beg you to leave unassailed by the shafts of your ridicule, in order that each may have his turn; each or rather either, for Agathon and Socrates are the only ones left.

Indeed, I am not going to attack you, said Eryximachus, for I thought your speech charming, and did I not know that Agathon and Socrates are masters in the art of love, I should be really afraid that they would have nothing to say, after the world of things which have been said already. But, for all that, I am not without hopes.

Socrates said: You played your part well, Eryximachus; but if you [194] were as I am now, or rather as I shall be when Agathon has spoken, you would, indeed, be in a great strait.

You want to cast a spell over me, Socrates, said Agathon, in the hope that I may be disconcerted at the expectation raised among the audience that I shall speak well.

I should be strangely forgetful, Agathon, replied Socrates, of the courage and magnanimity which you showed when your own compositions were about to be exhibited, and you came upon the stage with the actors and faced the vast theatre altogether undismayed, if I thought that your nevrves could be fluttered at a small party of friends.

Do you think, Socrates, said Agathon, that my head is so full of the theatre as not to know how much more formidable to a man of sense a few good judges are than many fools?

Nay, replied Socrates, I should be very wrong in attributing to you, Agathon, that or any other want of refinement. And I am quite aware that if you happened to meet with any whom you thought wise, you would care for their opinion much more than for that of the many. But then we, having been a part of the foolish many in the theatre, cannot be regarded as the select wise; though I know that if you chanced to be in the presence, not of one of ourselves, but of some really wise man, you would be ashamed of disgracing yourself before him—would you not?

Yes, said Agathon.

But before the many you would not be ashamed, if you thought that you were doing something disgraceful in their presence?

Here Phaedrus interrupted them, saying: Do not answer him, my dear Agathon; for if he can only get a partner with whom he can talk, especially a good-looking one, he will no longer care about the completion of our plan. Now I love to hear him talk; but just at present I must not forget the encomium on Love which I ought to receive from him and from every one. When you and he have paid your tribute to the god, then you may talk.

## The Speech of Agathon

Very good, Phaedrus, said Agathon; I see no reason why I should not proceed with my speech, as I shall have many other opportunities of conversing with Socrates. Let me say first how I ought to speak, and then speak:—

The previous speakers, instead of praising the god Love, or unfolding his nature, appear to have congratulated mankind on the benefits which he confers upon them. But I would rather praise the god first, and [195] then speak of his gifts; this is always the right way of praising everything. May I say without impiety or offence, that of all the blessed gods he is the most blessed because he is the fairest and best? And he is the fairest: for, in the first place, he is the youngest, and of his youth he is himself the witness, fleeing out of the way of age, who is swift enough, swifter truly than most of us like:—Love hates him and will not come near him; but youth and love live and move together—like to like, as the proverb says. Many things were said by Phaedrus about Love in which I agree with him; but I cannot agree that he is older than Iapetus and Kronos:—not so; I maintain him to be the youngest of the gods, and youthful ever. The ancient doings among the gods of which Hesiod and Parmenides spoke, if the tradition of them be true, were done of Necessity and not of Love; had Love been in those days, there would have been no chaining or mutilation of the gods, or other violence, but peace and sweetness, as there is now in heaven, since the rule of Love began. Love is young and also tender; he ought to have a poet like Homer to describe his tenderness, as Homer says of Ate, that she is a goddess and tender:—

"Her feet are tender, for she sets her steps,
Not on the ground but on the heads of
    men:"

herein is an excellent proof of her tenderness,—that she walks not upon the hard but upon the soft. Let us adduce a similar proof of the tenderness of Love; for he walks not upon the earth, nor yet upon the skulls of men, which are not so very soft, but in the hearts and souls of both gods and men, which are of all things the softest: in them he walks and dwells and makes his home. Not in every soul without exception, for where there is hardness he departs, where there is softness there he dwells; and nestling always with his feet and in all manner of ways in the softest of soft places, how can he be other than the softest of [196] all things? Of a truth he is the tenderest as well as the youngest, and also he is of flexile form; for if he were hard and without flexure he could not enfold all things, or wind his way into and out of every soul of man undiscovered. And a proof of his flexibility and symmetry of form is his grace, which is universally admitted to be in an especial manner the attribute of Love; ungrace and love are always at war with one another. The fairness of his complexion is revealed by his habitation among the flowers; for he dwells not amid bloomless or fading beauties, whether of body or soul or aught else, but in the place of flowers and scents, there he sits and abides. Concerning the beauty of the god I have said enough; and yet there remains much more which I might say. Of his virtue I have now to speak: his greatest glory is that he can neither do nor suffer wrong to or from any god or any man; for he suffers not by force if he suffers; force comes not near him, neither when he acts does he act by force. For all men in all things serve him of their own free will, and where there is voluntary agreement, there, as the laws which are the lords of the city say, is justice. And not only is he just but exceedingly temperate, for Temperance is the acknowledged ruler of the pleasures and desires, and no pleasure ever masters Love; he is their master and they are his servants; and if he conquers them he must be temperate indeed. As to courage, even the

God of War is no match for him; he is the captive and Love is the lord, for love, the love of Aphrodite, masters him, as the tale runs; and the master is stronger than the servant. And if he conquers the bravest of all others, he must be himself the bravest. Of his courage and justice and temperance I have spoken, but I have yet to speak of his wisdom; and according to the measure of my ability I must try to do my best. In the first place he is a poet (and here, like Eryximachus, I magnify my art), and he is also the source of poesy in others, which he could not be if he were not himself a poet. And at the touch of him every one becomes a poet,[9] even though he had no music in him before;[9] this also is a proof that Love is a good poet and accomplished in all the fine arts; for no one can give to another that which he has not himself, or teach that of which he has no knowledge. Who will deny that the creation of the animals is his doing? [197] Are they not all the works of his wisdom, born and begotten of him? And as to the artists, do we not know that he only of them whom love inspires has the light of fame?—he whom Love touches not walks in darkness. The arts of medicine and archery and divination were discovered by Apollo, under the guidance of love and desire; so that he too is a disciple of Love. Also the melody of the Muses, the metallurgy of Hephaestus, the weaving of Athene, the empire of Zeus over gods and men, are all due to Love, who was the inventor of them. And so Love set in order the empire of the gods—the love of beauty, as is evident, for with deformity Love has no concern. In the days of old, as I began by saying, dreadful deeds were done among the gods, for they were ruled by Necessity; but now since the birth of Love, and from the Love of the beauti-

ful, has sprung every good in heaven and earth. Therefore, Phaedrus, I say of Love that he is the fairest and best in himself, and the cause of what is fairest and best in all other things. And there comes into my mind a line of poetry in which he is said to be the god who

> "Gives peace on earth and calms the stormy deep,
> Who stills the winds and bids the sufferer sleep."

This is he who empties men of disaffection and fills them with affection, who makes them to meet together at banquets such as these: in sacrifices, feasts, dances, he is our lord—who sends courtesy and sends away discourtesy, who gives kindness ever and never gives unkindness; the friend of the good, the wonder of the wise, the amazement of the gods; desired by those who have no part in him, and precious to those who have the better part in him; parent of delicacy, luxury, desire, fondness, softness, grace; regardful of the good, regardless of the evil: in every word, work, wish, fear—saviour, pilot, comrade, helper; glory of gods and men, leader best and brightest: in whose footsteps let every man follow, sweetly singing in his honour and joining in that sweet strain with which love charms the souls of gods and men. Such is the speech, Phaedrus, half-playful, yet having a certain measure of seriousness, which, according to my ability, I dedicate to the god.

When Agathon had done speak- [198] ing, Aristodemus said that there was a general cheer; the young man was thought to have spoken in a manner worthy of himself, and of the god. And Socrates, looking at Eryximachus, said: Tell me, son of Acumenus, was there not reason in my fears? and was I not a true prophet when I said that Agathon would make a wonderful oration, and that I should be in a strait?

The part of the prophecy which concerns Agathon, replied Eryximachus, ap-

---

[9] A fragment of the *Sthenoboea* of Euripides.

pears to me to be true; but not the other part—that you will be in a strait.

## The Speech of Socrates

Why, my dear friend, said Socrates, must not I or any one be in a strait who has to speak after he has heard such a rich and varied discourse? I am especially struck with the beauty of the concluding words—who could listen to them without amazement? When I reflected on the immeasurable inferiority of my own powers, I was ready to run away for shame, if there had been a possibility of escape. For I was reminded of Gorgias, and at the end of his speech I fancied that Agathon was shaking at me the Gorginian or Gorgonian head of the great master of rhetoric, which was simply to turn me and my speech into stone, as Homer says,[10] and strike me dumb. And then I perceived how foolish I had been in consenting to take my turn with you in praising love, and saying that I too was a master of the art, when I really had no conception how anything ought to be praised. For in my simplicity I imagined that the topics of praise should be true, and that this being presupposed, out of the true the speaker was to choose the best and set them forth in the best manner. And I felt quite proud, thinking that I knew the nature of true praise, and should speak well. Whereas I now see that the intention was to attribute to Love every species of greatness and glory, whether really belonging to him or not, without regard to truth or falsehood—that was no matter; for the original proposal seems to have been not that each of you should really praise Love, but only that you should appear to praise him. And so you attribute to Love every imaginable form of praise which can be gathered anywhere; and you say that "he is all

this," and "the cause of all that," making him appear the fairest and best [199] of all to those who know him not, for you cannot impose upon those who know him. And a noble and solemn hymn of praise have you rehearsed. But as I misunderstood the nature of the praise when I said that I would take my turn, I must beg to be absolved from the promise which I made in ignorance, and which (as Euripides would say[11]) was a promise of the lips and not of the mind. Farewell then to such a strain: for I do not praise in that way; no, indeed, I cannot. But if you like to hear the truth about love, I am ready to speak in my own manner, though I will not make myself ridiculous by entering into any rivalry with you. Say then, Phaedrus, whether you would like to have the truth about love, spoken in any words and in any order which may happen to come into my mind at the time. Will that be agreeable to you?

Aristodemus said that Phaedrus and the company bid him speak in any manner which he thought best. Then, he added, let me have your permission first to ask Agathon a few more questions, in order that I may take his admissions as the premisses of my discourse.

I grant the permission, said Phaedrus: put your questions. Socrates then proceeded as follows:—

In the magnificent oration which you have just uttered, I think that you were right, my dear Agathon, in proposing to speak of the nature of Love first and afterwards of his works—that is a way of beginning which I very much approve. And as you have spoken so eloquently of his nature, may I ask you further, Whether love is the love of something or of nothing? And here I must explain myself: I do not want you to say that love is the love of a father or the love of a mother—that would be ridiculous; but to answer as you would,

---

[10] *Odyssey,* λ. 632.

[11] Eurip. *Hippolytus,* l. 612.

if I asked is a father a father of something? to which you would find no difficulty in replying, of a son or daughter: and the answer would be right.

Very true, said Agathon.

And you would say the same of a mother?

He assented.

Yet let me ask you one more question in order to illustrate my meaning: Is not a brother to be regarded essentially as a brother of something?

Certainly, he replied.

That is, of a brother or sister?

Yes, he said.

And now, said Socrates, I will ask about Love:—Is Love of something or of nothing?

Of something, surely, he replied. [200]

Keep in mind what this is, and tell me what I want to know—whether Love desires that of which love is.

Yes, surely.

And does he possess, or does he not possess, that which he loves and desires?

Probably not, I should say.

Nay, replied Socrates, I would have you consider whether "necessarily" is not rather the word. The inference that he who desires something is in want of something, and that he who desires nothing is in want of nothing, is in my judgment, Agathon, absolutely and necessarily true. What do you think?

I agree with you, said Agathon.

Very good. Would he who is great, desire to be great, or he who is strong, desire to be strong?

That would be inconsistent with our previous admissions.

True. For he who is anything cannot want to be that which he is?

Very true.

And yet, added Socrates, if a man being strong desired to be strong, or being swift desired to be swift, or being healthy desired to be healthy, in that case he might be thought to desire something which he already has or is. I give the example in order that we may avoid mis-

conception. For the possessors of these qualities, Agathon, must be supposed to have their respective advantages at the time, whether they choose or not; and who can desire that which he has? Therefore, when a person says, I am well and wish to be well, or I am rich and wish to be rich, and I desire simply to have what I have—to him we shall reply: "You, my friend, having wealth and health and strength, want to have the continuance of them; for at this moment, whether you choose or no, you have them. And when you say, I desire that which I have and nothing else, is not your meaning that you want to have what you now have in the future?" He must agree with us—must he not?

He must, replied Agathon.

Then, said Socrates, he desires that what he has at present may be preserved to him in the future, which is equivalent to saying that he desires something which is non-existent to him, and which as yet he has not got.

Very true, he said.

Then he and every one who desires, desires that which he has not already, and which is future and not present, and which he has not, and is not, and of which he is in want;—these are the sort of things which love and desire seek?

Very true, he said.

Then now, said Socrates, let us recapitulate the argument. First, is not love of something, and of something too which is wanting to a man?

Yes, he replied. [201]

Remember further what you said in your speech, or if you do not remember I will remind you: you said that the love of the beautiful set in order the empire of the gods, for that of deformed things there is no love—did you not say something of that kind?

Yes, said Agathon.

Yes, my friend, and the remark was a just one. And if this is true, Love is the love of beauty and not of deformity?

He assented.

And the admission has been already made that Love is of something which a man wants and has not?

True, he said.

Then Love wants and has not beauty?

Certainly, he replied.

And would you call that beautiful which wants and does not possess beauty?

Certainly not.

Then would you still say that love is beautiful?

Agathon replied: I fear that I did not understand what I was saying.

You made a very good speech, Agathon, replied Socrates; but there is yet one small question which I would fain ask:—Is not the good also the beautiful?

Yes.

Then in wanting the beautiful, love wants also the good?

I cannot refute you, Socrates, said Agathon:—Let us assume that what you say is true.

Say rather, beloved Agathon, that you cannot refute the truth; for Socrates is easily refuted.

And now, taking my leave of you, I will rehearse a tale of love which I heard from Diotima of Mantineia,[12] a woman wise in this and in many other kinds of knowledge, who in the days of old, when the Athenians offered sacrifice before the coming of the plague, delayed the disease ten years. She was my instructress in the art of love, and I shall repeat to you what she said to me, beginning with the admissions made by Agathon, which are nearly if not quite the same which I made to the wise woman when she questioned me: I think that this will be the easiest way, and I shall take both parts myself as well as I can.[13] As you, Agathon, suggested,[14] I must speak first of the being and nature of Love, and then of his works. First I said to her in nearly the same words

12 Cp. I. *Alcibiades.*
13 Cp. *Gorgias,* 505 E.
14 Supra, 195 A.

which he used to me, that Love was a mighty god, and likewise fair; and she proved to me as I proved to him that, by my own showing, Love was neither fair nor good. "What do you mean, Diotima," I said, "is love then evil and foul?" "Hush," she cried; "must that be foul which is not fair?" "Certainly," I said. "And is that which is not [202] wise, ignorant? do you not see that there is a mean between wisdom and ignorance?" "And what may that be?" I said. "Right opinion," she replied; "which, as you know, being incapable of giving a reason, is not knowledge (for how can knowledge be devoid of reason? nor again, ignorance, for neither can ignorance attain the truth), but is clearly something which is a mean between ignorance and wisdom." "Quite true," I replied. "Do not then insist," she said, "that what is not fair is of necessity foul, or what is not good evil; or infer that because love is not fair and good he is therefore foul and evil; for he is in a mean between them." "Well," I said, "Love is surely admitted by all to be a great god." "By those who know or by those who do not know? "By all." "And how, Socrates," she said with a smile, "can Love be acknowledged to be a great god by those who say that he is not a god at all?" "And who are they?" I said. "You and I are two of them," she replied. "How can that be?" I said. "It is quite intelligible," she replied; "for you yourself would acknowledge that the gods are happy and fair—of course you would—would you dare to say that any god was not?" "Certainly not," I replied. "And you mean by the happy, those who are the possessors of things good or fair?" "Yes." "And you admitted that Love, because he was in want, desires those good and fair things of which he is in want?" "Yes, I did." "But how can he be a god who has no portion in what is either good or fair?" "Impossible." "Then you see that you also deny the divinity of Love."

"What then is Love?" I asked; "Is he mortal?" "No." "What then?" "As in the former instance, he is neither mortal nor immortal, but in a mean between the two." "What is he, Diotima?" "He is a great spirit ($\delta\alpha\iota\mu\omega\nu$), and like all spirits he is intermediate between the divine and the mortal." "And what," I said, "is his power?" "He interprets," she replied, "between gods and men, conveying and taking across to the gods the prayers and sacrifices of men, and to men the commands and replies of the gods; he is the mediator who spans the chasm which divides them, and therefore in him all is bound together, and through him the arts of the prophet and the priest, their sacrifices and mysteries and charms, and all prophecy and incanta- [203] tion, find their way. For God mingles not with man; but through Love all the intercourse and converse of god with man, whether awake or asleep, is carried on. The wisdom which understands this is spiritual; all other wisdom, such as that of arts and handicrafts, is mean and vulgar. Now these spirits or intermediate powers are many and diverse, and one of them is Love." And who," I said, "was his father, and who his mother?" "The tale," she said, "will take time; nevertheless I will tell you. On the birthday of Aphrodite there was a feast of the gods, at which the god Poros or Plenty, who is the son of Metis or Discretion, was one of the guests. When the feast was over, Penia or Poverty, as the manner is on such occasions, came about the doors to beg. Now Plenty, who was the worse for nectar (there was no wine in those days), went into the garden of Zeus and fell into a heavy sleep; and Poverty considering her own straitened circumstances, plotted to have a child by him, and accordingly she lay down at his side and conceived Love, who partly because he is naturally a lover of the beautiful, and because Aphrodite is herself beautiful, and also because he was born on her birthday, is her follower and

attendant. And as his parentage is, so also are his fortunes. In the first place he is always poor, and anything but tender and fair, as the many imagine him; and he is rough and squalid, and has no shoes, nor a house to dwell in; on the bare earth exposed he lies under the open heaven, in the streets, or at the doors of houses, taking his rest; and like his mother he is always in distress. Like his father too, whom he also partly resembles, he is always plotting against the fair and good; he is bold, enterprising, strong, a mighty hunter, always weaving some intrigue or other, keen in the pursuit of wisdom, fertile in resources; a philosopher at all times, terrible as an enchanter, sorcerer, sophist. He is by nature neither mortal nor immortal, but alive and flourishing at one moment when he is in plenty, and dead at another moment, and again alive by reason of his father's nature. But that which is always flowing in is always flowing out, and so he is never in want and never in wealth; and, further, he is in a mean between ignorance and knowledge. The truth of the matter is this: No god is a philosopher or seeker after wisdom, for he is wise already; nor does any man who is wise seek after wisdom. Neither do the ignorant seek after wisdom. For herein is the evil of ignorance, that he who is neither good nor wise is [204] nevertheless satisfied with himself: he has no desire for that of which he feels no want." "But who then, Diotima," I said, "are the lovers of wisdom, if they are neither the wise nor the foolish?" "A child may answer that question," she replied; "they are those who are in a mean between the two; Love is one of them. For wisdom is a most beautiful thing, and Love is of the beautiful; and therefore Love is also a philosopher or lover of wisdom, and being a lover of wisdom is in a mean between the wise and the ignorant. And of this too his birth is the cause; for his father is wealthy and wise, and his mother poor and foolish.

Such, my dear Socrates, is the nature of the spirit Love. The error in your conception of him was very natural, and as I imagine from what you say, has arisen out of a confusion of love and the beloved, which made you think that love was all beautiful. For the beloved is the truly beautiful, and delicate, and perfect, and blessed; but the principle of love is of another nature, and is such as I have described."

I said: "O thou stranger woman, thou sayest well; but, assuming Love to be such as you say, what is the use of him to men?" "That, Socrates," she replied, "I will attempt to unfold: of his nature and birth I have already spoken; and you acknowledge that love is of the beautiful. But some one will say: Of the beautiful in what, Socrates and Diotima? —or rather let me put the question more clearly, and ask: When a man loves the beautiful, what does he desire?" I answered her "That the beautiful may be his." "Still," she said, "the answer suggests a further question: What is given by the possession of beauty?" "To what you have asked," I replied, "I have no answer ready." "Then," she said, "let me put the word 'good' in the place of the beautiful, and repeat the question once more: If he who loves loves the good, what is it then that he loves?" "The possession of the good," I said. "And what does he gain who possesses the good?" "Happiness," I replied; "there is less difficulty in answering that question." "Yes," she said, "the happy are made happy by the acquisition of good things. Nor is there any need [205] to ask why a man desires happiness; the answer is already final." "You are right," I said. "And is this wish and this desire common to all? and do all men always desire their own good, or only some men?—what say you?" "All men," I replied; "the desire is common to all." "Why, then," she rejoined, "are not all men, Socrates, said to love, but only some of them? whereas you say that all

men are always loving the same things." "I myself wonder," I said, "why this is." "There is nothing to wonder at," she replied; "the reason is that one part of love is separated off and receives the name of the whole, but the other parts have other names." "Give an illustration," I said. She answered me as followers: "There is poetry, which, as you know, is complex and manifold. All creation or passage of non-being into being is poetry or making, and the processes of all art are creative; and the masters of art are all poets or makers." "Very true." "Still," she said, "you know that they are not called poets, but have other names; only that portion of the art which is separated off from the rest, and is concerned with music and metre, is termed poetry, and they who possess poetry in this sense of the word are called poets." "Very true," I said. "And the same holds of love. For you may say generally that all desire of good and happiness is only the great and subtle power of love; but they who are drawn towards him by any other path, whether the path of money-making or gymnastics or philosophy, are not called lovers—the name of the whole is appropriated to those whose affection takes one form only—they alone are said to love, or to be lovers." "I dare say," I replied, "that you are right." "Yes," she added, "and you hear people say that lovers are seeking for their other half; but I say that they are seeking neither for the half of themselves, nor for the whole, unless the half or the whole be also a good. And they will cut off their own hands and feet and cast them away, if they are evil; for they love not what is their own, unless perchance there be some one who calls what belongs to him the good, and what belongs to another the evil. For there is nothing which men love [206] but the good. Is there anything?" "Certainly, I should say, that there is nothing." "Then," she said, "the simple truth is, that men love the good." "Yes,"

I said. "To which must be added that they love the possession of the good?" "Yes, that must be added." "And not only the possession, but the everlasting possession of the good?" "That must be added too." "Then love," she said, "may be described generally as the love of the everlasting possession of the good?" "That is most true."

"Then if this be the nature of love, can you tell me further," she said, "what is the manner of the pursuit? what are they doing who show all this eagerness and heat which is called love? and what is the object which they have in view? Answer me." "Nay, Diotima," I replied, "if I had known, I should not have wondered at your wisdom, neither should I have come to learn from you about this very matter." "Well," she said, "I will teach you:—The object which they have in view is birth in beauty, whether of body or soul." "I do not understand you," I said; "the oracle requires an explanation." "I will make my meaning clearer," she replied. "I mean to say, that all men are bringing to the birth in their bodies and in their souls. There is a certain age at which human nature is desirous of procreation—procreation which must be in beauty and not in deformity; and this procreation is the union of man and woman, and is a divine thing; for conception and generation are an immortal principle in the mortal creature, and in the inharmonious they can never be. But the deformed is always inharmonious with the divine, and the beautiful harmonious. Beauty, then, is the destiny or goddess of parturition who presides at birth, and therefore, when approaching beauty, the conceiving power is propitious, and diffusive, and benign, and begets and bears fruit: at the sight of ugliness she frowns and contracts and has a sense of pain, and turns away, and shrivels up, and not without a pang refrains from conception. And this is the reason why, when the hour of conception arrives, and

the teeming nature is full, there is such a flutter and ecstasy about beauty whose approach is the alleviation of the pain of travail. For love, Socrates, is not, as you imagine, the love of the beautiful only." "What then?" "The love of generation and of birth in beauty." "Yes," I said. "Yes, indeed," she replied. "But why of generation?" "Because to the mortal creature, generation is a sort of eternity and immortality," she replied; "and if, as has been already admitted, love is of the everlasting possession of the good, all men will necessarily desire immortality together with good: [207] Wherefore love is of immortality."

All this she taught me at various times when she spoke of love. And I remember her once saying to me, "What is the cause, Socrates, of love, and the attendant desire? See you not how all animals, birds, as well as beasts, in their desire of procreation, are in agony when they take the infection of love, which begins with the desire of union; whereto is added the care of offspring, on whose behalf the weakest are ready to battle against the strongest even to the uttermost, and to die for them, and will let themselves be tormented with hunger or suffer anything in order to maintain their young. Man may be supposed to act thus from reason; but why should animals have these passionate feelings? Can you tell me why?" Again I replied that I did not know. She said to me: "And do you expect ever to become a master in the art of love, if you do not know this?" "But I have told you already, Diotima, that my ignorance is the reason why I come to you; for I am conscious that I want a teacher; tell me then the cause of this and of the other mysteries of love." "Marvel not," she said, "if you believe that love is of the immortal, as we have several times acknowledged; for here again, and on the same principle too, the mortal nature is seeking as far as is possible to be everlasting and immortal: and this is only to be attained by generation, because generation always leaves behind a new existence in the place of the old. Nay even in the life of the same individual there is succession and not absolute unity: a man is called the same, and yet in the short interval which elapses between youth and age, and in which every animal is said to have life and identity, he is undergoing a perpetual process of loss and reparation—hair, flesh, bones, blood, and the whole body are always changing. Which is true not only of the body, but also of the soul, whose habits, tempers, opinions, desires, pleasures, pains, fears, never remain the same in any one of us, but are always coming and going; and equally true of knowledge, and what is still more surprising to us mortals, not only do [208] the sciences in general spring up and decay, so that in respect of them we are never the same; but each of them individually experiences a like change. For what is implied in the word 'recollection,' but the departure of knowledge, which is ever being forgotten, and is renewed and preserved by recollection, and appears to be the same although in reality new, according to that law of succession by which all mortal things are preserved, not absolutely the same, but by substitution, the old worn-out mortality leaving another new and similar existence behind—unlike the divine, which is always the same and not another? And in this way, Socrates, the mortal body, or mortal anything, partakes of immortality; but the immortal in another way. Marvel not then at the love which all men have of their offspring; for that universal love and interest is for the sake of immortality."

I was astonished at her words, and said: "Is this really true, O thou wise Diotima?" And she answered with all the authority of an accomplished sophist: "Of that, Socrates, you may be assured;—think only of the ambi-

tion of men, and you will wonder at the senselessness of their ways, unless you consider how they are stirred by the love of an immortality of fame. They are ready to run all risks greater far than they would have run for their children, and to spend money and undergo any sort of toil, and even to die, for the sake of leaving behind them a name which shall be eternal. Do you imagine that Alcestis would have died to save Admetus, or Achilles to avenge Patroclus, or your own Codrus in order to preserve the kingdom for his sons, if they had not imagined that the memory of their virtues, which still survives among us, would be immortal? Nay," she said, "I am persuaded that all men do all things, and the better they are the more they do them, in hope of the glorious fame of immortal virtue; for they desire the immortal.

"Those who are pregnant in the body only, betake themselves to women and beget children—this is the character of their love; their offspring, as they hope, will preserve their memory and give them the blessedness and immortality which they desire in the future. But souls which are pregnant—for there certainly are men who are more creative in their souls than in their [209] bodies—conceive that which is proper for the soul to conceive or contain. And what are these conceptions?—wisdom and virtue in general. And such creators are poets and all artists who are deserving of the name inventor. But the greatest and fairest sort of wisdom by far is that which is concerned with the ordering of states and families, and which is called temperance and justice. And he who in youth has the seed of these implanted in him and is himself inspired, when he comes to maturity desires to beget and generate. He wanders about seeking beauty that he may beget offspring—

for in deformity he will beget nothing —and naturally embraces the beautiful rather than the deformed body; above all when he finds a fair and noble and well-nurtured soul, he embraces the two in one person, and to such an one he is full of speech about virtue and the nature and pursuits of a good man; and he tries to educate him; and at the touch of the beautiful which is ever present to his memory, even when absent, he brings forth that which he had conceived long before, and in company with him tends that which he brings forth; and they are married by a far nearer tie and have a closer friendship than those who beget mortal children, for the children who are their common offspring are fairer and more immortal. Who, when he thinks of Homer and Hesiod and other great poets, would not rather have their children than ordinary human ones? Who would not emulate them in the creation of children such as theirs, which have preserved their memory and given them everlasting glory? Or who would not have such children as Lycurgus left behind him to be the saviours, not only of Lacedaemon, but of Hellas, as one may say? There is Solon, too, who is the revered father of Athenian laws; and many others there are in many other places, both among Hellenes and barbarians, who have given to the world many noble works, and have been the parents of virtue of every kind; and many temples have been raised in their honour for the sake of children such as their; which were never raised in honour of any one, for the sake of his mortal children. "These are the lesser mysteries of love, into which even you, Socrates, may enter; to the greater and more hidden ones which are the [210] crown of these, and to which, if you pursue them in a right spirit, they will lead, I know not whether you will be able to attain. But I will do my utmost to inform you, and do you follow if you can. For he who would proceed aright in this matter should begin in youth to visit beautiful forms; and first, if he be guided by his instructor aright, to love one such form only—out of that he should create fair thoughts; and soon he will of himself perceive that the beauty of one form is akin to the beauty of another; and then if beauty of form in general is his pursuit, how foolish would he be not to recognize that the beauty in every form is one and the same! And when he perceives this he will abate his violent love of the one, which he will despise and deem a small thing, and will become a lover of all beautiful forms; in the next stage he will consider that the beauty of the mind is more honourable than the beauty of the outward form. So that if a virtuous soul have but a little comeliness, he will be content to love and tend him, and will search out and bring to the birth thoughts which may improve the young, until he is compelled to contemplate and see the beauty of institutions and laws, and to understand that the beauty of them all is of one family, and that personal beauty is a trifle; and after laws and institutions he will go on to the sciences, that he may see their beauty, being not like a servant in love with the beauty of one youth or man or institution, himself a slave mean and narrow-minded, but drawing towards and contemplating the vast sea of beauty, he will create many fair and noble thoughts and notions in boundless love of wisdom; until on that shore he grows and waxes strong, and at last the vision is revealed to him of a single science, which is the science of beauty everywhere. To this I will proceed; please to give me your very best attention:

"He who has been instructed thus far in the things of love, and who has learned to see the beautiful in due order and succession, when he comes toward the end will suddenly perceive a nature of wondrous beauty (and this, Socrates, is the final cause of all our former [211] toils)—a nature which in the first place is everlasting, not growing and decaying, or waxing and waning; secondly, not fair in one point of view and foul in another, or at one time or in one relation or at one place fair, at another time or in another relation or at another place foul, as if fair to some and foul to others, or in the likeness of a face or hands or any other part of the bodily frame, or in any form of speech or knowledge, or existing in any other being, as for example, in an animal, or in heaven, or in earth, or in any other place; but beauty absolute, separate, simple, and everlasting, which without diminution and without increase, or any change, is imparted to the ever-growing and perishing beauties of all other things. He who from these ascending under the influence of true love, begins to perceive that beauty, is not far from the end. And the true order of going, or being led by another, to the things of love, is to begin from the beauties of earth and mount upwards for the sake of that other beauty, using these as steps only, and from one going on to two, and from two to all fair forms, and from fair forms to fair practices, and from fair practices to fair notions, until from fair notions he arrives at the notion of absolute beauty, and at last knows what the essence of beauty is. This, my dear Socrates," said the stranger of Mantineia, "is that life above all others which man should live, in the contemplation of beauty absolute; a beauty which if you once beheld, you would see not to be after the measure of gold, and garments, and fair boys and youths, whose presence now entrances you; and you and many a one would be content to live seeing them only and conversing with them without meat or drink, if that were possible—you only want to look at them and to be with

them. But what if man had eyes to see the true beauty—the divine beauty, I mean, pure and clear and unalloyed, not clogged with the pollutions of mortality and all the colours and vanities of human life—thither looking, and holding converse with the true beauty simple and divine? Remember how in [212] that communion only, beholding beauty with the eye of the mind, he will be enabled to bring forth, not images of beauty, but realities (for he has hold not of an image but of a reality), and bringing forth and nourishing true virtue to become the friend of God and be immortal, if mortal man may. Would that be an ignoble life?"

Such, Phaedrus—and I speak not only to you, but to all of you—were the words of Diotima; and I am persuaded of their truth. And being persuaded of them, I try to persuade others, that in the attainment of this end human nature will not easily find a helper better than love. And therefore, also, I say that every man ought to honour him as I myself honour him, and walk in his ways, and exhort others to do the same, and praise the power and spirit of love according to the measure of my ability now and ever.

The words which I have spoken, you, Phaedrus, may call an encomium of love, or anything else which you please.

When Socrates had done speaking, the company applauded, and Aristophanes was beginning to say something in answer to the allusion which Socrates had made to his own speech,[15] when suddenly there was a great knocking at the door of the house, as of revellers, and the sound of a flute-girl was heard. Agathon told the attendants to go and see who were the intruders. "If they are friends of ours," he said, "invite them in, but if not, say that the drinking is over." A little while afterwards they heard the voice of Alcibiades resounding in the court; he was in a great state

---

15 P. 205 E.

of intoxication, and kept roaring and shouting "Where is Agathon? Lead me to Agathon," and at length, supported by the flute-girl and some of his attendants, he found his way to them. "Hail, friends," he said, appearing at the door crowned with a massive garland of ivy and violets, his head flowing with ribands. "Will you have a very drunken man as a companion of your revels? Or shall I crown Agathon, which was my intention in coming, and go away? For I was unable to come yesterday, and therefore I am here to-day, carrying on my head these ribands, that taking them from my own head, I may crown the head of this fairest and wisest of men, as I may be allowed to call him. Will you laugh at me because I am drunk? Yet I know very well that I am speaking the truth, although you may laugh. [213] But first tell me; if I come in shall we have the understanding of which I spoke?[16] Will you drink with me or not?"

## The Speech of Alcibiades

The company were vociferous in begging that he would take his place among them, and Agathon specially invited him. Thereupon he was led in by the people who were with him; and as he was being led, intending to crown Agathon, he took the ribands from his own head and held them in front of his eyes; he was thus prevented from seeing Socrates, who made way for him, and Alcibiades took the vacant place between Agathon and Socrates, and in taking the place he embraced Agathon and crowned him. Take off his sandals, said Agathon, and let him make a third on the same couch.

By all means; but who makes the third partner in our revels? said Alcibiades, turning round and starting up as

---

16 Supra 212 D. Will you have a very drunken man? etc.

he caught sight of Socrates. By Heracles, he said, what is this? here is Socrates always lying in wait for me, and always, as his way is, coming out at all sorts of unsuspected places: and now, what have you to say for yourself, and why are you lying here, where I perceive that you have contrived to find a place, not by a joker or lover of jokes, like Aristophanes, but by the fairest of the company?

Socrates turned to Agathon and said: I must ask you to protect me, Agathon; for the passion of this man has grown quite a serious matter to me. Since I became his admirer I have never been allowed to speak to any other fair one, or so much as to look at them. If I do, he goes wild with envy and jealousy, and not only abuses me but can hardly keep his hands off me, and at this moment he may do me some harm. Please to see to this, and either reconcile me to him, or, if he attempts violence, protect me, as I am in bodily fear of his mad and passionate attempts.

There can never be reconciliation between you and me, said Alcibiades; but for the present I will defer your chastisement. And I must beg you, Agathon, to give me back some of the ribands that I may crown the marvellous head of this universal despot—I would not have him complain of me for crowning you, and neglecting him, who in conversation is the conqueror of all mankind; and this not only once, as you were the day before yesterday, but always. Whereupon, taking some of the ribands, he crowned Socrates, and again reclined.

Then he said: You seem, my friends, to be sober, which is a thing not to be endured; you must drink—for that was the agreement under which I was admitted—and I elect myself master of the feast until you are well drunk. Let us have a large goblet, Agathon, or rather, he said, addressing the attendant, bring me that wine-cooler. The wine-cooler which had caught his eye was a vessel holding more than two quarts—this he filled and emptied, and bade the attendant fill it again for Socrates. Ob- [214] serve, my friends, said Alcibiades, that this ingenious trick of mine will have no effect on Socrates, for he can drink any quantity of wine and not be at all nearer being drunk. Socrates drank the cup which the attendant filled for him.

Eryximachus said: What is this, Alcibiades? Are we to have neither conversation nor singing over our cups; but simply to drink as if we were thirsty?

Alcibiades replied: Hail, worthy son of a most wise and worthy sire!

The same to you, said Eryximachus; but what shall we do?

That I leave to you, said Alcibiades.

"The wise physician skilled our wounds to heal"[17]

shall prescribe and we will obey. What do you want?

Well, said Eryximachus, before you appeared we had passed a resolution that each one of us in turn should make a speech in praise of love, and as good a one as he could: the turn was passed round from left to right; and as all of us have spoken, and you have not spoken but have well drunken, you ought to speak, and then impose upon Socrates any task which you please, and he on his right hand neighbour, and so on.

That is good, Eryximachus, said Alcibiades; and yet the comparison of a drunken man's speech with those of sober men is hardly fair; and I should like to know, sweet friend, whether you really believe what Socrates was just now saying; for I can assure you that the very reverse is the fact, and that if I praise any one but himself in his presence, whether God or man, he will hardly keep his hands off me.

For shame, said Socrates.

Hold your tongue, said Alcibiades, for by Poseidon, there is no one else whom I will praise when you are of the company.

Well then, said Eryximachus, if you like praise Socrates.

What do you think, Eryximachus? said Alcibiades: shall I attack him and inflict the punishment before you all?

What are you about? said Socrates; are you going to raise a laugh at my expense? Is that the meaning of your praise?

I am going to speak the truth, if you will permit me.

I not only permit, but exhort you to speak the truth.

Then I will begin at once, said Alcibiades, and if I say anything which is not true, you may interrupt me if you will, and say "that is a lie," though my intention is to speak the truth. But you must not wonder if I speak any how as things come into my mind; for the fluent and orderly enumeration of all your singularities is not a task which is easy to a man in my condition.

And now, my boys, I shall praise [215] Socrates in a figure which will appear to him to be a caricature, and yet I speak, not to make fun of him, but only for the truth's sake. I say, that he is exactly like the busts of Silenus, which are set up in the statuaries' shops, holding pipes and flutes in their mouths; and they are made to open in the middle, and have images of gods inside them. I say also that he is like Marsyas the satyr. You yourself will not deny, Socrates, that your face is like that of a satyr. Aye, and there is a resemblance in other points too. For example, you are a bully, as I can prove by witnesses, if you will not confess. And are you not a flute-player? That you are, and a performer far more wonderful than Marsyas. He indeed with instruments used to charm the souls of men by the powers of his breath, and the players of his music do so still: for the melodies of Olympus[18] are derived

---

17 From Pope's Homer, *Il.* xi. 514.

18 Cp. Arist. *Pol.* viii. 5. 16.

from Marsyas who taught them, and these, whether they are played by a great master or by a miserable flute-girl, have a power which no others have; they alone possess the soul and reveal the wants of those who have need of gods and mysteries, because they are divine. But you produce the same effect with your words only, and do not require the flute; that is the difference between you and him. When we hear any other speaker, even a very good one, he produces absolutely no effect upon us, or not much, whereas the mere fragments of you and your words, even at second-hand, and however imperfectly repeated, amaze and possess the souls of every man, woman, and child who comes within hearing of them. And if I were not afraid that you would think me hopelessly drunk, I would have sworn as well as spoken to the influence which they have always had and still have over me. For my heart leaps within me more than that of any Corybantian reveller, and my eyes rain tears when I hear them. And I observe that many others are affected in the same manner. I have heard Pericles and other great orators, and I thought that they spoke well, but I never had any similar feeling; my soul was not stirred by them, nor was I angry at the thought of my own slavish state. But this Marsyas has often brought me to such a pass, that I have felt as if I could hardly endure the life which [216] I am leading (this, Socrates, you will admit) ; and I am conscious that if I did not shut my ears against him, and fly as from the voice of the siren, my fate would be like that of others,—he would transfix me, and I should grow old sitting at his feet. For he makes me confess that I ought not to live as I do, neglecting the wants of my own soul, and busying myself with the concerns of the Athenians; therefore I hold my ears and tear myself away from him. And he is the only person who ever made me ashamed, which you might think not to

be in my nature, and there is no one else who does the same. For I know that I cannot answer him or say that I ought not to do as he bids, but when I leave his presence the love of popularity gets the better of me. And therefore I run away and fly from him, and when I see him I am ashamed of what I have confessed to him. Many a time have I wished that he were dead, and yet I know that I should be much more sorry than glad, if he were to die: so that I am at my wit's end.

And this is what I and many others have suffered from the flute-playing of this satyr. Yet hear me once more while I show you how exact the image is, and how marvellous his power. For let me tell you; none of you know him; but I will reveal him to you; having begun, I must go on. See you how fond he is of the fair? He is always with them and is always being smitten by them, and then again he knows nothing and is ignorant of all things—such is the appearance which he puts on. Is he not like a Silenus in this? To be sure he is: his outer mask is the carved head of the Silenus; but, O my companions in drink, when he is opened, what temperance there is residing within! Know you that beauty and wealth and honour, at which the many wonder, are of no account with him, and are utterly despised by him: he regards not at all the persons who are gifted with them; mankind are nothing to him; all his life is spent in mocking and flouting at them. But when I opened him, and looked within at his serious purpose, I saw in him divine and golden images of such fascinating beauty that I was ready to do in a moment [217] whatever Socrates commanded: they may have escaped the observation of others, but I saw them. Now I fancied that he was seriously enamoured of my beauty, and I thought that I should therefore have a grand opportunity of hearing him tell what he knew, for I had a wonderful opinion of the attractions of my youth. In the prosecution of this design, when I next went to him, I sent away the attendant who usually accompanied me (I will confess the whole truth, and beg you to listen; and if I speak falsely, do you, Socrates, expose the falsehood). Well, he and I were alone together, and I thought that when there was nobody with us, I should hear him speak the language which lovers use to their loves when they are by themselves, and I was delighted. Nothing of the sort; he conversed as usual, and spent the day with me and then went away. Afterwards I challenged him to the palaestra; and he wrestled and closed with me several times when there was no one present; I fancied that I might succeed in this manner. Not a bit; I made no way with him. Lastly, as I had failed hitherto, I thought that I must take stronger measures and attack him boldly, and, as I had begun, not give him up, but see how matters stood between him and me. So I invited him to sup with me, just as if he were a fair youth, and I a designing lover. He was not easily persuaded to come; he did, however, after a while accept the invitation, and when he came the first time, he wanted to go away at once as soon as supper was over, and I had not the face to detain him. The second time, still in pursuance of my design, after we had supped, I went on conversing far into the night, and when he wanted to go away, I pretended that the hour was late and that he had much better remain. So he lay down on the couch next to me, the same on which he had supped, and there was no one but ourselves sleeping in the apartment. All this may be told without shame to any one. But what follows I could hardly tell you if I were sober. Yet as the proverb says, "In vino veritas," whether with boys, or without them;[19] and therefore I must

speak. Nor, again, should I be justified in concealing the lofty actions of Socrates when I come to praise him. Moreover I have felt the serpent's sting; and he who has suffered, as they say, is willing to tell his fellow-sufferers only, as they alone will be likely to understand him, and will not be extreme in judging of [218] the sayings or doings which have been wrung from his agony. For I have been bitten by a more than viper's tooth; I have known in my soul, or in my heart, or in some other part, that worst of pangs, more violent in ingenuous youth than any serpent's tooth, the pang of philosophy, which will make a man say or do anything. And you whom I see around me, Phaedrus and Agathon and Eryximachus and Pausanias and Aristodemus and Aristophanes, all of you, and I need not say Socrates himself, have had experience of the same madness and passion in your longing after wisdom. Therefore listen and excuse my doings then and my sayings now. But let the attendants and other profane and unmannered persons close up the doors of their ears.

When the lamp was put out and the servants had gone away, I thought that I must be plain with him and have no more ambiguity. So I gave him a shake, and I said: "Socrates, are you asleep?" "No," he said. "Do you know what I am meditating?" "What are you meditating?" he said. "I think," I replied, "that of all the lovers whom I have ever had you are the only one who is worthy of me, and you appear to be too modest to speak. Now I feel that I should be a fool to refuse you this or any other favour, and therefore I come to lay at your feet all that I have and all that my friends have, in the hope that you will assist me in the way of virtue, which I desire above all things, and in which I believe that you can help me better than any one else. And I should certainly have more reason to be ashamed of what wise men would say if I were

---

19 In allusion to the two proverbs, οἶνος καὶ παῖδες ἀληθεῖς, and οἶνος καὶ ἀλήθεια.

to refuse a favour to such as you, than of what the world, who are mostly fools, would say of me if I granted it." To these words he replied in the ironical manner which is so characteristic of him:—"Alcibiades, my friend, you have indeed an elevated aim if what you say is true, and if there really is in me any power by which you may become better; truly you must see in me some rare beauty of a kind infinitely higher than any which I see in you. And therefore, if you mean to share with me and to exchange beauty for beauty, you will have greatly the advantage of me; you will gain true beauty in return for appearance—like Diomede, gold in exchange for brass. But look again, sweet [219] friend, and see whether you are not deceived in me. The mind begins to grow critical when the bodily eye fails, and it will be a long time before you get old." Hearing this, I said: "I have told you my purpose, which is quite serious, and do you consider what you think best for you and me." "That is good," he said; "at some other time then we will consider and act as seems best about this and about other matters." Whereupon, I fancied that he was smitten, and that the words which I had uttered like arrows had wounded him, and so without waiting to hear more I got up, and throwing my coat about him crept under his threadbare cloak, as the time of year was winter, and there I lay during the whole night having this wonderful monster in my arms. This again, Socrates, will not be denied by you. And yet, notwithstanding all, he was so superior to my solicitations, so contemptuous and derisive and disdainful of my beauty—which really, as I fancied, had some attractions—hear, O judges; for judges you shall be of the haughty virtue of Socrates—nothing more happened, but in the morning when I awoke (let all the gods and goddesses be my witnesses) I arose as from the couch of a father or an elder brother.

What do you suppose must have been my feelings, after this rejection, at the thought of my own dishonour? And yet I could not help wondering at his natural temperance and self-restraint and manliness. I never imagined that I could have met with a man such as he is in wisdom and endurance. And therefore I could not be angry with him or renounce his company, any more than I could hope to win him. For I well knew that if Ajax could not be wounded by steel, much less he by money; and my only chance of captivating him by my personal attractions had failed. So I was at my wit's end; no one was ever more hopelessly enslaved by another. All this happened before he and I went on the expedition to Potidaea; there we messed together, and I had the opportunity of observing his extraordinary power of sustaining fatigue. His endurance was simply marvellous when, being cut off from our supplies, we were com- [220] pelled to go without food—on such occasions, which often happen in time of war, he was superior not only to me but to everybody; there was no one to be compared to him. Yet at a festival he was the only person who had any real powers of enjoyment; though not willing to drink, he could if compelled beat us all at that,—wonderful to relate! no human being had ever seen Socrates drunk; and his powers, if I am not mistaken, will be tested before long. His fortitude in enduring cold was also surprising. There was a severe frost, for the winter in that region is really tremendous, and everybody else either remained indoors, or if they went out had on an amazing quantity of clothes, and were well shod, and had their feet swathed in felt and fleeces: in the midst of this, Socrates with his bare feet on the ice and in his ordinary dress marched better than the other soldiers who had shoes, and they looked daggers at him because he seemed to despise them.

I have told you one tale, and now I

must tell you another, which is worth hearing,

"Of the doings and sufferings of the enduring man"

while he was on the expedition. One morning he was thinking about something which he could not resolve; he would not give it up, but continued thinking from early dawn until noon—there he stood fixed in thought; and at noon attention was drawn to him, and the rumour ran through the wondering crowd that Socrates had been standing and thinking about something ever since the break of day. At last, in the evening after supper, some Ionians out of curiosity (I should explain that this was not in winter but in summer), brought out their mats and slept in the open air that they might watch him and see whether he would stand all night. There he stood until the following morning; and with the return of light he offered up a prayer to the sun, and went his way.[20] I will also tell, if you please—and indeed I am bound to tell—of his courage in battle; for who but he saved my life? Now this was the engagement in which I received the prize of valour: for I was wounded and he would not leave me, but he rescued me and my arms; and he ought to have received the prize of valour which the generals wanted to confer on me partly on account of my rank, and I told them so (this, again, Socrates will not impeach or deny), but he was more eager than the generals that I and not he should have the prize. There was another occasion on which his behaviour was very remarkable—in the flight of [221] the army after the battle of Delium, where he served among the heavy-armed, —I had a better opportunity of seeing him than at Potidaea, for I was myself on horseback, and therefore comparatively out of danger. He and Laches were retreating, for the troops were in flight, and I met them and told them not to be discouraged, and promised to remain with them; and there you might see him, Aristophanes, as you describe,[21] just as he is in the streets of Athens, stalking like a pelican, and rolling his eyes, calmly contemplating enemies as well as friends, and making very intelligible to anybody, even from a distance, that whoever attacked him would be likely to meet with a stout resistance; and in this way he and his companion escaped—for this is the sort of man who is never touched in war; those only are pursued who are running away headlong. I particularly observed how superior he was to Laches in presence of mind. Many are the marvels which I might narrate in praise of Socrates; most of his ways might perhaps be paralleled in another man, but his absolute unlikeness to any human being that is or ever has been is perfectly astonishing. You may imagine Brasidas and others to have been like Achilles; or you may imagine Nestor and Antenor to have been like Pericles; and the same may be said of other famous men, but of this strange being you will never be able to find any likeness, however remote, either among men who now are or who ever have been—other than that which I have already suggested of Silenus and the satyrs; and they represent in a figure not only himself, but his words. For, although I forgot to mention this to you before, his words are like the images of Silenus which open; they are ridiculous when you first hear them; he clothes himself in language that is like the skin of the wanton satyr—for his talk is of pack-asses and smiths and cobblers and curriers, and he is always repeating the same things in the same words,[22] so that any ignorant or inexperienced person might feel disposed to laugh at him; [222] but he who opens the bust and sees what

---

[20] Cp. supra, 175 B.

[21] Aristoph. *Clouds*, 362.
[22] Cp. *Gorg.* 490, 491, 517.

is within will find that they are the only words which have a meaning in them, and also the most divine, abounding in fair images of virtue, and of the widest comprehension, or rather extending to the whole duty of a good and honourable man.

This, friends, is my praise of Socrates. I have added my blame of him for his ill-treatment of me; and he has ill-treated not only me, but Charmides the son of Glaucon, and Euthydemus the son of Diocles, and many others in the same way—beginning as their lover he has ended by making them pay their addresses to him. Wherefore I say to you, Agathon, "Be not deceived by him; learn from me and take warning, and do not be a fool and learn by experience, as the proverb says."

When Alcibiades had finished, there was a laugh at his outspokenness; for he seemed to be still in love with Socrates. You are sober, Alcibiades, said Socrates, or you would never have gone so far about to hide the purpose of your satyr's praises, for all this long story is only an ingenious circumlocution, of which the point comes in by the way at the end; you want to get up a quarrel between me and Agathon, and your notion is that I ought to love you and nobody else, and that you and you only ought to love Agathon. But the plot of this Satyric or Silenic drama has been detected, and you must not allow him, Agathon, to set us at variance.

I believe you are right, said Agathon, and I am disposed to think that his intention in placing himself between you and me was only to divide us; but he shall gain nothing by that move; for I will go and lie on the couch next to you.

Yes, yes, replied Socrates, by all means come here and lie on the couch below me.

Alas, said Alcibiades, how I am fooled by this man; he is determined to get the better of me at every turn. I do beseech you, allow Agathon to lie between us.

Certainly not, said Socrates, as you praised me, and I in turn ought to praise my neighbour on the right, he will be out of order in praising me again when he ought rather to be praised by me, and I must entreat you to consent to this, and not be jealous, for I have a great desire to praise the youth.          [223]

Hurrah! cried Agathon, I will rise instantly, that I may be praised by Socrates.

The usual way, said Alcibiades; where Socrates is, no one else has any chance with the fair; and now how readily has he invented a specious reason for attracting Agathon to himself.

Agathon arose in order that he might take his place on the couch by Socrates, when suddenly a band of revellers entered, and spoiled the order of the banquet. Some one who was going out having left the door open, they had found their way in, and made themselves at home; great confusion ensued, and every one was compelled to drink large quantities of wine. Aristodemus said that Eryximachus, Phaedrus, and others went away—he himself fell asleep, and as the nights were long took a good rest: he was awakened towards daybreak by a crowing of cocks, and when he awoke, the others were either asleep, or had gone away; there remained only Socrates, Aristophanes, and Agathon, who were drinking out of a large goblet which they passed round, and Socrates was discoursing to them. Aristodemus was only half awake, and he did not hear the beginning of the discourse; the chief thing which he remembered was Socrates compelling the other two to acknowledge that the genius of comedy was the same with that of tragedy, and that the true artist in tragedy was an artist in comedy also. To this they were constrained to assent, being drowsy, and not quite following the argument. And first of all Aristophanes dropped off, then, when the day was already dawning, Agathon. Socrates, having laid them to sleep, rose to depart; Aristodemus, as his manner was, following him. At the Lyceum he took a bath, and passed the day as usual. In the evening he retired to rest at his own home.

# PHAEDRUS (complete)

## I

*227A-230E   Introductory Conversation. The Scene on the Bank of the Ilissus*

SOCRATES. Where do you come [227] from, Phaedrus my friend, and where are you going?

PHAEDRUS. I've been with Lysias, Socrates, the son of Cephalus, and I'm off for a walk outside the wall, after a long morning's sitting there. On the instructions of our common friend Acumenus[1] I take my walks on the open roads; he tells me that is more invigorating than walking in the colonnades.

SOCR. Yes, he's right in saying so. But Lysias, I take it, was in town.   [B]

PH. Yes, staying with Epicrates, in that house where Morychus used to live, close to the temple of Olympian Zeus.

SOCR. Well, how were you occupied? No doubt Lysias was giving the company a feast of eloquence.

PH. I'll tell you, if you can spare time to come along with me and listen.

SOCR. What? Don't you realise that I should account it, in Pindar's words,[2] "above all business" to hear how you and Lysias passed your time?

PH. Lead on then.   [C]

SOCR. Please tell me.

PH. As a matter of fact the topic is appropriate for your ears, Socrates; for the discussion that engaged us may be said to have concerned love. Lysias, you must know, has described how a handsome boy was tempted, but not by a lover: that's the clever part of it: he maintains that surrender should be to one who is not in love rather than to one who is.

SOCR. Splendid! I wish he would add that it should be to a poor man rather than a rich one, an elderly man rather than a young one, and, in general, to ordinary folk like myself. What an attractive democratic theory that would [D] be! However, I'm so eager to hear about it that I vow I won't leave you even if you extend your walk as far as Megara, up to the walls and back again as recommended by Herodicus.[3]

PH. What do you mean, my good [228] man? Do you expect an amateur like me to repeat by heart, without disgracing its author, the work of the ablest writer of our day, which it took him weeks to compose at his leisure? That is far beyond me; though I'd rather have had the ability than come into a fortune.

SOCR. I know my Phaedrus; yes indeed, I'm as sure of him as of my own identity. I'm certain that the said Phaedrus didn't listen just once to Lysias's speech: time after time he asked him to repeat it to him, and Lysias was very ready to comply. Even that would not content him: in the end [B] he secured the script and began poring over the parts that specially attracted him; and thus engaged he sat there the

---

1 A well-known physician, father of Eryximachus, the physician who is one of the speakers in the *Symposium*.

2 *Isthm.* 1, 2.

3 Another physician, mentioned in *Protag.* 316D as a Megarian who afterwards settled at Selymbria in Thrace.

whole morning, until he grew weary and went for a walk. Upon my word, I believe he had learnt the whole speech by heart, unless it was a very long one; and he was going into the country to practise declaiming it. Then he fell in with one who has a passion for listening to discourses; and when he saw him he was delighted to think he would have someone to share his frenzied enthusiasm; so he asked him to join him on his way. But when the lover of discourses begged him to discourse, he became difficult, [c] pretending he didn't want to, though he meant to do so ultimately, even if he had to force himself on a reluctant listener. So beg him, Phaedrus, to do straightway what he will soon do in any case.

PH. Doubtless it will be much my best course to deliver myself to the best of my ability, for I fancy you will never let me go until I have given you some sort of a speech.

SOCR. You are quite right about my intention.

PH. Then here's what I will do: it [D] really is perfectly true, Socrates, that I have not got the words by heart; but I will sketch the general purport of the several points in which the lover and the non-lover were contrasted, taking them in order one by one, and beginning at the beginning.

SOCR. Very well, my dear fellow: but you must first show me what it is that you have in your left hand under your cloak; for I surmise that it is the actual discourse. If that is so, let me assure you of this, that much as I love you I am not altogether inclined to let you [E] practice your oratory on me when Lysias himself is here present. Come now, show it me.

PH. Say no more, Socrates; you have dashed my hope of trying out my powers on you. Well, where would you like us to sit for our reading?

SOCR. Let us turn off here and [229] walk along the Ilissus: then we can sit down in any quiet spot you choose.

PH. It's convenient, isn't it, that I

chance to be bare-footed: you of course always are so. There will be no trouble in wading in the stream, which is especially delightful at this hour of a summer's day.

SOCR. Lead on then, and look out for a place to sit down.

PH. You see that tall plane-tree over there?

SOCR. To be sure.

PH. There's some shade, and a [B] little breeze, and grass to sit down on, or lie down if we like.

SOCR. Then make for it.

PH. Tell me, Socrates, isn't it somewhere about here that they say Boreas seized Oreithuia from the river?

SOCR. Yes, that is the story.

PH. Was this the actual spot? Certainly the water looks charmingly pure and clear, it's just the place for girls to be playing beside the stream.

SOCR. No, it was about a quarter of [c] a mile lower down, where you cross to the sanctuary of Agra: there is, I believe, an altar dedicated to Boreas close by.

PH. I have never really noticed it; but pray tell me, Socrates, do you believe that story to be true?

SOCR. I should be quite in the fashion if I disbelieved it, as the men of science do: I might proceed to give a scientific account of how the maiden, while at play with Pharmaceia, was blown by a gust of Boreas down from the rocks hard by, and having thus met her death was said to have been seized by Boreas: though it may have happened on the [D] Areopagus, according to another version of the occurrence. For my part, Phaedrus, I regard such theories as no doubt attractive, but as the invention of clever, industrious people who are not exactly to be envied, for the simple reason that they must then go on and tell us the real truth about the appearance of Centaurs and the Chimaera, not to mention a whole host of such creatures, Gorgons and Pegasuses and countless other remarkable monsters of legend flocking in on them. If our sceptic, with his [E] somewhat crude science, means to reduce every one of them to the standard of probability, he'll need a deal of time for it. I myself have certainly no time for the business: and I'll tell you why, my friend: I can't as yet "know myself," as the inscription at Delphi enjoins; [230] and so long as that ignorance remains it seems to me ridiculous to inquire into extraneous matters. Consequently I don't bother about such things, but accept the current beliefs about them, and direct my inquiries, as I have just said, rather to myself, to discover whether I really am a more complex creature and more puffed up with pride than Typhon,[4] or a simpler, gentler being whom heaven has blessed with a quiet, un-Typhonic nature. By the way, isn't this the tree we were making for? [B]

PH. Yes, that's the one.

SOCR. Upon my word, a delightful resting-place, with this tall, spreading plane, and a lovely shade from the high branches of the agnus: now that it's in full flower, it will make the place ever so fragrant. And what a lovely stream under the plane-tree, and how cool to the feet! Judging by the statuettes and images I should say it's consecrated to Achelous and some of the Nymphs. And then too, isn't the freshness of the [C] air most welcome and pleasant: and the shrill summery music of the cicada-choir! And as crowning delight the grass, thick enough on a gentle slope to rest your head on most comfortably. In fact, my dear Phaedrus, you have been the stranger's perfect guide.

PH. Whereas you, my excellent friend, strike me as the oddest of men. Anyone would take you, as you say, for a stranger being shown the country by a guide instead of a native: never leaving town [D] to cross the frontier nor even, I believe,

so much as setting foot outside the walls.

SOCR. You must forgive me, dear friend; I'm a lover of learning, and trees and open country won't teach me anything, whereas men in the town do. Yet you seem to have discovered a recipe for getting me out. A hungry animal can be driven by dangling a carrot or a bit of green stuff in front of it: similarly if you proffer me volumes of speeches I don't doubt you can cart me all round Attica, and anywhere else you please. [E] Anyhow, now that we've got here I propose for the time being to lie down, and you can choose whatever posture you think most convenient for reading, and proceed.

PH. Here you are then.

II

## 230E-234C   The Speech of Lysias

You know how I am situated, and I have told you that I think it to our advantage that this should happen. Now I claim that I should not be refused what I ask simply because I am not your lover. Lovers, when their craving is [231] at an end, repent of such benefits as they have conferred: but for the other sort no occasion arises for regretting what has passed; for being free agents under no constraint, they regulate their services by the scale of their means, with an eye to their own personal interest. Again, lovers weigh up profit and loss accruing to their account by reason of their passion, and with the extra item of labour expended decided that they have long [B] since made full payment for favours received; whereas the non-lovers cannot allege any consequential neglect of their personal affairs, nor record any past exertions on the debit side, nor yet complain of having quarrelled with their relatives; hence, with all these troubles removed, all they have left to do is to devote their energies to such conduct as they conceive likely to gratify the other party.

---

4 Socrates connects the name of this hundred-headed monster with the verb τύφω, *to smoke*, and perhaps also with the noun τῦφος, *vanity, humbug.*

Again, it is argued that a lover [c] ought to be highly valued because he professes to be especially kind towards the loved one, and ready to gratify him in words and deeds while arousing the dislike of everyone else. If this is true, however, it is obvious that he will set greater store by the loved one of to-morrow than by that of to-day, and will doubtless do an injury to the old love if required by the new.

And really, what sense is there in lavishing what is so precious upon one labouring under an affliction which [D] nobody who knew anything of it would even attempt to remove? Why, the man himself admits that he is not sound, but sick; that he is aware of his folly, but cannot control himself; how then, when he comes to his senses, is he likely to approve of the intentions that he formed in his aberration?

And observe this: if you are to choose the best of a number of lovers, your choice will be only amongst a few; whereas a general choice of the person who most commends himself to you gives you a wide field, so that in that wide field you have a much better [E] prospect of finding someone worthy of your friendship.

Now maybe you respect established conventions, and anticipate odium if people get to hear about you; if so, it may be expected that a lover, conceiving that everyone will admire him as [232] he admires himself, will be proud to talk about it and flatter his vanity by declaring to all and sundry that his enterprise has been successful; whereas the other type, who can control themselves, will prefer to do what is best rather than shine in the eyes of their neighbours.

Again, a lover is bound to be heard about and seen by many people, consorting with his beloved and caring about little else; so that when they are observed talking to one another, the meeting is [B] taken to imply the satisfaction, actual or prospective, of their desires; whereas, with the other sort, no one ever thinks of putting a bad construction on their association, realising that a man must have someone to talk to by way of friendship or gratification of one sort or another.

And observe this: perhaps you feel troubled by the reflection that it is hard for friendship to be preserved, and that whereas a quarrel arising from other sources will be a calamity shared by both parties, one that follows the sacrifice of your all will involve a grievous hurt [c] to yourself; in that case it is doubtless the lover who should cause you the more alarm, for he is very ready to take offence, and thinks the whole affair is to his own hurt. Hence he discourages his beloved from consorting with anyone else, fearing that a wealthy rival may overreach him with his money, or cultured one outdo him with his intelligence: and he is perpetually on guard against the influence of those who possess other advantages. So by persuading you to become estranged from such rivals [D] he leaves you without a friend in the world; alternatively, if you look to your own interest and show more good sense than your lover, you will find yourself quarrelling with him. On the other hand, one who is not a lover, but has achieved what he asked of you by reason of his merit, will not be jealous of others who seek your society, but will rather detest those who avoid it, in the belief that the latter look down on him, whereas the former are serving his turn. Consequently the object of his attentions is far more likely to make friends than enemies [E] out of the affair.

And observe this: a lover more often than not wants to possess you before he has come to know your character or become familiar with your general personality; and that makes it uncertain whether he will still want to be your friend when his desires have waned; whereas in the other case, the fact [233] that the pair were already friends before the affair took place makes it probable that instead of friendship diminishing as the result of favours received, these favours will abide as a memory and promise of more to come.

And observe this; it ought to be for your betterment to listen to me rather than to a lover; for a lover commends anything you say or do even when it is amiss, partly from fear that he may offend you, partly because his passion impairs his own judgment. For the [B] record of Love's achievement is, first that, when things go badly, he makes a man count that an affliction which normally causes no distress: secondly that, when things go well, he compels his subjects to extol things that ought not to gratify them: which makes it fitting that they should be pitied far more than admired by the objects of their passion. On the other hand, if you listen to me, my intercourse with you will be a matter of ministering not to your immediate pleasure but to your future advantage; for I am the master of myself, rather than the victim of love; I do not [c] bring bitter enmity upon myself by resenting trifling offences: on the contrary it is only on account of serious wrongs that I am moved, and that but slowly, to mild indignation, pardoning what is done unintentionally, and endeavouring to hinder what is done of intent: for these are the tokens of lasting friendship. If however you are disposed to think that there can be no firm friendship save with a lover, you should reflect that in that case we should not set [D] store by sons, or fathers, or mothers, nor should we possess any trustworthy friends: no, it is not to erotic passion that we owe these, but to conduct of a different order.

Again, if we ought to favour those who press us most strongly, then in other matters too we should give our good offices not to the worthiest people but to the most destitute; for since their distress is the greatest, they will be the most thankful to us for relieving them. And observe this further consequence: when we give private banquets, the [E]

right people to invite will be not our friends but beggars and those in need of a good meal: for it is they that will be fond of us and attend upon us and flock to our doors: it is they that will be most delighted and most grateful and call down blessings on our heads. No: the proper course, surely, is to show favour not to the most importunate but to those most able to make us a return; not to mere beggars, but to the deserving; not to those who will regale [234] themselves with your youthful beauty, but to those who will let you share their prosperity when you are older; not to those who, when they have had their will of you, will flatter their vanity by telling the world, but to those who will keep a strict and modest silence; not to those who are devoted to you for a brief period, but to those who will continue to be your friends as long as you live; not to those who, when their passion is spent, will look for an excuse to turn against you, but to those who, when your beauty is past, will make that the time for displaying their own goodness.

Do you therefore be mindful of [B] what I have said and reflect that, while lovers are admonished by their friends and relatives for the wrongness of their conduct, the other sort have never been reproached by one of their family on the score of behaving to the detriment of their own interest.

Perhaps you will ask me whether I recommend you to accord your favours to all and sundry of this sort. Well, I do not suppose that even a lover would bid you to be favourable towards all and sundry lovers; in the first place a recipient would not regard it as merit- [c] ing so much gratitude, and in the second you would find it more difficult if you wished to keep your affairs concealed; and what is wanted is that the business should involve no harm, but mutual advantage.

And now I think I have said all that is needed; if you think I have neglected anything, and want more, let me know.

III

234C-237B *Criticism of Lysias Speech. Socrates Is Induced to Treat the Theme Himself*

PH. What do you think of the speech, Socrates? Isn't it extraordinarily fine, especially in point of language?

SOCR. Amazingly fine indeed, my [D] friend: I was thrilled by it. And it was you, Phaedrus, that made me feel as I did: I watched your apparent delight in the words as you read. And as I'm sure that you understand such matters better than I do, I took my cue from you, and therefore joined in the ecstasy of my right worshipful companion.

PH. Come, come! Do you mean to make a joke of it?

SOCR. Do you think I am joking, and don't mean it seriously?

PH. No more of that, Socrates: [E] tell me truly, as one friend to another, do you think there is anyone in Greece who could make a finer and more exhaustive speech on the same subject?

SOCR. What? Are you and I required to extol the speech not merely on the score of its author's lucidity and terseness of expression, and his consistently precise and well-polished vocabulary, but also for his having said what he ought? If we are, we shall have to allow it only on your account, for my feeble intelligence failed to appreciate it; I was only attending to it as a piece of rhetoric, [235] and as such I couldn't think that even Lysias himself would deem it adequate. Perhaps you won't agree with me, Phaedrus, but really it seemed to me that he said the same things several times over: maybe he's not very clever at expatiating at length on a single theme, or possibly he has no interest in such topics. In fact it struck me as an extravagant performance, to demonstrate his ability to say the same thing twice, in different words but with equal success.

PH. Not a bit of it, Socrates: the [B] outstanding feature of the discourse is just this, that it has not overlooked any important aspect of the subject, so making it impossible for anyone else to outdo what he has said with a fuller or more satisfactory oration.

SOCR. If you go as far as that I shall find it impossible to agree with you; if I were to assent out of politeness, I should be confuted by the wise men and women who in past ages have spoken and written on this theme.

PH. To whom do you refer? Where [C] have you heard anything better than this?

SOCR. I can't tell you off-hand; but I'm sure I have heard something better, from the fair Sappho maybe, or the wise Anacreon, or perhaps some prose writer. What ground, you may ask, have I for saying so? Good sir, there is something welling up within my breast, which makes me feel that I could find something different, and something better, to say. I am of course well aware it can't be anything originating in my own mind, for I know my own ignorance; so I suppose it can only be that it has been poured into me, through my ears, as [D] into a vessel, from some external source; though in my stupid fashion I have actually forgotten how, and from whom, I heard it.

PH. Well said! You move me to admiration. I don't mind your not telling me, even though I should press you, from whom and how you heard it, provided you do just what you say: you have undertaken to make a better speech than that in the book here and one of not less length which shall owe nothing to it; I in my turn undertake like the nine Archons to set up at Delphi a golden life-size statue, not only of [E] myself but of you also.

SOCR. How kind you are, Phaedrus, and what a pattern of golden-age simplicity, in supposing me to mean that Lysias has wholly missed the mark and that another speech could avoid all his points! Surely that couldn't be so even with the most worthless of writers. Thus, as regards the subject of the speech, do you imagine that anybody could argue that the non-lover should be favoured, rather than the lover, without praising the wisdom of the one and censuring the folly of the other? That he could dispense with these essential points, [236] and then bring up something different? No, no: surely we must allow such arguments, and forgive the orator for using them; and in that sort of field what merits praise is not invention, but arrangement; but when it comes to non-essential points, that are difficult to invent, we should praise arrangement and invention too.

PH. I agree: what you say seems fair enough. For my part, this is what I will do: I will allow you to take it for [B] granted that the lover is less sane than the non-lover: and for the rest, if you can replace what we have here by a fuller speech of superior merit, up with your statue in wrought gold beside the offering of the Cypselids at Olympia.

SOCR. Have you taken me seriously. Phaedrus, for teasing you with an attack on your darling Lysias? Can you possibly suppose that I shall make a real attempt to rival his cleverness with something more ornate?

PH. As to that, my friend, I've got you where I can return your fire. Assuredly you must do what you can in the [C] way of a speech, or else we shall be driven, like vulgar comedians, to capping each other's remarks. Beware: do not deliberately compel me to utter the words "Don't I know my Socrates? If not, I've forgotten my own identity," or "He wanted to speak, but made difficulties about it?" No: make up your mind that we're not going to leave this spot untiy you have delivered yourself of what you told me you had within your breast. We are by ourselves in a lonely place, and I am stronger and younger

than you: for all which reasons "mistake not thou my bidding"[5] and [D] please don't make me use force to open your lips.

SOCR. But, my dear good Phaedrus, it will be courting ridicule for an amateur like me to improvise on the same theme as an accomplished writer.

PH. Look here, I'll have no more of this affectation; for I'm pretty sure I have something to say which will compel you to speak.

SOCR. Then please don't say it.

PH. Oh, but I shall, here and now; and what I say will be on oath. I swear to you by—but by whom, by what [E] god? Or shall it be by this plane-tree? I swear that unless you deliver your speech here in its very presence, I will assuredly never again declaim nor report any other speech by any author whatsoever.

SOCR. Aha, you rogue! How clever of you to discover the means of compelling a lover of discourse to do your bidding!

PH. Then why all this twisting?

SOCR. I give it up, in view of what you've sworn. For how could I possibly do without such entertainment?

PH. Then proceed.                        [237]

SOCR. Well, do you know what I'm going to do?

PH. Do about what?

SOCR. I shall cover my head before I begin: then I can rush through my speech at top speed without looking at you and breaking down for shame.[6]

PH. You can do anything else you like, provided you make your speech.

SOCR. Come then, ye clear-voiced Muses, whether it be from the nature of

---

5 Pindar, *frag.* 94 (Bowra).
6 To Phaedrus Socrates's words here doubtless express apprehension that he will disgrace himself by an inferior performance, but the shame that Socrates really feels is, as transpires later (243B), due to his having been forced to adopt an unworthy conception of Eros.

your song, or from the musical people of Liguria that ye came to be so styled,[7] "assist the tale I tell" under compulsion by my good friend here, to the end that he may think yet more highly of one [B] dear to him, whom he already accounts a man of wisdom.

IV

## 237B-238C  Socrates Begins His Speech. A Definition of Love

SOCR. Well then, once upon a time there was a very handsome boy, or rather young man, who had a host of lovers; and one of them was wily, and had persuaded the boy that he was not in love with him, though really he was, quite as much as the others. And on one occasion, in pressing his suit he actually sought to convince him that he ought to favour a non-lover rather than a lover. And this is the purport of what he said:

My boy, if anyone means to deliberate successfully about anything, there is one thing he must do at the outset: he [C] must know what it is he is deliberating about; otherwise he is bound to go utterly astray. Now most people fail to realize that they don't know what this or that really is: consequently when they start discussing something, they dispense with any agreed definition, assuming that they know the thing; then later on they naturally find, to their cost, that they agree neither with each other nor with themselves. That being so, you and I would do well to avoid what we charge against other people; and as the question before us is whether one should preferably consort with a lover or a non-lover, we ought to agree upon a definition of love which shows its nature and its effects, so that we may have it before our minds as something to refer to while we discuss whether love is beneficial [D] or injurious.

Well now, it is plain to everyone that love is some sort of desire; and further we know that men desire that which is fair without being lovers. How then are we to distinguish one who loves from one who does not? We must go on to observe that within each one of us there are two sorts of ruling or guiding principle that we follow: one is an innate desire for pleasure, the other an acquired judgment that aims at what is best. Sometimes these internal guides are in accord, sometimes at variance: now one gains the mastery, now the other. [E] And when judgment guides us rationally towards what is best, and has the mastery, that mastery is called tem- [238] perance; but when desire drags us irrationally towards pleasure, and has come to rule within us, the name given to that rule is wantonness. But in truth wantonness itself has many names, as it has many branches or forms, and when one of these forms is conspicuously present in a man it makes that man bear its name, a name that it is no credit or distinction to possess. If it be in the matter of food that desire has the mastery over judgment of what is for the best, and over all other desires, it is called [B] gluttony, and the person in question will be called a glutton; or again if desire has achieved domination in the matter of drink, it is plain what term we shall apply to its subject who is led down that path; and no less plain what are the appropriate names in the case of other such persons and of other such desires, according as this one or that holds sway.

Now the reason for saying all this can hardly remain in doubt; yet even so a statement of it will be illuminating. When irrational desire, pursuing the en-

---

7 The suggested connexion between λιγύs (*clear-voiced*) and the Ligurian people is one of those etymological jests in which Plato often, and sometimes rather pointlessly, indulges.

joyment of beauty, has gained the mastery over judgment that prompts to right conduct, and has acquired from [c] other desires, akin to it, fresh strength to strain towards bodily beauty, that very strength provides it with its name: it is the strong passion called Love.

v

### 238C-241D Socrates Concludes His First Speech

socr. Well, Phaedrus my friend, do you think, as I do, that I am divinely inspired?

ph. Undoubtedly, Socrates, you have been vouchsafed a quite unusual eloquence.

socr. Then listen to me in silence. For truly there seems to be a divine presence in this spot, so that you must [d] not be surprised if, as my speech proceeds, I become as one possessed; already my style is not far from dithyrambic.

ph. Very true.

socr. But for that you are responsible. Still, let me continue; possibly the menace may be averted. However, that must be as God wills: our business is to resume our address to the boy:—

Very well then, my good friend: the true nature of that on which we have to deliberate has been stated and defined; and so, with that definition in mind, we may go on to say what advantage or [e] detriment may be expected to result to one who accords his favour to a lover and a non-lover respectively.

Now a man who is dominated by desire and enslaved to pleasure is of course bound to aim at getting the greatest possible pleasure out of his beloved; and what pleases a sick man[8] is anything that does not thwart him, whereas anything that is as strong as, or stronger than, himself gives him offence. Hence he will not, if he can avoid it, put up with a

---

8 Cf. 231d, 236a.

favourite that matches or outdoes [239] him in strength, but will always seek to make him weaker and feebler: and weakness is found in the ignorant, the cowardly, the poor speaker, the slow thinker, as against the wise, the brave, the eloquent, the quick-minded. All these defects of mind and more in the beloved are bound to be a source of pleasure to the lover: if they do not exist already as innate qualities, he will cultivate them, for not to do so means depriving himself of immediate pleasure. And of course he is bound to be jealous, constantly debarring the boy not only, to his great injury, from the advan- [b] tages of consorting with others, which would make a real man of him, but, greatest injury of all, from consorting with that which would most increase his wisdom; by which I mean divine philosophy: no access to that can possibly be permitted by the lover, for he dreads becoming thereby an object of contempt. And in general he must aim at making the boy totally ignorant and totally dependent on his lover, by way of securing the maximum of pleasure for himself, and the maximum of damage to the other.

Hence in respect of the boy's mind [c] it is anything but a profitable investment to have as guardian or partner a man in love.

After the mind, the body; we must see what sort of physical condition will be fostered, and how it will be fostered, in the boy that has become the possession of one who is under compulsion to pursue pleasure instead of goodness. We shall find him, of course, pursuing a weakling rather than a sturdy boy, one who has had a cosy, sheltered upbringing instead of being exposed to the open air, who has given himself up to a soft unmanly life instead of the toil and [d] sweat of manly exercise, who for lack of natural charm tricks himself out with artificial cosmetics, and resorts to all sorts of other similar practices which are too obvious to need further enumeration; yet before leaving the topic we may sum it up in a sentence: the boy will be of that physical type which in wartime, and other times that try a man's mettle, inspires confidence in his enemies and alarm in his friends, aye and in his very lovers too.

And now let us pass from these [E] obvious considerations and raise the next question: what advantage or detriment in respect of property and possessions shall we find resulting from the society and guardianship of a lover? Well, one thing is plain enough to anyone, and especially to the lover, namely that his foremost wish will be for the boy to be bereft of his dearest possessions, his treasury of kindness and ideal affection: father and mother, kinsmen and friends —he will want him to be robbed of them all, as likely to make difficulties [240] and raise objections to the intercourse which he finds so pleasant. If however the boy possesses property, in money or whatever it may be, he will reckon that he will not be so easy to capture, or if captured to manage; hence a lover is bound to nurse a grudge against one who possesses property, and to rejoice when he loses it. Furthermore he will want his beloved to remain as long as possible without wife or child or home, so as to enjoy for as long as may be his own delights.

There are, to be sure, other evils in life, but with most of them heaven has mixed some momentary pleasure: [B] thus in the parasite, a fearsome and most pernicious creature, nature has mingled a dash of pleasing wit or charm; a courtesan may well be branded as pernicious, not to mention many other similar creatures with their respective callings, yet in everyday life they can be agreeable; but a lover, besides being pernicious, is the most disagreeable of all men for a boy to spend his days with. There's

an old saying about "not matching [C] May with December," based, I suppose, on the idea that similarity of age tends to similarity of pleasures and consequently makes a couple good friends: still even with such a couple the association is apt to pall. Then again, in addition to the dissimilarity of age, there is that compulsion which is burdensome for anybody in any circumstances, but especially so in the relations of such a pair.

The elderly lover will not, if he can help it, suffer any desertion by his beloved by day or by night; he is [D] driven on by a compelling, goading power, lured by the continual promise of pleasure in the sight, hearing, touching or other physical experience of the beloved; to minister unfailingly to the boy's needs is his delight. But what pleasure or what solace will he have to offer to the beloved? How will he save him from experiencing the extremity of discomfort in those long hours at his lover's side, as he looks upon a face which years have robbed of its beauty, together with [E] other consequences which it is unpleasant even to hear mentioned, let alone to have continually to cope with in stark reality. And what of the suspicious precautions with which he is incessantly guarded, with whomsoever he associates, the unseasonable fulsome compliments to which he has to listen, alternating with reproaches which when uttered in soberness are hard to endure, but coming from one in his cups, in language of unlimited, undisguised coarseness, are both intolerable and disgusting?

To continue: if while his love lasts he is harmful and offensive, in later days, when it is spent, he will show his bad faith. He was lavish with promises, interspersed amongst his vows and entreaties, regarding those later days, contriving with some difficulty to secure his partner's endurance of an intercourse which even then was burdensome, [241] by holding out hopes of benefits to come.

But when the time comes for fulfilling the promises, a new authority takes the place within him of the former ruler: love and passion are replaced by wisdom and temperance: he has become a different person. But the boy does not realise it, and demands a return for what he gave in the past, reminding him of what had been done and said, as though he were talking to the same person; while the erstwhile lover, who has now acquired wisdom and temperance, cannot for very shame bring himself to declare that he has become a new man, nor yet see his way to redeeming [B] the solemn assurances and promises made under the old régime of folly; he fears that if he were to go on acting as before he would revert to his old character, his former self. So he runs away from his obligations as one compelled to default; it's "tails" this time instead of "heads,"[9] and he has to turn tail and rush away. But the boy must needs run after him, crying indignantly to high heaven: though from start to finish he has never understood that he ought not to have yielded to a lover inevitably devoid of reason, but far rather to one possessed of reason and not in love. He should have known that the wrong [C] choice must mean surrendering himself to a faithless, peevish, jealous and offensive captor, to one who would ruin his property, ruin his physique, and above all ruin his spiritual development, which is assuredly and ever will be of supreme value in the sight of gods and men alike.[10]

Let that then, my boy, be your lesson: be sure that the attentions of a lover carry no goodwill: they are no more than a glutting of his appetite, for

As wolf to lamb, so lover to his lad.  [D]

There, I knew I should,[11] Phaedrus. Not a word more shall you have from me: let that be the end of my discourse.

VI

## 241D-243E    Interlude, Leading to Socrates's Recantation

PH. Why, I thought you were only half-way through and would have an equal amount to say about the non-lover, enumerating his good points and showing that he should be the favoured suitor. Why is it, Socrates, that instead of that you break off?

SOCR. My dear good man, haven't you noticed that I've got beyond [E] dithyramb, and am breaking out into epic verse, despite my fault-finding? What do you suppose I shall do if I start extolling the other type? Don't you see that I shall clearly be possessed by those nymphs into whose clutches you deliberately threw me? I therefore tell you, in one short sentence, that to each evil for which I have abused the one party there is a corresponding good belonging to the other. So why waste [C] words? All has been said that needs saying about them both. And that being so, my story can be left to the fate appropriate to it, and I will take myself off across the river here before [242] you drive me to greater lengths.

PH. Oh, but you must wait until it gets cooler, Socrates. Don't you realise that it's just about the hour of "scorching moonday," as the phrase goes? Let us wait and discuss what we've heard; when it has got cool perhaps we will go.

SOCR. Phaedrus, your enthusiasm for discourse is sublime, and really moves me to admiration. Of the discourses pronounced during your lifetime no one, I fancy, has been responsible for [B]

---

[9] An allusion to the game called ὀστρακίνδα in which a shell was thrown into the air between two opposing sides, and according as it fell white or dark side uppermost one side had to run and the other to catch them.

[10] Cf. *Apol.* 29E, 30A-B.

[11] Socrates had feared that he would break out into inspired verse, 238D.

more than you, whether by delivering them yourself or by compelling others to do so by one means or another—with one exception, Simmias of Thebes: you are well ahead of all the rest. And now it seems that once more you are the cause of my having to deliver myself.

PH. It might be a lot worse! But how so? To what do you refer?

SOCR. At the moment when I was about to cross the river, dear friend, there came to me my familiar divine sign—which always checks me when on the point of doing something or [c] other—and all at once I seemed to hear a voice, forbidding me to leave the spot until I had made atonement for some offence to heaven. Now, you must know, I am a seer; not a very good one, it's true, but, like a poor scholar, good enough for my own purposes; hence I understand already well enough what my offence was. The fact is, you know, Phaedrus, the mind itself has a kind of divining power; for I felt disturbed some while ago as I was delivering that speech, and had a misgiving lest I might, in the words of Ibycus

By sinning in the sight of God win high
    renown from man.                      [D]

But now I realise my sin.

PH. And what is it?

SOCR. That was a terrible theory, Phaedrus, a terrible theory that you introduced and compelled me to expound.

PH. How so?

SOCR. It was foolish, and somewhat blasphemous; and what could be more terrible than that?

PH. I agree, if merits your description.

SOCR. Well, do you not hold Love to be a god, the child of Aphrodite?

PH. He is certainly said to be.

SOCR. But not according to Lysias, and not according to that discourse of yours which you caused my lips to utter [E] by putting a spell on them. If Love is, as he is indeed, a god or a divine being, he cannot be an evil thing: yet this pair of speeches treated him as evil. That then was their offence towards Love, to which was added the most exquisite folly of parading their pernicious rubbish as though it were good sense because it might deceive a few [243] miserable people and win their applause.

And so, my friend, I have to purify myself. Now for such as offend in speaking of gods and heroes there is an ancient mode of purification, which was known to Stesichorus, though not to Homer. When Stesichorus lost the sight of his eyes because of his defamation of Helen, he was not, like Homer, at a loss to know why: as a true artist he understood the reason, and promptly wrote the lines:

False, false the tale:
Thou never didst sail in the well-decked ships
    Nor come to the towers of Troy.   [B]

And after finishing the composition of his so-called Palinode he straightway recovered his sight. Now it's here that I shall show greater wisdom than these poets: I shall attempt to make my due palinode to Love before any harm comes to me for my defamation of him, and no longer veiling my head for shame, but uncovered.

PH. Nothing you could say, Socrates, would please me more.

SOCR. Yes, dear Phaedrus: you [c] understand how irreverent the two speeches were, the one in the book and that which followed. Suppose we were being listened to by a man of generous and humane character, who loved or had once loved another such as himself: suppose he heard us saying that for some triffling cause lovers conceive bitter hatred and a spirit of malice and injury towards their loved ones; wouldn't he be sure to think that we had been brought up among the scum of the people and had never seen a case of noble love? Wouldn't he utterly refuse to accept our vilification of Love?                              [D]

PH. Indeed, Socrates, he well might.

SOCR. Then out of respect for him, and in awe of Love himself, I should like to wash the bitter taste out of my mouth with a draught of wholesome discourse; and my advice to Lysias is that he should lose no time in telling us that, other things being equal, favour should be accorded to the lover rather than to the non-lover.

PH. Rest assured, that will be done. When you have delivered your encomium of the lover, I shall most certainly make Lysias compose a [E] new speech to the same purport.

SOCR. I'm sure of that, so long as you continue to be the man you are.

PH. Then you may confidently proceed.

SOCR. Where is that boy I was talking to? He must listen to me once more, and not rush off to yield to his non-lover before he hears what I have to say.

PH. Here he is, quite close beside you, whenever you want him.

VII

*243E-245C  Socrates Begins His
Second Speech. Three Types
of Divine Madness*

SOCR. Now you must understand, fair boy, that whereas the preceding discourse was by Phaedrus, son of Pythocles, of Myrrinous, that which I [224] shall now pronounce is by Stesichorus, son of Euphemus, of Himera.[12] This then is how it must run:

---

12 Thompson and, as we should expect, Hermeias before him, regard all these proper names as significant. Doubtless the last two are so: the speech will be εὔφημος as opposed to κακήγορος, and 'Ιμέραιος anticipates the "flood of passion" (ἵμερος) of 251c. But to find significance in the other four is a task best left to Neoplatonic subtlety.

"False is the tale" that when a lover is at hand favour ought rather to be accorded to one who does not love, on the ground that the former is mad, and the latter sound of mind. That would be right if it were an invariable truth that madness is an evil: but in reality, the greatest blessings come by way of madness, indeed of madness that is heaven-sent. It was when they were mad that the prophetess at Delphi [B] and the priestesses at Dodona achieved so much for which both states and individuals in Greece are thankful: when sane they did little or nothing. As for the Sibyl and others who by the power of inspired prophecy have so often foretold the future to so many, and guided them aright, I need not dwell on what is obvious to everyone. Yet it is in place to appeal to the fact that madness was accounted no shame nor disgrace by the men of old who gave things their names: otherwise they would not have connected that greatest of arts, whereby the future is discerned, with this [c] very word "madness," and named it accordingly. No, it was because they held madness to be a valuable gift, when due to divine dispensation, that they named that art as they did, though the men of to-day, having no sense of values, have put in an extra letter, making it not *manic* but *mantic*. That is borne out by the name they gave to the art of those sane prophets who inquire into the future by means of birds and other signs: the name was "oionoistic," which by its components indicated that the prophet attained understanding and information by a purely human activity of thought belonging to his own intelligence; though a younger generation has come to call it "oionistic," lengthening the quantity of the *o* to make it sound impressive. You see then what this [D] ancient evidence attests: corresponding to the superior perfection and value of the prophecy of inspiration over that of omen-reading, both in name and in fact, is the superiority of heaven-sent madness over man-made sanity.

And in the second place, when grievous maladies and afflictions have beset certain families by reason of some ancient sin, madness has appeared amongst them, and breaking out [E] into prophecy has secured relief by finding the means thereto, namely by recourse to prayer and worship; and in consequence thereof rites and means of purification were established, and the sufferer was brought out of danger, alike for the present and for the future. Thus did madness secure, for him that was maddened aright and possessed, deliverance from his troubles.

There is a third form of posses- [245] sion or madness, of which the Muses are the source. This seizes a tender, virgin soul and stimulates it to rapt passionate expression, especially in lyric poetry, glorifying the countless mighty deeds of ancient times for the instruction of posterity. But if any man come to the gates of poetry without the madness of the Muses, persuaded that skill alone will make him a good poet, then shall he and his works of sanity with him be brought to naught by the poetry of madness, and behold, their place is nowhere to be found.

Such then is the tale, though I [B] have not told it fully, of the achievements wrought by madness that comes from the gods. So let us have no fears simply on that score; let us not be disturbed by an argument that seeks to scare us into preferring the friendship of the sane to that of the passionate. For there is something more that it must prove if it is to carry the day, namely that love is not a thing sent from heaven for the advantage both of lover and beloved. What we have to prove is the opposite, namely that this sort of madness is a gift of the gods, fraught [C] with the highest bliss. And our proof

assuredly will prevail with the wise, though not with the learned.

Now our first step towards attaining the truth of the matter is to discern the nature of soul, divine and human, its experiences and its activities. Here then our proof begins.

VIII

## 245C-246A  *The Immortality of Soul*

All soul is immortal; for that which is ever in motion is immortal. But that which while imparting motion is itself moved by something else can cease to be in motion, and therefore can cease to live; it is only that which moves itself that never intermits its motion, inasmuch as it cannot abandon its own nature; moreover this self-mover is the source and first principle of motion for all other things that are moved. Now a first principle cannot come into [D] being: for while anything that comes to be must come to be from a first principle, the latter itself cannot come to be from anything whatsoever: if it did, it would cease any longer to be a first principle. Furthermore, since it does not come into being, it must be imperishable: for assuredly if a first principle were to be destroyed, nothing could come to be out of it, nor could anything bring the principle itself back into existence, seeing that a first principle is needed for anything to come into being.

The self-mover, then, is the first principle of motion: and it is as impossible that it should be destroyed as that it should come into being: were it otherwise, the whole universe, the whole of that which comes to be, would collapse into immobility, and never find [E] another source of motion to bring it back into being.

And now that we have seen that that which is moved by itself is immortal, we shall feel no scruple in affirming that precisely that is the essence and definition of soul, to wit self-motion. Any body that has an external source of motion is soulless; but a body deriving its motion from a source within itself is animate or *besouled,* which implies that the nature of soul is what has been said.

And if this last assertion is correct, namely that "that which moves itself" is precisely identifiable with soul, it must follow that soul is not born [246] and does not die.

## IX

### 246A-247C  Myth of the Soul. The Charioteer and Two Horses. The Procession of Souls

As to soul's immortality then we have said enough, but as to its nature there is this that must be said: what manner of thing it is would be a long tale to tell, and most assuredly a god alone could tell it; but what it resembles, that a man might tell in briefer compass: let this therefore be our manner of discourse. Let it be likened to the union of powers in a team of winged steeds and their winged charioteer. Now all the gods' steeds and all their charioteers are good, and of good stock; but with other beings it is not wholly so. With us men, in the first place, it is a pair of [B] steeds that the charioteer controls; moreover one of them is noble and good, and of good stock, while the other has the opposite character, and his stock is opposite. Hence the task of our charioteer is difficult and troublesome.

And now we must essay to tell how it is that living beings are called mortal and immortal. All soul has the care of all that is inanimate, and traverses the whole universe, though in ever-changing forms. Thus when it is perfect and winged it journeys on high and controls the whole world; but one that has [C]

shed its wings sinks down until it can fasten on something solid, and settling there it takes to itself an earthy body which seems by reason of the soul's power to move itself. This composite structure of soul and body is called a living being, and is further termed "mortal": "immortal" is a term applied on no basis of reasoned argument at all, but our fancy pictures the god whom we have never seen, nor fully conceived, as an immortal living being, possessed [D] of a soul and a body united for all time. Howbeit let these matters, and our account thereof, be as god pleases; what we must understand is the reason why the soul's wings fall from it, and are lost. It is on this wise.

The natural property of a wing is to raise that which is heavy and carry it aloft to the region where the gods dwell; and more than any other bodily part it shares in the divine nature, which is fair, wise and good, and [E] possessed of all other such excellences. Now by these excellences especially is the soul's plumage nourished and fostered, while by their opposites, even by ugliness and evil, it is wasted and destroyed. And behold, there in the heaven Zeus, mighty leader, drives his winged team: first of the host of gods and daemons he proceeds, ordering all things and caring therefor: and the host follows after him, marshalled in eleven companies. For Hestia abides alone in the gods' dwelling-place; [247] but for the rest, all such as are ranked in the number of the twelve as ruler gods lead their several companies, each according to his rank.

Now within the heavens are many spectacles of bliss upon the highways whereon the blessed gods pass to and fro, each doing his own work; and with them are all such as will and can follow them: for jealousy has no place in the choir divine. But at such times as they go to their feasting and banquet, behold they climb the steep ascent even unto the summit of the arch that supports the heavens; and easy is that ascent [B] for the chariots of the gods, for that they are well-balanced and readily guided; but for the others it is hard, by reason of the heaviness of the steed of wickedness, which pulls down his driver with his weight, except that driver have schooled him well.

And now there awaits the soul the extreme of her toil and struggling. For the souls that are called immortal, so soon as they are at the summit, come forth and stand upon the back of the world: and straightway the revolving heaven carries them round, and they [C] look upon the regions without.

x

## 247C-248E   The Soul's Vision of True Being. Its Fall and Incarnation

Of that place beyond the heavens none of our earthly poets has yet sung, and none shall sing worthily. But this is the manner of it, for assuredly we must be bold to speak what is true, above all when our discourse is upon truth. It is there that true Being dwells, without colour or shape, that cannot be touched; reason alone, the soul's pilot, can behold it, and all true knowledge is knowledge thereof. Now even as the mind of a god is nourished by reason and knowledge, so also is it with [D] every soul that has a care to receive her proper food; wherefore when at last she has beheld Being she is well content, and contemplating truth she is nourished and prospers, until the heaven's revolution brings her back full circle. And while she is borne round she discerns justice, its very self, and likewise temperance, and knowledge, not the knowledge that is neighbour to Becoming and varies with the various objects to which we commonly ascribe being, but the [E]

veritable knowledge of Being that veritably is. And when she has contemplated likewise and feasted upon all else that has true being, she descends again within the heavens and comes back home. And having so come, her charioteer sets his steeds at their manger, and puts ambrosia before them and draught of nectar to drink withal.

Such is the life of gods: of the [248] other souls that which best follows a god and becomes most like thereunto raises her charioteer's head into the outer region, and is carried round with the gods in the revolution, but being confounded by her steeds she has much ado to discern the things that are; another now rises, and now sinks, and by reason of her unruly steeds sees in part, but in part sees not. As for the rest, though all are eager to reach the heights and seek to follow, they are not able: sucked down as they travel they trample and tread upon one another, this one striving to outstrip that. Thus confusion ensues, and conflict and grievous [B] sweat: whereupon, with their charioteers powerless, many are lamed, and many have their wings all broken; and for all their toiling they are baulked, every one, of the full vision of Being, and departing therefrom, they feed upon the food of semblance.

Now the reason wherefore the souls are fain and eager to behold the Plain of Truth, and discover it, lies herein: to wit, that the pasturage that is proper to their noblest part comes from [C] that Meadow, and the plumage by which they are borne aloft is nourished thereby.

Hear now the ordinance of Necessity. Whatsoever soul has followed in the train of a god, and discerned something of truth, shall be kept from sorrow until a new revolution shall begin; and if she can do this always, she shall remain always free from hurt. But when she is not able so to follow, and sees none of it, but meeting with some mischance comes to be burdened with a load of forgetfulness and wrongdoing, and because of that burden sheds her wings and falls to the earth, then thus runs the law: in her first birth she shall not be planted in any brute [D] beast, but the soul that hath seen the most of Being shall enter into the human babe that shall grow into a seeker after wisdom or beauty, a follower of the Muses and a lover; the next, having seen less, shall dwell in a king that abides by law, or a warrior and ruler; the third in a statesman, a man of business or a trader; the fourth in an athlete, or physical trainer or physician; the fifth shall have the [E] life of a prophet or a mystery-priest; to the sixth that of a poet or other imitative artist shall be fittingly given; the seventh shall live in an artisan or farmer, the eighth in a sophist or demagogue, the ninth in a tyrant.

## XI

### 248E-249D  Reincarnation and Final Liberation of the Soul. The Philosopher's Privilege

Now in all these incarnations he who lives righteously has a better lot for his portion, and he who lives unrighteously a worse.[13] For a soul does not return to the place whence she came for ten thousand years, since in no lesser time can she regain her wings, save only his soul who has sought after wisdom [249] unfeignedly, or has conjoined his passion for a loved one with that seeking. Such a soul, if with three revolutions of a thousand years she has thrice chosen this philosophic life, regains thereby her wings, and speeds away after three thousand years; but the rest, when they have accomplished their first

life, are brought to judgment, and after the judgment some are taken to be punished in places of chastisement beneath the earth, while others are borne aloft by Justice to a certain region of the heavens, there to live in such manner as is merited by their past [B] life in the flesh. And after a thousand years these and those alike come to the allotment and choice of their second life, each choosing according to her will; then does the soul of a man enter into the life of a beast, and the beast's soul that was aforetime in a man goes back to a man again. For only the soul that has beheld truth may enter into this our human form: seeing that man must needs understand the language of Forms, passing from a plurality of [C] perceptions to a unity gathered together by reasoning; and such understanding is a recollection of those things which our souls beheld aforetime as they journeyed with their god, looking down upon the things which now we suppose to be, and gazing up to that which truly is.

Therefore is it meet and right that the soul of the philosopher alone[14] should recover her wings: for she, so far as may be, is ever near in memory to those things a god's nearness whereunto makes him truly god. Wherefore if a man makes right use of such means of remembrance, and ever approaches to the full vision of the perfect mysteries, he and he alone becomes truly perfect. Standing aside from the busy doings of mankind, and drawing nigh to the divine, he is rebuked by the [D] multitude as being out of his wits, for they know not that he is possessed by a deity.

---

13 These words refer not to the final destiny of the souls, but to the period of reward or punishment between two incarnations.

14 The word "alone" is strictly inconsistent with 248E 5-7, where it is implied that all souls ultimately regain their wings. But in the present sentence Plato is thinking only of events within a 10,000-year period, and giving the ground for his assertion that the philosopher alone can shorten the period of πτέρωσις.

XII

### 249D-250D  The Soul's Recollection of Ideal Beauty

Mark therefore the sum and substance of all our discourse touching the fourth sort of madness: to wit, that this is the best of all forms of divine possession, both in itself and in its sources, both for him that has it and for him that shares therein; and when he that loves beauty is touched by [E] such madness he is called a lover. Such an one, as soon as he beholds the beauty of this world, is reminded of true beauty, and his wings begin to grow; then is he fain to lift his wings and fly upward; yet he has not the power, but inasmuch as he gazes upward like a bird, and cares nothing for the world beneath, men charge it upon him that he is demented.

Now, as we have said, every human soul has, by reason of her nature, had contemplation of true Being: else would she never have entered into this human creature; but to be put in mind thereof by things here is not easy for every [250] soul; some, when they had the vision, had it but for a moment; some when they had fallen to earth consorted unhappily with such as led them to deeds of unrighteousness, wherefore they forgot the holy objects of their vision. Few indeed are left that can still remember much: but when these discern some likeness of the things yonder, they are amazed, and no longer masters of themselves, and know not what is come upon them by reason of their perception being dim.                              [B]

Now in the earthly likenesses of justice and temperance and all other prized possessions of the soul there dwells no lustre; nay, so dull are the organs wherewith men approach their images that hardly can a few behold that which is imaged; but with beauty it is otherwise. Beauty it was ours to see in all its brightness in those days when, amidst that happy company, we beheld with our eyes that blessed vision, ourselves in the train of Zeus, others following some other god; then were we all initiated into that mystery which is rightly accounted blessed beyond all others; whole and unblemished were we that did celebrate it, un- [C] touched by the evils that awaited us in days to come; whole and unblemished likewise, free from all alloy, steadfast and blissful were the spectacles on which we gazed in the moment of final revelation; pure was the light that shone around us, and pure were we, without taint of that prison-house which now we are encompassed withal, and call a body, fast bound therein as an oyster in its shell.

There let it rest then, our tribute to a memory that has stirred us to linger awhile on those former joys for which we yearn. Now beauty, as we said, [D] shone bright amidst these visions, and in this world below we apprehend it through the clearest of our senses, clear and resplendent. For sight is the keenest mode of perception vouchsafed us through the body; wisdom, indeed, we cannot see thereby—how passionate had been our desire for her, if she had granted us so clear an image of herself to gaze upon—nor yet any other of those beloved objects, save only beauty; for beauty alone this has been ordained, to be most manifest to sense and most lovely of them all.

XIII

### 250E-252C  Love as the Regrowing of the Soul's Wings

Now he whose vision of the mys- [E] tery is long past, or whose purity has been sullied, cannot pass swiftly hence to see Beauty's self yonder, when he beholds that which is called beautiful here; wherefore he looks upon it with no reverence, and surrendering to pleasure he essays to go after the fashion of a four-footed beast, and to beget offspring of the flesh; or consorting with wantonness he has no fear nor shame in running after unnatural pleasure. But when one who is fresh from the [251] mystery, and saw much of the vision, beholds a godlike face or bodily form that truly expresses beauty, first there comes upon him a shuddering and a measure of that awe which the vision inspired, and then reverence as at the sight of a god: and but for fear of being deemed a very madman he would offer sacrifice to his beloved, as to a holy image of deity. Next, with the passing of the shudder, a strange sweating and fever seizes him: for by reason of the stream of beauty entering in [B] through his eyes there comes a warmth, whereby his soul's plumage is fostered; and with that warmth the roots of the wings are melted, which for long had been so hardened and closed up that nothing could grow; then as the nourishment is poured in the stump of the wing swells and hastens to grow from the root over the whole substance of the soul: for aforetime the whole soul was furnished with wings. Meanwhile she throbs with ferment in every part, and even as a teething child [C] feels an aching and pain in its gums when a tooth has just come through, so does the soul of him who is beginning to grow his wings feel a ferment and painful irritation. Wherefore as she gazes upon the boy's beauty, she admits a flood of particles streaming therefrom—that is why we speak of a "flood of passion"[15]—whereby she is warmed and fostered; then has she respite from her anguish, and is filled with joy. But when she has been parted from him [D]

and become parched, the openings of those outlets at which the wings are sprouting dry up likewise and are closed, so that the wing's germ is barred off; and behind its bars, together with the flood aforesaid, it throbs like a fevered pulse, and pricks at its proper outlet; and thereat the whole soul round about is stung and goaded into anguish; howbeit she remembers the beauty of her beloved, and rejoices again. So between joy and anguish she is distraught at being in such strange case, perplexed and frenzied; with madness upon her she can neither sleep by night nor [E] keep still by day, but runs hither and thither, yearning for him in whom beauty dwells, if haply she may behold him. At last she does behold him, and lets the flood pour in upon her, releasing the imprisoned waters; then has she refreshment and respite from her stings and sufferings, and at that moment tastes a pleasure that is sweet beyond compare. Nor will she willingly give it up: above all others does [252] she esteem her beloved in his beauty: mother, brother, friends, she forgets them all: naught does she reck of losing worldly possessions through neglect: all the rules of conduct, all the graces of life, of which aforetime she was proud, she now disdains, welcoming a slave's estate and any couch where she may be suffered to lie down close beside her darling; for besides her reverence for the possessor of beauty she has found in him the only physician for her grievous suffering. [B]

Hearken, fair boy to whom I speak: this is the experience that men term love (ἔρως), but when you hear what the gods call it, you will probably smile at its strangeness. There are a couple of verses on love quoted by certain Homeric scholars from the unpublished works, the second of which is remarkably bold and a trifle astray in its quantities: they run as follows:

---

15 The suggestion is that ἵμερος is derived from ἱέναι + μέρη + ῥοή.

Eros, cleaver of air, in mortals' speech is
he named;
But, since he must grow wings, Pteros the
celestials call him.[16]

You may believe that or not, as [c]
you please; at all events the cause and
the nature of the lover's experience are
in fact what I have said.

XIV

## 252C-253C  The Various Types
of Lover

Now if he whom Love has caught be
amongst the followers of Zeus, he is
able to bear the burden of the winged
one with some constancy; but they that
attend upon Ares, and did range the
heavens in his train, when they are
caught by Love and fancy that their
beloved is doing them some injury, will
shed blood and not scruple to offer both
themselves and their loved ones in
sacrifice. And so does each lover live,
after the manner of the god in whose
company he once was, honouring [D]
him and copying him so far as may
be, so long as he remains uncorrupt and
is still living in his first earthly period;
and in like manner does he comport
himself towards his beloved and all his
other associates. And so each selects a
fair one for his love after his disposition,
and even as if the beloved himself were
a god he fashions for himself as it were
an image, and adorns it to be the object of his veneration and worship.

Thus the followers of Zeus seek [E]
a beloved who is Zeus-like in soul;
wherefore they look for one who is by
nature disposed to the love of wisdom

and the leading of men, and when
they have found him and come to love
him they do all in their power to foster
that disposition. And if they have not
aforetime trodden this path, they now
set out upon it, learning the way from
any source that may offer or finding it
for themselves; and as they follow up
the trace within themselves of the nature of their own god their task is [253]
made easier, inasmuch as they are
constrained to fix their gaze upon him,
and reaching out after him in memory
they are possesssed by him, and from
him they take their ways and manners
of life, in so far as a man can partake
of a god. But all this, mark you, they
attribute to the beloved, and the
draughts which they draw from Zeus
they pour out, like Bacchants, into the
soul of the beloved, thus creating in
him the closest possible likeness to the
god they worship.                    [B]

Those who were in the train of Hera
look for a royal nature, and when they
have found him they do unto him all
things in like fashion. And so it is with
the followers of Apollo and each other
god: every lover is fain that his beloved
should be of a nature like to his own
god; and when he has won him, he
leads him on to walk in the ways of
their god, and after his likeness, pattern-
ing himself thereupon and giving counsel and discipline to the boy. There is
no jealousy nor petty spitefulness in his
dealings, but his very act is aimed at
bringing the beloved to be every whit
like unto himself and unto the god [c]
of their worship.

So therefore glorious and blissful is
the endeavour of true lovers in that
mystery-rite, if they accomplish that
which they endeavour after the fashion
of which I speak, when mutual affection arises through the madness inspired
by love. But the beloved must needs be
captured: and the manner of that capture I will now tell.

---

16 For such double names cf. *Iliad* I, 404;
XIV, 291; XX, 74. The name given by the gods
is normally the more significant. It is uncertain whether the two lines are simply invented by Plato or modified from existing
lines fathered upon Homer, perhaps by some
Orphic writer.

xv

## 253C-256E   The Subjugation of Lust. Love and Counter-Love

In the beginning of our story we divided each soul into three parts, two being like steeds and the third like a charioteer. Well and good. Now of the steeds, so we declare, one is good and the other is not; but we have not [D] described the excellence of the one nor the badness of the other, and that is what must now be done. He that is on the more honourable side is upright and clean-limbed, carrying his neck high, with something of a hooked nose: in colour he is white, with black eyes: a lover of glory, but with temperance and modesty: one that consorts with genuine renown, and needs no whip, being driven by the word of command alone. The other is crooked of frame, a massive jumble of a creature, with [E] thick short neck, snub nose, black skin, and grey eyes; hot-blooded, consorting with wantonness and vainglory; shaggy of ear, deaf, and hard to control with whip and goad.

Now when the driver beholds the person of the beloved, and causes a sensation of warmth to suffuse the whole soul, he begins to experience a tickling or pricking of desire; and [254] the obedient steed, constrained now as always by modesty, refrains from leaping upon the beloved; but his fellow, heeding no more the driver's goad or whip, leaps and dashes on, sorely troubling his companion and his driver, and forcing them to approach the loved one and remind him of the delights of love's commerce. For a while they struggle, indignant that he should force [B] them to a monstrous and forbidden act; but at last, finding no end to their evil plight, they yield and agree to do his bidding. And so he draws them on, and now they are quite close and behold the spectacle of the beloved flashing upon them. At that sight the driver's memory goes back to that form of Beauty, and he sees her once again enthroned by the side of Temperance upon her holy seat; then in awe and reverence he falls upon his back, and therewith is compelled to pull the reins so violently that he brings both steeds down on their haunches, the good [C] one willing and unresistant, but the wanton sore against his will. Now that they are a little way off, the good horse in shame and horror drenches the whole soul with sweat, while the other, contriving to recover his wind after the pain of the bit and his fall, bursts into angry abuse, railing at the charioteer and his yoke-fellow as cowardly treacherous deserters. Once again he tries to force them to advance, and when [D] they beg him to delay awhile he grudgingly consents. But when the time appointed is come, and they feign to have forgotten, he reminds them of it, struggling and neighing and pulling until he compels them a second time to approach the beloved and renew their offer; and when they have come close, with head down and tail stretched out he takes the bit between his teeth and shamelessly plunges on. But the driver, with resentment even stronger than before, like a racer recoiling from the [E] starting-rope, jerks back the bit in the mouth of the wanton horse with an even stronger pull, bespatters his railing tongue and his jaws with blood, and forcing him down on legs and haunches delivers him over to anguish.

And so it happens time and again, until the evil steed casts off his wantonness; humbled in the end, he obeys the counsel of his driver, and when he sees the fair beloved is like to die of fear. Wherefore at long last the soul of the lover follows after the beloved with reverence and awe.

Thus the loved one receives all [255] manner of service, as peer of the gods, from a lover that is no pretender but loves in all sincerity; of his own nature, too, he is kindly disposed to him who pays such service. Now it may be that in time past he has been misled, by his schoolfellows or others, who told him that it is shameful to have commerce with a lover, and by reason of this he may repel his advances; nevertheless as time goes on ripening age and the ordinance of destiny together lead him to welcome the other's society; for assuredly fate does not suffer one evil [B] man to be friend to another, nor yet one good man to lack the friendship of another.

And now that he has come to welcome his lover and to take pleasure in his company and converse, it comes home to him what a depth of kindliness he has found, and he is filled with amazement, for he perceives that all his other friends and kinsmen have nothing to offer in comparison with this friend in whom there dwells a god. So as he continues in this converse and society, and comes close to his lover in the gymnasium and elsewhere, that flowing stream which Zeus, as the lover of [C] Ganymede, called the "flood of passion," pours in upon the lover; and part of it is absorbed within him, but when he can contain no more the rest flows away outside him; and as a breath of wind or an echo, rebounding from a smooth hard surface, goes back to its place of origin, even so the stream of beauty turns back and re-enters the eyes of the fair beloved; and so by the natural channel it reaches his soul and gives it fresh vigour, watering the roots of the wings and quickening them to growth: whereby the soul of the beloved, in [D] its turn, is filled with love. So he loves, yet knows not what he loves: he does not understand, he cannot tell what has come upon him; like one that has caught a disease of the eye from another, he cannot account for it, not realising that his lover is as it were a mirror in which he beholds himself. And when the other is beside him, he shares his respite from anguish; when he is absent, he likewise shares his

longing and being longed for; since he possesses that counter-love which is the image of love, though he supposes it to be friendship rather than love, [E] and calls it by that name. He feels a desire, like the lover's yet not so strong, to behold, to touch, to kiss him, to share his couch: and now ere long the desire, as one might guess, leads to the act.

So when they lie side by side, the wanton horse of the lover's soul would have a word with the charioteer, claiming a little guerdon for all his trouble. The like steed in the soul of the beloved has no word to say, but [256] swelling with desire for he knows not what embraces and kisses the lover, in grateful acknowledgment of all his kindness. And when they lie by one another, he is minded not to refuse to do his part in gratifying his lover's entreaties; yet his yoke-fellow in turn, being moved by reverence and heedfulness, joins with the driver in resisting. And so, if the victory be won by the higher elements of mind guiding them into the ordered rule of the philosophic life, their days on earth will be blessed with happiness and concord; for the power of evil in the soul has been [B] subjected, and the power of goodness liberated: they have won self-mastery and inward peace. And when life is over, with burden shed and wings recovered they stand victorious in the first of the three rounds in that truly Olympic struggle; nor can any nobler prize be secured whether by the wisdom that is of man or by the madness that is of god.

But if they turn to a way of life [C] more ignoble and unphilosophic, yet covetous of honour, then mayhap in a careless hour, or when the wine is flowing, the wanton horses in their two souls will catch them off their guard, bring the pair together, and choosing that part which the multitude account blissful achieve their full desire. And this once done, they continue therein, albeit but rarely, seeing that their minds are not wholly set thereupon. Such a pair as this also are dear friends, but not so dear as that other pair, one to another, both in the time of their love and when love is past; for they feel that they have exchanged the most [D] binding pledges, which it were a sin to break by becoming enemies. When death comes they quit the body wingless indeed, yet eager to be winged, and therefore they carry off no mean reward for their lovers' madness: for it is ordained that all such as have taken the first steps on the celestial highway shall no more return to the dark pathways beneath the earth, but shall walk together in a life of shining bliss, and be furnished in due time with like plumage the one to the other, be- [E] cause of their love.

### XVI

## 256E-257B  The Speech Concluded. A Prayer for Lysias and Phaedrus

These then, my boy, are the blessings great and glorious which will come to you from the friendship of a lover. He who is not a lover can offer a mere acquaintance flavoured with worldly wisdom, dispensing a niggardly measure of worldly goods; in the soul to which he is attached he will engender an ignoble quality extolled by the multitude as virtue, and condemn it to [257] float for nine thousand years hither and thither, around the earth and beneath it, bereft of understanding.

Thus then, dear God of Love, I have offered the fairest recantation and fullest atonement that my powers could compass; some of its language, in particular, was perforce poetical, to please Phaedrus. Grant me thy pardon for what went before, and thy favour for what ensued: be merciful and gracious, and take not from me the lover's talent wherewith thou hast blest, me neither let it wither by reason of thy displeasure, but grant me still to increase in the esteem of the fair. And if anything that Phaedrus and I said earlier [B] sounded discordant to thy ear, set it down to Lysias, the only begetter of that discourse; and staying him from discourses after this fashion turn him towards the love of wisdom, even as his brother Polemarchus has been turned. Then will his loving disciple here present no longer halt between two opinions, as now he does, but live for Love in singleness of purpose with the aid of philosophical discourse.

### XVII

## 257B-258E  Preliminary Consideration of Speech-Writing

PH. If that be for our good, Socrates, I join in your prayer for it. And I have this long while been filled with ad- [C] miration for your speech as a far finer achievement than the one you made before. It makes me afraid that I shall find Lysias cutting a poor figure, if he proves to be willing to compete with another speech of his own. The fact is that only the other day, my dear good sir, one of our politicians was railing at him and reproaching him on this very score, constantly dubbing him a "speech-writer"; so possibly we shall find him desisting from further composition to preserve his reputation.

SOCR. What a ridiculous line to take, young man! And how utterly you misjudge our friend, if you suppose him [D] to be such a timid creature! Am I to believe you really do think that the person you speak of meant his raillery as a reproach?

PH. He gave me that impression, Socrates; and of course you know as well as I do that the men of greatest influence and dignity in political life are reluctant to write speeches and bequeath to posterity compositions of their own, for fear of the verdict of later ages, which might pronounce them Sophists.[17]

socr. Phaedrus, you are unaware that the expression "Pleasant Bend" comes from the long bend in the Nile: and [E] besides the matter of the Bend you are unaware that the proudest of politicians have the strongest desire to write speeches and bequeath compositions; why, whenever they write a speech, they are so pleased to have admirers that they put in a special clause at the beginning with the names of the persons who admire the speech in question.

ph. What do you mean? I don't understand.

socr. You don't understand that [258] when a politician begins a composition the first thing he writes is the name of his admirer.

ph. Is it?

socr. Yes, he says maybe "Resolved by the Council" or "by the People" or by both: and then "Proposed by so-and-so"—a pompous piece of self-advertisement on the part of the author; after which he proceeds with what he has to say, showing off his own wisdom to his admirers, sometimes in a very lengthy composition. This sort of thing amounts, don't you think, to composing a speech?

ph. Yes, I think it does.          [B]

socr. Then if the speech holds its ground, the author quits the scene rejoicing; but if it is blotted out, and he loses his status as a recognised speech-writer, he goes into mourning, and his friends with him.

ph. Quite so.

socr. Which clearly implies that their attitude to the profession is not one of disdain, but of admiration.

ph. To be sure.

socr. Tell me then: when an orator, or a king, succeeds in acquiring the power of a Lycurgus, a Solon or a [C] Darius, and so winning immortality among his people as a speech-writer, doesn't he deem himself a peer of the gods while still living, and do not people of later ages hold the same opinion of him when they contemplate his writings?

ph. Yes, indeed.

socr. Then do you suppose that anyone of that type, whoever he might be, and whatever his animosity towards Lysias, could reproach him simply on the ground that he writes?

ph. What you say certainly makes that improbable; for apparently he would be reproaching what he wanted to do himself.

socr. Then the conclusion is ob- [D] vious, that there is nothing shameful in the mere writing of speeches.

ph. Of course.

socr. But in speaking and writing shamefully and badly, instead of as one should, that is where the shame comes in, I take it.

ph. Clearly.

socr. Then what is the nature of good writing and bad? Is it incumbent on us, Phaedrus, to examine Lysias on this point, and all such as have written or mean to write anything at all, whether in the field of public affairs or private, whether in the verse of the poet or the plain speech of prose?

ph. Is it incumbent! Why, life [E] itself would hardly be worth living save for pleasures like this: certainly not for those pleasures that involve previous pain, as do almost all concerned with the body, which for that reason are rightly called slavish.

XVIII

*258E-259D   Interlude.*
*The Myth of the Cicadas*

socr. Well, I suppose we can spare the time; and I think too that the cicadas overhead, singing after their wont in the hot sun and conversing with one an-

---

[17] The implication is that most prose works hitherto had come from the pens of Sophists; and a glance at the relevant *testimonia* in Diels-Kranz, Vors. II, makes this easy to believe.

other, don't fail to observe us as [259] well. So if they were to see us two behaving like ordinary folk at midday, not conversing but dozing lazy-minded under their spell, they would very properly have the laugh of us, taking us for a pair of slaves that had invaded their retreat like sheep, to have their midday sleep beside the spring. If however they see us conversing and steering clear of their bewitching siren-song, they might feel respect for us and grant us that [B] boon which heaven permits them to confer upon mortals.

PH. Oh, what is that? I don't think I have heard of it.

SOCR. Surely it is unbecoming in a devotee of the Muses not to have heard of a thing like that! The story is that once upon a time these creatures were men—men of an age before there were any Muses: and that when the latter came into the world, and music made its appearance, some of the people of those days were so thrilled with pleasure that they went on singing, and quite [C] forgot to eat and drink until they actually died without noticing it. From them in due course sprang the race of cicadas, to which the Muses have granted the boon of needing no sustenance right from their birth, but of singing from the very first, without food or drink, until the day of their death: after which they go and report to the Muses how they severally are paid honour amongst mankind, and by whom. So for those whom they report as having honoured Terpsichore in the dance they win that [D] Muse's favour; for those that have worshipped in the rites of love the favour of Erato; and so with all the others, according to the nature of the worship paid to each. To the eldest, Calliope, and to her next sister Urania, they tell of those who live a life of philosophy and so do honour to the music of those twain whose theme is the heavens and all the story of gods and men, and whose song is the noblest of them all.

Thus there is every reason for us not to yield to slumber in the noontide, but to pursue our talk.

PH. Of course we must pursue it.

XIX

## 259E-261A   Rhetoric and Knowledge

SOCR. Well, the subject we proposed for inquiry just now was the nature of good and bad speaking and writing: so we are to inquire into that.

PH. Plainly.

SOCR. Then does not a good and successful discourse presuppose a knowledge in the mind of the speaker of the truth about his subject?

PH. As to that, dear Socrates, what I have heard is that the intending orator is under no necessity of understand- [260] ing what is truly just, but only what is likely to be thought just by the body of men who are to give judgment; nor need he know what is truly good or noble, but what will be thought so; since it is on the latter, not the former, that persuasion depends.

SOCR. "Not to be lightly rejected,"[18] Phaedrus, is any word of the wise; perhaps they are right: one has to see. And in particular this present assertion must not be dismissed.

PH. I agree.

SOCR. Well, here is my suggestion for discussion.

PH. Yes?

SOCR. Suppose I tried to persuade [B] you to acquire a horse to use in battle against the enemy, and suppose that neither of us knew what a horse was, but I knew this much about you, that Phaedrus believes a horse to be that tame animal which possesses the largest ears.

PH. A ridiculous thing to suppose, Socrates.

SOCR. Wait a moment: suppose I con-

---

[18] A quotation from *Iliad* II, 361.

tinued to urge upon you in all seriousness, with a studied encomium of a donkey, that it was what I called it, a horse: that it was highly important for you to possess the creature, both at home and in the field: that it was just the animal to ride on into battle, and that it was [c] handy, into the bargain, for carrying your equipment and so forth.

PH. To go to that length would be utterly ridiculous.

SOCR. Well, isn't it better to be a ridiculous friend than a clever enemy?[19]

PH. I suppose it is.

SOCR. Then when a master of oratory, who is ignorant of good and evil, employs his power of persuasion on a community as ignorant as himself, not by extolling a miserable donkey as being really a horse, but by extolling evil as being really good: and when by studying the beliefs of the masses he persuades them to do evil instead of good, what kind of crop do you think his oratory [D] is likely to reap from the seed thus sown?

PH. A pretty poor one.

SOCR. Well now, my good friend, have we been too scurrilous in our abuse of the art of speech? Might it not retort: "Why do you extraordinary people talk such nonsense? I never insist on ignorance of the truth on the part of one who would learn to speak; on the contrary, if my advice goes for anything, it is that he should only resort to me after he has come into possession of truth; what I do however pride myself on is that without my aid knowledge of what is true will get a man no nearer to mastering the art of persuasion."

PH. And will not such a retort be [E] just?

SOCR. Yes, if the arguments advanced against oratory sustain its claim to be an art. In point of fact, I fancy I can hear certain arguments advancing, and protesting that the claim is false, that it is no art, but a knack that has nothing to do with art: inasmuch as there is, as the Spartans put it, no "soothfast" art of speech, nor assuredly will there ever be one, without a grasp of truth.[20]

PH. We must have these argu- [261] ments, Socrates. Come, bring them up before us, and examine their purport.

SOCR. Come hither then, you worthy creatures, and impress upon Phaedrus, who is so blessed in his offspring,[21] that unless he gets on with his philosophy he will never get on as a speaker on any subject; and let Phaedrus be your respondent.

PH. I await their questions.

### XX

### 261A-264E    Knowledge of Resemblances and Differences

SOCR. Must not the art of rhetoric, taken as a whole, be a kind of influencing of the mind by means of words, not only in courts of law and other public gatherings, but in private places also? And must it not be the same art that is concerned with great issues and small, its right employment commanding no [B] more respect when dealing with important matters than with unimportant? Is that what you have been told about it?

PH. No indeed, not exactly that: it is principally, I should say, to lawsuits that an art of speaking and writing is applied —and of course to public harangues also. I know of no wider application.

---

[19] The meaning is that the obviously ridiculous mistakes of a well-intentioned speaker are likely to do less harm that the mistakes of an ill-intentioned one who is clever enough to disguise his ignorance and so escape ridicule.

[20] The point urged here is that knowledge of truth must be part and parcel of the art of rhetoric, if it is really to be an art: knowledge cannot be something preliminary or extraneous which the orator can presume in his audience to start with, as had just been suggested by the apologist of rhetoric.

[21] The allusion is to Phaedrus as begetter of discourses: cf. 242A-B.

soCR. What? Are you acquainted only with the "Arts" or manuals of oratory by Nestor and Odysseus, which they composed in their leisure hours at Troy? Have you never heard of the work of Palamedes?

PH. No, upon my word, nor of [c] Nestor either; unless you are casting Gorgias for the role of Nestor, with Odysseus played by Thrasymachus, or maybe Theodorus.

soCR. Perhaps I am. But anyway we may let them be, and do you tell me, what is it that the contending parties in lawcourts do? Do they not in fact contend with words, or how else should we put it?

PH. That is just what they do.

soCR. About what is just and unjust?

PH. Yes.

soCR. And he who possesses the art of doing this can make the same thing appear to the same people now just, now unjust, at will?                              [D]

PH. To be sure.

soCR. And in public harangues, no doubt, he can make the same things seem to the community now good, and now the reverse of good?

PH. Just so.

soCR. Then can we fail to see that the Palamedes of Elea[22] has an art of speaking, such that he can make the same things appear to his audience like and unlike, or one and many, or again at rest and in motion?

PH. Indeed he can.

soCR. So contending with words is a practice found not only in lawsuits and public harangues but, it seems, [E] wherever men speak we find this single art, if indeed it is an art, which enables people to make out everything to be like

everything else, within the limits of possible comparison, and to expose the corresponding attempts of others who disguise what they are doing.

PH. How so, pray?

soCR. I think that will become clear if we put the following question. Are we misled when the difference between two things is wide, or narrow?

PH. When it is narrow.                         [262]

soCR. Well then, if you shift your ground little by little, you are more likely to pass undetected from so-and-so to its opposite than if you do so at one bound.

PH. Of course.

soCR. It follows that anyone who intends to mislead another, without being misled himself, must discern precisely the degree of resemblance and dissimilarity between this and that.

PH. Yes, that is essential.

soCR. Then if he does not know the truth about a given thing, how is he going to discern the degree of resemblance between that unknown thing and other things?

PH. It will be impossible.                       [B]

soCR. Well now, when people hold beliefs contrary to fact, and are misled, it is plain that the error has crept into their minds through the suggestion of some similarity or other.

PH. That certainly does happen.

soCR. But can anyone possibly master the art of using similarities for the purpose of bringing people round, and leading them away from the truth about this or that to the opposite of the truth, or again can anyone possibly avoid this happening to himself, unless he has knowledge of what the thing in question really is?

PH. No, never.

soCR. It would seem to follow, my [c] friend, that the art of speech displayed by one who has gone chasing after beliefs, instead of knowing the truth, will be a comical sort of art, in fact no art at all.

PH. I dare say.

---

22 I.e., Zeno, whose method of argument was to show that an opponent's thesis led to two contradictory consequences. For the contradictory pairs here mentioned cf. *Parm.* 127E 6, 129B 5 and 129E 1; and see F. M. Cornford, *Plato and Parmenides*, pp. 57-9.

SOCR. Then would you like to observe some instances of what I call the presence and absence of art in that speech of Lysias which you are carrying, and in those which I have delivered?

PH. Yes, by all means: at present our discussion is somewhat abstract, for want of adequate illustrations.

SOCR. Why, as to that it seems a stroke of luck that in the two speeches we have a sort of illustration of the way in [D] which one who knows the truth can mislead his audience by playing an oratorical joke on them. I myself, Phaedrus, put that down to the local deities, or perhaps those mouthpieces of the Muses that are chirping over our heads have vouchsafed us their inspiration; for of course I don't lay claim to any oratorical skill myself.

PH. I dare say that is so: but please explain your point.

SOCR. Well, come along: read the beginning of Lysias's speech.

PH. "You know how I am situated, [E] and I have told you that I think it to our advantage that the thing should be done. Now I claim that I should not be refused what I ask simply because I am not your lover. Lovers repent when—"

SOCR. Stop. Our business is to indicate where the speaker is at fault, and shows absence of art, isn't it?

PH. Yes. [263]

SOCR. Well now, is not the following assertion obviously true, that there are some words about which we all agree, and others about which we are at variance?

PH. I think I grasp your meaning, but you might make it still plainer.

SOCR. When someone utters the word "iron" or "silver," we all have the same object before our minds, haven't we?

PH. Certainly.

SOCR. But what about the words "just" and "good"? Don't we diverge, and dispute not only with one another but with our own selves?

PH. Yes indeed.

SOCR. So in some cases we agree, and in others we don't. [B]

PH. Quite so.

SOCR. Now in which of the cases are we more apt to be misled, and in which is rhetoric more effective?

PH. Plainly in the case where we fluctuate.

SOCR. Then the intending student of the art of rhetoric ought, in the first place, to make a systematic division of words, and get hold of some mark distinguishing the two kinds of words, those namely in the use of which the multitude are bound to fluctuate, and those in which they are not.

PH. To grasp that, Socrates, would [C] certainly be an excellent piece of discernment.

SOCR. And secondly, I take it, when he comes across a particular word he must realise what it is, and be swift to perceive which of the two kinds the thing he proposes to discuss really belongs to.

PH. To be sure.

SOCR. Well then, shall we reckon love as one of the disputed terms, or as one of the other sort?

PH. As a disputed term, surely. Otherwise can you suppose it would have been possible for you to say of it what you said just now, namely that it is harmful both to the beloved and the lover, and then to turn round and say that it is really the greatest of goods?

SOCR. And excellent point. But now [D] tell me this, for thanks to my inspired condition I can't quite remember: did I define love at the beginning of my speech?

PH. Yes indeed, and immensely thorough you were about it.

SOCR. Upon my word, you rate the Nymphs of Achelous and Pan, son of Hermes, much higher as artists in oratory than Lysias, son of Cephalus. Or am I quite wrong? Did Lysias at the beginning of his discourse on love compel us to conceive of it as a certain definite entity, with a meaning he had himself decided upon? And did he proceed to [E] bring all his subsequent remarks, from first to last, into line with that meaning? Shall we read his first words once again?

PH. If you like; but what you are looking for isn't there.

SOCR. Read it out, so that I can listen to the author himself.

PH. "You know how I am situated, and I have told you that I think it to our advantage that the thing should be done. Now I claim that I should not be refused what I ask simply because I [264] am not your lover. Lovers, when their craving is at an end, repent of such benefits as they have conferred."

SOCR. No: he doesn't seem to get anywhere near what we are looking for: he goes about it like a man swimming on his back, in reverse, and starts from the end instead of the beginning; his opening words are what the lover would naturally say to his boy only when he had finished. Or am I quite wrong, dear Phaedrus?

PH. I grant you, Socrates, that the [B] substance of his address is really a peroration.

SOCR. And to pass to other points: doesn't his matter strike you as thrown out at haphazard? Do you find any cogent reason for his next remark, or indeed any of his remarks, occupying the place it does? I myself, in my ignorance, thought that the writer, with a fine abandon, put down just what came into his head. Can you find any cogent principle of composition which he observed in setting down his observations in this particular order?

PH. You flatter me in supposing that I am competent to see into his mind with all that accuracy.                           [C]

SOCR. Well, there is one point at least which I think you will admit, namely that any discourse ought to be constructed like a living creature, with its own body, as it were; it must not lack either head or feet; it must have a middle and extremities so composed as

to suit each other and the whole work.

PH. Of course.

SOCR. Then ask yourself whether that is or is not the case with your friend's speech. You will find that it is just like the epitaph said to have been carved on the tomb of Midas the Phrygian.

PH. What is that, and what's wrong with it?                                        [D]

SOCR. It runs like this:

A maid of bronze I stand on Midas' tomb,
So long as waters flow and trees grow tall,
Abiding here on his lamented grave,
I tell the traveller Midas here is laid.

I expect you notice that it makes no [E] difference what order the lines come in.

PH. Socrates, you are making a joke of our speech!

### XXI

### 264E-266B   Dialectic Method
### as Exhibited in Preceding Speeches

SOCR. Well, to avoid distressing you, let us say no more of that—though indeed I think it provides many examples which it would be profitable to notice, provided one were chary of imitating them—and let us pass to the other speeches; for they, I think, presented a certain feature which everyone desirous of examining oratory would do well to observe.

PH. To what do you refer?       [265]

SOCR. They were of opposite purport, one maintaining that the lover should be favoured, the other the non-lover.

PH. Yes, they did so very manfully.

SOCR. I thought you were going to say —and with truth—madly; but that reminds me of what I was about to ask. We said, did we not, that love is a sort of madness?

PH. Yes.

SOCR. And that there are two kinds of madness, one resulting from human ailments, the other from a divine disturbance of our conventions of conduct.

PH. Quite so.                              [B]

SOCR. And in the divine kind we distinguished four types, ascribing them to four gods: the inspiration of the prophet to Apollo, that of the mystic to Dionysus, that of the poet to the Muses, and a fourth type which we declared to be the highest, the madness of the lover, to Aphrodite and Eros; moreover we painted, after a fashion, a picture of the lover's experience, in which perhaps we attained some degree of truth, though we may well have sometimes gone astray; the blend resulting in a discourse which had some claim to plausibility, or shall we say a mythical hymn of praise, in [c] due religious language, a festal celebration of my master and yours too, Phaedrus, that god of love who watches over the young and fair.

PH. It certainly gave me great pleasure to listen to it.

SOCR. Then let us take one feature of it, the way in which the discourse contrived to pass from censure to encomium.

PH. Well now, what do you make of that?

SOCR. For the most part I think our festal hymn has really been just a festive entertainment; but we did casually allude to a certain pair of procedures, and it would be very agreeable if we [D] could seize their significance in a scientific fashion.

PH. What procedures do you mean?

SOCR. The first is that in which we bring a dispersed plurality under a single form, seeing it all together: the purpose being to define so-and-so, and thus to make plain whatever may be chosen as the topic for exposition. For example, take the definition given just now of love: whether it was right or wrong, at all events it was that which enabled our discourse to achieve lucidity and consistency.

PH. And what is the second procedure you speak of, Socrates?

SOCR. The reverse of the other, [E] whereby we are enabled to divide into forms, following the objective articulation; we are not to attempt to hack off

parts like a clumsy butcher, but to take example from our two recent speeches. The single general form which they postulated was irrationality; next, on the analogy of a single natural body [266] with its pairs of like-named members, right arm or leg, as we say, and left, they conceived of madness as a single objective form existing in human beings: wherefore the first speech divided off a part on the left, and continued to make divisions, never desisting until it discovered one particular part bearing the name of "sinister" love, on which it very properly poured abuse. The other speech conducted us to the forms of madness which lay on the right-hand side, and upon discovering a type of love that shared its name with the other but was divine, displayed it to our view and extolled it as the source of the greatest [B] goods that can befall us.[23]

---

23 There are serious difficulties in this paragraph. Socrates speaks as though the generic concept of madness (τὸ ἄφρον, παράγνοια, μανία) had been common to his two speeches, and there had been a formal divisional procedure followed in both of them. Neither of these things is true. . . .

It must therefore be admitted that Socrates's account of the dialectical procedure followed in his speeches is far from exact. Nevertheless it may be said to be substantially true: for it is true to the spirit and implication of what has happened: it describes how the two speeches might naturally be schematised when taken together as part of a design which has gradually unfolded itself. A writer with more concern for exact statement than Plato had, would have made Socrates say something to the following effect: "I can illustrate these two procedures, Collection and Division, by reference to my two speeches; if you think of them together, you will agree that I was in fact, though not explicitly, operating with a generic concept, μανία, under which I contrived to subsume two sorts of ἔρως: though I grant you that my actual procedure was very informal, and in particular that I tended to leap from genus to *infima species*, without any clear indication of intermediate species."

It should further be remembered that the word μανία did occur in Socrates's first speech, although more or less casually. . . .

PH. That is perfectly true.

SOCR. Believe me, Phaedrus, I am myself a lover of these divisions and collections, that I may gain the power to speak and to think; and whenever I deem another man able to discern an objective unity and plurality, I follow "in his footsteps where he leadeth as a god." Furthermore—whether I am right or wrong in doing so, God alone knows —it is those that have this ability whom for the present I call dialecticians.

## XXII

### 266C-269C   The Technique of Existing Rhetoric

SOCR. But now tell me what we ought to call them if we take instruction from Lysias and yourself. Or is what I have been describing precisely that art of oratory thanks to which Thrasymachus and the rest of them have not only made themselves masterly orators, but can do the same for anyone else who cares to bring offerings to these princes amongst men?

PH. Doubtless they behave like princes, but assuredly they do not possess the kind of knowledge to which you refer. No, I think you are right in calling the procedure that you have described dialectical; but we still seem to be in the dark about rhetoric.

SOCR. What? Can there really be [D] anything of value that admits of scientific acquisition despite the lack of that procedure? If so, you and I should certainly not disdain it, but should explain what this residuum of rhetoric actually consists in.

PH. Well, Socrates, of course there is plenty of matter in the rhetorical manuals.

SOCR. Thank you for the reminder. The first point, I suppose, is that a speech must begin with a Preamble. You are referring, are you not, to such niceties of the art?

PH. Yes.                                    [E]

SOCR. And next comes Exposition accompanied by Direct Evidence; thirdly Indirect Evidence, fourthly Probabilities; besides which there are the Proof and Supplementary Proof mentioned by the Byzantine master of rhetorical artifice.

PH. You mean the worthy Theodorus?

SOCR. Of course; and we are to [267] have a Refutation and Supplementary Refutation both for prosecution and defence. And can we leave the admirable Evenus of Paros out of the picture, the inventor of Covert Allusion and Indirect Compliment and (according to some accounts) of the Indirect Censure in mnemonic verse? A real master, that. But we won't disturb the rest of Tisias and Gorgias, who realised that probability deserves more respect than truth, who could make trifles seem important and important points trifles by the force of their language, who dressed up novel- [B] ties as antiques and vice versa, and found out how to argue concisely or at interminable length about anything and everything. This last accomplishment provoked Prodicus once to mirth when he heard me mention it: he remarked that he and he alone had discovered what sort of speeches the art demands: to wit, neither long ones nor short, but of fitting length.

PH. Masterly, Prodicus!

SOCR. Are we forgetting Hippias? I think Prodicus's view would be supported by the man of Elis.

PH. No doubt.

SOCR. And then Polus: what are we to say of his *Muses' Treasury of Phrases* with its Reduplications and Maxims [C] and Similes, and of words *à la* Licymnius which that master made him a present of as a contribution to his fine writing?

PH. But didn't Protagoras in point of fact produce some such works, Socrates?

SOCR. Yes, my young friend: there is his *Correct Diction*, and many other excellent works. But to pass now to the application of pathetic language to the poor and aged, the master in that style seems to me to be the mighty man of

Chalcedon, who was also expert at rousing a crowd to anger and then soothing them down again with his [D] spells, to quote his own saying; while at casting aspersions and dissipating them, whatever their source, he was unbeatable.

But to resume: on the way to conclude a speech there seems to be general agreement, though some call it Recapitulation and others by some other name.

PH. You mean the practice of reminding the audience towards the end of a speech of its main points?

SOCR. Yes. And now if you have anything further to add about the art of rhetoric—

PH. Only a few unimportant points.

SOCR. If they are unimportant, [268] we may pass them over. But let us look at what we have got in a clearer light, to see what power the art possesses, and when.

PH. A very substantial power, Socrates, at all events in large assemblies.

SOCR. Yes indeed. But have a look at it, my good sir, and see whether you discern some holes in the fabrics, as I do.

PH. Do show them me.

SOCR. Well, look here: Suppose someone went up to your friend Eryximachus, or his father Acumenus, and said "I know how to apply such treatment to a patient's body as will induce warmth or coolness, as I choose: I can make [B] him vomit, if I see fit, or go to stool, and so on and so forth. And on the strength of this knowledge I claim to be a competent physician, and to make a competent physician of anyone to whom I communicate this knowledge." What do you imagine they would have to say to that?

PH. They would ask him, of course, whether he also knew which patients ought to be given the various treatments, and when, and for how long.

SOCR. Then what if he said "Oh, no: but I expect my pupils to manage

what you refer to by themselves?" [C]

PH. I expect they would say "The man is mad: he thinks he has made himself a doctor by picking up something out of a book, or coming across some common drug or other, without any real knowledge of medicine."

SOCR. Now suppose someone went up to Sophocles or Euripides and said he knew how to compose lengthy dramatic speeches about a trifling matter, and quite short ones about a matter of moment; that he could write pathetic passages when he chose, or again passages of intimidation and menace, and so forth; and that he considered that by [D] teaching these accomplishments he could turn a pupil into a tragic poet.

PH. I imagine that they too would laugh at anyone who supposed that you could make a tragedy otherwise than by so arranging such passages as to exhibit a proper relation to one another and to the whole of which they are parts.

SOCR. Still I don't think they would abuse him rudely, but rather treat him as a musician would treat a man who fancied himself to be a master of harmony simply because he knew how to produce the highest possible note and the lowest possible on his strings. The musician would not be so rude as to say "You miserable fellow, you're off your [E] head": but rather, in the gentler language befitting his profession "My good sir, it is true that one who proposes to become a master of harmony must know the things you speak of: but it is perfectly possible for one who has got at far as yourself to have not the slightest real knowledge of harmony. You are acquainted with what has to be learnt before studying harmony: but of harmony itself you know nothing."

PH. Perfectly true.

SOCR. Similarly then Sophocles [269] would tell the man who sought to show off to himself and Euripides that what he knew was not tragic composition but its antecedents; and Acumenus would make the same distinction between medicine and the antecedents of medicine.

PH. I entirely agree.

SOCR. And if "mellifluous" Adrastus, or shall we say Pericles, were to hear of those admirable artifices that we were referring to just now—the Brachylogies and Imageries and all the rest of them, which we enumerated and deemed it necessary to examine in a clear light— are we to suppose that they would address those who practise and teach this sort of thing, under the name of the art of rhetoric, with the severity you and I displayed, and in rude, coarse [B] language? Or would they, in their ampler wisdom, actually reproach us and say "Phaedrus and Socrates, you ought not to get angry, but to make allowances for such people; it is because they are ignorant of dialectic that they are incapable of properly defining rhetoric, and that in turn leads them to imagine that by possessing themselves of the requisite antecedent learning they have discovered the art itself. And so they [C] teach these antecedents to their pupils, and believe that that constitutes a complete instruction in rhetoric; they don't bother about employing the various artifices in such a way that they will be effective, or about organising a work as a whole: that is for the pupils to see to for themselves when they come to make speeches."

## XXIII

### 269C-272B  Philosophy
### and Rhetoric. Pericles's Debt
### to Anaxagoras

PH. Well yes, Socrates: I dare say that does more or less describe what the teachers and writers in question regard as the art of rhetoric; personally I think what you say is true. But now by what means and from what source can one attain the art of the true rhetorician, [D] the real master of persuasion?

SOCR. If you mean how can one become a finished performer, then prob- ably—indeed I might say undoubtedly— it is the same as with anything else: if you have an innate capacity for rhetoric, you will become a famous rhetorician, provided you also acquire knowledge and practice; but if you lack any of these three you will be correspondingly unfinished. As regards the art itself (as distinct from the artist) I fancy that the line of approach adopted by Lysias and Thrasymachus is not the one I have in view.

PH. Then what is?

SOCR. I am inclined to think, my [E] good friend, that it was not surprising that Pericles became the most finished exponent of rhetoric there has ever been.

PH. Why so?

SOCR. All the great arts need supplementing by a study of Nature: your artist must cultivate garrulity and high- [270] flown speculation; from that source alone can come the mental elevation and thoroughly finished execution of which you are thinking; and that is what Pericles acquired to supplement his inborn capacity. He came across the right sort of man, I fancy, in Anaxagoras, and by enriching himself with high speculation and coming to recognise the nature of wisdom and folly—on which topics of course Anaxagoras was always discoursing—he drew from that source and applied to the art of rhetoric what was suitable thereto.

PH. How do you mean?

SOCR. Rhetoric is in the same case [B] as medicine, don't you think?

PH. How so?

SOCR. In both cases there is a nature that we have to determine, the nature of body in the one, and of soul in the other, if we mean to be scientific and not content with mere empirical routine when we apply medicine and diet to induce health and strength, or words and rules of conduct to implant such convictions and virtues as we desire.

PH. You are probably right, Socrates.

SOCR. Then do you think it possible [C] to understand the nature of the soul satisfactorily without taking it as a whole?

PH. If we are to believe Hippocrates the Asclepiad, we can't understand even the body without such a procedure.

SOCR. No, my friend, and he is right. But we must not just rely on Hippocrates: we must examine the assertion and see whether it accords with the truth.

PH. Yes.

SOCR. Then what is it that Hippocrates and the truth have to say on this matter of nature? I suggest that the way to [D] reflect about the nature of anything is as follows: first, to decide whether the object in respect of which we desire to have scientific knowledge, and to be able to impart it to others, is simple or complex; secondly, if it is simple, to inquire what natural capacity it has of acting upon another thing, and through what means; or by what other thing, and through what means, it can be acted upon; or, if it is complex, to enumerate its parts and observe in respect of each what we observe in the case of the simple object, to wit what its natural capacity, active or passive, consists in.

PH. Perhaps so, Socrates.

SOCR. Well, at all events, to pursue an inquiry without doing so would be like a blind man's progress. Surely we [E] mustn't make out that any sort of scientific inquirer resembles a blind or deaf person. No, it is plain that if we are to address people scientifically, we shall show them precisely what is the real and true nature of that object on which our discourse is brought to bear. And that object, I take it, is the soul.

PH. To be sure.

SOCR. Hence the speaker's whole [271] effort is concentrated on that, for it is there that he is attempting to implant conviction. Isn't that so?

PH. Yes.

SOCR. Then it is plain that Thrasymachus, or anyone else who seriously proffers a scientific rhetoric, will, in the first place, describe the soul very precisely, and let us see whether it is single and uniform in nature or, analogously to the body, complex; for to do that is, we maintain, to show a thing's nature.

PH. Yes, undoubtedly.

SOCR. And secondly he will describe what natural capacity it has to act upon what, and through what means, or by what it can be acted upon.

PH. Quite so.

SOCR. Thirdly, he will classify the [B] types of discourse and the types of soul, and the various ways in which souls are affected, explaining the reasons in each case, suggesting the type of speech appropriate to each type of soul, and showing what kind of speech can be relied on to create belief in one soul and disbelief in another, and why.

PH. I certainly think that would be an excellent procedure.

SOCR. Yes: in fact I can assure you, my friend, that no other scientific method of treating either our present [C] subject or any other will ever be found, whether in the models of the schools or in speeches actually delivered. But the present-day authors of manuals of rhetoric, of whom you have heard, are cunning folk who know all about the soul but keep their knowledge out of sight. So don't let us admit their claim to write scientifically until they compose their speeches and writings in the way we have indicated.

PH. And what way is that?

SOCR. To give the actual words would be troublesome; but I am quite ready to say how one ought to compose if he means to be as scientific as possible.

PH. Then please do.

SOCR. Since the function of oratory is in fact to influence men's souls, the intending orator must know what types [D] of soul there are. Now these are of a determinate number, and their variety results in a variety of individuals. To the types of soul thus discriminated there corresponds a determinate number of types of discourse. Hence a certain type of hearer will be easy to persuade by a certain type of speech to take such-and-such action for such-and-such reason, while another type will be hard to persuade. All this the orator must fully understand; and next he must watch it actually occurring, exemplified in men's conduct, and must cultivate a keenness of perception in following it, if he is [E] going to get any advantage out of the previous instruction that he was given in the school. And when he is competent to say what type of man is susceptible to what kind of discourse; when, further, he can, on catching sight of so-and-so, tell himself "That is the man, that [272] character now actually before me is the one I heard about in school, and in order to persuade him of so-and-so I have to apply *these* arguments in *this* fashion"; and when, on top of all this, he has further grasped the right occasions for speaking and for keeping quiet, and has come to recognise the right and the wrong time for the Brachylogy, the Pathetic Passage, the Exacerbation and all the rest of his accomplishments, then and not till then has he well and truly achieved the art. But if in his speaking or teaching or writing he fails in any of these requirements, he may tell you that he has the art of speech, but one [B] mustn't believe all one is told.

And now maybe our author will say "Well, what of it, Phaedrus and Socrates? Do you agree with me, or should we accept some other account of the art of speech?"

PH. Surely we can't accept any other, Socrates; still it does seem a considerable business.

### XXIV

### 272B-274B  The True Method
### of Rhetoric. Its Difficulty
### and Its Justification

SOCR. You are right, and that makes it necessary thoroughly to overhaul all our arguments, and see whether there is some easier and shorter way of arriving at the art; we don't want to waste effort in [C] going off on a long rough road, when we might take a short smooth one. But if you can help us at all through what you have heard from Lysias or anyone else, do try to recall it.

PH. As far as trying goes, I might; but I can suggest nothing on the spur of the moment.

SOCR. Then would you like me to tell you something I have heard from those concerned with these matters?

PH. Why, yes.

SOCR. Anyhow, Phaedrus, we are told that even the devil's advocate ought to be heard.

PH. Then you can put his case.    [D]

SOCR. Well, they tell us that there is no need to make such a solemn business of it, or fetch such a long compass on an uphill road. As we remarked at the beginning of this discussion, there is, they maintain, absolutely no need for the budding orator to concern himself with the truth about what is just or good conduct, nor indeed about who are just and good men whether by nature or education. In the lawcourts nobody cares a rap for the truth about these matters, but only about what is plausible. And that is the same as what is prob- [E] able, and is what must occupy the attention of the would-be master of the art of speech. Even actual facts ought sometimes not to be stated, if they don't tally with probability; they should be replaced by what is probable, whether in prosecution or defence; whatever you say, you simply must pursue this probability they talk of, and can say good-bye to the truth for ever. Stick to that all through [273] your speech, and you are equipped with the art complete.

PH. Your account, Socrates, precisely reproduces what is said by those who claim to be experts in the art of speech. I remember that we did touch briefly on this sort of contention a while ago; and the professionals regard it as a highly important point.

SOCR. Very well then, take Tisias himself; you have thumbed him carefully, so let Tisias tell us this: does he maintain that the probable is anything other than that which commends itself to the multitude? [B]

PH. How could it be anything else?

SOCR. Then in consequence, it would seem, of that profound scientific discovery he laid down that if a weak but brave man is arrested for assaulting a strong but cowardly one, whom he has robbed of his cloak or some other garment, neither of them ought to state the true facts; the coward should say that the brave man didn't assault him single-handed, and the brave man should contend that there were only the two of them, and then have recourse to the famous plea "How could a little fellow like me have attacked a big fellow [C] like him?" Upon which the big fellow will not avow his own poltroonery but will try to invent some fresh lie which will probably supply his opponent with a means of refuting him. And similar "scientific" rules are given for other cases of the kind. Isn't that so, Phaedrus?

PH. To be sure.

SOCR. Bless my soul! It appears that he made a brilliant discovery of a buried art, your Tisias, or whoever it really was and whatever he is pleased to be called after. But, my friend, shall we or shall we not say to him—

PH. Say what? [D]

SOCR. This: "In point of fact, Tisias, we have for some time before you came on the scene been saying that the multitude get their notion of probability as the result of a likeness to truth; and we explained just now that these likenesses can always be best discovered by one who knows the truth. Therefore if you have anything else to say about the art of speech, we should be glad to hear it; but if not we shall adhere to the point we made just now, namely that unless the aspirant to oratory can on the one hand list the various natures amongst his prospective audiences, and on the other

divide things into their kinds and em- [E] brace each individual thing under a single form, he will never attain such success as is within the grasp of mankind. Yet he will assuredly never acquire such competence without considerable diligence, which the wise man should exert not for the sake of speaking to and dealing with his fellow-men, but that he may be able to speak what is pleasing to the gods, and in all his dealings to do their pleasure to the best of his ability. For you see, Tisias, what we are told by those wiser than ourselves is true, that a man of sense ought never to study [274] the gratification of his fellow-slaves, save as a minor consideration, but that of his most excellent masters. So don't be surprised that we have to make a long detour: it is because the goal is glorious, though not the goal you think of." Not but what those lesser objects also, if you would have them, can best be attained (so our argument assures us) as a consequence of the greater.

PH. Your project seems to be excellent, Socrates, if only one could carry it out.

SOCR. Well, when a man sets his hand to something good, it is good that he should take what comes to him. [B]

PH. Yes, of course.

SOCR. Then we may feel that we have said enough about the art of speech, both the true art and the false?

PH. Certainly.

XXV

*274B-278B The Superiority of the Spoken Word. Myth of the Invention of Writing*

SOCR. But there remains the question of propriety and impropriety in writing, that is to say the conditions which make it proper or improper. Isn't that so?

PH. Yes.

SOCR. Now do you know how we may best please God, in practice and in theory, in this matter of words?

PH. No indeed. Do you?

SOCR. I can tell you the tradition [c] that has come down from our forefathers, but they alone know the truth of it. However, if we could discover that for ourselves, should we still be concerned with the fancies of mankind?

PH. What a ridiculous question! But tell me the tradition you speak of.

SOCR. Very well. The story is that in the region of Naucratis in Egypt there dwelt one of the old gods of the country, the god to whom the bird called Ibis is sacred, his own name being Theuth. He it was that invented number and calculation, geometry and astronomy, not to [D] speak of draughts and dice, and above all writing. Now the king of the whole country at that time was Thamus, who dwelt in the great city of Upper Egypt which the Greeks call Egyptian Thebes, while Thamus they call Ammon. To him came Theuth, and revealed his arts, saying that they ought to be passed on to the Egyptians in general. Thamus asked what was the use of them all: and when Theuth explained, he condemned what he thought the bad points and praised [E] what he thought the good. On each art, we are told, Thamus had plenty of views both for and against; it would take too long to give them in detail, but when it came to writing Theuth said "Here, O king, is a branch of learning that will make the people of Egypt wiser and improve their memories: my discovery provides a recipe for memory and wisdom." But the king answered and said "O man full of arts, to one is it given to create the things of art, and to another to judge what measure of harm and of profit they have for those that shall employ them. And so it is that you, by reason of your tender regard for the writing that [275] is your offspring, have declared the very opposite of its true effect. If men learn this, it will implant forgetfulness in their souls: they will cease to exercise memory because they rely on that which is written, calling things to remembrance no

longer from within themselves, but by means of external marks; what you have discovered is a recipe not for memory, but for reminder. And it is no true wisdom that you offer your disciples, but only its semblance; for by telling them of many things without teaching them you will make them seem to know much, while for the most part they know [B] nothing; and as men filled, not with wisdom, but with the conceit of wisdom, they will be a burden to their fellows."

PH. It is easy for you, Socrates, to make up tales from Egypt or anywhere else you fancy.[24]

SOCR. Oh, but the authorities of the temple of Zeus at Dodona, my friend, said that the first prophetic utterances came from an oak-tree. In fact the people of those days, lacking the wisdom of you young people, were content in their simplicity to listen to trees or rocks, provided these told the truth. For you [c] apparently it makes a difference who the speaker is, and what country he comes from: you don't merely ask whether what he says is true or false.

PH. I deserve your rebuke, and I agree that the man of Thebes is right in what he said about writing.

SOCR. Then anyone who leaves behind him a written manual, and likewise anyone who takes it over from him, on the supposition that such writing will provide something reliable and permanent, must be exceedingly simple-minded; he must really be ignorant of Ammon's utterance, if he imagines that written

---

24 The little myth of Theuth and Thamus is, like that of the cicadas, apparently Plato's own invention, though of course the personages belong to Egyptian history or legend. The inventor of writing in Greek legend was Prometheus; but he was unsuitable for Plato's purpose, since it would have been difficult to make anyone play against him the part that Thamus plays against Theuth. And in any case it was natural enough for Plato to go to Egypt for a tale of pre-history, just as in a later dialogue he goes to an Egyptian priest for his story of Atlantis.

words can do anything more than remind one who knows that which the writing is concerned with.                [D]

PH. Very true.

SOCR. You know, Phaedrus, that's the strange thing about writing, which makes it truly analogous to painting. The painter's products stand before us as though they were alive: but if you question them, they maintain a most majestic silence. It is the same with written words: they seem to talk to you as though they were intelligent, but if you ask them anything about what they say, from a desire to be instructed, they go on telling you just the same thing for ever. And once a thing is put in writing, the composition, whatever it may be, [E] drifts all over the place, getting into the hands not only of those who understand it, but equally of those who have no business with it; it doesn't know how to address the right people, and not address the wrong. And when it is ill-treated and unfairly abused it always needs its parent to come to its help, being unable to defend or help itself.

PH. Once again you are perfectly right.

SOCR. But now tell me, is there [276] another sort of discourse, that is brother to the written speech, but of unquestioned legitimacy? Can we see how it originates, and how much better and more effective it is than the other?

PH. What sort of discourse have you now in mind, and what is its origin?

SOCR. The sort that goes together with knowledge, and is written in the soul of the learner: that can defend itself, and knows to whom it should speak and to whom it should say nothing.

PH. You mean no dead discourse, but the living speech, the original of which the written discourse may fairly be called a kind of image.

SOCR. Precisely. And now tell me [B] this: if a sensible farmer had some seeds to look after and wanted them to bear fruit, would he with serious intent plant them during the summer in a garden of Adonis,[25] and enjoy watching it producing fine fruit within eight days? If he did so at all, wouldn't it be in a holiday spirit, just by way of pastime? For serious purposes wouldn't he behave like a scientific farmer, sow his seeds in suitable soil, and be well content if they came to maturity within eight months?

PH. I think we may distinguish as [C] you say, Socrates, between what the farmer would do seriously and what he would do in a different spirit.

SOCR. And are we to maintain that he who has knowledge of what is just, honourable and good has less sense than the farmer in dealing with his seeds?

PH. Of course not.

SOCR. Then it won't be with serious intent that he "writes them in water"[26] or that black fluid we call ink, using his pen to sow words that can't either speak in their own defense or present the truth adequately.

PH. It certainly isn't likely.

SOCR. No, it is not. He will sow his [D] seed in literary gardens, I take it, and write when he does write by way of pasttime, collecting a store of refreshment both for his own memory, against the day "when age oblivious comes," and for all such as tread in his footsteps; and he will take pleasure in watching the tender plants grow up. And when other men resort to other pastimes, regaling themselves with drinking-parties and such like, he will doubtless prefer to indulge in the recreation I refer to.

PH. And what an excellent one it [E] is, Socrates! How far superior to the other sort is the recreation that a man finds in words, when he discourses about justice and the other topics you speak of.

SOCR. Yes indeed, dear Phaedrus. But far more excellent, I think, is the serious treatment of them, which employs the

_____

25 A pot or window-box for forcing plants at the festival of Adonis.

26 A proverbial phrase for useless labour.

art of dialectic. The dialectician selects a soul of the right type, and in it he plants and sows his words founded on knowledge, words which can defend both themselves and him who planted [277] them, words which instead of remaining barren contain a seed whence new words grow up in new characters; whereby the seed is vouchsafed immortality, and its possessor the fullest measure of blessedness that man can attain unto.

PH. Yes, that is a far more excellent way.

SOCR. Then now that that has been settled, Phaedrus, we can proceed to the other point.

PH. What is that?

SOCR. The point that we wanted to look into before we arrived at our present conclusion. Our intention was to examine the reproach levelled against Lysias on the score of speech-writing, and therewith the general question of speech-writing and what does and [B] does not make it an art. Now I think we have pretty well cleared up the question of art.

PH. Yes, we did think so, but please remind me how we did it.

SOCR. The conditions to be fulfilled are these: first, you must know the truth about the subject that you speak or write about: that is to say, you must be able to isolate it in definition, and having so defined it you must next understand how to divide it into kinds, until you reach the limit of division; secondly, you must have a corresponding discernment of the nature of the soul, discover the type [C] of speech appropriate to each nature, and order and arrange your discourse accordingly, addressing a variegated soul in a variegated style that ranges over the whole gamut of tones, and a simple soul in a simple style. All this must be done if you are to become competent, within human limits, as a scientific practitioner of speech, whether you propose to expound or to persuade. Such is the clear purport of all our foregoing discussion.

PH. Yes, that was undoubtedly how we came to see the matter.

SOCR. And now to revert to our [D] other question, whether the delivery and composition of speeches is honourable or base, and in what circumstances they may properly become a matter of reproach, our earlier conclusions have, I think, shown—

PH. Which conclusions?

SOCR. They have shown that any work, in the past or in the future, whether by Lysias or anyone else, whether composed in a private capacity or in the role of a public man who by proposing a law becomes the author of a political composition, is a matter of reproach to its author (whether or no the reproach is actually voiced) if he regards it as containing important truth of permanent validity. For ignorance of what is a waking vision and what is a mere dream-image of justice and in-[E] justice, good and evil, cannot truly be [E] acquitted of involving reproach, even if the mass of men extol it.

PH. No indeed.

SOCR. On the other hand, if a man believes that a written discourse on any subject is bound to contain much that is fanciful: that nothing that has ever been written whether in verse or prose merits much serious attention—and for that matter nothing that has ever been spoken in the declamatory fashion which aims at mere persuasion without any questioning or exposition: that in reality such compositions are, at the best, a means of reminding those who know the [278] truth: that lucidity and completeness and serious importance belong only to those lessons on justice and honour and goodness that are expounded and set forth for the sake of instruction, and are veritably written in the soul of the listener: and that such discourses as these ought to be accounted a man's own legitimate children—a title to be applied primarily to such as originate within the man himself, and secondarily to such of their sons and brothers as have grown [B] up aright in the souls of other men: the man, I say, who believes this, and disdains all manner of discourse other than this, is, I would venture to affirm, the man whose example you and I would pray that we might follow.

PH. My own wishes and prayers are most certainly to that effect.

### XXVI

### 278B-279C  Messages to Lysias and Isocrates

SOCR. Then we may regard our literary pastime[27] as having reached a satisfactory conclusion. Do you now go and tell Lysias that we two went down to the stream where is the holy place of the Nymphs, and there listened to words which charged us to deliver a message, first to Lysias and all other composers [C] of discourses, secondly to Homer and all others who have written poetry whether to be read or sung, and thirdly to Solon and all such as are authors of political compositions under the name of laws: to wit, that if any of them has done his work with a knowledge of the truth, can defend his statements when challenged, and can demonstrate the inferiority of his writings out of his own mouth, he ought not to be designated by a name drawn from those writings, but by one that indicates his serious pursuit.     [D]

PH. Then what names would you assign him?

SOCR. To call him wise, Phaedrus, would, I think, be going too far: the epithet is proper only to a god; a name that would fit him better, and have more seemliness, would be "lover of wisdom," or something similar.

PH. Yes, that would be quite in keeping.

SOCR. On the other hand, one who has nothing to show of more value than the literary works on whose phrases he spends hours, twisting them this way and that, pasting them together and pull- [E] ing them apart,[28] will rightly, I suggest, be called a poet or speech-writer or lawwriter.

PH. Of course.

SOCR. Then that is what you must tell your friend.

PH. But what about yourself? What are you going to do? You too have a friend who should not be passed over.

SOCR. Who is that?

PH. The fair Isocrates. What will be your message to him, Socrates, and what shall we call him?

SOCR. Isocrates is still young, Phaedrus, but I don't mind telling you the future I prophesy for him.     [279]

PH. Oh, what is that?

SOCR. It seems to me that his natural powers give him a superiority over anything that Lysias has achieved in literature, and also that in point of character he is of a nobler composition; hence it would not surprise me if with advancing years he made all his literary predecessors look like very small fry; that is, supposing him to persist in the actual type of writing in which he engages at present; still more so, if he should become dissatisfied with such work, and a sublimer impulse lead him to do greater things. For that mind of his, Phaedrus, contains an innate tincture of philosophy.

Well then, there's the report I con- [B] vey from the gods of this place to Isoc-

---

27 The reference is probably not to the whole dialogue, but to the discussion from 274A 6 onwards.

28 Dionysius of Halicarnassus (*de comp. verb.* p. 208, Reiske) tells us that Plato continued throughout his life "combing and curling" (κτενίζων καὶ βοστρυχίζων) his dialogues, and that at his death a tablet was found with numerous variants of the opening sentence of the *Republic*; cf. also Diog. Laert. III, 37. It is possible that the present sentence reflects the impatience of Plato the philosopher with Plato the meticulous literary artist.

rates my beloved, and there's yours for your beloved Lysias.

PH. So be it. But let us be going, now that it has become less oppressively hot.

SOCR. Oughtn't we first to offer a prayer to the divinities here?

PH. To be sure.

SOCR. Dear Pan, and all ye other gods that dwell in this place, grant that I may become fair within, and that such outward things as I have may not war [c] against the spirit within me. May I count him rich who is wise; and as for gold, may I possess so much of it as only a temperate man might bear and carry with him.

Is there anything more we can ask for, Phaedrus? The prayer contents me.

PH. Make it a prayer for me too, since friends have all things in common.

SOCR. Let us be going.

# THE LATER PLATO

## PARMENIDES (in part : 127-136)

### 127A-D  Antiphon Repeats
### Pythodorus' Account
### of the Meeting

According to Antiphon, then, this was Pythodorus' account. Zeno and Parmenides once came to Athens for the [B] Great Panathenaea. Parmenides was a man of distinguished appearance. By that time he was well advanced in years, with hair almost white; he may have been sixty-five. Zeno was nearing forty, a tall and attractive figure. It was said that he had been Parmenides' favourite. They were staying with Pythodorus outside the walls in the Ceramicus. Socrates and [C] a few others came there, anxious to hear a reading of Zeno's treatise, which the two visitors had brought for the first time to Athens. Socrates was then quite young. Zeno himself read it to them; Parmenides at the moment had gone out. The reading of the arguments was very nearly over when Pythodorus himself came in, accompanied by Parmenides [D]

and Aristoteles, the man who was afterwards one of the Thirty; so they heard only a small part of the treatise. Pythodorus himself, however, had heard it read by Zeno before.

### 127D-128E  The Contents
### and Charactar of Zeno's Treatise

When Zeno had finished, Socrates asked him to read once more the first hypothesis of the first argument. He did so, and Socrates asked: What does this statement mean, Zeno? "If things are [E] many," you say, "they must be both like and unlike. But that is impossible: unlike things cannot be like, nor like things unlike." That is what you say, isn't it?

Yes, replied Zeno.

And so, if unlike things cannot be like or like things unlike, it is also impossible that things should be a plurality; if many things did exist, they would have impossible attributes. Is this the precise purpose of your arguments—to maintain, against everything that is commonly said, that things are not a plurality? Do you regard every one of your arguments as evidence of exactly that conclusion, and so hold that, in each argument in your treatise, you are giving just one more proof that a plurality does not exist? Is that what you mean, or am I [128] understanding you wrongly?

No, said Zeno, you have quite rightly understood the purpose of the whole treatise.

I see, Parmenides, said Socrates, that Zeno's intention is to associate himself with you by means of his treatise no less intimately than by his personal attachment. In a way, his book states the same position as your own; only by varying the form he tries to delude us into thinking that his thesis is a different one. You assert, in your poem, that the All is one; and for this you advance admirable proofs. Zeno, for his part, asserts that it is not a plurality; and he too has many weighty proofs to bring forward. You assert unity, he asserts no plurality; each expresses himself in such a way that your arguments seem to have nothing in common, though really they come to very much the same thing. That is why your exposition and his seem to be rather over the heads of outsiders like ourselves.

Yes, Socrates, Zeno replied; but [c] you have not quite seen the real character of my book. True, you are as quick as a Spartan hound to pick up the scent and follow the trail of the argument; but there is a point you have missed at the outset. The book makes no pretence of disguising from the public the fact that it was written with the purpose you describe, as if such deception were something to be proud of. What you have pointed out is only incidental; the book is in fact a sort of defence of Parmenides' argument against those who try to [D] make fun of it by showing that his supposition, that there is a One, leads to many absurdities and contradictions. This book, then, is a retort against those

who assert a plurality. It pays them back in the same coin with something to spare, and aims at showing that, on a thorough examination, their own supposition that there is a plurality leads to even more absurd consequences than the hypothesis of the One. It was written in that controversial spirit in my young days; and someone copied it surreptitiously, so that I had not even the chance to consider whether it should see the light or not. [E] That is where you are mistaken Socrates; you imagine it was inspired, not by a youthful eagerness for controversy, but by the more dispassionate aims of an older man; though, as I said, your description of it was not far wrong.

### 128E-130A   Socrates Offers the Theory of Separate Forms as Explaining How One Thing Can Have Two Contrary Characters

I accept that, said Socrates, and I have no doubt it is as you say. But tell me this. Do you not recognise that [129] there exists, just by itself, a Form of Likeness and again another contrary Form, Unlikeness itself, and that of these two Forms you and I and all the things we speak of as "many" come to partake? Also, that things which come to partake of Likeness come to be alike in that respect and just in so far as they do come to partake of it, and those that come to partake of Unlikeness come to be unlike, while those which come to partake of both come to be both? Even if all things come to partake of both, contrary as they are, and by having a share in both are at once like and unlike one another, what is there surprising in that? If one could point to things which are simply "alike" or "unlike" proving to be unlike or alike, that no doubt would be a portent; but when things which have a share in both are shown to have both characters, I see nothing strange in that, Zeno; nor yet in a proof that all things are one by having a share in unity and at the same time many by sharing in plurality. But if anyone can prove that what is simply Unity itself is many or that Plurality itself is one, then I shall [c] begin to be surprised.

And so in all other cases; if the kinds or Forms themselves were shown to have these contrary characters among themselves, there would be good ground for astonishment; but what is there surprising in someone pointing out that I am one thing and also many? When he wants to shown that I am many things, he can  say that my right side is a different thing from my left, my front from my back, my upper parts from my lower, since no doubt I do partake of plurality. When he wants to prove that I am one thing, he will say that I am one person among the seven of us, [d] since I partake also of unity. So both statements are true. Accordingly, if anyone sets out to show about things of this kind—sticks and stones, and so on —that the same thing is many and one, we shall say that what he is proving is that *something* is many and one, not that Unity is many or that Plurality is one; he is not telling us anything wonderful, but only what we should all admit. But, as I said just now, if he begins by distinguishing the Forms apart just by themselves—Likeness, for instance, and Unlikeness, Plurality and Unity, Rest and Motion, and all the [e] rest—and then shows that these Forms among themselves can be combined with, or separate from, one another, then, Zeno, I should be filled with admiration. I am sure you have dealt with this subject very forcibly; but, as I say, my admiration would be much greater if anyone could show that these same perplexities are everywhere involved in the Forms themselves—among the objects we apprehend in reflection, just as you and Parmenides have shown [130] them to be involved in the things we see.

## 130A-E  *Parmenides Criticises the Theory of Forms*

### (1) What Classes of Things Have Forms ?

While Socrates was speaking, Pythodorus said he was expecting every moment that Parmenides and Zeno would be annoyed; but they listened very attentively and kept on exchanging glances and smiles in admiration of Socrates. When he ended, Parmenides expressed this feeling: Socrates, he said, your eagerness for discussion is admirable. And now tell me: have you yourself drawn this distinction you speak of and separated apart on the one side Forms themselves and on the other the things that share in them? Do you believe that there is such a thing as Likeness itself apart from the likeness that we possess, and so on with Unity and Plurality and all the terms in Zeno's argument that you have just been listening to?

Certainly I do, said Socrates.
And also in cases like these, asked Parmenides: is there, for example, a Form of Rightness or of Beauty or of Goodness, and all of such things?

Yes.
And again, a Form of Man, apart from ourselves and all other men like us—a Form of Man as something by itself? Or a Form of Fire or of Water?

I have often been puzzled about those things, Parmenides, whether one should say that the same thing is true in their case or not.

Are you also puzzled, Socrates, about cases that might be thought absurd, such as hair or mud or dirt or any other trivial and undignified objects? Are you doubtful whether or not to assert that each of these has a separate Form distinct from things like those we handle?                                          [d]

Not at all, said Socrates; in these

cases, the things are just the things we see; it would surely be too absurd to suppose that they have a Form. All the same, I have sometimes been troubled by a doubt whether what is true in one case may not be true in all. Then, when I have reached that point, I am driven to retreat, for fear of tumbling into a bottomless pit of nonsense. Anyhow, I get back to the things which we were just now speaking of as having Forms, and occupy my time with thinking about them.

That, replied Parmenides, is be- [E] cause you are still young, Socrates, and philosophy has not yet taken hold of you so firmly as I believe it will some day. You will not despise any of these objects then; but at present your youth makes you still pay attention to what the world will think.

## (2) Objections to          [130E-131E]
## Participation

### (a) A THING CANNOT CONTAIN EITHER THE FORM AS A WHOLE OR A PART OF IT

(*Parmenides continues.*) However that may be, tell me this. You say you hold that there exist certain Forms, of which these other things come to partake and so to be called after their names: by coming to partake of Likeness or Largeness or Beauty or Justice, [131] they become like or large or beautiful or just?

Certainly, said Socrates.

Then each thing that partakes receives as its share either the Form as a whole or a part of it? Or can there be any other way of partaking besides this?

No, how could there be?

Do you hold, then, that the Form as a whole, a single thing, is in each of the many, or how?

Why should it not be in each, Parmenides?

If so, a Form which is one and [B] the same will be at the same time, as

a whole, in a number of things which are separate, and consequently will be separate from itself.

No, it would not, replied Socrates, if it were like one and the same day, which is in many places at the same time and nevertheless is not separate from itself. Suppose any given Form is in them all at the same time as one and the same thing in that way.

I like the way you make out that one and the same thing is in many places at once, Socrates. You might as well spread a sail over a number of people and then say that the one sail as a whole was over them all. Don't you think that is a fair analogy?

Perhaps it is.                          [C]

Then would the sail as a whole be over each man, or only a part over one, another part over another?

Only a part.

In that case, Socrates, the Forms themselves much be divisible into parts, and the things which have a share in them will have a part for their share. Only a part of any given Form, and no longer the whole of it, will be in each thing.

Evidently, on that showing.

Are you, then, prepared to assert that we shall find the single Form actually being divided? Will it still be one?

Certainly not.

No, for consider this. Suppose it is Largeness itself that you are going to divide into parts, and that each of the many large things is to be large by [D] virtue of a part of Largeness which is smaller than Largeness itself. Will not that seem unreasonable?

It will indeed.

And again, if it is Equality that a thing receives some small part of, will that part, which is less than Equality itself, make its possessor equal to something else?

No, that is impossible.

Well, take Smallness: is one of us to have a portion of Smallness, and is Smallness to be larger than that portion, which is a part of it? On this supposition again Smallness itself will be larger, and anything to which the portion taken is added will be smaller, [E] and larger, than it was before.

That cannot be so.

Well then, Socrates, how are the other things going to partake of your Forms, if they can partake of them neither in part nor as wholes?

Really, said Socrates, it seems no easy matter to determine in any way.

(b) THE THIRD MAN   [131E-132B]

Again, there is another question.

What is that?

How do you feel about this? I [132] imagine your ground for believing in a single Form in each case is this: when it seems to you that a number of things are large, there seems, I suppose, to be a certain single character which is the same when you look at them all; hence you think that Largeness is a single thing.

True, he replied.

But now take Largeness itself and the other things which are large. Suppose you look at all these in the same way in your mind's eye, will not yet another unity make its appearance—a Largeness by virtue of which they all appear large?

So it would seem.

If so, a second Form of Largeness will present itself, over and above Largeness itself and the things that share in it; and again, covering all these, yet another, which will make all of them [B] large. So each of your Forms will no longer be one, but an indefinite number.

*These objections cannot be met by making the Form a thought in a mind.* [132B-C]

But, Parmenides, said Socrates, may it not be that each of these Forms is a thought, which cannot properly exist anywhere but in a mind. In that way each of them can be one and the statements that have just been made would no longer be true of it.

Then, is each Form one of these thoughts and yet a thought of nothing?

No, that is impossible.

So it is a thought of something?

Yes.

Of something that is, or of something that is not? [C]

Of something that is.

In fact, of some *one* thing which that thought observes to cover all the cases, as being a certain single character?

Yes.

Then will not this thing that is thought of as being one and always the same in all cases be a Form?

That again seems to follow.

And besides, said Parmenides, according to the way in which you assert that the other things have a share in the Forms, must you not hold either that each of those things consists of thoughts, so that all things think, or else that they are thoughts which nevertheless do not think?

That too is unreasonable, replied Socrates.

*Can the objections be met by making the Forms patterns of which there are likenesses in things?* [132C-133A]

(*Socrates continues.*) But, Parmenides, the best I can make of the matter is this: that these Forms are as it were patterns fixed in the nature of things; the other things are made in their image and are likenesses; and this participation they come to have in the Forms is nothing but their being made in their image.

Well, if a thing is made in the image of the Form, can that Form fail to be like the image of it, in so far as the image was made in its likeness? If a thing is like, must it not be like something that is like it?

It must.

And must not the thing which is [E] like share with the thing that is like it in one and the same thing (character)?

Yes.

And will not that in which the like things share, so as to be alike, be just the Form itself that you spoke of?

Certainly.

If so, nothing can be like the Form, nor can the Form be like anything. Otherwise a second Form will always make its appearance over and above the first Form; and if that second Form is like anything, yet a third; and [133] there will be no end to this emergence of fresh Forms, if the Form is to be like the thing that partakes of it.

Quite true.

It follows that the other things do not partake of Forms by being like them; we must look for some other means by which they partake.

So it seems.

## (3) Will Not the Separate Forms Be Unknowable by Us?          [133A-134E]

You see then, Socrates, said Parmenides, what great difficulties there are in asserting their existence as Forms just by themselves?

I do indeed.

I assure you, then, you have as [B] yet hardly a notion of how great they will be, if you are going to set up a single Form for every distinction you make among things.

How so?

The worst difficulty will be this, though there are plenty more. Suppose someone should say that the Forms, if they are such as we are saying they must be, cannot even be known. One could not convince him that he was mistaken in that objection, unless he chanced to be a man of wide experience and natural ability, and were willing to follow one through a long and remote train of argument. Otherwise there would be no way of convincing a man who [C] maintained that the Forms were unknowable.

Why so, Parmenides?

Because, Socrates, I imagine that you

or anyone else who asserts that each of them has a real being "just by itself," would admit, to begin with, that no such real being exists in our world.

True; for how could it then be just by itself?

Very good, said Parmenides. And further, those Forms which are what they are with reference to one another, have their being in such references among themselves, not with reference to those likenesses (or whatever we are to call them) in our world, which we possess and so come to be called by their [D] several names. And, on the other hand, these things in our world which bear the same names as the Forms are related among themselves, not to the Forms; and all the names of that sort that they bear have reference to one another, not to the Forms.

How do you mean? asked Socrates.

Suppose, for instance, one of us is master or slave of another; he is not, of course, the slave of Master itself, the essential Master, nor, if he is a master, is he master of Slave itself, the essential Slave, but, being a man, is master [E] or slave of another man; whereas Mastership itself is what it is (mastership) of Slavery itself, and Slavery itself is slavery to Mastership itself. The significance of things in our world is not with reference to things in that other world, nor have these their significance with reference to us; but as I say, the things in that world are what they are with reference to one another and towards one another; and so likewise are the things in our world. You see what I mean?

Certainly I do.

And similarly Knowledge itself, [134] the essence of Knowledge, will be knowledge of that Reality itself, the essentially real.

Certainly.

And again any given branch of Knowledge in itself will be knowledge of some department of real things as it is in itself, will it not?

Yes.

Whereas the knowledge in our world will be knowledge of the reality in our world; and it will follow again that each branch of knowledge in our world must be knowledge of some department of [B] thing that exist in our world.

Necessarily.

But, as you admit, we do not possess the Forms themselves, nor can they exist in our world.

No.

And presumably the Forms, just as they are in themselves, are known by the Form of Knowledge itself?

Yes.

The Form which we do not passess.

True.

Then, none of the Forms is known by us, since we have no part in Knowledge itself.

Apparently not.

So Beauty itself or Goodness itself and all the things we take as Forms in themselves, are unknowable to us.

I am afraid that is so.

Then here is a still more formidable consequence for you to consider.

What is that?

You will grant, I suppose, that if there is such a thing as a Form, Knowledge itself, it is much more perfect than the knowledge in our world; and so with Beauty and all the rest.

Yes.

And if anything has part in this Knowledge itself, you would agree that a god has a better title than anyone else to possess the most perfect knowledge?

Undoubtedly.

Then will the god, who possesses [D] Knowledge itself, be able to know the things in our world?

Why not?

Because we have agreed that those Forms have no significance with reference to things in our world, nor have things in our world any significance with reference to them. Each set has it only among themselves.

Yes, we did.

Then if this most perfect Mastership and most perfect Knowledge are in the gods' world, the gods' Mastership can never be exercised over us, nor their [E] Knowledge know us or anything in our world. Just as we do not rule over them by virtue of rule as it exists in our world and we know nothing that is divine by our knowledge, so they, on the same principle, being gods, are not our masters nor do they know anything of human concerns.

But surely, said Socrates, an argument which would deprive the gods of knowledge, would be too strange.

*The Forms are admitted* [134E-135C] *to be necessary for all thought and discourse.*

And yet, Socrates, Parmenides went on, these difficulties and many more besides are inevitably involved in the Forms, if these characters of things [135] really exist and one is going to distinguish each Form as a thing just by itself. The result is that the hearer is perplexed and inclined either to question their existence, or to contend that, if they do exist, they must certainly be unknowable by our human nature. Moreover, there seems to be some weight in these objections, and, as we were saying, it is extraordinarily difficult to convert the objector. Only a man of exceptional gifts will be able to see that a Form, or essence just by itself, does exist in each case; and it will require someone still more remarkable to discover it and to instruct [B] another who has thoroughly examined all these difficulties.

I admit that, Parmenides; I [135B] quite agree with what you are saying.

But on the other hand, Parmenides continued, if, in view of all these difficulties and others like them, a man refuses to admit that Forms of things exist or to distinguish a definite Form in every case, he will have nothing on which to fix his thought, so long as he will not allow that each thing has [c] a character which is always the same; and in so doing he will completely destroy the significance of all discourse. But of that consequence I think you are only too well aware.

True.

### 135C-136E   Transition
### to the Second Part

What are you going to do about philosophy, then? Where will you turn while the answers to these questions remain unknown?

I can see no way out at the present moment.

That is because you are undertaking to define "Beautiful," "Just," "Good," and other particular Forms, too soon, before you have had a preliminary [D] training. I noticed that the other day when I heard you talking here with Aristoteles. Believe me, there is something noble and inspired in your passion for argument; but you must make an effort and submit yourself, while you are still young, to a severer training in what the world calls idle talk and condemns as useless. Otherwise, the truth will escape you.

What form, then, should this exercise take, Parmenides?

The form that Zeno used in the treatise you have been listening to. With this exception: there was one thing you said to him which impressed me [E] very much: you would not allow the survey to be confined to visible things or to range only over that field; it was to extend to those objects which are specially apprehended by discourse and can be regarded as Forms.

Yes, because in that other field there seems to be no difficulty about showing that things are both like and unlike and have any other character you please.

You are right. But there is one thing more you must do. If you want to be thoroughly exercised, you must not merely make the supposition that such and such a thing *is* and then consider the consequences; you must also [136] take the supposition that that same thing *is not.*

How do you mean?

Take, if you like, the supposition that Zeno made: *"If there is a plurality of things."* You must consider what consequences must follow both for those many things with reference to one another and to the One, and also for the One with reference to itself and to the many. Then again, on the supposition that *there is not a plurality,* you must consider what will follow both for the One and for the many, with reference to themselves and to each other. . . .

# THEAETETUS (in part)

PERSONS OF THE DIALOGUE

SOCRATES   THEAETETUS   THEODORUS

• • •

SOCRATES. Do you fancy it is a [148c] small matter to discover the nature of knowledge? Is it not one of the hardest questions?

THEAETETUS. One of the very hardest, I should say.

SOCR. You may be reassured, then, about Theodorus' account of you, and set your mind on finding a definition of knowledge, as of anything else, [D] with all the zeal at your command.

THEAET. If it depends on my zeal,

Socrates, the truth will come to light.

SOCR. Forward, then, on the way you have just shown so well. Take as a model your answer about the roots: just as you found a single character to embrace all that multitude, so now try to find a single formula that applies to the many kinds of knowledge.

THEAET. But I assure you, Soc- [E] rates, I have often set myself to study that problem, when I heard reports of the questions you ask. But I cannot persuade myself that I can give any satisfactory solution or that anyone has ever stated in my hearing the sort of answer you require. And yet I cannot get the question out of my mind.

### Socrates' Art of Midwifery

SOCR. My dear Theaetetus, that is because your mind is not empty or barren. You are suffering the pains of travail.

THEAET. I don't know about that, Socrates. I am only telling you how I feel.

SOCR. How absurd of you, never [149] to have heard that I am the son of a midwife, a fine buxom woman called Phaenarete!

THEAET. I have heard that.

SOCR. Have you also been told that I practise the same art?

THEAET. No, never.

SOCR. It is true, though; only don't give away my secret. It is not known that I possess this skill; so the ignorant world describes me in other terms as an eccentric person who reduces people to hopeless perplexity. Have you been told that too?

THEAET. I have.

SOCR. Shall I tell you the reason?

THEAET. Please do.

SOCR. Consider, then, how it is with all midwives; that will help you to understand what I mean. I dare say you know that they never attend other women in childbirth so long as they themselves can conceive and bear children, but only when they are too old for that.

THEAET. Of course.

SOCR. They said that is because Artemis, the patroness of childbirth, is herself childless; and so, while she did not allow barren women to be midwives, because it is beyond the power of human nature to achieve skill with- [C] out any experience, she assigned the privilege to women who were past childbearing, out of respect to their likeness to herself.

THEAET. That sounds likely.

SOCR. And it is more than likely, is it not, that no one can tell so well as a midwife whether women are pregnant or not?

THEAET. Assuredly.

SOCR. Moreover, with the drugs and incantations they administer, midwives can either bring on the pains of travail or allay them at their will, make a [D] difficult labour easy, and at an early stage cause a miscarriage if they so decide.

THEAET. True.

SOCR. Have you also observed that they are the cleverest match-makers, having an unerring skill in selecting a pair whose marriage will produce the best children?

THEAET. I was not aware of that.

SOCR. Well, you may be sure they pride themselves on that more than on cutting the umbilical cord. Consider the knowledge of the sort of plant or [E] seed that should be sown in any given soil; does not that go together with skill in tending and harvesting the fruits of the earth? They are not two different arts?

THEAET. No, the same.

SOCR. And so with a woman; skill in the sowing is not to be separated from skill in the harvesting?

THEAET. Probably not.

SOCR. No; only, because there is [150]

that wrong and ignorant way of bringing together man and woman which they call pandering, midwives, out of self-respect, are shy even of matchmaking, for fear of falling under the accusation of pandering. Yet the genuine midwife is the only successful matchmaker.

THEAET. That is clear.

SOCR. All this, then, lies within the midwife's province; but her performance falls short of mine. It is not the way of women sometimes to bring forth real children, sometimes mere phantoms, [B] such that it is hard to tell the one from the other. If it were so, the highest and noblest task of the midwife would be to discern the real from the unreal, would it not?

THEAET. I agree.

SOCR. My art of midwifery is in general like theirs; the only difference is that my patients are men, not women, and my concern is not with the body but with the soul that is in travail of birth. And the highest point of my art is the power to prove by every test whether the offspring of a young [C] man's thought is a false phantom or instinct with life and truth. I am so far like the midwife, that I cannot myself give birth to wisdom; and the common reproach is true, that, though I question others, I can myself bring nothing to light because there is no wisdom in me. The reason is this: heaven constrains me to serve as a midwife, but has debarred me from giving birth. So of myself I have no sort of wisdom, nor [D] has any discovery ever been born to me as the child of my soul. Those who frequent my company at first appear, some of them, quite unintelligent; but, as we go further with our discussions, all who are favoured by heaven make progress at a rate that seems surprising to others as well as to themselves, although it is clear that they have never learnt anything from me; the many admirable truths they bring to birth have been discovered by themselves from within. But the delivery is heaven's work and mine.

The proof of this is that many [E] who have not been conscious of my assistance but have made light of me, thinking it was all their own doing, have left me sooner than they should, whether under others' influence or of their own motion, and thenceforward suffered miscarriage of their thoughts through falling into bad company; and they have lost the children of whom I had delivered them by bringing them up badly, caring more for false phantoms than for the true; and so at last their lack of understanding has become apparent to themselves and to every- [151] one else. Such a one was Aristides, son of Lysimachus, and there have been many more. When they come back and beg for a renewed of our intercourse with extravagant protestations, sometimes the divine warning that comes to me forbirds it; with others it is permitted, and these begin again to make progress. In yet another way, those who seek my company have the same experience as a woman with child: they suffer the pains of labour and, by night and day, are full of distress far greater than a woman's; and my art has power to bring on these pangs or to allay [B] them. So it fares with these; but there are some, Theaetetus, whose minds, as I judge, have never conceived at all. I see that they have no need of me and with all goodwill I seek a match for them. Without boasting unduly, I can guess pretty well whose society will profit them. I have arranged many of these matches with Prodicus, and with other men of inspired sagacity.

And now for the upshot of this long discourse of mine. I suspect that, as you yourself believe, your mind is in labour with some thought it has conceived. Accept, then, the ministration of a midwife's son who himself practises his [C] mother's art, and do the best you can to answer the questions I ask. Perhaps when I examine your statements I may judge one or another of them to be an unreal phantom. If I then take the abortion from you and cast it away, do not be savage with me like a woman robbed of her first child. People have often felt like that towards me and been positively ready to bite me for taking away some foolish notion they have conceived. They do not see that I am doing them a kindness. They have not learnt that no divinity is ever ill-disposed towards [D] man, nor is such action on my part due to unkindness; it is only that I am not permitted to acquiesce in falsehood and suppress the truth.

So, Theaetetus, start again and try to explain what knowledge is. Never say it is beyond your power; it will not be so, if heaven wills and you take courage.

## Theaetetus Identifies Knowledge with Perception

THEAET. Well, Socrates, with such encouragement from a person like you, it would be a shame not to do one's best to say what one can. It seems to me that one who knows something is perceiving the thing he knows, and, so [E] far as I can see at present, knowledge is nothing but perception.

SOCR. Good; that is the right spirit in which to express one's opinion. But now suppose we examine your offspring together, and see whether it is a mere wind-egg or has some life in it. Perception, you say, is knowledge?

THEAET. Yes.

SOCR. The account you give of the nature of knowledge is not, by any means, to be despised. It is the same that was given by Protagoras, [152] though he stated it in a somewhat different way. He says, you will remember, that "man is the measure of all things—alike of the being of things that are and of the not-being of things that are not." No doubt you have read that.

THEAET. Yes, often.

SOCR. He puts it in this sort of way, doesn't he?—that any given thing "is to me such as it appears to me, and is to you such as it appears to you," you and I being men.

THEAET. Yes, that is how he puts it.

SOCR. Well, what a wise man says [B] is not likely to be nonsense. So let us follow up his meaning. Sometimes, when the same wind is blowing, one of us feels chilly, the other does not; or one may feel slightly chilly, the other quite cold.

THEAET. Certainly.

SOCR. Well, in that case are we to say that the wind in itself is cold or not cold? Or shall we agree with Protagoras that it is cold to the one who feels chilly, and not to the other?

THEAET. That seems reasonable.

SOCR. And further that it so "appears" to each of us?

THEAET. Yes.

SOCR. And "appears" means that he "perceives" it so?

THEAET. True.

SOCR. "Appearing," then, is the [C] same thing as "perceiving," in the case of what is hot or anything of that kind. They *are* to each man such as he *perceives* them.

THEAET. So it seems.

SOCR. Perception, then, is always of something that *is*, and, as being knowledge, it is infallible.

THEAET. That is clear.

• • •

SOCR. ... When we say that I, being of the height you see, without gaining or losing in size, may within a year be taller (as I am now) than a youth like you, and later on be shorter, not because I have lost anything in bulk, but [C] because you have grown. For apparently I am later what I was not before, and yet have not become so; for without the process of becoming the result is impossible, and I could not be in process of becoming shorter without losing some of my bulk. I could give you countless other examples, if we are to accept these. For I think you follow me, Theaetetus; I fancy, at any rate, such puzzles are not altogether strange to you.

THEAET. No; indeed it is extraordinary how they set me wondering whatever they can mean. Sometimes I get quite dizzy with thinking of them.

SOCR. That shows that Theodorus [D] was not wrong in his estimate of your nature. This sense of wonder is the mark of the philosopher. Philsophy indeed has no other origin, and he was a good genealogist who made Iris the daughter of Thaumas.[1] Do you now begin to see the explanation of all this which follows from the theory we are attributing to Protagoras? Or is it not yet clear?

THEAET. I can't say it is yet.

SOCR. Then perhaps you will be grateful if I help you to penetrate to the truth concealed in the thoughts of a man—or, I should say, of men—of such distinction.[2]          (E)

THEAET. Of course I shall be very grateful.

SOCR. Then just take a look round and make sure that none of the uninitiate overhears us. I mean by the uninitiate the people who believe that nothing is real save what they can grasp with their hands and do not admit that actions or processes or anything invisible can count as real.

THEAET. They sound like a very hard and repellent sort of people.[3]          [156]

· · ·

---

[1] The *Cratylus* connects Iris with εἴρειν (408B), and εἴρειν (λέγειν) with dialectic (398D). So Iris (philosophy) is daughter of Thaumas (wonder).

[2] Observe the hints that the coming theory is one that "we are attributing" to Protagoras, and not to him alone.

[3] Like the physical bodies in whose reality they believe, with their essential property of hardness and resistance to touch.

SOCR. You have an absolute pas- [161] sion for discussion, Theodorus. I like the way you take me for a sort of bag full or arguments, and imagine I can easily pull out a proof to show that our conclusion is wrong. You don't see [B] what is happening: the arguments never come out of me, they always come from the person I am talking with. I am only at a slight advantage in having the skill to get some account of the matter from another's wisdom and entertain it with fair treatment. So now, I shall not give any explanation myself, but try to get it out of our friend.

THEOD. That is better, Socrates; do as you say.

· · ·

## Objections to a Simple Identification of Perceiving and Knowing

· · ·

SOCR. Let us look at it in this [163A] way, then—this question whether knowledge and perception are, after all, the same thing or not. For that, you remember, was the point to which our whole discussion was directed, and it was for its sake that we stirred up all this swarm of queer doctrines, wasn't it?

THEAET. Quite true.

SOCR. Well, are we going to agree [B] that, whenever we perceive something by sight or hearing, we also at the same time know it? Take the case of a foreign language we have not learnt. Are we to say that we do not hear the sounds that foreigners utter, or that we both hear and know what they are saying? Or again, when we don't know our letters, are we to maintain that we don't see them when we look at them, or that, since we see them, we do know them?

THEAET. We shall say, Socrates, that we know just so much of them as we do see or hear. The shape and colour of the letters we both see and know; we hear and at the same time know the rising and falling accents of the [C] voice; but we neither perceive by sight and hearing nor yet know what a schoolmaster or an interpreter could tell us about them.

SOCR. Well done, Theaetetus. I had better not raise objections to that, for fear of checking your growth. But look, here is another objection threatening. How are we going to parry it?

THEAET. What is that?

SOCR. It is this. Suppose someone [D] to ask: "Is it possible for a man who has once come to know something and still preserves a memory of it, not to know just that thing that he remembers at the moment when he remembers it?" This is, perhaps, rather a long-winded way of putting the question. I mean: Can a man who has become acquainted with something and remembers it, not know it?

THEAET. Of course not, Socrates; the supposition is monstrous.

SOCR. Perhaps I am talking nonsense, then. But consider: you call seeing "perceiving," and sight "perception," don't you?

THEAET. I do.

SOCR. Then, according to our [E] earlier statement, a man who sees something acquires from that moment knowledge of the thing he sees?

THEAET. Yes.

SOCR. Again, you recognise such a thing as memory?

THEAET. Yes.

SOCR. Memory of nothing, or of something?

THEAET. Of something, surely.

SOCR. Of what one has become acquainted with and perceived—that sort of things?

THEAET. Of course.

SOCR. So a man sometimes remembers what he has seen?

THEAET. He does.

SOCR. Even when he shuts his eyes? Or does he forget when he shuts them?

THEAET. No, Socrates; that would be a monstrous thing to say.

SOCR. All the same, we shall have [164] to say it, if we are to save our former statement. Otherwise, it goes by the board.

THEAET. I certainly have a suspicion that you are right, but I don't quite see how. You must tell me.

SOCR. In this way. One who sees, we say, acquires knowledge of what he sees, because it is agreed that sight or perception and knowledge are the same thing.

THEAET. Certainly.

SOCR. But suppose this man who sees and acquires knowledge of what he has seen, shuts his eyes; then he remembers the thing, but does not see it. Isn't that so?

THEAET. Yes.

SOCR. But "does not see it" means [B] "does not know it," since "sees" and "knows" mean the same.

THEAET. True.

SOCR. Then the conclusion is that a man who has come to know a thing and still remembers it does not know it, since he does not see it; and we said that would be a monstrous conclusion.

THEAET. Quite true.

SOCR. Apparently, then, if you say that knowledge and perception are the same thing, it leads to an impossibility.

THEAET. So it seems.

SOCR. Then we shall have to say they are different.

THEAET. I suppose so.

•  •  •

## Defence of Protagoras    [165E-168C]

SOCR. ...Now, perhaps, you may wonder what argument Protagoras will find to defend his position. Shall we try to put it into words?

THEAET. By all means.

SOCR. No doubt, then, Protagoras will make all the points we have put forward in our attempt to defend him, and [166] at the same time will come to close quarters with the assailant, dismissing us with contempt.[4] "Your admirable Socrates," he will say, "finds a little boy who is scared at being asked whether one and the same person can remember and at the same time not know one and the same thing. When the child is frightened into saying No, because he cannot foresee the consequence, Socrates turns the conversation so as to make a figure of fun of my unfortunate self. You take things much too easily, Socrates. The truth of the matter is this: when you ask someone questions in order to canvass some opinion of mine and he is found tripping, then I am refuted only if his answers are such as I should have given; if they are different, it is he [B] who is refuted, not I. For instance, do you think you will find anyone to admit that one's present memory of a past impression is an impression of the same character as one had during the original experience, which is now over? It is nothing of the sort. Or again, will anyone shrink from admitting that it is possible for the same person to know and not to know the same thing? Or, if he is frightened of saying that, will he ever allow that a person who is changed is the *same* as he was before the change occurred; or rather, that he is *one* person at all, and not several, indeed an infinite succession of persons, provided change goes on happening—if we are [c] really to be on the watch against one another's attempts to catch at words? 'No,' he will say; 'show a more generous spirit by attacking what I actually say; and prove, if you can, that we have not, each one of us, his peculiar perceptions, or that, granting them to be peculiar, it would not follow that what appears to

each becomes—or is, if we may use the word 'is'—for him alone to whom it appears. With this talk of pigs and baboons, you are behaving like a pig yourself,[5] and, what is more, you tempt your [D] hearers to treat my writings in the same way, which is not fair.

"For I do indeed assert that the truth is as I have written: each one of us is a measure of what is and of what is not; but there is all the difference in the world between one man and another just in the very fact that what is and appears to one is different from what is and appears to the other. And as for wisdom and the wise man, I am very far from saying they do not exist. By a wise man I mean precisely a man who can change any one of us, when what is bad appears and is to him, and make what is good appear and be to him. In this statement, again, don't set off in chase of words, but let me explain [E] still more clearly what I mean. Remember how it was put earlier in the conversation: to the sick man his food appears sour and is so; to the healthy man it is and appears the opposite. Now there is no call to represent either of the two as wiser—that cannot be—nor is the sick man to be pronounced unwise [167] because he thinks[6] as he does, or the healthy man wise because he thinks differently. What is wanted is a change to the opposite condition, because the other state is better.

"And so too in education a change has

---

[4] Protagoras will both (τε) urge, as we have done for him, that we are talking claptrap (162D), that verbal disputation is futile (164B) and we must use words more carefully (165A), and (καὶ) will come to grips (not with us, but) with the sophistic skirmisher and his armoury of eristic cavils, despising us for our feeble surrender to such weapons.

[5] The pig, in Greek, is an emblem of stupidity (ἀμαθία). *Lach.* 169D: "Would not any pig know..." Cic. *Ac. Post.* i, 5, 18: *non sus docet Minervam.* This remark is less offensive than the English sounds.

[6] "Thinks," "judges" (δοξάξει), here replaces "appears" (φαίνεσθαι). What is meant is the judgment stating the fact of a sense-impression: "This food seems and is to me sour." If Socrates' earlier expression, "what every man believes as the result of perception" (ὃ ἂν δι' αἰσθήσεως δοξάζῃ, 161D) is restricted to such judgments, they are not ignorant or foolish judgments; nor are they false.

to be effected from the worse condition to the better; only, whereas the physician produces a change by means of drugs, the sophist does it by discourse. It is not that a man makes someone who previously thought what is false think what is true (for it is not possible either to think the thing that is not or to think anything but what one experiences, [B] and all experiences are true); rather, I should say, when someone by reason of a depraved condition of mind has thoughts of a like character, one makes him, by reason of a sound condition, think other and sound thoughts, which some people ignorantly call true, whereas I should say that one set of thoughts is better than the other, but not in any way truer.[7] And as for the wise, my dear Socrates, so far from calling them frogs, I call them, when they have to do with the body, physicians, and when they have to do with plants, husbandmen. For I assert that husbandmen too, when plants are sickly and have depraved sensations, substitute for these sensations that are [c] sound and healthy;[8] and moreover that wise and honest public speakers substitute in the community sound for unsound views of what is right. For I hold that whatever practices seem right and laudable to any particular State are so,

for that State, so long as it holds by them. Only, when the practices are, in any particular case, unsound for them, the wise man substitutes others that are and appear sound. On the same principle the sophist, since he can in the same manner guide his pupils in the way they should go, is wise and worth a con- [D] siderable fee to them when their education is completed. In this way it is true both that some men are wiser than others and that no one thinks falsely; and you, whether you like it or not, must put up with being a measure, since by these considerations my doctrine is saved from shipwreck. Now if you can dispute this doctrine in principle, do so by argument stating the case on the other side, or by asking questions, if you prefer that method, which has no terrors for a man of sense; on the contrary it ought to be specially agreeable to him. Only there is this rule to be observed: [E] do not conduct your questioning unfairly. It is very unreasonable that one who professes a concern for virtue should be constantly guilty of unfairness in argument. Unfairness here consists in not observing the distinction between a debate and a conversation. A debate need not be taken seriously and one may trip up an opponent to the best of one's power; but a conversation should be taken in earnest; one should help out the other party and bring home to him only those slips and fallacies that are due to [168] himself or to his earlier instructors. If you follow this rule, your associates will lay the blame for their confusions and perplexities on themselves and not on you; they will like you and court your society, and disgusted with themselves, will turn to philosophy, hoping to escape from their former selves and become different men. But if, like so many, you take the opposite course, you will reach the opposite result: instead of turning your companions to philosophy, you [B] will make them hate the whole business when they get older. So, if you will take

---

[7] The text is doubtful. The best sense is obtained by taking τίς (167A, 7) as the subject of a single sentence from ἐπεὶ (A, 6) to οὐδέν (B, 4). Read πονηρᾷ and χρηστῇ (sc. ψυχῆς ἕξει, with W.) and omit τὰ φαντάσματα (with Diels, Vors.[4] ii, 225). It is the sophist, not the χρηστὴ ἕξις, that "makes" the change to sound thoughts. The reading χρηστὴ will then be explained as an attempt to provide the ἐποίησε following it with a subject, made by someone who did not see that τίς (governing the earlier ἐποίησε, (. 7) is still the subject.

[8] Omitting τε καὶ αληθεῖς. Diels' suggestion (Vors.[4] ii, 225) ὥστε καὶ ἀληθεῖς gives a wrong sense, for the unhealthy sensations are also true. The conjectures ἀληθείας (Schleiermacher), ἕξεις (Diès), πάθας (Richards) are not convincing.

my advice, you will meet us in the candid spirit I spoke of, without hostility or contentiousness, and honestly consider what we mean when we say that all things are in motion and that what seems also is, to any individual or community. The further question whether knowledge is, or is not, the same thing as perception, you will consider as a consequence of these principles, not (as you did just now) basing your argu- [c] ment on the common use of words and phrases, which the vulgar twist into any sense they please and so perplex one another in all sorts of ways.'

∙ ∙ ∙

## Criticism of Protagoras' Doctrine as Extended to All Judgments

SOCR. Let us begin, then, by [169D] coming to grips with the doctrine at the same point as before. Let us see whether or not our discontent was justified, when we criticised it as making every individual self-sufficient in wisdom. Protagoras then conceded that some people were superior in the matter of what is better or worse, and these, he said, were wise. Didn't he?

THEOD. Yes.

SOCR. If he were here himself to make that admission, instead of our conceding it for him in our defence, there would [E] be no need to reopen the question and make sure of our ground; but, as things are, we might be said to have no authority to make the admission on his behalf. So it will be more satisfactory to come to a more complete and clear agreement on this particular point; for it makes a considerable difference, whether this is so or not.

THEOD. That is true.

SOCR. Let us, then, as briefly as possible, obtain his agreement, not through any third person, but from his own statement.                                    [170]

THEOD. How?

SOCR. In this way. He says—doesn't

he?—that what seems true[9] to anyone is true for him to whom it seems so?

THEOD. He does.

SOCR. Well now, Protagoras, we are expressing what seems true to a man, or rather to all men, when we say that everyone without exception holds that in some respects he is wiser than his neighbours and in others they are wiser than he. For instance, in moments of great danger and distress, whether in war or in sickness or at sea, men regard as a god anyone who can take control of the [B] situation and look to him as a saviour, when his only point of superiority is his knowledge. Indeed, the world is full of people looking for those who can instruct and govern men and animals and direct their doings, and on the other hand of people who think themselves quite competent to undertake the teaching and governing. In all these cases what can we say, if not that men do hold that wisdom and ignorance exist among them?

THEOD. We must say that.

SOCR. And they hold that wisdom lies in thinking truly, and ignorance in false belief?

THEOD. Of course.                                    [c]

SOCR. In that case, Protagoras, what are we to make of your doctrine? Are we to say that what men think is always true, or that it is sometimes true and sometimes false? From either supposition it results that their thoughts are not always true, but both true and false. For consider, Theodorus. Are you, or is any Protagorean, prepared to maintain that no one regards anyone else as ignorant or as making false judgments?

THEOD. That is incredible, Socrates.

SOCR. That, however, is the inevit- [D] able consequence of the doctrine which makes man the measure of all things.

THEOD. How so?

---

9 τὸ δοκοῦν here, as the context shows, mean "what seems true." Since Protagoras' maxim covered judgment, the interpretation is perfectly fair.

socr. When you have formed a judgment on some matter in your own mind and express an opinion about it to me, let us grant that, as Protagoras' theory says, it is true for you; but are we to understand that it is impossible for us, the rest of the company, to pronounce any judgment upon your judgment; or, if we can, that we always pronounce your opinion to be true? Do you not rather find thousands of opponents who set their opinion against yours on every occasion and hold that your judgment and belief are false?

THEOD. I should just think so, Soc- [E] rates; thousands and tens of thousands, as Homer says; and they give me all the trouble in the world.

socr. And what then? Would you have us say that in such a case the opinion you hold is true for yourself and false for these tens of thousands?

THEOD. The doctrine certainly seems to imply that.

socr. And what is the consequence for Protagoras himself? Is it not this: supposing that not even he believed in man being the measure and the world in general did not believe it either—as in fact it doesn't—then this Truth which he wrote would not be true for any- [171] one? If, on the other hand, he did believe it, but the mass of mankind does not agree with him, then, you see, it is more false than true by just so much as the unbelievers outnumber the believers.

THEOD. That follows, if its truth or falsity varies with each individual opinion.

socr. Yes, and besides that it involves a really exquisite conclusion.[10] Protagoras, for his part, admitting as he does that everybody's opinion is true, must acknowledge the truth of his opponents' belief about his own belief, where they think he is wrong.

THEOD. Certainly.

socr. That is to say, he would [B] acknowledge his own belief to be false, if he admits that the belief of those who think him wrong is true?

THEOD. Necessarily.

socr. But the others, on their side, do not admit to themselves that they are wrong.

THEOD. No.

socr. Whereas Protagoras, once more, according to what he has written, admits that this opinion of theirs is as true as any other.

THEOD. Evidently.

socr. On all hands, then, Protagoras included, his opinion will be disputed, or rather Protagoras will join in the general consent—when he admits to an opponent the truth of his contrary opinion, [C] from that moment Protagoras himself will be admitting that a dog or the man in the street is not a measure of anything whatever that he does not understand. Isn't that so?

THEOD. Yes.

socr. Then, since it is disputed by everyone, the Truth of Protagoras is true to nobody—to himself no more than to anyone else.

THEOD. We are running my old friend too hard, Socrates.

socr. But it is not clear that we are outrunning the truth, my friend. Of course it is likely that, as an older [D] man, he was wiser than we are; and if at this moment he could pop his head up through the ground there as far as to the neck, very probably he would expose me thoroughly for talking such nonsense and you for agreeing to it, before he sank out of sight and took to his heels. However, we must do our best with such lights as we have and continue to say what we think.

•   •   •

## Digression: The Philosopher

THEOD. What do you mean, Socrates?                                    [174]

---

10 Sextus, *Math.* vii, 389, says that an argument of this form, known as "turning the tables" ($\pi\epsilon\rho\iota\tau\rho\sigma\pi\acute{\eta}$), was used against Protagoras by Democritus, as well as by Plato here.

SOCR. The same thing as the story about the Thracian maidservant who exercised her wit at the expense of Thales, when he was looking up to study the stars and tumbled down a well. She scoffed at him for being so eager to know what was happening in the sky that he could not see what lay at his feet. Anyone who gives his life to philosophy is open to such mockery. It is true that he is unaware what his next-door [B] neighbour is doing, hardly knows, indeed, whether the creature is a man at all; he spends all his pains on the question, what man is, and what powers and properties distinguish such a nature from any other.[11] You see what I mean, Theodorus?

THEOD. Yes; and it is true.

SOCR. And so, my friend, as I said at first, on a public occasion or in private company, in a law court or anywhere [C] else, when he is forced to talk about what lies at his feet or is before his eyes, the whole rabble will join the maidservants in laughing at him, as from inexperience he walks blindly and stumbles into every pitfall. His terrible clumsiness makes him seem so stupid. He cannot engage in an exchange of abuse,[12] for, never having made a study of anyone's peculiar weaknesses, he has no personal scandals to bring up; so in his helplessness he looks a fool. When people vaunt their own or other men's [D] merits, his unaffected laughter makes him conspicuous and they think he is frivolous. When a despot or king is eulogised, he fancies he is hearing some keeper of swine or sheep or cows being congratulated on the quantity of milk he has squeezed out of his flock; only he reflects that the animal that princes tend and milk is more given than sheep or cows to nurse a sullen grievance, and

that a herdsman of this sort, penned up in his castle, doomed by sheer press of work to be as rude and uncultivated [E] as the shepherd in his mountain fold. He hears of the marvellous wealth of some landlord who owns ten thousand acres or more; but that seems a small matter to one accustomed to think of the earth as a whole. When they harp upon birth—some gentleman who can point to seven generations of wealthy ancestors—he thinks that such commendation must come from men of purblind vision, too uneducated to keep their eyes fixed [175] on the whole or to reflect that any man has had countless myriads of ancestors and among them any number of rich men and beggars, kings and slaves, Greeks and barbarians. To pride oneself on a catalogue of twenty-five progenitors going back to Heracles, son of Amphitryon, strikes him as showing a strange pettiness of outlook. He laughs at a man who cannot rid his mind of foolish vanity by reckoning that be- [B] fore Amphitryon there was a twenty-fifth ancestor, and before him a fiftieth, whose fortunes were as luck would have it. But in all these matters the world has the laugh of the philosopher, partly because he seems arrogant, partly because of his helpless ignorance in matters of daily life.

THEOD. Yes, Socrates, that is exactly what happens.

SOCR. On the other hand, my friend, when the philosopher drags the other upwards to a height at which he may [C] consent to drop the question "What injustice have I done to you or you to me?" and to think about justice and injustice in themselves, what each is, and how they differ from one another and from anything else;[13] or to stop quoting poetry about the happiness of kings or of men with gold in store and think about the meaning of kingship and the

---

[11] A clear allusion to the theory of Forms. The real object of knowledge is the Form "Man," not individual men.

[12] A constant feature of forensic speeches at Athens.

[13] The moral Forms are here openly mentioned, and there are allusions to the allegory of the Cave in *Rep.* vi.

whole question of human happiness and misery, what their nature is, and how humanity can gain the one and escape the other—in all this field, when that small, shrewd, legal mind has to render an account, then the situation is re- [D] versed. Now it is he who is dizzy from hanging at such an unaccustomed height and looking down from mid-air. Lost and dismayed and stammering, he will be laughed at, not by maidservants or the uneducated—they will not see what is happening—but by everyone whose breeding has been the antithesis of a slave's.

Such are the two characters, Theodorus. The one is nursed in freedom and leisure, the philosopher, as you call [E] him. He may be excused if he looks foolish or useless when faced with some menial task, if he cannot tie up bedclothes into a neat bundle or flavour a dish with spices and a speech with flattery. The other is smart in the dispatch of all such services, but has not learnt to wear his cloak like a gentleman, or caught the accent of discourse that will rightly celebrate the true life of [176] happiness for gods and men.

THEOD. If you could convince everyone, Socrates, as you convince me, there would be more peace and fewer evils in the world.

SOCR. Evils, Theodorus, can never be done away with, for the good must always have its contrary; nor have they any place in the divine world; but they must needs haunt this region of our mortal nature. That is why we should make all speed to take flight from this world to the other; and that means becoming like the divine so far as we [B] can, and that again is to become righteous with the help of wisdom. But it is no such easy matter to convince men that the reasons for avoiding wickedness and seeking after goodness are not those which the world gives. The right motive is not that one should seem innocent and good—that is no better, to my thinking, than an old wives' tale—but let us state

the truth in this way. In the divine [C] there is no shadow of unrighteousness, only the perfection of righteousness; and nothing is more like the divine than any one of us who becomes as righteous as possible. It is here that a man shows his true spirit and power or lack of spirit and nothingness. For to know this is wisdom and excellence of the genuine sort; not to know it is to be manifestly blind and base. All other forms of seeming power and intelligence in the rulers of society are as mean and vulgar as the mechanic's skill in handicraft. If a [D] man's words and deeds are unrighteous and profane, he had best not persuade himself that he is a great man because he sticks at nothing, glorying in his shame as such men do when they fancy that others say of them: They are no fools, no useless burdens to the earth, but men of the right sort to weather the storms of public life. Let the truth be told: they are what they fancy they are not, all the more for deceiving themselves; for they are ignorant of the very thing it most concerns them to know— the penalty of injustice. This is not, as they imagine, stripes and death, which do not always fall on the wrong-doer, but a penalty that cannot be escaped.    [E]

THEOD. What penalty is that?

SOCR. There are two patterns, my friend, in the unchangeable nature of things, one of divine happiness, the other of godless misery—a truth to which their folly makes them utterly blind, un- [177] aware that in doing injustice they are growing less like one of these patterns and more like the other. The penalty they pay is the life they lead, answering to the pattern they resemble. But if we tell them that, unless they rid themselves of their superior cunning, that other region which is free from all evil will not receive them after death, but here on earth they will dwell for all time in some form of life resembling their own and in the society of things as evil as themselves, all this will sound like foolishness to such strong and unscrupulous minds.

THEOD. So it will, Socrates.

SOCR. I have good reason to know [B] it, my friend. But there is one thing about them: when you get them alone and make them explain their objections to philosophy, then, if they are men enough to face a long examination without running away, it is odd how they end by finding their own arguments unsatisfying; somehow their flow of eloquency runs dry, and they become as speechless as an infant.

All this, however, is a digression; we must stop now, and dam the flood of topics that threatens to break in and [c] drown our original argument. With your leave, let us go back to where we were before.

THEOD. For my part, I rather prefer listening to your digressions, Socrates; they are easier to follow at my time of life. However, let us go back, if you like.

• • •

## Thinking

SOCR. Do you accept my de- [189E] scription of the process of thinking?

THEAET. How do you describe it?

SOCR. As a discourse that the mind carries on with itself about any subject it is considering. You must take this explanation as coming from an ignoramus; but I have a notion that, when the mind is thinking, it is simply talking to itself, asking questions and answering them, and saying Yes or No. When it reaches a decision—which may come slowly [190] or in a sudden rush—when doubt is over and the two voices affirm the same thing, then we call that its "judgment." So I should describe thinking as discourse, and judgment as a statement pronounced, not aloud to someone else, but silently to oneself.[14]

THEAET. I agree.

SOCR. It seems, then, that when a person thinks of one thing as another, he is

_____
14 This account of the process of thinking and judgment is repeated in the Sophist 263, see below.

affirming to himself that the one is the other.

• • •

## Conclusion                  [210]

SOCR. So, apparently, to the question, What is knowledge? our definition will reply: "Correct belief together with knowledge of a differentness"; for, according to it, "adding an account" will come to that.

THEAET. So it seems.

SOCR. Yes; and when we are inquiring after the nature of knowledge, nothing could be sillier than to say that it is correct belief together with a _knowledge_ of differentness or of anything whatever.

So, Theaetetus, neither perception, nor true belief, nor the addition of an "account" to true belief can be knowledge.                                   [B]

THEAET. Apparently not.

SOCR. Are we in labour, then, with any further child, my friend, or have we brought to birth all we have to say about knowledge?

THEAET. Indeed we have; and for my part I have already, thanks to you, given utterance to more than I had in me.

SOCR. All of which our midwife's skill pronounces to be mere wind-eggs and not worth the rearing?

THEAET. Undoubtedly.

SOCR. Then supposing you should ever henceforth try to conceive afresh, Theaetetus, if you succeed, your embryo [c] thoughts will be the better as a consequence of to-day's scrutiny; and if you remain barren, you will be gentler and more agreeable to your companions, having the good sense not to fancy you know what you do not know. For that, and no more, is all that my art can effect; nor have I any of that knowledge possessed by all the great and admirable men of our own day or of the past. But this midwife's art is a gift from heaven; my mother had it for women, and I [D] for young men of a generous spirit and for all in whom beauty dwells.

Now I must go to the portico of the

King Archon to meet the indictment
which Meletus has drawn up against me.

But to-morrow morning, Theodorus, let
us meet here again.

## THE SOPHIST (in part : 216-18, 234-end)

PERSONS OF THE DIALOGUE

THEODORUS     *A* STRANGER *from Elea*
SOCRATES       THEAETETUS

### Introductory Conversation

THEODORUS. Here we are, Socra- [216]
tes, faithful to our appointment of yesterday; and, what is more, we have
brought a guest with us. Our friend here
is a native of Elea; he belongs to the
school of Parmenides and Zeno, and is
devoted to philosophy.

SOCRATES. Perhaps, Theodorus, it is no
ordinary guest but some god that you
have brought us unawares. Homer[1] [B]
tells us that gods attend upon the goings
of men of mercy and justice; and not
least among them the God of Strangers
comes to mark the orderly or lawless
doings of mankind. Your companion may
be one of those higher powers, who intends to observe and expose our weakness in philosophic discourse, like a very
spirit of refutation.

THEOD. That is not our friend's way,
Socrates; he is more reasonable than the
devotees of verbal dispute. I should not
call him a god by any means; but there
is something divine about him: I [C]
would say that of any philosopher.

SOCR. And rightly, my friend; but one
might almost say that the type you mention is hardly easier to discern than the
god. Such men—the genuine, not the
sham philosophers—as they go from city
to city surveying from a height the life
beneath them, appear, owing to the
world's blindness, to wear all sorts of
shapes. To some they seem of no account,
to others above all worth; now they wear

the guise of statesmen, now of sophists;
and sometimes they may give the im- [D]
pression of simply being mad. But if our
guest will allow me, I should like to ask
him what his countrymen thought and
how they used these names.          [217]

THEOD. What names?

SOCR. Sophist, Statesman, Philosopher.

THEOD. What is your question exactly?
What sort of difficulty about these names
have you in mind?

SOCR. This: did they think of all these
as a single type, or as two, or did they
distinguish three types and attach one of
the three corresponding names to each?

THEOD. I imagine you are quite welcome to the information. Is not that so,
sir?

STRANGER. Yes, Theodorus, perfect- [B]
ly welcome; and the answer is not difficult. They thought of them as three
different types; but it is not so short and
easy a task to define each one of them
clearly.

THEOD. As luck would have it, Socrates, you have hit upon a subject closely
allied to one on which we were pressing
him with questions before we came here.
He tried to put us off with the same
excuse he has just made to you, though
he admits he has been thoroughly instructed and has not forgotten what he
heard.

SOCR. Do not deny us, then, the [C]
first favour we ask. Tell us this much:
which do you commonly prefer—to discourse at length by yourself on any matter you wish to make clear, or to use the
method of asking questions, as Parmenides himself did on one occasion in
developing some magnificent arguments
in my presence, when I was young and
he quite an elderly man?

---

[1] *Odyssey* ix, 270, and xvii, 483.

STR. When the other party to the [D] conversation is tractable and gives no trouble, to address him is the easier course; otherwise, to speak by oneself.

SOCR. Then you may choose any of the company you will; they will all follow you and respond amenably. But if you take my advice, you will choose one of the younger men—Theaetetus here or any other you may prefer.

STR. I feel some shyness, Socrates, at the notion that, at my first meeting with you and your friends, instead of exchanging our ideas in the give and take of ordinary conversation, I should [E] spin out a long discourse by myself or even address it to another, as if I were giving a display of eloquence.[2] For indeed the question you have just raised is not so easy a matter as one might suppose, on hearing it so simply put, but it calls for a very long discussion. On the other hand, to refuse you and your friends a request, especially one put to me in such terms as you have used, strikes me as a breach of civility in a guest. That Theaetetus should be the other party to our conversation is a [218] proposal which my earlier talk with him, as well as your recommendation, makes exceedingly welcome.

THEAETETUS. Then do as you say, sir; you will, as Socrates said, be conferring a favour on us all.

STR. On this point, Theaetetus, no more need be said; the discussion from now onwards must, it seems, be carried on with you. But if the long task should after all weigh heavy on you, your

friends here, not I, must bear the blame.

THEAET. I do not feel at this mo- [B] ment as if I should sink under it; but should something of that sort happen, we will call in Socrates' namesake here, who is of my own age and shares my pursuits. He is quite used to working out most questions with me.

STR. A good suggestion: that shall be for you to consider as our conversation goes forward. What now concerns us both is our joint inquiry. We had better, I think, begin by studying the Sophist and try to bring his nature to light in a clear formula.                              [C]

*        *        *

STR. About the Sophist: tell me, is it now clear that he is a sort of wizard, an imitator of real things—or are we [235] still uncertain whether he may not possess genuine knowledge of all the things he seems capable of disputing about?

THEAET. He cannot, sir. It is clear enough from what has been said that he is one of those whose province is play.

STR. Then we may class him as a wizard and an imitator of some sort.

THEAET. Certainly.

*Division of Image-making into two species*                        [235A-236C]

STR. Come then, it is now for us to see that we do not again relax the pursuit of our quarry. We may say that we have [B] him enveloped in such a net as argument provides for hunting of this sort. He cannot shuffle out of this.

THEAET. Out of what?

STR. Out of being somewhere within the class of illusionists.[3]

THEAET. So far I quite agree with you.

STR. Agreed then that we should at once quarter the ground by dividing the art of Image-making, and if, as soon as

---

[2] Three alternative procedures are suggested: (1) an unbroken monologue, such as the rhetorical Sophists preferred; (2) an exposition "addressed to another," *i.e.* cast in the form of questions, to which the respondent merely answers "yes" or "no" as required (ὑπακούειν), like the young Aristotle in the *Parmenides*; (3) a genuine conversation, to which the respondent makes a real contribution. The Stranger's preference for the third marks that he understands "dialectic" as Plato understood it.

[3] θαυματοποιῶν means specially the puppet-showman, but it is used here to cover all species of "imitators"—artists and poets as well as Sophists. (cf. 224A). They are all "creators of *eidola*."

we descend into that enclosure, we meet with the Sophist at bay, we should [c] arrest him on the royal warrant of reason, report the capture, and hand him over to the sovereign.[4] But if he should find some lurking-place among the subdivisions of this art of imitation, we must follow hard upon him, constantly dividing the part that gives him shelter, until he is caught. In any event there is no fear that he or any other kind shall ever boast of having eluded a process of investigation so minute and so comprehensive.

THEAET. Good; that is the way to go to work.

STR. Following, then, the same method of division as before, I seem once more to make out two forms of imitation; [D] but as yet I do not feel able to discover in which of the two the type we are seeking is to be found.

THEAET. Make your division first, at any rate, and tell us what two forms you mean.

STR. One art that I see contained in it is the making of likenesses (eikastiké). The perfect example of this consists in creating a copy that conforms to the proportions of the original in all three dimensions and giving moreover the proper colour to every part.          [E]

THEAET. Why, is not that what all imitators try to do?

STR. Not those sculptors or painters whose works are of colossal size. If they were to reproduce the true proportions of a well-made figure,[5] as you know, the upper parts would look tco small, and the lower too large, because we see the one at a distance, the other close at hand.                     [236]

THEAET. That is true.

STR. So artists, leaving the truth to take care of itself, do in fact put into the images they make, not the real proportions, but those that will appear beautiful.

THEAET. Quite so.

STR. The first kind of image, then, being like the original, may fairly be called a likeness (eikon).

THEAET. Yes.

STR. And the corresponding sub- [B] division of the art of imitation may be called by the name we used just now— Likeness-making.

THEAET. It may.

STR. Now, what are we to call the kind which only appears to be a likeness of a well-made figure because it is not seen from a satisfactory point of view, but to a spectator with eyes that could fully take in so large an object would not be even like the original it professes to resemble? Since it seems to be a likeness, but is not really so, may we not call it a semblance (phantasma)?

THEAET. By all means.

STR. And this is a very extensive class, in painting and in imitation of all [c] sorts.

THEAET. True.

STR. So the best name for the art which creates, not a likeness, but a

---

4 Apelt illustrates the allusion to the Persian method (called "draw-netting," σαγηνεία) of sweeping up the whole population of a district by means of a line of soldiers holding hands and marching across it. It is several times mentioned by Herodotus (e.g. vi, 31); and Plato (Laws 698D) says that Datis, ten years before Salamis, sent word to Athens that he had captured all the Eretrians by this method, under Darius' orders (the "royal warrant") to transport all Eretrians and Athenians to Persia. The method is an admirable image for the procedure of the last section which has drawn the notion of Image-making or Imitation like a net around all the types called "Sophists" collected for review. The net also includes other "imitators," all the varieties of artist.

5 "Well-made" (καλῶν), because what is in question is not improving the proportions of an ill-made model to conform to canons of beauty, but altering the proportions which are really beautiful so as to keep the appearance of beauty. Apelt mentions that, in the Epicurean inscription on a wall at Oenoanda, the letters in the top lines are cut larger than those in the lower, so that all may look the same size from below.

semblance will be Semblance-making (*phantastiké*).

THEAET. Quite so.

STR. These, then, are the two forms of image-making I meant—the making of likenesses and the making of semblances.

THEAET. Good.

*Statement of the problems of unreal appearances and of falsity in speech and thought* [236c-237b]

STR. Yes; but even now I cannot see clearly how to settle the doubt I then expressed: under which of the two arts (likeness-making and semblance-making) we must place the Sophist. It is really surprising how hart it is to get a clear view of the man. At this very [D] moment he has, with admirable cleverness, taken refuge in a class[6] which baffles investigation.

THEAET. So it seems.

STR. You assent, but do you recognise the class I mean, or has the current of the argument carried you along to agree so readily from force of habit?

THEAET. How? What are you referring to?

STR. The truth is, my friend, that we are faced with an extremely difficult question. This "appearing" or "seem- [E] ing" without really "being" and the saying of something which yet is not true— all these expressions have always been and still are deeply involved in perplexity. It is extremely hard, Theaetetus, to find correct terms in which one may say or think that falsehoods have a real existence, without being caught in a contradiction by the mere utterance of such words.[7] [237]

THEAET. Why?

STR. The audacity of the statement

lies in its implication that "what is not" has being; for in no other way could a falsehood come to have being. But, my young friend, when we were of your age the great Parmenides from beginning to end testified against this, constantly telling us what he also says in his poem:

"Never shall this be proved—that things that are not are; but do thou, in thy inquiry, hold back thy thought from this way."[8]

So we have the great man's testimony, [B] and the best way to obtain a confession of the truth may be to put the statement itself to a mild degree of torture.[9] So, if it makes no difference to you, let us begin by studying it on its own merits.

THEAET. I am at your disposal. As for the argument, you must consider the way that will best lead to a conclusion, and take me with you along it.

STR. It shall be done.

I

## The Worlds of Reality and Appearance

(*a*) *The totally unreal* [237b-239c]

STR. (*continues*) Now tell me: we do not hesitate to utter the phrase "that which has no sort of being"?[10]

THEAET. Surely not.

STR. Then setting aside disputation for its own sake[11] and playing with words, suppose one of this company were seri-

---

6 Namely "unreal appearance and falsity."

7 Falsehoods being "things which are not," as the Stranger next remarks. A common equivalent of "speaking falsely" is "saying the thing that is not," see *Theaet.* 1884 ff. (p. 114). Campbell correctly interprets the construction. ψευδῆ is placed where it stands for emphasis.

8 *Parmenides*, frag. 7.

9 The statement itself (that falsehood, or what is not, really exists) is compared to a slave belonging to the *other* party in the suit, against whom Parmenides has borne witness. The immediate sequel submits this statement (not Parmenides) to examination. Parmenides' own statement will be put to the question later (τὸν τοῦ πατρὸς Παρμενίδου ἀναγκαῖον ... βασανίζειν, 241D).

10 τὸ μηδαμῶς ὄν, the "totally unreal" or "absolute nonentity." We can "utter this phrase" (φθέγγεσθαι), but it will be shown to have no meaning.

11 The problems to be stated had figured in Eristic debate, but our purpose is to face the real difficulties seriously.

ously required to concentrate his mind and tell us to what this name can be [c] applied—"that which is not." Of what thing or of what sort of thing should we expect him to use it himself, and what would he indicate by it to the inquirer?

THEAET. That is a hard question. It is scarcely for a person like me to find an answer at all.

STR. Well, this much is clear at any rate: that the term "what is not" must not be applied to anything that exists.

THEAET. Certainly not.

STR. And since it cannot be applied to what exists, neither can it properly be applied to "something."

THEAET. How so?

STR. Surely we can see that this [D] expression "something" is always used of a thing that exists. We cannot use it just by itself in naked isolation from everything that exists, can we?

THEAET. No.

STR. Is your assent due to the reflection that to speak of "something" is to speak of "some *one* thing"?[12]

THEAET. Yes.

STR. Because you will admit that "something" stands for one thing, as "some things" for two or more.

THEAET. Certainly.

STR. So it seems to follow neces- [E] sarily that to speak of what is not "something" is to speak of no thing at all.

THEAET. Necessarily.

STR. Must we not even refuse to allow that in such a case a person is *saying*

something, though he may be speaking of nothing? Must we not assert that he is not even saying anything when he sets about uttering the sounds "a thing that is not"?

THEAET. That would certainly bring the argument to the last pitch of perplexity.

STR. "No time for boasting yet." [238] There is more to come, in fact the chief of all the difficulties and the first, for it goes to the very root of the matter.

THEAET. How do you mean? Do not hesitate to state it.

STR. When a thing exists, I suppose something else that exists may be attributed to it.

THEAET. Certainly.

STR. But can we say it is possible for something that exists to be attributed to what has no existence?

THEAET. How could it be?

STR. Well, among things that exist we include number in general.

THEAET. Yes, number must exist, if anything does.                                [B]

STR. We must not, then, so much as attempt to attach either plurality or unity in number of the non-existent.

THEAET. That would certainly seem to be wrong, according to our argument.

STR. How then can anyone utter the words "things which are not," or "that which is not," or even conceive such things in his mind at all, apart from number?

THEAET. How do you mean?

STR. When we speak of *"things* that are not," are we not undertaking to attribute plurality to them?                [c]

THEAET. Yes.

STR. And unity, when we speak of *"that* which is not"?

THEAET. Clearly.

STR. And yet we admit that it is not justifiable or correct to set about attaching something that exists to the non-existent.

THEAET. Quite true.

STR. You see the inference then: one cannot legitimately utter the words, or

---

12 The accident that English confines "some *one*" and "no *one*" to persons, "some*thing*," "*nothing*" to things, makes translation awkward. Greek has (1) τις, "some" (masc. someone, neut. something) with (in poetry) its contradictory οὔτις "not-some" (masc. no-one, neut. nothing); and (2) οὐδείς "not even one" (masc. no-one, neut. no-thing) with its regular contradictory εἴς γέ τις, at least *some* one" (masc. *some*one, neut. *some*thing), which is used here, and has to be rendered "some *one* thing," in order to introduce the word "one."

speak or think of that which just simply is not; it is unthinkable, not to be spoken of or uttered or expressed.[13]

THEAET. Quite true.

STR. Perhaps then I was mistaken [D] in saying just now that I was going to state the greatest difficulty it presents; whereas there is a worse one still that we can formulate.

THEAET. What is that?

STR. I am surprised you do not see from the very phrases I have just used that the non-existent reduces even one who is refuting its claims[14] to such straits that, as soon as he sets about doing so, he is forced to contradict himself.

THEAET. How? Explain more clearly.

STR. You must not look to me for illumination. I who laid it down that the non-existent could have neither [E] unity nor plurality, have not only just now but at this very moment spoken of it as one thing: for I am saying "*the* non-existent." You see what I mean?

THEAET. Yes.

STR. And again a little while ago I was speaking of its *being* a thing not to be uttered or spoken of or expressed. Do you follow?

THEAET. Yes, of course.

STR. Well, then, in trying to apply that term "being" to it, was I not contradicting what I said before?[15]          [239]

THEAET. Evidently.

STR. And again in applying the term "the," was I not addressing it as singular?[16]

THEAET. Yes.

STR. And again in speaking of it as "a thing not to be expressed or spoken of or uttered," I was using language as if referring to a single thing.

THEAET. Certainly.

STR. Whereas we are admitting that, if we are to speak strictly, we ought not to specify it as either one thing or many or even to call it "it" at all; for even that appellation means ascribing to it the character of singleness.

THEAET. Quite so.

STR. In that case there is nothing [B] to be said for me. I shall be found to have had the worst of it, now and all along, in my criticism of the non-existent. Accordingly, as I said, we must not look to anything I have to say for the correct way of describing the non-existent; we must turn to you for that. Come along now.

THEAET. What do you mean?

STR. Come, you are young; show your spirit and make the best effort you can. Try, without attributing being or unity or plurality to the nonexistent, to find some form of words describing it correctly.

THEAET. I should need an extra- [C] ordinary zeal for such an enterprise in face of what has happened to you.

(*b*) *Definition of* eidolon [239c-242B] *and the problem of false statement and belief*

STR. Well, if you agree, we will leave ourselves out of account; and until we meet with someone who can perform this feat, let us say that the Sophist with extreme cunning has found an impenetrable lurking-place.[17]

THEAET. It certainly seems so.

---

13 ἄλογον not "irrational," but "incapable of being expressed in discourse" (λόγος). There is no *meaning* conveyed (cf. *Parm.* 142A). ἄρρητον means that there is nothing for the words to *refer to*. Plato is echoing Parmenides' warning against the "Way of Not-Being," "to leave that way as unthinkable, unnameable; for it is no true way" (frag. 8, 15).

14 Refuting any claim it might make to "being." I cannot even deny its existence without contradicting myself by speaking of it at all.

15 The reference is to 238A: nothing that has existence must be attributed to the non-existent. "Being" (τὸ εἶναι) is something that exists, in the same sense that number exists.

16 Read τὸ "τὸ" for τοῦτο

17 It must be remembered that the various senses of "that which is not" are only gradually being disclosed. The Sophist does not lurk in the region of nonentity, above dealt with, but in the field of the not wholly read and the false which we are now entering.

STR. Accordingly, if we are going to say he possesses an art of creating "semblances," he will readily take advan- [D] tage of our handling our arguments in this way to grapple with us and turn them against ourselves. When we call him a maker of images, he will ask what on earth we mean in speaking of an "image" at all. So we must consider, Theaetetus, how this truculent person's question is to be answered.

THEAET. Clearly we shall say we mean images in water or in mirrors, and again images made by the draughtsman or the sculptor, and any other things of that sort.

STR. It is plain, Theaetetus, that you have never seen a Sophist.          [E]

THEAET. Why?

STR. He will make as though his eyes were shut or he had no eyes at all.

THEAET. How so?

STR. When you offer him your answer in such terms, if you speak of something to be found in mirrors or in sculpture, he will laugh at your words, as implying that he can see. He will profess to [240] know nothing about mirrors or water or even eyesight, and will confine his question to what can be gathered from discourse.

THEAET. Namely?

STR. The common character in all these things you mentioned and thought fit to call by a single name when you used the expression "image" as one term covering them all. State it, then, and hold your ground against the man without yielding an inch.

THEAET. Well, sir, what could we say an image was, if not another thing of the same sort, copied from the real thing?

STR. "Of the same sort"? Do you [2] mean another real thing, or what does "of the same sort" signify?

THEAET. Certainly not real, but like it.

STR. Meaning by "real" a thing that really exists.

THEAET. Yes.

STR. And by "not real" the opposite of real?

THEAET. Of course.

STR. Then by what is "like" you mean what has not real existence,[18] if you are going to call it "not real."

THEAET. But it has some sort of existence.

STR. Only not real existence, according to you.

THEAET. No; except that it is really a likeness.

STR. So, not having real existence, it really is what we call a likeness?[19]

THEAET. Real and unreal do seem [C] to be combined in that perplexing way, and very queer it is.

STR. Queer indeed. You see that now again by dovetailing them together in this way our hydra-headed Sophist has forced us against our will to admit that "what is not" has some sort of being.

THEAET. Yes, I do.

STR. And what now? How can we define his art without contradicting ourselves?

THEAET. How do you mean? What sort of contradiction do you fear?

STR. When we say that he deceives [D] with that semblance we spoke of and that his art is a practice of deception, shall we be saying that, as the effect of his art, our mind thinks what is false, or what shall we mean?

THEAET. Just that. What else could we mean?

STR. And false thinking, again, will be thinking things contrary to the things that are?[20]

_____

18 Reading ὀυκ ὄντως [ὀυκ] ὄν with Burnet and others.

19 Reading ὀυκ ὂν ἄρα [ὀυκ] ὄντως The subject "it" is, as in the previous sentences, τό ἐοικός, i.e. εἴδωλον the term we are defining. The paradox lies in saying that an εἴ δωλον, which is not real, really is a likeness.

20 "The things that are." "The facts" would be a more natural translation, but at this stage it seems better to keep the vaguer expression. "Things that are not" (falsehoods) are things which are contrary to the facts and yet must have some sort of being, for we have already said that we cannot think sheer nonentity.

THEAET. Yes.

STR. You mean, then, by false thinking, thinking things that are not?

THEAET. Necessarily.

STR. Does that mean thinking that [E] things that are not, are not, or that things that are not in any way, in some way are?

THEAET. It must at least mean thinking that things that are not[21] are in some way, if anyone is ever to be in error even to the smallest extent.

STR. And also surely thinking that things which certainly[22] are, are not in any way at all?

THEAET. Yes.

STR. That also is error?

THEAET. Yes, that also.

STR. And a false statement,[23] I suppose, is to be regarded in the same light, as stating that things that are, are [241] not, and that things that are not, are.

THEAET. Yes. How else could it be false?

STR. Hardly in any other way. But the Sophist will deny that. How could a sensible man agree, when the admissions we made earlier are set beside this one? We understand, Theaetetus, what he is referring to?

THEAET. Of course we understand. He will say that we are contradicting what was said just now, when we have the [B] face to say that falsehoods exist in thoughts and in statements; for we are constantly being obliged to attribute

what has being to what is not, after agreeing just now that this was altogether impossible.[24]

STR. Your recollection is correct. But you must now consider what we are to do about the Sophist; for if we pursue our search for him by ranking him under the art of the illusionists and creators of error, you see what an easy opening we offer to many perplexities and counterattacks.

THEAET. I do.

STR. They are almost without num- [3] ber and we have stated only a small fraction of them.

THEAET. If that is so, it looks as if it were impossible to catch the Sophist.

STR. What then? Are we to lose heart and give up now?

THEAET. I don't think we ought to, if we have the least chance of being able to lay hands on him somehow.

STR. Then I may count on your indulgence, and, as you now say, you will be content if we can by some twist free ourselves, even to the least extent, from the grip of so powerful an argument?

THEAET. By all means.

STR. Then I have another still more pressing request.                          [D]

THEAET. What is that?

STR. That you will not think I am turning into a sort of parricide.

THEAET. In what way?

STR. We shall find it necessary in self-defence to put to the question that pronouncement of father Parmenides, and establish by main force[25] that what is not, in some respect has being, and conversely that what is, in a way is not.

THEAET. It is plain that the course of the argument requires us to maintain that at all costs.

---

21 Theaetetus does not repeat the Stranger's suggestion τὰ μηδαμῶς ὄντα, but correctly substitutes τὰ μὴ ὄντα, things which are *not the fact,* but are not (as μηδαμῶς might suggest) sheer nonentities.

22 πάντως, "in any case": "things which *certainly* have being" (not παντελῶς, "things which have the *fullest* sort of being or reality"). The whole means "denying any existence to facts which certainly do exist."

23 "Statement" is the best rendering for λόγος not "proposition," because of its modern uses. For Plato a "statement" is simply the utterance in speech of a judgment made by the mind in its silent dialogue with itself (263E, and *Theaet.* 189E, 206D, 208C).

24 This is the "earlier admission" referred to: "Nothing that exists (such as "Being") must be attributed to the non-existent" (238A), an admission already recalled at 238E.

25 βιάζεσθαι may allude to Parmenides' own word δαμῇ (δαμάζω) in the lines quoted above.

STR. Plain enough for the blind to [E] see, as they say. Unless these propositions are either refuted or accepted, anyone who talks of false statements or false judgment as being images or likenesses or copies or semblances, or of any of the arts concerned with such things, can hardly escape becoming a laughing-stock by being forced to contradict himself.

THEAET. Quite true.

STR. That is why we must now [242] dare to lay unfilial hands on that pronouncement, or else, if some scruple holds us back, drop the matter entirely.

THEAET. As for that, we must let no scruple hinder us.

STR. In that case, for the third time, I have a small favour to ask.

THEAET. You have only to mention it.

STR. I believe I confessed just now that on this point the task of refutation has always proved too much for my powers, and still does so.

THEAET. You did say that.

STR. Well, that confession, I am afraid, may make you think me scatter-brained when at every turn I shift my [B] position to and fro. It is for your satisfaction that we shall attempt to refute the pronouncement, if we can refute it.

THEAET. Then you may take it that I shall never think you are overstepping the limits by entering on your refutation and proof. So far as that goes, you may proceed with an easy mind.

*(c) The perfectly Real. What does "real" mean?*[26]          [242B-244B]

STR. Come then, where is one to make a start on so hazardous a theme? I think I see the path we must inevitably follow.

THEAET. And that is——?

STR. To take first things that are [C]

now supposed to be quite clear[27] and see whether we are not in some confusion about them and too easily reaching conclusions on the assumption that we understand them well enough.

THEAET. Tell me more plainly what you mean.

STR. It strikes me that Parmenides and everyone else who has set out to determine how many real things there are and what they are like, have discoursed to us in rather an off-hand fashion.

THEAET. How so?

STR. They each and all seem to treat us as children to whom they are telling a story. According to one there are three real things, some of which now carry on a sort of warfare with one another, [D] and then make friends and set about marrying and begetting and bringing up their children. Another tells us that there are two—Moist and Dry, or Hot and Cold—whom he marries off, and makes them set up house together.[28] In our part of the world the Eleatic set, who hark back to Xenophanes or even earlier, unfold their tale on the assumption that what we call "all things" are only one thing. Later, certain Muses in Ionia and Sicily perceived that safety lay rather in combining both accounts and saying [E] that the real is both many and one and is held together by enmity and friendship. "In parting asunder it is always being drawn together" say the stricter[29]

---

26 In the coming section τὸ ὄν will be translated by "the real" or "reality." This sense of the word has emerged from the contrast between the "sort of existence" belonging to an *eidolon*, and the real existence of the ὄντως ὄν.

27 Namely, the meaning of "real," a word we all use and imagine we understand.

28 Plato recognises in the pre-Socratic systems the presence of mythical images, especially the two most important: the sex-imagery of the cosmic Eros, and the warfare of opposed "powers" (such as Hot and Cold). These images of Love and Strife can be traced all through the ancient science of nature, and survive even in Atomism as the Venus and Mars of Lucretius.

29 The stricter Muses of Ionia represent the philosophy of Heracleitus. It was a main point of his doctrine that the Harmony of Opposite essentially involves a tension or strife that is never resolved. There is no peace without war.

of these Muses. The milder[30] relax the rule that this should always be so and tell us of alternate states, in which [243] the universe is now one and at peace through the power of Love, and now many and at war with itself owing to some sort of Strife.

In all this, whether any one of them has told the truth or not is a hard question, and it is in bad taste to find fault so grossly with men of long-established fame. But one observation may be made without offence.

THEAET. And that is——?

STR. That they have shown too little consideration for ordinary people like ourselves in talking over our heads. [B] Each school pursues its own argument to the conclusion without caring whether we follow what they say or get left behind.

THEAET. How do you mean?

STR. When one or another of them in his discourse uses these expressions "there really are" or "have come to be" or "are coming to be" "many things" or "one thing" or "two," or again another speaks[31] of "Hot being mixed with Cold," assuming "combinations" and "separations," do you, Theaetetus understand a single word they say? Speaking for myself, when I was younger I thought I understood quite clearly when someone spoke of this thing that is now puzzling us—"the unreal." But now you see how completely perplexed we are about that.

THEAET. I do.                         [C]

STR. Possibly, then, our minds are in

the same state of confusion about reality. We profess to be quite at our ease about the real and to understand the word when it is spoken though we may not understand the unreal, when perhaps we are equally in the dark about both.

THEAET. Perhaps.

STR. And we may take it that the same is true of the other expressions I have just mentioned.

THEAET. Certainly.

STR. The general run of these expressions we will consider later, if we so decide. We must begin now with the [D] chief and most important of them all.

THEAET. Which is that? Of course you mean we ought to begin by studying "reality" and finding out what those who use the word think it stands for.

STR. You have hit my meaning precisely, Theaetetus; I do mean that we must take this line. Imagine them here before us, and let us put this question: "You who say that Hot and Cold or some such pair *really are* all things, what exactly does this expression convey [E] that you apply to both when you say that they both are 'real' or each of them is 'real'? How are we to understand this 'reality' you speak of? Are we to suppose it is a third thing alongside the other two and that the All is no longer, as you say, two things, but three? For surely you do not give the name 'reality' to one of the two and then say that both alike are real; for then there will be only one thing, whichever of the two it may be, and not two."

THEAET. True.

STR. "Well then, do you intend to give the name 'reality' to the pair of them?"

THEAET. Perhaps.

STR. "But that again," we shall [244] object, "will clearly be speaking of your two things as one."

THEAET. You are quite right.

STR. "We are completely puzzled, then, and you must clear up the question for us, what you do intend to signify when you use the word 'real.' Obviously you

---

[30] The milder Muses of Sicily (Empedocles) recognised a Reign of Love (without Strife) and, at the opposite pole, a Reign of Strife (without Love). Between these polar states, worlds come into being and pass away. In one half of the cycle a world is formed by Love gaining upon Strife, in the other, by Strife gaining upon Love.

[31] Reading ἄλλος εἴπῃ (Rademacher, Diès) for ἄλλοθί πῃ, which is pointless, whether it means "elsewhere in his discourse" or "elsewhere in the universe."

must be quite familiar with what you mean, whereas we, who formerly imagined we knew, are now at a loss. First, then, enlighten us on just this point, so that we may not fancy we understand what you have to tell us, when in fact we are as far as possible from under- [B] standing."

If we put our case in that way to these people and to any others who say that the All is more than one thing, will there be anything unwarrantable in our request?

THEAET. Not at all.

### Criticism of Parmenides' [244B-245E] One Real Being

STR. Again, there are those who say that the All is one thing. Must we not do our best to find out what they mean by "reality"?

THEAET. Surely.

STR. Let them answer this question, then: "You say, we understand, that there is only one thing?" "We do," they will reply, won't they?

THEAET. Yes.

STR. "And there is something to which you give the name *real?*"

THEAET. Yes.

STR. "Is it the same thing as that [C] to which you give the name *one?* Are you applying two names to the same thing, or what do you mean?"

THEAET. What will their next answer be?

STR. Obviously, Theaetetus, it is not so very easy for one who has laid down their fundamental assertion to answer this question or any other.

THEAET. How so?

STR. In the first place, it is surely absurd for him to admit the existence of *two* names, when he has laid down that there is no more than one thing.

THEAET. Of course.

STR. And further, it is equally [D] absurd to allow anyone to assert that a name can have any existence, when that would be inexplicable.

THEAET. How is it inexplicable?

STR. If, on the one hand, he assumes that the name is different from the thing, he is surely speaking of *two* things.

THEAET. Yes.

STR. Whereas, if he assumes that the name is the same as the thing, either he will have to say it is not the name of anything, or if he says it is the name of something, it will follow that the name is merely a name of a name and of nothing else whatsoever.

THEAET. That is so.

STR. . . . [32]

THEAET. Necessarily.

STR. And what of "the whole"? Will they say that this is other than their "one real thing" or the same?

THEAET. Certainly that is the same. [E] In fact they do say so.

STR. Then if it is a whole—as indeed Parmenides says:[33]

---

[32] The dilemma stated in the Stranger's last two speeches is complete. It has been shown that the very existence of a name is inexplicable, whether it be distinct from the thing or identical with it. This argument applies equally to the name "real" and to the name "one," and there is no need for any special application of it to the name "one." The speech here omitted is corrupt. It looks as if it might be intended to make that special application; but since that is not wanted, it is impossible to restore the sense with any probability. The oldest evidence for the text is Simplicius, *Phys.* 89: καὶ τὸ ἕν γε ἑνὸς ἓν (ἕν om. D) ὂν μόνον καὶ τοῦ ὀνόματος αὐτὸ ἓν ὄν. This (including ἕν) agrees with the Bodleian (B) of Plato. The view that ἑνὸς ἕν can mean "unity of a unity" is rightly rejected by Ritter (*N. Unters.* 15), who adopts the reading of T: καὶ τὸ ἕν γε ἑνὸς ὂν μόνον (SC. ὄνομα συμβήσεται), καὶ τοῦτο ὀνόματος, αὐτὸ ⟨τὸ?⟩ ἓν ὄν, "And it will result too that One (they talk of) will be the name of itself only, and *that* the name (not of a different objective reality, but) of a name (the name "one"), while yet it is the One itself." The last words here are barely intelligible, and the whole statement seems to have no point. If the speech, together with Theaetetus' previous reply οὕτως, were simply omitted, it would not be missed.

[33] Frag. 8, 43.

"Every way like the mass of a well-rounded sphere, evenly balanced from the midst in every direction; for there must not be something more nor something less here than there"—

if the real is like that, it has a middle and extremities, and consequently it must have parts, must it not?

THEAET. It must.

STR. Well, if a thing is divided [245] into parts, there is nothing against its having the property of unity as applied to the aggregate of all the parts and being in that way one, as being a sum or whole.

THEAET. Of course.

STR. On the other hand, the thing which has these properties cannot be just Unity itself, can it?

THEAET. Why not?

STR. Surely Unity in the true sense and rightly defined must be altogether without parts.

THEAET. Yes, it must.

STR. Whereas a thing such as we [B] described, consisting of several parts, will not answer to that definition.

THEAET. I see.

STR. Then, (A) is the Real one and a whole in the sense that it has the property of unity, or (B) are we to say that the Real is not a whole at all?

THEAET. That is a hard choice.

STR. Quite true. For if (A) the real has the property of being in a sense one, it will evidently not be the same thing as Unity, and so all things will be more than one.

THEAET. Yes.

STR. And again (B) if the Real is [C] not a whole by virtue of having this property of unity while (a) at the same time Wholeness itself is real, it follows that the Real falls short of itself.

THEAET. Certainly.

STR. So, on this line of argument too, the Real will be deprived of reality and will not be a thing that is.

THEAET. Yes.

STR. And further, once more all things will be more than one, since Reality on the one side and Wholeness on the other have now each a distinct nature.

THEAET. Yes.

STR. But if, (b) on the other hand, there is no such thing as Wholeness at all, not only are the same things true of the Real, but also that, besides not being a thing that really is, it could never even become such.

THEAET. Why not?                              [D]

STR. Whenever a thing comes into being, at that moment it has come to be as a whole; accordingly, if you do not reckon unity or wholeness among real things, you have no right to speak of either being or coming-into-being as having any existence.

THEAET. That seems perfectly true.

STR. And further, what is not a whole cannot have any definite number either; for if a thing has a definite number, it must amount to that number, whatever it may be, as a whole.

THEAET. Assuredly.

STR. And countless other difficul- [E] ties, each involved in measureless perplexity, will arise, if you say that the real is either two things or only one.

THEAET. That is plain enough from those we have had a glimpse of now. One leads to another, and each carries us further into a wilderness of doubt about every theory as it is mentioned.

*The Battle of Gods and* [245E-246E] *Giants: Idealists and Materialists*

STR. So much, then, for those who give an exact account of what is real or unreal. We have not gone through them all, but let this suffice. Now we must turn to look at those who put the matter in a different way, so that, from a complete review of all, we may see that reality is just as hard to define as unreality.

THEAET. We had better go on, then, to their position.

STR. What we shall see[34] is [246A]

34 καὶ μήν, as in tragedy, where a person on the stage calls attention to the entry of a fresh character.

something like a Battle of Gods and Giants going on between them over their quarrel about reality.

THEAET. How so?

STR. One party is trying to drag everything down to earth out of heaven and the unseen, literally grasping rocks and trees in their hands; for they lay hold upon every stock and stone and strenuously affirm that real existence belongs only to that which can be handled and offers resistance to the touch. They define reality as the same thing a body, [B] and as soon as one of the opposite party asserts that anything without a body is real, they are utterly contemptuous and will not listen to another word.

THEAET. The people you describe are certainly a formidable crew. I have met quite a number of them before now.

STR. Yes, and accordingly their adversaries are very wary in defending their position somewhere in the heights of the unseen, maintaining with all their force that true reality consists in certain intelligible and bodiless Forms. In the clash of argument they shatter and pulverise those bodies which their opponents [c] wield, and what those others allege to be true reality they call, not real being, but a sort of moving process of becoming. On this issue an interminable battle is always going on between the two camps.

THEAET. True.

STR. Suppose, then, we challenge each party in turn to render an account of the reality they assert.

THEAET. How shall we do so?

STR. It will be easier to obtain from those who place reality in Forms, because they are more civilised; harder, [D] from those whose violence would drag everything down to the level of body— perhaps, all but impossible. However, I think I see the right way to deal with them.

THEAET. What is that?

STR. Best of all, if it were anyhow possible, would be to bring about a real change of heart; but if that is beyond our power, to imagine them reformed and assume them willing to moderate their present lawlessness in answering our questions. The better a man's character is, the more force there will be in any agreement you make with him. However, we are not concerned with them so much as with our search for the truth.

THEAET. You are quite right.          [E]

*A mark of the real is of-* [246E-248A] *fered for the materialists' acceptance*

STR. Well then, call upon these reformed characters to oblige you with an answer, and you shall act as their spokesman.

THEAET. I will.

STR. Let them tell us, then, whether they admit that there is such a thing as a mortal living creature.

THEAET. Of course they do.

STR. And they will agree that it is a body animated by a soul?

THEAET. Certainly.

STR. Taking a soul to be something real?

THEAET. Yes.                          [247]

STR. Again, they allow that one soul may be just, another unjust, or one wise, another foolish?

THEAET. Naturally.

STR. And that any soul comes to be just or the reverse by possessing justice or the reverse, which is present in it?

THEAET. Yes, they agree to that too.

STR. But surely they will admit that whatever can come to be present in a thing or absent from it is certainly a real thing.

THEAET. Yes.

STR. Granted, then, that justice or [B] wisdom or any other sort of goodness or badness is real, and moreover that a soul in which they come to exist is real, do they maintain that any one of these things is visible and tangible, or are they all invisible?

THEAET. They can hardly say that any one of them is visible.

STR. And do they really assert that

something that is not visible has a body?

THEAET. That question they do not answer as a whole without a distinction. The soul itself, they think, does possess a sort of body;[35] but when it comes to wisdom or any of the other things you asked about, they have not the face either to accept the inference that [c] they have no place among real things or to persist in maintaining that they are all bodies.

STR. That shows, Theaetetus, that they are genuinely reformed characters. The Giants among them, of the true earth-born breed, would not stick at any point; they would hold out to the end, that whatever they cannot squeeze between their hands is just nothing at all.

THEAET. I dare say that describes their state of mind.

STR. Let us question them further, then; for it is quite enough for our purpose if they consent to admit that [d] even a small part of reality is bodiless. They must now tell us this: when they say that these bodiless things and the other things which have body are alike "real," what common character that emerges as covering both sets of things have they in view? It is possible they may be at a loss for an answer. If that is their state of mind, you must consider whether they would accept at our suggestion a description of the real and agree to it.

THEAET. What description? Perhaps we can tell, if you will state it.

STR. I suggest that anything has [e] real being, that is so constituted as to possess any sort of power either to affect anything else or to be affected, in however small a degree, by the most insignificant agent, though it be only once. I am proposing as a mark to distinguish

real things, that they are nothing but power.[36]

THEAET. Well, they accept that, having for the moment no better suggestion of their own to offer.

STR. That will do; for later on [248] both they and we perhaps may change our minds. For the present, then, let us take it that this agreement stands between us and the one party.

THEAET. It does.

*The Idealists must con-* [248A-249D] *cede that reality includes some changing things*

STR. Let us turn, then, to the opposite party, the friends of Forms. Once more you shall act as their spokesman.

THEAET. I will.

STR. We understand that you make a distinction between "Becoming" and "Real being" and speak of them as separate. Is that so?

THEAET. Yes.

STR. And you say that we have intercourse with[37] becoming by means of the body through sense, whereas we have intercourse with Real being by means of the soul through reflection. And Real being, you say, is always in the same unchanging state, whereas Becoming is variable.

---

35 The soul had been regarded both popularly and by philosophers before Plato as consisting of a subtle and invisible kind of matter. The Atomists continued to maintain that it was composed of atoms, like everything else; only its atoms were round and so specially mobile.

36 Τίθεμαι γὰρ ὅρον ὁρίζειν τὰ ὄντα ὡς ἔστιν οὐκ ἄλλο τι πλὴν δύναμις. The construction is difficult. I think the sentence ought to mean that the mark of real things (not the real things themselves) is nothing but power. This sense could be obtained if we could translate: "I am proposing a mark to distinguish real things—that there is nothing else but power (to serve as such a mark)" *or* "that *it* (the mark) is nothing but power." But neither rendering seems defensible.

37 κοινωνεῖν ("are in touch with," Taylor) is chosen as a neutral word covering all forms of cognition, the usual words (εἰδέναι, γιγνώσκειν, ἐπίστασθαι, αἰσθάνεσθαι, etc.) being too much specialised and associated either with knowledge to the exclusion of sensation and perception or *vice versa*. κοινωνεῖν is "to enter into relations with." It is used of social and business intercourse, and also of sexual intercourse. . . .

THEAET. We do.                          [B]

STR. Admirable. But now what are we to take you as meaning by this expression "intercourse" which you apply to both? Don't you mean what we described a moment ago?

THEAET. What was that?

STR. The experiencing an effect or the production of one, arising, as the result of some power, from things that encounter one another. Perhaps, Theaetetus, you may not be able to catch their answer to this, but I, who am familiar with them, may be more successful.

THEAET. What have they to say, then?

STR. They do not agree to the prop- [C] osition we put just now to the earth-born Giants about reality.

THEAET. You mean—?

STR. We proposed as a sufficient mark of real things the presence in a thing of the power of being acted upon or of acting in relation to however insignificant a thing.

THEAET. Yes.

STR. Well, to that they reply that a power of acting and being acted upon belongs to Becoming, but neither of these powers is compatible with Real being.

THEAET. And there is something in that answer?

STR. Something to which we must [D] reply by a request for more enlightenment. Do they acknowledge further that the soul knows and Real being is known?

THEAET. Certainly they agree to that.

STR. Well, do you agree that knowing or being known is an action, or is it experiencing an effect, or both? Or is one of them experiencing an effect, the other an action? Or does neither of them come under either of these heads at all?[38]

THEAET. Evidently neither; otherwise our friends would be contradicting what they said earlier.

STR. I see what you mean. They [E] would have to say this:[39] If knowing is to be acting on something, it follows that what is known must be acted upon[40] by it; and so, on this showing, Reality when it is being known by the act of knowledge must, in so far as it is known, be changed owing to being so acted upon; and that, we say, cannot happen to the changeless.

THEAET. Exactly.

STR. But tell me, in heaven's name: are we really to be so easily convinced that change, life, soul, understanding have no place in that which is perfectly real—that it has neither life nor [249] thought, but stands immutable in solemn aloofness, devoid of intelligence?

THEAET. That, sir, would be a strange doctrine to accept.

STR. But can we say it has intelligence without having life?

THEAET. Surely not.

STR. But if we say it contains both, can we deny that it has soul in which they reside?

THEAET. How else could it possess them?

STR. But then, if it has intelligence, life, and soul, can we say that a living thing remains at rest in complete changelessness?

THEAET. All that seems to me unreasonable.                          [B]

STR. In that case we must admit that what changes and change itself are real things.

THEAET. Certainly.

STR. From this, however, it follows, Theaetetus, first, that, if all things are

---

38 The Stranger puts all the possible ways of regarding knowing. He does not suggest that it must be an action, not a being-acted-upon, but that it may be either, or both, or neither. The Idealists in their next reply take up only one of these suggestions—that knowing is an action—and object to that.

39 ΞΕ. μανθάνω τόδε γε (SC. λέγοιεν ἄν). What follows is put into the mouths of the Idealists, who state their objection to regarding knowing as an action. They ignore the possibility that knowing is an affection of the soul, acted upon by the object.

40 Of "affected"—a rendering that more clearly implies suffering some change.

unchangeable[41] no intelligence can really exist anywhere in anything with regard to any object.

THEAET. Quite so.

STR. And, on the other hand, if we allow that all things are moving and changing, on that view equally we shall be excluding intelligence from the class of real things.

THEAET. How so?

·STR. Do you think that, without rest, there could ever be anything that abides constant in the same condition and in the same respects?                    [c]

THEAET. Certainly not.

STR. And without such objects can you make out that intelligence exists or could ever exist anywhere?

THEAET. It would be quite impossible.

STR. Well then, all the force of reasoning must be enlisted to oppose anyone who tries to maintain any assertion about anything at the same time that he suppresses knowledge or understanding or intelligence.

THEAET. Most certainly.

STR. On these grounds, then, it seems that only one course is open to the philosopher who values knowledge and the rest above all else. He must refuse to accept from the champions either [D] of the One or of the many Forms[42] the doctrine that all Reality is changeless; and he must turn a deaf ear to the other party who represent Reality as everywhere changing. Like a child begging for "both," he must declare that Reality

---

41 The point is that, if the *whole* of Reality excludes change, intelligence (which involves life and therefore change) will have no real existence *anywhere*.

42 As Ritter (*Platon* ii, 132) remarks, no one could ever have doubted that the Friends of Forms include the Platonic Socrates of the *Phaedo* and *Republic*, if the temporal sequence of the dialogues had been correctly determined earlier than it was. Ritter himself identifies the Friends of Forms with members of the Academy who took the doctrines of personal immortality and of bodiless Forms, as set forth in the *Phaedo*, more seriously and literally than Plato himself intended.

or the sum of things is both at once—all that is unchangeable and all that is in change.

THEAET. Perfectly true.

*Transition. What does the* [249D-251A] *idealist mean by "real"?*

STR. Well then, does it not look now as if we had fairly caught reality within the compass of our description?

THEAET. Certainly it does.

STR. And yet—oh dear, Theaetetus, what if I say after all that I think it is just at this point that we shall come to see how baffling this question of reality is?

THEAET. How so? Why do you say that?                                           [E]

STR. My good friend, don't you see that now we are wholly in the dark about it, though we fancy we are talking good sense?

THEAET. I certainly thought so, and I don't at all understand how we can be deceived about our condition.

STR. Then consider these last conclusions of ours more carefully, and whether, when we agree to them, we might not fairly be posed with the same [250] question we put earlier to those who said that the sum of things "really is" Hot and Cold.

THEAET. You must remind me what that question was.

STR. By all means; and I will try to do it by questioning you in the same way as I questioned them, so that we may get a little further at the same time.

THEAET. Very good.

STR. Come along then. When you speak of Movement and Rest, these are things completely opposed to one another, aren't they?

THEAET. Of course.

STR. At the same time you say of both and of each severally, that they are real?

THEAET. I do.                                    [B]

STR. And when you admit that they are real, do you mean that either or both are in movement?

THEAET. Certainly not.

STR. Then, perhaps, by saying both are real you mean they are both at rest?

THEAET. No, how could I?

STR. So, then, you conceive of reality (realness) as a third thing over and above these two; and when you speak of both as being real, you mean that you are taking both movement and rest together as embraced by reality and fixing your attention on their common association with reality?

THEAET. It does seem as if we [c] discerned reality as a third thing, when we say that movement and rest are real.

STR. So reality is not motion and rest "both at once," but something distinct from them.

THEAET. Apparently.

STR. In virtue of its own nature, then, reality is neither at rest nor in movement.

THEAET. I suppose so.

STR. If so, where is the mind to turn for help if one wants to reach any clear and certain conclusion about reality?

THEAET. Where indeed?

STR. It seems hard to find help in [D] any quarter. If a thing is not in movement, how can it not be at rest? Or how can what is not in any way at rest fail to be in movement? Yet reality is now revealed to us as outside both alternatives. Is that possible?

THEAET. As impossible as anything could be.

STR. Then there is one thing that ought to be remembered at this point.

THEAET. And that is—?

STR. That we were completely puzzled when we were asked to what the name "unreal" should be applied. You remember?

THEAET. Of course.

STR. And now we are in no less perplexity about reality?                    [E]

THEAET. In even greater, I should say, sir, if that be possible.

STR. Let us take it, then, that our difficulty is now completely stated. But since reality and unreality are equally puzzling, there is henceforward some

hope that any light, whether dim or bright, thrown upon the one will illuminate the other to an equal degree; and if, on the other hand, we cannot get [251] sight of either, at any rate we will make the best we can of it under these conditions and force a passage through the argument with both elbows at once.

THEAET. Very good.

## II

## The Combination of Forms and the Problem of Negative Statements

*Exclusion of the trivial ques-* [251A-C] *tion, how one individual thing can have many names*

STR. Let us explain, then, how it is that we call the same thing—whatever is in question at the moment—by several names.

THEAET. For instance? Give me an example.

STR. Well, when we speak of a man we give him many additional names: we attribute to him colours and shapes and sizes and defects and good qualities; and in all these and countless other statements we say he is not merely a "man" but also "good" and any number of [B] other things. And so with everything else: we take any given thing as one and yet speak of it as many and by many names.

THEAET. True.

STR. And thereby, I fancy, we have provided a magnificent entertainment for the young and for some of their elders who have taken to learning late in life. Anyone can take a hand in the game and at once object that many things cannot be one, nor one thing many; indeed, they delight in forbidding us to speak of a man as "good"; we must only speak of a good as good, and of [C] the man as man. I imagine, Theaetetus, you often meet with these enthusiasts, sometimes elderly men who, being poorly endowed with intelligence, gape with wonder at these discoveries and fancy they have lighted here on the very treasure of complete wisdom.

THEAET. I have indeed.

*Proof that some Forms will combine, others will not*          [251c-252e]

STR. Well then, we want our argument to be addressed to all alike who have ever had anything to say about existence; so let us take it that the [D] questions we shall put now are intended not only for these people but for all those others whom we have been conversing with earlier.

THEAET. And what are the questions?

STR. Are we not to attach Existence to Motion and Rest, nor anything else to anything else, but rather to treat them in our discourse as incapable of any blending or participation in one another? Or are we to lump them all together as capable of association with one another? Or shall we say that this is true of some and not of others? Which of these possibilities shall we say they prefer, Theaetetus?          [E]

THEAET. I am not prepared to answer that on their behalf.

STR. Then why not answer the questions one at a time and see what are the consequences in each case?

THEAET. Very good.

STR. And first, if you like, let us suppose them to say that nothing has any capacity for combination with anything else for any purpose. Then Movement and Rest will have no part in Existence.

THEAET. No.          [252]

STR. Well then, will either of them exist, if it has no association with Existence?

THEAET. No, it will not exist.

STR. That admission seems to make short work of all theories; it upsets at one blow those who have a universe in motion, and those who make it a motionless unity, and all who say their realities exist in Forms that are always the same

in all respects;[43] for they all attribute existence to things, some saying they really *are* in movement, some that they really *are* at rest.

THEAET. Quite so.

STR. And further, those who make [B] all things come together at one time and separate at another, whether they bring innumerable things into a unity and out of a unity, or divide things into and combine them out of a limited set of elements; no matter whether they suppose this to happen in alternation or to be going on all the time—however it may be, all this would be meaningless if there is no blending at all.[44]

THEAET. True.

STR. Moreover, the greatest absurdity of all results from pursuing the theory of those very people who will not allow one thing to share in the quality of another and so be called by its name.

THEAET. How so?          [c]

STR. Why, in referring to anything they cannot help using the words "being" and "apart" and "from the others" and "by itself" and any number more. They cannot refrain from these expressions or from connecting them in their statements, and so need not wait for others to refute them; the foe is in their own household, as the saying goes, and, like that queer fellow Eurycles,[45] they carry about with them wherever they go a voice in their own bellies to contradict them.

THEAET. True; your comparison is [D] very much to the purpose.

---

[43] The three classes mentioned above (249B) at the end of the argument with the idealists. The earlier philosophers are recalled in the next speech.

[44] "No blending" means no blending of Forms. If no Form partakes of any other, the statements that "Motion exists" and "Rest exists" are either false or meaningless. If that is so, it follows that physical things cannot partake of Motion or of Rest; and this is fatal to all cosmologies.

[45] A ventriloquist, mentioned by Aristophanes.

STR. Well, suppose we allow that all are capable of combining with one another.

THEAET. Even I can dispose of that suggestion.

STR. How?

THEAET. Because then Movement itself would come to a complete standstill, and again Rest itself would be in movement, if each were to supervene upon the other.

STR. And that is to the last degree impossible—that Movement should come to be at rest and Rest be in motion?

THEAET. Surely.

STR. Then only the third choice is left.

THEAET. Yes.

STR. And observe that one of these alternatives must be true: either all [E] will blend, or none, or some will and some will not.

THEAET. Certainly.

STR. And two of the three have been found impossible.

THEAET. Yes.

STR. Whoever, then, wishes to give a right answer will assert the remaining one.

THEAET. Quite so.

*The texture of philosophic discourse*[46]
[252E-253C]

STR. Then since some will blend, some not, they might be said to be in the same case with the letters of the [253] alphabet. Some of these cannot be conjoined, others will fit together.

THEAET. Of course.

STR. And the vowels are specially good at combination—a sort of bond pervading them all, so that without a vowel the others cannot be fitted together.

THEAET. That is so.

STR. And does everyone[47] know which

can combine with which, or does one need an art to do it rightly?

THEAET. It needs art.

STR. And that art is—?

THEAET. Grammar.

STR. Again, is it not the same with sounds of high or low pitch? To [B] possess the art of recognising the sounds that can or can not be blended is to be a musician; if one doesn't understand that, one is unmusical.

THEAET. True.

STR. And we shall find differences of the same sort between competence and incompetence in any other art.

THEAET. Of course.

STR. Well, now that we have agreed that the Kinds stand towards one another in the same way as regards blending, is not some science needed as a guide on the voyage of discourse, if one is to succeed in pointing out which Kinds are consonant, and which are incompatible with one another; also, whether there are certain Kinds that pervade [c] them all and connect them so that they can blend, and again, where there are divisions (separations), whether there are certain others that traverse wholes and are responsible for the division?

THEAET. Surely some science is needed—perhaps the most important of all.

*Description of the science of Dialectic*
[253C-254B]

STR. And what name shall we give to this science? Or—good gracious, Theaetetus, have we stumbled unawares upon the free man's knowledge and, in seeking for the Sophist, chanced to find the Philosopher first?

THEAET. How do you mean?

STR. Dividing according to Kinds, not taking the same Form for a different [D] one or a different one for the same—is not that the business of the science of Dialectic?

THEAET. Yes.

STR. And the man who can do that discerns clearly *one* Form everywhere

---

46 *Rep.* vi, 511B. The phrase "texture of discourse" is based on Plato's later remark that "all discourse depends on the weaving together (συμπλοκή) of Forms" (259E below).

47 In Burnet's text (1899) πῶς is misprinted for πᾶς.

extended throughout many, where each one lies apart, and *many* Forms, different from one another, embraced from without by one Form; and again *one* Form connected in a unity through many wholes, and *many* Forms, entirely marked off apart. That means knowing how to distinguish, Kind by Kind, in [E] what ways the several Kinds can or can not combine.

THEAET. Most certainly.

STR. And the only person, I imagine, to whom you would allow this mastery of Dialectic is the pure and rightful lover of wisdom.

THEAET. To whom else could it be allowed?

STR. It is, then, in some such region as this that we shall find the Philosopher now or later, if we should look for him. He too may be difficult to see clear- [254] ly; but the difficulty in his case is not the same as in the Sophist's.

THEAET. What is the difference?

STR. The Sophist takes refuge in the darkness of Not-being, where he is at home and has the knack of feeling his way; and it is the darkness of the place that makes him so hard to perceive.

THEAET. That may well be.

STR. Whereas the Philosopher, whose thoughts constantly dwell upon the nature of reality, is difficult to see because his region is so bright; for the eye of the vulgar soul cannot endure to keep [B] its gaze fixed on the divine.

THEAET. That may well be no less true.

STR. Then we will look more closely at the Philosopher presently, if we are still in the mind to do so; meanwhile clearly we must not loosen our grip on the Sophist until we have studied him thoroughly.

THEAET. I entirely agree.

*Three of the most important Forms, selected for purposes of illustration: Existence, Motion, Rest* [254B-D]

STR. Now that we are agreed, then,

that some of the Kinds will combine with one another and some will not, and that some combine to a small extent, others with a large number, while some pervade all and there is nothing against their being combined with everything, let [C] us next follow up the argument in this way. We will not take all the Forms, for fear of getting confused in such a multitude, but choose out some of those that are recognised as most (*or* very) important, and consider first their several natures and then how they stand in respect of being capable of combination with one another. In this way, though we may not be able to conceive Being and Not-being with perfect clearness, we may at least give as satisfactory an account of them as we can under the conditions of our present inquiry,[48] and see if there is any opening allowing us [D] to assert that what is not, *really is* what is not, and to escape unscathed.

THEAET. Yes, we had better do that.

STR. Now, among the Kinds, those we were just now discussing—Existence itself and Rest and Motion—*are* very important.[49]

THEAET. Quite so.

[48] Possibly a hint that in what follows we shall not draw all the distinctions that a complete account would require, or at least not emphasise those which do not directly bear on the conclusion desired.

[49] This sentence is usually mistranslated, μέγιστα being rendered as if it were τὰ μέγιστα and taken as subject; e.g., Campbell: "*The most important kinds are those which we have just been considering.*" The point is important because all these renderings mean that Existence, Motion, and Rest are *the* most important kinds. Plato does not assert this. The previous speech said that we would select "*some* of those that are recognised as most (or very) important." The present speech tells us which these "some" are; but they are only *some* of the most important, not *the* most important. The subject is ἃ νυνδὴ διῇμεν: μέγιστα is predicate, standing first for emphasis and because it provides the link with the former speech. We might translate: "Now this description 'most important' (or 'very im-

STR. And observe, we say that two of the three will not blend with one another.[50]

THEAET. Certainly.

STR. Whereas Existence can be blended with both; for surely they both exist.

THEAET. Of course.

STR. So they make three in all.

*Two further Forms, Sameness and Difference, distinct from these three and all-pervading*                     [254D-255E]

STR. And each one of them (Existence, Motion, Rest) is *different* from the other two[51] and the *same* as itself.

THEAET. That is so.                         [E]

STR. But what do we mean by these words we have just used—"same" and "different"? Are they a pair of Kinds distinct from those three, though always necessarily blending with them, so that we must consider the Forms as five in all, not three? Or, when we say "same" or "different," are we unconsciously using a name that belongs to one or [255] another of those three Kinds?

THEAET. Possibly.

STR. Well, Motion and Rest at any rate cannot be (identical with) Difference or Sameness.

THEAET. Why not?

STR. Neither Motion nor Rest can be (identical with) anything that we say of both of them in common.

THEAET. Why?

STR. Because Motion would then be at rest, and Rest in motion; for whichever of the two (Motion or Rest) becomes applicable to both (by being identified with either Sameness or Difference, which *are* applicable to both) will force the other (Rest or Motion) to change to the contrary of its own nature, as thus coming to partake of its contrary. [B]

THEAET. Quite so.

STR. But both do partake of Sameness or Difference.

THEAET. Yes.

STR. Then we must not say that Sameness or Difference is (identical with) Motion, nor yet with Rest.[52]

THEAET. No.

STR. Are we, however, to think of Existence and Sameness as a single thing?

---

portant') among the Kinds does apply to those we have been discussing, namely Existence, Rest, Motion." Accordingly, we take those as the "*some*" we said we would take. But there are others of the highest importance, as the earlier speech implied. Sameness and Difference, presently added, are equally important, and actually "wider" than Motion and Rest, being "all-pervading" like Existence. These speeches leave open the possibility that there may be any number of other μέγιστα γένη, which we do not require to mention for our purpose. The consequences of mistranslation will be noted presently.

50 The Motion will not blend with Rest was remarked at 252D. The point of these sentences is that Existence, Motion, Rest, are three distinct Forms, no one of them identical with any other.

51 This statement at once notes that Difference is distinct from Incompatibility; for Motion and Rest are not incompatible with Existence.

52 This argument is highly compressed and somewhat obscure even with the additions I have interpolated in the translation. We want to prove that neither the word "Motion" (or "being in motion") nor the word "Rest" (or "being at rest") can mean the same thing as either the word "Sameness" (or "being the same") or the word "Different" (or "being different"). The proof is (1) We know that

Motion blends with Sameness
Rest      "      "   Sameness
Motion   "      "   Difference
Rest      "      "   Difference.

(2) We now say: Anything that can be asserted of (blends with) both Motion and Rest —and Sameness and Difference do blend with both—cannot be identical with either. (3) For suppose (for example) that Motion is identical with Sameness. Then "Motion" can be substituted for "Sameness" in any statement. So the second statement above ("Rest blends with Sameness") becomes "Rest blends with Motion." But this is false. Therefore Motion is not identical with Sameness. The same proof holds of all the other identifications of Motion with Difference, Rest with Difference, Rest with Sameness.

THEAET. Perhaps.

STR. But if "Existence" and "Sameness" have no difference in meaning, once more, when we say that Motion [c] and Rest both "exist," we shall thereby be speaking of them as being "the same."

THEAET. But that is impossible.

STR. Then Sameness and Existence cannot be one thing.

THEAET. Hardly.

STR. We may, then, set down Sameness as a fourth Form, additional to our three.

THEAET. Certainly.

STR. And are we to call Difference a fifth? Or must we think of Difference and Existence as two names for a single Kind?

THEAET. Perhaps.

STR. But I suppose you admit that, among things that exist, some are always spoken of as being what they are[53] just in themselves, others as being what they are with reference to other things.

THEAET. Of course.

STR. And what is different is always [D] so called with reference to another thing, isn't it?

THEAET. That is so.

STR. It would not be so, if Existence and Difference were not very different things. If Difference partook of both characters[54] as Existence does, there would sometimes be, within the class of different things, something that was different not with reference to another thing. But in fact we undoubtedly find that whatever is different, as a necessary consequence, is what it is with reference to another.

THEAET. It is as you say.

STR. Then we must call the nature [E] of Difference a fifth among the Forms we are singling out.

THEAET. Yes.

STR. And moreover we shall say that this nature pervades all the Forms; for each one is different from the rest, not by virtue of its own nature, but because it partakes of the character of Difference.

THEAET. Quite so.

*A review of true statements involving the five Forms shows that there are any number of true statements asserting that "what is" in a sense "is not" [255E-257A]*

STR. Now, then, taking our five Kinds one by one, let us make some statements about them.

THEAET. What statements?

STR. First about Motion: let us say that Motion is altogether different from Rest. Or is that not so?

THEAET. It is so.

STR. So Motion is not Rest.

THEAET. Not in any sense.[55]

STR. But Motion *is* (exists), by virtue of partaking of Existence.          [256]

THEAET. Yes.

STR. And once more Motion is different from the Same (Sameness).[56]

THEAET. No doubt.

STR. So Motion is not the Same (Sameness).

THEAET. No.

STR. But on the other hand, Motion, we said, is the same as itself, because everything partakes of the Same (Sameness).[57]

THEAET. Certainly.

STR. Motion, then, is both the same and not the Same: we must admit that without boggling at it. For when we say it is "the same" and "not the Same"

---

53 The addition of the words "being what they are" is justified by the statement below (D7) that what is different *is what it is* (τοῦθ' ὅπερ ἐστὶν) with reference to another thing.

54 I.e. τὸ καθ' αὑτό and τὸ πρὸς ἄλλο. Note that Existence, which *includes* both these Forms, is said to *partake* of both. This is one of the places which show that "partaking" is symmetrical in the case of Forms.

55 Possibly "*altogether* different" and "not *in any sense*" mean that Motion and Rest are not only different but also incompatible.

56 In Greek the appearance of contradiction is increased by ταὐτὸν meaning both "Sameness" and "the same."

57 Reading αὐτὴ ... πᾶν ταὐτοῦ with Madvig.

we are not using the expression in the [B] same sense: we call it "the same" on account of its participation in the Same with reference to itself; but we call it "not the Same" because of its combination with Difference, a combination that separates it off from the Same (Sameness) and makes it not the Same but different, so that we have the right to say this time that it is "not the Same."

THEAET. Certainly.

STR. So too, supposing Motion itself did in any way participate in Rest, there would be nothing outrageous in speaking of it as stationary. <But it does not in fact participate in Rest at all.

THEAET. No, it does not.

STR. Whereas it does participate both in Sameness and in Difference, so that it is correct to speak of it as both the same and not the Same.>

THEAET. Perfectly correct, provided that we are to agree that some of the Kinds will blend with one another, some will not.

STR. Well, that is a conclusion we [C] proved at an earlier stage, when we showed that such was indeed their nature.

THEAET. Of course.[58]

---

[58] I understand the argument here as follows. We have just said that Motion is the same and not the same (as partaking of Difference). The sounds like a contradiction: how can what is the same partake of Difference? "Same" and "Different" sound as if they were contraries and so incompatible, like Motion and Rest, which are contraries and incompatible. But suppose Motion and Rest were merely different, not incompatible: then Motion could partake of Rest and be called stationary. That is impossible because Motion and Rest are in fact incompatible. But the sameness which Motion has towards itself and the difference it has towards other things are not incompatible. So there is no contradiction in saying Motion is the same and not the same. (Cf. Brochard, *Études*, 143.)

If this is the meaning, the text is intolerably elliptical and obscure....

Other critics suppose that Plato is suggesting that there is, after all, a sense in which

STR. To go back to our statements, then: is Motion different from Different (Difference), just as it was other than the Same (Sameness) and other than Rest?

THEAET. Necessarily.

STR. Motion, then, in a sense is not Different, and also is different, in accordance with the argument we stated just now.

THEAET. True.

STR. What, then of the next point? Are we to say that Motion is different from three of the four, but not from the [D] fourth, when we have agreed that there were five Kinds in the field we set before us for examination?

THEAET. How can we? We cannot allow that their number is less than it was shown to be.

STR. So we may fearlessly contend that Motion is different from Existence.

THEAET. Without the smallest fear.

STR. In fact, it is clear that Motion really is a thing that is not (Existence) and a thing that is, since it partakes of Existence.

THEAET. Perfectly clear.

STR. It must, then, be possible for "that which is not" (*i.e.* is different from Existence) to be (to exist), not only in the case of Motion but of all the other Kinds. For in the case of them all [E] the nature of Difference makes each one of them different from Existence and so makes it a thing that "is not"; and hence we shall be right to speak of them all on the same principle as things that in this sense "*are not*," and again, because they partake of Existence, to say that they "*are*" (exist) and call them things that have been (existence).

---

Motion does partake of Rest, *e.g.* the uniform motion of a sphere in the same place (Dies), or because Motion partakes of stability in that it can be measured and described (Ritter, *N. Unt.* 61). But I agree with Brochard that the reference to earlier statements asserting that Motion and Rest are incompatible excludes such interpretations.

THEAET. No doubt.

STR. So, in the case of every one of the Forms there is much that it *is* and an indefinite number of things that it *is not*.[59]

THEAET. So it appears.

STR. And, moreover, Existence [257] itself must be called different from the rest.

THEAET. Necessarily.

STR. We find, then, that Existence likewise "is not" in as many respects as there are other things; for, not being those others, while it *is* its single self, it *is not* all that indefinite number of other things.

THEAET. That is so.

STR. Then we must not boggle even at that conclusion, granted that Kinds are of a nature to admit combination with one another. If anyone denies that, he must win over our earlier arguments to his side before he tries to win over their consequences.

THEAET. That is a fair demand.

*There are also any number of true statements asserting that "what is not" in a sense "is"*                    [257B-258c]

STR. Now let us mark this.

THEAET. Yes?

STR. When we speak of "that which is not," it seems that we do not mean something contrary to what exists but only something that is different.

THEAET. How?

STR. In the same way that when, for example, we speak of something as "not tall," we may just as well mean by that phrase "what is equal" as "what is short," mayn't we?[60]

THEAET. Certainly.

STR. So, when it is asserted that a negative signifies a contrary, we shall not agree, but admit no more than this: [c] that the prefix "not" indicates something different from the words that follow—or rather from the things designated by the words pronounced after the negative.

THEAET. Exactly.

STR. And here, if you agree, is a point for us to consider.

THEAET. Namely?

STR. The nature of the Different (Difference)[61] appears to the parcelled out, in the same way as knowledge.

THEAET. How so?

STR. Knowledge also is surely one, but each part of it that commands a certain field is marked off and given a special [D] name proper to itself. Hence language recognises many arts and forms of knowledge.[62]

THEAET. Certainly.

STR. And the same thing is true of the parts of the single nature of the Different.

THEAET. Perhaps; but shall we explain how?

STR. There exists a part of the Different that is set in contrast to the Beautiful?

THEAET. Yes.

STR. Are we to say it is nameless, or has it a special name?

THEAET. It has. Whenever we use the expression "not Beautiful," the thing we mean is precisely that which is different from the nature of the Beautiful.

STR. Then tell me this.

THEAET. What?                                    [E]

STR. May we not say that the *existence*

---

[59] This means that many affirmative statements are true of any Form, and also any number of negative statements, expressing its difference from other Forms. This conclusion is next applied to Existence itself.

[60] "Short" is the contrary of "tall"; but "equal" is not; so the equal is different from the tall, not contrary. Similarly "the notbeautiful" is not necessarily "the ugly."

[61] The ambiguity of θάτερον in all this section—"the different" (that which is different) and "Difference itself"—will be discussed below. [Cornford's discussion has been omitted, but see note 65 below. W.K.]

[62] Knowledge and its species are a mere illustration. There is no suggestion that the species of knowledge correspond to "parts of the Different." Every Form is a part of the Different, but there is not a species of knowledge for every Form.

of the not-Beautiful is constituted by its being marked off from a single definite Kind among existing things and again set in contrast with something that exists?

THEAET. Yes.

STR. So it appears that the not-Beautiful is an instance of something that exists being set in contrast to something that exists.

THEAET. Perfectly.

STR. What then? On this showing has the non-Beautiful any less claim than the Beautiful to be a thing that exists?

THEAET. None whatever.

STR. And so the not-Tall must be said to exist just as much as the Tall [258] itself.

THEAET. Just as much.

STR. And we must also put the not-Just[63] on the same footing as the Just with respect to the fact that the one exists no less than the other.

THEAET. Certainly.

STR. And we shall say the same of all the rest, since we have seen that the nature of the Different is to be ranked among things that exist, and, once it exists, its parts also must be considered as existing just as much as anything else.

THEAET. Of course.

STR. So, it seems, when a part of the nature of the Different and a part of the nature of the Existent (Existence) [B] are set in contrast to one another, the contrast is, if it be permisssible to say so, as much a reality as Existence itself; it does not mean what is contrary to "existent," but only what is different from that Existent.

THEAET. That is quite clear.

STR. What name are we to give it, then?

THEAET. Obviously this is just that "what-is-not" which we were seeking for the sake of the Sophist.

_____
63 The "not-Just" is not "the unjust," but any Form that is different from "the Just." ... Note that the moral Forms (Beautiful, Just) once more appear alongside the rest.

STR. Has it then, as you say, an existence inferior to none of the rest in reality? May we now be bold to say that "that which is not" unquestionably *is* a thing that has a nature of its own— [C] just as the Tall was tall and the Beautiful was beautiful, so too with the not-Tall and the not-Beautiful—and in that sense "that which is not" also, on the same principle, both was and *is* what-is-not, a single Form to be reckoned among the many realities? Or have we any further doubts with regard to it, Theaetetus?

THEAET. None at all.

*Conclusion: We have re-* [258c-259d] *futed Parmenides' dogma that "what is" cannot in any sense not-be, and that "what is not" cannot in any sense be*

STR. You see, then, that in our disobedience to Parmenides we have trespassed far beyond the limits of his prohibition.

THEAET. In what way?

STR. In pushing forward on our quest, we have shown him results in a field which he forbade us even to explore.

THEAET. How?

STR. He says, you remember,      [D]

"Never shall this be proved, that things that are not, are; but keep back thy thought from this way of inquiry."

THEAET. Yes, he does say that.

STR. Whereas we have not merely shown that things that are not, are, but we have brought to light the real character of "not-being." We have shown that the nature of the Different has [E] existence and is parcelled out over the whole field of existent things with reference to one another; and of every part of it that is set in contrast to "that which is" we have dared to say that precisely that *is really* "that which is not."

THEAET. Yes, sir, and I think what we have said is perfectly true.

STR. Then let no one say that it is the contrary of the existent that we mean by "what is not," when we make bold to say that "what is not" exists. So far as any contrary of the existent is concerned, we have long ago[64] said good-bye to the question whether there is such a [259] thing or not and whether any account can be given of it or none whatsoever.

But with respect to the "what-is-not" that we have now asserted to exist, an opponent must either convince us that our account is wrong by refuting it, or, so long as he proves unable to do that, he must accept our statements:

that the Kinds blend with one another;

that Existence and Difference pervade them all, and pervade one another;

that Difference (or the Different),[65] by partaking of Existence, is by virtue of that participation, but on the other hand is not that Existence of which it partakes, but is different; and since it is different from Existence (or an existent), quite clearly it must be possible[66] that it should be a thing that is not;[67]

and again, Existence, having a part [B] in Difference, will be different from all the rest of the Kinds; and, because it is different from them all, it is not any one of them nor yet all the others put together, but is only itself,[68] with the con-

sequence, again indisputable, that Existence is not myriads upon myriads of things, and that all the other Kinds in the same way, whether taken severally or all together, in many respects are and in many respects are not.

THEAET. True.

STR. And if anyone mistrusts these apparent contradictions, he should study the question and produce some better [C] explanation that we have now given; whereas if he imagines he has discovered an embarrassing puzzle and takes delight in reducing argument to a tug of war, he is wasting his pains on a triviality, as our present argument declares. There is nothing clever in such a discovery, nor is it hard to make; what is hard and at the same time worth the pains is something different.

THEAET. And that is——?

STR. What I said before: leaving such quibbling alone as leading nowhere,[69] to be able to follow our statements step by step and, in criticising the assertion that a different thing is the same or the [D] same thing is different in a certain sense, to take account of the precise sense and the precise respect in which they are said to be one or the other. Merely to show that in some unspecified way the same is different or the different is the same, the tall short, the like unlike, and to take pleasure in perpetually parading such contradictions in argument—that is not genuine criticism, but may be recognised as the callow offspring of a too recent contact with reality.

THEAET. I quite agree.

---

64 At 238c, where τὸ μηδαμῶς ὄν, "the simply non-existent," was dismissed as not to be spoken or thought of. There are no true statements saying that any Form does not exist. But it is true of every Form other than Existence itself that it is not (identical with) Existence.

65 As before, θάτερον is verbally ambiguous and the formula covers the two statements: (1) that the Form Difference is not (the same as) Existence, but is (exists); (2) that the different (that which is not so-and-so) is not (the same as) a thing that is (viz. a certain existent, the so-and-so differs from), but is a thing that is (an, existent).

66 ἔστιν ἐξ ἀνάγκης εἶναι, "It is possible, necessarily, for it to be." Cf 256D, ἔστιν ἐξ ἀνάγκης ... εἶναι, in the same sense.

67 I.e. (1) Difference is not Existence; and (2) the different is not some other definite existent with which it is contrasted.

68 Here the distinction between the Form

Existence as discussed in all this section and the Existent (the Real, the whole world of real Forms) is clearly recognised. The corresponding statements are: (1) Existence is not (the same as any other Form), but is (the same as) itself; (2) the Existent (any Form or group of Forms) is not (the same as) any other existent, but is (exists).

69 ἀνήνυτα (Badham) "seems to be the most probable correction of δυνατὰ yet proposed.

III

## False Speaking and Thinking

*Introductory statement of* [259D-261C]
*the problem*

STR. Yes, my friend, and the attempt
to separate everything from every other
thing not only strikes a discordant [E]
note but amounts to a crude defiance of
the philosophic Muse.

THEAET. Why?

STR. This isolation of everything from
everything else means a complete aboli-
tion of all discourse; for any discourse
we can have owes its existence to the
weaving together of Forms.

THEAET. True.

STR. Observe, then, how oppor- [260]
tune was our struggle with those sepa-
ratists, when we forced them to allow
one Form to blend with another.

THEAET. In what respect?

STR. In respect of securing the position
of discourse as one of the kinds of things
that exist. To rob us of discourse would
be to rob us of philosophy. That would
be the most serious consequence; but,
besides that, we need at the present moment to come to an agreement about the
nature of discourse, and if its very existence had been taken from us, we
should naturally not be able to dis- [B]
course any further. And that would have
happened, if we had yielded the point
that there is no blending of any one
Form with another.

THEAET. That is certainly true. But I
do not understand why we need an
agreement about discourse at the present
moment.

STR. I may be able to suggest a line of
thought that will help you to understand.

THEAET. What is that?

STR. We saw the "not being" is a
single kind among the rest, dispersed
over the whole field of realities.

THEAET. Yes.

STR. We have next to consider whether
it blends with thinking and discourse.

THEAET. Why that?

STR. If it does not blend with them, [C]
everything must be true; but if it does,
we shall have false thinking and discourse; for thinking or saying "what is
not" comes, I suppose, to the same thing
as falsity in thought and speech.

THEAET. Yes.

STR. And if falsity exists, deception is
possible.

THEAET. Yes.

STR. And once deception exists, images and likenesses and appearance will
be everywhere rampant.

THEAET. Of course.

STR. And the Sophist, we said, had [D]
taken refuge somewhere in that region,
but then he had denied the very existence of falsity: no one could either think
or say "what is not," because what is not
never has any sort of being.

THEAET. So he said.

STR. But now that "what is not" has
been found to have its share in existence,
perhaps he will not fight with us further
on that point. On the other hand, he
may perhaps say that some things partake of not-being, some do not, and that
speech and thinking are among those
that do not; and so once more he might
contend that the art of creating im- [E]
ages and semblances, where we say he
is to be found, has no existence at all,
since thought and speech have no share
in not-being, and without that combination there is no such thing as falsity.

That is why we must begin by investigating the nature of discourse and
thinking and appearance, in order that
we may then make out their combination with not-being and so prove [261]
that falsity exists, and by that proof pin
down the Sophist there, if he is amenable to capture, or else let him go and
pursue our search in some other Kind.

THEAET. Certainly, sir, what we said
at the outset about the Sophist seems

true: that he is a hard sort of beast to hunt down. Evidently he possesses a whole armoury of problems, and every time that he puts one forward to shield him, we have to fight our way through it before we can get at him. So now, hardly have we got the better of his defence that "what is not" cannot exist, when another obstacle is raised in our [B] path: we must, it seems, prove that falsity exists both in speech and thought, and after that perhaps something else, and so on. It looks as if the end would never be in sight.

STR. A man should be of good courage, Theaetetus, if he can make only a little headway at each step. If he loses heart then, what will he do in another case where he cannot advance at all or even perhaps loses ground? No city, as they say, will surrender to so faint a [C] summons. And now that we have surmounted the barrier you speak of, we may have already taken the highest wall and the rest may be easier to capture.

THEAET. That is encouraging.

*Every statement is a complex of heterogeneous elements (name and verb)*                   [261C-262E]

STR. Then, as I said, let us take first statement[70] and judgment, so as to establish clearly whether not-being has any point of contact with them, or both are altogether true and there is never falsity in either.

THEAET. Very good.

STR. Now, remembering what we [D] said about Forms and letters,[71] let us consider words in the same way. The

solution of our present problem promises to lie in that quarter.

THEAET. What are you going to ask me about words?

STR. Whether they all fit together, or none of them, or some will and some will not.

THEAET. That is plain enough: some will, some will not.

STR. You mean perhaps something like this: words which, when spoken in succession, signify something, do fit [E] together, while those which mean nothing when they are strung together, do not.

THEAET. What do you mean?

STR. What I supposed you had in your mind when you gave your assent.[72] The signs we use in speech to signify being are surely of two kinds.

THEAET. How?

STR. One kind called "names," the other "verbs."                        [262]

THEAET. Give me a description of each.

STR. By "verb" we mean an expression which is applied to actions.

THEAET. Yes.

STR. And by a "name" the spoken sign applied to what performs these actions.

THEAET. Quite so.

STR. Now a statement never consists solely of names spoken in succession, nor yet of verbs apart from names.

THEAET. I don't follow that.

STR. Evidently you had something [B] else in mind when you agreed with me just now; because what I meant was just this: that these words spoken in a

---

70 "Statement." So far λόγος has been translated "discourse"; but the following analysis is concerned with what Aristotle calls the ἀποφαντικὸς λόγος a statement which can and must be either true or false, as distinct from questions, prayers, etc. A "judgment" (as explained later) is here equivalent to an unspoken statement made by the mind in its internal dialogue with itself.

71 At 253A.

72 Probably what Theaetetus had in mind was the combination of Forms in affirmative statements and the incompatibility of Forms expressed by negative statements, which was illustrated by the fitting-together (συναρμόττειν) or not fitting of vowels and consonants at 253A. But the Stranger is referring only to the illustration and is thinking of the fact that a statement cannot consist of a combination of two nouns only or of two verbs only, any more than a word can consist of two consonants without a vowel.

string in this way do not make a statement.

THEAET. In what way?

STR. For example, "walks runs sleeps,"[73] and so on with all the other verbs signifying actions—you may utter them all one after another, but that does not make a statement.

THEAET. Naturally.

STR. And again, if you say "lion stag horse" and any other names given to things that perform actions, such a [C] string never makes up a statement. Neither in this example nor in the other do the sounds uttered signify any action performed or not performed or nature of anything that exists or does not exist,[74] until you combine verbs with names. The moment you do that, they fit together and the simplest combination becomes a statement of what might be called the simplest and briefest kind.

THEAET. Then how do you make a statement of that kind?

STR. When one says "A man understands," do you agree that this is a statement of the simplest and shortest possible kind?

THEAET. Yes. [D]

STR. Because now it gives information about facts or events in the present or past or future: it does not merely name something but gets you somewhere by weaving together verbs with names. Hence we say it "states" something, not merely "names" something, and in fact

---

[73] The inverted commas in Burnet's text between βαδίζει and καθεύδει (and below, between λέων and ἵπποι) should be omitted.

[74] πρᾶξιν οὐδ' ἀπραξίαν refers to the former example (ἐκείνως) of the verbs, which does not state that any action is actually performed, or not performed, by any agent. οὐδὲ οὐσίαν ὄντος οὐδὲ μὴ ὄντος refers to the latter example (οὕτως) of the string of names, which does not state that there actually exists (ὄντος), or does not exist, anything with the nature (οὐσία) expressed by any of the names. This does not mean that the words themselves have no meaning, and are senseless noises; but that such concatenations are not statements of fact, do not refer (or profess to refer) to any actual fact or event.

it is this complex that we mean by the word "statement."

THEAET. True.

STR. And so, just as some things fit together, some do not, so with the signs of speech: some do not fit, but those [E] that do fit make a statement.

THEAET. Quite so.

*Every statement is about something and is either true or false* [262E]

STR. Now another small point.

THEAET. Yes?

STR. Whenever there is a statement, it must be about something; it cannot be about nothing.

THEAET. That is so.

STR. And must it not have a certain character?[75]

THEAET. Of course.

*The definition of true* [262E-263B] *statement*

STR. Now let us fix our attention on ourselves.

THEAET. We will.

STR. I will make a statement to you, then, putting together a thing with an action by means of a name and a verb. You are to tell me what the statement is about.

THEAET. I will do my best. [263]

STR. "Theaetetus sits"—not a lengthy statement, is it?

THEAET. No, of very modest length.

STR. Now it is for you to say what it is about—to whom it belongs.

THEAET. Clearly about me: it belongs to me.

STR. Now take another.

THEAET. Namely——?

STR. "Theaetetus (whom I am talking to at this moment)[76] flies."

THEAET. That too can only be described as belonging to me and about me.

---

[75] That "character" or "quality" means truth or falsity, here as at *Philebus* 37B, is obvious from what follows (263A, B).

[76] Not an imaginary Theaetetus or Theaetetus at some other moment, but the real Theaetetus here and now.

STR. And moreover we agree that any statement must have a certain character.

THEAET. Yes.                                    [B]

STR. Then what sort of character can we assign to each of these?

THEAET. One is false, the other true.

STR. And the true one states about you the things that are (or the facts) as they are.

THEAET. Certainly.

*The definition of false state-* [263B-D]
*ment.*

STR. Whereas the false statement states about you things *different* from the things that are.

THEAET. Yes.

STR. And accordingly states *things that are-not* as being.

THEAET. No doubt.

STR. Yes, but things that *exist*, different from things that *exist* in your case. For we said that in the case of everything there are many things that are and also many that are not.

THEAET. Quite so.

STR. So the second statement I [c] made about you, in the first place, according to our definition of the nature of a statement, must itself necessarily be one of the shortest possible.

THEAET. So we agreed just now.

STR. And secondly it must be about something.

THEAET. Yes.

STR. And if it is not about you, it is not about anything else.

THEAET. Certainly.

STR. And if it were about nothing, it would not be a statement at all; for we pointed out that there could not be a statement that was a statement about nothing.

THEAET. Quite true.

STR. So what is stated about you, [D] but so that what is different is stated as the same or what is not as what is—a combination of verbs and names answering to that description finally seems to be really and truly a false statement.

THEAET. Perfectly true.

*Judgment being simply* [263D-264B] *unspoken statement, false judgment and false "appearing" are possible*

STR. And next, what of thinking and judgment and appearing? Is it not now clear that all these things occur in our minds both as false and as true?

THEAET. How so?

STR. You will see more easily if you begin by letting me give you an account of their nature and how each differs [E] from the others.

THEAET. Let me have it.

STR. Well, thinking and discourse[77] are the same thing, except that what we call thinking is, precisely, the inward dialogue carried on by the mind with itself without spoken sound.

THEAET. Certainly.

STR. Whereas the stream which flows from the mind through the lips with sound is called discourse.

THEAET. True.

STR. And further there is a thing[78] which we know occurs in discourse.

THEAET. Namely?

STR. Assertion and denial.[79]

THEAET. Yes.

STR. Then when this occurs in [264] the mind in the course of silent thinking, can you call it anything but judgment?

---

[77] Thinking (διάνοια) and discource (λόγος) are both used in the wide sense which includes, not only judgment (δόξα) and statement (λόγος), which must be true or false, but all forms of thinking and speech, questions, commands, etc. The account of thinking as unspoken discourse at *Theaet.* 189E [see above] and 206D [not included in this volume], is here briefly repeated.

[78] αὐτό, BT should be retained: "a thing (presently to be mentioned)." Cf αὐτὰ at *Theaet.* 207D (Campbell).

[79] φάσις and ἀπόφασις cover (1) affirmation and negation, which appear in the affirmative or negative form of the spoken statement, and (2) the mental acts of assent and dissent— saying "yes" and "no"—to questions which the mind puts to itself, as described at *Theaet.* 190A. φάσκουσα καὶ οὐ φάσκουσα [see above]. Judgment was there defined as the mind's final decision when all doubt and debate is over.

THEAET. No.

STR. And suppose judgment occurs, not independently, but by means of perception, the only right name for such a state of mind is "appearing."

THEAET. Yes.

STR. Well then, since we have seen that there is true and false statement, and of these mental processes we have found thinking to be a dialogue of the mind with itself, and judgment to be [B] the conclusion of thinking, and what we mean by "it appears" a blend of perception and judgment, it follows that these also, being of the same nature as statement, must be, some of them and on some occasions, false.

THEAET. Of course.

STR. You see, then, that we have discovered the nature of false judgment and false statement sooner than we expected just now when we feared there would be no end to the task we were setting ourselves in the search for them.

THEAET. I do.

*Transition, connecting these* [264B-D] *results with the interrupted Division of Image-making*

STR. Then let us not lose courage for what remains to be done. Now that these matters are cleared up, let us recall [C] our earlier divisions by forms.

THEAET. Which do you mean?

STR. We distinguished two forms of Image-making: the making of likenesses and the making of semblances.

THEAET. Yes.

STR. And we said we were puzzled to tell under which of these two we should place the Sophist.

THEAET. We did.

STR. And to increase our perplexity we were plunged in a whirl of confusion by the apparition of an argument that called in question all these terms and disputed the very existence of any copy or image or semblance, on the ground that falsity never has any sort of existence anywhere.                          [D]

THEAET. True.

STR. But now that we have brought to light the existence of false statement and of false judgment, it is possible that there should be imitations of real things and that this condition of mind [false judgment] should account for the existence of an art of deception.

THEAET. Yes, it is.

STR. And we agreed earlier that the Sophist does come under one or other of the two kinds mentioned.

THEAET. Yes.

*The Sophist as a species* [264D-268D] *of Image-maker*[80]

---

[80] The final Table of Division is as follows:

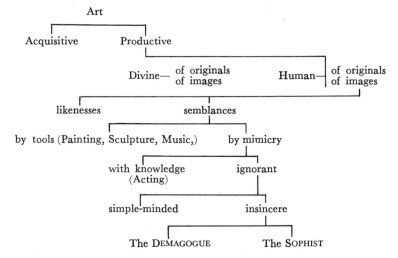

STR. Now, then, let us set to work again and, as we divide the Kind proposed in two, keep to the right-hand [E] section at each stage. Holding fast to the characters of which the Sophist partakes until we have stripped off all that he has in common with others and left only the nature that is peculiar to him, let us so make that nature plain, in the first place to ourselves, and secondly to [265] others whose temperament finds a procedure of this sort congenial.

THEAET. Very good.

STR. Well, we began by dividing Art into Productive and Acquisitive.

THEAET. Yes.

STR. And under the head of the Acquisitive we had glimpses of the Sophist in the arts of hunting, contention, trafficking, and other kinds of that sort.[81]

THEAET. Certainly.

STR. But now that he has been included under an art of Imitation, clearly we must start by dividing into two [B] the Productive branch of Art. For Imitation is surely a kind of production, though it be only a production of images, as we say, not of originals of every sort. Is that not so?

THEAET. Assuredly.

STR. Let us begin, then, by recognising two kinds of Production.

THEAET. What are they?

STR. The one Divine, the other Human.

THEAET. I don't understand yet.

STR. Production—to recall what we said at the outset—we defined as any power that can bring into existence what did not exist before.

THEAET. I remember.

STR. Now take all mortal animals [C] and also all things that grow—plants that grow above the earth from seeds and roots, and lifeless bodies compacted beneath the earth, whether fusible or not fusible. Must we not attribute the coming into being of these things out of not-being to divine craftsmanship and nothing else? Or are we to fall in with the belief that is commonly expressed?

THEAET. What belief do you mean?

STR. That Nature gives birth to them as a result of some spontaneous cause that generates without intelligence. Or shall we say that they come from a cause which, working with reason and art, is divine and proceeds from divinity?

THEAET. Perhaps because I am young, I often shift from one belief to the other; but at this moment, looking at your face and believing you to hold that these things have a divine origin, I too am convinced.

STR. Well said, Theaetetus. If I thought you were the sort of person that might believe otherwise in the future, I should now try by force of persuasion to make you accept that account. But I can see clearly that, without any arguments of mine, your nature will come of [E] itself to the conclusion which you tell me attracts you at this moment. So I will let that pass: I should be wasting time. I will only lay it down that the products of Nature, as they are called, are works of divine art, as things made out of them by man are works of human art. Accordingly there will be two kinds of Production, one human, the other divine.

THEAET. Good.

STR. Once more, then, divide each of these two into two parts.

THEAET. How?

STR. As you have just divided the [266] whole extent of Production horizontally, now divide it vertically.

THEAET. Be it so.

STR. The result is four parts in all: two on our side, human; two on the side of the gods, divine.

---

81 This reference to the five tentative Divisions of the Acquisitive branch is significant. They only provided "glimpses" or indistinct visions of various types called sophists, not the essential feature. With ἐφαντάζετο compare φανταζόμενον used of the figure indistinctly seen at a distance, *Philebus* 38c. The third main branch of Art, the Separative (διακριτική), from which was derived the Cathartic method of Socrates in Division VI, is here ignored. It gave us no glimpse of the Sophist.

THEAET. Yes.

STR. And taking the divisions made in the first way (horizontally: divine and human), one section of each part will be the production of originals, and the remaining two sections will be best described as production of images. So we have a second division of Production on that principle (originals and images).

THEAET. Explain once more how [B] each of the two parts (divine and human) is divided.

STR. Ourselves, I take it, and all other living creatures and the elements of natural things—fire, water, and their kindred—are all originals, the offspring, as we are well assured, of divine workmanship. Is it not so?

THEAET. Yes.

STR. And every one of these products is attended by images which are not the actual thing, and which also owe their existence to divine contrivance.

THEAET. You mean——?

STR. Dream images, and in daylight all those naturally produced semblances which we call "shadow" when dark [C] patches interrupt the light, or a "reflection" when the light belonging to the eye meets and coalesces with light belonging to something else on a bright and smooth surface and produces a form yielding a perception that is the reverse of the ordinary direct view.

THEAET. There are, indeed, these two products of divine workmanship: the original and the image that in every case accompanies it.[82]

STR. And what of our human art?

Must we not say that in building it produces an actual house, and in painting a house of a different sort, as it were a man-made dream for waking eyes?

THEAET. Certainly.                        [D]

STR. And so in all cases, we find once more twin products of our own productive activity in pairs—one an actual thing, the other an image.

THEAET. I understand better now, and I recognise two forms of production, each of them twofold: divine and human according to one division, and according to the other a production of actual things and of some sort of likenesses.

STR. Let us remind ourselves, then, that of this production of images there were to be two kinds, one producing [E] likenesses, the other semblances, provided that falsity should be shown to be a thing that really is false and of such a nature as to have a place among existing things.

THEAET. Yes, it was to be so.

STR. And that has now been shown; so on that ground shall we now reckon the distinction of these two forms as beyond dispute?

THEAET. Yes.

STR. Once more, then, let us [267] divide in two the kind that produces semblances.

THEAET. How?

STR. There is the semblance produced by means of tools, and another sort where the producer of the semblance takes his own person as an instrument.

THEAET. How do you mean?

STR. When someone uses his own person or voice to counterfeit your traits or speech, the proper name for creating such a semblance is, I take it, Mimicry.

THEAET. Yes.

STR. Let us reserve that section, then, under the name of mimicry, and indulge ourselves so far as to leave all the rest [B] for someone else to collect into a unity and give it an appropriate name.

THEAET. So be it.

STR. But there is still ground for thinking that mimicry is of two sorts. Let me put it before you.

---

82 These originals and images make up the contents of the visible world (ὁρατά or δοξαστά of *Rep.* vi, where they are described in similar terms, 510A). They are the work of the divine craftsman of the *Timaeus*, who fashions the visible world after the pattern of the Forms. The Forms themselves, which are not created, are, of course, not mentioned here. But the Platonist will recall that the actual things here called originals are themselves only copies or images of the Forms. They are those *eidola* whose ambiguous existence still remains a problem.

THEAET. Do.

STR. Some mimics know the thing they are impersonating, other do not; and could we find a more important distinction than that of knowing from not knowing?

THEAET. No.

STR. And the mimicry we have just mentioned goes with knowledge; for to impersonate you, one must be acquainted with you and your traits.

THEAET. Of course.                    [c]

STR. And what of the traits of Justice and of virtue generally? Are there not many who, having no knowledge of virtue but only some sort of opinion about it, zealously set about making it appear that they embody virtue as they conceive it, mimicking it as effectively as they can in their words and actions?

THEAET. Only too many.

STR. And are they always unsuccessful in appearing to be virtuous when they are not really virtuous at all? Do they not rather succeed perfectly?

THEAET. They do.

STR. We must, then, distinguish [D] the ignorant mimic from the other, who has knowledge.

THEAET. Yes.

STR. Where, then, must we look for a suitable name for each? No doubt it is hard to find one, because the ancients, it would seem, suffered from a certain laziness and lack of discrimination with regard to the division of Kinds by forms, and not one of them even tried to make such divisions, with the result that there is a serious shortage of names. However, though the expression may seem daring, for purposes of distinction let us call mimicry guided by opinion "conceit- [E] mimicry," and the sort that is guided by knowledge "mimicry by acquaintance."

THEAET. So be it.

STR. It is the former, then, that concerns us; for the Sophist was not among those who have knowledge, but he has a place among mimics.

THEAET. Certainly.

STR. Then let us take this conceit-mimic and see if his metal rings sound or there is still a crack in it somewhere.

THEAET. Let us do so.

STR. Well, there is a gaping [268] crack. There is the simple-minded type who imagines that what he believes is knowledge, and an opposite type who is versed in discussion, so that his attitude betrays no little misgiving and suspicion that the knowledge he has the air of possessing in the eyes of the world is really ignorance.

THEAET. Certainly both the types you describe exist.

STR. We may, then, set down one of these mimics as sincere, the other as insincere.

THEAET. So it appears.

STR. And the insincere—is he of two kinds or only one?

THEAET. That is for you to consider.

STR. I will; and I can clearly make [B] out a pair of them. I see one who can keep up his dissimulation publicly in long speeches to a large assembly. The other uses short arguments in private and forces others to contradict themselves in conversation.

THEAET. Very true.

STR. And with whom shall we identify the more long-winded type—with the Statesman or with the demagogue?

THEAET. The demagogue.

STR. And what shall we call the other —wise man or Sophist?

THEAET. We cannot surely call him [c] wise, because we set him down as ignorant; but as a mimic of the wise man he will clearly assume a title derived from his, and I now see that here at last is the man who must be truly described as the real and genuine Sophist.

STR. Shall we, then, as before collect all the elements of his description, from the end to the beginning,[83] and draw our threads together in a knot?

---

[83] The construction of the final definition is obscured by the effort to frame it so as to mention all the specific differences in order "from the end to the beginning" (productive art).

THEAET. By all means.

STR. The art of contradiction-making, descended from an insincere kind of conceited mimicry, of the semblance-making breed, derived from image-making, distinguished as a portion, not divine [c] but human, of production, that presents a shadow-play of words—such is the blood and lineage which can, with perfect truth, be assigned to the authentic Sophist.

THEAET. I entirely agree.

# TIMAEUS (in part)

PERSONS OF THE DIALOGUE

CRITIAS     SOCRATES     TIMAEUS

•  •  •

CRITIAS. I will submit to you the [27A] plan we have arranged for your entertainment, Socrates. We decided that Timaeus shall speak first. He knows more of astronomy than the rest of us and has made knowledge of the nature of the universe his chief object; he will begin with the birth of the world and end with the nature of man.

•  •  •

TIMAEUS. We must in my judgment, first make this distinction: what is that which is always real and has no becoming, and what is that which is always becoming and is never real? That [28] which is apprehensible by thought with a rational account is the thing that is always unchangeably real; whereas that which is the object of belief together with unreasoning sensation is the thing that becomes and passes away, but never has real being. Again, all that becomes must needs become by the agency of some cause; for without a cause nothing can come to be. Now whenever the maker of anything looks to that which is always unchanging and uses a model of that description in fashioning the form and quality of his work, all that he thus accomplishes must be good. If he [B] looks to something that has come to be and uses a generated model, it will not be good.

So concerning the whole Heaven or World—let us call it by whatsoever name may be most acceptable to it[1]— we must ask the question which, it is agreed, must be asked at the outset of inquiry concerning anything: Has it always been, without any source of becoming; or has it come to be, starting from some beginning? It has come to be; for it can be seen and touched and it has body, and all such things are sensible; and as we saw, sensible things, that are to be apprehended by belief together [c] with sensation, are things that become and can be generated. But again, that which becomes, we say, must necessarily become by the agency of some cause. The maker and father of this universe it is a hard task to find, and having found him it would be impossible to declare him to all mankind. Be that as it may, we must go back to this question about the world: After which of the two models did its builder frame it—after that which is always in the same unchanging state, [29] or after that which has come to be? Now if this world is good and its maker is good, clearly he looked to the eternal; on the contrary supposition (which cannot be spoken without blasphemy), to that which has come to be. Everyone, then, must see that he looked to the eternal; for the world is the best of things that have become, and he is the

---

1 "Heaven" (οὐρανός) is used throughout the dialogue as a synonym of cosmos, the entire world, not the sky.

best of causes. Having come to be, then, in this way, the world has been fashioned on the model of that which is comprehensible by rational discourse and understanding and is always in the same state.

Again, these things being so, our [B] world must necessarily be a likeness of something. Now in every matter it is of great moment to start at the right point in accordance with the nature of the subject. Concerning a likeness, then, and its model we must make this distinction: an account is of the same order as the things which it sets forth—an account of that which is abiding and stable and discoverable by the aid of reason will itself be abiding and unchangeable (so far as it is possible and it lies in the nature of an account to be incontrovertible and irrefutable, there must be no falling short of that); while an ac- [C] count of what is made in the image of that other, but is only a likeness, will itself be but likely, standing to accounts of the former kind in a proportion: as reality is to becoming, so is truth to disbelief. If then, Socrates, in many respects concerning many things—the gods and the generation of the universe—we prove unable to render an account at all points entirely consistent with itself and exact, you must not be surprised. If we can furnish accounts no less likely than any other, we must be content, remembering that I who speak and you my judges are only human, and con- [D] sequently it is fitting that we should, in these matters, accept the likely story and look for nothing further.

SOCRATES. Excellent, Timaeus; we must certainly accept it as you say. Your prelude we have found exceedingly acceptable; so now go on to develop your main theme.

TIM. Let us, then, state for what reason becoming and this universe were framed by him who framed them. [E] He was good; and in the good no jealousy in any matter can ever arise. So, being without jealousy, he desired that all things should come as near as possible to being like himself. That this is the supremely valid principle of becoming and of the order of the world, we shall most surely be right to accept from men of understanding. Desiring, then, [30] that all things should be good and, so far as might be, nothing imperfect, the god took over all that is visible—not at rest, but in discordant and unordered motion—and brought it from disorder into order, since he judged that order was in every way the better.

Now it was not, nor can it ever be, permitted that the work of the supremely good should be anything but that which is best. Taking thought, therefore, he found that, among things that are by [B] nature visible, no work that is without intelligence will ever be better than one that has intelligence, when each is taken as a whole, and moreover that intelligence cannot be present in anything apart from soul. In virtue of this reasoning, when he framed the universe, he fashioned reason within soul and soul within body, to the end that the work he accomplished might be by nature as excellent and perfect as possible. This, then, is how we must say, according to the likely account, that this world came to be, by the god's providence, in very [C] truth a living creature with soul and reason.

This being premised, we have now to state what follows next: What was the living creature in whose likeness he framed the world? We must not suppose that it was any creature that ranks only as a species; for no copy of that which is incomplete can ever be good. Let us rather say that the world is like, above all things, to that Living Creature of which all other living creatures, severally and in their families, are parts. For that embraces and contains within itself all [D] the intelligible living creatures, just as this world contains ourselves and all other creatures that have been formed as things visible. For the god, wishing to make this world most nearly like that intelligible thing which is best and in every way complete, fashioned it as a single visible living creature, containing within itself all living things whose nature is of the same order.

Have we, then, been right to call [31] it one Heaven, or would it have been true rather to speak of many and indeed of an indefinite number? One we must call it, if we are to hold that it was made according to its pattern. For that which embraces all the intelligible living creatures that there are, cannot be one of a pair; for then there would have to be yet another Living Creature embracing those two, and they would be parts of it; and thus our world would be more truly described as a likeness, not of them, but of that other which would embrace them. Accordingly, to the end that this world may be like the completely Living Creature in respect of its uniqueness, [B] for that reason its maker did not make two worlds nor yet an indefinite number; but this Heaven has come to be and is and shall be hereafter one and unique.

Now that which comes to be must be bodily, and so visible and tangible; and nothing can be visible without fire, or tangible without something solid, and nothing is solid without earth. Hence the god, when he began to put together the body of the universe, set about making it of fire and earth. But two things alone cannot be satisfactorily united without a third; for there must be some bond [c] oetween them drawing them together. And of all bonds the best is that which makes itself and the terms it connects a unity in the fullest sense; and it is of the nature of a continued geometrical proportion to effect this most perfectly. For whenever, of three numbers, the [32] middle one between any two that are either solids (cubes?) or squares is such that, as the first is to it, so is it to the

last, and conversely as the last is to the middle, so is the middle to the first, then since the middle becomes first and last, and again the last and first becomes middle, in that way all will necessarily come to play the same part toward one another, and by so doing they will all make a unity.

Now if it had been required that the body of the universe should be a plane surface with no depth, a single mean would have been enough to connect its companions and itself; but in fact [B] the world was to be solid in form, and solids are always conjoined, not by one mean, but by two. Accordingly the god set water and air between fire and earth, and made them, so far as was possible, proportional to one another, so that as fire is to air, so is air to water, and as air is to water, so is water to earth, and thus he bound together the frame of a world visible and tangible.

For these reasons and from such [c] constituents, four in number, the body of the universe was brought into being, coming into concord by means of proportion, and from these it acquired Amity, so that coming into unity with itself it became indissoluble by any other save him who bound it together.

Now the frame of the world took up the whole of each of these four; he who put it together made it consist of all the fire and water and air and earth, leaving no part or power of any one of them outside. This was his intent: first, that it might be in the fullest measure a living being whole and complete, of [D] complete parts; next, that it might be single, nothing being left over, out of which such another might come into [33] being; and moreover that it might be free from age and sickness. For he perceived that, if a body be composite, when hot things and cold and all things that have strong powers beset that body and attack it from without, they bring it to untimely dissolution and cause it to waste away by bringing upon it sickness and age. For this reason and so considering, he fashioned it as a single whole consisting of all these wholes, complete and free from age and sickness.

And for shape he gave it that which [B] is fitting and akin to its nature. For the living creature that was to embrace all living creatures within itself, the fitting shape would be the figure that comprehends in itself all the figures there are; accordingly, he turned its shape rounded and spherical, equidistant every way from center to extremity—a figure the most perfect and uniform of all; for he judged uniformity to be immeasurably better than its opposite. And all round on the outside he made it perfectly smooth, for several reasons. It had no [C] need of eyes, for nothing visible was left outside; nor of hearing, for there was nothing outside to be heard. There was no surrounding air to require breathing, nor yet was it in need of any organ by which to receive food into itself or to discharge it again when drained of its juices. For nothing went out or came into it from anywhere, since there was nothing: it was designed to feed itself on its own waste and to act and be acted upon entirely by itself and within itself; because its framer thought that it [D] would be better self-sufficient, rather than dependent upon anything else.

It had no need of hands to grasp with or to defend itself, nor yet of feet or anything that would serve to stand upon; so he saw no need to attach to it these limbs to no purpose. For he assigned to it the motion proper to its bodily form, namely, that one of the [34] seven which above all belongs to reason and intelligence; accordingly, he caused it to turn about uniformly in the same place and within its own limits and made it revolve round and round; he took from it all the other six motions and gave it no part in their wanderings. And since for this revolution it needed no feet, he made it without feet or legs.

All this, then, was the plan of the god who is forever for the god who was sometime to be. According to this [B] plan he made it smooth and uniform, everywhere equidistant from its center, a body whole and complete, with complete bodies for its parts. And in the center he set a soul and caused it to extend throughout the whole and further wrapped its body round with soul on the outside; and so he established one world alone, round and revolving in a circle, solitary but able by reason of its excellence to bear itself company, needing no other acquaintance or friend but sufficient to itself. On all these accounts the world which he brought into being was a blessed god.

Now this soul, though it comes later in the account we are now attempting, was not made by the god younger than the body; for when he joined them together, he would not have suffered the elder [C] to be ruled by the younger. There is in us too much of the casual and random, which shows itself in our speech; but the god made soul prior to body and more venerable in birth and excellence, to be the body's mistress and governor.

•  •  •

When the father who had begotten it saw it set in motion and alive, a shrine brought into being for the everlasting gods, he rejoiced and being well pleased he took thought to make it yet more like its pattern. So as that pattern is the Living Being that is forever existent, he sought to make this universe also like it, so far as might be, in that respect. [37D] Now the nature of that Living Being was eternal, and this character it was impossible to confer in full completeness on the generated thing. But he took thought to make, as it were, a moving likeness of eternity; and, at the same time that he ordered the Heaven, he made, of eternity that abides in unity, an everlasting likeness moving according to number—that to which we have given the name Time.

For there were no days and nights, months and years, before the Heaven came into being; but he planned that they should now come to be at the [E] same time that the Heaven was framed. All these are parts of Time, and "was" and "shall be" are forms of time that have come to be; we are wrong to transfer them unthinkingly to eternal being. We say that it was and is and shall be; but "is" alone really belongs to it and describes it truly; "was" and "shall be" are properly used of becoming which proceeds in time, for they [38] are motions. But that which is forever in the same state immovably cannot be becoming older or younger by lapse of time, nor can it ever become so; neither can it now have been, nor will it be in the future; and in general nothing belongs to it of all that Becoming attaches to the moving things of sense; but these have come into being as forms of time, which images eternity and revolves according to number. And besides we make statements like these: that what is past *is* past, what happens now *is* [B] happening now, and again that what will happen *is* what will happen, and that the nonexistent *is* nonexistent: no one of these expressions is exact. But this, perhaps, may not be the right moment for a precise discussion of these matters.

Be that as it may, Time came into being together with the Heaven, in order that, as they were brought into being together, so they may be dissolved together, if ever their dissolution should come to pass; and it is made after the pattern of the ever-enduring nature, in order that it may be as like that [C] pattern as possible; for the pattern is a thing that has being for all eternity, whereas the Heaven has been and is and shall be perpetually throughout all time.

. . .

As concerning the other divinities, to know and to declare their generation is too high a task for us; we must trust those who have declared it in former times: being, as they said, descendants of gods, they must, no doubt, have had certain knowledge of their own ancestors. We cannot, then, mistrust the children of gods, though they speak without [E] probable or necessary proofs; when they profess to report their family history, we must follow established usage and accept what they say. Let us, then, take on their word this account of the generation of these gods. As children of Earth and Heaven were born Oceanus and Tethys; and of these Phorkys and Cronos and Rhea and all their company; and of Cronos and Rhea, Zeus and Hera and all their brothers and sisters whose [41] names we know; and of these yet other offspring.

Be that as it may, when all the gods had come to birth—both all that revolve before our eyes and all that reveal themselves in so far as they will—the author of this universe addressed them in these words:

"Gods, of gods whereof I am the maker and of works the father, those which are my own handiwork are indissoluble, save with my consent. Now, although whatsoever bond has been fastened may be unloosed, yet only an evil will [B] could consent to dissolve what has been well fitted together and is in a good state; therefore, although you, having come into being, are not immortal nor indissoluble altogether, nevertheless you shall not be disssolved nor taste of death, finding my will a bond yet stronger and more sovereign than those wherewith you were bound together when you came to be.

"Now, therefore, take heed to this that I declare to you. There are yet left mortal creatures of three kinds that have not been brought into being. If these be not born, the Heaven will be imperfect; for it will not contain all the kinds of living being, as it must if it is to be perfect and complete. But if I [C] myself gave them birth and life, they would be equal to gods. In order, then, that mortal things may exist and this All may be truly all, turn according to your own nature to the making of living creatures, imitating my power in generating you. In so far as it is fitting that something in them should share the name of the immortals, being called divine and ruling over those among them who at any time are willing to follow after righteousness and after you —that part, having sown it as seed and made a beginning, I will hand over to you. For the rest, do you, weaving mortal to immortal, make living beings; [D] bring them to birth, feed them, and cause them to grow; and when they fail, receive them back again."

Having said this, he turned once more to the same mixing bowl wherein he had mixed and blended the soul of the universe, and poured into it what was left of the former ingredients, blending them this time in somewhat the same way, only no longer so pure as before, but second or third in degree of purity. And when he had compounded the whole, he divided it into souls equal in number with the stars, and distributed them, each soul to its several star. There mounting them as it were in chariots, [E] he showed them the nature of the universe and declared to them the laws of Destiny. There would be appointed a first incarnation one and the same for all, that none might suffer disadvantage at his hands; and they were to be sown into the instruments of time, each one into that which was meet for it, and to be born as the most god- [42] fearing of living creatures; and human nature being twofold, the better sort was that which should thereafter be called "man."

Whensoever, therefore, they should of necessity have been implanted in bodies, and of their bodies some part should always be coming in and some part passing out, there must needs be innate in them, first, sensation, the same for

all, arising from violent impressions; second, desire blended with pleasure and pain, and besides these fear and anger and all the feelings that accompany these and all that are of a contrary [B] nature: and if they should master these passions, they would live in righteousness; if they were mastered by them, in unrighteousness.

And he who should live well for his due span of time should journey back to the habitation of his consort star and there live a happy and congenial life; but failing of this, he should shift at his second birth into a woman; and if in this condition he still did not cease [C] from wickedness, then according to the character of his depravation, he should constantly be changed into some beast of a nature resembling the formation of that character, and should have no rest from the travail of these changes, until letting the revolution of the Same and uniform within himself draw into its train all that turmoil or fire and water and air and earth that had later grown about it, he should control its [D] irrational turbulence by discourse of reason and return once more to the form of his first and best condition.

When he had delivered to them all these ordinances, to the end that he might be guiltless of the future wickedness of any one of them, he sowed them, some in the Earth, some in the Moon, some in all the other instruments of time. After this sowing he left it to the newly made gods to mold mortal bodies, to fashion all that part of a human soul that there was still need to add and all that these things entail, and to govern [E] and guide the mortal creature to the best of their powers, save in so far as it should be a cause of evil to itself.

•  •  •

I will try to give an explanation of all these matters in detail, no less probable than another, but more so, starting from the beginning in the same manner as before. So now once again at the outset of our discourse let us call upon a protecting deity to grant us safe passage through a strange and unfamiliar exposition to the conclusion that [48E] probability dictates; and so let us begin once more.

Our new starting point in describing the universe must, however, be a fuller classification than we made before. We then distinguished two things; but now a third must be pointed out. For our earlier discourse the two were sufficient: one postulated as model, intelligible and always unchangingly real; second, a copy of this model, which becomes [49] and is visible. A third we did not then distinguish, thinking that the two would suffice; but now, it seems, the argument compels us to attempt to bring to light and describe a form difficult and obscure. What nature must we, then, conceive it to possess and what part does it play? This, more than anything else: that it is the Receptacle—as it were, the nurse—of all Becoming.

True, however, as this statement is, it needs to be put in clearer language; and that is hard, in particular because to that end it is necessary to raise a [B] previous difficulty about fire and the things that rank with fire. It is hard to say, with respect to any one of these, which we ought to call really water rather than fire, or indeed which we should call by any given name rather than by all the names together or by each severally, so as to use language in a sound and trustworthy way. How, then, and in what terms are we to speak of this matter, and what is the previous difficulty that may be reasonably stated?

In the first place, take the thing we now call water. This, when it is compacted, we see (as we imagine) becoming earth and stones, and this same [c] thing, when it is dissolved and dispersed, becoming wind and air; air becoming fire by being inflamed; and, by a reverse process, fire, when condensed

and extinguished, returning once more to the form of air, and air coming together again and condensing as mist and cloud; and from these, as they are yet more closely compacted, flowing water; and from water once more earth and stones: and thus, as it appears, they transmit in a cycle the process of passing into one another. Since, then, in this way no one of these things ever makes its appearance as the *same* thing, [D] which of them can we steadfastly affirm to be *this*—whatever it may be—and not something else, without blushing for ourselves? It cannot be done; but by far the safest course is to speak of them in the following terms. Whenever we observe a thing perpetually changing—fire, for example—in every case we should speak of fire not as "this," but as "what is of such and such a quality," nor of water as "this," but always as "what is of such and such a quality"; nor must we speak of anything else as having some permanence, among all the things we indicate by the expres- [E] sions "this" or "that," imagining we are pointing out some definite thing. For they slip away and do not wait to be described as "that" or "this" or by any phrase that exhibits them as having permanent being. We should not use these expressions of any of them, but "that which is of a certain quality and has the same sort of quality as it perpetually recurs in the cycle"—that is the description we should use in the case of each and all of them. In fact, we must give the name "fire" to that which is at all times of such and such a quality; and so with anything else that is in process of becoming. Only in speaking of that *in* which all of them are always coming to be, making their appearance and again vanishing out of it, may we use the words "this" or "that"; we must [50] not apply any of these words to that which is of some quality—hot or cold or any of the opposites—or to any combination of these opposites.

But I must do my best to explain this thing once more in still clearer terms.

Suppose a man had molded figures of all sorts out of gold, and were unceasingly to remold each into all the rest: then, if you should point to one of them and ask what it was, much the safest [B] answer in respect of truth would be to say "gold," and never to speak of a triangle or any of the other figures that were coming to be in it as things that have being, since they are changing even while one is asserting their existence. Rather one should be content if they so much as consent to accept the description "what is of such and such a quality" with any certainty. Now the same thing must be said of that nature which receives all bodies. It must be called always the same; for it never departs at all from its own character; since it is always receiving all things, and never in any way whatsoever takes on [c] any character that is like any of the things that enter it: by nature it is there as a matrix for everything, changed and diversified by the things that enter it, and on their account it *appears* to have different qualities at different times; while the things that pass in and out are to be called copies of the eternal things, impressions taken from them in a strange manner that is hard to express: we will follow it up on another occasion.

Be that as it may, for the present [D] we must conceive three things: that which becomes; that in which it becomes; and the model in whose likeness that which becomes is born. Indeed we may fittingly compare the Recipient to a mother, the model to a father, and the nature that arises between them to their offspring. Further we must observe that, if there is to be an impress presenting all diversities of aspect, the thing itself in which the impress comes to be situated, cannot have been duly prepared unless it is free from all those characters which it is to receive from elsewhere. For if it were like any one of the things that come in upon it, then, when [E] things of contrary or entirely different nature came, in receiving them it would reproduce them badly, intruding its own features alongside. Hence that which is to receive in itself all kinds must be free from all characters; just like the base which the makers of scented ointments skillfully contrive to start with: they make the liquids that are to receive the scents as odorless as possible. Or again, anyone who sets about taking impressions of shapes in some soft substance allows no shape to show itself there beforehand, but begins by making the surface as smooth and level as he can, In the same way, that which is duly to [51] receive over its whole extent and many times over all the likenesses of the intelligible and eternal things ought in its own nature to be free of all the characters. For this reason, then, the mother and Receptacle of what has come to be visible and otherwise sensible must not be called earth or air or fire or water, nor any of their compounds or components; but we shall not be deceived if we call it a nature invisible and characterless, all-receiving, partaking in some very puzzling way of the intelli- [B] gible and very hard to apprehend. So far as its nature can be arrived at from what has already been said, the most correct account of it would be this: that part of it which has been made fiery appears at any time as fire; the part that is liquefied as water; and as earth or air such parts as receive likenesses of these.

But in pressing our inquiry about them, there is a question that must rather be determined by argument. Is there such a thing as "Fire just in itself" or any of the other things which we are always describing in such terms, as things that "are just in themselves"? [c] Or are the things we see or otherwise perceive by the bodily senses the only things that have such reality, and has nothing else, over and above these, any sort of being at all? Are we talking idly whenever we say that there is such a thing as an intelligible Form of anything? Is this nothing more than a word?

Now it does not become us either to dismiss the present question without trial or verdict, simply asseverating that it is so, nor yet to insert a lengthy digression into a discourse that is already [D] long. If we could see our way to draw a distinction of great importance in few words, that would best suit the occasion. My own verdict, then, is this. If intelligence and true belief are two different kinds, then these things—Forms that we cannot perceive but only think of— certainly exist in themselves; but if, as some hold, true belief in no way differs from intelligence, then all the things we perceive through the bodily senses must be taken as the most certain reality. Now we must affirm that they are two dif- [E] ferent things, for they are distinct in origin and unlike in nature. The one is produced in us by instruction, the other by persuasion; the one can always give a true account of itself, the other can give none; the one cannot be shaken by persuasion, whereas the other can be won over; and true belief, we must allow, is shared by all mankind, intelligence only by the gods and a small number of men.

This being so, we must agree that there is, first, the unchanging Form, ungenerated and indestructible, which [52] neither receives anything else into itself from elsewhere nor itself enters into anything else anywhere, invisible and otherwise imperceptible; that, in fact, which thinking has for its object.

Second is that which bears the same name and is like that Form; is sensible; is brought into existence; is perpetually in motion, coming to be in a certain place and again vanishing out of it; and is to be apprehended by belief involving perception.

Third is Space, which is everlasting, not admitting destruction; providing a situation for all things that come into [B] being, but itself apprehended without the senses by a sort of bastard reasoning, and hardly an object of belief.

This, indeed, is that which we look upon as in a dream and say that anything that is must needs be in some place and occupy some room, and that what is not somewhere in earth or heaven is nothing. Because of this dreaming state, we prove unable to rouse ourselves and to draw all these distinction and others akin to them, even in the case of the [C] waking and truly existing nature, and so to state the truth: namely that, whereas for an image, since not even the very principle on which it has come into being belongs to the image itself, but it is the ever moving semblance of something else, it is proper that it should come to be *in* something else, clinging in some sort of existence on pain of being nothing at all; on the other hand that which has real being has the support of the exactly true account, which declares that, so long as the two things are different, neither can ever come to be in the [D] other in such a way that the two should become at once one and the same thing and two.

Let this, then, be given as the tale summed according to my judgment: that there are Being, Space, Becoming— three distinct things—even before the Heaven came into being. Now the nurse of Becoming, being made watery and fiery and receiving the characters of earth and air, and qualified by all the other affections that go with these, [E] had every sort of diverse appearance to the sight; but because it was filled with powers that were neither alike nor evenly balanced, there was no equipoise in any region of it; but it was everywhere swayed unevenly and shaken by these things, and by its motion shook them in turn. And they, being thus moved, were perpetually being separated and carried in different directions; just as when things are shaken and winnowed by means of winnowing baskets and other instruments for cleaning corn, the [53] dense and heavy things go one way, while the rare and light are carried to another place and settle there. In the same way at that time the four kinds were shaken by the Recipient, which itself was in motion like an instrument for shaking, and it separated the most unlike kinds farthest apart from one another, and thrust the most alike closest together; whereby the different kinds came to have different regions, even [B] before the ordered whole consisting of them came to be. Before that, all these kinds were without proportion or measure. Fire, water, earth, and air possessed indeed some vestiges of their own nature, but were altogether in such a condition as we should expect for anything when deity is absent from it. Such being their nature at the time when the ordering of the universe was taken in hand, the god then began by giving them a distinct configuration by means of shapes and numbers. That the god framed them with the greatest possible perfection, which they had not before, must be taken, above all, as a principle we constantly assert.

...But as it was, the artificers who brought us into being reckoned whether they should make a long-lived but inferior race or one with a shorter life but nobler, and agreed that everyone [75c] must on all accounts prefer the shorter and better life to the longer and worse.

· · ·

When the conjoined bonds of the triangles in the marrow no longer hold out under the stress, but part asunder, they let go in their turn the bonds of the soul; and she, when thus set free in the course of nature, finds pleasure in taking wing to fly away. For whereas all that is against nature is painful, what takes place in the natural way is [81E] pleasant. So death itself, on this principle, is painful and contrary to nature when it results from disease or wounds,

but when it comes to close the natural course of old age, it is, of all deaths, the least distressing and is accompanied rather by pleasure than by pain.

· · ·

And now, it would seem, we have [E] fairly accomplished the task laid upon us at the outset: to tell the story of the universe so far as to the generation of man: For the manner in which the other living creatures have come into being, brief mention shall be enough, where there is no need to speak at length; so shall we, in our own judgment, rather preserve due measure in our account of them.

Let this matter, then, be set forth as follows. Of those who were born as men, all that were cowardly and spent their life in wrongdoing were, according to the probable account, transformed [91] at the second birth into women: for this reason it was at that time that the gods constructed the desire of sexual intercourse, fashioning one creature instinct with life in us, and another in women. The two were made by them in this way. From the conduit of our drink, where it receives liquid that has passed through the lungs by the kidneys into the bladder and ejects it with the air that presses upon it, they pierced an opening communicating with the compact marrow which runs from the head down the neck and along the spine and has, indeed, in our earlier discourse been called [B] "seed." This marrow, being instinct with life and finding an outlet, implanted in the part where this outlet was a lively appetite for egress and so brought it to completion as an Eros of begetting. Hence it is that in men the privy member is disobedient and self-willed, like a creature that will not listen to reason, and because of frenzied appetite bent upon carrying all before it. In women again, for the same reason, what is [C] called the matrix or womb, a living creature within them with a desire for childbearing, if it be left long unfruitful beyond the due season, is vexed and aggrieved, and wandering throughout the body and blocking the channels of the breath, by forbidding respiration brings the sufferer to extreme distress and causes all manner of disorders; until at last the Eros of the one and the Desire of the other bring the pair together, [D] pluck as it were the fruit from the tree and sow the plowland of the womb with living creatures still unformed and too small to be seen, and again differentiating their parts nourish them till they grow large within, and thereafter by bringing them to the light of day accomplish the birth of the living creature. Such is the origin of women and of all that is female.

Birds were made by transformation: growing feathers instead of hair, they came from harmless but light-witted men, who studied the heavens but imagined in their simplicity that the surest evidence in these matters comes through the eye. [E]

Land animals came from men who had no use for philosophy and paid no heed to the heavens because they had lost the use of the circuits in the head and followed the guidance of those parts of the soul that are in the breast. By reason of these practices they let their forelimbs and heads be drawn down to earth by natural affinity and there supported, and their heads were lengthened out and took any sort of shape into [92] which their circles were crushed together through inactivity. On this account their kind was born with four feet or with many, heaven giving to the more witless the greater number of points of support, that they might be all the more drawn earthward. The most senseless, whose whole bodies were stretched at length upon the earth, since they had no further need of feet, the gods made footless, crawling over the ground.

The fourth sort, that live in water, [B] came from the most foolish and stupid of all. The gods who remolded their form thought these unworthy any more to breathe the pure air, because their souls were polluted with every sort of transgression; and in place of breathing the fine and clean air, they thrust them down to inhale the muddy water of the depths. Hence came fishes and shellfish and all that lives in the water: in penalty for the last extreme of folly they are assigned the last and lowest habitation. These are the principles on which, now as then, all living creatures change one into another, shifting their place with [C] the loss or gain of understanding or folly.

Here at last let us say that our discourse concerning the universe has come to its end. For having received in full its complement of living creatures, mortal and immortal, this world has thus become a visible living creature embracing all that are visible and an image of the intelligible, a perceptible god, supreme in greatness and excellence, in beauty and perfection, this Heaven single in its kind and one.

## LAWS, Book X (in part)

PERSONS OF THE DIALOGUE

*An* ATHENIAN *Stranger*
CLEINIAS, *a Cretan*

ATHENIAN. Now we have to determine what is to be the punishment of those who speak or act insolently toward the Gods. But first we must give them an admonition which may be in the following terms:—No one who in obedience to the laws believed that there were Gods, ever intentionally did any unholy act, or uttered any unlawful word; but he who did must have supposed one of three things,—either that they did not exist,—which is the first possibility, or secondly, that, if they did, they took no care of man, or thirdly, that they were easily appeased and turned aside from their purpose by sacrifices and prayers.

CLEINIAS. What shall we say or do to these persons?

ATH. My good friend, let us first hear the jests which I suspect that they in their superiority will utter against us.

CLE. What jests?

ATH. They will make some irreverent speech of this sort:—"O inhabitants of Athens, and Sparta, and Cnosus," they will reply, "in that you speak truly; for some of us deny the very existence of the Gods, while others, as you say, are of the opinion that they do not care about us; and others that they are turned from their course by gifts. Now we have a right to claim, as you yourself allowed, in the matter of laws, that before you are hard upon us and threaten us, you should argue with us and convince us— you should first attempt to teach and persuade us that there are Gods by reasonable evidences, and also that they are too good to be unrighteous, or to be propitiated, or turned from their course by gifts. For when we hear such things said of them by those who are esteemed to be the best of poets, and orators, and prophets, and priests, and by innumerable others, the thoughts of most of us are not set upon abstaining from unrighteous acts, but upon doing them and atoning for them. When lawgivers profess that they are gentle and not stern, we think that they should first of all use persuasion to us, and show us the existence of Gods, if not in a better manner than other men, at any rate in a truer; and who knows but that we shall hearken to you? If then our request is a fair one, please to accept our challenge."

CLE. But is there any difficulty in proving the existence of the Gods?

ATH. How would you prove it? [886]

CLE. How? In the first place, the earth and the sun, and the stars and the universe, and the fair order of the seasons, and the division of them into years and months, furnish proofs of their existence; and also there is the fact that all Hellenes and barbarians believe in them.

ATH. I fear, my sweet friend, though I will not say that I much regard, the contempt with which the profane will be likely to assail us. For you do not understand the nature of their complaint, and you fancy that they rush into impiety only from a love of sensual pleasure.

CLE. Why, Stranger, what other reason is there?

ATH. One which you who live in a different atmosphere would never guess.

CLE. What is it?

ATH. A very grievous sort of ignorance which is imagined to be the greatest wisdom.

CLE. What do you mean?

ATH. At Athens there are tales preserved in writing which the virtue of your state, as I am informed, refuses to admit. They speak of the Gods in prose as well as verse, and the oldest of them tell of the origin of the heavens and of the world, and not far from the beginning of their story they proceed to narrate the birth of the Gods, and how after they were born they behaved to one another. Whether these stories have in other ways a good or a bad influence, I should not like to be severe upon them, because they are ancient; but, looking at them with reference to the duties of children to their parents, I cannot praise them, or think that they are useful, or at all true. Of the words of the ancients I have nothing more to say; and I should wish to say of them only what is pleasing to the Gods. But as to our younger generation and their wisdom, I cannot let them off when they do mischief. For do but mark the effect of their words: when you and I argue for the existence of the Gods, and produce the sun, moon, stars, and earth, claiming for them a divine being, if we would listen to the aforesaid philosophers we should say that they are earth and stones only, which can have no care at all of human affairs, and that all religion is a cooking up of words and a make-believe.

CLE. One such teacher, O Stranger, would be bad enough, and you imply that there are many of them, which is worse.

ATH. Well, then; what shall we [887] say or do?—Shall we assume that some one is accusing us among unholy men, who are trying to escape from the effect of our legislation; and that they say of us—How dreadful that you should legislate on the supposition that there are Gods! Shall we make a defence of ourselves?

. . .

The duty of the legislator is and always will be to teach you the truth of these matters.                        [888]

. . .

I must repeat the singular argument of those who manufacture the soul according to their own impious notions; they affirm that which is the first cause of the generation and destruction of all things, to be not first, but last, and that which is last to be first, and hence they have fallen into error about the true nature of the Gods.

CLE. Still I do not understand [892] you.

ATH. Nearly all of them, my friends, seem to be ignorant of the nature and power of the soul, especially in what relates to her origin: they do not know that she is among the first of things, and before all bodies, and is the chief author of their changes and transpositions. And if this is true, and if the soul is older than the body, must not the things which are of the soul's kindred be of necessity prior to those which appertain to the body?

CLE. Certainly.

ATH. Then thought and attention and mind and art and law will be prior to that which is hard and soft and heavy and light; and the great and primitive works and actions will be works of art; they will be the first, and after them will come nature and works of nature, which however is a wrong term for men to apply to them; these will follow, and will be under the government of art and mind.

CLE. But why is the word "nature" wrong?

ATH. Because those who use the term mean to say that nature is the first creative power; but if the soul turn out to be the primeval element, and not fire or air, then in the truest sense and beyond other things the soul may be said to exist by nature; and this would be true if you proved that the soul is older than the body, but not otherwise.

. . .

Holding fast to the rope we will venture upon the depths of the argument. When questions of this sort are asked of me, my safest answer would appear to be as follows:—Some one says to me, "O Stranger, are all things at rest and nothing in motion, or is the exact opposite of this true, or are some things in motion and others at rest?"—To this I shall reply that some things are in motion and others at rest. "And do not things which move move in a place, and are not the things which are at rest at rest in a place?" Certainly. "And some move or rest in one place and some in more places than one?" You mean to say, we shall rejoin, that those things which rest at the centre move in one place, just as the circumference goes round of globes which are said to be at rest? "Yes." And we observe that, in the revolution, the motion which carries round the larger and the lesser circle at the same time is proportionally distributed to greater and smaller, and is greater and smaller in a certain proportion. Here is a wonder which might be thought an impossibility, that the same motion should impart swiftness and slowness in due proportion to larger and lesser circles. "Very true." And when you speak of bodies moving in many places, you seem to me to mean those which move from one place to another, and sometimes have one centre of motion and sometimes more than one because they turn upon their axis; and whenever they meet anything, if it be stationary, they are divided by it; but if they get in the midst between bodies which are approaching and moving towards the same spot from opposite directions, they unite with them. "I admit the truth of what you are saying." Also when they unite they grow, and when they are divided they waste away,—that is, supposing the constitution of each to remain, or if that fails, then there is a second reason of their dissolution. "And when are all things created and [894] how?" Clearly, they are created when the first principle receives increase and attains to the second dimension, and from this arrives at the one which is neighbour to this, and after reaching the third becomes perceptible to sense. Everything which is thus changing and moving is in process of generation; only when at rest has it real existence, but when passing into another state it is destroyed utterly. Have we not mentioned all motions that there are, and comprehended them under their kinds and numbered them with the exception, my friends, of two?

CLE. Which are they?

ATH. Just the two, with which our present enquiry is concerned.

CLE. Speak plainer.

ATH. I suppose that our enquiry has reference to the soul?

CLE. Very true.

ATH. Let us assume that there is a motion able to move other things, but not to move itself;—that is one kind;

and there is another kind which can move itself as well as other things, working in composition and decomposition, by increase and diminution and generation and destruction,—that is also one of the many kinds of motion.

CLE. Granted.

ATH. And we will assume that which moves other, and is changed by other, to be the ninth, and that which changes itself and others, and is co-incident with every action and every passion, and is the true principle of change and motion in all that is,—that we shall be inclined to call the tenth.

CLE. Certainly.

ATH. And which of these ten motions ought we to prefer as being the mightiest and most efficient?

CLE. I must say that the motion which is able to move itself is ten thousand times superior to all the others.

ATH. Very good; but may I make one or two corrections in what I have been saying?

CLE. What are they?

ATH. When I spoke of the tenth sort of motion, that was not quite correct.

CLE. What was the error?

ATH. According to the true order, the tenth was really the first in generation and power; then follows the second, which was strangely enough termed the ninth by us.

CLE. What do you mean?

ATH. I mean this: when one thing changes another, and that another, of such will there be any primary changing element? How can a thing which is moved by another ever be the beginning of change? Impossible. But when the self-moved changes other, and that again other, and thus thousands upon tens of thousands of bodies are set in mo- [895] tion, must not the beginning of all this motion be the change of the self-moving principle?

CLE. Very true, and I quite agree.

ATH. Or, to put the question in another way, making answer to ourselves:

—If, as most of these philosophers have the audacity to affirm, all things were at rest in one mass, which of the above-mentioned principles of motion would first spring up among them?

CLE. Clearly the self-moving; for there could be no change in them arising out of any external cause; the change must first take place in themselves.

ATH. Then we must say that self-motion being the origin of all motions, and the first which arises among things at rest as well as among things in motion, is the eldest and mightiest principle of change, and that which is changed by another and yet moves other is second.

CLE. Quite true.

ATH. At this stage of the argument let us put a question.

CLE. What question?

ATH. If we were to see this power existing in any earthy, watery, or fiery substance, simple or compound—how should we describe it?

CLE. You mean to ask whether we should call such a self-moving power life?

ATH. I do.

CLE. Certainly we should.

ATH. And when we see soul in anything, must we not do the same—must we not admit that this is life?

CLE. We must.

ATH. And now, I beseech you, reflect; —you would admit that we have a three-fold knowledge of things?

CLE. What do you mean?

ATH. I mean that we know the essence, and that we know the definition of the essence, and the name,—these are the three; and there are two questions which may be raised about anything.

CLE. How two?

ATH. Sometimes a person may give the name and ask the definition; or he may give the definition and ask the name. I may illustrate what I mean in this way.

CLE. How?

ATH. Number like some other things is capable of being divided into equal parts; when thus divided, number is named "even," and the definition of the name "even" is "number divisible into two equal parts"?

CLE. True.

ATH. I mean, that when we are asked about the definition and give the name, or when we are asked about the name and give the definition—in either case, whether we give name or definition, we speak of the same thing, calling "even" the number which is divided into two equal parts.

CLE. Quite true.

ATH. And what is the definition [896] of that which is named "soul"? Can we conceive of any other than that which has been already given—the motion which can move itself?

CLE. You mean to say that the essence which is defined as the self-moved is the same with that which has the name soul?

ATH. Yes; and if this is true, do we still maintain that there is anything wanting in the proof that the soul is the first origin and moving power of all that is, or has become, or will be, and their contraries, when she has been clearly shown to be the source of change and motion in all things?

CLE. Certainly not; the soul as being the source of motion, has been most satisfactorily shown to be the oldest of all things.

ATH. And is not that motion which is produced in another, by reason of another, but never has any self-moving power at all, being in truth the change of an inanimate body, to be reckoned second, or by any lower number which you may prefer?

CLE. Exactly.

ATH. Then we are right, and speak the most perfect and absolute truth, when we say that the soul is prior to the body, and that the body is second and comes afterwards, and is born to obey the soul, which is the ruler?

CLE. Nothing can be more true.

ATH. Do you remember our old admission, that if the soul was prior to the body the things of the soul were also prior to those of the body?

CLE. Certainly.

ATH. Then characters and manners, and wishes and reasonings, and true opinions, and reflections, and recollections are prior to length and breadth and depth and strength of bodies, if the soul is prior to the body.

CLE. To be sure.

ATH. In the next place, must we not of necessity admit that the soul is the cause of good and evil, base and honourable, just and unjust, and of all other opposites, if we suppose her to be the cause of all things?

CLE. We must.

ATH. And as the soul orders and inhabits all things that move, however moving, must we not say that she orders also the heavens?

CLE. Of course.

ATH. One soul or more? More than one—I will answer for you;—at any rate, we must not suppose that there are less than two—one the author of good, and the other of evil.

CLE. Very true.

. . .

ATH. If, my friend, we say that the whole path and movement of heaven, and of all that is therein, is by nature akin to the movement and revolution and calculation of mind, and proceeds by kindred laws, then, as is plain, we must say that the best soul takes care of the world and guides it along the good path.                              [897]

. . .

CLE. And judging from what has been said, Stranger, there would be impiety in asserting that any but the most perfect soul or souls carries round the [898] heavens.

. . .

ATH. Either the soul which moves the sun this way and that, resides within the circular and visible body, like the soul which carries us about every way; or the soul provides herself with an ex- [899] ternal body of fire or air, as some affirm, and violently propels body by body; or thirdly, she is without such a body, but guides the sun by some extraordinary and wonderful power.

CLE. Yes, certainly; the soul can only order all things in one of these three ways.

ATH. And this soul of the sun, which is therefore better than the sun, whether taking the sun about in a chariot to give light to men, or acting from without, or in whatever way, ought by every man to be deemed a God.

CLE. Yes, by every man who has the least particle of sense.

ATH. And of the stars too, and of the moon, and of the years and months and seasons, must we not say in like manner, that since a soul or souls having every sort of excellence are the causes of all of them, those souls are Gods, whether they are living beings and reside in bodies, and in this way order the whole heaven, or whatever be the place and mode of their existence;—and will any one who admits all this venture to deny that all things are full of Gods?

CLE. No one, Stranger, would be such a madman.

ATH. And now, Megillus and Cleinias, let us offer terms to him who has hitherto denied the existence of the Gods, and leave him.

CLE. What terms?

ATH. Either he shall teach us that we were wrong in saying that the soul is the original of all things, and arguing accordingly; or, if he be not able to say anything better, then he must yield to us and live for the remainder of his life in the belief that there are Gods.—Let us see, then, whether we have said enough or not enough to those who deny that there are Gods.

CLE. Certainly,—quite enough, Stranger.

ATH. Then to them we will say no more. And now we are to address him who, believing that there are Gods, believes also that they take no heed of human affairs: To him we say,—O thou best of men, in believing that there are Gods you are led by some affinity to them, which attracts you towards your kindred and makes you honour and believe in them. But the fortunes of evil and unrighteous men in private as well as public life, which, though not really happy, are wrongly counted happy in the judgment of men, and are celebrated both by poets and prose writers—these draw you aside from your natural [900] piety. Perhaps you have seen impious men growing old and leaving their children's children in high offices, and their prosperity shakes your faith—you have known or heard or been yourself an eye-witness of many monstrous impieties, and have beheld men by such criminal means from small beginnings attaining to sovereignty and the pinnacle of greatness; and considering all these things you do not like to accuse the Gods of them, because they are your relatives; and so from some want of reasoning power, and also from an unwillingness to find fault with them, you have come to believe that they exist indeed, but have no thought or care of human things. Now, that your present evil opinion may not grow to still greater impiety, and that we may if possible use arguments which may conjure away the evil before it arrives, we will add another argument to that originally addressed to him who utterly denied the existence of the Gods. And do you, Megillus and Cleinias, answer for the young man as you did before; and if any impediment comes in our way, I will take the word out of your mouths, and carry you over the river as I did just now.

CLE. Very good; do as you say, and we will help you as well as we can.

ATH. There will probably be no dif-

ficulty in proving to him that the Gods care about the small as well as about the great. For he was present and heard what was said, that they are perfectly good, and that the care of all things is most entirely natural to them.

CLE. No doubt he heard that.

ATH. Let us consider together in the next place what we mean by this virtue which we ascribe to them. Surely we should say that to be temperate and to possess mind belongs to virtue, and the contrary to vice?

CLE. Certainly.

ATH. Yes; and courage is a part of virtue, and cowardice of vice?

CLE. True.

ATH. And the one is honourable, and the other dishonourable?

CLE. To be sure.

ATH. And the one, like other meaner things, is a human quality, but the Gods have no part in anything of the sort?

CLE. That again is what everybody will admit.

ATH. But do we imagine carelessness and idleness and luxury to be virtues? What do you think?

CLE. Decidedly not.

ATH. They rank under the opposite class?

CLE. Yes.

ATH. And their opposites, there- [901] fore, would fall under the opposite class?

CLE. Yes.

ATH. But are we to suppose that one who possesses all these good qualities will be luxurious and heedless and idle, like those whom the poet compares to sting-less drones?[1]

CLE. And the comparison is a most just one.

ATH. Surely God must not be supposed to have a nature which He Himself hates?—he who dares to say this sort of thing must not be tolerated for a moment.

---

[1] Hesiod, *Works and Days*, 307.

CLE. Of course not. How could He have?

ATH. Should we not on any principle be entirely mistaken in praising any one who has some special business entrusted to him, if he have a mind which takes care of great matters and no care of small ones? Reflect; he who acts in this way, whether he be God or man, must act from one of two principles.

CLE. What are they?

ATH. Either he must think that the neglect of the small matters is of no consequence to the whole, or if he knows that they are of consequence, and he neglects them, his neglect must be attributed to carelessness and indolence. Is there any other way in which his neglect can be explained? For surely, when it is impossible for him to take care of all, he is not negligent if he fails to attend to these things great or small, which a God or some inferior being might be wanting in strength or capacity to manage?

CLE. Certainly not.

ATH. Now, then, let us examine the offenders, who both alike confess that there are Gods, but with a difference,— the one saying that they may be appeased, and the other that they have no care of small matters: there are three of us and two of them, and we will say to them,—In the first place, you both acknowledge that the Gods hear and see and know all things, and that nothing can escape them which is matter of sense and knowledge:—do you admit this?

CLE. Yes.

ATH. And do you admit also that they have all power which mortals and immortals can have?

CLE. They will, of course, admit this also.

. . .

ATH. Let us say to the youth:— [903] The ruler of the universe has ordered all things with a view to the excellence and preservation of the whole, and each part,

as far as may be, has an action and passion appropriate to it. Over these, down to the least fraction of them, ministers have been appointed to preside, who have wrought out their perfection with infinitesimal exactness. And one of these portions of the universe is thine own, unhappy man, which, however little, contributes to the whole; and you do not seem to be aware that this and every other creation is for the sake of the whole, and in order that the life of the whole may be blessed; and that you are created for the sake of the whole, and not the whole for the sake of you. For every physician and every skilled artist does all things for the sake of the whole, directing his effort towards the common good, executing the part for the sake of the whole, and not the whole for the sake of the part. And you are annoyed because you are ignorant of how what is best for you happens to you and to the universe, as far as the laws of the common creation admit. Now, as the soul combining first with one body and then with another undergoes all sorts of changes, either of herself, or through the influence of another soul, all that remains to the player of the game is that he should shift the pieces; sending the better nature to the better place, and the worse to the worse, and so asigning to them their proper portion.

. . .

The formation of qualities he left to the wills of individuals. For every one of us is made pretty much what he is by the bent of his desires and the nature of his soul.

CLE. Yes, that is probably true.

ATH. Then all things which have a soul change, and possess in themselves a principle of change, and in changing move according to law and to the order of destiny: natures which have undergone a lesser change move less and on the earth's surface, but those which have suffered more change and have become more criminal sink into the abyss, that is to say, into Hades and other places in the world below, of which the very names terrify men, and which they picture to themselves as in a dream, both while alive and when released from the body. And whenever the soul receives more of good or evil from her own energy and the strong influence of others —when she has communion with divine virtue and becomes divine, she is carried into another and better place, which is perfect in holiness; but when she has communion with evil, then she also changes the place of her life.

"This is the justice of the Gods who inhabit Olympus."[2]

O youth or young man, who fancy that you are neglected by the Gods, know that if you become worse you shall go to the worse souls, or if better, to the better, and in every succession of life and death you will do and suffer what like may fitly suffer at the hands of like. This is [905] the justice of heaven, which neither you nor any other unfortunate will ever glory in escaping, and which the ordaining powers have specially ordained; take good heed thereof, for it will be sure to take heed of you. If you say:—I am small and will creep into the depths of the earth, or I am high and will fly up to heaven, you are not so small or so high but that you shall pay the fitting penalty, either here or in the world below or in some still more savage place whither you shall be conveyed. . . . For I think that we have sufficiently proved the existence of the Gods, and that they care for men:—The other notion that they are appeased by the wicked, and take gifts, is what we must not concede to any one, and what every man should disprove to the utmost of his power.

• • •

2 Hom. *Odyss.* xix. 43.

ATH. And shall we say that those who guard our noblest interests, and are the best of guardians, are inferior in virtue to dogs, and to men even of moderate excellence, who would never betray justice for the sake of gifts which unjust men impiously offer them?

CLE. Certainly not; nor is such a notion to be endured, and he who holds this opinion may be fairly singled out and characterized as of all impious men the wickedest and most impious.

ATH. Then are the three assertions— that the Gods exist, and that they take care of men, and that they can never be persuaded to do injustice, now sufficiently demonstrated? May we say that they are?

CLE. You have our entire assent to your words.

ATH. I have spoken with vehemence because I am zealous against evil men; and I will tell you, dear Cleinias, why I am so. I would not have the wicked think that, having the superiority in argument, they may do as they please and act according to their various imaginations about the Gods; and this zeal has led me to speak too vehemently; but if we have at all succeeded in persuading the men to hate themselves and love their opposites, the prelude of our laws about impiety will not have been spoken in vain.

CLE. So let us hope; and even if we have failed, the style of our argument will not discredit the lawgiver.

ATH. After the prelude shall follow a discourse, which will be the interpreter of the law; this shall proclaim to all impious persons that they must depart from their ways and go over to the pious. And to those who disobey, let the law about impiety be as follows:—If a man be guilty of any impiety in word or deed, any one who happens to be present shall give information to the magistrates, in aid of the law; and if a magistrate, after receiving information, refuses to act, he shall be tried for impiety at the instance of any one who is willing to vindicate the laws; and if any one be cast, the court shall estimate the punishment of each act of impiety; and let all such criminals be imprisoned. There shall be three prisons in the [908] state: the first of them is to be the common prison in the neighborhood of the agora for the safe-keeping of the generality of offenders; another is to be in the neighborhood of the nocturnal council, and is to be called the "House of Reformation"; another, to be situated in some wild and desolate region in the centre of the country, shall be called by some name expressive of retribution. Now, men fall into impiety from three causes, which have been already mentioned, and from each of these causes arise two sorts of impiety, in all six, which are worth distinguishing, and should not all have the same punishment. For he who does not believe in the Gods, and yet has a righteous nature, hates the wicked and dislikes and refuses to do injustice, and avoids unrighteous men, and loves the righteous. But they who besides believing that the world is devoid of Gods are intemperate, and have at the same time good memories and quick wits, are worse; although both of them are unbelievers, much less injury is done by the one than by the other. The one may talk loosely about the Gods and about sacrifices and oaths, and perhaps by laughing at other men he may make them like himself, if he be not punished. But the other who holds the same opinions and is called a clever man, is full of stratagem and deceit—men of this class deal in prophecy and jugglery of all kinds, and out of their ranks sometimes come tyrants and demagogues and generals and hierophants of private mysteries and the Sophists, as they are termed, with their ingenious devices. There are many kinds of unbelievers, but two only, for whom legislation is required; one the hypocritical sort, whose crime is deserv-

ing of death many times over, while the other needs only bonds and admonition. In like manner also the notion that the Gods take no thought of men produces two other sorts of crimes, and the notion that they may be propitiated produces two more. Assuming these divisions, let those who have been made what they are only from want of understanding, and not from malice or [909] an evil nature, be placed by the judge in the House of Reformation, and ordered to suffer imprisonment during a period of not less than five years. And in the meantime let them have no intercourse with the other citizens, except with the members of the nocturnal council, and with them let them converse with a view to the improvement of their soul's health. And when the time of their imprisonment has expired, if any of them be of sound mind let him be restored to sane company, but if not, and if he be condemned a second time, let him be punished with death. As to that class of monstrous natures who not only believe that there are no Gods, or that they are negligent, or to be propitiated, but in contempt of mankind conjure the souls of the living and say that they can conjure the dead and promise to charm the Gods with sacrifices and prayers, and will utterly overthrow individuals and whole houses and states for the sake of money—let him who is guilty of any of these things be condemned by the court to be bound according to law in the prison which is in the centre of the land, and let no freeman ever approach him, but let him receive the rations of food appointed by the guardians of the law from the hands of the public slaves; and when he is dead let him be cast beyond the borders unburied, and if any freeman assist in burying him, let him pay the penalty of impiety to any one who is willing to bring a suit against him. But if he leaves behind him children who are fit to be citizens, let the guardians of orphans take care of them, just as they would of any other orphans, from the day on which their father is convicted.

In all these cases there should be one law, which will make men in general less liable to transgress in word or deed, and less foolish, because they will not be allowed to practise religious rites contrary to law. And let this be the simple form of the law:—No man shall have sacred rites in a private house. When he would sacrifice, let him go to the temples and hand over his offerings to the priests and priestesses, who see to the sanctity of such things, and let him pray himself, and let any one who pleases join with him in prayer. The reason of this is as follows:—Gods and temples are not easily instituted, and to establish them rightly is the work of a mighty intellect. And women especially, and men too, when they are sick or in danger, or in any sort of difficulty, or again on their receiving any good fortune, have a way of consecrating the occasion, vowing sacrifices, and promising shrines to Gods, demigods, and [910] sons of Gods; and when they are awakened by terrible apparitions and dreams or remember visions, they find in altars and temples the remedies of them, and will fill every house and village with them, placing them in the open air, or wherever they may have had such visions; and with a view to all these cases we should obey the law. The law has also regard to the impious, and would not have them fancy that by secret performance of these actions—by raising temples and by building altars in private houses, they can propitiate the God secretly with sacrifices and prayers, while they are really multiplying their crimes infinitely, bringing guilt from heaven upon themselves, and also upon those who permit them, and who are better men than they are; and the consequence is that the whole state reaps the fruit of their impiety, which, in a certain sense, is deserved. Assuredly God will not blame the legislator, who will enact the following law:—No one shall possess shrines of the Gods in private houses, and he who is found to possess them, and perform any sacred rites not publicly authorized,—supposing the offender to be some man or woman who is not guilty of any other great and impious crime,—shall be informed against by him who is acquainted with the fact, which shall be announced by him to the guardians of the law; and let them issue orders that he or she shall carry away their private rites to public temples, and if they do not persuade them, let them inflict a penalty on them until they comply. And if a person is proven guilty of impiety, not merely from childish levity, but such as grown-up men may be guilty of, whether he have sacrificed publicly or privately to any Gods, let him be punished with death, for his sacrifice is impure. Whether the deed has been done in earnest, or only from childish levity, let the guardians of the law determine, before they bring the matter into court and prosecute the offender for impiety.

# EPILOGUE

*EPISTLE VII (in part : 324-26, 330-31, 341)*

In the days of my youth my experience was the same as that of many others. I thought that as soon as I should become my own master I would immediately enter into public life. But it so happened, I found, that the following changes occurred in the political situation.

In the government then existing, reviled as it was by many, a revolution took place; and the revolution was headed by fifty-one leaders, of whom eleven were in the City and ten in the Piraeus—each of these sections dealing with the market and with all municipal matters requiring management—and Thirty were established as irresponsible rulers of all. Now of these some were actually connexions and acquaintances of mine; and indeed they invited me at once to join their administration, thinking it would be congenial. The feelings I then experienced, owing to my youth, were in no way surprising: for I imagined that they would ad- minister the State by leading it out of an unjust way of life into a just way, and consequently I gave my mind to them very diligently, to see what they would do. And indeed I saw how these men within a short time caused men to look back on the former government as a golden age; and above all how they treated my aged friend Socrates, whom I would hardly scruple to call the most just of men then living, when they tried to send him, along with others, after one of the citizens, to fetch him by force that he might be put to death—their object being that Socrates, whether he wished or no, might be made to share in their political actions; he, however, refused to obey and risked the uttermost penalties rather than be a partaker in their unholy deeds. So when I beheld all these actions and others of a similar grave kind, I was indignant, and I withdrew myself from the evil practices then going on. But in no long time the power of the Thirty was overthrown together with the whole of the government which then existed. Then once again I was really, though less urgently, impelled with a desire to take part in public and political affairs. Many deplorable events, however, were still happening in those times, troublous as they were, and it was not surprising that in some instances, during these revolutions, men were avenging themselves on their foes too fiercely; yet, notwithstanding, the exiles who then returned exercised no little moderation. But, as ill-luck would have it, certain men of authority summoned our comrade Socrates before the law-courts, laying a charge against him which was most unholy, and which Socrates of all men least deserved; for it was on the charge of impiety that those men summoned him and the rest condemned and slew him—the very man who on the former occasion, when they themselves had the misfortune to be in exile, had refused to take part in the unholy arrest of one of the friends of the men then exiled.

When, therefore, I considered all this, and the type of men who were administering the affairs of State, with their laws too and their customs, the more I considered them and the more I advanced in years myself, the more difficult appeared to me the task of managing affairs of State rightly. For it was impossible to take action without friends and trusty companions; and these it was not easy to find ready to hand, since our State was no longer managed according to the principles and institutions of our forefathers; while to acquire other new friends with any facility was a thing impossible. Moreover, both the written laws and the customs were being corrupted, and that with surprising rapidity. Consequently, although at first I was filled with an ardent desire to engage in public affairs, when I considered all this and saw how things were shifting about anyhow in all directions, I finally became dizzy;

and although I continued to consider by what means some betterment could be brought about not only in these matters but also in the government as a whole, yet as regards political action I kept constantly waiting for an opportune moment; until, finally, looking at all the States which now exist, I perceived that one and all they are badly governed; for the state of their laws is such as to be almost incurable without some marvellous overhauling and good luck to boot. So in my praise of the right philosophy I was compelled to declare that by it one is enabled to discern all forms of justice both political and individual. Wherefore the classes of mankind (I said) will have no cessation from evils until either the class of those who are right and true philosophers attains political supremacy, or else the class of those who hold power in the States becomes, by some dispensation of Heaven, really philosophic [cf. *Republic* 437].

. . .

Ought not the doctor that is giving counsel to a sick man who is indulging in a mode of life that is bad for his health to try first of all to change his life, and only proceed with the rest of his advice if the patient is willing to obey? But should he prove unwilling, then I would esteem him both manly and a true doctor if he withdraws from advising a patient of that description, and contrariwise unmanly and unskilled if he continues to advise.[1] So too with a State, whether it has one ruler or many, if so be that it asks for some salutary advice when its government is duly proceeding by the right road, then it is the act of a judicious man to give advice to such people. But in the case of those who altogether exceed the

---

[1] For the comparison of the political adviser to a physician *cf. Rep.* 425 E ff., *Laws* 720 A ff.

bounds of right government and wholly refuse to proceed in its tracks, and who warn their counsellor to leave the government alone and not disturb it, on pain of death if he does disturb it, while ordering him to advise as to how all that contributes to their desires and appetites may most easily and quickly be secured for ever and ever—then, in such a case, I should esteem unmanly the man who continued to engage in counsels of this kind, and the man who refused to continue manly.

This, then, being the view I hold, whenever anyone consults me concerning any very important affair relating to his life—the acquisition of wealth, for instance, or the care of his body or his soul,—if I believe that he is carrying on his daily life in a proper way, or that he will be willing to obey my advice in regard to the matters disclosed, then I give counsel readily and do not confine myself to some merely cursory reply. But if he does not ask my advice at all or plainly shows that he will in no wise obey his adviser, I do not of my own instance come forward to advise such an one, nor yet to compel him, not even were he my own son. To a slave, however, I would give advice, and if he refused it I would use compulsion. But to a father or mother I deem it impious to apply compulsion, unless they are in the grip of the disease of insanity; but if they are living a settled life which is pleasing to them, though not to me, I would neither irritate them with vain exhortations nor yet minister to them with flatteries by providing them with means to satisfy appetites of a sort such that I, were I addicted to them, would refuse to live. So likewise it behooves the man of sense to hold, while he lives, the same view concerning his own State: if it appears to him to be ill governed he ought to speak, if so be that his speech is not likely to prove fruitless nor to cause his death; but he ought not to apply violence to his fatherland in the form of a political revolution, whenever it is impossible to establish the best kind of polity without banishing and slaughtering citizens, but rather he ought to keep quiet and pray for what is good both for himself and for his State.

. . .

I know indeed that certain others have written about these same subjects; but what manner of men they are not even themselves know. But thus much I can certainly declare concerning all these writers, or prospective writers, who claim to know the subjects which I seriously study, whether as hearers of mine or of other teachers, or from their own discoveries; it is impossible, in my judgement at least, that these men should understand anything about this subject. There does not exist, nor will there ever exist, any treatise of mine dealing therewith. For it does not at all admit of verbal expression like other studies, but, as a result of continued application to the subject itself and communion therewith, it is brought to birth in the soul on a sudden, as light that is kindled by a leaping spark, and thereafter it nourishes itself. Notwithstanding, of thus much I am certain, that the best statement of these doctrines in writing or in speech would be my own statement; and further, that if they should be badly stated in writing, it is I who would be the person most deeply pained. And if I had thought that these subjects ought to be fully stated in writing or in speech to the public, what nobler action could I have performed in my life than that of writing what is of great benefit to mankind and bringing forth to the light for all men the nature of reality? But were I to undertake this task it would not, as I think, prove a good thing for men, save for some few who are able to discover the truth themselves with but little instruction; for as to the rest, some it would most unseasonably fill with a mistaken contempt, and others with an overweening and empty aspiration, as though they had learnt some sublime mysteries.

.   .   .

### part three

# ARISTOTLE

I

Aristotle was born at Stagira, on the borders of Macedonia, in 384 B.C. For twenty years, beginning in 367, he was a student in Plato's Academy; but, as he said, he loved the truth more than he loved Plato, and he had no mind to remain a mere disciple. It is said that he left Athens when Plato made his nephew Speusippus his successor as head of the Academy, in 347. Around 343 he was called to Macedonia by king Philip to tutor the king's son, Alexander. Ten years later, Alexander had conquered all of Greece and overthrown the Persian Empire. By that time Aristotle had returned to Athens, where he presided over his own school, the so-called Lyceum. Because he liked to do some of his teaching while walking up and down under the colonnades with some of his more advanced students, his school and his philosophy were also called peripatetic. Charged with impiety when he was just over sixty, he fled Athens "lest," as he put it, "the Athenians sin twice against philosophy." A year later, in 322, he died.

There is no doubt that after Plato, he was the most influential philosopher of all time. He dominated later medieval philosophy to such an extent that St. Thomas referred to him simply as *philosophus,* "the philosopher." Thomism and contemporary Catholic philosophy are unthinkable without him. Logic, as taught until about the time of the second World War, was essentially Aristotle's logic. His *Poetics* is still one of the classics of literary criticism, and his dicta about tragedy are still widely accepted. In metaphysics and ethics, criticism of his views has spread since Bacon and Descartes inaugurated modern philosophy, hurling their defiance at him; but for all that, the problems he saw, the distinctions he introduced, and the terms he

279

defined are still central in many, if not most, discussions. His influence and prestige, like Plato's, are international and not confined to any school. Without him, Western philosophy might be very different.

His extant works lack the literary grace of Plato's. He, too, is said to have written dialogues, but they have not survived. What we have are often crabbed, extremely difficult, but generally highly interesting notes. There is a great deal of overlapping, repetition, and no dearth of apparent contradictions. Even one who is loath to violate the philosophic and artistic integrity of a complete work finds that we simply do not have works from Aristotle's hand that are complete in that sense. Still, there is no need to paste together snippets from here and there to piece together a system.

Over half of the following selections comes from Aristotle's *Metaphysics:* five of its fourteen books are offered complete, and about half of Book V is included. In the first book (A), he introduces his conception of the four kinds of causes (formal, material, efficient, and final), and reviews the history of philosophy to his own time. In the fourth (*Γ*) he speaks of the study of being as such, of substance, of the law of contradiction and the law of excluded middle, and discusses and criticizes the teaching of Protagoras. In the fifth book (*Δ*) he furnishes a "Philosophical Lexicon" and defines thirty terms or groups of terms. Only half of this "dictionary" is offered here. Book VII (*Z*) deals with substance and related notions. Book nine (*Θ*) is devoted to the distinction between potency and actuality. The twelfth book (*Λ*) has been called "in some ways the most impressive of all" by W. D. Ross. It employs many of the conceptions introduced previously, such as substance, actuality, and potency, and then argues to a first mover, to whom a large number of other unmoved movers are added in short order, before we are offered Aristotle's conception of the divine as contemplating itself.

Scholars agree that the books of the *Metaphysics* represent a collection of notes and treatises, not a finished work. Many of the best consider Book V (*Δ*) an independent work, earlier than most of the rest, and regard XII (*Λ*) as a separate treatise, too. XII.8, with its many unmoved movers, has been relegated to a later phase in Aristotle's development.

The first five chapters of Aristotle's *Categories* help to clear up all kinds of questions about his conception of substance; and they add a few other interesting points as well.

The *Posterior Analytics*, which deals with the forms of argument and inquiry, is divided into two books. From the first, Chapters 1-3, 8-10, and 31 are offered here. Of these three sections, the first deals with the need for pre-existent knowledge, the nature of scientific knowledge, the conditions of demonstration, and the meaning of contradiction, enunciation, proposition, basic truth, thesis, axiom, hypothesis, and definition. In Chapter 8, Aristotle argues that only eternal connections can be demonstrated; in Chapter 9, that demonstrations must proceed from the basic premises peculiar to each science, except in the case of subalternate sciences. In Chapter 10, he distinguishes the different kinds of basic truth. Chapters 1 and 2 of Book II, reproduced here, consider the four possible forms of inquiry and argue that they all concern the middle term. And in Chapter 19, the last Chapter of the whole work, he discusses how the individual mind comes to know the basic truths.

Of Aristotle's many works on science, two are represented in the following pages. From the *Physics*, three sections have been selected: In Book II, Chapter 8, Aristotle argues that nature is purposeful; in Book IV, Chapters 10 through 14, he offers a noteworthy discussion of time; and in Book VI, Chapter 9, he attempts to refute Zeno's arguments against the possibility of motion.

From the first book of *On the Heavens* (often cited as *De Caelo*), Chapters 2 and 3 are offered. Here the four elements that we know from the pre-Socratics—earth, water, air, and fire—are found insufficient, and Aristotle adds a fifth, sometimes called aither.

Next, we turn to Aristotle's work *On the Soul* (also known as *De Anima*). In the first three chapters of the second book, Aristotle defines the soul and distinguishes its faculties. In Chapters 4 and 5 of the third and last book, the passive and the active mind are discussed.

The *Nicomachean Ethics* is still considered one of the greatest works, if not the single most important one, in the whole field of ethics. The comprehensive selections from it include Aristotle's discussions of the subject matter and nature of ethics, of the good for man, of moral virtue, of the mean, of the conditions of responsibility for an action, of pride, vanity, humility, and the great-souled man (Aristotle's ideal), of the superiority of loving over being loved, of friendship and self-love, and finally of human happiness.

The last selection comprises the first fifteen (of twenty-six) chapters of the famous *Poetics*. This is still a standard work of literary criticism, if not *the* standard work. This is not to say that everybody agrees with Aristotle, although it is astonishing how many critics do. But no other work in this field has elicited so much discussion. The discussion of diction in some of the later chapters, here omitted, is scarcely comprehensible in translation (at least the original Greek words or lines have to be furnished in parentheses or notes), and much of the rest abounds in brief allusions to a great number of plays: those who have read all of these plays will surely want to read the whole of the *Poetics*, while those who have not will not find the later chapters as rewarding as the fifteen reproduced here.

II

The translation of *Categories* is that of J. L. Ackrill, published by the Clarendon Press, Oxford, in 1963.

The translation of the *Posterior Analytics* used here is that of G. R. G. Mure; it comes from *The Works of Aristotle*, translated into English under the editorship of W. D. Ross, and published by the Oxford University Press. The translation of the *Metaphysics* is by W. D. Ross himself.

The next four translations are taken from The Loeb Classical Library, founded by James Loeb and published by the Harvard University Press, in Cambridge, Massachusetts, and by William Heinemann Ltd., in London. In over two hundred volumes, which are available singly, The Loeb Classical Library offers scholarly editions of the original texts of the great Greek and Latin works of classical antiquity, with exceedingly faithful and readable English translations on facing pages. Top scholars have contributed translations with introductions and notes. The names of the translators of the selections offered here are as follows:

*Physics*, Philip H. Wicksteed and Francis M. Cornford; *On the Heavens*, W. K. C. Guthrie; *On the Soul*, W. S. Hett; and *Nicomachean Ethics*, H. Rackham.

The translation of the *Poetics* is that of S. H. Butcher. Those who want to go on to read the whole work will find much helpful material in G. M. A. Grube's version.

The marginal page numbers, with their "a" and "b," are the same in all scholarly editions, regardless of language. They are therefore used in all scholarly citations of Aristotle. They will be found at the top of the following pages, as part of the running heads.

The student who seeks further guidance will find W. D. Ross's *Aristotle* (published in paperback by Meridian Books) particularly helpful.

# CATEGORIES

## Chapter 1

1ª1. When things have only a name in common and the definition of being which corresponds to the name is different, they are called *homonymous.* Thus, for example, both a man and a picture are animals. These have only a name in common and the definition of being which corresponds to the name is different; for if one is to say what being an animal is for each of them, one will give two distinct definitions.

1ª6. When things have the name in common and the definition of being which corresponds to the name is the same, they are called *synonymous.* Thus, for example, both a man and an ox are animals. Each of these is called by a common name, "animal," and the def-

inition of being is also the same; for if one is to give the definition of each— what being an animal is for each of them—one will give the same definition.

1ª12. When things get their name from something, with a difference of ending, they are called *paronymous* Thus, for example, the grammarian gets his name from grammar, the brave get theirs from bravery.

## Chapter 2

1ª16. Of things that are said, some involve combination while others are said without combination. Examples of those involving combination are "man runs," "man wins"; and of those without combination "man," "ox," "runs," "wins."

1a20. Of things there are: (*a*) some are *said of* a subject but are not *in* any subject. For example, man is said of a subject, the individual man, but is not in any subject. (*b*) Some are in a subject but are not said of any subject. (By "in a subject" I mean what is in something, not as a part, and cannot exist separately from what it is in.) For example, the individual knowledge-of-grammar is in a subject, the soul, but is not said of any subject; and the individual white is in a subject, the body (for all colour is in a body), but is not said of any subject. (*c*) Some are both said of a subject and in a subject. For example, knowledge is in a subject, the soul, and is also said of a subject, knowledge-of-grammar. (*d*) Some are neither in a subject nor said of a subject, for example, the individual man or individual horse—for nothing of this sort is either in a subject or said of a subject. Things that are individual and numerically one are, without exception, not said of any subject, but there is nothing to prevent some of them from being in a subject—the individual knowledge-of-grammar is one of the things in a subject.

## Chapter 3

1b10. Whenever one thing is predicated of another as of a subject, all things said of what is predicated will be said of the subject also. For example, man is predicated of the individual man, and animal of man; so animal will be predicated of the individual man also—for the individual man is both a man and an animal.

1b16. The differentiae of genera which are different[1] and not subordinate one to the other are themselves different in kind. For example, animal and knowledge: footed, winged, aquatic,

two-footed, are differentiae of animal, but none of these is a differentia of knowledge; one sort of knowledge does not differ from another by being two-footed. However, there is nothing to prevent genera subordinate one to the other from having the same differentiae. For the higher are predicated of the genera below them, so that all differentiae of the predicated genus will be differentiae of the subject also.

## Chapter 4

1b25. Of things said without any combination, each signifies either substance or quantity or qualification or a relative or where or when or being-in-a-position or having or doing or being-affected. To give a rough idea, examples of substance are man, horse; of quantity: four-foot, five-foot; of qualification: white, grammatical; of a relative: double, half, larger; of where: in the Lyceum, in the market-place; of when: yesterday, last-year; of being-in-a-position: is-lying, is-sitting; of having: has-shoes-on, has-armour-on; of doing: cutting, burning; of being-affected: being-cut, being-burned.

2a4. None of the above is said just by itself in any affirmation, but by the combination of these with one another an affirmation is produced. For every affirmation, it seems, is either true or false; but of things said without any combination none is either true or false (e.g. "man," "white," "runs," "wins").

## Chapter 5

2a11. A *substance*—that which is called a substance most strictly, primarily, and most of all—is that which is neither said of a subject nor in a subject, e.g. the individual man or the individual horse. The species in which the things primarily called substances are, are

---

[1] Read τῶν ἑτέρων γενῶν.

called *secondary substances,* as also are the genera of these species. For example, the individual man belongs in a species, man, and animal is a genus of the species; so these—both man and animal— are called secondary substances.

2ª19. It is clear from what has been said that if something is said of a subject both its name and its definition are necessarily predicated of the subject. For example, man is said of a subject, the individual man, and the name is of course predicated (since you will be predicating man of the individual man), and also the definition of man will be predicated of the individual man (since the individual man is also a man). Thus both the name and the definition will be predicated of the subject. But as for things which are in a subject, in most cases neither the name nor the definition is predicated of the subject. In some cases there is nothing to prevent the name from being predicated of the subject, but it is impossible for the definition to be predicated. For example, white, which is in a subject (the body), is predicated of the subject; for a body is called white. But the definition of white will never be predicated of the body.

2ª34. All the other things are either said of the primary substances as subjects or in them as subjects. This is clear from an examination of cases. For example, animal is predicated of man and therefore also of the individual man; for were it predicated of none of the individual men it would not be predicated of man at all. Again, colour is in body and therefore also in an individual body; for were it not in some individual body it would not be in body at all. Thus all the other things are either said of the primary substances as subjects or in them as subjects. So if the pirmary substances did not exist it would be impossible for any of the other things to exist.

2ᵇ7. Of the secondary substances the species is more a substance than the genus, since it is nearer to the primary substance. For if one is to say of the primary substance what it is, it will be more informative and apt to give the species than the genus. For example, it would be more informative to say of the individual man that he is a man than that he is an animal (since the one is more distinctive of the individual man while the other is more general); and more informative to say of the individual tree that it is a tree than that it is a plant. Further, it is because the primary substances are subjects for all the other things and all the other things are predicated of them or are in them, that they are called substances most of all. But as the primary substances stand to the other things, so the species stands to the genus: the species is a subject for the genus (for the genera are predicated of the species but the species are not predicated reciprocally of the genera). Hence for this reason too the species is more a substance than the genus.

2ᵇ22. But of the species themselves —those which are not genera—one is no more a substance than another: it is no more apt to say of the individual man that he is a man than to say of the individual horse that it is a horse. And similarly of the primary substances one is no more a substance than another: the individual man is no more a substance than the individual ox.

2ᵇ29. It is reasonable that, after the primary substances, their species and genera should be the only other things called (secondary) substances. For only they, of things predicated, reveal the primary substance. For if one is to say of the individual man what he is, it will be in place to give the species or the genus (though more informative to give man than animal); but to give any of the other things would be out of place —for example, to say "white" or "runs" or anything like that. So it is reasonable that these should be the only other things called substances. Further, it is because the primary substances are subjects for everything else that they are called substances most strictly. But as the primary substances stand to everything else, so the species and genera of the primary substances stand to all the rest: all the rest are predicated of these. For if you will call the individual man grammatical it follows that you will call both a man and an animal grammatical; and similarly in other cases.

3ᵃ7. It is a characteristic common to every substance not to be in a subject. For a primary substance is neither said of a subject nor in a subject. And as for secondary substances, it is obvious at once that they are not in a subject. For man is said of the individual man as subject but is not in a subject: man is not *in* the individual man. Similarly, animal also is said of the individual man as subject but animal is not *in* the individual man. Further, while there is nothing to prevent the name of what is in a subject from being sometimes predicated of the subject, it is impossible for the definition to be predicated. But the definition of the secondary substances, as well as the name, is predicated of the subject: you will predicate the definition of man of the individual man, and also that of animal. No substance, therefore, is in a subject.

3ᵃ21. This is not, however, peculiar to substance; the differentia also is not in a subject. For footed and two-footed are said of man as subject but are not in a subject; neither two-footed nor footed is *in* man. Moreover, the definition of the differentia is predicated of that of which the differentia is said. For example, if footed is said of man the definition of footed will also be predicated of man; for man is footed.

3ᵃ29. We need not be disturbed by

any fear that we may be forced to say that the parts of a substance, being in a subject (the whole substance), are not substances. For when we spoke of things *in a subject* we did not mean things belonging in something as *parts*.

3ᵃ33. It is a characteristic of substances and differentiae that all things called from them are so called synonymously. For all the predicates from them are predicated either of the individuals or of the species. (For from a primary substance there is no predicate, since it is said of no subject; and as for secondary substances, the species is predicated of the individual, the genus both of the species and of the individual. Similarly, differentiae too are predicated both of the species and of the individuals.) And the primary substances admit the definition of the species and of the genera, and the species admits that of the genus; for everything said of what is predicated will be said of the subject also. Similarly, both the species and the individuals admit the definition of the differentiae. But synonymous things were precisely those with both the name in common and the same definition. Hence all the things called from substances and differentiae are so called synonymously.

3ᵇ10. Every substance seems to signify a certain "this." As regards the primary substances, it is indisputably true that each of them signifies a certain "this"; for the thing revealed is individual and numerically one. But as regards the secondary substances, though it appears from the form of the name—when one speaks of man or animal—that a secondary substance likewise signifies a certain "this," this is not really true; rather, it signifies a certain qualification, for the subject is not, as the primary substance is, one, but man and animal are said of many things. However, it does not signify simply a certain qualification, as white does. White signifies nothing but a qualification, whereas the species and the genus mark off the qualification of substance—they signify substance of a certain qualification. (One draws a wider boundary with the genus than with the species, for in speaking of animal one takes in more than in speaking of man.)

3ᵇ24. Another characteristic of substances is that there is nothing contrary to them. For what would be contrary to a primary substance? For example, there is nothing contrary to an individual man, nor yet is there anything contrary to man or to animal. This, however, is not peculiar to substance but holds of many other things also, for example, of quantity. For there is nothing contrary to four-foot or to ten or to anything of this kind—unless someone were to say that many is contrary to few or large to small; but still there is nothing contrary to any *definite* quantity.

3ᵇ33. Substance, it seems, does not admit of a more and a less. I do not mean that one substance is not more a substance than another (we have said that it is), but that any given substance is not called more, or less, that which it is. For example, if this substance is a man, it will not be more a man or less a man either than itself or than another man. For one man is not more a man than another, as one pale thing is more pale than another and one beautiful thing more beautiful than another. Again, a thing is called more, or less, such-and-such than itself; for example, the body that is pale is called more pale now than before, and the one that is hot is called more, or less, hot. Substance, however, is not spoken of thus. For a man is not called more a man now than before, nor is anything else that is a substance. Thus substance does not admit of a more and a less.

4ᵃ10. It seems most distinctive of substance that what is numerically one and the same is able to receive contraries. In no other case could one bring forward anything, numerically one, which is able to receive contraries. For example, a colour which is numerically one and the same will not be black and white, nor will numerically one and the same action be bad and good; and similarly with everything else that is not substance. A substance, however, numerically one and the same, is able to receive contraries. For example, an individual man—one and the same—becomes pale at one time and dark at another, and hot and cold, and bad and good. Nothing like this is to be seen in any other case.

4ᵃ22. But perhaps someone might object and say that statements and beliefs are like this. For the same statement seems to be both true and false. Suppose, for example, that the statement that somebody is sitting is true; after he has got up this same statement will be false. Similarly with beliefs. Suppose you believe truly that somebody is sitting; after he has got up you will believe falsely if you hold the same belief about him. However, even if we were to grant this, there is still a difference in the *way* contraries are received. For in the case of substances it is by themselves changing that they are able to receive contraries. For what has become cold instead of hot, or dark instead of pale, or good instead of bad, has changed (has altered); similarly in other cases too it is by itself undergoing change that each thing is able to receive contraries. Statements and beliefs, on the other hand, themselves remain completely unchangeable in every way; it is because the *actual thing* changes that the contrary comes to belong to them. For the statement that somebody is sitting remains the same; it is because of a change in the actual thing that it comes to be true at one time and false at another. Similarly with beliefs. Hence at least the *way* in which it is able to receive contraries—through a change in itself—would be distinctive of substance, even if we were to grant that beliefs and statements are able to receive contraries. However, this is not true. For it is not because they themselves receive anything that statements and beliefs are said to be able to receive contraries, but because of what has happened to something else. For it is because the actual thing exists or does not exist that the statement is said to be true or false, not because it is able itself to receive contraries. No statement, in fact, or belief is changed at all by anything. So, since nothing happens in them, they are not able to receive contraries. A substance, on the other hand, is said to be able to receive contraries because it itself receives contraries. For it receives sickness and health, and paleness and darkness; and because it itself receives the various things of this kind it is said to be able to receive contraries. It is, therefore, distinctive of substance that what is numerically one and the same is able to receive contraries. This brings to an end our discussion of substance.

• • •

# POSTERIOR ANALYTICS

## Book I

1. All instruction given or re- [71ᵃ] ceived by way of argument proceeds from pre-existent knowledge. This becomes evident upon a survey of all species of such instruction. The mathematical sciences and all other speculative disciplines are acquired in this way, and so are the two forms of dialectical reasoning, syllogistic and inductive: for each of these latter makes use of old knowledge to impart new, the syllogism assuming an audience that accepts its premises, induction exhibiting the universal as implicit in the clearly known particular. Again, the persuasion exerted by rhetorical arguments is in principle the same, since they use either example, a kind of induction, or enthymeme, a form of syllogism.

The pre-existent knowledge required is of two kinds. In some cases admission of the fact must be assumed, in others comprehension of the meaning of the term used, and sometimes both assumptions are essential. Thus, we assume that every predicate can be either truly affirmed or truly denied of any subject, and that "triangle" means so and so; as regards "unit" we have to make the double assumption of the meaning of the word and the existence of the thing. The reason is that these several objects are not equally obvious to us. Recognition of a truth may in some cases contain as factors both previous knowledge and also knowledge acquired simultaneously with that recognition—knowledge, this latter, of the particulars actually falling under the universal and therein already virtually known. For example, the student knew beforehand that the angles of every triangle are equal to two right angles; but it was only at the actual moment at which he was being led on to recognize this as true in the instance before him that he came to know "this figure inscribed in the semicircle" to be a triangle. For some things (viz. the singulars finally reached which are not predicable of anything else as subject) are only learnt in this way, i.e. there is here no recognition through a middle of a minor term as subject to a major. Before he was led on to recognition or before he actually drew a conclusion, we should perhaps say that in a manner he knew, in a manner not.

If he did not in an unqualified sense of the term *know* the existence of this triangle, how could he *know* without qualification that its angles were equal to two right angles? No: clearly he *knows* not without qualification but only in the sense that he *knows* universally. If this distinction is not drawn, we are faced with the dilemma in the *Meno:* either a man will learn nothing or what he already knows; for we cannot accept the solution which some people offer. A man is asked. "Do you, or do you not, know that every pair is even?" He says he does know it. The questioner then produces a particular pair, of the existence, and so *a fortiori* of the evenness, of which he was unaware. The solution which some people offer is to assert that they do not know that every pair is even, but only that everything which they know to be a pair is even: yet what they know [71ᵇ] to be even is that of which they have demonstrated evenness, i e. what they made the subject of their premiss, viz. not merely every triangle or number which they know to be such, but any and every number or triangle without reservation. For no premiss is ever couched in the form "every number which you know to be such," or "every rectilinear figure which you know to be such": the predicate is always construed as applicable to any and every instance of the thing. On the other hand, I imagine there is nothing to prevent a man in one sense knowing what he is learning, in another not knowing it. The strange thing would be, not if in some sense he knew what he was learning, but if he were to know it in that precise sense and manner in which he was learning it.

2. We suppose ourselves to possess unqualified scientific knowledge of a thing, as opposed to knowing it in the accidental way in which the sophist knows, when we think that we know the cause on which the fact depends, as the cause of that fact and of no other, and, further, that the fact could not be other than it is. Now that scientific knowing is something of this sort is evident—witness both those who falsely claim it and those who actually possess it, since the former merely imagine themselves to be, while the latter are also actually, in the condition described. Consequently the proper object of unqualified scientific knowledge is something which cannot be other than it is.

There may be another manner of knowing as well—that will be discussed later. What I now assert is that at all events we do know by demonstration. By demonstration I mean a syllogism productive of scientific knowledge, a syllogism, that is, the grasp of which is *eo ipso* such knowledge. Assuming then that my thesis as to the nature of scientific knowing is correct, the premisses of demonstrated knowledge must be true, primary, immediate, better known than and prior to the conclusion, which is further related to them as effect to cause. Unless these conditions are satisfied, the basic truths will not be "appropriate" to the conclusion. Syllogism there may indeed be without these conditions, but such syllogism, not being productive of scientific knowledge, will not be demonstration. The premisses must be true: for that which is non-existent cannot be known—we cannot know, e.g., that the diagonal of a square is commensurate with its side. The premisses must be primary and indemonstrable; otherwise they will require demonstration in order to be known, since to have knowledge, if it be not accidental knowledge, of things which are demonstrable, means precisely to have a demonstration of them. The premisses must be the causes of the conclusion, better known than it, and prior to it; its causes, since we possess scientific knowledge of a thing only when we know its cause; prior, in order to be causes; antecedently known, this antecedent knowledge being not our more understanding of the meaning, but knowledge of the fact as well. Now "prior" and "better known" are ambiguous terms, for there is a difference between what is prior and better known in the order of being and what is [72ᵃ] prior and better known to man. I mean that objects nearer to sense are prior and better known to man; objects without qualification prior and better known are those further from sense. Now the most universal causes are furthest from sense and particular causes are nearest to sense, and they are thus exactly opposed to one another. In saying that the premisses of demonstrated knowledge must be primary, I mean that they must be the "appropriate" basic truths, for I identify primary premiss and basic truth. A "basic truth" in a demonstration is an immediate proposition. An immediate proposition is one which has no other proposition prior to it. A proposition is either part of an enunciation, i.e. it predicates a single attribute of a single subject. If a proposition is dialectical, it assumes either part indifferently; if it is demonstrative, it lays down one part to the definite exclusion of the other because that part is true. The term "enunciation" denotes either part of a contradiction indifferently. A contradiction is an opposition which of its own nature excludes a middle. The part of a contradiction which conjoins a predicate with a subject is an affirmation; the part disjoining them is a negation. I call an immediate basic truth of syllogism a "thesis" when, though it is not susceptible of proof by the teacher, yet ignorance of it does not constitute a total bar to progress on the part of the pupil: one which the pupil must know if he is to learn anything whatever is an axiom. I call it an axiom because there are such truths and we give them the name of axioms *par excellence*. If a thesis assumes one part or the other of an enunciation, i.e. asserts either the existence or the non-existence of a subject, it is a hypothesis; if it does not so assert, it is a definition. Definition *is* a "thesis" or a "laying something down," since the arithmetician lays it down that to be a unit is to be quantitatively indivisible; but it is not a hypothesis, for to define

what a unit is is not the same as to affirm its existence.

Now since the required ground of our knowledge—i.e. of our conviction—of a fact is the possession of such a syllogism as we call demonstration, and the ground of the syllogism is the facts constituting its premisses, we must not only know the primary premisses—some if not all of them—beforehand, but know them better than the conclusion: for the cause of an attribute's inherence in a subject always itself inheres in the subject more firmly than that attribute; e.g. the cause of our loving anything is dearer to us than the object of our love. So since the primary premisses are the cause of our knowledge—i.e. if our conviction—it follows that we know them better—that is, are more convinced of them—than their consequences, precisely because our knowledge of the latter is the effect of our knowledge of the premisses. Now a man cannot believe in anything more than in the things he knows, unless he has either actual knowledge of it or something better than actual knowledge. But we are faced with this paradox if a student whose belief rests on demonstration has not prior knowledge; a man must believe in some, if not in all, of the basic truths more than in the conclusion. Moreover, if a man sets out to acquire the scientific knowledge that comes through demonstration, he must not only have a better knowledge of the basic truths and a firmer conviction of them than of the connexion which is being demonstrated: more than this, [72ᵇ] nothing must be more certain or better known to him than these basic truths in their character as contradicting the fundamental premisses which lead to the opposed and erroneous conclusion. For indeed the conviction of pure science must be unshakable.

3. Some hold that, owing to the necessity of knowing the primary premisses, there is no scientific knowledge. Others think there is, but that all truths are

demonstrable. Neither doctrine is either true or a necessary deduction from the premisses. The first school, assuming that there is no way of knowing other than by demonstration, maintain that an infinite regress is involved, on the ground that if behind the prior stands no primary, we could not know the posterior through the prior (wherein they are right, for one cannot traverse an infinite series) : if on the other hand—they say —the series terminates and there are primary premisses, yet these are unknowable because incapable of demonstration, which according to them is the only form of knowledge. And since thus one cannot know the primary premisses, knowledge of the conclusions which follow from them is not pure scientific knowledge nor properly knowing at all, but rests on the mere supposition that the premisses are true. The other party agree with them as regards knowing, holding that it is only possible by demonstration, but they see no difficulty in holding that all truths are demonstrated, on the ground that demonstration may be circular and reciprocal.

Our own doctrine is that not all knowledge is demonstrative: on the contrary, knowledge of the immediate premisses is independent of demonstration. (The necessity of this is obvious; for since we must know the prior premisses from which the demonstration is drawn, and since the regress must end in immediate truths, those truths must be indemonstrable.) Such, then, is our doctrine, and in addition we maintain that besides scientific knowledge there is its originative source which enables us to recognize the definitions.

Now demonstration must be based on premisses prior to and better known than the conclusion; and the same things cannot simultaneously be both prior and posterior to one another: so circular demonstration is clearly not possible in the unqualified sense of "demonstration," but only possible if "demonstration" be extended to include that other method of argument which rests on a distinction between truths prior to us and truths without qualification prior, i.e. the method by which induction produces knowledge. But if we accept this extension of its meaning, our definition of unqualified knowledge will prove faulty; for there seem to be two kinds of it. Perhaps, however, the second form of demonstration, that which proceeds from truths better known to us, is not demonstration in the unqualified sense of the term.

The advocates of circular demonstration are not only faced with the difficulty we have just stated: in addition their theory reduces to the mere statement that if a thing exists, then it does exist— an easy way of proving anything. That this is so can be clearly shown by taking three terms, for to constitute the circle it makes no difference whether many terms or few or even only two are taken. Thus by direct proof, if $A$ is, $B$ must be; if $B$ is, $C$ must be; therefore if $A$ is, $C$ must be. Since then—by the circular proof—if $A$ is, $B$ must be, and if $B$ is, $A$ must be, $A$ may be substituted for $C$ [73ᵃ] above. Then "if $B$ is, $A$ must be" = "if $B$ is, $C$ must be," which above gave the conclusion "if $A$ is, $C$ must be": but $C$ and $A$ have been identified. Consequently the upholders of circular demonstration are in the position of saying that if $A$ is, $A$ must be—a simple way of proving anything. Moreover, even such circular demonstration is impossible except in the case of attributes that imply one another, viz. "peculiar" properties.

Now, it has been shown that the positing of one thing—be it one term or one premiss—never involves a necessary consequent: two premisses constitute the first and smallest foundation for drawing a conclusion at all and therefore a fortiori for the demonstrative syllogism of science. If, then, $A$ is implied in $B$ and $C$, and $B$ and $C$ are reciprocally implied in one another and in $A$, it is possible, as has been shown in my writings on the syllogism, to prove all the assumptions on which the original conclusion rested, by circular demonstration in the first figure. But it has also been shown that in the other figures either no conclusion is possible, or at least none which proves both the original premisses. Propositions the terms of which are not convertible cannot be circularly demonstrated at all, and since convertible terms occur rarely in actual demonstrations, it is clearly frivolous and impossible to say that demonstration is reciprocal and that therefore everything can be demonstrated.

. . .

8. It is also clear that if the premisses from which the syllogism proceeds are commensurately universal, the conclusion of such demonstration—demonstration, i.e., in the unqualified sense—must also be eternal. Therefore no attribute can be demonstrated nor known by strictly scientific knowledge to inhere in perishable things. The proof can only be accidental, because the attribute's connexion with its perishable subject is not commensurately universal but temporary and special. If such a demonstration is made, one premiss must be perishable and not commensurately universal (perishable because only if it is perishable will the conclusion be perishable; not commensurately universal, because the predicate will be predicable of some instances of the subject and not of others); so that the conclusion can only be that a fact is true at the moment—not commensurately and universally. The same is true of definitions, since a definition is either a primary premiss or a conclusion of a demonstration, or else only differs from a demonstration in the order of its terms. Demonstration and science of merely frequent occurrences—e.g. of eclipse as happening to the moon—are, as such, clearly eternal: whereas so far as they are not eternal they are not fully

commensurate. Other subjects too have properities attaching to them in the same way as eclipse attaches to the moon.

9. It is clear that if the conclusion is to show an attribute inhering as such, nothing can be demonstrated except from its "appropriate" basic truths. Consequently a proof even from true, indemonstrable, and immediate premisses does not constitute knowledge. Such proofs are like Bryson's method of squaring the circle; for they operate by taking as their middle a common character —a character, therefore, which the [76ª] subject may share with another—and consequently they apply equally to subjects different in kind. They therefore afford knowledge of an attribute only as inhering accidentally, not as belonging to its subject as such: otherwise they would not have been applicable to another genus.

Our knowledge of any attribute's connexion with a subject is accidental unless we know that connexion through the middle term in virtue of which it inheres, and as an inference from basic premisses essential and "appropriate" to the subject—unless we know, e.g., the property of possessing angles equal to two right angles as belonging to that subject in which it inheres essentially, and as inferred from basic premisses essential and "appropriate" to that subject: so that if that middle term also belongs essentially to the minor, the middle must belong to the same kind as the major and minor terms. The only exceptions to this rule are such cases as theorems in harmonics which are demonstrable by arithmetic. Such theorems are proved by the same middle terms as arithmetical properties, but with a qualification—the fact falls under a separate science (for the subject genus is separate), but the reasoned fact concerns the superior science, to which the attributes essentially belong. Thus, even these apparent exceptions show that no attribute is strictly demonstrable except from its "appropriate" basic truths, which, however, in the case of these sciences have the requisite identity of character.

It is no less evident that the peculiar basic truths of each inhering attribute are indemonstrable; for basic truths from which they might be deduced would be basic truths of all that is, and the science to which they belonged would possess universal sovereignty. This is so because he knows better whose knowledge is deduced from higher causes, for his knowledge is from prior premises when it derives from causes themselves uncaused: hence, if he knows better than others or best of all, his knowledge would be science in a higher or the highest degree. But, as things are, demonstration is not transferable to another genus with such exceptions as we have mentioned of the application of geometrical demonstrations to theorems in mechanics or optics, or of arithmetical demonstrations to those of harmonics.

It is hard to be sure whether one knows or not; for it is hard to be sure whether one's knowledge is based on the basic truths appropriate to each attribute —the differentia of true knowledge. We think we have scientific knowledge if we have reasoned from true and primary premises. But that is not so: the conclusion must be homogeneous with the basic facts of the science.

10. I call the basic truths of every genus those elements in it the existence of which cannot be proved. As regards both these primary truths and the attributes dependent on them the meaning of the name is assumed. The fact of their existence as regards the primary truths must be assumed; but it has to be proved of the remainder, the attributes. Thus we assume the meaning alike of unity, straight, and triangular; but while as regards unity and magnitude we as-

sume also the fact of their existence, in the case of the remainder proof is required.

Of the basic truths used in the demonstrative sciences some are peculiar to each science, and some are common, but common only in the sense of analogous, being of use only in so far as they fall within the genus constituting the province of the science in question.

Peculiar truths are, e.g., the definitions of line and straight; common truths are such as "take equals from equals and equals remain." Only so much of these common truths is required as falls [76ᵇ] within the genus in question: for a truth of this kind will have the same force even if not used generally but applied by the geometer only to magnitudes, or by the arithmetician only to numbers. Also peculiar to a science are the subjects the existence as well as the meaning of which it assumes, and the essential attributes of which it investigates, e.g. in arithmetic units, in geometry points and lines. Both the existence and the meaning of the subjects are assumed by these sciences; but of their essential attributes only the meaning is assumed. For example arithmetic assumes the meaning of odd and even, square and cube, geometry that of incommensurable, or of deflection or verging of lines, whereas the existence of these attributes is demonstrated by means of the axioms and from previous conclusions as premises. Astronomy too proceeds in the same way. For indeed every demonstrative science has three elements: (1) that which it posits, the subject genus whose essential attributes it examines; (2) the so-called axioms, which are primay premises of its demonstration; (3) the attributes, the meaning of which it assumes. Yet some sciences may very well pass over some of these elements; e.g. we might not expressly posit the existence of the genus if its existence were obvious (for instance, the existence of hot and cold is more evident than that of number); or we might omit to assume expressly the meaning of the attributes if it were well understood. In the same way the meaning of axioms, such as "Take equals from equals and equals remain," is well known and so not expressly assumed. Nevertheless in the nature of the case the essential elements of demonstration are three: the subject, the attributes, and the basic premisses.

That which expresses necessary self-grounded fact, and which we must necessarily believe, is distinct both from the hypotheses of a science and from illegitimate postulate—I say "must believe," because all syllogism, and therefore a fortiori demonstration, is addressed not to the spoken word, but to the discourse within the soul, and though we can always raise objections to the spoken word, to the inward discourse we cannot always object. That which is capable of proof but assumed by the teacher without proof is, if the pupil believes and accepts it, hypothesis, though only in a limited sense hypothesis—that is, relatively to the pupil; if the pupil has no opinion or a contrary opinion on the matter, the same assumption is an illegitimate postulate. Therein lies the distinction between hypothesis and illegitimate postulate: the latter is the contrary of the pupil's opinion, demonstrable, but assumed and used without demonstration.

The definitions—viz. those which are not expressed as statements that anything is or is not—are not hypotheses: but it is in the premisses of a science that its hypotheses are contained. Definitions require only to be understood, and this is not hypothesis—unless it be contended that the pupil's hearing is also an hypothesis required by the teacher. Hypotheses, on the contrary, postulate facts on the being of which depends the being of the fact inferred. Nor are the geometer's hypotheses false, as some have held, urging that one must not employ falsehood and that the geometer

is uttering falsehood in stating that the line which he draws is a foot long or straight, when it is actually neither. [77ᵃ] The truth is that the geometer does not draw any conclusion from the being of the particular line of which he speaks, but from what his diagrams symbolize. A further distinction is that all hypotheses and illegitimate postulates are either universal or particular, whereas a definition is neither.

. . .

31. Scientific knowledge is not possible through the act of perception. Even if perception as a faculty is of "the such" and not merely of a "this somewhat," yet one must at any rate actually perceive a "this somewhat," and at a definite present place and time: but that which is commensurately universal and true in all cases one cannot perceive, since it is not "this" and it is not "now"; if it were, it would not be commensurately universal—the term we apply to what is always and everywhere. Seeing, therefore, that demonstrations are commensurately universal and universals imperceptible, we clearly cannot obtain scientific knowledge by the act of perception: nay, it is obvious that even if it were possible to perceive that a triangle has its angles equal to two right angles, we should still be looking for a demonstration—we should not (as some say) possess knowledge of it; for perception must be of a particular, whereas scientific knowledge involves the recognition of the commensurate universal. So if we were on the moon, and saw the earth shutting out the sun's light, we should not know the cause of the eclipse: we should perceive the present fact of the eclipse, but not the reasoned fact at [88ᵃ] all, since the act of perception is not of the commensurate universal. I do not, of course, deny that by watching the frequent recurrencce of this event we might, after tracking the commensurate universal, possess a demonstration, for

the commensurate universal is elicited from the several groups of singulars.

The commensurate universal is precious because it makes clear the cause; so that in the case of facts like these which have a cause other than themselves universal knowledge is more precious than sense-perceptions and than intuition. (As regards primary truths there is of course a different account to be given.) Hence it is clear that knowledge of things demonstrable cannot be acquired by perception, unless the term perception is applied to the possession of scientific knowledge through demonstration. Nevertheless certain points do arise with regard to connexions to be proved which are referred for their explanation to a failure in sense-perception: there are cases when an act of vision would terminate our inquiry, not because in seeing we should be knowing, but because we should have elicited the universal from seeing; if, for example, we saw pores in the glass and the light passing through, the reason of the kindling would be clear to us because we should at the same time see it in each instance and intuit that it must be so in all instances.

### Book II

1. The kinds of question we ask are as many as the kinds of things which we know. They are in fact four:—(1) whether the connexion of an attribute with a thing is a fact, (2) what is the reason of the connexion, (3) whether a thing exists, (4) what is the nature of the thing. Thus, when our question concerns a complex of thing and attribute and we ask whether the thing is thus or otherwise qualified—whether, e.g., the sun suffers eclipse or not—then we are asking as to the fact of a connexion. That our inquiry ceases with the discovery that the sun does suffer eclipse is an indication of this; and if

we know from the start that the sun suffers eclipse, we do not inquire whether it does so or not. On the other hand, when we know the fact we ask the reason; as, for example, when we know that the sun is being eclipsed and that an earthquake is in progress, it is the reason of eclipse or earthquake into which we inquire.

Where a complex is concerned, then, those are the two questions we ask; but for some objects of inquiry we have a different kind of question to ask, such as whether there is or is not a centaur or a God. (By "is or is not" I mean "is or is not, without further qualification"; as opposed to "is or is not [e.g.] white.") On the other hand, when we have ascertained the thing's existence, we inquire as to its nature, asking, for instance, "what, then, is God?" or "what is man?"

2. These, then, are the four kinds of question we ask, and it is in the answers to these questions that our knowledge consists.

Now when we ask whether a connexion is a fact, or whether a thing without qualification *is*, we are really asking whether the connexion or the thing has a "middle"; and when we have ascertained either that the connexion is a fact or that the thing *is*—i.e. ascertained either the partial or the unqualified being of the thing—and are proceeding to ask the reason of the [90a] connexion or the nature of the thing, then we are asking what the "middle" is.

(By distinguishing the fact of the connexion and the existence of the thing as respectively the partial and the unqualified being of the thing I mean that if we ask "does the moon suffer eclipse?" or "does the moon wax?" the question concerns a part of the thing's being; for what we are asking in such questions is whether a thing is this or that, i.e. has or has not this or that attribute: whereas, if we ask whether the moon or night exists, the question concerns the unqualified being of a thing.)

We conclude that in all our inquiries we are asking either whether there is a "middle" or what the "middle" is: for the "middle" here is precisely the cause, and it is the cause that we seek in all our inquiries. Thus, "Does the moon suffer eclipse?" means "Is there or is there not a cause producing eclipse of the moon?" and when we have learnt that there is, our next question is, "What, then, is this cause?"; for the cause through which a thing *is*—not *is this or that*, i.e. has this or that attribute, but without qualification *is*—and the cause through which it is—not *is* without qualification, but *is this or that* as having some essential attribute or some accident—are both alike the "middle." By that which *is* without qualification I mean the subject, e.g. moon or earth or sun or triangle; by that which a subject *is* (in the partial sense) I mean a property, e.g. eclipse, equality or inequality, interposition or non-interposition. For in all these examples it is clear that the nature of the thing and the reason of the fact are identical: the question "What is eclipse?" and its answer "The privation of the moon's light by the interposition of the earth" are identical with the question "What is the reason of eclipse?" or "Why does the moon suffer eclipse?" and the reply "because of the failure of light through the earth's shutting it out." Again, for "What is a concord? A commensurate numerical ratio of a high and a low note," we may substitute "What reason makes a high and a low note concordant? Their relation according to a commensurate numerical ratio." "Are the high and the low note concordant?" is equivalent to "Is their ratio commensurate?"; and when we find that it is commensurate, we ask "What, then, is their ratio?"

Cases in which the "middle" is sensible show that the object of our inquiry is always the "middle": we inquire, because we have not perceived it, whether there is or is not a "middle" causing e.g. an eclipse. On the other hand, if we were on the moon we should not be inquiring either as to the fact or the reason, but both fact and reason would be obvious simultaneously. For the act of perception would have enabled us to know the universal too; since, the present fact of an eclipse being evident, perception would then at the same time give us the present fact of the earth's screening the sun's light, and from this would arise the universal.

Thus, as we maintain, to know a thing's nature is to know the reason why it is; and this is equally true of things in so far as they are said without qualification to *be* as opposed to being possessed of some attribute, and in so far as they are said to be possessed of some attribute such as equal to two right angles, or greater or less.

•   •   •

19. As regards syllogism and demonstration, the definition of, and the conditions required to produce each of them, are now clear, and with that also the definition of, and the conditions required to produce, demonstrative knowledge, since it is the same as demonstration. As to the basic premisses, how they become known and what is the developed state of knowledge of them is made clear by raising some preliminary problems.

We have already said that scientific knowledge through demonstration is impossible unless a man knows the primary immediate premisses. But there are questions which might be raised in respect of the apprehension of these immediate premisses: one might not only ask whether it is of the same kind as the apprehension of the conclusions, but also whether there is or is not scientific knowledge of both; or scientific knowledge of the latter, and of the former a different kind of knowledge; and, further, whether the developed states of knowledge are not innate but come to be in us, or are innate but at first unnoticed. Now it is strange if we possess them from birth; for it means that we possess apprehensions more accurate than demonstration and fail to notice them. If on the other hand we acquire them and do not previously possess them, how could we apprehend and learn without a basis of pre-existent knowledge? For that is impossible, as we used to find in the case of demonstration. So it emerges that neither can we possess them from birth, nor can they come to be in us if we are without knowledge of them to the extent of having no such developed state at all. Therefore we must possess a capacity of some sort, but not such as to rank higher in accuracy than these developed states. And this at least is an obvious characteristic of all animals, for they possess a congenital discriminative capacity which is called sense-perception. But though sense-perception is innate in all animals, in some the sense-impression comes to persist, in others it does not. So animals in which this persistence does not come to be have either no knowledge at all outside the act of perceiving, or no knowledge of objects of which no impression persists; animals in which it does come into being have perception and can continue to retain the sense-impression in the soul: and when [100$^a$] such persistence is frequently repeated a further distinction at once arises between those which out of the persistence of such sense-impressions develop a power of systematizing them and those which do not. So out of sense-perception comes to be what we call memory, and out of frequently repeated memories of the same thing develops experience; for a number of memories constitute a single experience. From experience again—i.e. from the universal now stabilized in its entirety within the soul, the one beside the many which is a single identity within them all—originate the skill of the craftsman and the knowledge of the man of science, skill in the sphere of coming to be and science in the sphere of being.

We conclude that these states of knowledge are neither innate in a determinate form, nor developed from other higher states of knowledge, but from sense-perception. It is like a rout in battle stopped by first one man making a stand and then another, until the original formation has been restored. The soul is so constituted as to be capable of this process.

Let us now restate the account given already, though with insufficient clearness. When one of a number of logically indiscriminable particulars has made a stand, the earliest universal is present in the soul: for though the act of sense-perception is of the particular, its content is universal—is man, for example, not the man Callias. A fresh stand [100$^b$] is made among these rudimentary universals, and the process does not cease until the indivisible concepts, the true universals, are established: e.g. such and such a species of animal is a step towards the genus animal, which by the same process is a step towards a further generalization.

Thus it is clear that we must get to know the primary premises by induction; for the method by which even sense-perception implants the universal is inductive. Now of the thinking states by which we grasp truth, some are unfailingly true, others admit of error—opinion, for instance, and calculation, whereas scientific knowing and intuition are always true: further, no other kind of thought except intuition is more accurate than scientific knowledge, whereas primary premises are more knowable than demonstrations, and all scientific knowledge is discursive. From these considerations it follows that there will be no scientific knowledge of the primary premisses, and since except intuition nothing can be truer than scientific knowledge, it will be intuition that apprehends the primary premisses—a result which also follows from the fact that demonstration cannot be the originative source of demonstration, nor, consequently, scientific knowledge of scientific knowledge. If, therefore, it is the only other kind of true thinking except scientific knowing, intuition will be the originative source of scientific knowledge. And the originative source of science grasps the original basic premiss, while science as a whole is similarly related as originative source to the whole body of fact.

# METAPHYSICS

## Book A (I)

1. All men by nature desire to [980ª] know. An indication of this is the delight we take in our senses; for even apart from their usefulness they are loved for themselves; and above all others the sense of sight. For not only with a view to action, but even when we are not going to do anything, we prefer seeing (one might say) to everything else. The reason is that this, most of all the senses, makes us know and brings to light many differences between things.

By nature animals are born with the faculty of sensation, and from sensation memory is produced in some of them, though not in others. And therefore the former are more intelligent and [980ᵇ] apt at learning than those which cannot remember; those which are incapable of hearing sounds are intelligent though they cannot be taught, e.g. the bee, and any other race of animals that may be like it; and those which besides memory have this sense of hearing can be taught.

The animals other than man live [30] by appearances and memories, and have but little of connected experience; but the human race lives also by art and reasonings. Now from memory experience is produced in men; for the several memories of the same thing produce finally the capacity for a single experience. And experience seems pretty much like [981ª] science and art, but really science and art come to men *through* experience; for "experience made art," as Polus says,[1] "but inexperience luck." Now art arises when from many notions gained by experience one universal judgement about a class of objects is produced. For to have a judgement that when Callias was ill of this disease this did him good, and similarly in the case of Socrates and in many individual cases, is a matter of experience; but to judge that it has done good to all persons of a certain constitution, marked off [10] in one class, when they were ill of this disease, e.g. to phlegmatic or bilious people when burning with fever—this is a matter of art.

With a view to action experience seems in no respect inferior to art, and men of experience succeed even better than those who have theory without experience. (The reason is that experience is knowledge of individuals, art of universals, and actions and productions are all concerned with the individual; for the physician does not cure *man*, except in an incidental way, but Callias or Socrates or some other called by some such individual name, who happens to be a [20] man. If, then, a man has the theory with-

---

1 Cf. Pl. *Gorg.* 448 c, 462 ᴮᴄ.

out the experience, and recognizes the universal but does not know the individual included in this, he will often fail to cure; for it is the individual that is to be cured.) But yet we think that *knowledge* and *understanding* belong to art rather than to experience, and we suppose artists to be wiser than men of experience (which implies that Wisdom depends in all cases rather on knowledge); and this because the former know the cause, but the latter do not. For men of experience know that the thing [30] is so, but do not know why, while the others know the "why" and the cause. Hence we think also that the master-workers in each craft are more honourable and know in a truer sense and are wiser than the manual workers, [981ᵇ] because they know the causes of the things that are done (we think the manual workers are like certain lifeless things which act indeed, but act without knowing what they do, as fire burns—but while the lifeless things perform each of their functions by a natural tendency, the labourers perform them through habit); thus we view them as being wiser not in virtue of being able to act, but of having the theory for themselves and knowing the causes. And in general it is a sign of the man who knows and of the man who does not know, that the former can teach, and therefore we think art more truly knowledge than experience is; for artists can teach, and men of mere experience cannot.

Again, we do not regard any of [10] the senses as Wisdom; yet surely these give the most authoritative knowledge of particulars. But they do not tell us the "why" of anything—e.g. why fire is hot; they only say *that* it is hot.

At first he who invented any art whatever that went beyond the common perceptions of man was naturally admired by men, not only because there was something useful in the inventions, but because he was thought wise and superior to the rest. But as more arts

were invented, and some were directed to the necessities of life, others to recreation, the inventors of the latter were naturally always regarded as wiser than the inventors of the former, because their branches of knowledge did not aim at utility. Hence when all such inven- [20] tions were already established, the sciences which do not aim at giving pleasure or at the necessities of life were discovered, and first in the places where men first began to have leisure. This is why the mathematical arts were founded in Egypt; for there the priestly caste was allowed to be at leisure.

We have said in the *Ethics*[2] what the difference is between art and science and the other kindred faculties; but the point of our present discussion is this, that all men suppose what is called Wisdom to deal with the first causes and the principles of things; so that, as has been said before, the man of experience is [30] thought to be wiser than the possessors of any sense-perception whatever, the artist wiser than the men of experience, the master-worker than the mechanic, and the theoretical kinds of knowledge to be more of the nature of Wisdom than the productive. Clearly then Wis- [982ª] dom is knowledge about certain principles and causes.

2. Since we are seeking this knowledge, we must inquire of what kind are the causes and the principles, the knowledge of which is Wisdom. If one were to take the notions we have about the wise man, this might perhaps make the answer more evident. We suppose first, then, that the wise man knows all things, as far as possible, although he has not knowledge of each of them in detail; [10] secondly, that he who can learn things that are difficult, and not easy for man to know, is wise (sense-perception is common to all, and therefore easy and no mark of Wisdom); again, that he

—————

2 1139ᵇ 14–1141ᵇ 8.

who is more exact and more capable of teaching the causes is wiser, in every branch of knowledge; and that of the sciences, also, that which is desirable on its own account and for the sake of knowing it is more of the nature of Wisdom than that which is desirable on account of its results, and the superior science is more of the nature of Wisdom than the ancillary; for the wise man must not be ordered but must order, and he must not obey another, but the less wise must obey *him*.

Such and so many are the notions, [20] then, which we have about Wisdom and the wise. Now of these characteristics that of knowing all things must belong to him who has in the highest degree universal knowledge; for he knows in a sense all the instances that fall under the universal. And these things, the most universal, are on the whole the hardest for men to know; for they are farthest from the senses. And the most exact of the sciences are those which deal most with first principles; for those which involve fewer principles are more exact than those which involve additional principles, e.g. arithmetic than geometry. But the science which investigates causes is also *instructive*, in a higher degree, for the people who instruct us are those who tell the causes of each thing. [30] And understanding and knowledge pursued for their own sake are found most in the knowledge of that which is most knowable (for he who chooses to know for the sake of knowing will choose most readily that which is most [982ᵇ] truly knowledge, and such is the knowledge of that which is most knowable); and the first principles and the causes are most knowable; for by reason of these, and from these, all other things come to be known, and not these by means of the things subordinate to them. And the science which knows to what end each thing must be done is the most authoritative of the sciences, and more authoritative than any ancillary science;

and this end is the good of that thing, and in general the supreme good in the whole of nature. Judged by all the tests we have mentioned, then, the name in question falls to the same science; this must be a science that investigates the first principles and causes; for the [10] good, i.e. the end, is one of the causes.

That it is not a science of production is clear even from the history of the earliest philosophers. For it is owing to their wonder that men both now begin and at first began to philosophize; they wondered originally at the obvious difficulties, then advanced little by little and stated difficulties about the greater matters, e.g. about the phenomena of the moon and those of the sun and of the stars, and about the genesis of the universe. And a man who is puzzled and wonders thinks himself ignorant (whence even the lover of myth is in a sense a lover of Wisdom, for the myth is composed of wonders); therefore since [20] they philosophized in order to escape from ignorance, evidently they were pursuing science in order to know, and not for any utilitarian end. And this is confirmed by the facts; for it was when almost all the necessities of life and the things that make for comfort and recreation had been secured, that such knowledge began to be sought. Evidently then we do not seek it for the sake of any other advantage; but as the man is free, we say, who exists for his own sake and not for another's, so we pursue this as the only free science, for it alone exists for its own sake.

Hence also the possession of it might be justly regarded as beyond human power; for in many ways human nature is in bondage, so that according to [30] Simonides "God alone can have this privilege," and it is unfitting that man should not be content to seek the knowledge that is suited to him. If, then, there is something in what the poets [983ª] say, and jealously is natural to the divine power, it would probably occur in this case above all, and all who excelled in this knowledge would be unfortunate. But the divine power cannot be jealous (nay, according to the proverb, "bards tell many a lie"), nor should any other science be thought more honourable than one of this sort. For the most divine science is also most honourable; and this science alone must be, in two ways, most divine. For the science which it would be most meet for God to have is a divine science, and so is any science that deals with divine objects; and this science alone has both these qualities; for (1) God is thought to be among the causes of all things and to be a first principle, and (2) such a science either God alone can have, or God above [10] all others. All the sciences, indeed, are more necessary than this, but none is better.

Yet the acquisition of it must in a sense end in something which is the opposite of our original inquiries. For all men begin, as we said, by wondering that things are as they are, as they do about self-moving marionettes, or about the solstices or the incommensurability of the diagonal of a square with the side; for it seems wonderful to all who have not yet seen the reason, that there is a thing which cannot be measured even by the smallest unit. But we must end in the contrary and, according to the proverb, the better state, as is the case in these instances too when men learn the cause; for there is nothing which would surprise a geometer so much as if the [20] diagonal turned out to be commensurable.

We have stated, then, what is the nature of the science we are searching for, and what is the mark which our search and our whole investigation must reach.

3. Evidently we have to acquire knowledge of the original causes (for we say we know each thing only when we think we recognize its first cause),

and causes are spoken of in four senses. In one of these we mean the substance, i.e. the essence (for the "why" is reducible finally to the definition, and the ultimate "why" is a cause and principle) ; in another the matter or sub- [30] stratum, in a third the source of the change, and in a fourth the cause opposed to this, the purpose and the good (for this is the end of all genera- [983ᵇ] tion and change). We have studied these causes sufficiently in our work on nature,[3] but yet let us call to our aid those who have attacked the investigation of being and philosophized about reality before us. For obviously they too speak of certain principles and causes; to go over their views, then, will be of profit to the present inquiry, for we shall either find another kind of cause, or be more convinced of the correctness of those which we now maintain.

Of the first philosophers, then, most thought the principles which were of the nature of matter were the only principles of all things. That of which all things that are consist, the first from which they come to be, the last into which they are resolved (the substance remaining, but changing in its [10] modifications), this they say is the element and this the principle of things, and therefore they think nothing is either generated or destroyed, since this sort of entity is always conserved, as we say Socrates neither comes to be absolutely when he comes to be beautiful or musical, nor ceases to be when he loses these characteristics, because the substratum, Socrates himself, remains. Just so they say nothing else comes to be or ceases to be; for there must be some entity—either one or more than one—from which all other things come to be, it being conserved.

Yet they do not all agree as to the number and the nature of these [20] principles. Thales, the founder of this

---

3 *Phys.* ii. 3, 7.

type of philosophy, says the principle is water (for which reason he declared that the earth rests on water), getting the notion perhaps from seeing that the nutriment of all things is moist, and that heat itself is generated from the moist and kept alive by it (and that from which they come to be is a principle of all things). He got his notion from this fact, and from the fact that the seeds of all things have a moist nature, and that water is the origin of the nature of moist things.

Some[4] think that even the ancients who lived long before the present generation, and first framed accounts of the gods, had a similar view of na- [30] ture; for they made Ocean and Tethys the parents of creation,[5] and described the oath of the gods as being by water,[6] to which they give the name of Styx; for what is oldest is most honourable, and the most honourable thing is that by which one swears. It may per- [984ᵃ] haps be uncertain whether this opinion about nature is primitive and ancient, but Thales at any rate is said to have declared himself thus about the first cause. Hippo no one would think fit to include among these thinkers, because of the paltriness of his thought.

Anaximenes and Diogenes make air prior to water, and the most primary of the simple bodies, while Hippasus of Metapontium and Heraclitus of Ephesus say this of fire, and Empedocles says it of the four elements (adding a fourth— earth—to those which have been named); for these, he says, always remain and do not come to be, except [10] that they come to be more or fewer, being aggregated into one and segregated out of one.

Anaxagoras of Clazomenae, who, though older than Empedocles, was later in his philosophical activity, says the

principles are infinite in number; for he says almost all the things that are made of parts like themselves, in the manner of water or fire, are generated and destroyed in this way, only by aggregation and segregation, and are not in any other sense generated or destroyed, but remain eternally.

From these facts one might think that the only cause is the so-called material cause; but as men thus advanced, the very facts opened the way for them and joined in forcing them to investigate the subject. However true is may be that all generation and destruction [20] proceed from some one or (for that matter) from more elements, why does this happen and what is the cause? For at least the substratum itself does not make itself change; e.g. neither the wood nor the bronze causes the change of either of them, nor does the wood manufacture a bed and the bronze a statue, but something else is the cause of the change. And to seek this is to seek the second cause, as *we* should say—that from which comes the beginning of the movement. Now those who at the very beginning set themselves to this kind of inquiry, and said the substratum was one,[7] were not at all dissatisfied with themselves; but some at least of those who maintain it to be one[8]—as though defeated by this search for the sec- [30] ond cause—say the one and nature as a whole is unchangeable not only in respect of generation and destruction (for this is a primitive belief, and all agreed in it), but also of all other change; and this view is peculiar to them. Of those who said the universe was one, [984ᵇ] then, none succeeded in discovering a cause of this sort, except perhaps Parmenides, and he only inasmuch as he supposes that there is not only one but also in some sense two causes. But for those who make more elements[9] it

---

4 The reference is probably to Plato (*Crat.* 402 B, *Theaet.* 152 E, 162 D, 180 C).

5 Hom. *Il.* vix, 201, 246.

6 Ibid. ii. 755, xiv. 271, xv. 37.

7 Thales, Anaximenes, and Heraclitus.

8 The Eleatics.

9 The reference is probably to Empedocles.

is more possible to state the second cause, e.g. for those who make hot and cold, or fire and earth, the elements; for they treat fire as having a nature which fits it to move things, and water and earth and such things they treat in the contrary way.

When these men and the principles of this kind had had their day, as the latter were found inadequate to generate the nature of things men were again forced by the truth itself, as we said,[10] to inquire into the next kind of [10] cause. For it is not likely either that fire or earth or any such element should be the reason why things manifest goodness and beauty both in their being and in their coming to be, or that those thinkers should have supposed it was; nor again could it be right to entrust so great a matter to spontaneity and chance. When one man[11] said, then, that reason was present—as in animals, so throughout nature—as the cause of order and of all arrangement, he seemed like a sober man in contrast with the random talk of his predecessors. We know that Anaxagoras certainly adopted these views, but Hermotimus of Clazomenae is credited with expressing them earlier. Those who thought thus [20] stated that there is a principle of things which is at the same time the cause of beauty, and that sort of cause from which things acquire movement.

4. One might suspect that Hesiod was the first to look for such a thing—or some one else who put love or desire among existing things as a principle, as Parmenides, too, does; for he, in constructing the genesis of the universe, says:—

Love first of all the Gods she planned.

And Hesiod says:—

First of all things was chaos made, and then

Broad-breasted earth, . . .
And love, 'mid all the gods pre-eminent,

which implies that among existing [30] things there must be from the first a cause which will move things and bring them together. How these thinkers should be arranged with regard to priority of discovery let us be allowed to decide later;[12] but since the contraries of the various forms of good were also perceived to be present in nature—not only order and the beautiful, but also disorder and the ugly, and bad [985a] things in greater number than good, and ignoble things than beautiful— therefore another thinker introduced friendship and strife, each of the two the cause of one of these two sets of qualities. For if we were to follow out the view of Empedocles, and interpret it according to its meaning and not to its lisping expression, we should find that friendship is the cause of good things, and strife of bad. Therefore, if we said that Empedocles in a sense both mentions, and is the first to mention, the bad and the good as principles, we should perhaps be right, since the cause of all goods is the good itself.

These thinkers, as we say, evident- [10] ly grasped, and to this extent, two of the causes which we distinguished in our work on nature[13]—the matter and the source of the movement—vaguely, however, and with no clearness, but as untrained men behave in fights; for they go round their opponents and often strike fine blows, but they do not fight on scientific principles, and so too these thinkers do not seem to know what they say; for it is evident that, as a rule, they make no use of their causes except to a small extent. For Anaxagoras uses reason as a *deus ex machina* for the making of the world, and when he is at a loss to tell from what cause something neces-

---

10 a 18.
11 Anaxagoras.

12 The promise is not fulfilled.
13 *Phys.* ii. 3, 7.

sarily is, then he drags reason in, [20] but in all other cases ascribes events to anything rather than to reason.[14] And Empedocles, though he uses the causes to a greater extent than this, neither does so sufficiently nor attains consistency in their use. At least, in many cases he makes love segregate things, and strife aggregate them. For whenever the universe is dissolved into its elements by strife, fire is aggregated into one, and so is each of the other elements; but whenever again under the influence of love they come together into one, the parts must again be segregated out of each element.

Empedocles, then, in contrast with his predecessors, was the first to introduce the dividing of this cause, not positing one source of movement, but [30] different and contrary sources. Again, he was the first to speak of four material elements; yet he does not *use* four, [985ᵇ] but treats them as two only; he treats fire by itself, and its opposites—earth, air, and water—as one kind of thing. We may learn this by study of his verses.

This philosopher then, as we say, has spoken of the principles in this way, and made them of this number. Leucippus and his associate Democritus say that the full and the empty are the elements, calling the one being and the other non-being—the full and solid being being, the empty non-being (whence they say being no more is than non-being, because the solid no more is than the empty); and they make these the material causes of things. And as those who make the [10] underlying substance one generate all other things by its modifications, supposing the rare and the dense to be the sources of the modifications, in the same way these philosophers say the differences in the elements are the causes of all other qualities. These differences, they say, are three—shape and order and position. For they say the real is differen-

tiated only by "rhythm" and "inter-contact" and "turning"; and of these rhythm is shape, inter-contact is order, and turning is position; for A differs from N in shape, AN from NA in order, ⊟ from H in position. The question of movement—whence or how it is to belong to things—these thinkers, like the others, lazily neglected.

Regarding the two causes, then, as we say, the inquiry seems to have [20] been pushed thus far by the early philosophers.

5. Contemporaneously with these philosophers and before them, the so-called Pythagoreans, who were the first to take up mathematics, not only advanced this study, but also having been brought up in it they thought its principles were the principles of all things. Since of these principles numbers are by nature the first, and in numbers they seemed to see many resemblances to the things that exist and come into being—more than in fire and earth and water (such and such a modification of numbers being justice, another being soul and reason, another being oppor- [30] tunity—and similarly almost all other things being numerically expressible); since, again, they saw that the modifications and the ratios of the musical scales were expressible in numbers;—since, then, all other things seemed in their whole nature to be modelled on numbers, and numbers seemed to be [986ᵃ] the first things in the whole of nature, they supposed the elements of numbers to be the elements of all things, and the whole heaven to be a musical scale and a number. And all the properties of numbers and scales which they could show to agree with the attributes and parts and the whole arrangement of the heavens, they collected and fitted into their scheme; and if there was a gap anywhere, they readily made additions so as to make their whole theory coherent. E.g. as the number 10 is

---

14 Cf. Pl. *Phaedo*, 98 ʙᴄ, *Laws*, 967 ʙ–ᴅ.

thought to be perfect and to comprise the whole nature of numbers, they [10] say that the bodies which move through the heavens are ten, but as the visible bodies are only nine, to meet this they invent a tenth—the "counter-earth." We have discussed these matters more exactly elsewhere.[15]

But the object of our review is that we may learn from these philosophers also what they suppose to be the principles and how these fall under the causes we have named. Evidently, then, these thinkers also consider that number is the principle both as matter for things and as forming both their modifications and their permanent states, and hold that the elements of number are the even and the odd, and that of these the latter is limited, and the former unlimited; and that the One proceeds from both of these (for it is both even and odd), and number from the [20] One; and that the whole heaven, as has been said, is numbers.

Other members of this same school say there are ten principles, which they arrange in two columns of cognates—limit and unlimited, odd and even, one and plurality, right and left, male and female, resting and moving, straight and curved, light and darkness, good and bad, square and oblong. In this way Alcmaeon of Croton seems also to have conceived the matter, and either he got this view from them or they got it from him; for he expressed himself simi- [30] larly to them. For he says most human affairs go in pairs, meaning not definite contrarieties such as the Pythagoreans speak of, but any chance contrarieties, e.g. white and black, sweet and bitter, good and bad, great and small. He threw out indefinite suggestions about the other contrarieties, but the Pythagoreans declared both how many [986ᵇ] and which their contrarieties are.

From both these schools, then, we

can learn this much, that the contraries are the principles of things; and how many these principles are and which they are, we can learn from one of the two schools. But how these principles can be brought together under the causes we have named has not been clearly and articulately stated by them; they seem, however, to range the elements under the head of matter; for out of these as immanent parts they say substance is composed and moulded.

From these facts we may sufficiently perceive the meaning of the ancients who said the elements of nature were more than one; but there are some who spoke of the universe as if it were [10] one entity, though they were not all alike either in the excellence of their statement or in its conformity to the facts of nature. The discussion of them is in no way appropriate to our present investigation of causes, for they do not, like some of the natural philosophers, assume being to be one and yet generate it out of the one as out of matter, but they speak in another way; those others add change, since they generate the universe, but these thinkers say the universe is unchangeable. Yet *this* much is germane to the present inquiry: Parmenides seems to fasten on that which is one in definition, Melissus on that which is one in matter, for which reason the former says that it is limited, the [20] latter that it is unlimited; while Xenophanes, the first of these partisans of the One (for Parmenides is said to have been his pupil), gave no clear statement, nor does he seem to have grasped the nature of either of these causes, but with reference to the whole material universe he says the One is God. Now these thinkers, as we said, must be neglected for the purposes of the present inquiry—two of them entirely, as being a little too naïve, viz. Xenophanes and Melissus; but Parmenides seems in places to speak with more insight. For, claiming that, besides the existent, nothing non-existent

---

15 *De Caelo*, ii. 13.

exists, he thinks that of necessity one thing exists, viz. the existent and nothing else (on this we have spoken more clearly in our work on nature),[16] [30] but being forced to follow the observed facts, and supposing the existence of that which is one in definition, but more than one according to our sensations, he now posits two causes and two principles, calling them hot and cold, i.e. fire and earth; and of these he ranges the [987ᵃ] hot with the existent, and the other with the nonexistent.

From what has been said, then, and from the wise men who have now sat in council with us, we have got thus much—on the one hand from the earliest philosophers, who regard the first principle as corporeal (for water and fire and such things are bodies), and of whom some suppose that there is one corporeal principle, others that there are more than one, but both put these under the head of matter; and on the other hand from some who posit both this cause and besides this the sources of movement, which we have got from some as single and from others as twofold.

Down to the Italian school, then, and apart from it, philosophers have [10] treated these subjects rather obscurely, except that, as we said, they have in fact used two kinds of cause, and one of these—the source of movement— some treat as one and others as two. But the Pythagoreans have said in the same way that there are two principles, but added this much, which is peculiar to them, that they thought that finitude and infinity were not attributes of certain other things, e.g. of fire or earth or anything else of this kind, but that infinity itself and unity itself were the substance of the things of which they are predicated. This is why number was the substance of all things. On this subject, [20] then, they expressed themselves thus;

and regarding the question of essence they began to make statements and definitions, but treated the matter too simply. For they both defined superficially and thought that the first subject of which a given definition was predicable was the substance of the thing defined, as if one supposed that "double" and "2" were the same, because 2 is the first thing of which "double" is predicable. But surely to be double and to be 2 are not the same; if they are, one thing will be many[17]—a consequence which they actually drew.[18] From the earlier philosophers, then, and from their successors we can learn thus much.

6. After the systems we have named came the philosophy of Plato, which [30] in most respects followed these thinkers, but had peculiarities that distinguished it from the philosophy of the Italians. For, having in his youth first become familiar with Cratylus and with the Heraclitean doctrines (that all sensible things are ever in a state of flux and there is no knowledge about them), these views he held even in later [987ᵇ] years. Socrates, however, was busying himself about ethical matters and neglecting the world of nature as a whole but seeking the universal in these ethical matters, and fixed thought for the first time on definitions; Plato accepted his teaching, but held that the problem applied not to sensible things but to entities of another kind—for this reason, that the common definition could not be a definition of any sensible thing, as they were always changing. Things of this other sort, then, he called Ideas, and sensible things, he said, were all named after these, and in virtue of a relation to these; for the many existed by participation in the Ideas that have the same name as they. Only the name "par- [10]

16 *Phys.* i. 3.

17 I.e. 2 will be each of several things whose definition is predicable of it.

18 E.g. 2 was identified both with opinion and with daring.

ticipation" was new; for the Pythagoreans say that things exist by "imitation" of numbers, and Plato says they exist by participation, changing the name. But what the participation or the imitation of the Forms could be they left an open question.

Further, besides sensible things and Forms he says there are the objects of mathematics, which occupy an intermediate position, differing from sensible things in being eternal and unchangeable, from Forms in that there are many alike, while the Form itself is in each case unique.

Since the Forms were the causes of all other things, he thought their elements were the elements of all things. As [20] matter, the great and the small were principles; as essential reality, the One; for from the great and the small, by participation in the One, come the Numbers.

But he agreed with the Pythagoreans in saying that the One is substance and not a predicate of something else; and in saying that the Numbers are the causes of the reality of other things he agreed with them; but positing a dyad and constructing the infinite out of great and small, instead of treating the infinite as one, is peculiar to him; and so is his view that the Numbers exist apart from sensible things, while *they* say that the things themselves are Numbers, and do not place the objects of mathematics between Forms and sensible things. His divergence from the Pythagoreans in making the One [30] and the Numbers separate from things, and his introduction of the Forms, were due to his inquiries in the region of definitions (for the earlier thinkers had no tincture of dialectic), and his making the other entity besides the One a dyad was due to the belief that the numbers, except those which were prime, could be neatly produced out of the dyad as out of some plastic material.

Yet what *happens* is the con- [988ᵃ]

trary; the theory is not a reasonable one. For they make many things out of the matter, and the form generates only once, but what we observe is that one table is made from one matter, while the man who applies the form, though he is one, makes many tables. And the relation of the male to the female is similar; for the latter is impregnated by one copulation, but the male impregnates many females; yet these are analogues of those first principles.

Plato, then, declared himself thus on the points in question; it is evident from what has been said that he has used only two causes, that of the essence and the material cause (for the Forms are the causes of the essence of all other [10] things, and the One is the cause of the essence of the Forms); and it is evident what the underlying matter is, of which the Forms are predicated in the case of sensible things, and the One in the case of Forms, viz. that this is a dyad, the great and the small. Further, he has assigned the cause of good and that of evil to the elements, one to each of the two, as we say[19] some of his predecessors sought to do, e.g. Empedocles and Anaxagoras.

7. Our review of those who have spoken about first principles and reality and of the way in which they have spoken, has been concise and sum- [20] mary; but yet we have learnt *this* much from them, that of those who speak about "principle" and "cause" no one has mentioned any principle except those which have been distinguished in our work on nature,[20] but all evidently have some inkling of *them*, though only vaguely. For some speak of the first principle as matter, whether they suppose one or more first principles, and whether they suppose this to be a body or to be incorporeal; e.g. Plato spoke of the great and the small, the Italians of

[19] Cf. 984ᵇ 15–19, 32–ᵇ 10.
[20] *Phys.* ii. 3, 7.

the infinite, Empedocles of fire, earth, water, and air, Anaxagoras of the infinity of things composed of similar parts. These, then, have all had a notion of this kind of cause, and so have all [30] who speak of air or fire or water, or something denser than fire and rarer than air; for some have said the prime element is of this kind.

These thinkers grasped this cause only; but certain others have mentioned the source of movement, e.g. those who make friendship and strife, or reason, or love, a principle.

The essence, i.e. the substantial reality, no one has expressed distinctly. It is hinted at chiefly by those who believe in the Forms; for they do not sup- [988ᵇ] pose either that the Forms are the matter of sensible things, and the One the matter of the Forms, or that they are the source of movement (for they say these are causes rather of immobility and of being at rest), but they furnish the Forms as the essence of every other thing, and the One as the essence of the Forms.

That for whose sake actions and changes and movements take place, they assert to be a cause in a way, but not in this way, i.e. not in the way in which it is its *nature* to be a cause. For those who speak of reason or friendship class these causes as goods; they do not speak, however, as if anything that exists either existed or came into being for the sake of these, but as if movements started [10] from these. In the same way those who say the One of the existent is the good, say that it is the cause of substance, but not that substance either is or comes to be for the sake of this. Therefore it turns out that in a sense they both say and do not say the good is a cause; for they do not call it a cause *qua* good but only incidentally.

All these thinkers, then, as they cannot pitch on another cause, seem to testify that we have determined rightly both how many and of what sort the causes are. Besides this it is plain that when the causes are being looked for, either all four must be sought thus or they must be sought in one of these four ways. Let us next discuss the possible [20] difficulties with regard to the way in which each of these thinkers has spoken, and with regard to his situation relatively to the first principles.

8. Those, then, who say the universe is one and posit one kind of thing as matter, and as corporeal matter which has spatial magnitude, evidently go astray in many ways. For they posit the elements of bodies only, not of incorporeal things, though there are also incorporeal things. And in trying to state the causes of generation and destruction, and in giving a physical account of all things, they do away with the cause of movement. Further, they err in not positing the substance, i.e. the essence, as the cause of anything, and besides this in lightly calling any of the simple bodies except earth the first principle, with- [30] out inquiring how they are produced out of one another,—I mean fire, water, earth, and air. For some things are produced out of each other by combination, others by separation, and this makes the greatest difference to their priority and posteriority. For (1) in a way the property of being most elementary of all would seem to belong to the first thing from which they are produced by combination, and *this* property would [989ᵃ] belong to the most fine-grained and subtle of bodies. For this reason those who make fire the principle would be most in agreement with this argument. But each of the other thinkers agrees that the element of corporeal things is of this sort. At least none of those who named one element claimed that earth was the element, evidently because of the coarseness of its grain. (Of the other three elements each has found some judge on its side; for some maintain that fire, others that water, others

that air is the element. Yet why, after all, do they not name earth also, as most men do? For people say all things are earth. And Hesiod says earth was produced [10] first of corporeal things; so primitive and popular has the opinion been.) According to this argument, then, no one would be right who either says the first principle is any of the elements other than fire, or supposes it to be denser than air but rarer than water. But (2) if that which is later in generation is prior in nature, and that which is concocted and compounded is later in generation, the contrary of what we have been saying must be true—water must be prior to air, and earth to water.

So much, then, for those who posit one cause such as we mentioned; but [20] the same is true if one supposes more of these, as Empedocles says the matter of things is four bodies. For he too is confronted by consequences some of which are the same as have been mentioned, while others are peculiar to him. For we see these bodies produced from one another, which implies that the same body does not always remain fire or earth (we have spoken about this in our works on nature[21]); and regarding the cause of movement and the question whether we must posit one or two, he must be thought to have spoken neither correctly nor altogether plausibly. And in general, change of quality is necessarily done away with for those who speak thus, for on their view cold will not come from hot nor hot from cold. For if it did there would be something that accepted the contraries themselves, and there would be some one entity that became fire and water, which Empedocles denies.

As regards Anaxagoras, if one [30] were to suppose that he said there were two elements, the supposition would accord thoroughly with an argument which Anaxagoras himself did not state articulately, but which he must have accepted if any one had led him on to it.

---

21 *De Caelo*, iii. 7.

True, to say that in the beginning all things were mixed is absurd both on other grounds and because it follows that they must have existed before in an unmixed form, and because nature [989ᵇ] does not allow any chance thing to be mixed with any chance thing, and also because on this view modifications and accidents could be separated from substances (for the same things which are mixed can be separated); yet if one were to follow him up, piecing together what he means, he would perhaps be seen to be somewhat modern in his views. For when nothing was separated out, evidently nothing could be truly asserted of the substance that then existed. I mean, e.g., that it was neither white nor black, nor grey nor any other colour, but of necessity colourless; for if it had been coloured, it would have had one of these colours. And similarly, [10] by this same argument, it was flavourless, nor had it any similar attribute; for it could not be either of any quality or of any size, nor could it be any definite kind of thing. For if it were, one of the particular forms would have belonged to it, and this is impossible, since all were mixed together; for the particular form would necessarily have been already separated out, but he says all were mixed except reason, and this alone was unmixed and pure. From this it follows, then, that he must say the principles are the One (for this is simple and unmixed) and the Other, which is of such a nature as we suppose the indefinite to be before it is defined and partakes of some form. Therefore, while expressing himself neither rightly nor clearly, he means something like what the later thinkers say and what is now more clearly [20] seen to be the case.

But these thinkers are, after all, at home only in arguments about generation and destruction and movement; for it is practically only of this sort of substance that they seek the principles and the causes. But those who extend their vision to all things that exist, and of existing things suppose some to be perceptible and others not perceptible evidently study both classes, which is all the more reason why one should devote some time to seeing what is good in their views and what bad from the standpoint of the inquiry we have now before us.

The "Pythagoreans" treat of principles and elements stranger than those of the physical philosophers (the reason is [30] that they got the principles from non-sensible things, for the objects of mathematics, except those of astronomy, are of the class of things without movement); yet their discussions and investigations are all about nature; for they generate the heavens, and with regard to their parts and attributes and [990ᵃ] functions they observe the phenomena, and use up the principles and the causes in explaining these, which implies that they agree with the others, the physical philosophers, that the *real* is just all that which is perceptible and contained by the so-called "heavens." But the causes and the principles which they mention are, as we said, sufficient to act as steps even up to the higher realms of reality, and are more suited to these than to theories about nature. They do not tell us at all, however, how there can be movement if limit and unlimited and odd and even are the only things assumed, or how without movement [10] and change there can be generation and destruction, or the bodies that move through the heavens can do what they do.

Further, if one either granted them that spatial magnitude consists of these elements, or this were proved, still how would some bodies be light and others have weight? To judge from what they assume and maintain they are speaking no more of mathematical bodies than of perceptible; hence they have said nothing whatever about fire or earth or the other bodies of this sort, I suppose because they have nothing to say which applies *peculiarly* to perceptible things.

Further, how are we to combine the beliefs that the attributes of number, and number itself, are causes of what exists and happens in the heavens both [20] from the beginning and now, and that there is no other number than this number out of which the world is composed? When in one particular region they place opinion and opportunity, and, a little above or below, injustice and decision or mixture, and allege, as proof, that each of these is a number, and that there happens to be already in this place a plurality of the extended bodies composed of numbers, because these attributes of number attach to the various places—this being so, is this number, which we must suppose each of these abstractions to be, the same number which is exhibited in the material universe, or is it another than this? Plato says it is different; yet even he [30] thinks that both these bodies and their causes arc numbers, but that the *intelligible* numbers are causes, while the others are *sensible*.

9. Let us leave the Pythagoreans for the present; for it is enough to have touched on them as much as we have done. But as for those who posit the Ideas as causes, firstly, in seeking [990ᵇ] to grasp the causes of the things around us, they introduced others equal in number to these, as if a man who wanted to count things thought he would not be able to do it while they were few, but tried to count them when he had added to their number. For the Forms are practically equal to—or not fewer than —the things, in trying to explain which these thinkers proceeded from them to the Forms. For to each thing there answers an entity which has the same name and exists apart from the substances, and so also in the case of all other groups there is a one over many, whether the many are in this world or are eternal.

Further, of the ways in which we prove that the Forms exist, none is convincing; for from some no inference [10] necessarily follows, and from some arise

Forms even of things of which we think there are no Forms. For according to the arguments from the existence of the sciences there will be Forms of all things of which there are sciences, and according to the "one over many" argument there will be Forms even of negations, and according to the argument that there is an object for thought even when the thing has perished, there will be Forms of perishable things; for we have an image of these. Further, of the more accurate arguments, some lead to Ideas of relations, of which we say there is no independent class, and others introduce the "third man."

And in general the arguments for the Forms destroy the things for whose existence we are more zealous than for the existence of the Ideas; for it follows that not the dyad but number is first, i.e. that the relative is prior to the [20] absolute—besides, all the other points on which certain people by following out the opinions held about the Ideas have come into conflict with the principles of the theory.

Further, according to the assumption on which our belief in the Ideas rests, there will be Forms not only of substances but also of many other things (for the concept is single not only in the case of substances but also in the other cases, and there are sciences not only of substance but also of other things, and a thousand other such difficulties confront them). But according to the necessities of the case and the opinions held about the Forms, if Forms can be shared in there must be Ideas of substances only. For they are not shared in incidentally, but a thing must share in its Form as [30] in something not predicated of a subject (by "being shared in incidentally" I mean that e.g. if a thing shares in "double itself," it shares also in "eternal," but incidentally; for "eternal" happens to be predicable of the "double"). Therefore the Forms will be substance; but the same terms indicate substance in this and in the ideal world (or what will

be the meaning of saying that [991ᵃ] there is something apart from the particulars—the one over many?). And if the Ideas and the particulars that share in them have the same form, there will be something common to these; for why should "2" be one and the same in the perishable 2's or in those which are many but eternal, and not the same in the "2 itself" as in the particular 2? But if they have not the same form, they must have only the name in common, and it is as if one were to call both Callias and a wooden image a "man," without observing any community between them.[22]

Above all one might discuss the question what on earth the Forms contribute to sensible things, either to those that are eternal or to those that come into being and cease to be. For they cause [10] neither movement nor any change in them. But again they help in no wise either towards the knowledge of the other things (for they are not even the substance of these, else they would have been in them), or towards their being, if they are not *in* the particulars which share in them; though if they were, they might be thought to be causes, as white causes whiteness in a white object by entering into its composition. But this argument, which first Anaxagoras and later Eudoxus and certain others used, is very easily upset; for it is not difficult to collect many insuperable objections to such a view.

But, further, all other things cannot come from the Forms in any of the usual senses of "from." And to say that [20] they are patterns and the other things share in them is to use empty words and poetical metaphors. For what is it that works, looking to the Ideas? And anything can either be, or become, like another without being copied from it, so that whether Socrates exists or not a man like Socrates might come to be; and

---

22 With 990ᵇ 2–991ᵃ 8 cf. xiii. 1078ᵇ 34– 1079ᵇ 3.

evidently this might be so even if Socrates were eternal. And there will be several patterns of the same thing, and therefore several Forms; e.g. "animal" and "two-footed" and also "man himself" will be Forms of man. Again, the Forms are patterns not only of sensible things, but of Forms themselves also; [30] i.e. the genus, as genus of various species, will be so; therefore the same thing will be pattern and copy.

Again, it would seem impossible [991ᵇ] that the substance and that of which it is the substance should exist apart; how, therefore, could the Ideas, being the substances of things, exist apart? In the *Phaedo*[23] the case is stated in this way— that the Forms are causes both of being and of becoming; yet when the Forms exist, still the things that share in them do not come into being, unless there is something to originate movement; and many other things come into being (e.g. a house or a ring) of which we say there are no Forms. Clearly, therefore, even the other things can both be and come into being owing to such causes as produce the things just mentioned.[24]

Again, if the Forms are numbers, how can they be causes? Is it because existing things are other numbers, e.g. one [10] number is man, another is Socrates, another Callias? Why then are the one set of numbers causes of the other set? It will not make any difference even if the former are eternal and the latter are not. But if it is because things in this sensible world (e.g. harmony) are ratios of numbers, evidently the things between which they are ratios are some one class of things. If, then, this—the matter—is some definite thing, evidently the numbers themselves too will be ratios of something to something else. E.g. if Callias is a numerical ratio between fire and earth and water and air, his Idea also will be a number of certain other

underlying things; and man-himself, whether it is a number in a sense or not, will still be a numerical ratio of certain things and not a number proper, nor will it be a kind of number merely be- [20] cause it is a numerical ratio.

Again, from many numbers one number is produced, but how can one Form come from many Forms? And if the number comes not from the many numbers themselves but from the units in them, e.g. in 10,000, how is it with the units? If they are specifically alike, numerous absurdities will follow, and also if they are not alike (neither the units in one number being themselves like one another nor those in other numbers being all like to all); for in what will they differ, as they are without quality? This is not a plausible view, nor is it consistent with our thought on the matter.

Further, they must set up a second kind of number (with which arithmetic deals), and all the objects which are called "intermediate" by some thinkers; and how do these exist or from what principles do they proceed? Or why must they be intermediate between the [30] things in this sensible world and the things-themselves?

Further, the units in 2 must each come from a prior 2; but this is impossible.

Further, why is a number, when taken all together, one?                    [992ᵃ]

Again, besides what has been said, if the units are *diverse* the Platonists should have spoken like those who say there are four, or two, elements; for each of these thinkers gives the name of element not to that which is common, e.g. to body, but to fire and earth, whether there is something common to them, viz. body, or not. But in fact the Platonists speak as if the One were *homogeneous* like fire or water; and if this is so, the numbers will not be substances. Evidently, if there is a One-itself and this is a first principle, "one" is being used in more than one sense; for otherwise the theory is impossible.

23  100 C–E.
24  With 991ᵃ 8–ᵇ 9 cf. xiii. 1079ᵇ 12–1080ᵃ 8.

When we wish to reduce sub- [10] stances to their principles, we state that lines come from the short and long (i.e. from a kind of small and great), and the plane from the broad and narrow, and body from the deep and shallow. Yet how then can either the plane contain a line, or the solid a line or a plane? For the broad and narrow is a different class from the deep and shallow. There- fore, just as number is not present in these, because the many and few are dif- ferent from these, evidently no other of the higher classes will be present in the lower. But again the broad is not a genus which includes the deep, for then the solid would have been a species of plane.[25] Further, from what principle will the presence of the *points* in the line be derived? Plato even used to object to this class of things as being a geo- [20] metrical fiction. He gave the name of principle of the line—and this he often posited—to the indivisible lines. Yet these must have a limit; therefore the argument from which the existence of the line follows proves also the existence of the point.

In general, though philosophy seeks the cause of perceptible things, we have given this up (for we say nothing of the cause from which change takes its start), but while we fancy we are stating the substance of perceptible things, we as- sert the existence of a second class of substances, while our account of the way in which they are the substances of perceptible things is empty talk; for "sharing," as we said before,[26] means nothing.

Nor have the Forms any connexion with what we see to be the cause in the case of the arts, that for whose sake [30] both all mind and the whole of nature are operative[27]—with this cause which we assert to be one of the first principles; but mathematics has come to be identical with philosophy for modern thinkers, though they say that it should be studied for the sake of other things.[28]

Further, one might suppose that the substance which according to them un- derlies as matter is too mathe- [992ᵇ] matical, and is a predicate and differen- tia of the substance, i.e. of the matter, rather than the matter itself; i.e. the great and the small are like the rare and the dense which the physical philoso- phers speak of, calling these the primary differentiae of the substratum; for these are a kind of excess and defect. And regarding movement, if the great and the small are to *be* movement, evidently the Forms will be moved; but if they are not to be movement, whence did movement come? The wholy study of nature has been annihilated.

And what is thought to be easy—to show that all things are one—is not done; for what is proved by the [10] method of setting out instances[29] is not that all things are one but that there is a One-itself,—if we grant all the assump- tions. And not even this follows, if we do not grant that the universal is a genus; and this in some cases it cannot be.

Nor can it be explained either how the lines and planes and solids that come after the numbers exist or can exist, or what significance they have; for these can neither be Forms (for they are not numbers), nor the intermediates (for those are the objects of mathematics), nor the perishable things. This is evident- ly a distinct fourth class.

In general, if we search for the ele- ments of existing things without dis- tinguishing the many senses in which things are said to exist, we cannot find them, especially if the search for the elements of which things are made is conducted in this manner. For it is [20] surely impossible to discover what "act-

---

25With 992ª 10–19 cf. xiii. 1085ª 9–19.
26 991ª 20–22.
27 *Sc.* the final cause.

28 Cf. Plato, *Rep.* vii. 531 ᴅ, 533 ʙ–ᴇ.
29 For this Platonic method cf. vii. 1031ᵇ 21, xiii. 1086ᵇ 9, viv. 1090ª 17.

ing" or "being acted on," or "the straight," is made of, but if elements can be discovered at all, it is only the elements of substances; therefore either to seek the elements of all existing things or to think one has them is incorrect.

And how could we *learn* the elements of all things? Evidently we cannot start by knowing anything before. For as he who is learning geometry, though he may know other things before, knows none of the things with which the science deals and about which he is to learn, so is it in all other cases. Therefore if there is a science of all things, such as some assert to exist, he who is learning this will know nothing before. Yet all learning is by means of premisses which are [30] (either all or some of them) known before—whether the learning be by demonstration or by definitions; for the elements of the definition must be known before and be familiar; and learning by induction proceeds similarly. But again, if the science were actually innate, [993ᵃ] it were strange that we are unaware of our possession of the greatest of sciences.

Again, how is one to *come to know* what all things are made of, and how is this to be made *evident?* This also affords a difficulty; for there might be a conflict of opinion, as there is about certain syllables; some say *za* is made of *s* and *d* and *a*, while others say it is a distinct sound and none of those that are familiar.

Further, how could we know the objects of sense without having the sense in question? Yet we ought to, if the elements of which all things consist, as complex sounds consist of the ele- [10] ments proper to sound, are the same.

10. It is evident, then, even from what we have said before, that all men seem to seek the causes named in the *Physics*,[30] and that we cannot name any beyond these; but they seek these vaguely; and though in a sense they have all

been described before, in a sense they have not been described at all. For the earliest philosophy is, on all subjects, like one who lisps, since it is young and in its beginnings. For even Empedocles says bone exists by virtue of the ratio in it. Now this is the essence and the substance of the thing. But it is similarly necessary that flesh and each of the other tissues should be the ratio of its elements, or that not one of them should; for it [20] is on account of this that both flesh and bone and everything else will exist, and not on account of the matter, which *he* names—fire and earth and water and air. But while he would necessarily have agreed if another had said this, he has not said it clearly.

On those questions our views have been expressed before; but let us return to enumerate the difficulties that might be raised on those same points;[31] for perhaps we may get from them some help towards our later difficulties.

## Book Γ (IV)

1. There is a science which in- [1003ᵃ] vestigates being as being and the attributes which belong to this in virtue of its own nature. Now this is not the same as any of the so-called special sciences; for none of these others treats universally of being as being. They cut off a part of being and investigate the attribute of this part; this is what the mathematical sciences for instance do. Now since we are seeking the first principles and the highest causes, clearly there must be some thing to which these belong in virtue of its own nature. If then those who sought the elements of existing things were seeking these same principles, it is necessary that the elements must [30] be elements of being not by accident but just because it *is* being. Therefore it is of being as being that we also must grasp the first causes.

---

30 ii. 3, 7.

31 The reference is to Bk. iii.

2. There are many senses in which a thing may be said to "be," but all that "is" is related to one central point, one definite kind of thing, and is not said to "be" by a mere ambiguity. Everything which is healthy is related to health, one thing in the sense that it preserves health, another in the sense that it produces it, another in the sense that it is a symptom of health, another because it is capable of it. And that which is medical [1003ᵇ] is relative to the medical art, one thing being called medical because it possesses it, another because it is naturally adapted to it, another because it is a function of the medical art. And we shall find other words used similarly to these. So, too, there are many senses in which a thing is said to be, but all refer to one starting-point; some things are said to be because they are substances, others because they are affections of substance, others because they are a process towards substance, or destructions or privations or qualities of substance, or productive or generative of substance, or of things which are relative to substance, or negations of one of these things or of substance itself. It is for this reason that [10] we say even of non-being that it *is* non-being. As, then, there is one science which deals with all healthy things, the same applies in the other cases also. For not only in the case of things which have one common notion does the investigation belong to one science, but also in the case of things which are related to one common nature: for even these in a sense have one common notion. It is clear then that it is the work of one science also to study the things that are, *qua* being.—But everywhere science deals chiefly with that which is primary, and on which the other things depend, and in virtue of which they get their names. If, then, this is substance, it will be of substances that the philosopher must grasp the principles and the causes.

Now for each one class of things, as there is one perception, so there is one science, as for instance grammar, [20] being one science, investigates all articulate sounds. Hence to investigate all the species of being *qua* being is the work of a science which is generically one, and to investigate the several species is the work of the specific parts of the science.

If, now, being and unity are the same and are one thing in the sense that they are implied in one another as principle and cause are, not in the sense that they are explained by the same definition (though it makes no difference even if we suppose them to be like that—in fact this would even strengthen our case) ; for "one man" and "man" are the same thing, and so are "existent man" and "man," and the doubling of the words in "one man and one *existent* man" does not express anything different (it is clear that the two things are not separated either in coming to be or in ceasing to be) ; and similarly "*one* existent man" adds nothing to "existent man," so [30] that it is obvious that the addition in these cases means the same thing, and unity is nothing apart from being; and if, further, the substance of each thing is one in no merely accidental way, and similarly is from its very nature something that *is*:—all this being so, there must be exactly as many species of being as of unity. And to investigate the essence of these is the work of a science which is generically one—I mean, for instance, the discussion of the same and the similar and the other concepts of this sort; and nearly all contraries may be referred to this origin; let us take them as having been investigated [1004ª] in the "Selection of Contraries."

And there are as many parts of philosophy as there are kinds of substance, so that there must necessarily be among them a first philosophy and one which follows this. For being falls immediately into genera; for which reason the sciences too will correspond to these genera. For the philosopher is like the mathematician, as that word is used; for mathematics also has parts, and there is a first and a second science and other successive ones within the sphere of mathematics.[1]

Now since it is the work of one science to investigate opposites, and plurality is opposed to unity—and it belongs to [10] one science to investigate the negation and the privation because in both cases we are really investigating the one thing of which the negation or the privation is a negation or privation (for we either say simply that that thing is not present, or that it is not present in some particular class; in the latter case difference is present over and above what is implied in negation; for negation means just the absence of the thing in question, while in privation there is also employed an underlying nature of which the privation is asserted):—in view of all these facts, the contraries of the concepts we named above, the other and the dissimilar and the unequal, and everything else which is derived either from these or from plurality and unity, must fall within the province of the science above named. And contrariety is one of these con- [20] cepts; for contrariety is a kind of difference, and difference is a kind of otherness. Therefore, since there are many senses in which a thing is said to be one, these terms also will have many senses, but yet it belongs to one science to know them all; for a term belongs to different sciences not if it has different senses, but if it has not one meaning *and* its definitions cannot be referred to one central meaning. And since all things are referred to that which is primary, as for instance all things which are called one are referred to the primary one, we must say that this holds good also of the same and the other and of contraries in general; so that after distinguishing the various senses of each, we must then explain by reference to what is primary in the case of each of the predicates in question, saying how they are related to it; for some will be called what they are [30] called because they possess it, others because they produce it, and others in other such ways.

It is evident, then, that it belongs to one science to be able to give an account of these concepts as well as of substance (this was one of the questions in our book of problems),[2] and that it is the function of the philosopher to be [1004ᵇ] able to investigate all things. For if it is not the function of the philosopher, who is it who will inquire whether Socrates and Socrates seated are the same thing, or whether one thing has one contrary, or what contrariety is, or how many meanings it has? And similarly with all other such questions. Since, then, these are essential modifications of unity *qua* unity and of being *qua* being, not *qua* numbers or lines or fire, it is clear that it belongs to this science to investigate both the essence of these concepts and their properties. And those who study these properties err not by leaving the sphere of philosophy,[3] but by forgetting that substance, of which they have no correct idea, is prior to these other things. For number *qua* number has peculiar [10] attributes, such as oddness and evenness, commensurability and equality, excess and defect, and these belong to numbers either in themselves or in relation to one another. And similarly the solid and the motionless and that which is in motion and the weightless and that which has weight have other peculiar properties. So too there are certain properties peculiar to being as such, and it is about these that the philosopher has to investigate the truth.—An indication of this may be mentioned:—dialecticians and sophists assume the same guise as the philosopher, for sophistic is Wisdom which exists only

---

[1] With 1004ᵃ 2–9 cf. iii. 995ᵇ 10–13, 997ᵃ 15–25, vi. 1.

[2] I.e. iii. 995ᵇ 18–27, 997ᵃ 25–34.
[3] *Sc.* which they do not do.

in semblance, and dialecticians embrace all things in their dialectic, and be- [20] ing is common to all things; but evidently their dialectic embraces these subjects because these are proper to philosophy. —For sophistic and dialectic turn on the same class of things as philosophy, but this differs from dialectic in the nature of the faculty required and from sophistic in respect of the purpose of the philosophic life. Dialectic is merely critical where philosophy claims to know, and sophistic is what appears to be philosophy but is not.

Again, in the list of contraries one of the two columns is privative, and all contraries are reducible to being and non-being, and to unity and plurality, as for instance rest belongs to unity and movement to plurality. And nearly all thinkers agree that being and sub- [30] stance are composed of contraries; at least all name contraries as their first principles—some name odd and even,[4] some hot and cold,[5] some limit and the unlimited,[6] some love and strife.[7] And all the others as well are evidently reducible to unity and plurality [1005ᵃ] (this reduction we must take for granted), and the principles stated by other thinkers fall entirely under these as their genera. It is obvious then from these considerations too that it belongs to one science to examine being *qua* being. For all things are either contraries or composed of contraries, and unity and plurality are the starting-points of all contraries. And these belong to one science, whether they have or have not one single meaning. Probably the truth is that they have not; yet even if "one" has several meanings, the other meanings will be related to the primary meaning (and similarly in the case of the contraries), even if being or unity is not a universal and the same in every

instance or is not separable from the particular instances (as in fact it probably is not; the unity is in some cases [10] that of common reference, in some cases that of serial succession). And for this reason it does not belong to the geometer to inquire what is contrariety or completeness or unity or being or the same or the other, but only to presuppose these concepts and reason from this starting-point.—Obviously then it is the work of one science to examine being *qua* being, and the attributes which belong to it *qua* being, and the same science will examine not only substances but also their attributes, both those above named and the concepts "prior" and "posterior," "genus" and "species," "whole" and "part," and the others of this sort.[8]

3. We must state whether it belongs to one or to different sciences to inquiry into the truths which are in mathematics called axioms, and into substance. Evidently, the inquiry into these also [20] belongs to one science, and that the science of the philosopher; for these truths hold good for everything that is, and not for some special genus apart from others. And all men use them, because they are true of being *qua* being and each genus has being. But men use them just so far as to satisfy their purposes; that is, as far as the genus to which their demonstrations refer extends. Therefore since these truths clearly hold good for all things *qua* being (for this is what is common to them), to him who studies being *qua* being belongs the inquiry into these as well. And for this reason no one who is conducting a special inquiry tries to say anything [30] about their truth or falsity—neither the geometer nor the arithmetician. Some natural philosophers indeed have done so, and their procedure was intelligible enough; for they thought that they alone were inquiring about the whole of nature

---

4 The Pythagoreans.
5 Parmenides in the "Way of Opinion."
6 The Platonists.
7 Empedocles.

---

8 With 1003ᵇ 22–1005ᵃ 18 cf. iii. 995ᵇ 18–27, 997ᵃ 25–34. With the whole ch. cf.

and about being. But since there is one kind of thinker who is above even the natural philosopher (for nature is only one particular genus of being), the discussion of these truths also will belong to him whose inquiry is universal and deals with primary substance. [1005ᵇ] Physics also is a kind of Wisdom, but it is not the first kind.[9]—And the attempts of some of those who discuss the terms on which truth should be accepted,[10] are due to a want of training in logic; for they should know these things already when they come to a special study, and not be inquiring into them while they are listening to lectures on it.

Evidently then it belongs to the philosopher, i.e. to him who is studying the nature of all substance, to inquire also into the principles of syllogism. But he who knows best about each genus must be able to state the most certain principles of his subject, so that he whose subject is existing things *qua* existing [10] must be able to state the most certain principles of all things. This is the philosopher, and the most certain principle of all is that regarding which it is impossible to be mistaken; for such a principle must be both the best known (for all men may be mistaken about things which they do not know), and non-hypothetical. For a principle which every one must have who understands anything that is, is not a hypothesis; and that which every one must know who knows anything, he must already have when he comes to a special study. Evidently then such a principle is the most certain of all; which principle this is, let us proceed to say. It is, that the same attribute cannot at the same time belong and not belong to the same subject and in the same respect; we must presuppose, [20] to guard against dialectical objections, any further qualifications which might be added. This, then, is the most certain of all principles, since it answers to the

definition given above. For it is impossible for any one to believe the same thing to be and not to be, as some think Heraclitus says. For what a man says, he does not necessarily believe; and if it is impossible that contrary attributes should belong at the same time to the same subject (the usual qualifications must be presupposed in this premiss too), and if an opinion which contradicts another is contrary to it, obviously it is impossible for the same man at the same time to believe the same thing to be and not to be; for if a man [30] were mistaken on this point he would have contrary opinions at the same time. It is for this reason that all who are carrying out a demonstration reduce it to this as an ultimate belief; for this is naturally the starting-point even for all the other axioms.[11]

4. There are some who, as we said,[12] both themselves assert that it is possible for the same thing to be and not to be, and say that people can judge this to be the case.[13] And among others [1006ᵃ] many writers about nature use this language. But we have now posited that it is impossible for anything at the same time to be and not to be, and by this means have shown that this is the most indisputable of all principles.—Some indeed demand that even this shall be demonstrated, but this they do through want of education, for not to know of what things one should demand demonstration, and of what one should not, argues want of education. For it is impossible that there should be demonstration of absolutely everything (there would be an infinite regress, so that there would still be no demonstration); but if there are things of which one should [10] not demand demonstration, these per-

----

9 With 1005ᵃ 19–ᵇ2 cf. xi. 4.

10 The reference may be to Antisthenes.

11 With ch. 3 cf. iii. 995ᵇ 6–10, 996ᵇ 26–997ᵃ 15. With 1005ᵇ 8–34 cf. xi. 1061ᵇ 34–1062ᵃ 2 (with 1005ᵇ 23–6 cf. 1062ᵃ 31–5).

12 Apparently a loose reference to 1005ᵇ 23–5.

13 The Megaric school may be referred to.

sons could not say what principle they maintain to be more self-evident than the present one.

We can, however, demonstrate negatively even that this view is impossible, if our opponent will only say something; and if he says nothing, it is absurd to seek to give an account of our views to one who cannot give an account of anything, in so far as he cannot do so. For such a man, as such, is from the start no better than a vegetable. Now negative demonstration I distinguish from demonstration proper, because in a demonstration one might be thought to be begging the question, but if another person is responsible for the assumption we shall have negative proof not demonstration.[14] The starting-point for all such arguments is not the demand that our opponent shall say that something either is or is not (for this one might per- [20] haps take to be a begging of the question), but that he shall say something which is *significant* both for himself and for another; for this is necessary, if he really is to say anything. For, if he means nothing, such a man will not be capable of reasoning, either with himself or with another. But if any one grants this, demonstration will be possible; for we shall already have something definite. The person responsible for the proof, however, is not he who demonstrates but he who listens; for while disowning reason he listens to reason. And again he who admits this has admitted that something is true apart from demonstration [so that not everything will be "so and not so"].

First then this at least is obviously true, that the word "be" or "not be" has a definite meaning, so that not every- [30] thing will be "so and not so."[15]—Again, if "man" has one meaning, let this be "two-footed animal"; by having one

meaning I understand this:—if "man" means "X," then if A is a man "X" will be what "being a man" means for him. (It makes no difference even if one were to say a word has several meanings, if only they are limited in number; [1006ᵇ] for to each definition there might be assigned a different word. For instance, we might say that "man" has not one meaning but several, one of which would have one definition, viz. "two-footed animal," while there might be also several other definitions if only they were limited in number; for a peculiar name might be assigned to each of the definitions. If, however, they were not limited but one were to say that the word has an infinite number of meanings, obviously reasoning would be impossible; for not to have one meaning is to have no meaning, and if words have no meaning our reasoning with one another, and indeed with ourselves, has been annihilated; for it is impossible to think of anything if we do not think [10] of one thing; but if this *is* possible, one name might be assigned to this thing.)

Let it be assumed then, as was said at the beginning,[16] that the name has a meaning and has one meaning; it is impossible, then, that "being a man" should mean precisely "not being a man," if "man" not only signifies something about one subject but also has one significance (for we do not identify "having one significance" with "signifying something about one subject," since on *that* assumption even "musical" and "white" and "man" would have had one significance, so that all things would have been one; for they would all have had the same significance).

And it will not be possible to be and not to be the same thing, except in virtue of an ambiguity, just as if one whom we call "man," others were to call "notman"; but the point in question is [20]

---

[14] With ll. 5–18 cf. xi. 1062ª 2–5.
[15] For "so and not so" cf. Pl. *Theaet.* 183 A.

[16] a 21, 31.

not this, whether the same thing can at the same time be and not be a man in name, but whether it can in fact.—Now if "man" and "not-man" mean nothing different, obviously "not being a man" will mean nothing different from "being a man"; so that "being a man" will be "not being a man"; for they will be one. For being one means this—being related as "raiment" and "dress" are, if their definition is one. And if "being a man" and "being a not-man" are to be one, they must mean one thing. But it was shown earlier[17] that they mean different things.—Therefore, if it is true to say of anything that it is a man, it must be a two-footed animal (for this was what "man" meant[18]); and if this is necessary, it is impossible that the same [30] thing should not at that time be a two-footed animal; for this is what "being necessary" means—that it is impossible for the thing not to be. It is, then, impossible that it should be at the same time true to say the same thing is a man and is not a man.

The same account holds good with regard to "not being a man," for "being a man" and "being a not-man" [1007ᵃ] mean different things, since even "being white" and "being a man" are different; for the former terms are much more opposed, so that they must *a fortiori* mean different things. And if any one says that "*white*" means one and the same thing as "man," again we shall say the same as what was said before,[19] that it would follow that *all* things are one, and not only opposites. But if this is impossible, then what we have maintained will follow, if our opponent will only answer our question.

And if, when one asks the question simply, he adds the contradictories, he is not answering the question. For [10] there is nothing to prevent the same

thing from being both a man and white and countless other things: but still, if one asks whether it is or is not true to say that this is a man, our opponent must give an answer which means one thing, and not add that "it is also white and large." For, besides other reasons, it is impossible to enumerate its accidental attributes, which are infinite in number; let him, then, enumerate either all or none. Similarly, therefore, even if the same thing is a thousand times a man and a not-man, he must not, in answering the question whether this is a man, add that it is also at the same time a not-man, unless he is bound to add also all the other accidents, all that the subject is or is not; and if he does this, he is not observing the rules of argument.[20]

And in general those who say this [20] do away with substance and essence. For they must say that all attributes are accidents, and that there is no such thing as "being essentially a man" or "an animal." For if there is to be any such thing as "being essentially a man" this will not be "being a not-man" or "not being a man" (yet these are negations of it[21]); for there was one thing which it meant, and this was the substance of something. And denoting the substance of a thing means that the essence of the thing is nothing else. But if its being essentially a man is to be the same as either being essentially a not-man or essentially not being a man, then its essence *will* be something else. Therefore our opponents must say that there cannot be such a definition of anything, but that all attributes are accidental; for this [30] is the distinction between substance and accident—"white" is accidental to man, because though he is white, whiteness is not his essence. But if *all* statements are accidental, there will be nothing primary

---

17 ll. 11-15.
18 In ᵃ 31 f.
19 1006ᵇ 17.

20 With 1006ᵃ 18–1007ᵃ cf. xi. 1062ᵃ 5–20 (with 1006ᵇ 28–34 cf. 1062ᵃ 20–3).
21 *Sc.* and hence (on the view attacked) should be compatible with it.

about which they are made, if the accidental always implies predication about a subject. The predication, then, [1007ᵇ] must go on *ad infinitum*. But this is impossible; for not even more than two terms can be combined in accidental predication. For (1) an accident is not an accident of an accident, unless it be because both are accidents of the same subject. I mean, for instance, that the white is musical and the latter is white, only because both are accidental to man. But (2) Socrates is musical, not in this sense, that both terms are accidental to something else. Since then some predicates are accidental in this and some in that sense, (*a*) those which are accidental in the latter sense, in which white is accidental to Socrates, cannot form an infinite series in the upward direction;[22] e.g. Socrates the white has not yet another accident; for no unity can be [10] got out of such a sum. Nor again (*b*) will "white" have another term accidental to it, e.g. "musical." For this is no more accidental to that than that is to this; and at the same time we have drawn the distinction, that while some predicates are accidental in this sense, others are so in the sense in which "musical" is accidental to Socrates; and the accident is an accident of an accident not in cases of the latter kind, but only in cases of the other kind, so that not *all* terms will be accidental.[23] There must, then, even so be something which denotes substance. And if this is so, it has been shown that contradictories cannot be predicated at the same time.

Again, if all contradictory statements are true of the same subject at the same time, evidently all things will be one. For the same thing will be a trireme, a wall, and a man, if of everything it is pos- [20]

sible either to affirm or to deny anything (and this premiss must be accepted by those who share the views of Protagoras). For if any one thinks that the man is not a trireme, evidently he is not a trireme; so that he also *is* a trireme, if, as they say, contradictory statements are both true. And we thus get the doctrine of Anaxagoras, that all things are mixed together; so that nothing really exists. They seem, then, to be speaking of the indeterminate, and, while fancying themselves to be speaking of being, they are speaking about non-being; for it is that which exists potentially and not in complete reality that is indeterminate. But they *must* predicate of every subject the affirmation or the negation of every attribute. For it is absurd if of each [30] subject its own negation is to be predicable, while the negation of something else which cannot be predicated of it is not to be predicable of it; for instance, if it is true to say of a man that he is not a man, evidently it is also true to say that he is either a trireme or not a trireme. If, then, the affirmative[24] can be predicated, the negative must be predicable too; and if the affirmative is not predicable, the negative, at least, will be more predicable than the nega- [1008ᵃ] tive of the subject itself. If, then, even the latter negative is predicable, the negative of "trireme" will be also predicable; and, if this is predicable, the affirmative will be so too.[25]

Those, then, who maintain this view are driven to this conclusion, and to the further conclusion that it is not necessary either to assert or to deny. For if it is true that a thing is a man and a not-man, evidently also it will be neither a man nor a not-man. For to the two assertions there answer two negations, and if the former[26] is treated as a single

---

[22] I.e. in the direction of predicates, which are naturally wider or higher than the subject.

[23] Sense (1) reduces to sense (2), and in this an infinite number of accidents combined together is impossible; there must be substance somewhere.

[24] *Sc.* "trireme."

[25] With 1007ᵇ 18–1008ᵃ 2 cf. xi. 1062ᵃ 23–30.

[26] *Sc.* that the thing is a man and a not-man.

proposition compounded out of two, the latter also is a single proposition opposite to the former.[27]

Again, either the theory is true in all cases, and a thing is both white and not-white, and existent and non-existent, and all other assertions and negations are similarly compatible, or the [10] theory is true of some statements and not of others. And if not of all, the exceptions will be contradictories of which admittedly only one is true; but if of all, again either the negation will be true whenever the assertion is, and the assertion true wherever the negation is, or the negation will be true where the assertion is, but the assertion not always true where the negation is. And (*a*) in the latter case there will be something which fixedly *is not,* and this will be an indisputable belief; and if non-being is something indisputable and knowable, the opposite assertion will be more knowable. But (*b*) if it is equally possible also to assert all that it is possible to deny, one must either be saying what is true when one separates the predicates (and says, for instance, that a thing is [20] white, and again that it is not-white), or not. And if (i) it is not true to apply the predicates separately, our opponent is not saying what he professes to say, and also nothing at all exists, but how could nonexistent things speak or walk, as he does? Also all things would on this view be one, as has been already said,[28] and man and God and trireme and their contradictories will be the same. For if contradictories can be predicated alike of each subject, one thing will in no wise differ from another; for if it differ, this difference will be something true and peculiar to it. And (ii) if one may with truth apply the predicates separately, the above-mentioned result follows none the less, and, further, it follows that all would then be right and all

would be in error, and our opponent himself confesses himself to be in [30] error.—And at the same time our discussion with him is evidently about nothing at all; for he says nothing. For he says neither "yes" nor "no," but "yes and no"; and again he denies both of these and says "neither yes nor no"; for otherwise there would already be something definite.

Again, if when the assertion is true, the negation is false, and when this is true, the affirmation is false, it will not be possible to assert and deny the same thing truly at the same time. But [1008ᵇ] perhaps they might say this was the very question at issue.

Again, is he in error who judges either that the thing is so or that it is not so, and is he right who judges both? If he is right, what can they mean by saying that the nature of existing things is of this kind? And if he is not right, but more right than he who judges in the other way, being will already be of a definite nature, and this will be true, and not at the same time also not true. But if all are alike both wrong and right, one who is in this condition will not be able either to speak or to say any- [10] thing intelligible; for he says at the same time both "yes" and "no." And if he makes no judgement but "thinks" and "does not think," indifferently, what difference will there be between him and a vegetable?—Thus, then, it is in the highest degree evident that neither any one of those who maintain this view nor any one else is really in this position. For why does a man walk to Megara and not stay at home, when he thinks he ought to be walking there? Why does he not walk early some morning into a well or over a precipice, if one happens to be in his way? Why do we observe him guarding against this, evidently because he does not think that falling in is alike good and not good? Evidently, then, he judges one thing to be better and another worse. And if this is so, he

---

27 With ll. 6–7 cf. **xi.** 1062ᵃ 36–ᵇ 7.

28 1006ᵇ 17, 1007ᵃ 6.

must also judge one thing to be a man and another to be not-a-man, one [20] thing to be sweet and another to be not-sweet. For he does not aim at and judge all things alike, when, thinking it desirable to drink water or to see a man, he proceeds to aim at these things; yet he *ought,* if the same thing were alike a man and not-a-man. But, as was said, there is no one who does not obviously avoid some things and not others. Therefore, as it seems, all men make unqualified judgement, if not about all things, still about what is better and worse.[29] And if this is not knowledge but opinion, they should be all the more anxious about the truth, as a sick man should be more anxious about his health than [30] one who is healthy; for he who has opinions is, in comparison with the man who knows, not in a healthy state as far as the truth is concerned.

Again, however much all things may be "so and not so," still there is a more and a less in the nature of things; for we should not say that two and three are equally even, nor is he is who thinks four things are five equally wrong with him who thinks they are a thousand. If then they are not equally wrong, obviously one is less wrong and therefore more right. If then that which has more of any quality is nearer the norm, there must be some truth to which the more true is nearer. And even if there [1009ᵃ] is not, still there is already something better founded and liker the truth, and we shall have got rid of the unqualified doctrine which would prevent us from determining anything in our thought.

5. From the same opinion proceeds the doctrine of Protagoras, and both doctrines must be alike true or alike untrue. For on the one hand, if all opinions and appearances are true, all statements must be at the same time true and false. For many men hold beliefs in which they conflict with one another, and think those mistaken who have [10] not the same opinions as themselves; so that the same thing must both be and not be. And on the other hand, if this is so, all opinions must be true; for those who are mistaken and those who are right are opposed to one another in their opinions; if, then, reality is such as the view in question supposes, all will be right in their beliefs.

Evidently, then, both doctrines proceed from the same way of thinking. But the same method of discussion must not be used with all opponents; for some need persuasion, and others compulsion. Those who have been driven to this position by difficulties in their thinking can easily be cured of their ignorance; for it is not their expressed [20] argument but their thought that one has to meet. But those who argue for the sake of argument can be cured only by refuting the argument as expressed in speech and in words.[30]

Those who really feel the difficulties have been led to this opinion by observation of the sensible world. (1) They think that contradictories or contraries are true at the same time, because they see contraries coming into existence out of the same thing. If, then, that which is not cannot come to be, the thing must have existed before as both contraries alike, as Anaxagoras says all is mixed in all, and Democritus too; for *he* says the void and the full exist alike in every [30] part, and yet one of these is being, and the other non-being.[31] To those, then, whose belief rests on these grounds, we shall say that in a sense they speak rightly and in a sense they err. For "that which is" has two meanings, so that in some sense a thing can come to be out of that which is not, while in some sense

---

[29] With ll. 12–27 cf. xi. 1063ᵃ 28–35.

[30] With ll. 16–22 cf. xi. 1063ᵇ 7–16.
[31] With ll. 6–16, 22–30 cf. xi .1062ᵇ 12–24.

it cannot, and the same thing can at the same time be in being and not in being —but not in the same respect. For the same thing can be potentially at the same time two contraries, but it cannot actually.[32] And again we shall ask them to believe that among existing things there is also another kind of substance to which neither movement nor destruction nor generation at all belongs.

And (2) similarly some have [1009ᵇ] inferred from observation of the sensible world the truth of appearances. For they think that the truth should not be determined by the large or small number of those who hold a belief, and that the same thing is thought sweet by some when they taste it, and bitter by others, so that if all were ill or all were mad, and only two or three were well or sane, these would be thought ill and mad, and not the others.

And again, they say that many of the other animals receive impressions contrary to ours; and that even to the senses of each individual, things do not always seem the same. Which, then, of these impressions are true and [10] which are false is not obvious; for the one set is no more true than the other, but both are alike. And this is why Democritus, at any rate, says that either there is no truth or to us at least it is not evident.

And in general it is because these thinkers suppose knowledge to be sensation, and this to be a physical alteration, that they say that what appears to our senses must be true; for it is for these reasons that both Empedocles and Democritus and, one may almost say, all the others have fallen victims to opinions of this sort. For Empedocles says that when men change their condition they change their knowledge;

For wisdom increases in men according to what is before them.

And elsewhere he says that

So far as their nature changed, so far to them always                              [20]
Came changed thoughts into mind.

And Parmenides also expresses himself in the same way:

For as at each time the much-bent limbs are composed,
So is the mind of men; for in each and all men
'Tis one thing thinks—the substance of their limbs:
For that of which there is more is thought.

A saying of Anaxagoras to some of his friends is also related—that things would be for them such as they supposed them to be. And they say that Homer also evidently had this opinion, because he made Hector, when he was unconscious from the blow, lie "thinking other thoughts"—which implies that even those who are bereft of [30] thought have thoughts, though not the same thoughts. Evidently, then, if both are forms of knowledge, the real things also are at the same time "both so and not so."[33] And it is in this direction that the consequences are most difficult. For if those who have seen most of such truth as is possible for us (and these are those who seek and love it most)—if these have such opinions and express these views about the truth, is it not natural that beginners in philosophy should lose heart? For to seek the truth would be to follow flying game.

But the reason why these thinkers held this opinion is that while [1010ᵃ] they were inquiring into the truth of that which is, they thought "that which is" was identical with the sensible world; in this, however, there is largely present the nature of the indeterminate —of that which exists in the peculiar sense which we have explained;[34] and

---

[32] With ll. 30–6 cf. xi. 1062ᵇ 24–33.

[33] With ᵃ 38–ᵇ 33 cf. xi. 1063ᵃ 35–ᵇ 7.
[34] Cf. 1009ᵃ 32.

therefore, while they speak plausibly, they do not say what is true (for it is fitting to put the matter so rather than as Epicharmus put it against Xenophanes[35]). And again, because they saw that all this world of nature is in movement, and that about that which changes no true statement can be made, they said that of course, regarding that which everywhere in every respect is changing, nothing could truly be affirmed. It was this belief that blossomed into the [10] most extreme of the views above mentioned, that of the professed Heracliteans, such as was held by Cratylus, who finally did not think it right to say anything but only moved his finger, and criticized Heraclitus for saying that it is impossible to step twice into the same river; for *he* thought one could not do it even once.

But we shall say in answer to this argument also, that while there is some justification for their thinking that the changing when it is changing, does not exist, yet it is after all disputable; for that which is losing a quality has something of that which is being lost, and of that which is coming to be, something must already be. And in general if a thing is perishing, there will be present something that exists; and if a [20] thing is coming to be, there must be something from which it comes to be and something by which it is generated, and this process cannot go on *ad infinitum*.—But, leaving these arguments, let us insist on this, that it is not the same thing to change in quantity and in quality. Grant that in quantity a thing is not constant; still it is in respect of its form that we know each thing.[36]— And again, it would be fair to criticize those who hold this view for asserting about the whole material universe what they saw only in a minority even of sensible things. For only that region of the sensible world which immediately [30] surrounds us is always in process of destruction and generation; but this is—so to speak—not even a fraction of the whole, so that it would have been juster to acquit this part of the world because of the other part, than to condemn the other because of this.[37]—And again, obviously we shall make to them also the same reply that we made long ago;[38] we must show them and persuade them that there is something whose nature is changeless. Indeed, those who say that things at the same time are and are not, should in consequence say that all things are at rest rather than that they are in movement; for there is nothing into which they can change, since all attributes belong already to all subjects.

Regarding the nature of truth, we must maintain that not every- [1010ᵇ] thing which appears is true; firstly, because even if sensation—at least of the object peculiar to the sense in question— is not false, still appearance is not the same as sensation.—Again, it is fair to express surprise at our opponents' raising the question whether magnitudes are as great, and colours are of such a nature, as they appear to people at a distance, or as they appear to those close at hand, and whether they are such as they appear to the healthy or to the sick, and whether those things are heavy which appear so to the weak or those which appear so to the strong, and those things true which appear to the sleeping or to the waking. For obviously they do not think these to be open questions; no one, at [10] least, if when he is in Libya he has fancied one night that he is in Athens, starts for the concert hall.—And again with regard to the future, as Plato says,[39] surely the opinion of the physician and that of the ignorant man are not equally

35 Epicharmus may have said that Xenophanes' views were "neither plausible nor true," or that they were "true but not plausible."
36 With ll. 22–5 cf. xi. 1063ᵃ 22–8.

37 With ll. 25–32 cf. xi. 1063ᵃ 10–17.
38 Cf. 1009ᵃ 36–8.
39 Cf. *Theaetetus* 178 B–179 A.

weighty, for instance, on the question whether a man will get well or not.— And again, among sensations themselves the sensation of a foreign object and that of the appropriate object, or that of a kindred object and that of the object of the sense in question,[40] are not equally authoritative, but in the case of colour sight, not taste, has the authority, and in the case of flavour taste, not sight; each of which senses never says at the same time of the same object that it simultaneously is "so and not so."— But not even at different times does one sense disagree about the quality, but [20] only about that to which the quality belongs. I mean, for instance, that the same wine might seem, if either it or one's body changed, at one time sweet and at another time not sweet; but at least the sweet, such as it is when it exists, has never yet changed, but one is always right about it, and that which is to be sweet is of necessity of such and such a nature.[41] Yet all these views destroy this necessity, leaving nothing to be of necessity, as they leave no essence of anything; for the necessary cannot be in this way and also in that, so that if anything is of necessity, it will not be "both so and not so."

And, in general, if only the sensible exists, there would be nothing if [30] animate things were not; for there would be no faculty of sense. Now the view that neither the sensible qualities nor the sensations would exist is doubtless true (for they are affections of the perceiver), but that the substrata which cause the sensation should not exist even apart from sensation is impossible. For sensation is surely not the sensation of itself, but there is something beyond the sensation, which must be prior to the sensation; for that which moves is prior in nature to that which is moved, and if

they are correlative terms, this is [1011ᵃ] no less the case.

6. There are, both among those who have these convictions and among those who merely profess these views, some who raise a difficulty by asking, who is to be the judge of the healthy man, and in general who is likely to judge rightly on each class of questions. But such inquiries are like puzzling over the question whether we are now asleep or awake. And all such questions have the same meaning. These people demand that a reason shall be given for everything;[42] for they seek a starting-point, and they seek to get this by demonstration, while it is obvious from their [10] actions that they have no conviction. But their mistake is what we have stated it to be; they seek a reason for things for which no reason can be given; for the starting-point of demonstration is not demonstration.

These, then, might be easily persuaded of this truth, for it is not difficult to grasp; but those who seek merely compulsion in argument seek what is impossible; for they demand to be allowed to contradict themselves—a claim which contradicts itself from the very first.[43] —But if not all things are relative, but some are self-existent, not everything that appears will be true; for that which appears is apparent to some one; so that he who says all things that appear are true, makes all things [20] relative. And, therefore, those who ask for an irresistible argument, and at the same time demand to be called to account for their views, must guard themselves by saying that the truth is not that what appears exists, but that what appears exists *for him to whom* it appears, and *when,* and *to the sense to which,* and *under the conditions under which* it appears. And if they give an

---

[40] E.g. the awareness which smell gives us of savour and of odour respectively.
[41] With ll. 1–26 cf. xi. 1062ᵇ 33–1063ᵃ 10.

[42] The reference may be to Antisthenes.
[43] With ll. 3–16 cf. xi. 1063ᵇ 7–16.

account of their view, but do not give it in this way, they will soon find themselves contradicting themselves. For it is possible that the same thing may appear to be honey to the sight, but not to the taste, and that, since we have two eyes, things may not appear the same to each, if their sight is unlike. For to those who for the reasons named some time [30] ago[44] say what appears is true, and therefore that all things are alike false and true, for things do not appear either the same to all men or always the same to the same man, but often have contrary appearances at the same time (for touch says there are two objects when we cross our fingers, while sight says there is one),[45]—to these we shall say "yes, but not to the same sense and in the same part of it and under the same conditions and at the same time," so that what appears will be with [1011$^b$] these qualifications true. But perhaps for this reason those who argue thus not because they feel a difficulty but for the sake of argument, should say that this is not true, but true for this man. And as has been said [46] before, they must make everything relative—relative to opinion and perception, so that nothing either has come to be or will be without some one's first thinking so. But if things *have* come to be or will be,[47] evidently not all things will be relative to opinion.— Again, if a thing is one, it is in relation to one thing or to a definite number of things; and if the same thing is both half and equal, it is not to the double that the equal is correlative.[48] If, then, in relation to that which thinks, man and that which is thought are the same, man [10] will not be that which thinks, but only

that which is thought. And if each thing is to be relative to that which thinks, that which thinks will be relative to an infinity of specifically different things.

Let this, then, suffice to show (1) that the most indisputable of all beliefs is that contradictory statements are not at the same time true, and (2) what consequences follow from the assertion that they are, and (3) why people do assert this. Now since it is impossible that contradictories should be at the same time true of the same thing, obviously contraries also cannot belong at the same time to the same thing. For of contraries, one is a privation no less than it is a contrary—and a privation of the essential nature; and privation is the denial of a predicate to a determinate genus. If, then, it is impossible to affirm [20] and deny truly at the same time, it is also impossible that contraries should belong to a subject at the same time, unless both belong to it in particular relations, or one in a particular relation and one without qualification.[49]

7. But on the other hand there cannot be an intermediate between contradictories, but of one subject we must either affirm or deny any one predicate. This is clear, in the first place, if we define what the true and the false are. To say of what is that it is not, or of what is not that it is, is false, while to say of what is that it is, and of what is not that it is not, is true; so that he who says of anything that it is, or that it is not, will say either what is true or what is false; but neither what is nor what is not is said to be or not to be.[50]—Again, the intermediate between the contradictories will be so either in the way [30]

<hr/>

44 Cf. 1009$^a$ 38–1010$^a$ 15.
45 With ll. 31–4 cf. xi. 1062$^b$ 33–1063$^a$ 10.
46 a 19 f.
47 *Sc.* without some one's first thinking so.
48 *Sc.* but the equal to the equal, the half to the double.

<hr/>

49 With ll. 17–22 cf. xi. 1063$^b$ 17–19.
50 *Sc.* by those who say there is an intermediate between contradictories. Hence such a statement is neither true nor false, which is absurd.

in which grey is between black and white,[51] or as that which is neither man nor horse is between man and horse. (*a*) If it were of the latter kind, it could not change into the extremes (for change is from not-good to good, or from good to not-good), but as a matter of fact when there is an intermediate it is always observed to change into the extremes. For there is no change except to opposites[52] and to their intermediates. (*b*) But if it is really intermediate,[53] in this way too there would have to be a change to white, which was not from not-white; but as it is, this is never seen.—Again, every object of understanding or [1012ᵃ] reason the understanding either affirms or denies—this is obvious from the definition—whenever it says what is true or false. When it connects in one way by assertion or negation, it says what is true, and when it does so in another way, what is false.—Again, there must be an intermediate between *all* contradictories, if one is not arguing merely for the sake of argument; so that it will be possible for a man to say what is neither true nor untrue, and there will be a middle between that which is and that which is not, so that there will also be a kind of change intermediate between generation and destruction.—Again, in all classes in which the negation of an attribute involves the assertion of its contrary, even in these there will be an intermediate; for instance, in the sphere of num- [10] bers there will be number which is neither odd nor not-odd. But this is impossible, as is obvious from the definition.—Again, the process will go on *ad infinitum*, and the number of realities will be not only half as great again, but even greater. For again it will be possible

to deny this intermediate with reference both to its assertion and to its negation,[54] and this new term will be some definite thing; for its essence is something different.—Again, when a man, on being asked whether a thing is white, says "no," he has denied nothing except that it is; and its not being is a negation.

Some people have acquired this opinions as other paradoxical opinions have been acquired; when men cannot refute eristical arguments, they give in to the argument and agree that the con- [20] clusion is true. This, then, is why some express this view; others do so because they demand a reason for everything.[55] And the starting-point in dealing with all such people is definition. Now the definition rests on the necessity of their meaning something; for the form of words of which the word is a sign will be its definition.[56]—While the doctrine of Heraclitus, that all things are and are not, seems to make everything true, that of Anaxagoras, that there is an intermediate between the terms of a contradiction, seems to make everything false; for when things are mixed, the mixture is neither good nor not-good, so that one cannot say anything that is true.

8. In view of these distinctions it is obvious that the one-sided theories which some people express about all things cannot be valid—on the one hand the [30] theory that nothing is true (for, say they, there is nothing to prevent every statement from being like the statement "the diagonal of a square is commensurate with the side"), on the other hand the theory that everything is true. These views are practically the same as that of

---

[51] Though of course it differs from this case in being between contradictories, not contraries.

[52] *Sc.* contrary, not contradictory opposites.

[53] *Sc.* as grey is between black and white.

[54] I.e. if there is a term *B* which is neither *A* nor not-*A*, there will be a new term *C* which is neither *B* nor not-*B*.

[55] The reference may be to Antisthenes.

[56] With 1011ᵇ 23–1012ᵃ 24 cf. xi. 1063ᵇ 19–24.

Heraclitus; for he who says that "all things are true and all are false" also makes each of these statements [1012ᵇ] separately, so that since they are impossible, the double statement must be impossible too.—Again, there are obviously contradictories which cannot be at the same time true—nor on the other hand can all statements be false; yet this would *seem* more possible in the light of what has been said.—But against all such views we must postulate, as we said above,[57] not that something is or is not, but that something has a meaning, so that we must argue from a definition, viz. by assuming what falsity or truth means. If that which it is true to affirm is nothing other than that which it is false to deny, it is impossible that all statements should be false; for one side of the contradiction must be true. [10] Again, if it is necessary with regard to everything either to assert or to deny it, it is impossible that both should be false; for it is *one* side of the contradiction that is false.—Therefore all such views are also exposed to the often expressed objection, that they destroy themselves. For he who says that everything is true makes even the statement contrary to his own true, and therefore his own not true (for the contrary statement denies that it is true), while he who says everything is false makes himself also false.[58]—And if the former person excepts the contrary statement, saying it alone is not true, while the latter excepts his own as being not false, none the less they are driven to postulate [20] the truth or falsity of an infinite number of statements; for that which says the true statement is true is true, and this process will go on to infinity.

Evidently, again, those who say all things are at rest are not right, nor are those who say all things are in move-

ment. For if all things are at rest, the same statements will always be true and the same always false—but this obviously changes; for he who makes a statement, himself at one time was not and again will not be. And if all things are in motion, nothing will be true; everything therefore will be false. But it has been shown that this is impossible. Again, it must be that which is that changes; for change is from something to something. But again it is not the case that all things are at rest or in motion *sometimes*, and nothing *for ever*; for there is some- [30] thing which always moves the things that are in motion, and the first mover is itself unmoved.

## Book Δ (V)

2. "Cause" means (1) that [1013ᵃ] from which, as immanent material, a thing comes into being, e.g. the bronze is the cause of the statue and the silver of the saucer, and so are the classes which include these. (2) The form or pattern, i.e. the definition of the essence, and the classes which include this (e.g. the ratio 2:1 and number in general are causes of the octave), and the parts included in the definition. (3) That from which the change or the resting from change first begins; e.g. the adviser is a cause of [30] the action, and the father a cause of the child, and in general the maker a cause of the thing made and the change-producing of the changing. (4) The end, i.e. that for the sake of which a thing is; e.g. health is the cause of walking. For "Why does one walk?" we say; "that one may be healthy"; and in speaking thus we think we have given the cause. The same is true of all the means that intervene before the end, when something else has put the process in motion, as e.g. thinning or purging or drugs or instruments intervene before health [1013ᵇ] is reached; for all these are for the sake of the end, though they differ from one

---

57 Cf. 1006ᵃ 18–22.

58 With ᵃ 24–ᵇ 18 cf. xi. 1063ᵇ 24–35 (with ᵇ 13–18 cf. 1062ᵇ 7–9).

another in that some are instruments and others are actions.

These, then, are practically all the senses in which causes are spoken of, and as they are spoken of in several senses it follows both that there are several causes of the same thing, and in no accidental sense (e.g. both the art of sculpture and the bronze are causes of the statue not in respect of anything else but *qua* statue; not, however, in the same way, but the one as matter and the other as source of the movement), and that things can be causes of one another (e.g. exercise of good condition, and the latter of exercise; not, however, in the same way, but the one as end and the [10] other as source of movement).—Again, the same thing is the cause of contraries; for that which when present causes a particular thing, we sometimes charge, when absent, with the contrary, e.g. we impute the shipwreck to the absence of the steersman, whose presence was the cause of safety; and both—the presence and the privation—are causes as sources of movement.

All the causes now mentioned fall under four senses which are the most obvious. For the letters are the cause of syllables, and the material is the cause of manufactured things, and fire and earth and all such things are the causes of bodies, and the parts are causes of the whole, and the hypotheses are [20] causes of the conclusion, in the sense that they are that out of which these respectively are made; but of these some are cause as the *substratum* (e.g. the parts), others as the *essence* (the whole, the synthesis, and the form). The semen, the physician, the adviser, and in general the agent, are all *sources of change* or of rest. The remainder are causes as the *end* and the good of the other things; for that for the sake of which other things are tends to be the best and the end of the other things; let us take it as making no difference whether we call it good or apparent good.

These, then, are the causes, and this is the number of their kinds, but the *varieties* of causes are many in number, though when summarized these also are comparatively few. Causes are [30] spoken of in many senses, and even of those which are of the same kind some are causes in a prior and others in a posterior sense, e.g. both "the physician" and "the professional man" are causes of health, and both "the ratio 2:1" and "number" are causes of the octave, and the classes that include any particular cause are always causes of the particular effect. Again, there are accidental causes and the classes which include these; e.g. while in one sense "the sculptor" causes the statue, in another sense "Polyclitus" causes it, because the sculptor happens to be Polyclitus; and the classes [1014ᵃ] that include the accidental cause are also causes, e.g. "man"—or in general "animal"—is the cause of the statue, because Polyclitus is a man, and man is an animal. Of accidental causes also some are more remote or nearer than others, as, for instance, if "the white" and musical" were called causes of the statue, and not only "Polyclitus" or "man." But besides all these varieties of causes, whether proper or accidental, some are called causes as being able to act, others as acting; e.g. the cause of the house's being built is a builder, or a builder who is building.—The same variety of language will be found with regard to [10] the effects of causes; e.g. a thing may be called the cause of this statue or of a statue or in general of an image, and of this bronze or of bronze or of matter in general; and similarly in the case of accidental effects. Again, both accidental and proper causes may be spoken of in combination; e.g. we may say not "Polyclitus" nor "the sculptor," but "Polyclitus the sculptor."

Yet all these are but six in number, while each is spoken of in two ways; for (A) they are causes either as the individual, or as the genus, or as the accidental, or as the genus that includes the accidental, and these either as combined, or as taken simply; and (B) all may be taken as acting or as having a capac- [20] ity. But they differ inasmuch as the acting causes, i.e. the individuals, exist, or do not exist, simultaneously with the things of which they are causes, e.g. this particular man who is healing, with this particular man who is recovering health, and this particular builder with this particular thing that is being built; but the potential causes are not always in this case; for the house does not perish at the same time as the builder.

.  .  .

4. "Nature" means (1) the [1014ᵇ] genesis of growing things—the meaning which would be suggested if one were to pronounce the *y* in *physis* long.¹ (2) That immanent part of a growing thing, from which its growth first proceeds. (3) The source from which the primary movement in each natural object is [20] present in it in virtue of its own essence. Those things are said to grow which derive increase from something else by contact and either by organic unity, or by organic adhesion as in the case of embryos. Organic unity differs from contact; for in the latter case there need not be anything besides the contact, but in organic unities there is something identical in both parts, which makes them grow together instead of merely touching, and be one in respect of continuity and quantity, though not of quality.—(4) "Nature" means the primary material of which any natural object consists or out of which it is made, which is relatively unshaped and cannot be changed from its own potency, as e.g. bronze is said to be the nature of a statue and of bronze utensils, and wood the nature of wooden things; and so in [30]

all other cases; for when a product is made out of these materials, the first matter is preserved throughout. For it is in this way that people call the elements of natural objects also their nature, some naming fire, others earth, others air, others water, others something else of the sort, and some naming more than one of these, and others all of them.—(5) "Nature" means the *essence* of natural objects as with those who say the nature is the primary mode of composition or as Empedocles says:—

Nothing that is has a nature,    [1015ª]
But only mixing and parting of the mixed,
And nature is but a name given them by men.

Hence as regards the things that are or come to be by nature, though that *from which* they naturally come to be or are is already present, we say they have not their nature yet, unless they have their form or shape. That which comprises both of these² exists *by* nature, e.g. the animals and their parts; and not only is the first matter nature (and this in two senses, either the first, counting from the thing, or the first in general; e.g. in the case of works in bronze, bronze is first with reference to them, but in general perhaps water is first, if all things that can be melted are water), but also the form or essence, which is the end of [10] the process of becoming.—(6) By an extension of meaning from this sense of "nature" every essence in general has come to be called a "nature," because the nature of a thing is one kind of essence.

From what has been said, then, it is plain that nature in the primary and strict sense is the essence of things which have in themselves, as such, a source of movement; for the matter is called the nature because it is qualified to receive this, and processes of becoming and growing are called nature because they

---

¹ This (i.e. "growth") is the etymological sense of *physis*. *Phuesthai*, "to grow," has *u* long in most of its forms.

² Matter and form.

are movements proceeding from this. And nature in this sense is the source of the movement of natural objects, being present in them somehow, either potentially or in complete reality.

5. We call "necessary" (1) (*a*) [20] that without which, as a condition, a thing cannot live; e.g. breathing and food are necessary for an animal; for it is incapable of existing without these (*b*) the conditions without which good cannot be or come to be, or without which we cannot get rid or be freed of evil; e.g. drinking the medicine is necessary in order that we may be cured of disease, and a man's sailing to Aegina is necessary in order that he may get his money. —(2) The compulsory and compulsion, i.e. that which impedes and tends to hinder, contrary to impulse and purpose. For the compulsory is called necessary (whence the necessary is painful, as Evenus says: "For every necessary thing is ever irksome"), and compulsion is a form of necessity, as Sophocles says: [30] "'But force necessitates me to this act." And necessity is held to be something that cannot be persuaded—and rightly, for it is contrary to the movement which accords with purpose and with reasoning.—(3) We say that that which cannot be otherwise is necessarily as it is. And from this sense of "necessary" all the others are somehow derived; for a thing is said to do or suffer what is necessary in the sense of compulsory, only when it cannot act according to its im- [1015b] pulse because of the compelling force— which implies that necessity is that because of which a thing cannot be otherwise; and similarly as regards the conditions of life and of good; for when in the one case good, in the other life and being, are not possible without certain conditions, these are necessary, and this kind of cause is a sort of necessity. Again, demonstration is a necessary thing because the conclusion cannot be otherwise, if there has been demonstration in

the unqualified sense; and the causes of this necessity are the first premisses, i.e. the fact that the propositions from which the syllogism proceeds cannot be otherwise.

Now some things owe their necessity to something other than themselves; others do not, but are themselves [10] the source of necessity in other things. Therefore the necessary in the primary and strict sense is the simple; for this does not admit of more states than one, so that it cannot even be in one state and also in another; for if it did it would already be in more than one. If, then, there are any things that are eternal and unmovable, nothing compulsory or against their nature attaches to them.

. . .

7. Things are said to "be" (1) [1017a] in an accidental sense, (2) by their own nature.

(1) In an accidental sense, e.g., we say "the righteous doer is musical," and "the man is musical," and "the musician is a man," just as we say "the musician builds," because the builder happens [10] to be musical or the musician to be a builder; for here "one thing is another" means "one is an accident of another." So in the cases we have mentioned; for when we say "the man is musical" and "the musician is a man," or "he who is pale is musical" or "the musician is pale," the last two mean that both attributes are accidents of the same thing; the first that the attribute is an accident of that which *is*; while "the musical is a man" means that "musical" is an accident of a man. (In this sense, too, the not-pale is said to *be*, because that of which it is an accident *is*.) Thus when one thing is said in an accidental sense to be another, this is either because both belong to the same thing, and this [20] *is*, or because that to which the attribute belongs *is*, or because the subject which has an attribute that of which it is itself predicated, itself *is*.

(2) The kinds of essential being are precisely those that are indicated by the figures of predication;[3] for the senses of "being" are just as many as these figures. Since, then, some predicates indicate what the subject is, others its quality, others quantity, others relation, others activity or passivity, others its "where," others its "when," "being" has a meaning answering to each of these. For there is no difference between "the man is recovering" and "the man recovers," nor between "the man is walking" or [30] "cutting" and "the man walks" or "cuts"; and similarly in all other cases.

(3) Again, "being" and "is" mean that a statement is true, "not being" that it is not true but false—and this alike in the case of affirmation and of negation; e.g. "Socrates *is* "musical" means that this is true, or "Socrates *is* not-pale" means that this is true; but "the diagonal of the square *is not* commensurate with the side" means that it is false to say it is.

(4) Again, "being" and "that which is" mean that some of the things we have mentioned "are" potential- [1017ᵇ] ly, others in complete reality. For we say both of that which sees potentially and of that which sees actually, that it is "seeing," and both of that which can actualize its knowledge and of that which is actualizing it, that it knows, and both of that to which rest is already present and of that which can rest, that it rests. And similarly in the case of substances; we say the Hermes is in the stone, and the half of the line is in the line, and we say of that which is not yet ripe that it is corn. *When* a thing is potential and when it is not yet potential must be explained elsewhere.[4]

8. We call "substance" (1) the [10] simple bodies, i.e. earth and fire and water and everything of the sort, and in general bodies and the things composed of them, both animals and divine beings, and the parts of these. All these are called substance because they are not predicated of a subject but everything else is predicated of them.—(2) That which, being present in such things as are not predicated of a subject, is the cause of their being, as the soul is of the being of an animal.—(3) The parts which are present in such things, limiting them and marking them as individuals, and by whose destruction the whole is destroyed, as the body is by the destruction of the plane, as some[5] say, and the plane by the destruction of [20] the line; and in general number is thought by some[6] to be of this nature; for if it is destroyed, they say, nothing exists, and it limits all things.—(4) The essence, the formula of which is a definition, is also called the substance of each thing.

It follows, then, that "substance" has two senses, (*A*) the ultimate substratum, which is no longer predicated of anything else, and (*B*) that which, being a "this," is also separable[7]—and of this nature is the shape or form of each thing.

9. "The same" means (1) that which is the same in an accidental sense, e.g. "the pale" and "the musical" are the same because they are accidents of the same thing, and "a man" and "musical" because the one is an accident of the other; and "the musical" is "a man" because it is an accident of the man. (The complex entity is the same as either [30] of the simple ones and each of these is the same as it; for both "the man" and "the musical" are said to be the same as "the musical man," and this the same

---

3 I.e. the categories.
4 ix. 7.

5 The Pythagoreans and Plato.
6 The Pythagoreans and Plato.
7 Cf. viii. 1042ᵃ 29.

as they.) This is why all of these statements are made not universally; for it is
not true to say that *every* man is the
same as "the musical" (for universal
attributes belong to things in virtue of
their own nature, but accidents do not
belong to them in virtue of their own
nature); but of the individuals [1018a]
the statements are made without qualification. For "Socrates" and "musical
Socrates" are thought to be the same;
but "Socrates" is not predicable of more
than one subject, and therefore we do
not say "every Socrates" as we say "every
man."

Some things are said to be the same
in this sense, others (2) are the same by
their own nature, in as many senses as
that which is one by its own nature is
so; for both the things whose matter is
one either in kind or in number, and
those whose essence is one, are said to
be the same. Clearly, therefore, sameness
is a unity of the being either of more
than one thing or of one thing when it
is treated as more than one, i.e. when we
say a thing is the same as itself; for we
treat it as two.

Things are called "other" if either [10]
their kinds or their matters or the definitions of their essence are more than
one; and in general "other" has meanings opposite to those of "the same."

"Different" is applied (1) to those
things which though other are the same
in some respect, only not in number but
either in species or in genus or by analogy; (2) to those whose genus is other,
and to contraries, and to all things that
have their otherness in their essence.

Those things are called "like" which
have the same attributes in every respect, and those which have more attributes the same than different, and those
whose quality is one; and that which
shares with another thing the greater
number or the more important of the
attributes (each of them one of two contraries) in respect of which things are

capable of altering, is like that other
thing.[8] The senses of "unlike" are opposite to those of "like."

10. The term "opposite" is ap- [20]
plied to contradictories, and to contraries, and to relative terms, and to
privation and possession, and to the extremes from which and into which
generation and dissolution take place;
and the attributes that cannot be present
at the same time in that which is receptive of both, are said to be opposed—
either themselves or their constituents.
Grey and white colour do not belong at
the same time to the same thing; hence
their constituents are opposed.[9]

The term "contrary" is applied (1) to
those attributes differing in genus which
cannot belong at the same time to the
same subject, (2) to the most different
of the things in the same genus, (3) to
the most different of the attributes in
the same recipient subject, (4) to the
most different of the things that fall [30]
under the same faculty, (5) to the
things whose difference is greatest either
absolutely or in genus or in species. The
other things that are called contrary are
so called, some because they possess contraries of the above kind, some because
they are receptive of such, some because
they are productive of or susceptible to
such, or are producing or suffering
them, or are losses or acquisitions, or
possessions or privations, of such. Since
"one" and "being" have many senses,
the other terms which are derived from
these, and therefore "same," "other,"
and "contrary," must correspond, so that
they must be different for each category.

---

8 Such attributes are hot and cold, wet and
dry, rough and smooth, hard and soft, white
and black, sweet and bitter. The more important pairs of contraries, in Aristotle's view,
are the first two.

9 We cannot say grey and white are opposites, but we say the constituents of grey
(black and white) are opposites.

The term "other in species" is applied to things which being of the same genus are not subordinate the one to the other, or which being in the same genus have a difference,[10] or which have a [1018ᵇ] contrariety in their substance; and contraries are other than one another in species (either all contraries or those which are so called in the primary sense[11]), and so are those things whose definitions differ in the *infima species* of the genus (e.g. man and horse are indivisible in genus but their definitions are different), and those which being in the same substance have a difference. "The same in species" has the various meanings opposite to these.

11. The words "prior" and "posterior" are applied (1) to some things (on the assumption that there is a first, i.e. a beginning, in each class) because they are nearer some beginning deter- [10] mined either absolutely and by nature, or by reference to something or in some place or by certain people; e.g. things are prior in place because they are nearer either to some place determined by nature (e.g. the middle or the last place), or to some chance object; and that which is farther is posterior.—Other things are prior in time; some by being farther from the present, i.e. in the case of past events (for the Trojan war is prior to the Persian, because it is farther from the present), others by being nearer the present, i.e. in the case of future events (for the Nemean games are prior to the Pythian, if we treat the present as beginning and first point, because they are nearer the present).—Other things are prior in movement; for that which is nearer the first mover is prior (e.g. [20] the boy is prior to the man); and the prime mover also is a beginning absolutely.—Others are prior in power; for that which exceeds in power, i.e. the more powerful, is prior; and such is that according to whose will the other—i.e. the posterior—must follow, so that if the prior does not set it in motion the other does not move, and if it sets it in motion it does move; and here will is a beginning.—Others are prior in arrangement; these are the things that are placed at intervals in reference to some one definite thing according to some rule, e.g. in the chorus the second man is prior to the third, and in the lyre the second lowest string is prior to the lowest; for in the one case the leader and in the other the middle string is the beginning.

These, then, are called prior in [30] this sense, but (2) in another sense that which is prior for knowledge is treated as also absolutely prior; of these, the things that are prior in definition do not coincide with those that are prior in relation to perception. For in definition universals are prior, in relation to perception individuals. And in definition also the accident is prior to the whole, e.g. "musical" to "musical man," for the definition cannot exist as a whole without the part; yet musicalness cannot exist unless there is some one who is musical.

(3) The attributes of prior things are called prior, e.g. straightness is prior to smoothness; for one is an attribute of a line as such, and the other of a surface.

Some things then are called [1019ᵃ] prior and posterior in this sense, others (4) in respect of nature and substance, i.e. those which can be without other things, while the others cannot be without *them*—a distinction which Plato used. (If we consider the various senses of "being," firstly the subject is prior, so that substance is prior; secondly, according as potency or complete reality is taken into account, different things are prior, for some things are prior in respect of potency, others in respect of complete reality, e.g. in potency the half line is prior to the whole line, and the part to

---

10 This definition is wider than the previous one, since it includes species subordinate one to the other.

11 Cf. ᵃ 25–31 in distinction from 31–35.

the whole, and the matter to the concrete substance, but in complete reality these are posterior; for it is only when the whole has been dissolved that [10] they will exist in complete reality.) In a sense, therefore, all things that are called prior and posterior are so called with reference to this fourth sense; for some things can exist without others in respect of generation, e.g. the whole without the parts, and others in respect of dissolution, e.g. the part without the whole. And the same is true in all other cases.

12. "Potency" means (1) a source of movement or change, which is in another thing than the thing moved or in the same thing *qua* other; e.g. the art of building is a potency which is not in the thing built, while the art of healing, which is a potency, may be in the man healed, but not in him *qua* healed. "Potency" then means the source, in general, of change or movement in another thing or in the same thing *qua* other, and also (2) the source of a [20] thing's being moved by another thing or by itself *qua* other. For in virtue of that principle, in virtue of which a patient suffers anything, we call it "capable" of suffering; and this we do sometimes if it suffers anything at all, sometimes not in respect of everything it suffers, but only if it suffers a change for the better.— (3) The capacity of performing this well or according to intention; for sometimes we say of those who merely can walk or speak but not well or not as they intend, that they cannot speak or walk. So too (4) in the case of passivity.—(5) The states in virtue of which things are absolutely impassive or unchangeable, or not easily changed for the worse, are called potencies; for things are broken and crushed and bent and in general destroyed not by having a potency [30] but by not having one and by lacking something, and things are impassive with respect to such processes if they are scarcely and slightly affected by them, because of a "potency" and because they "can" do something and are in some positive state.

"Potency" having this variety of meanings, so too the "potent" or "capable" in one sense will mean that which can begin a movement (or a change in general, for even that which can bring things to rest is a "potent" thing) in another thing or in itself *qua* other; and in one sense that over which something else has such a potency; and in [1019ᵇ] one sense that which has a potency of changing into something, whether for the worse or for the better (for even that which perishes is thought to be "capable" of perishing, for it would not have perished if it had not been capable of it; but, as a matter of fact, it has a certain disposition and cause and principle which fits it to suffer this; sometimes it is thought to be of this sort because it has something, sometimes because it is deprived of something; but if privation is in a sense "having" or "habit," everything will be capable by having something, so that things are capable both by having a positive habit and principle, and by having the privation of this, if it is possible to *have* a privation; and if privation is *not* in a sense "habit," [10] "capable" is used in two distinct senses) ; and a thing is capable in another sense because neither any other thing, nor itself *qua* other, has a potency or principle which can destroy it. Again, all of these are capable either merely because the thing might chance to happen or not to happen, or because it might do so *well*. This sort of potency is found even in lifeless things, e.g. in instruments; for we say one lyre can speak, and another cannot speak at all, if it has not a good tone.

Incapacity is privation of capacity—i.e. of such a principle as has been described—either in general or in the case of something that would naturally have the capacity, or even at the time when it would naturally already have it; for the senses in which we should call a boy and a man and a eunuch "incapable of begetting" are distinct.—Again, to either kind of capacity there is an opposite incapacity—both to that which only *can* produce movement and to that [20] which can produce it well.

Some things, then, are called *adunata* in virtue of this kind of incapacity, while others are so in another sense; i.e. both *dunaton* and *adunaton* are used as follows. The impossible is that of which the contrary is of necessity true, e.g. that the diagonal of a square is commensurate with the side is impossible, because such a statement is a falsity of which the contrary is not only true but also necessary; that it is commensurate, then, is not only false but also of necessity false. The contrary of this, the possible, is found when it is not necessary that the contrary is false, e.g. that a man should be seated is possible; for that he is not seated is not of necessity false. The [30] possible, then, in one sense, as has been said, means that which is not of necessity false; in one, that which is true; in one, that which may be true.—A "potency" or "power"[12] in geometry is so called by a change of meaning.—These senses of "capable" or "possible" involve no reference to potency. But the senses which involve a reference to potency all refer to the primary kind of potency; [1020ᵃ] and this is a source of change in another thing or in the same thing *qua* other. For other things are called "capable," some because something else has such a potency over them, some because it has not, some because it has it in a particular way. The same is true of the things that are incapable. Therefore the proper definition of the primary kind of potency will be "a source of change in another thing or in the same thing *qua* other."

13. "Quantum" means that which is divisible into two or more constituent

parts of which each is by nature a "one" and a "this." A quantum is a plurality if it is numerable, a magnitude if it [10] is measurable. "Plurality" means that which is divisible potentially into non-continuous parts, "magnitude" that which is divisible into continuous parts; of magnitude, that which is continuous in one dimension is length, in two breadth, in three depth. Of these, limited plurality is number, limited length is a line, breadth a surface, depth a solid.

Again, some things are called quanta in virtue of their own nature, others incidentally; e.g. the line is a quantum by its own nature, the musical is one incidentally. Of the things that are quanta by their own nature some are so as substances, e.g. the line is a quantum (for "a certain kind of quantum" is present in the definition which states what it is), and others are modifications and states of this kind of substance, e.g. much and little, long and short, broad and narrow, deep and shallow, heavy [20] and light, and all other such attributes. And also great and small, and greater and smaller, both in themselves and when taken relatively to each other, are by their own nature attributes of what is quantitative; but these names are transferred to other things also. Of things that are quanta incidentally, some are so called in the sense in which it was said that the musical and the white were quanta, viz. because that to which musicalness and whiteness belong is a quantum, and some are quanta in the way in which movement and time are so; for these also are called quanta [30] of a sort and continuous because the things of which these are attributes are divisible. I mean not that which is moved, but the space through which it is moved; for because that is a quantum movement also is a quantum, and because this is a quantum time is one.

14. "Quality" means (1) the differentia of the essence, e.g. man is an animal of a certain quality because he is

---

12 The reference is to squares and cubes.

two-footed, and the horse is so because it is four-footed; and a circle is a figure of particular quality because it is without angles—which shows that the [1020ᵇ] essential differentia is a quality.—This, then, is one meaning of quality—the differentia or the essence, but (2) there is another sense in which it applies to the unmovable objects of mathematics, the sense in which the numbers have a certain quality, e.g. the composite numbers which are not in one dimension only, but of which the plane and the solid are copies (these are those which have two or three factors); and in general that which exists in the essence of numbers besides quantity is quality; for the essence of each is what it is once, e.g. that of 6 is not what it is twice or thrice, but what it is once; for 6 is once 6.

(3) All the modifications of substances that move (e.g. heat and cold, whiteness and blackness, heaviness and lightness, and the others of the sort) [10] in virtue of which, when they change, bodies are said to alter. (4) Quality in respect of virtue and vice and, in general, of evil and good.

Quality, then, seems to have practically two meanings, and one of these is the more proper. The primary quality is the differentia of the essence, and of this the quality in numbers is a part; for it is a differentia of essences, but either not of things that move or not of them *qua* moving. Secondly, there are the modifications of things that move, *qua* moving, and the differentiae of movements. Virtue and vice fall among these modifications; for they indicate differentiae of the movement or activity, according to which the things in motion act or [20] are acted on well or badly; for that which can be moved or act in one way is good, and that which can do so in another—the contrary—way is vicious. Good and evil indicate quality especially in living things, and among these especially in those which have purpose.

•  •  •

17. "Limit" means (1) the last [1022ᵃ] point of each thing, i.e. the first point beyond which it is not possible to find any part, and the first point within which every part is; (2) the form, whatever it may be, of a spatial magnitude or of a thing that has magnitude; (3) the end of each thing (and of this nature is that towards which the movement and the action are, not that from which they are—though sometimes it is both, that from which and that to which the movement is, i.e. the final cause); (4) the substance of each thing, and the essence of each; for this is the limit of knowledge; and if of knowledge, of the [10] object also. Evidently, therefore, "limit" has as many senses as "beginning," and yet more; for the beginning is a limit, but not every limit is a beginning.

•  •  •

21. "Affection" means (1) a [1022ᵇ] quality in respect of which a thing can be altered, e.g. white and black, sweet and bitter, heaviness and lightness, and all others of the kind.—(2) The actualization of these—the already accomplished alterations.—(3) Especially, injurious alteration and move- [20] ments, and, above all, painful injuries.—(4) Misfortunes and painful experiences when on a large scale are called affections.

22. We speak of "privation" (1) if something has not one of the attributes which a thing might naturally have, even if this thing itself would not naturally have it; e.g. a plant is said to be "deprived" of eyes.—(2) If, though either the thing itself or its genus would naturally have an attribute, it has it not; e.g. a blind man and a mole are in different senses "deprived" of sight; the latter in contrast with its genus,[13] the former in contrast with his own normal nature.—(3) If, though it would nat-

•  •  •

---

13 I.e. "animal."

urally have the attribute, and when it would naturally have it, it has it not; for blindness is a privation, but one is not "blind" at any and every age, but only if one has not sight at the age at which one would naturally have it. [30] Similarly a thing is called blind if it has not sight in the medium in which, and in respect of the organ in respect of which, and with reference to the object with reference to which, and in the circumstances in which, it would naturally have it.—(4) The violent taking away of anything is called privation.

Indeed there are just as many kinds of privations as there are of words with negative prefixes; for a thing is called unequal because it has not equality though it would naturally have it, and invisible either because it has no colour at all or because it has a poor colour, and apodous either because it has no feet at all or because it has imperfect feet. Again, a privative term may be used because the thing has little of the attribute (and this means having [1023ᵃ] it in a sense imperfectly), e.g. "kernelless"; or because it has it not easily or not well (e.g. we call a thing uncuttable not only if it cannot be cut but also if it cannot be cut easily or well); or because it has not the attribute at all; for it is not the one-eyed man but he who is sightless in both eyes that is called blind. This is why not every man is "good" or "bad," "just" or "unjust," but there is also an intermediate state.

## Book Z (VII)

1. There are several senses in [1028ᵃ] which a thing may be said to "be," [10] as we pointed out previously in our book on the various senses of words;[1] for in one sense the "being" meant is "what a thing is" or a "this," and in another sense it means a quality or quantity or one of the other things that are pred-

icated as these are. While "being" has all these senses, obviously that which "is" primarily is the "what," which indicates the substance of the thing. For when we say of what quality a thing is, we say that it is good or bad, not that it is three cubits long or that it is a man; but when we say *what* it is, we do not say "white" or "hot" or "three cubits long," but "a man" or "a god." And all other things are said to be because they are, some of them, quantities of that which *is* in this primary sense, others qualities of it, others affections of it, and others some other determination of it. And so one might even raise the question [20] whether the words "to walk," "to be healthy," "to sit" imply that each of these things is existent, and similarly in any other case of this sort; for none of them is either self-subsistent or capable of being separated from substance, but rather, if anything, it is that which walks or sits or is healthy that is an existent thing. Now these are seen to be more real because there is something definite which underlies them (i.e. the substance or individual), which is implied in such a predicate; for we never use the word "good" or "sitting" without implying this. Clearly then it is in virtue of this category that each of the others also *is*. Therefore that which is primarily, i.e. not in a qualified sense but without qualification, must be substance.      [30]

Now there are several senses in which a thing is said to be first; yet substance is first in every sense—(1) in definition, (2) in order of knowledge, (3) in time. For (3) of the other categories none can exist independently, but only substance. And (1) in definition also this is first; for in the definition of each term the definition of its substance must be present. And (2) we think we know each thing most fully, when we know what it is, e.g. what man is or what fire is, rather than when we know its quality, its quantity, or its place; since we know each of these predicates also, [1028ᵇ]

---

1 Cf. v. 7.

only when we know *what* the quantity or the quality *is*.

And indeed the question which was raised of old and is raised now and always, and is always the subject of doubt, viz. what being is, is just the question, what is substance? For it is this that some[2] assert to be one, others more than one, and that some[3] assert to be limited in number, others[4] unlimited. And so we also must consider chiefly and primarily and almost exclusively what that is which *is* in *this* sense.

2. Substance is thought to belong most obviously to bodies; and so we say that not only animals and plants and their parts are substances, but also natural bodies such as fire and water and [10] earth and everything of the sort, and all things that are either parts of these or composed of these (either of parts or of the whole bodies), e.g. the physical universe and its parts, stars and moon and sun. But whether these alone are substances, or there are also others, or only some of these, or others as well, or none of these but only some other things, are substances, must be considered. Some[5] think the limits of body, i.e. surface, line, point, and unit, are substances, and more so than body or the solid.

Further, some do not think there is anything substantial besides sensible things, but others think there are eternal substances which are more in number and more real; e.g. Plato posited two kinds of substance—the Forms and the objects of mathematics—as well as a [20] third kind, viz. the substance of sensible bodies. And Speusippus made still more kinds of substance, beginning with the One, and assuming principles for each kind of substance, one for numbers, another for spatial magnitudes, and then

another for the soul; and by going on in this way he multiplies the kinds of substance. And some[6] say Forms and numbers have the same nature, and the other things come after them—lines and planes—until we come to the substance of the material universe and to sensible bodies.

Regarding these matters, then, we must inquire which of the common statements are right and which are not right, and what substances there are, and whether there are or are not any besides sensible substances, and how sensible [30] substances exist, and whether there is a substance capable of separate existence (and if so why and how) or no such substance, apart from sensible substances; and we must first sketch the nature of substance.

3. The word "substance" is applied, if not in more senses, still at least to four main objects; for both the essence and the universal and the genus are thought to be the substance of each thing, and fourthly the substratum. Now the substratum is that of which everything else is predicated, while it is itself not predicated of anything else. And so we must first determine the nature of this; [1029ᵃ] for that which underlies a thing primarily is thought to be in the truest sense its substance. And in one sense matter is said to be of the nature of substratum, in another, shape, and in a third, the compound of these. (By the matter I mean, for instance, the bronze, by the shape the pattern of its form, and by the compound of these the statue, the concrete whole.) Therefore if the form is prior to the matter and more real, it will be prior also to the compound of both, for the same reason.

We have now outlined the nature of substance, showing that it is that which is not predicated of a stratum, but of which all else is predicated. But we must

---

2 The schools of Miletus and Elea.
3 The Pythagoreans and Empedocles.
4 Anaxagoras and the Atomists.
5 The Pythagoreans.

6 The school of Xenocrates.

not merely state the matter thus; for this is not enough. The statement itself is obscure, and further, on this view, *matter* becomes substance. For if [10] this is not substance, it baffles us to say what else is. When all else is stripped off evidently nothing but matter remains. For while the rest are affections, products, and potencies of bodies, length, breadth, and depth are quantities and not substances (for a quantity is not a substance), but the substance is rather that to which these belong primarily. But when length and breadth and depth are taken away we see nothing left unless there is something that is bounded by these; so that to those who consider the question thus matter alone must seem to be substance. By matter I mean that which in itself is neither a particular [20] thing nor of a certain quantity nor assigned to any other of the categories by which being is determined. For there is something of which each of these is predicated, whose being is different from that of each of the predicates (for the predicates other than substance are predicated of substance, while substance is predicated of matter). Therefore the ultimate substratum is of itself neither a particular thing nor of a particular quantity nor otherwise positively characterized; nor yet is it the negations of these, for negations also will belong to it only by accident.

If we adopt this point of view, then, it follows that matter is substance. But this is impossible; for both separability and "thisness" are thought to belong chiefly to substance. And so form and the compound of form and matter would be thought to be substance, rather [30] than matter. The substance compounded of both, i.e. of matter and shape, may be dismissed; for it is posterior and its nature is obvious. And matter also is in a sense manifest. But we must inquire into the third kind of substance; for this is the most perplexing.

Some of the sensible substances are generally admitted to be substances, so that we must look first among these. For it is an advantage to advance to that which is more knowable. For [1029ᵇ] learning proceeds for all in this way— through that which is less knowable by nature to that which is more knowable; and just as in conduct our task is to start from what is good for each and make what is without qualification good good for each, so it is our task to start from what is more knowable to oneself and make what is knowable by nature knowable to oneself. Now what is knowable and primary for particular sets of people is often knowable to a very small extent, and has little or nothing of reality. But yet one must start from that which [10] is barely knowable but knowable to oneself, and try to know what is knowable without qualification, passing, as has been said, by way of those very things which one does know.

4. Since at the start[7] we distinguished the various marks by which we determine substance, and one of these was thought to be the essence, we must investigate this. And first let us make some linguistic remarks about it. The essence of each thing is what it is said to be *propter se*.[8] For being you is not being musical, since you are not by your very nature musical. What, then, you are by your very nature is your essence.

Nor yet is the whole of this the essence of a thing; not that which is *propter se* as white is to a surface, because being a surface is not *identical* with being white. But again the combination of both— "being a white surface"—is not the essence of surface, because "surface" itself is added. The formula, therefore, in which the term itself is not present but its meaning is expressed, this is the [20]

---

7 1028ᵇ 33–6.

8 It seems convenient here to translate thus the phrase translated in v. 18 as "in virtue of itself."

formula of the essence of each thing. Therefore if to be a white surface is to be a smooth surface,[9] to be white and to be smooth are one and the same.[10]

But since there are also compounds answering to the other categories (for there is a substratum for each category, e.g. for quality, quantity, time, place, and motion), we must inquire whether there is a formula of the essence of each of them, i.e. whether to these compounds also there belongs an essence, e.g. to "white man." Let the compound be denoted by "cloak." What is the essence of cloak? But, it may be said, this also is not a *propter se* expression. We reply that there are just two ways in which a predicate may fail to be true of a [30] subject *propter se*, and one of these results from the addition, and the other from the omission, of a determinant. *One* kind of predicate is not *propter se* because the term that is being defined is combined with another determinant, e.g. if in defining the essence of white one were to state the formula of white *man*; the *other* because in the subject another determinant is combined with that which is expressed in the formula, e.g. if "cloak" meant "white man," and one were to define cloak as white; white man is white indeed, but its essence is not to be white.                    [1030ᵃ]

But is being-a-cloak an essence at all? Probably not. For the essence is precisely what something *is*; but when an attribute is asserted of a subject other than itself, the complex is not precisely what some "this" *is*, e.g. white man is not precisely what some "this" *is*, since this-ness belongs only to substances. Therefore there is an essence only of those things whose formula is a definition. But

we have a definition not where we have a word and a formula identical in meaning (for in that case all formulae or sets of words would be definitions; for there will be some name for any set of words whatever, so that even the *Iliad* will be a definition[11]), but where there is a formula of something primary; and primary things are those which do [10] not imply the predication of one element in them of another element. Nothing, then, which is not a species of a genus will have an *essence*—only species will have it, for these are thought to imply not merely that the subject participates in the attribute and has it as an affection, or has it by accident; but for everything else as well, if it has a name, there will be *formula of its meaning*—viz. that this attribute belongs to this subject; or instead of a simple formula we shall be able to give a more accurate one; but there will be no definition nor essence.

Or has "definition," like "what a thing is," several meanings? "What a thing is" in one sense means substance and the "this," in another one or other of the predicates, quantity, quality, [20] and the like. For as "is" belongs to all things, not however in the same sense, but to one sort of thing primarily and to others in a secondary way, so too "what a thing is" belongs in the simple sense to substance, but in a limited sense to the other categories. For even of a quality we might ask what it is, so that quality also is a "what a thing is"—not in the simple sense, however, but just as, in the case of that which is not, some say,[12] emphasizing the linguistic form, that that which is not *is*—not *is* simply, but *is* nonexistent; so too with quality.

We must no doubt inquire how we should express ourselves on each point, but certainly not more than how the facts actually stand. And so now also,

---

9 I.e. this identification does not give the essence of "surface" (for "suface" is repeated) but it gives the essence of "white," since this is not repeated but replaced by an equivalent.

10 I.e. compounds of substance with the other categories.

11 *Sc.* of the word "Iliad."

12 Cf. Pl. *Soph.* 237, 256 ff.

since it is evident what language we use, essence will belong, just as "what a thing is" does, primarily and in the simple sense to substance, and in a [30] secondary way to the other categories also—not essence in the simple sense, but the essence of a quality or of a quantity. For it must be either by an equivocation that we say these *are,* or by adding to and taking from the meaning of "are" (in the way in which that which is not known may be said to be known[13])— the truth being that we use the word neither ambiguously nor in the same sense, but just as we apply the word "medical" by virtue of a *reference* to one and the same thing, not *meaning* one and the same thing, nor yet [1030ᵇ] speaking ambiguously; for a patient and an operation and an instrument are called medical neither by an ambiguity nor with a single meaning, but with reference to a common end. But it does not matter at all in which of the two ways one likes to describe the facts; this is evident, that definition and essence in the primary and simple sense belong to substances. Still they belong to other things as well, only not in the primary sense. For if we suppose this it does not follow that there is a definition of every word which means the same as any formula; it must mean the same as a particular kind of formula; and this condition is satisfied if it is a formula of something which is one, not by continuity like the *Iliad* or the things that are one by [10] being bound together, but in one of the main senses of "one," which answer to the senses of "is"; now "that which is" in one sense denotes a "this," in another a quantity, in another a quality. And so there can be a formula or definition even of white man, but not in the sense in which there is a definition either of white or of a substance.

5. It is a difficult question, if one denies that a formula with an added

determinant is a definition, whether any of the terms that are not simple but coupled will be definable. For we *must* explain them by adding a determinant. E.g. there is the nose, and concavity, and snubness, which is compounded out of the two by the presence of the one in the other, and it is not by *accident* that the nose has the attribute either of concavity or of snubness, but in virtue of its nature; nor do they attach to it as whiteness does to Callias, or to man [20] (because Callias, who happens to be a man, is white), but as "male" attaches to animal and "equal" to quantity, and as all so-called "attributes *propter se*" attach to their subjects. And such attributes are those in which is involved either the *formula* or the *name* of the subject of the particular attribute, and which cannot be explained without this; e.g. white can be explained apart from man, but not female apart from animal. Therefore there is either no essence and definition of any of these things, or if there is, it is in another sense, as we have said.[14]

But there is also a second difficulty about them. For if snub nose and concave nose are the same thing, snub and concave will be the same thing; but if snub and concave are not the same [30] (because it is impossible to speak of snubness apart from the thing of which it is an attribute *propter se,* for snubness is concavity-*in-a-nose*), either it is impossible to say "snub nose" or the same thing will have been said twice, concave-nose nose; for snub nose will be concave-nose nose. And so it is absurd that such things should have an essence; if they have, there will be an infinite regress; for in snub-nose nose yet another "nose" will be involved.

Clearly, then, only substance is [1031ª] definable. For if the other categories also are definable, it must be by addition of a determinant, e.g. the qualitative is defined thus, and so is the odd, for it can-

13 I.e. it is known to be unknown.

14 a 17–b 13.

not be defined apart from number; nor can female be defined apart from animal. (When I say "by addition" I mean the expressions in which it turns out that we are saying the same thing twice, as in these instances.) And if this is true, coupled terms also, like "odd number," will not be definable (but this escapes our notice because our formulae are not accurate). But if these also are definable, either it is in some other way or, as we said,[15] definition and essence must be said to have more than one sense. Therefore in one sense nothing [10] will have a definition and nothing will have an essence, except substances, but in another sense other things will have them. Clearly, then, definition is the formula of the essence, and essence belongs to substances either alone or chiefly and primarily and in the unqualified sense.

6. We must inquire whether each thing and its essence are the same or different. This is of some use for the inquiry concerning substance; for each thing is thought to be not different from its substance, and the essence is said to be the substance of each thing.

Now in the case of accidental unities the two would be generally thought to be different, e.g. white man would [20] be thought to be different from the essence of white man. For if they are the same, the essence of man and that of white man are also the same; for a man and a white man are the same thing, as people say, so that the essence of white man and that of man would be also the same. But perhaps it does not follow that the essence of accidental unities should be the same as that of the simple terms. For the extreme terms are not in the same way identical with the middle term. But perhaps this might be thought to follow, that the extreme terms, the accidents, should turn out to be the same, e.g. the essence of white

and that of musical; but this is not actually thought to be the case.

But in the case of so-called self-subsistent things, is a thing necessarily the same as its essence? E.g. if there are some substances which have no other substances nor entities prior to them [30] —substances such as some assert the Ideas to be?—If the essence of good is to be different from good-itself, and the essence of animal from animal-itself, and the essence of being from being-itself, there will, firstly, be other sub- [1031ᵇ] stances and entities and Ideas besides those which are asserted, and, secondly, these others will be prior substances, if essence is substance. And if the posterior substances and the prior are severed from each other, (a) there will be no knowledge of the former,[16] and (b) the latter[17] will have no being. (By "several" I mean, if the good-itself has not the essence of good, and the latter has not the property of being good.) For (a) there is knowledge of each thing only when we know its essence. And (b) the case is the same for other things as for the good; so that if the essence of good is not good, neither is the essence of reality real, nor the essence of unity one. And all essences alike exist or none [10] of them does; so that if the essence of reality is not real, neither is any of the others. Again, that to which the essence of good does not belong[18] is not good.— The good, then, must be one with the essence of good, and the beautiful with the essence of beauty, and so with all things which do not depend on something else but are self-subsistent and primary. For it is enough if they are this, even if they are not Forms; or rather, perhaps, even if they are Forms. (At the same time it is clear that if there are Ideas such as some people say there are, it will not be substratum that is substance; for these must be substances, but

---

15 1030ª 17–ᵇ 13.

16 The Ideas or things-themselves.
17 The essences.
18 I.e. the Idea of good (l. 5).

not predicable of substratum; for if they were they would exist only by being participated in.[19])

Each thing itself, then, and its essence are one and the same in no merely accidental way, as is evident both from the preceding arguments and because to *know* each thing, at least, is just to [20] know its essence, so that even by the exhibition of instances it becomes clear that both must be one.

(But of an accidental term, e.g. "the musical" or "the white," since it has two meanings, it is not true to say that it itself is identical with its essence; for both that to which the accidental quality belongs, and the accidental quality, are white, so that in a sense the accident and its essence are the same, and in a sense they are not; for the essence of white is not the same as the man[20] or the white man, but it is the same as the attribute white.)

The absurdity of the separation would appear also if one were to assign a name to each of the essences; for there would be yet another essence besides the original one, e.g. to the essence of horse [30] there will belong a second essence.[21] Yet why should not some things be their essences from the start, since essence is substance? But indeed not only are a thing and its essence one, but the formula of them is also the same, as is clear even from what has been said; [1032ᵃ] for it is not by accident that the essence of one, and the one, are one. Further, if they are to be different, the process will go on to infinity; for we shall have (1) the essence of one, and (2) the one, so that to terms of the former kind the same argument will be applicable.[22]

Clearly, then, each primary and self-subsistent thing is one and the same as its essence. The sophistical objections to this position, and the question whether Socrates and to be Socrates are the same thing, are obviously answered by the same solution; for there is no difference either in the standpoint from which the question would be asked, or in that from which one could answer it success- [10] fully. We have explained, then, in what sense each thing is the same as its essence and in what sense it is not.

7. Of things that come to be, some come to be by nature, some by art, some spontaneously. Now everything that comes to be comes to be by the agency of something and from something and comes to be something. And the something which I say it comes to be may be found in any category; it may come to be either a "this" or of some size or of some quality or somewhere.

Now natural comings to be are the comings to be of those things which come to be by nature; and that out of which they come to be is what we call matter; and that by which they come to be is something which exists naturally; and the something which they come to be is a man or a plant or one of the things of this kind, which we say are substances if anything is—all things [20] produced either by nature or by art have matter; for each of them is capable both of being and of not being, and this capacity is the matter in each—and, in general, both that from which they are produced is nature, and the type according to which they are produced is nature (for that which is produced, e.g. a plant or an animal, has a nature), and so is that by which they are produced—the so-called "formal" nature, which is specifically the same (though this is in another individual); for man begets man.

Thus, then, are natural products produced; all other productions are called "makings." And all makings proceed either from art or from a faculty or from

19 I.e. as immanent in particulars.

20 *Sc.* who is white.

21 *Sc.* and so *ad infinitum*. As an infinite process is absurd, why take the first step that commits you to it—why say that the essence of horse is separate from the horse?

22 I.e. if the essence of one is different from the one, the essence of the essence of one is different from the essence of one.

thought.[23] Some of them happen also spontaneously or by luck[24] just as natural products sometimes do; for there [30] also the same things sometimes are produced without seed as well as from seed. Concerning these cases, then, we must inquire later,[25] but from art proceed the things of which the form is in the soul of the artist. (By form I mean the essence of each thing and its pri- [1032ᵇ] mary substance.) For even contraries have in a sense the same form; for the substance of a privation is the opposite substance, e.g. health is the substance of disease (for disease is the absence of health) ; and health is the formula in the soul or the knowledge of it. The healthy subject is produced as the result of the following train of thought:—since *this* is health, if the subject is to be healthy *this* must first be present, e.g. a uniform state of body, and if this is to be present, there must be heat; and the physician goes on thinking thus until he reduces the matter to a final something which he himself can produce. Then the process from this point onward, i.e. the process towards health, is called a [10] "making." Therefore it follows that in a sense health comes from health and house from house, that with matter from that without matter; for medical art and the building art are the form of health and of the house, and when I speak of substance without matter I mean the essence.

Of the productions or processes one part is called thinking and the other making—that which proceeds from the starting-point and the form is thinking, and that which proceeds from the final step of the thinking is making. And each of the other, intermediate, things is produced in the same way. I mean, for instance, if the subject is to be healthy his bodily state must be made uniform.

What then does being made uniform imply? This or that. And this depends on his being made warm. What does this imply? Something else. And this [20] something is present potentially; and what is present potentially is already in the physician's power.

The active principle then and the starting-point for the process of becoming healthy is, if it happens by art, the form in the soul, and if spontaneously, it is that, whatever it is, which starts the making,[26] for the man who makes by art, as in healing the starting-point is perhaps the production of warmth (and this the physician produces by rubbing). Warmth in the body, then, is either a part of health or is followed (either directly or through several intermediate steps) by something similar which is a part of health; and this, viz. that which produces the part of health, is the limiting-point[27] —and so too with a house (the stones are the limiting-point here) and in all other cases.

Therefore, as the saying goes, it [30] is impossible that anything should be produced if there were nothing existing before. Obviously then some part of the result will pre-exist of necessity; for the matter is a part; for this is present in the process and it is this that becomes something. But is the matter an element even in the *formula?* We certain- [1033ª] ly describe in both ways[28] what brazen circles are; we describe both the matter by saying it is brass, and the form by saying that it is such and such a figure; and figure is the proximate genus in which it is placed. The brazen circle, then, has its matter *in its formula.*

As for that out of which as matter they are produced, some things are said, when

23 Cf. vi. 1025ᵇ 22.
24 For the theory of these cf. *Phys.* ii. 5, 6.
25 Cf. ᵇ 23–30, 1034ª 9–21, ᵇ 4–7.

26 *Sc.* not the thinking, cf. ll. 15-17.
27 I.e. the minimum necessary basis.
28 From the proportion established, warmth : health : : stones : house, and from the next paragraph, it would appear that warmth is treated as the matter which when specialized in a particular way becomes health.

they have been produced, to be not that but "thaten"; e.g. the statue is not gold but golden. And a healthy man is not said to be that from which he has come. The reason is that though a thing comes both from its privation and from its substratum, which we call its matter (e.g. what becomes healthy is both a [10] man and an invalid), it is said to come rather from its privation (e.g. it is from an invalid rather than from a man that a healthy subject is produced). And so the healthy subject is not said to *be* an invalid, but to be a man, and the man is said to be healthy. But as for the things whose privation is obscure and nameless, e.g. in brass the privation of a particular shape or in bricks and timber the privation of arrangement as a house, the thing is thought to be produced *from* these materials, as in the former case the healthy man is produced *from* an invalid. And so, as there also a thing is not said to be that from which it comes, here the statue is not said to be wood but is said by a verbal change to be wooden, not brass but brazen, not gold but golden, and the house is said to be not bricks but bricken (though we [20] should not say without qualification, if we looked at the matter carefully, even that a statue is produced from wood or a house from bricks, because coming to be implies change in that from which a thing comes to be, and not permanence). It is for this reason, then, that we use this way of speaking.

8. Since anything which is produced is produced by something (and this I call the starting-point of the production), and from something (and let this be taken to be not the privation but the matter; for the meaning we attach to this has already[29] been explained), and since something is produced (and this is either a sphere or a circle or whatever

else it may chance to be), just as we do not make the substratum (the brass), so we do not make the sphere, except incidentally, because the brazen sphere is a sphere and we make the former. [30] For to make a "this" is to make a "this" out of the substratum in the full sense of the word.[30] (I mean that to make the brass round is not to make the round or the sphere, but something else, i.e. to produce this form in something different from itself. For if we make the form, we must make it out of something else; for this was assumed.[31] E.g. we make [1033ᵇ] a brazen sphere; and that in the sense that out of this, which is brass, we make this other, which is a sphere.) If, then, we also make the substratum itself, clearly we shall make it in the same way, and the processes of making will regress to infinity. Obviously then the form also,[32] or whatever we ought to call the shape present in the sensible thing, is not produced, nor is there any production of it, nor is the essence produced; for this is that which is made to be in something else either by art or by nature or by some faculty. But that there is a *brazen sphere,* this we make. For we make it out of brass and the sphere; we [10] bring the form into this particular matter, and the result is a brazen sphere. But if the essence of sphere in general is to be produced, something must be produced out of something. For the product will always have to be divisible, and one part must be this and another that; I mean the one must be matter and the other form. If, then, a sphere is "the figure whose circumference is at all points equidistant from the centre," part of this will be the medium in which the thing made will be, and part will be in that medium, and the whole will be the thing produced, which corresponds to

---

29 Cf. 1032ᵃ 17.

30 I.e. including form as well as matter (cf. 1029ᵃ 3).

31 a 25.

32 *Sc.* as well as the matter.

the brazen sphere. It is obvious, then, from what has been said, that that which is spoken of as form or substance is not produced, but the concrete thing which gets its name from this is produced, and that in everything which is generated matter is present, and one part of the thing is matter and the other form.

Is there, then, a sphere apart from the individual spheres or a house apart from the bricks? Rather we may say that [20] no "this" would ever have been coming to be, if this had been so, but that the "form" means the "such," and is not a "this"—a definite thing; but the artist makes, or the father begets, a "such" out of a "this"; and when it has been begotten, it is a "this such."[33] And the whole "this," Callias or Socrates, is analogous to "this brazen sphere," but man and animal to "brazen sphere" in general. Obviously, then, the cause which consists of the Forms (taken in the sense in which some maintain the existence of the Forms, i.e. if they are something apart from the individuals) is useless, at least with regard to comings-to-be and to substances; and the Forms need not, for this reason at least, be self-subsistent substances. In some cases indeed it is even obvious that the begetter is of [30] the same kind as the begotten (not, however, the *same* nor one in number, but in form), i.e. in the case of natural products (for man begets man), unless something happens contrary to nature, e.g. the production of a mule by a horse. (And even these cases are similar; for that which would be found to be common to horse and ass, the genus next above them, has not received a name, but it would doubtless be both, [1034ᵃ] in fact something like a mule.) Obviously, therefore, it is quite unnecessary to set up a Form as a pattern (for we should have looked for Forms in these

cases if in any; for these are substances if anything is so); the begetter is adequate to the making of the product and to the causing of the form in the matter. And when we have the whole, such and such a form in this flesh and in these bones, this is Callias or Socrates; and they are different in virtue of their matter (for that is different), but the same in form; for their form is indivisible.

9. The question might be raised, why some things are produced spontaneously as well as by art, e.g. health, while others are not, e.g. a house. The reason is that in some cases the matter which [10] governs the production in the making and producing of any work of art, and in which a part of the product is present —some matter is such as to be set in motion by itself and some is not of this nature, and of the former kind some can move itself in the particular way required, while other matter is incapable of this; for many things can be set in motion by themselves but not in some particular way, e.g. that of dancing. The things, then, whose matter is of this sort, e.g. stones, cannot be moved in the particular way required,[34] except by something else, but in another way they can move themselves—and so it is with fire. Therefore some things will not exist apart from some one who has the art of making them, while others will; for motion will be started by these things which have not the art but can themselves [20] be moved by other things which have not the art or with a motion starting from a part of the product.[35]

And it is clear also from what has been said that in a sense every product of art is produced from a thing which shares its name (as natural products are produced), or from a part of itself which shares its name (e.g. the house is pro-

---

[33] I.e. the artist, or the father, turns a mere piece of matter into a qualified piece of matter.

[34] *Sc.* for building.

[35] I.e. an element of it pre-existing in the things themselves (cf. 1032ᵇ 26–1033ᵃ I, 1034ᵃ 12).

duced from a house, *qua* produced by reason; for the art of building is the form of the house), or from something which contains a part of it—if we exclude things produced by accident; for the cause of the thing's producing the product directly *per se* is a part of the product. The heat in the movement[36] caused heat in the body, and this is either health, or a part of health, or is followed by a part of health or by health itself. And so it is said to cause health, because it causes that to which health attaches as a consequence.

Therefore, as in syllogisms, sub- [30] stance[37] is the starting-point of everything. It is from "what a thing is" that syllogisms start; and from it also we now find processes of production to start.

Things which are formed by nature are in the same case as these products of art. For the seed is productive in the same way as the things that work by art; for it has the form potentially, and that from which the seed comes has in [1034ᵇ] a sense the same name as the offspring —only in a sense, for we must not expect parent and offspring always to have exactly the same name, as in the production of "human being" from "human being"; of a "woman" also can be produced by a "man"—unless the offspring be an imperfect form; which is the reason why the parent of a mule is not a mule.[38] The natural things which (like the artificial objects previously considered[39]) can be produced spontaneously are those whose matter can be moved even by itself in the way in which the seed usually moves it; those things which have not such matter cannot be produced except from the parent animals themselves.

But not only regarding substance does our argument prove that its form does not come to be, but the argument applies to all the primary classes alike, i.e. quantity, quality, and the other categories. For as the brazen sphere comes to be, but not the sphere nor the [10] brass, and so too in the case of brass itself, if it comes to be, it is its concrete unity that comes to be (for the matter and the form must always exist before), so is it both in the case of substance and in that of quality and quantity and the other categories likewise; for the quality does not come to be, but the wood of that quality, and the quantity does not come to be, but the wood or the animal of that size. But we may learn from these instances a peculiarity of substance, that there must exist beforehand in complete reality another substance which produces it, e.g. an animal if an animal is produced; but it is not necessary that a quality or quantity should pre-exist otherwise than potentially.

10. Since a definition is a formula, and every formula has parts, and as [20] the formula is to the thing, so is the part of the formula to the part of the thing, the question is already being asked whether the formula of the parts must be present in the formula of the whole or not. For in some cases the formulae of the parts are seen to be present, and in some not. The formula of the circle does not include that of the segments, but that of the syllable includes that of the letters; yet the circle is divided into segments as the syllable is into letters.— And further if the parts are prior to the whole, and the acute angle is a part of the right angle and the finger a part of the animal, the acute angle will be [30] prior to the right angle and the finger to the man. But the latter are thought to be prior; for in formula the parts are explained by reference to them, and in respect also of the power of existing apart from each other the wholes are prior to the parts.

---

36 *Sc.* of the rubber's hand.
37 I.e. essence.
38 Cf. 1033ᵇ 33.
39 Cf. ᵃ 9–32.

Perhaps we should rather say that "part" is used in several senses. One of these is "that which measures another thing in respect of quantity." But let this sense be set aside; let us inquire about the parts of which *substance* consists. If then matter is one thing, form [1035a] another, the compound of these a third, and both the matter and the form and the compound are substance, even the matter is in a sense called part of a thing, while in a sense *it* is not, but only the elements of which the formula of the form consists. E.g. of concavity flesh (for this is the matter in which it is produced) is not a part, but of snubness it is a part; and the bronze is a part of the concrete statue, but not of the statue when this is spoken of in the sense of the form. (For the form, or thing as having form, should be said to be the thing, but the material element by itself must never be said to be so.) And so the formula of the circle does not include that of the segments, but the [10] formula of the syllable includes that of the letters; for the letters are parts of the formula of the form, and not matter, but the segments are parts in the sense of matter on which the form supervenes; yet they are nearer the form than the bronze is when roundness is produced in bronze. But in a sense not even every kind of letter will be present in the formula of the syllable, e.g. particular waxen letters or the letters as movements in the air; for in these also we have already something that is part of the syllable only in the sense that it is its perceptible matter. For even if the line when divided passes away into its halves, or the man into bones and muscles and flesh, it does not follow that they are composed of these as parts of their essence, but rather as matter; and these are parts of the concrete thing, but [20] not also of the form, i.e. of that to which the formula refers; wherefore also they are not present in the formulae. In one kind of formula, then, the formula of

such parts will be present, but in another it must not be present, where the formula does not refer to the concrete object. For it is for this reason that some things have as their constituent principles parts into which they pass away, while some have not. Those things which are the form and the matter taken together, e.g. the snub, or the bronze circle, pass away into these materials, and the matter is a part of them; but those things which do not involve matter but are without matter, and whose formulae are formulae of the form only, do not pass away— either not at all or at any rate not in this way. Therefore these materials are principles and parts of the concrete [30] things, while of the form they are neither parts nor principles. And therefore the clay statue is resolved into clay and the ball into bronze and Callias into flesh and bones, and again the circle into its segments; for there is a sense of "circle" in which it involves matter. For "circle" is used ambiguously, meaning both the circle, unqualified, and the in- [1935b] dividual circle, because there is no name peculiar to the individuals.

The truth has indeed now been stated, but still let us state it yet more clearly, taking up the question again. The parts of the formula, into which the formula is divided, are prior to it, either all or some of them. The formula of the right angle, however, does not include the formula of the acute, but the formula of the acute includes that of the right angle; for he who defines the acute uses the right angle; for the acute is "less than a right angle." The circle and the semicircle also are in a like relation; for the semicircle is defined by the circle; and so is the finger by the whole [10] body, for a finger is "such and such a part of a man." Therefore the parts which are of the nature of matter, and into which as its matter a thing is divided, are posterior; but those which are of the nature of parts of the formula, and of the substance according to its formula, are prior, either all or some of them. And since the soul of animals (for this is the substance of a living being) is their substance according to the formula, i.e. the form and the essence of a body of a certain kind (at least we shall define each part, if we define it well, not without reference to its function, and this cannot belong to it without perception[40]), so that the parts of soul are prior, either all or some of them, to the concrete "animal," and so too with each individual animal; and the body and [20] its parts are posterior to this, the essential substance, and it is not the substance but the concrete thing that is divided into these parts as its matter:—this being so, to the concrete thing these are in a sense prior, but in a sense they are not. For they cannot even exist if severed from the whole; for it is not a finger in any and every state that is the finger of a living thing, but a dead finger is a finger only in name. Some parts are neither prior nor posterior to the whole, i.e. those which are dominant and in which the formula, i.e. the essential substance, is immediately present, e.g. perhaps the heart or the brain; for it does not matter in the least which of the two has this quality. But man and horse and terms which are thus applied to individuals, but universally, are not substance but something composed of this particular formula and this par- [30] ticular matter treated as universal; and as regards the individual, Socrates already includes in him ultimate individual matter; and similarly in all other cases. "A part" may be a part either of the form (i.e. of the essence), or of the compound of the form and the matter, or of the matter itself. But only the parts of the form are parts of the formula, and the formula is of the universal; [1036ᵃ] for "being a circle" is the same as the circle, and "being a soul" the same as

the soul. But when we come to the concrete thing, e.g. *this* circle, i.e. one of the individual circles, whether perceptible or intelligible (I mean by intelligible circles the mathematical, and by perceptible circles those of bronze and of wood) —of these there is no definition, but they are known by the aid of intuitive thinking or of perception; and when they pass out of this complete realization it is not clear whether they exist or not; but they are always stated and recognized by means of the universal formula. But matter is unknowable in itself. And some matter is perceptible and some intelligible, perceptible matter being [10] for instance bronze and wood and all matter that is changeable, and intelligible matter being that which is present in perceptible things not *qua* perceptible, i.e. the objects of mathematics.

We have stated, then, how matters stand with regard to whole and part, and their priority and posteriority. But when any one asks whether the right angle and the circle and the animal are prior, or the things into which they are divided and of which they consist, i.e. the parts, we must meet the inquiry by saying that the question cannot be answered simply. For if even bare soul is the animal or[41] the living thing, or the soul of each individual is the individual itself, and "being a circle" is the circle, and "being a right angle" and the essence of the right angle is the right angle, then the whole in one sense must be called posterior to the part in one sense, i.e. to the parts included in the formula and to the parts of the in- [20] dividual right angle (for both the material right angle which is made of bronze, and that which is formed by individual lines, are posterior to their parts); while the immaterial right angle is posterior to the parts included in the formula, but prior to those included in

---

[40] And therefore not without soul.

[41] *Sc.* to put it more widely so as to include the vegetable world.

the particular instance, and the question must not be answered simply. If, however, the soul is something different and is not identical with the animal, even so some parts must, as we have maintained, be called prior and others must not.

11. Another question is naturally raised, viz. what sort of parts belong to the form and what sort not to the form, but to the concrete thing. Yet if this is not plain it is not possible to define any thing; for definition is of the universal and of the form. If then it is not evident what sort of parts are of the nature [30] of matter and what sort are not, neither will the formula of the thing be evident. In the case of things which are found to occur in specifically different materials, as a circle may exist in bronze or stone or wood, it seems plain that these, the bronze or the stone, are no part of the essence of the circle, since it is found apart from them. Of things which are *not* seen to exist apart, there is no reason why the same may not be true, just as if all circles that had ever been [1036ᵇ] seen were of bronze; for none the less the bronze would be no part of the form; but it is hard to eliminate it in thought. E.g. the form of man is always found in flesh and bones and parts of this kind; are these then also parts of the form and the formula? No, they are matter; but because man is not found also in other matters we are unable to perform the abstraction.

Since this is thought to be possible, but it is not clear *when* it is the case, some people,[42] already raise the question even in the case of the circle and the triangle, thinking that it is not right to define these by reference to lines and to the continuous, but that all these are [10] to the circle or the triangle as flesh and bones are to man, and bronze or stone to the statue; and they reduce all things

to numbers, and they say the formula of "line" is that of "two." And of those who assert the Ideas some[43] make "two" the line-itself, and others make in the Form of the line; for in some cases they say the Form and that of which it is the Form are the same, e.g. "two" and the Form of two; but in the case of "line" they say this is no longer so.

It follows then that there is one Form for many things whose form is evidently different (a conclusion which confronted the Pythagoreans also) ; and it is possible to make one thing the Form-itself of all, and to hold that the others are not Forms; but thus all things will be [20] one.

We have pointed out, then, that the question of definitions contains some difficulty, and why this is so. And so to reduce all things thus to Forms and to eliminate the matter is useless labour; for some things surely are a particular form in a particular matter, or particular things in a particular state. And the comparison which Socrates the younger[44] used to make in the case of "animal"[45] is not sound; for it leads away from the truth, and makes one suppose that man can possibly exist without his parts, as the circle can without the bronze. But the case is not similar; for an animal is something perceptible, and it is not possible to define it without reference to movement—nor, therefore, without reference to the parts' being in a certain state. For it is not a hand in any and [30] every state that is a part of man, but only when it can fulfil its work, and therefore only when it is alive; if it is not alive it is not a part.

Regarding the objects of mathematics, why are the formulae of the parts not parts of the formulae of the wholes; e.g. why are not the semicircles included in

---

42 Aristotle is thinking of Pythagoreans.

43 This probably inludes Plato himself.

44 Cf. Pl. *Theaet.* 147 D; *Soph.* 218 B; *Pol.* 257 C; *Epp.* 358 D.

45 Cf a 34–b 7.

the formula of the circle? It cannot be said, "because these parts are perceptible things"; for they are not. But perhaps this makes no difference; for even some things which are not perceptible must have matter; indeed there is some [1037ª] matter in everything which is not an essence and a bare form but a "this." The semicircles, then, will not be parts of the universal circle, but will be parts of the individual circles, as has been said before;[46] for while one kind of matter is perceptible, there is another which is intelligible.

It is clear also that the soul is the primary substance and the body is matter, and man or animal is the compound of both taken universally; and "Socrates" or "Coriscus," if even the soul of Socrates may be called Socrates,[47] has two meanings (for some mean by such a term the soul, and others mean the concrete thing), but if "Socrates" or "Coriscus" means simply this particular soul and this particular body, the individual is analogous to the universal in its composition.[48]

Whether there is, apart from the [10] matter of such substances, another kind of matter, and one should look for some substance other than these, e.g. numbers or something of the sort, must be considered later.[49] For it is for the sake of this that we are trying to determine the nature of perceptible substances as well, since in a sense the inquiry about perceptible substances is the work of physics, i.e. of second philosophy; for the physicist must come to know not only about the matter, but also about the substance expressed in the formula, and even more than about the other. And in the case of definitions, how the elements in the formula are parts of the defi-

nition, and why the definition is one formula (for clearly the thing is one, but in virtue of *what* is the thing one, [20] although it has parts?)—this must be considered later.[50]

What the essence is and in what sense it is independent, has been stated universally in a way which is true of every case,[51] and also why the formula of the essence of some things contains the parts of the thing defined, while that of others does not. And we have stated that in the formula of the substance the material parts will not be present (for they are not even parts of the substance in that sense, but of the concrete substance; but of *this* there is in a sense a formula, and in a sense there is not; for there is no formula of it with its matter, for this is indefinite, but there is a formula of it with reference to its primary substance —e.g. in the case of man the formula of the soul—for the substance is the indwelling form, from which and the matter the so-called concrete substance is derived;[52] e.g. concavity is a form of this sort, for from this and the nose arise "snub nose" and "snubness"); but in the concrete substance, e.g. a snub nose or Callias, the matter also will be present.[53] And we have stated that the essence and the thing itself are in some cases the same; i.e. in the case of primary [1037ᵇ] substances, e.g. curvature and the essence of curvature, if this is primary. (By a "primary" substance I mean one which does not imply the presence of something in something else, i.e. in something that underlies it which acts as matter.) But things which are of the nature of matter, or of wholes that include matter, are not the same as their essences, nor are accidental unities like that of "Socrates" and "musical"; for these are the same only by accident.[54]

---

46 1035ª 30–ᵇ 3.
47 Cf. 1036ª 16–17, viii. 1043ᵇ 2–4.
48 I.e. as man = soul + body, Socrates = this soul + this body.
49 Cf. xiii, xiv.

50 Cf. vii. 12, viii. 6.
51 Ch. 4.
52 Chs. 10, 11.
53 Ch. 5.
54 Ch. 6.

12. Now let us treat first of definition, in so far as we have not treated of it in the *Analytics*;[55] for the problem stated in them[56] is useful for our inquiries concerning substance. I mean this problem: —wherein can consist the unity of [10] that, the formula of which we call a definition, as for instance, in the case of man, "twofooted animal"; for let this be the formula of man. Why, then, is this one, and not many, viz. "animal" *and* "two-footed"? For in the case of "man" and "pale" there is a plurality when one term does not belong to the other, but a unity when it does belong and the subject, man, has a certain attribute; for then a unity is produced and we have "the pale man." In the present case, on the other hand,[57] one does not share in the other; the genus is not thought to share in its differentiae (for then the same thing would share in contraries; for the differentiae by which the genus is divided are contrary). [20] And even if the genus does share in them, the same argument applies, since the differentiae present in man are many, e.g. endowed with feet, two-footed, featherless. Why are these one and not many? Not because they are present in one thing; for on this principle a unity can be made out of *all* the attributes of a thing. But surely all the attributes in the definition *must* be one; for the definition is a single formula and a formula of substance, so that it must be a formula of some one thing; for substance means a "one" and a "this," as we maintain.

We must first inquire about definitions reached by the method of divisions. There is nothing in the definition except the first-named genus and the differentiae. The other genera are the first genus and along with this the differentiae that are taken with it, e.g. the first

may be "animal," the next "animal which is two-footed," and again "animal which is two-footed and featherless," and similarly if the definition includes more terms. And in general it makes [1038$^a$] no difference whether it includes many or few terms—nor, therefore, whether it includes few or simply two; and of the two the one is differentia and the other genus; e.g. in "two-footed animal" "animal" is genus, and the other is differentia.

If then the genus absolutely does not exist apart from the species-of-a-genus, or if it exists but exists as matter (for the voice is genus and matter, but its differentiae make the species, i.e. the letters, out of it), clearly the definition is the formula which comprises the differentiae.

But it is also necessary that the division be by the differentia *of the differentia*; e.g. "endowed with feet" is a differentia of "animal," again the differentia of "animal endowed with feet" must [10] be of it *qua* endowed with feet. Therefore we must not say, if we are to speak rightly, that of that which is endowed with feet one part has feathers and one is featherless (if we do this we do it through incapacity); we must divide it only into cloven-footed and not-cloven; for these are differentiae in the foot; cloven-footedness is a form of footedness. And the process wants always to go on so till it reaches the species that contain no differences. And then there will be as many kinds of foot as there are differentiae, and the kinds of animals endowed with feet will be equal in number to the differentiae. If then this is so, clearly the *last* differentia will be the substance of the thing and its definition, since it is not right to state the same [20] things more than once in our definitions; for it is superfluous. And this does happen; for when we say "animal endowed with feet and two-footed" we have said nothing other than "animal having feet, having two feet"; and if we divide this

---

55 Cf. *An. Post.* ii. 3–10, 13.

56 Cf. *ib.* 97$^a$ 29.

57 That of "animal" and "two-footed."

by the proper division, we shall be saying the same thing more than once—as many times as there are differentiae.

If then a differentia of a differentia be taken at each step, one differentia—the last—will be the form and the substance; but if we divide according to accidental qualities, e.g. if we were to divide that which is endowed with feet into the white and the black, there will be as many differentiae as there are cuts. Therefore it is plain that the definition is the formula which contains the differentiae, or, according to the right method, the last of these. [30] This would be evident, if we were to change the order of such definitions, e.g. of that of man, saying "animal which is two-footed and endowed with feet"; for "endowed with feet" is superfluous when "two-footed" has been said. But there is no order in the substance; for how are we to think the one element posterior and the other prior? Regarding the definitions, then, which are reached by the method of divisions, let this suffice as our first attempt at stating their nature.

13. Let us return to the subject [1038ᵇ] of our inquiry, which is substance. As the substratum and the essence and the compound of these are called substance, so also is the universal. About two of these we have spoken; both about the essence[58] and about the substratum,[59] of which we have said[60] that it underlies in two senses, either being a "this"—which is the way in which an animal underlies its attributes—or as the matter underlies the complete reality. The universal also is thought by some to be in the fullest sense a cause, and a principle; therefore let us attack the discussion of this point also. For it seems impossible that any universal term should be the name of a substance. For firstly the substance of

each thing is that which is peculiar to it, which does not belong to anything [10] else; but the universal is common, since that is called universal which is such as to belong to more than one thing. Of which individual then will this be the substance? Either of all or of none; but it cannot be the substance of all. And if it is to be the substance of one, this one will be the others also; for things whose substance is one and whose essence is one are themselves also one.

Further, substance means that which is not predicable of a subject, but the universal is predicable of some subject always.

But perhaps the universal, while it cannot be substance in the way in which the essence is so, can be present in this; e.g. "animal" can be present in "man" and "horse." Then clearly it is a formula of the essence. And it makes no difference if it is not a formula of everything that is in the substance; for none the [20] less the universal will be the substance of something, as "man" is the substance of the individual man in whom it is present, so that the same result will follow once more; for the universal, e.g. "animal," will be the substance of that in which it is present as something peculiar to it. And further it is impossible and absurd that the "this," i.e. the substance, if it consists of parts, should not consist of substances nor of what is a "this," but of quality; for that which is not substance, i.e. the quality, will then be prior to substance and to the "this." Which is impossible; for neither in formula nor in time nor in coming to be can the modifications be prior to the substance; for then they will also be separable from it. Further, Socrates will contain a substance present in a substance, so that this will be the substance of two things. And in general it follows, if man and such things are sub- [30] stance, that none of the elements in their formulae is the substance of anything, nor does it exist apart from the species

---

58 Chs. 4–6, 10–12.
59 Ch. 3.
60 1029ª 2–3, 23–4.

or in anything else; I mean, for instance, that no "animal" exists apart from the particular kinds of animal, nor does any other of the elements present in formulae exist apart.

If, then, we view the matter from these standpoints, it is plain that no universal attribute is a substance, and this is plain also from the fact that no common predicate indicates a "this," but rather a "such." If not, many difficulties follow and especially the "third [1039ᵃ] man."[61]

The conclusion is evident also from the following consideration. A substance cannot consist of substances present in it in complete reality; for things that are thus in complete reality two are never in complete reality one, though if they are *potentially* two, they can be one (e.g. the double line consists of two halves— potentially; for the complete realization of the halves divides them from one another); therefore if the substance is one, it will not consist of substances present, in it and present in this way, which Democritus describes rightly; he says one thing cannot be made out of two nor [10] two out of one; for he identifies substances with his indivisible magnitudes. It is clear therefore that the same will hold good of number, if number is a synthesis of units, as is said by some;[62] for two is either not one, or there is no unit present in it in complete reality.

But our result involves a difficulty. If no substance can consist of universals because a universal indicates a "such," not a "this," and if no substance can be composed of substances existing in complete reality, every substance would be incomposite, so that there would not even be a formula of any substance. But it is *thought* by all and was stated long ago[63] that it is either only, or primarily, substance that can be defined; yet now

it seems that not even substance can. [20] There cannot, then, be a definition of anything; or in a sense there can be, and in a sense there cannot. And what we are saying will be plainer from what follows.[64]

14. It is clear also from these very facts what consequence confronts those who say the Ideas are substances capable of separate existence, and at the same time make the Form consist of the genus and the differentiae. For if the Forms exist and "animal" is present in "man" and "horse," it is either one and the same in number, or different. (In formula it is clearly one; for he who states the formula will go through the same formula in either case.) If then there [30] is a "man-in-himself" who is a "this" and exists apart, the parts also of which he consists, e.g. "animal" and "two-footed," must indicate "thises," and be capable of separate existence, and substances; therefore "animal," as well as "man," must be of this sort.

Now (1) if the "animal" in "the horse" and in "man" is one and the same, as you are with yourself, (a) how will the one in things that exist apart be one, and how will this "animal" [1039ᵇ] escape being divided even from itself?

Further, (b) if it is to share in "two-footed" and "many-footed," an impossible conclusion follows; for contrary attributes will belong at the same time to it, although it is one and a "this." If it is not to share in them, what is the relation implied when one says the animal is two-footed or possessed of feet? But perhaps the two things are "put together" and are "in contact," or are "mixed." Yet all these expressions are absurd.

But (2) suppose the Form to be different in each species. Then there will be practically an infinite number of things whose *substance* is "animal"; for it is not

---

61 Cf. i. 990ᵇ 17.
62 Thales is said to have defined number as "a system of units."
63 Cf. 1031ᵃ 11–14.

64 Cf. vii. 15, viii. 6.

by accident that "man" has "animal" for one of its elements. Further, many things will be "animal-itself." For (i) the "animal" in each species will be the [10] substance of the species; for it is after nothing else that the species is called; if it were, that other would be an element in "man," i.e. would be the genus of man. And further, (ii) all the elements of which "man" is composed will be Ideas. None of them, then, will be the Idea of one thing and the substance of another; this is impossible. The "animal," then, present in each species of animals will be animal-itself. Further, from what is this "animal" in each species derived, and how will it be derived from animal-itself? Or how can this "animal," whose essence is simply animality, exist apart from animal-itself?

Further, (3) in the case of sensible things both these consequences and others still more absurd follow. If, then, these consequences are impossible, clearly there are not Forms of sensible things in the sense in which some maintain their existence.

15. Since substance is of two [20] kinds, the concrete thing and the formula (I mean that one kind of substance is the formula taken with the matter, while another kind is the formula in its generality), substances in the former sense are capable of destruction (for they are capable also of generation), but there is no destruction of the formula in the sense that it is ever in course of being destroyed (for there is no generation of it either; the being of house is not generated, but only the being of *this* house), but without generation and destruction formulae are and are not; for it has been shown[65] that no one begets nor makes these. For this reason, also, there is neither definition of nor demonstration about sensible individual substances, because they have matter whose nature is such that they are capable both

of being and of not being; for which reason all the individual instances of [30] them are destructible. If then demonstration is of necessary truths and definition is a scientific process, and if, just as knowledge cannot be sometimes knowledge and sometimes ignorance, but the state which varies thus is opinion, so too demonstration and definition cannot vary thus, but it is opinion that deals with that which can be otherwise than as it is, clearly there can neither be [1040ᵃ] definition of nor demonstration about sensible individuals. For perishing things are obscure to those who have the relevant knowledge, when they have passed from our perception; and though the formulae remain in the soul unchanged, there will no longer be either definition or demonstration. And so when one of the definition-mongers defines any individual, he must recognize that his definition may always be overthrown; for it is not possible to define such things.

Nor is it possible to define any Idea. For the Idea is, as its supporters say, an individual, and can exist apart; and the formula must consist of words; and he who defines must not invent a word [10] (for it would be unknown), but the established words are common to all the members of a class; these then must apply to something besides the thing defined; e.g. if one were defining you, he would say "an animal which is lean" or "pale," or something else which will apply also to some one other than you. If any one were to say that perhaps all the attributes taken apart may belong to many subjects, but together they belong only to this one, we must reply first that they belong also to both the elements; e.g. "two-footed animal" belongs to animal and to the two-footed. (And in the case of eternal entities[66] this is even necessary, since the elements are prior to and parts of the compound; nay more, they can also exist apart, if "man" can exist apart. For either neither or both

---

[65] Ch. 8.

[66] I.e. the Ideas.

can. If, then, neither can, the genus [20] will not exist apart from the various species; but if it does, the differentia will also.) Secondly, we must reply that "animal" and "two-footed" are prior in being to "two-footed animal"; and things which are prior to others are not destroyed when the others are.

Again, if the Ideas consist of Ideas (as they must, since elements are simpler than the compound), it will be further necessary that the elements also of which the Idea consists, e.g. "animal" and "two-footed," should be predicated of many subjects. If not, how will they come to be known? For there will then be an Idea which cannot be predicated of more subjects than one. But this is not thought possible—every Idea is thought to be capable of being shared.

As has been said,[67] then, the impossibility of defining individuals escapes notice in the case of eternal things, especially those which are unique, like the sun or the moon. For people err not [30] only by adding attributes whose removal the sun would survive, e.g. "going round the earth" or "night-hidden" (for from their view it follows that if it stands still or is visible,[68] it will no longer be the sun; but it is strange if this is so; for "the sun" means a certain *substance*); but also by the mention of attributes which can belong to another subject; e.g. if another thing with the stated attributes comes into existence, clearly it will be a sun; the formula there- [1040ᵇ] fore is general. But the sun was supposed to be an individual, like Cleon or Socrates. After all, why does not one of the supporters of the Ideas produce a definition of an Idea? It would become clear, if they tried, that what has now been said is true.

16. Evidently even of the things that are thought to be substances, most are only potencies—both the parts of animals

(for none of them exists separately; and when they *are* separated, then too they exist, all of them, merely as matter) and earth and fire and air; for none of them is a unity, but as it were a mere heap, till they are worked up and some unity is made out of them. One might [10] most readily suppose the parts of living things and the parts of the soul nearly related to them to turn out to be both, i.e. existent in complete reality as well as in potency, because they have sources of movement in something in their joints; for which reason some animals live when divided. Yet all the parts must exist only potentially, when they are one and continuous by nature—not by force or by growing into one, for such a phenomenon is an abnormality.

Since the term "unity" is used like the term "being," and the substance of that which is one is one, and things whose substance is numerically one are numerically one, evidently neither unity nor being can be the substance of things, just as being an element or a principle cannot be the substance, but we ask [20] what, then, the principle is, that we may reduce the thing to something more knowable. Now of these concepts "being" and "unity" are more substantial than "principle" or "element" or "cause," but not even the former are substance, since in general nothing that is common is substance; for substance does not belong to anything but to itself and to that which has it, of which it is the substance. Further, that which is one cannot be in many places at the same time, but that which is common is present in many places at the same time; so that clearly no universal exists apart from its individuals.

But those who say the Forms exist, in one respect are right, in giving the Forms separate existence, *if* they are substances; but in another respect they are not right, because they say the one over many [30] is a Form. The reason for their doing this is that they cannot declare what are the substances of this sort, the imperish-

67 Cf. 1. 17.
68 *Sc.* at night.

able substances which exist apart from the individual and sensible substances. They make them, then, the same in kind as the perishable things (for this kind of substance we know)—"man-himself" and "horse-itself," adding to the sensible things the word "itself." Yet even if we had not seen the stars, none the less, I suppose, would they have been [1041ᵃ] eternal substances apart from those which we knew; so that now also if we do not know what non-sensible substances there are, yet it is doubtless necessary that there should *be* some.—Clearly, then, no universal term is the name of a substance, and no substance is composed of substances.

17. Let us state what, i.e. what kind of thing, substance should be said to be, taking once more another starting-point; for perhaps from this we shall get a clear view also of that substance which exists apart from sensible substances. Since, then, substance is a principle and a cause, let us pursue it from this start- [10] ing-point. The "why" is always sought in this form—"why does one thing attach to some other?" For to inquire why the musical man is a musical man, is either to inquire—as we have said—why the man is musical, or it is something else. Now "why a thing is itself" is a meaningless inquiry (for [to give meaning to the question "why"] the fact or the existence of the thing must already be evident—e.g. that the moon is eclipsed—but the fact that a thing is itself is the single reason and the single cause to be given in answer to all such questions as "why the man is man, or the musician musical,"⁶⁹ unless one were to answer "because each thing is inseparable from itself, and its being one just meant this"; this, however, is common to all things and is a short and easy way with the question). But we *can* in-

quire why man is an animal of such [20] and such a nature. This, then, is plain, that we are not inquiring why he who is a man is a man. We are inquiring, then, why something is predicable of something (that it is predicable must be clear; for if not, the inquiry is an inquiry into nothing). E.g. why does it thunder? This is the same as "why is sound produced in the clouds?" Thus the inquiry is about the predication of one thing of another. And why are these things, i.e. bricks and stones, a house? Plainly we are seeking the cause. And this is the essence (to speak abstractly), which in some cases is the end, e.g. perhaps in the case of a house or a bed, and in some cases is the first mover; for this also [30] is a cause. But while the efficient cause is sought in the case of genesis and destruction, the final cause is sought in the case of being also.

The object of the inquiry is most easily overlooked where one term is not expressly predicated of another (e.g. when we inquire "what man is"), because we do not distinguish and do not [1041ᵇ] say definitely that certain elements make up a certain whole. Blt we must articulate our meaning before we begin to inquire; if not, the inquiry is on the border-line between being a search for something and a search for nothing. Since we must have the existence of the thing as something given, clearly the question is *why* the matter is some definite thing; e.g. why are these materials a house? Because that which was the essence of a house is present. And why is this individual thing, or this body having this form, a man? Therefore what we seek is the cause, i.e. the form, by reason of which the matter is some definite thing; and this is the substance of the thing. Evidently, then, in the case of *simple* terms no inquiry nor teaching [10] is possible; our attitude towards such things is other than that of inquiry.

Since that which is compounded out of something so that the whole is one,

---

69 *Sc.* and therefore in this case, when the fact is known, there is no question as to the "why."

not like a heap but like a syllable—now the syllable is not its elements, *ba* is not the same as *b* and *a*, nor is flesh fire and earth (for when these are separated the wholes, i.e. the flesh and the syllable, no longer exist, but the elements of the syllable exist, and so do fire and earth); the syllable, then, is something—not only its elements (the vowel and the consonant) but also something else, and the flesh is not only fire and earth or the hot and the cold, but also something else:—if, then, that something must itself be either an element or composed of elements, (1) if it is an element the same argu- [20] ment will again apply; for flesh will consist of this and fire and earth and something still further, so that the process will go on to infinity. But (2) if it is a compound, clearly it will be a compound not of one but of more than one (or else that one will be the thing itself), so that again in this case we can use the same argument as in the case of flesh or of the syllable. But it would seem that this "other" is something, and not an element, and that it is the *cause* which makes *this* thing flesh and *that* a syllable. And similarly in all other cases. And this is the *substance* of each thing (for this is the primary cause of its being); and since, while some things are not substances, as many as are substances are formed in accordance with a nature of their own and by a process of nature, their substance would seem to be this kind of "nature,"⁷⁰ which is not an [30] element but a principle. An *element*, on the other hand, is that into which a thing is divided and which is present in it as matter; e.g. *a* and *b* are the elements of the syllable.

### Book Θ (IX)

1. We have treated¹ of that [1045ᵇ] which *is* primarily and to which all the other categories of being are referred— i.e. of substance. For it is in virtue of the concept of substance that the [30] others also are said to be—quantity and quality and the like; for all will be found to involve the concept of substance, as we said in the first part of our work.² And since "being" is in one way divided into individual thing, quality, and quantity, and is in another way distinguished in respect of potency and complete reality, and of function, let us now add a discussion of potency and complete reality. And first let us explain potency in the strictest sense, which is, however, not the most *useful* for our present [1046ᵃ] purpose. For potency and actuality extend beyond the cases that involve a reference to motion. But when we have spoken of this first kind, we shall in our discussions of actuality³ explain the others kinds of potency as well.

We have pointed out elsewhere⁴ that "potency" and the word "can" have several senses. Of these we may neglect all the potencies that are so called by an equivocation. For some are called so by analogy, as in geometry we say one thing is or is not a "power" of another by virtue of the presence or absence of some relation between them. But all potencies that conform to the same type are originative sources of some kind, and are called potencies in reference to [10] one primary kind of potency, which is an originative source of change in another thing or in the thing itself *qua* other. For one kind is a potency of being acted on, i.e. the originative source, in the very thing acted on, of its being passively changed by another thing or by itself *qua* other; and another kind is a state of insusceptibility to change for the worse and to destruction by another thing or by the thing itself *qua* other by virtue of an originative source of change. In all

---

⁷⁰ *Sc.* the formal cause. Cf. v. 1014ᵇ 36 in contrast with ib. 27.
¹ Cf. vii, viii.

² Cf. vii. 1.
³ Cf. ix. 1048ᵃ 27–ᵇ 6.
⁴ Cf. v. 12.

these definitions is implied the formula of potency in the primary sense.—And again these so-called potencies are potencies either of merely acting or being acted on, or of acting or being acted on *well*, so that even in the formulae of the latter the formulae of the prior kinds of potency are somehow implied.

Obviously, then, in a sense the potency of acting and of being acted on is one (for a thing may be "capable" [20] either because it can itself be acted on or because something else can be acted on by it), but in a sense the potencies are different. For the one is in the thing acted on; it is because it contains a certain originative source, and because even the matter is an originative source, that the thing acted on is acted on, and one thing by one, another by another; for that which is oily can be burnt, and that which yields in a particular way can be crushed;[5] and similarly in all other cases. But the other potency is in the agent, e.g. heat and the art of building are present, one in that which can produce heat and the other in the man who can build. And so, in so far as a thing is an organic unity, it cannot be acted on by itself; for it is one and not two different things. And "impotence" and "impotent" stand for the privation which is contrary to potency of this sort, so [30] that every potency belongs to the same subject and refers to the same process as a corresponding impotence. Privation has several senses; for it means (1) that which has not a certain quality and (2) that which might naturally have it but has not it, either (*a*) in general or (*b*) when it might naturally have it, and either (*α*) in some particular way, e.g. when it has not it completely, or (*β*) when it has not it at all. And in certain cases if things which naturally have a quality lose it by violence, we say they have suffered privation.

2. Since some such originative sources are present in soulless things, and others in things possessed of soul, and in soul, and in the rational part of the soul, clearly some potencies will be [1046ᵇ] non-rational and some will be accompanied by a rational formula. This is why all arts, i.e. all productive forms of knowledge, are potencies; they are originative sources of change in another thing or in the artist himself considered as other.

And each of those which are accompanied by a rational formula is alike capable of contrary effects, but one non-rational power produces one effect; e.g. the hot is capable only of heating, but the medical art can produce both disease and health. The reason is that science is a rational formula, and the same rational formula explains a thing and its privation, only not in the same way; and in a sense it applies to both, but in a sense it applies rather to the positive fact. [10] Therefore such sciences must deal with contraries, but with one in virtue of their own nature and with the other not in virtue of their nature; for the rational formula applies to one object in virtue of that object's nature, and to the other, in a sense, accidentally. For it is by denial and removal that it exhibits the contrary; for the contrary is the primary privation, and this is the removal of the positive term. Now since contraries do not occur in the same thing, but science is a potency which depends on the possession of a rational formula, and the soul possesses an originative source of movement; therefore, while the wholesome produces only health and the calorific only heat and the frigorific only cold, the scientific man produces [20] both the contrary effects. For the rational formula is one which applies to both, though not in the same way, and it is a soul which possesses an originative source

---

5 I.e. the event would not happen if the passive factor were different. What is oily cannot necessarily be crushed, nor what is yielding burnt.

of movement; so that the soul will start both processes from the same originative source, having linked them up with the same thing.[6] And so the things whose potency is according to a rational formula act contrariwise to the things whose potency is non-rational; for the products of the former are included under one originative source, the rational formula.

It is obvious also that the potency of merely doing a thing or having it done to one is implied in that of doing it or having it done *well*, but the latter is not always implied in the former; for he who does a thing well must also do it, but he who does it merely need not also do it well.

3. There are some who say, as the Megaric school does, that a thing "can" act only when it is acting, and when it is not acting it "cannot" act, e.g. that he who is not building cannot build, [30] but only he who is building, when he is building; and so in all other cases. It is not hard to see the absurdities that attend this view.

For it is clear that on this view a man will not be a builder unless he is building (for to be a builder is to be able to build), and so with the other arts. If, then, it is impossible to have such arts if one has not at some time learnt and acquired them, and it is then impossible not to have them if one has not sometime lost them (either by forget- [1047ᵃ] fulness or by some accident or by time; for it cannot be by the destruction of the *object*,[7] for that lasts for ever), a man will not have the art when he has ceased to use it, and yet he may immediately build again; how then will he have got the art? And similarly with regard to lifeless things; nothing will be either cold or hot or sweet or perceptible

at all if people are not perceiving it; so that the upholders of this view will have to maintain the doctrine of Protagoras.[8] But, indeed, nothing will even have perception if it is perceiving, i.e. exercising its perception. If, then, that is blind which has not sight though it would naturally have it, when it would naturally have it and when it still exists, the same people will be blind many times in the day—and deaf too.

Again, if that which is deprived [10] of potency is incapable, that which is not happening will be incapable of happening; but he who says of that which is incapable of happening either that it is or that it will be will say what is untrue; for this is what incapacity meant. Therefore these views do away with both movement and becoming. For that which stands will always stand, and that which sits will always sit, since if it is sitting it will not get up; for that which, as we are told, cannot get up will be incapable of getting up. But we cannot say this, so that evidently potency and actuality are different (but these views make potency and actuality the same, and so it is no small thing they are seeking to annihilate), so that it is possible that a thing may be capable [20] of being and not *be*, and capable of not being and yet *be*, and similarly with the other kinds of predicate; it may be capable of walking and yet not walk, or capable of not walking and yet walk. And a thing is capable of doing something if there will be nothing impossible in its having the actuality of that of which it is said to have the capacity. I mean, for instance, if a thing is capable of sitting and it is open to it to sit, there will be nothing impossible in its actually sitting; and similarly if it is capable of being moved or moving, or of standing or making to stand, or of being or coming to be, or of not being or not coming to be.

---

6 I.e. with the rational formula.

7 The object of knowledge is always a form, which is eternal. The matter which makes things perishable is no object for knowledge.

8 Cf. iv. 5, 6.

The word "actuality," which we [30] connect with "complete reality," has, in the main, been extended from movements to other things; for actuality in the strict sense is thought to be identical with movement. And so people do not assign movement to non-existent things, though they do assign some other predicates. E.g. they say that non-existent things are objects of thought and desire, but not that they are moved; and this because, while *ex hypothesi* they do not actually exist, they would have to exist actually if they were moved. For of non-existent things some exist potentially; but they do not *exist*, because [1047ᵇ] they do not exist in complete reality.

4. If what we have described[9] is identical with the capable or convertible with it, evidently it cannot be true to say "this is capable of being but will not be," which would imply that the things *in*capable of being would on this showing vanish. Suppose, for instance, that a man—one who did not take account of that which is incapable of being—were to say that the diagonal of the square is capable of being measured but will not be measured, because a thing may well be capable of being or coming to be, and yet not be or be about to be. But from the premises this necessarily follows, that if we actually supposed that which is not, but is capable of being, to be or to have come to be, there [10] will be nothing impossible in this; but the result *will* be impossible, for the measuring of the diagonal is impossible. For the false and the impossible are *not* the same; that you are standing now is false, but that you should be standing is not impossible.

At the same time it is clear that if, when $A$ is real, $B$ must be real, then, when $A$ is possible, $B$ also must be possible. For if $B$ need not be possible, there is nothing to prevent its not being possible. Now let $A$ be supposed possible.

Then, when $A$ was possible, we agreed that nothing impossible followed if $A$ were supposed to be real; and then $B$ must of course be real. But we supposed $B$ to be impossible. Let it be impos- [20] sible, then. If then, $B$ is impossible, $A$ also must be so. But the first *was* supposed impossible; therefore the second also is impossible. If, then, $A$ is possible, $B$ also will be possible, if they were so related that if $A$ is real, $B$ must be real. If, then, $A$ and $B$ being thus related,[10] $B$ is not possible on this condition,[11] $A$ and $B$ will not be related as was supposed.[12] And if when $A$ is possible, $B$ must be possible, then if $A$ is real, $B$ also must be real For to say that $B$ must be possible, if $A$ is possible, means this, that if $A$ is real both at the time when and in the way in which it was supposed capable of being real, $B$ also must then and in that way be real.          [30]

5. As all potencies are either innate, like the senses, or come by practice, like the power of playing the flute, or by learning, like artistic power, those which come by practice or by rational formula we must acquire by previous exercise but this is not necessary with those which are not of this nature and which imply passivity.

Since that which is "capable" is capable of something and at some time and in some way (with all the other qualifications which must be present [1048ª] in the definition), and since some things can produce change according to a rational formula and their potencies involve such a formula, while other things are non-rational and their potencies are non-rational, and the former potencies must be in a living thing, while the latter can be both in the living and in the lifeless; as regards potencies of the latter

---

9 Cf. 1047ª 24–26.

10 *Sc.* so related that if the reality of $A$ implies the reality of $B$ the possibility of $A$ implies the possibility of $B$.

11 *Sc.* if $A$ possible.

12 *Sc.* so related that the reality of $A$ implies the reality of $B$.

kind, when the agent and the patient meet in the way appropriate to the potency in question, the one must act and the other be acted on, but with the former kind of potency this is not necessary. For the non-rational potencies are all productive of one effect each, but the rational produce contrary effects, so that if they produced their effects necessarily they would produce contrary effects at the same time; but this is impossible. There must, then, be something else [10] that decides; I mean by this, desire or will. For whichever of two things the animal desires decisively, it will do, when it is present, and meets the passive object, in the way appropriate to the potency in question. Therefore everything which has a rational potency, when it desires that for which it has a potency and in the circumstances in which it has the potency, must do this. And it has the potency in question when the passive object is present and is in a certain state; if not it will not be able to act. (To add the qualification "if nothing external prevents it" is not further necessary; for it has the potency on the terms on which this is a potency of acting, and it is this not in all circumstances but on certain conditions, among which will be the exclusion of external hindrances; for these are [20] barred by some of the positive qualifications.) And so even if one has a rational wish, or an appetite, to do two things or contrary things at the same time, one will not do them; for it is not on these terms that one has the potency for them, nor is it a potency of doing both at the same time, since one will do the things which it is a potency of doing, on the terms on which one has the potency.

6. Since we have treated[13] of the kind of potency which is related to movement, let us discuss actuality—what, and what kind of thing, actuality is. For in the course of our analysis it will also become clear, with regard to the potential, that we not only ascribe potency to that whose nature it is to move something else, or to be moved by something else, either without qualification or in some particular way, but also use the word in another sense, which is the reason of the inquiry in the course of which we have discussed these previous senses also. Actuality, then, is the [30] existence of a thing not in the way which we express by "potentially"; we say that potentially, for instance, a statue of Hermes is in the block of wood and the half-line is in the whole, because it might be separated out, and we call even the man who is not studying a man of science, if he is capable of studying; the thing that stands in contrast to each of these exists actually. Our meaning can be seen in the particular cases by induction, and we must not seek a definition of everything but be content to grasp the analogy, that it is as that which is building is to that which is capable of building, and the waking to the sleeping, and that which is [1048ᵇ] seeing to that which has its eyes shut but has sight, and that which has been shaped out of the matter to the matter, and that which has been wrought up to the unwrought. Let actuality be defined by one member of this antithesis, and the potential by the other. But all things are not said in the *same sense* to exist actually, but only by analogy—as $A$ is in $B$ or to $B$, $C$ is in $D$ or to $D$; for some are as movement to potency, and the others as substance to some sort of matter.

But also the infinite and the void and all similar things are said to exist potentially and actually in a different sense from that which applies to many [10] other things, e.g. to that which sees or walks or is seen. For of the latter class these predicates can at some time be also truly asserted without qualification; for the seen is so called sometimes because it is being seen, sometimes because

---

13 Cf. ix. 1-5.

it is capable of being seen. But the infinite does not exist potentially in the sense that it will ever actually have separate existence; it exists potentially only for knowledge. For the fact that the process of dividing never comes to an end ensures that this activity exists potentially, but not that the infinite exists separately.

Since of the actions which have a limit none is an end but all are relative to the end, e.g. the removing of fat, or fat-removal, and the bodily parts themselves when one is making them [20] thin are in movement in this way (i.e. without being already that at which the movement aims), this is not an action or at least not a complete one (for it is not an end); but that movement in which the end is present is an action. E.g. at the same time we are seeing and have seen, are understanding and have understood, are thinking and have thought (while it is not true that at the same time we are learning and have learnt, or are being cured and have been cured). At the same time we are living well and have lived well, and are happy and have been happy. If not, the process would have had sometime to cease, as the process of making thin ceases: but, as things are, it does not cease; we are living and have lived. Of these processes, then, we must call the one set movements, and the other actualities. For every movement is incomplete—making thin, learning, walking, building; these are movements, and incomplete at that. For it is not true that at the [30] same time a thing is walking and has walked, or is building and has built, or is coming to be and has come to be, or is being moved and has been moved, but what is being moved is different from what has been moved, and what is moving from what has moved. But it is the same thing that at the same time has seen and is seeing, or is thinking and has thought. The latter sort of process, then, I call an actuality, and the former a movement.

7. What, and what kind of thing, the actual is, may be taken as explained by these and similar considerations. But we must distinguish when a thing exists potentially and when it does not; for it is not at any and every time. E.g. is earth potentially a man? No— [1049ᵃ] but rather when it has already become seed, and perhaps not even then. It is just as it is with being healed; not everything can be healed by the medical art or by luck, but there is a certain kind of thing which is capable of it, and only this is potentially healthy. And (1) the delimiting mark of that which as a result of *thought* comes to exist in complete reality from having existed potentially is that if the agent has willed it it comes to pass if nothing external hinders, while the condition on the other side—viz. in that which is healed—is that nothing in it hinders the result. It is on similar terms that we have what is potentially a house; if nothing in the thing acted on—i.e. in the matter—prevents it from becoming a house, and [10] if there is nothing which must be added or taken away or changed, this is potentially a house; and the same is true of all other things the source of whose becoming is external. And (2) in the cases in which the source of the becoming is in the very thing which comes to be, a thing is potentially all those things which it will be of itself if nothing external hinders it. E.g. the seed is not yet potentially a man; for it must be deposited in something other than itself and undergo a change. But when through its own motive principle it has already got such and such attributes, in this state it is already potentially a man; while in the former state it needs another motive principle, just as earth is not yet potentially a statue (for it must first change in order to become brass).

It seems that when we call a thing not something else but "thaten"—e.g. a casket is not "wood" but "wooden," and wood is not "earth" but "earthen," [20] and again earth will illustrate our point if it is similarly not something else but "thaten"—that other thing is always potentially (in the full sense of that word) the thing which comes after it in this series. E.g. a casket is not "earthen" nor "earth," but "wooden"; for this is potentially a casket and this is the matter of a casket, wood in general of a casket in general, and this particular wood of this particular casket. And if there is a first thing, which is no longer, in reference to something else, called "thaten," this is prime matter; e.g. if earth is "airy" and air is not "fire" but "fiery," fire is prime matter, which is not a "this." For the subject or substratum is differentiated by being a "this" or not being one; i.e. the substratum of *modifications* is, e.g., a man, i.e. a body and a soul, while the modification is "musical" or "pale." (The subject is called, when music comes [30] to be present in it, not "music" but "musical," and the man is not "paleness" but "pale," and not "ambulation" or "movement" but "walking" or "moving"—which is akin to the "thaten.") Wherever this is so, then, the ultimate subject is a substance; but when this is not so but the predicate is a *form* and a "this," the ultimate subject is matter and material substance. And it is only right that "thaten" should be used with reference both to the matter and to the accident; for both are indeterminates.                                    [1049ᵇ]

We have stated, then, when a thing is to be said to exist potentially and when it is not.

8. From our discussion of the various senses of "prior,"[14] it is clear that actuality is prior to potency. And I mean by potency not only that definite kind which is said to be a principle of change in another thing or in the thing itself regarded as other, but in general every principle of movement or of rest. For nature also is in the same genus as poten-

cy; for it is a principle of movement —not, however, in something else [10] but in the thing itself *qua* itself. To all such potency, then, actuality is prior both in formula and in substantiality; and in time it is prior in one sense, and in another not.

(1) Clearly it is prior in formula; for that which is in the primary sense potential is potential because it is possible for it to become active; e.g. I mean by "capable of building" that which can build, and by "capable of seeing" that which can see, and by "visible" that which can be seen. And the same account applies to all other cases, so that the formula and the knowledge of the one must precede the knowledge of the other.

(2) In time it is prior in this sense: the actual which is identical in species though not in number with a potentially existing thing is prior to it. I mean that to this particular man who now exists actually and to the corn and to the seeing subject the matter and the [20] seed and that which is capable of seeing, which are potentially a man and corn and seeing, but not yet actually so, are prior in time; but prior in time to these are other actually existing things, from which they were produced. For from the potentially existing the actually existing is always produced by an actually existing thing, e.g. man from man, musician by musician; there is always a first mover, and the mover already exists actually. We have said in our account of substance[15] that everything that is produced is something produced from something and by something, and that the same in species as it.

This is why it is thought impossible to be a builder if one has built nothing or a harper if one has never played the harp; for he who learns to play the [30] harp learns to play it by playing it, and all other learners do similarly. And thence arose the sophistical quibble, that

---

one who does not possess a science will be doing that which is the object of the science; for he who is learning it does not possess it. But since, of that which is coming to be, some part must have come to be, and, of that which, in general, is changing, some part must have changed (this is shown in the treatise on movement[16]), he who is learning must, it would seem, possess some [1050a] part of the science. But *here* too, then, it is clear that actuality is in this sense also, viz. in order of generation and of time, prior to potency.

But (3) it is also prior in substantiality; firstly, (*a*) because the things that are posterior in becoming are prior in form and in substantiality (e.g. man is prior to boy and human being to seed; for the one already has its form, and the other has not), and because everything that comes to be moves towards a principle, i.e. an end (for that for the sake of which a thing is, is its principle, and the becoming is for the sake of the end), and the actuality is the end, and it is for the sake of this that the potency is acquired. For [10] animals do not see in order that they may have sight, but they have sight that they may see. And similarly men have the art of building that they may build, and theoretical science that they may theorize; but they do not theorize that they may have theoretical science, except those who are learning by practice; and these do not theorize except in a limited sense, or because they have no need to theorize. Further, matter exists in a potential state, just because it may come to its form; and when it exists *actually*, then it is in its form. And the same holds good in all cases, even those in which the end is a movement. And so, as teachers think they have achieved their end when they have exhibited the pupil at work, nature does likewise. For if this is not the case, we shall have

Pauson's Hermes over again, since [20] it will be hard to say about the knowledge, as about the figure in the picture, whether it is within or without.[17] For the action is the end, and the actuality is the action. And so even the *word* "actuality" is derived from "action," and points to the complete reality.

And while in some cases the exercise is the ultimate thing (e.g. in sight the ultimate thing is seeing, and no other product besides this results from sight), but from some things a product follows (e.g. from the art of building there results a house as well as the act of building), yet none the less the act is in the former case the end and in the latter more of an end then the potency is. For the act of building is realized in the thing that is being built, and comes to be, and is, at the same time as the house.

Where, then, the result is some- [30] thing apart from the exercise, the actuality is in the thing that is being made, e.g. the act of building is in the thing that is being built and that of weaving in the thing that is being woven, and similarly in all other cases, and in general the movement is in the thing that is being moved; but where there is no product apart from the actuality, the actuality is present in the agents, e.g. the act of seeing is in the seeing subject and that of theorizing in the theorizing subject and the life is in the soul (and therefore well-being also; for it is a certain kind of life).          [1050b]

Obviously, therefore, the substance or form is actuality. According to this argument, then, it is obvious that actuality is prior in substantial being to potency; and as we have said,[18] one actuality always precedes another in time right back to the actuality of the eternal prime mover.

---

16 Cf. *Phys.* vi. 6.

17 The reference is apparently to a tricky painting in which the figure was painted so as to stand out in high relief.
18 1049b 17–29.

But (*b*) actuality is prior in a stricter sense also; for eternal things are prior in substance to perishable things, and no eternal thing exists potentially. The reason is this. Every potency is at one and the same time a potency of the opposite; for, while that which is not capable of being present in a subject cannot be present, everything that [10] is capable of being may possibly not be actual. That, then, which is capable of being may either be or not be; the same thing, then, is capable both of being and of not being. And that which is capable of not being may possibly not be; and that which may possibly not be is perishable, either in the full sense, or in the precise sense in which it is said that it possibly may not be, i.e. in respect either of place or of quantity or quality; "in the full sense" means "in respect of substance." Nothing, then, which is in the full sense imperishable is in the full sense potentially existent (though there is nothing to prevent its being so in some respect, e.g. potentially of a certain quality or in a certain place); all imperishable things, then, exist actually. Nor can anything which is of *necessity* exist potentially; yet these things are primary; for if these did not exist, nothing would exist. Nor does eternal movement, if there be such, exist [20] potentially; and, if there is an eternal *mobile*, it is not in motion in virtue of a potentiality, except in respect of "whence" and "whither" (there is nothing to prevent its having matter which makes it capable of movement in various directions). And so the sun and the stars and the whole heaven are ever active, and there is no fear that they may sometime stand still, as the natural philosophers fear they may.[19] Nor do they tire in this activity; for movement is not for them, as it is for perishable things, connected with the potentiality

for opposites, so that the continuity of the movement should be laborious; for it is that kind of substance which is matter and potency, not actuality, that causes this.

Imperishable things[20] are imitated by those that are involved in change, e.g. earth and fire. For these also are ever active; for they have their movement of themselves and in themselves.[21] But [30] the other potencies, according to our previous discussion,[22] are all potencies for opposites; for that which can move another in this way can also move it not in this way, i.e. if it acts according to a rational formula; and the same *non-rational* potencies will produce opposite results by their presence or absence.

If, then, there are any entities or substances such as the dialecticians[23] say the Ideas are, there must be something much more scientific than science-itself and something more mobile than movement-itself; for these will be more of the nature of actualities, while [1051ᵃ] science-itself and movement-itself are potencies for these.[24]

Obviously, then, actuality is prior both to potency and to every principle of change.

9. That the actuality is also better and more valuable than the good potency is evident from the following argument. Everything of which we say that it can do something, is alike capable of contraries, e.g. that of which we say that it can be well is the same as that which can be ill, and has both potencies at once; for the same potency is a potency of health and illness, of rest and motion,

---

19 E.g. Empedocles (cf. *De Caelo*, 284ᵃ 24-6).

20 *Sc.* the heavenly bodies.
21 I.e. they are both movers and moved.
22 Cf. ᵇ 8-12.
23 The Platonists are meant; cf. i. 987ᵇ 31.
24 The Idea, being the universal apart from its special manifestations, will be a potentiality, and will therefore be inferior to the corresponding particulars—e.g. the Idea of science will be inferior to particular acts of scientific thought.

of building and throwing down, of being built and being thrown down. The capacity for contraries, then, is present at the same time; but contraries can- [10] not be present at the same time, and the actualities also cannot be present at the same time, e.g. health and illness. Therefore, while the good must be one of them, the capacity is both alike, or neither; the actuality, then, is better. Also in the case of bad things the end or actuality must be worse than the potency; for that which "can" is both contraries alike. Clearly, then, the bad does not exist apart from bad things; for the bad is in its nature posterior to the potency.[25] And therefore we may also say that in the things which are from the beginning, i.e. in eternal things, there is nothing bad, nothing defec- [20] tive, nothing perverted (for perversion is something bad).[26]

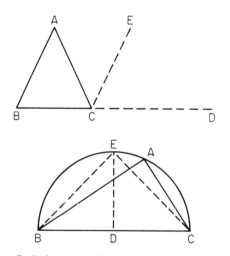

It is by an activity also that geometrical constructions are discovered; for we find them by dividing. If the figures had been already divided, the constructions would have been obvious; but as it is they are present only potentially. Why are the angles of the triangle equal to two right angles? Because the angles about one point are equal to two right angles. If, then, the line parallel to the side had been already drawn upwards, the reason would have been evident to any one as soon as he saw the figure. Why is the angle in a semicircle in all cases a right angle? If three lines are equal—the two which form the base, and the perpendicular from the centre— the conclusion is evident at a glance to one who knows the former proposition. Obviously, therefore, the potentially existing constructions are discovered [30] by being brought to actuality; the reason is that the geometer's thinking is an actuality; so that the potency proceeds from an actuality; and therefore it is by making constructions that people come to know them (though the single actuality is later in generation than the corresponding potency).

10. The terms "being" and "non-being" are employed firstly with reference to the categories, and secondly with reference to the potency or actuality of these or their non-potency or non-actuality, and thirdly in the sense [1051ᵇ] of true and false. This depends, on the side of the objects, on their being combined or separated, so that he who thinks the separated to be separated and the combined to be combined has the truth, while he whose thought is in a state contrary to that of the objects is in error. This being so, when is what is called truth or falsity present, and when is it not? We must consider what we mean by these terms. It is not because we think truly that you are pale, that you *are* pale, but because you are pale we who say this have the truth. If, then, some things are always combined and cannot be separated, and others are always separated and cannot be com- [10] bined, while others are capable either of combination or of separation, "being"

²⁵ *Sc.* while the eternal and substantial must be better than the potency.

²⁶ The paragraph seems to be directed against Plato: cf. *Rep.* 402 C, 476 A, *Theaet.* 176 E, *Laws* 896 E, 898 C.

is being combined and one, and "not being" is being not combined but more than one. Regarding contingent facts, then, the same opinion or the same statement comes to be false and true, and it is possible for it to be at one time correct and at another erroneous; but regarding things that cannot be otherwise opinions are not at one time true and at another false, but the same opinions are always true or always false.

But with regard to *incomposites*, what is being or not being, and truth or falsity? A thing of this sort is not composite, so as to "be" when it is compounded, and not to "be" if it is separated, like "that the wood is [20] white" or "that the diagonal is incommensurable"; nor will truth and falsity be still present in the same way as in the previous cases. In fact, as truth is not the same in these cases, so also being is not the same; but (*a*) truth or falsity is as follows—contact and assertion are truth (assertion not being the same as affirmation), and ignorance is non-contact. For it is not possible to be in *error* regarding the question what a thing is, save in an accidental sense; and the same holds good regarding non-composite substances (for it is not possible to be in error about them). And they all exist actually, not potentially; for otherwise they would have come to be and ceased to be; but, as it is, being itself does not come to be (nor cease to be); for if it had done so it would [30] have had to come out of something. About the things, then, which are essences and actualities, it is not possible to be in error, but only to know them or not to know them. But we do inquire what they are, viz. whether they are of such and such a nature or not.

(*b*) As regards the *"being"* that answers to truth and the "non-being" that answers to falsity, in one case there is truth if the subject and the attribute are really combined, and falsity if they are not combined; in the other case, if the object is existent it exists in a particular way, and if it does not exist in [1052<sup>a</sup>] this way it does not exist at all.<sup>27</sup> And truth means knowing these objects, and falsity does not exist, nor error, but only ignorance—and not an ignorance which is like blindness; for blindness is akin to a total absence of the faculty of thinking.

It is evident also that about unchangeable things there can be no error in respect of time, if we assume them to be unchangeable. E.g. if we suppose that the triangle does not change, we shall not suppose that at one time its angles are equal to two right angles while at another time they are not (for that would imply change). It is possible, however, to suppose that one member of such a class has a certain attribute and another has not; e.g. while we *may* suppose that no even number is prime, we *may* suppose that some are and some are not. But regarding a numerically single number not even this form of error is possible; for we cannot in this case [10] suppose that one instance has an attribute and another has not, but whether our judgement be true or false, it is implied that the fact is eternal.

## Book Λ (XII)

1. The subject of our injury is substance; for the principles and the [1069<sup>a</sup>] causes we are seeking are those of substances. For if the universe is of the nature of a whole, substance is its first part; and if it coheres merely by [20] virtue of serial succession, on this view also substance is first, and is succeeded by quality, and then by quantity. At the same time these latter are not even being in the full sense, but are qualities and movements of it—or else even the not-white and the not-straight would be being; at least we say even these *are*, e.g.

---

27 I.e. we have not here *A* and *B*, which may or may not be combined, but *A*, which if it exists at all exists as *A*.

"there is not white."[1] Further, none of the categories other than substance can exist apart. And the early philosophers also in practice testify to the primacy of substance; for it was of substance that they sought the principles and elements and causes. The thinkers of the present[2] day tend to rank universals as substances (for genera are universals, and these they tend to describe as principles and substances, owing to the abstract nature of their inquiry); but the thinkers of old ranked particular things as substances, e.g. fire and earth, not what is common to both, body.

There are three kinds of substance— one that is sensible (of which [30] one subdivision is eternal and another is perishable; the latter is recognized by all men, and includes e.g. plants and animals), of which we must grasp the elements, whether one or many; and another that is immovable, and this certain thinkers assert to be capable of existing apart, some dividing it into two, others identifying the Forms and the objects of mathematics, and others positing, of these two, only the objects of mathematics.[3] The former two kinds of substance are the subject of physics (for they imply movement); but the [1069ᵇ] third kind belongs to another science, if there is no principle common to it and to the other kinds.

2. Sensible substance is changeable. Now if change proceeds from opposites or from intermediates, and not from all opposites (for the voice is not-white [but it does not therefore change to white]), but from the contrary, there must be something underlying which changes into the contrary state; for the *contraries*

do not change. Further, something persists, but the contrary does not persist; there is, then, some third thing besides the contraries, viz. the matter. Now since changes are of four kinds—either in respect of the "what" or of the quality or of the quantity or of the place, and change in respect of "thisness" is [10] simple generation and destruction, and change in quantity is increase and diminution, and change in respect of an affection is alteration, and change of place is motion, changes will be from given states into those contrary to them in these several respects. The matter, then, which changes must be capable of both states. And since that which "is" has two senses, we must say that everything changes from that which is potentially to that which is actually, e.g. from potentially white to actually white, and similarly in the case of increase and diminution. Therefore not only can a thing come to be, incidentally, out of that which is not, but also all things come to be out of that which is, but is potentially, and is not actually. And this is the "One" of Anaxagoras; for [20] instead of "all things were together"— and the "Mixture" of Empedocles and Anaximander and the account given by Democritus—it is better to say "all things were together potentially but not actually." Therefore these thinkers seem to have had some notion of matter. Now all things that change have matter, but different matter; and of eternal things those which are not generable but are movable in space have matter—not matter for generation, however, but for motion from one place to another.

One might raise the question from what sort of non-being generation proceeds; for "non-being" has three senses. If, then, one form of non-being exists potentially, still it is not by virtue of a potentiality for any and every thing, but different things come from different things; nor is it satisfactory to say that "all things were together"; for they [30]

---

[1] This is an implication of the ordinary type of judgement, "*x* is not white."

[2] The Platonists.

[3] The three views appear to have been held respectively by Plato, Xenocrates, and Speusippus.

differ in their matter, since otherwise why did an infinity of things come to be, and not one thing? For "reason" is one, so that if matter also were one, that must have come to be in actuality which the matter was in potency.[4] The causes and the principles, then, are three, two being the pair of contraries of which one is definition and form and the other is privation, and the third being the matter.

3. Note, next, that neither the matter nor the form comes to be—and I mean the last matter and form. For everything that changes is something and is changed by something and into something. That by which it is [1070a] changed is the immediate mover; that which is changed, the matter; that into which it is changed, the form. The process, then, will go on to infinity, if not only the bronze comes to be round but also the round or the bronze comes to be; therefore there must be a stop.

Note, next, that each substance comes into being out of something that shares its name. (Natural objects and other things both rank as substances). For things come into being either by art or by nature or by luck or by spontaneity. Now art is a principle of movement in something other than the thing moved, nature is a principle in the thing itself (for man begets man), and the other causes are privations of these two.

There are three kinds of substance— the matter, which is a "this" in appearance (for all things that are [10] characterized by contact and not by organic unity are matter and substratum, e.g. fire, flesh, head; for these are all matter, and the last matter is the matter of that which is in the full sense substance); the nature, which is a "this" or positive state towards which movement takes place; and again, thirdly, the particular substance which

is composed of these two, e.g. Socrates or Callias. Now in some cases the "this" does not exist apart from the composite substance, e.g. the form of house does not so exist, unless the art of building exists apart (nor is there generation and destruction of these forms, but it is in another way that the house apart from its matter, and health, and all ideals of art, exist and do not exist); but if the "this" exists apart from the concrete thing, it is only in the case of natural objects. And so Plato was not far wrong when he said that there are as many Forms as there are kinds of natural object (if there *are* Forms distinct from [20] the things of this earth). The moving causes exist as things preceding the effects, but causes in the sense of definitions are simultaneous with their effects. For when a man is healthy, then health also exists; and the shape of a bronze sphere exists at the same time as the bronze sphere. (But we must examine whether any form also survives afterwards. For in some cases there is nothing to prevent this; e.g. the soul may be of this sort—not all soul but the reason; for presumably it is impossible that *all* soul should survive.) Evidently then there is no necessity, on this ground at least, for the existence of the Ideas. For man is begotten by man, a given man by an individual father; and similarly in the arts; for the medical art is the formal cause of health.                    [30]

4. The causes and the principles of different things are in a sense different, but in a sense, if one speaks universally and analogically, they are the same for all. For one might raise the question whether the principles and elements are different or the same for substances and for relative terms, and similarly in the case of each of the categories. But it would be paradoxical if they were the same for all. For then from the same elements will proceed relative terms and substances. What then will this common

---

[4] *Sc.* an undifferentiated unity.

element be? For (1) (*a*) there [1070ᵇ] is nothing common to and distinct from substance and the other categories, viz. those which are predicated; but an element is prior to the things of which it is an element. But again (*b*) substance is not an element in relative terms, nor is any of these an element in substance. Further, (2) how can all things have the same elements? For none of the elements can be the same as that which is composed of elements, e.g. *b* or *a* cannot be the same as *ba*. (None, therefore, of the intelligibles, e.g. being or unity, is an element; for these are predicable of each of the compounds as well.) None of the elements, then, will be either a substance or a relative term; but it must be one or other. All things, then, have not the same elements.

Or, as we are wont to put it, in a [10] sense they have and in a sense they have not; e.g. perhaps the elements of perceptible bodies are, as *form*, the hot, and in another sense the cold, which is the *privation*; and, as *matter*, that which directly and of itself potentially has these attributes; and substances comprise both these and the things composed of these, of which these are the principles, or any unity which is produced out of the hot and the cold, e.g. flesh or bone; for the product must be different from the elements. These things then have the same elements and principles (though specifically different things have specifically different elements); but *all* things have not the same elements in this sense, but only analogically; i.e. one might say that there are three principles —the form, the privation, and the matter. But each of these is different for each class; e.g. in colour they are [20] white, black, and surface, and in day and night they are light, darkness, and air.

Since not only the elements present in a thing are causes, but also something external, i.e. the moving cause, clearly while "principle" and "element" are different both are causes, and "principle"

is divided into these two kinds⁵ and that which acts as producing movement or rest is a principle and a substance. Therefore analogically there are three elements, and four causes and principles; but the elements are different in different things, and the proximate moving cause is different for different things. Health, disease, body; the moving cause is the medical art. Form, disorder of a particular kind, bricks; the moving cause is the building art. And since the [30] moving cause in the case of natural things is—for man, for instance, man, and in the products of thought the form or its contrary, there will be in a sense three causes, while in a sense there are four. For the medical art is in some sense health, and the building art is the form of the house, and man begets man;⁶ further, besides these there is that which as first of all things moves all things.

5. Some things can exist apart and some cannot, and it is the former that are substances. And therefore all [1071ᵃ] things have the same causes,⁷ because, without substances, modifications and movements do not exist. Further, these causes will probably be soul and body, or reason and desire and body.

And in yet another way, analogically identical things are principles, i.e. actuality and potency; but these also are not only different for different things but also apply in different ways to them. For in some cases the same thing exists at one time actually and at another potentially, e.g. wine or flesh or man does so. (And these two fall under the above-named causes.⁸ For the form exists

---

⁵ I.e. the principles which are elements and those which are not.
⁶ I.e. the efficient cause is identical with the formal.
⁷ I.e. the causes of substance are the causes of all things.
⁸ I.e. the division into potency and actuality stands in a definite relation to the previous division into matter, form, and privation.

actually, if it can exist apart, and so does the complex of form and matter, and the privation, e.g. darkness or disease; but the matter exists potential- [10] ly; for this is that which can become qualified either by the form or by the privation.) But the distinction of actuality and potentiality applies in another way to cases where the matter of cause and of effect is not the same, in some of which cases the form is not the same but different; e.g. the cause of man is (1) the elements in man (viz. fire and earth as matter, and the peculiar form), and further (2) something else outside, i.e. the father, and (3) besides these the sun and its oblique course, which are neither matter nor form nor privation of man nor of the same species with him, but moving causes.

Further, one must observe that some causes can be expressed in universal terms, and some cannot. The proximate principles of all things are the "this" which is proximate in actuality, and another which is proximate in potentiality.⁹ The universal causes, then, of which we spoke¹⁰ do not *exist*. For it is the [20] individual that is the originative principle of the individuals. For while man is the originative principle of man universally, there *is* no universal man, but Peleus is the originative principle of Achilles, and your father of you, and this particular *b* of this particular *ba*, though *b* in general is the originative principle of *ba* taken without qualification.

Further, if the causes of substances are the causes of all things, yet different things have different causes and elements, as was said;¹¹ the causes of things that are not in the same class, e.g. of colours and sounds, of substances and quantities, are different except in an analogical sense; and those of things in the same species are different, not in species, but in the sense that the causes of different individuals are different, your matter and form and moving cause being different from mine, while in their universal definition they are the same. And if we inquire what are the principles or elements of substances and rela- [30] tions and qualities—whether they are the same or different—clearly when the names of the causes are used in several senses the causes of each are the same, but when the senses are distinguished the causes are not the same but different, except that in the following senses the causes of all are the same. They are (1) the same or analogous in this sense, that matter, form, privation, and the moving cause are common to all things; and (2) the causes of substances may be treated as causes of all things in this sense, that when substances are removed all things are removed; further, (3) that which is first in respect of complete reality is the cause of all things. But in another sense there are different first causes, viz. all the contraries which are neither generic nor ambiguous terms; and, further, the matters of different things are different. We have stated, then, what are [1071ᵇ] the principles of sensible things and how many they are, and in what sense they are the same and in what sense different.

6. Since there were¹² three kinds of substance, two of them physical and one unmovable, regarding the latter we must assert that it is necessary that there should be an eternal unmovable substance. For substances are the first of existing things, and if they are all destructible, all things are destructible. But it is impossible that movement should either have come into being or cease to be (for it must always have existed), or that time should. For there could not

---

⁹ E.g. the proximate causes of a child are the individual father (who on Aristotle's view is the efficient and contains the formal cause) and the germ contained in the individual mother (which is the material cause).
¹⁰ In l. 17.
¹¹ In 1070ᵇ 17.

¹² Cf. 1069ª 30.

be a before and an after if time did not exist. Movement also is continuous, then, in the sense in which time is; for time is either the same thing as movement or an attribute of movement. And there [10] is no continuous movement except movement in place, and of this only that which is circular is continuous.

But if there is something which is capable of moving things or acting on them, but is not actually doing so, there will not necessarily be movement; for that which has a potency need not exercise it. Nothing, then, is gained even if we suppose eternal substances, as the believers in the Forms do, unless there is to be in them some principle which can cause change; nay, even this is not enough, nor is another substance besides the Forms enough; for if it is not to *act*, there will be no movement. Further, even if it acts, this will not be enough, if its essence is potency; for there will not be *eternal* movement, since that which is 'potentially may possibly not be. There must, then, be such a princi- [20] ple, whose very essence is actuality. Further, then, these substances must be without matter; for they must be eternal, if *anything* is eternal. Therefore they must be actuality.

Yet there is a difficulty; for it is thought that everything that acts is able to act, but that not everything that is able to act acts, so that the potency is prior. But if this is so, nothing that is need be; for it is possible for all things to be capable of existing but not yet to exist.

Yet if we follow the theologians who generate the world from night, or the natural philosophers who say that "all things were together,"[13] the same impossible result ensues. For how will there be movement, if there is no actually existing cause? Wood will surely not move itself—the carpenter's art must act [30] on it; nor will the menstrual blood nor

the earth set themselves in motion, but the seeds must act on the earth and the *semen* on the menstrual blood.

This is why some suppose eternal actuality—e.g. Leucippus[14] and Plato;[15] for they say there is always movement. But why and what this movement is they do not say, nor, if the world moves in this way or that, do they tell us the cause of its doing so. Now nothing is moved at random, but there must always be something present to move it; e.g. as a matter of fact a thing moves in one way by nature, and in another by force or through the influence of reason or something else. (Further, what sort of movement is primary? This makes a vast difference.) But again for Plato, at least, it is not permissible to name here that which he sometimes supposes to [1072ᵃ] be the source of movement—that which moves itself;[16] for the soul is later, and coeval with the heavens, according to his account.[17] To suppose potency prior to actuality, then, is in a sense right, and in a sense not; and we have specified these senses.[18] That actuality is prior is testified by Anaxagoras (for his "reason" is actuality) and by Empedocles in his doctrine of love and strife, and by those who say that there is always movement, e.g. Leucippus. Therefore chaos or night did not exist for an infinite time, but the same things have always existed (either passing through a cycle of changes or obeying some other law), since actuality is prior to potency. If, then, there is a constant cycle, something must always remain,[19] acting in the same way. [10] And if there is to be generation and destruction, there must be something else[20] which is always acting in different

---

13 Anaxagoras.

14 Cf. *De Caelo*, iii. 300ᵇ 8.
15 Cf. *Timaeus*, 30 A.
16 Cf. *Phaedrus*, 245 c; Laws, 894 E.
17 Cf. *Timaeus*, 34 B.
18 Cf. 1071ᵇ 22–26.
19 I.e. the sphere of the fixed stars.
20 I.e. the sun. *Cf. De Gen. et Corr.* ii. 336ᵃ 23 ff.

ways. This must, then, act in one way in virtue of itself, and in another in virtue of something else—either of a third agent, therefore, or of the first. Now it must be in virtue of the first. For otherwise this again causes the motion both of the second agent and of the third. Therefore it is better to say "the first." For it was the cause of eternal uniformity; and something else is the cause of variety, and evidently both together are the cause of eternal variety. This, accordingly, is the character which the motions actually exhibit. What need then is there to seek for other principles?

7. Since (1) this is a possible account of the matter, and (2) if it were not true, the world would have proceeded out of night and "all things together" and out of non-being, these difficul- [20] ties may be taken as solved. There is, then, something which is always moved with an unceasing motion, which is motion in a circle; and this is plain not in theory only but in fact. Therefore the first heaven[21] must be eternal. There is therefore also something which moves it. And since that which is moved and moves is intermediate, there is something which moves without being moved, being eternal, substance, and actuality. And the object of desire and the object of thought move in this way; they move without being moved. The primary objects of desire and of thought are the same. For the apparent good is the object of appetite, and the real good is the primary object of rational wish. But desire is consequent on opinion rather than opinion on desire; for the thinking is the [30] starting-point. And thought is moved by the object of thought, and one of the two columns of opposites is in itself the object of thought; and in this, substance is first, and in substance, that which is simple and exists actually. (The one and

the simple are not the same; for "one" means a measure, but "simple" means that the thing itself has a certain nature.) But the beautiful, also, and that which is in itself desirable are in the same column; and the first in any class is always best, or analogous to the best.

That a final cause may exist [1072ᵇ] among unchangeable entities is shown by the distinction of its meanings. For the final cause is (a) some being for whose good an action is done, and (b) something at which the action aims; and of these the latter exists among unchangeable entities though the former does not. The final cause, then, produces motion as being loved, but all other things move by being moved.

Now if something is moved it is capable of being otherwise than as it is. Therefore if its actuality is the primary form of spatial motion, then in so far as it is subject to change, in *this* respect it is capable of being otherwise—in place, even if not in substance. But since there is something which moves while itself unmoved, existing actually, this can in no way be otherwise than as it is. For motion in space is the first of the kinds of change, and motion in a circle the first kind of spatial motion; and this [10] the first mover *produces*.[22] The first mover, then, exists of necessity; and in so far as it exists by necessity, its mode of being is good, and it is in this sense a first principle. For the necessary has all these senses—that which is necessary perforce because it is contrary to the natural impulse, that without which the good is impossible, and that which cannot be otherwise but can exist only in a single way.

On such a principle, then, depend the heavens and the world of nature. And

---

21 I.e. the outer sphere of the universe, that in which the fixed stars are set.

22 If it had any movement, it would have the first. But it produces this and therefore cannot share in it; for if it did, we should have to look for something that is prior to the first mover and imparts this motion to it.

it is a life such as the best which we enjoy, and enjoy for but a short time (for it is ever in this state, which we cannot be), since its actuality is also pleasure. (And for this reason[23] are waking, perception, and thinking most pleasant, and hopes and memories are so on account of these.) And thinking in itself deals with that which is best in itself, and that which is thinking in the fullest sense with that which is best in the fullest sense. And thought thinks on itself [20] because it shares the nature of the object of thought; for it becomes an object of thought in coming into contact with and thinking its objects, so that thought and object of thought the same. For that which is *capable* of receiving the object of thought, i.e. the essence, is thought. But it is *active* when it *possesses* this object. Therefore the possession rather than the receptivity is the divine element which thought seems to contain, and the act of contemplation is what is most pleasant and best. If, then, God is always in that good state in which we sometimes are, this compels our wonder; and if in a better this compels it yet more. And God *is* in a better state. And life also belongs to God; for the actuality of thought is life, and God is that actuality; and God's self-dependent actuality is life most good and eternal. We say therefore that God is a living being, eternal, most good, so that life and duration continuous and eternal belong to God; for this *is* God.

Those whose suppose, as the Pythagoreans[24] and Speusippus[25] do, that [30] supreme beauty and goodness are not present in the beginning, because the beginnings both of plants and of animals are *causes*, but beauty and completeness

are in the *effects* of these,[26] are wrong in their opinion. For the seed comes from other individuals which are prior and complete, and the first thing is not seed but the complete being; e.g. we must say that before the seed there is a [1073ᵃ] man—not the man produced from the seed, but another from whom the seed comes.

It is clear then from what has been said that there is a substance which is eternal and unmovable and separate from sensible things. It has been shown also that this substance cannot have any magnitude, but is without parts and indivisible (for it produces movement through infinite time, but nothing finite has infinite power; and, while every magnitude is either infinite or finite, it cannot, for the above reason, have finite magnitude, and it cannot have in- [10] finite magnitude because there is no infinite magnitude at all). But it has also been shown that it is impassive and unalterable; for all the other changes are posterior to[27] change of place.

8. It is clear, then, why these things are as they are. But we must not ignore the question whether we have to suppose one such substance or more than one, and if the latter, how many; we must also mention, regarding the opinions expressed by others, that they have said nothing about the number of the substances that can even be clearly stated. For the theory of Ideas has no special discussion of the subject; for those who speak of Ideas say the Ideas are numbers, and they speak of numbers now as unlimited, now[28] as limited by the number 10; but as for the reason why there should be just so many [20]

---

23 *Sc.* because they are activities or actualities.

24 Cf. 1075ᵃ 36.

25 Cf. vii. 1028ᵇ 21, xiv. 1091ᵃ 34, 1092ᵃ 11.

26 I.e. the animal or plant is more beautiful and perfect than the seed.

27 I.e. impossible without.

28 The reference is to Plato (cf. *Phys.* 206ᵇ 32).

numbers, nothing is said with any demonstrative exactness. We however must discuss the subject, starting from the presuppositions and distinctions we have mentioned. The first principle or primary being is not movable either in itself or accidentally, but produces the primary eternal and single movement. But since that which is moved must be moved by something, and the first mover must be in itself unmovable, and eternal movement must be produced by something eternal and a single movement by a single thing, and since we see that besides the simple spatial movement of the universe, which we say the first and [30] unmovable substance produces, there are other spatial movements—those of the planets—which are eternal (for a body which moves in a circle is eternal and unresting; we have proved these points in the physical treaties²⁹), each of *these* movements also must be caused by a substance both unmovable in itself and eternal. For the nature of the stars³⁰ is eternal just because it is a certain kind of substance, and the mover is eternal and prior to the moved, and that which is prior to a substance must be a substance. Evidently, then, there must be substances which are of the same number as the movements of the stars, and in their nature eternal, and in themselves unmovable, and without magnitude, for the reason before mentioned.³¹

That the movers are sub- [1073ᵇ] stances, then, and that one of these is first and another second according to the same order as the movements of the stars, is evident. But in the number of the movements we reach a problem which must be treated from the standpoint of that one of the mathematical

sciences which is most akin to philosophy—viz. of astronomy; for this science speculates about substance which is perceptible but eternal, but the other mathematical sciences, i.e. arithmetic and geometry, treat of no substance. That the movements are more numerous than the bodies that are moved is evident to those who have given moderate attention to the matter; for each of the [10] planets has more than one movement. But as to the actual number of these movements, we now—to give some notion of the subject—quote what some of the mathematicians say, that our thought may have some definite number to grasp; but, for the rest, we must partly investigate for ourselves, partly learn from other investigators, and if those who study this subject form an opinion contrary to what we have now stated, we must esteem both parties indeed, but follow the more accurate.

Eudoxus supposed that the motion of the sun or of the moon involves, in either case, three spheres, of which the first is the phere of the fixed stars, and the second moves in the circle which runs along the middle of the zodiac, [20] and the third in the circle which is inclined across the breadth of the zodiac; but the circle in which the moon moves is inclined at a greater angle than that in which the sun moves. And the motion of the planets involves, in each case, four spheres, and of these also the first and second are the same as the first two mentioned above (for the sphere of the fixed stars is that which moves all the other spheres, and that which is placed beneath this and has its movement in the circle which bisects the zodiac is common to all), but the *poles* of the third sphere of each planet are in the circle which bisects the zodiac, and the motion of the fourth sphere is in the circle which is inclined at an angle to the equator of the third sphere; and the poles of the third sphere are different

---

²⁹ Cf. Phys. viii. 8, 9; *De Caelo*, i. 2, ii. 3–8.

³⁰ This is to be understood as a general term including both fixed stars and planets.

³¹ Cf. ll. 5–11.

for each of the other planets, but [30] those of Venus and Mercury are the same.

Callippus made the position of the spheres the same as Eudoxus did, but while he assigned the same number as Eudoxus did to Jupiter and to Saturn, he thought two more spheres should be added to the sun and two to the moon, if one is to explain the observed facts; and one more to each of the other planets.

But it is necessary, if all the spheres combined are to explain the observed facts, that for each of the planets [1074a] there should be other spheres (one fewer than those hitherto assigned) which counteract those already mentioned and bring back to the same position the outermost sphere of the star which in each case is situated below[32] the star in question; for only thus can all the forces at work produce the observed motion of the planets. Since, then, the spheres involved in the movement of the planets themselves are—eight for Saturn and Jupiter and twenty-five for the others, and of these only those involved in the movement of the lowest-situated planet need not be counteracted, the spheres which counteract those of the outermost two planets will be six in number, and the spheres which counteract those of the next four planets will be sixteen; therefore the number of all the [10] spheres—both those which move the planets and those which counteract these—will be fifty-five. And if one were not to add to the moon and to the sun the movements we mentioned,[33] the whole set of spheres will be forty-seven in number.

Let this, then, be taken as the number of the spheres, so that the unmovable substances and principles also may

probably be taken as just so many; the assertion of *necessity* must be left to more powerful thinkers. But if there can be no spatial movement which does not conduce to the moving of a star, and if further every being and every substance which is immune from change and in virtue of itself has attained to the best must be considered an end, there can be no other being apart from these we have named, but this must be [20] the number of the substances. For if there are others, they will cause change as being a final cause of movement; but there cannot *be* other movements besides those mentioned. And it is reasonable to infer this from a consideration of the bodies that are moved; for if everything that moves is for the sake of that which is moved, and every movement belongs to something that is moved, no movement can be for the sake of itself or of another movement, but all the movements must be for the sake of the stars. For if there is to be a movement for the sake of a movement, this latter also will have to be for the sake of something else; so that since [30] there cannot be an infinite regress, the end of every movement will be one of the divine bodies which move through the heaven.

(Evidently there is but one heaven. For if there are many heavens as there are many men, the moving principles, of which each heaven will have one, will be one in form but in *number* many. But all things that are many in number have matter; for one and the same definition, e.g. that of man, applies to many things, while Socrates is one. But the primary essence has not matter; for it is complete reality. So the unmovable first mover is one both in definition and in number; so too, therefore, is that which is moved always and continuously; therefore there is one heaven alone.)

Our forefathers in the most re- [1074b] mote ages have handed down to their posterity a tradition, in the form of a

---

[32] I.e. inwards from, the universe being thought of as a system of concentric spheres encircling the earth.

[33] In 1073b 35, 38–1074a 4.

myth, that these bodies are gods and that the divine encloses the whole of nature. The rest of the tradition has been added later in mythical form with a view to the persuasion of the multitude and to its legal and utilitarian expediency; they say these gods are in the form of men or like some of the other animals, and they say other things consequent on and similar to these which we have mentioned. But if one were to separate the first point from these additions and take it alone—that they thought the first substances to be [10] gods, one must regard this as an inspired utterance, and reflect that, while probably each art and each science has often been developed as far as possible and has again perished, these opinions, with others, have been preserved until the present like relics of the ancient treasure. Only thus far, then, is the opinion of our ancestors and of our earliest predecessors clear to us.

9. The nature of the divine thought involves certain problems; for while thought is held to be the most divine of things observed by us, the question how it must be situated in order to have that character involves difficulties. For if it thinks of nothing, what is there here of dignity? It is just like one who sleeps. And if it thinks, but this depends on something else, then (since that which is its substance is not the act of thinking, but a potency) it cannot be the best substance; for it is through [20] thinking that its value belongs to it. Further, whether its substance is the faculty of thought or the act of thinking, what does it think of? Either of itself or of something else; and if of something else, either of the same thing always or of something different. Does it matter, then, or not, whether it thinks of the good or of any chance thing? Are there not some things about which it is incredible that it should think? Evidently, then, it thinks of that which is most

divine and precious, and it does not change; for change would be change for the worse, and this would be already a movement. First, then, if "thought" is not the act of thinking but a potency, it would be reasonable to suppose that the continuity of its thinking, is wearisome to it. Secondly, there would evidently be something else more precious than thought, viz. that which is thought of. For both thinking and the act of [30] thought will belong even to one who thinks of the worst thing in the world, so that if this ought to be avoided (and it ought, for there are even some things which it is better not to see than to see), the act of thinking cannot be the best of things. Therefore it must be of itself that the divine thought thinks (since it is the most excellent of things), and its thinking is a thinking on thinking.

But evidently knowledge and perception and opinion and understanding have always something else as their object, and themselves only by the way. Further, if thinking and being thought of are different, in respect of which does goodness belong to thought? For to *be* an act of thinking and to *be* an object of thought are not the same thing. We answer that in some cases the knowledge is the object. In the productive [1075ᵃ] sciences it is the substance or essence of the object, matter omitted, and in the theoretical sciences the definition or the act of thinking is the object. Since, then, thought and the object of thought are not different in the case of things that have not matter, the divine thought and its object will be the same, i.e. the thinking will be one with the object of its thought.

A further question is left—whether the object of the divine thought is composite; for if it were, thought would change in passing from part to part of the whole. We answer that everything which has not matter is indivisible—as human thought, or rather the thought of composite beings, is in a certain period of time (for it does not possess the good at this moment or at that, but its best, being something *different* from it, is attained only in a whole period [30] of time), so throughout eternity is the thought which has *itself* for its object.

10. We must consider also in which of two ways the nature of the universe contains the good and the highest good, whether as something separate and by itself, or as the order of the parts. Probably in both ways, as an army does; for its good is found both in its order and in its leader, and more in the latter; for he does not depend on the order but it depends on him. And all things are ordered together somehow, but not all alike—both fishes and fowls and plants; and the world is not such that one thing has nothing to do with another, but they are connected. For all are ordered together to one end, but it is as in a house, where the freemen are least at liberty to act at random, but all [20] things or most things are already ordained for them, while the slaves and the animals do little for the common good, and for the most part live at random; for this is the sort of principle that constitutes the nature of each. I mean, for instance, that all must at least come to be dissolved into their elements,[34] and there are other functions similarly in which all share for the good of the whole.

We must not fail to observe how many impossible or paradoxical results confront those who hold different views from our own, and what are the views of the subtler thinkers, and which views are attended by fewest difficulties. All make all things out of contraries. But neither "all things" nor "out of contraries" is right; nor do these thinkers tell us how all the things in which the contraries are present can be made out of the contraries; for contraries are not

affected by one another. Now for [30] us this difficulty is solved naturally by the fact that there is a third element.[35] These thinkers however make one of the two contraries matter; this is done for instance by those who make the unequal matter for the equal, or the many matter for the one.[36] But this also is refuted in the same way; for the one matter which underlies any pair of contraries is contrary to nothing. Further, all things, except the one, will, on the view we are criticizing, partake of evil; for the bad itself is one of the two elements. But the other school[37] does not treat the good and the bad even as principles; yet in all things the good is in the highest degree a principle. The school we first mentioned is right in saying that it is a principle, but *how* the good is a principle they do not say —whether as end or as mover or as form.

Empedocles[38] also has a para- [1075ᵇ] doxical view; for he identifies the good with love, but this is a principle both as mover (for it brings things together) and as matter (for it is part of the mixture). Now even if it happens that the same thing is a principle both as matter and as mover, still the being, at least, of the two is not the same. In which respect then is love a principle? It is paradoxical also that strife should be imperishable; the nature of his "evil" is just strife.

Anaxagoras makes the good a motive principle; for his "reason" moves things. But it moves them for an end, which must be something other than it, except according to *our* way of stating the case; for, on our view, the medical art is in a sense health. It is paradoxical also [10] not to suppose a contrary to the good, i.e. to reason. But all who speak of the contraries make no use of the contraries,

---

34 *Sc.* in order that higher forms of being may be produced by new combinations of the elements.

35 I.e. the substratum.

36 The reference is to Platonists.

37 The reference is to the Pythagoreans and Speusippus; cf. xii. 1072ᵇ 31.

38 Cf. i. 985ᵃ 4.

unless we bring their views into shape. And why some things are perishable and others imperishable, no one tells us; for they make all existing things out of the same principles. Further, some make existing things out of the non-existent; and others to avoid the necessity of this make all things one.

Further, why should there always be becoming and what is the cause of becoming?—this no one tells us. And those who suppose two principles must suppose another, a superior principle, and so must those who believe in the Forms; for why did things come to participate, or why do they participate, in the Forms? And all other thinkers[39] are [20] confronted by the necessary consequence that there is something contrary to Wisdom, i.e. to the highest knowledge; but *we* are not. For there is nothing contrary to that which is primary; for all contraries have matter, and things that have matter exist only potentially; and the ignorance which is contrary to any knowledge leads to an object contrary to the object of the knowledge; but what is primary has no contrary.

Again, if besides sensible things no others exist, there will be no first principle, no order, no becoming, no heavenly bodies, but each principle will have a principle before it, as in the accounts of the theologians and all the natural philosophers. But if the Forms or the numbers are to exist, they will be causes of nothing; or if not that, at least not of movement. Further, how is extension, i.e. a *continuum*, to be produced out of unextended parts? For number will not, either as mover or as form, produce a *continuum*. But again there cannot [30] be any *contrary* that is also essentially a productive or moving principle; or it would be possible not to be.[40] Or at least its action would be posterior to its potency. The world, then, would not be eternal. But it is; one of these premises, then, must be denied. And we have said how this must be done.[41] Further, in virtue of what the numbers, or the soul and the body, or in general the form and the thing, are one—of this no one tells us anything; nor can any one tell, unless he says, as we do, that the mover makes them one. And those who say[42] mathematical number is first and go on to generate one kind of substance after another and give different principles for each, make the substance of the universe a mere series of episodes (for [1076ᵃ] one substance has no influence on another by its existence or non-existence), and they give us many governing principles; but the world refuses to be governed badly.

"The rule of many is not good; one ruler let there be."[43]

# PHYSICS

## Book II
## (Chapter VIII: On Purpose in Nature)

### Chapter VIII

We must now consider why Nature is to be ranked among causes that are final, that is to say purposeful; and further we must consider what is meant by "necessity" when we are speaking of Nature. For thinkers are for ever referring things to necessity as a cause, and explaining that, since hot and cold and

---

39 The special reference is to Plato; cf. *Rep.* 477.

40 Since contraries must contain matter, and matter implies potentiality and contingency.

41 Cf. 1071ᵇ 19, 20.

42 Speusippus is meant; cf. vii. 1028ᵇ 21, xiv. 1090ᵇ 13–20.

43 Cf. *Iliad*, ii. 204.

so forth are what they are, this or that exists or comes into being "of necessity"; for even if one or another of them alleges some other cause, such as "Sympathy and Antipathy" or "Mind," he straight away drops it again, after a mere acknowledgement.

So here the question rises whether we have any reason to regard Nature as making for any goal at all, or as seeking any one thing as preferable to any other. Why not say, it is asked, that Nature acts as Zeus drops the rain, not to make the corn grow, but of necessity (for the rising vapour must needs be condensed into water by the cold, and must then descend, and incidentally, when this happens, the corn grows), just as, when a man loses his corn on the threshing-floor, it did not rain on purpose to destroy the crop, but the result was merely incidental to the raining? So why should it not be the same with natural organs like the teeth? Why should it not be a coincidence that the front teeth come up with an edge, suited to dividing the food, and the back ones flat and good for grinding it, without there being any design in the matter? And so with all other organs that seem to embody a purpose. In cases where a coincidence brought about such a combination as might have been arranged on purpose, the creatures, it is urged, having been suitably formed by the operation of chance, survived; otherwise they perished, and still perish, as Empedocles says of his "man-faced oxen."

Such and suchlike are the arguments which may be urged in raising this problem; but it is impossible that this should really be the way of it. For all these phenomena and all natural things are either constant or normal, and this is contrary to the very meaning of luck or chance. No one assigns it to chance or to a remarkable coincidence if [199ᵃ] there is abundant rain in the winter,

though he would if there were in the dog-days; and the other way about, if there were parching heat. Accordingly, if the only choice is to assign these occurrences either to coincidence or to purpose, and if in these cases chance coincidence is out of the question, then it must be purpose. But, as our opponents themselves would admit, these occurrences are all natural. There is purpose, then, in what is, and in what happens, in Nature.

Further, in any operation of human art, where there is an end to be achieved, the earlier and successive stages of the operation are performed for the purpose of realizing that end. Now, when a thing is produced by Nature, the earlier stages in every case lead up to the final development in the same way as in the operation of art, and *vice versa,* provided that no impediment balks the process. The operation is directed by a purpose; we may, therefore, infer that the natural process was guided by a purpose to the end that is realized. Thus, if a house were a natural product, the process would pass through the same stages that it in fact passes through when it is produced by art; and if natural products could also be produced by art, they would move along the same line that the natural process actually takes. We may therefore say that the earlier stages are for the purpose of leading to the later. Indeed, as a general proposition, the arts either, on the basis of Nature, carry things further than Nature can, or they imitate Nature. If, then, artificial processes are purposeful, so are natural processes too; for the relation of antecedent to consequent is identical in art and in Nature.

This principle comes out most clearly when we consider the other animals. For their doings are not the outcome of art (design) or of previous research or deliberation; so that some raise the question whether the works of spiders and ants and so on should be attributed to intelligence or to some similar faculty. And then, descending step by step, we find that plants too produce organs subservient to their perfect development —leaves, for instance, to shelter the fruit. Hence, if it is by nature and also for a purpose that the swallow makes her nest and the spider his web, and that plants make leaves for the sake of the fruit and strike down (and not up) with their roots in order to get their nourishment, it is clear that causality of the kind we have described is at work in things that come about or exist in the course of Nature.

Also, since the term "nature" is applied both to material and to form, and since it is the latter that constitutes the goal, and all else is for the sake of that goal, it follows that the form is the final cause.

Now there are failures even in the arts (for writers make mistakes in writing and physicians administer the wrong dose); so that analogous failures in Nature may evidently be anticipated as possible. Thus, if in art there are cases in which the correct procedure serves a purpose, and attempts that fail [199ᵇ] are aimed at a purpose but miss it, we may take it to be the same in Nature, and monstrosities will be like failures of purpose in Nature. So if, in the primal combinations, such "ox-creatures" as could not reach an equilibrium and goal, should appear, it would be by the miscarriage of some principle, as monstrous births are actually produced now by abortive developments of sperm. Besides, the sperm must precede the formation of the animal, and Empedocles' "primal all-generative" is no other than such sperm.

In plants, too, though they are less elaborately articulated, there are manifest indications of purpose. Are we to suppose, then, that as there were "ox-creatures man-faced" so also there were "vine-growths olive-bearing"? Incongruous as such a thing seems, it ought to follow if we accept the principle in the case of animals. Moreover, it ought still to be a matter of chance what comes up when you sow this seed or that.

In general, the theory does away with the whole order of Nature, and indeed with Nature's self. For natural things are exactly those which do move continuously, in virtue of a principle inherent in themselves, towards a determined goal; and the final development which results from any one such principle is not identical for any two species, nor yet is it any random result; but in each there is always a tendency towards an identical result, if nothing interferes with the process. A desirable result and the means to it may also be produced by chance, as for instance we say it was "by luck" that the stranger came and ransomed the prisoner before he left, where the ransoming is done as if the man had come for that purpose, though in fact he did not. In this case the desirable result is incidental; for, as we have explained, chance is an incidental cause. But when the desirable result is effected invariably or normally, it is not an incidental or chance occurrence; and in the course of Nature the result always is achieved either invariably or normally, if nothing hinders. It is absurd to suppose that there is no purpose because in Nature we can never detect the moving power in the act of deliberation. Art, in fact, does not deliberate either, and if the shipbuilding art were incorporate in the timber, it would proceed by nature in the same way in which it now proceeds by art. If purpose, then, is inherent in art, so is it in Nature also. The best illustration is the case of a man being his own physician, for Nature is like that—agent and patient at once.

That Nature is a cause, then, and a goal-directed cause, is above dispute.

## Book IV
### (Chapters X-XIV : On Time)

### Chapter X

The subject of inquiry next in succession is "time." It will be well to begin with the questions which general reflections suggest as to its existence or non-existence and its nature.

The following considerations might make one suspect either that there is really no such thing as time, or at least that it has only an equivocal and obscure existence.

1. Some of it is past and no [218ᵃ] longer exists, and the rest is future and does not yet exist; and time, whether limitless or any given length of time we take, is entirely made up of the no-longer and not-yet; and how can we conceive of that which is composed of non-existents sharing in existence in any way?

2. Moreover, if anything divisible exists, then, so long as it is in existence, either all its parts or some of them must exist. Now time is divisible into parts, and some of these were in the past and some will be in the future, but none of them exists. The present "now" is not part of time at all, for a part measures the whole, and the whole must be made up of the parts, but we cannot say that time is made up of "nows."

3. Nor is it easy to see whether the "now" that appears to divide the past and the future (a) is always one and the same or (b) is perpetually different.

(b) For if it is perpetually different, and if no two sectional parts of time can exist at once (unless one includes the other, the longer the shorter), and if the "now" that is not, but was, must have ceased to be at *some* time or other, so also no two "nows" can exist together, but the past "now" must have perished

before there was any other "now." Now it cannot have ceased to be when it was itself the "now," for that is just when it existed; but it is impossible that the past "now" should have perished in any other "now" but itself. For we must lay it down as an axiom that there can be no next "now" to a given "now," any more than a next point to a given point. So that if it did not perish in the next "now," but in some subsequent one, it would have been in existence coincidently with the countless "nows" that lie between the "now" in which it was and the subsequent "now" in which we are supposing it to perish; which is impossible.

(a) But neither can it continuously persist in its identity. For nothing which is finite and divisible is bounded by a single limit, whether it be continuous in one dimension only or in more than one; but the "now" is a time limit, and if we take any limited period of time, it must be determined by two limits, which cannot be identical. Again, if simultaneity in time, and not being before or after, means coinciding and being in the very "now" wherein they coincide, then, if the before and the after were both in the persistently identical "now" we are discussing, what happened ten thousand years ago would be simultaneous with what is happening to-day, and nothing would be before or after anything else.

Let this suffice as to the problems raised by considering the properties of time.

But what time really is and under what category it falls, is no more revealed by anything that has come down to us from earlier thinkers than it is by the considerations that have just been urged. For (a) some have identified time with the revolution of the all-embracing heaven, and (b) some with that heavenly sphere itself. But (a) a partial revolution is time just as [218ᵇ] much as a whole one is, but it is not just as much a revolution; for any finite portion of time is a portion of a revolution, but is not a revolution. Moreover, if there were more universes than one, the reentrant circumlation of each of them would be time, so that several different times would exist at once. And (*b*) as to those who declare the heavenly sphere itself to be time, their only reason was that all things are contained "in the celestial sphere" and also occur "in time," which is too childish to be worth reducing to absurdities more obvious than itself.

Now the most obvious thing about time is that it strikes us as some kind of "passing along" and changing; but if we follow this clue, we find that, when any particular thing changes or moves, the movement or change is in the moving or changing thing itself or occurs only where that thing is; whereas "the passage of time" is current everywhere alike and is in relation with everything. And further, all changes may be faster or slower, but not so time; for fast and slow are defined by time, "faster" being more change in less time, and "slower" less in more. But time cannot measure time thus, as though it were a distance (like the space passed through in motion) or a qualitative modification, as in other kinds of change. It is evident, therefore, that time is not identical with movement; nor, in this connexion, need we distinguish between movement and other kinds of change.

## Chapter XI

On the other hand, time cannot be disconnected from change; for when we experience no changes of consciousness, or, if we do, are not aware of them, no time seems to have passed, any more than it did to the men in the fable who "slept with the heroes" in Sardinia, when they awoke; for under such circumstances we fit the former "now" on to the later, making them one and the same and eliminating the interval between them, because we did not perceive it. So, just as there would be no time if there were no distinction between this "now" and that "now," but it were always the same "now"; in the same way there appears to be no time between two "nows" when we fail to distinguish between them. Since, then, we are not aware of time when we do not distinguish any change (the mind appearing to abide in a single indivisible and undifferentiated state), whereas if we perceive and distinguish changes, then we say that time has elapsed, it is clear that time cannot be discon- [219ᵃ] nected from motion and change.

Plainly, then, time is neither identical with movement nor capable of being separated from it.

In our attempt to find out what time is, therefore, we must start from the question, in what way it pertains to movement. For when we are aware of movement we are thereby aware of time, since, even if it were dark and we were conscious of no bodily sensations, but something were "going on" in our minds, we should, from that very experience, recognize the passage of time. And conversely, whenever we recognize that there has been a lapse of time, we by that act recognize that something "has been going on." So time must either itself be movement, or if not, must pertain to movement; and since we have seen that it is not identical with movement, it must pertain to it in some way.

Well then, since anything that moves from a "here" to a "there," and magnitude as such is continuous, movement is dependent on magnitude; for it is because magnitude is continuous that movement is so also, and because movement is continuous so is time; for (excluding differences of velocity) the time occupied is conceived as proportionate to the distance moved over. Now, the primary significance of before-and-afterness is the local one of "in front of" and "behind." There it is applied to order of position; but since there is a before-and-after in magnitude, there must also be a before-and-after in movement in analogy with them. But there is also a before-and-after in time, in virtue of the dependence of time upon motion. Motion, then, is the objective seat of before-and-afterness both in movement and in time; but conceptually the before-and-afterness is distinguishable from movement. Now, when we determine a movement by defining its first and last limit, we also recognize a lapse of time, for it is when we are aware of the measuring of motion by a prior and posterior limit that we may say time has passed. And our determination consists in distinguishing between the initial limit and the final one, and seeing that what lies between them is distinct from both; for when we distinguish between the extremes and what is between them, and the mind pronounces the "nows" to be two—an initial and a final one—it is then that we say that a certain time has passed; for that which is determined either way by a "now" seems to be what we mean by time. And let this be accepted and laid down.

Accordingly, when we perceive a "now" in isolation, that is to say not as one of two, an initial and a final one in the motion, nor yet as being a final "now" of one period and at the same time the initial "now" of a succeeding period, then no time seems to have elapsed, for neither has there been any corresponding motion. But when we perceive a distinct before and after, then we speak of time; for this is just what time is, the calculable measure [219ᵇ] or dimension of motion with respect to before-and-afterness.

Time, then, is not movement, but that by which movement can be numerically estimated. To see this, reflect that we estimate any kind of more-and-lessness

by number; so, since we estimate all more-or-lessness on some numerical scale and estimate the more-or-lessness of motion by time, time is a scale on which something (to wit, movement) can be numerically estimated. But now, since "number" has two meanings (for we speak of the "numbers" that are counted in the thing in question, and also of the "numbers" by which we count them and in which we calculate), we are to note that time is the countable thing that we are counting not the numbers we count in—which two things are different.

And as motion is a continuous flux, so is time; but at any given moment time is the same everywhere, for the "now" itself is identical in its essence, but the relations into which it enters differ in different connexions, and it is the "now" that marks off time as before and after. But this "now," which is identical everywhere, itself retains its identity in one sense, but does not in another; for inasmuch as the point in the flux of time which it marks is changing (and so to mark it is its essential function) the "now" too differs perpetually, but inasmuch as at every moment it is performing its essential function of dividing the past and future it retains its identity. For there is a dependent sequence, as we have shown, of movement upon magnitude and (we may add) of time upon movement; and the moving object, by which we become aware of movement and its before-and-afterness, may be regarded as a point; and throughout its course this—whether point or stone or what you like—retains its identity, but its relations alter: as the Sophists distinguish between Koriscos in the Lyceum and Koriscos in the market-place, so this moving object also is different in so far as it is perpetually marking a different position. And as time follows the analogy of movement, so does the "now" of time follow the analogy of the moving object, since it is by the moving object that we come to know the before-and-after in motion, and it is in virtue of the countableness of its before-and-afters that the "now" exists; so that the "now," wherever found in the before-and-afters, is identical (for it is simply the mark of the before-and-afters in motion), but the before-and-afternesses it marks differ; though the nature of the "now" depends on the markableness of any before-and-after in general, not on the specific before-and-after marked by it. And it is this specifically related "now" that is nearest to our apprehension, just as motion-change is apprehended through the changing object, and translation through the translated object, for this object is a concrete thing, which motion is not. There is a sense, then, in which what we mean when we say "now" is always the same, and a sense in which it is now, just as is the case with anything that is in motion.

It is evident, too, that neither would time be if there were no "now," nor would "now" be if there were no time; for they belong to each other as [220ᵃ] the moving thing and the motion do, so that whatever ticks off the position of the one ticks off the other. For time is the dimension proper to motion, and the "now" corresponds to the moving object as the numerical monad.

So, too, time owes its continuity to the "now," and yet is divided by reference to it, since in this respect also the analogy with the translation and the object translated holds good; for the movement or translation is one and continuous in virtue of the identity of the translated object—not its identity *qua* object (for it would preserve that if it stopped) but its unbroken identity *qua* "the thing that is being moved"; and it is this that also marks the division between the movement before and the movement after. And there is an analogy also between such a "body that is being moved" and a point; for it is

a point that both constitutes (by its movement) the continuity of the line it traces and also marks the end of the line that is behind and the beginning of the line in front. If, however, one ascribes the latter function to it, regarding the one point in two capacities— as the end of one section of the line and the beginning of another—it must have been arrested, since its identity in this "statical" relation must be preserved. But the "now," as it follows the object in motion, marks a perpetually different position, so that time is not counted as if by one and the same point,—since each point in it so counted is a double point, being end and beginning at once, —but rather as the two extremities of the line, and not as *parts* of it, for the reason already stated (that, if one were to count the dividing point in its two capacities that would involve a pause), and because it is obvious that the "now" is not a portion of time, just as the division of motion is not part of motion any more than points are of a line; it is the two sections that are *parts* of the one line. The "now," therefore, as a limit is not time but is incidental to time, while as the numerator it is a number; for limits are limits only of the particular thing they limit, whereas the number 10, for instance, pertains equally to the ten horses (say) the sum of which it has defined, and to anything else numerable.

That time, then, is the dimension of movement in its before-and-afterness, and is continuous (because movement is so), is evident.

## Chapter XII

The dyad is the smallest possible *abstract number*. In one sense there is no smallest possible number, but in another sense there is; for, whatever line you take for the unit, two is the smallest number of such units, but in magnitude there is no minimum, for any line whatever may itself be divided into smaller lines. So too with time, "two" is the smallest possible number of time units, but there is no smallest possible time unit itself that may be selected.

Observe too that we do not speak of time itself as "swift or slow," but as consisting of "many or few" of the units in which it is counted, or as "long [220ᵇ] and short" when we regard it as a continuum. It would not be swift or slow, even if we supposed it to be the counter that counts, not the dimension that is counted (which it really is); for abstract numbers are in no case swift or slow, though the counting of them may be.

Moreover, though time is identical everywhere simultaneously, it is not identical if taken twice successively; for the change it measures, likewise, is one when considered as present but not one if considered as partly past and partly future. And time considered numerically is concrete, not abstract; whereby follows that it changes from the former to the latter "now," inasmuch as these "nows" themselves are different; just as the number of a hundred horses is identical with that of a hundred men, but the horses enumerated are different from the men enumerated. Now note further that as there may be movement (of rotation to wit) that covers the same course over and over again, in like manner we mark off time by the year or by spring or autumn.

And not only do we measure the length of uniform movement by time, but also the length of time by uniform movement, since they mutually determine each other; for the time taken determines the length moved over (the time units corresponding to the space units), and the length moved over determines the time taken. And when we call time "much" or "little" we are estimating it in units of uniform motion, as we measure the "number" of anything we count by the units we count it

in—the number of horses, for example, by taking one horse as our unit. For when we are told the number of horses, we know how many there are in the troop; and by counting how many there are, horse by horse, we know their number. And so too with time and uniform motion, for we measure them by each other either way. And this is only natural, for movement corresponds to linear magnitude, and time to movement, in being a quantity, in being continuous, and in being divisible; for it is from linear magnitude that motion takes on these qualities, and from motion that time does. That we do measure linear magnitude by movement, and *vice versa*, is evidenced from our saying that it is a great "way" if it is a great "walk," or *vice versa*. So too with time and movement: we speak of a "long walk" taking a "long time," or *vice versa*.

It is by reference to the stand- [221ᵃ] ard unit of time that we determine the relative velocity of two several motions. For we ask what distance either motion has covered during the lapse of the standard unit of time, and pronounce the motion itself fast or slow in proportion as that distance is great or small. But that same standard unit of time measures the duration of a motion. So the way in which a motion exists in time is by both itself and its duration being measured by time. For time measures both the motion and its duration by the same act, and its duration being so measured constitutes it as existing in time. But it is obvious that other things as well as motion exist in time because their existence too is measured by time.

For this phrase "existing in time" is ambiguous. It may mean (1) existing when time also exists, or (2) it may mean "in time" in a sense analogous to that in which we say that certain things exist "in number"; and this phrase again is ambiguous, for it may mean (*a*) that they exist in number as parts or affections of it, or generally that they pertain to it in some way or other, or (*b*) it may mean that they themselves can be counted.

Now (2) taking time as a number scale, (*a*) the "now" and the "before" and suchlike exist in time as the monad and the odd and even exist in number (for these latter pertain to number just in the same way in which the former pertain to time); but (*b*) events have their places in time in a sense analogous to that in which any numbered group of things exist in number (*i.e.*, in such and such a definite number), and such things as these are *embraced* in number (*i.e.*, in time) as things that have locality are embraced in their places.

And it is further evident (1) that to be in existence while time is in existence does not constitute being "in time," just as neither is a thing constituted as in motion or in a place because a motion and place exist while it does. For if this constitutes being "*in*" a thing, everything would be in anything, and the universe in a grain of millet, because a grain of millet exists while the universe is in existence. But this latter is an incidental coincidence; whereas when a thing is said to exist in time, it follows of necessity that there should be time while this thing exists, and if it exists in motion, it follows of necessity that there should be motion while it exists.

And since what exists in time exists in it as number (that is to say, as countable), you can take a time longer than anything that exists in time. So we must add that for things to exist in time they must be embraced by time, just as with other cases of being "in" something; for instance, things that are in places are embraced by place. And it will follow that they are in some respect affected by time, just as we are wont to say that time crumbles things, and that everything grows old under the power of time and is forgotten through the lapse of time. But we do not say that we have learnt,

or that anything is made new or beautiful, by the mere lapse of time; for we regard time in itself as destroying [221ᵇ] rather than producing, for what is counted in time is movement, and movement dislodges whatever it affects from its present state. From all this it is clear that things which exist eternally, as such, are not in time; for they are not embraced by time, nor is their duration measured by time. This is indicated by their not suffering anything under the action of time as though they were within its scope.

And since time is the measure of a motion, it will also incidentally be the measure of rest; for all rest is in time. For a thing being in motion necessitates that it should be moving, but its being in time does not; for time is not identical with motion, but is that in terms of which motion is counted, and even if a thing is at rest, it may be countable by the same count as motion. For not everything that is unmoved is at rest, but that only which by its nature is capable of moving but now lacks its actual motion, as we have already noted. But a thing existing in number means that it "has" a number and that its existence is measured by that number; and so too in the case of time. And time will measure that which is in motion and that which is at rest, *as such*; for it is their motion and their rest of which it determines the amount. So that the thing in motion is not measured by time in all respects in its capacity of a quantum, but in so far as its motion is defined in quantity; hence that which is neither in motion nor at rest is not in time, since to be "in time" means to be measured by time, and it is motion and rest of which time is the measure.

Clearly, then, not all non-existences are in time, but only such as might exist; for instance, the commensurability of the diagonal and the side does not exist, but its non-existence is not temporal. For, as a general proposition, if time is the measure of motion on its own account and of anything else only by incidental coincidence, obviously everything whose existence it measures must have its existence in rest or in motion. Accordingly, whatever is destructible or generable, or (more broadly) sometimes existing and sometimes not, must be embraced by time; for there must be some time great enough to exceed the time of their duration and therefore the time which measures their being. Among non-existents, on the other hand, those which are embraced by time either once were [222$^a$] (as Homer once existed) or will be (e.g., some future event), according as they are embraced by time on one or the other side of the present moment, or, if they are embraced in both directions, they can be either past or future; whereas those which are not in any way embraced by time neither were nor are nor will be. Non-existents of this latter kind are all those things whose opposites eternally exist; for instance, the incommensurability of the diagonal eternally exists, and therefore is not in time. And it follows that neither is its commensurability in time; hence it is *eternally* non-existent, inasmuch as it is a contradiction of what is eternally existent; whereas things of which the opposite does not exist eternally may either be or not be, and so they can come into existence and vanish from it.

## Chapter XIII

We have said that it is through the "now" that time is continuous, for it holds time past and future time together; and in its general character of "limit" it is at once the beginning of time to come and the end of time past. But in the case of the "now" this is not so obvious as in that of the stationary point; for, as well as actually continuing, it potentially divides time. And in this potentiality one "now" differs from another, but in its actual holding of time continuously to-

gether it always remains the same, as in the parallel case of mathematical lines traced by moving points, in which case the point too, if arrested as a divider, is not conceived as retaining its identity with the tracing point or another arrested point; for if we are dividing the line, the point differs at every division, but if we regard the line as a single undivided one, the point that traces it is the same all along. Thus too the "now" of time is a divider in mental potentiality, but a continuing unifier as the coincident end-term and beginning-term of past and future time; and these two capacities of potential divider and actual uniter pertain to the same actual "now" and on the same count of its being two limits at once, but its essential and defined functioning in the one capacity differs from that in the other.

This is one of the meaning of "now," but it is also used for "not far off in time." "He will come now," if he will come to-day; "He has come but now," if he came to-day. But we do not speak so of the Trojan war or Deucalion's flood; though time is continuous between us and these events, they are not near.

"Sometimes" is used when we wish to be no more definite than that the present "now" comes after it or the reverse. When was Troy taken? "Sometime" in the past. When will the flood be? "Sometime" in the future. There will be a measurable stretch of time from now onwards to that, or there has been one from that to now.

And since there is no time-ago or time-to-come that was not, or will not be, "some time" off, it would seem that all time is limited. Will it come to an end, then? Surely not; for if motion is everlasting, so is time. Is it, then, always a different stretch of time that continues the succession, or the same stretch of time taken repeatedly? As to this, evidently it must conform to motion; for whichever of these kinds of counting applies to motion must apply to time.

And besides, since the "now" is [222ᵇ] the final limit and the initial limit of time, but not of the same time, but the final limit of time past and the initial limit of time to come, it must present a relation analogous to the kind of identity between the convexity and the concavity of the same circumference, which necessitates a difference between that with respect to which it bears the one character and that with respect to which it bears the other. So too, since every "now" is at once the initial limit and the final limit of a stretch of time, the two stretches must be different; for the same "now" cannot be both the beginning and the end of the same thing, for, if so, it would be both of two contradictories in the same subject at once. Neither, then, will time ever come to an end, for it is always at a beginning.

We say "already" (*ēdē*) for any time close enough to the indivisible "now" of the absolute present. "When do you take your walk?" "I am starting already," or "I have already taken it." But the phrase only applies to the near future or past; so that we should not say "Troy has already fallen." Another term for the near past is "just now" (*arti*). "When did you arrive?" "Just now," if it was near to the instantaneous "now" at which you speak; but "some time ago" (*palai*) if the interval is considerable; and "suddenly" (*exaiphnēs*) if the passage of time is so short as to be imperceptible.

All change is in its nature a "passing away." And it is "in time" that everything begins and ceases to be; so some have called it the wisest of things, because it brings all knowledge, but the Pythagorean Paron said it was the most ignorant, because it is in time too that everything is forgotten, and he was nearer the mark. Indeed, it is evident that the mere passage of time itself is destructive rather than generative, as we said earlier; because change is primarily a "passing away." So it is only incidentally that time is the cause of the things coming into being and existing. A sufficient indication of this may be found in the fact that nothing comes into being without being started by some cause and reacting to it, but things perish without anything being stirred, and it is a kind of perishing without apparent provocation that we especially attribute to time. But yet, after all, it is not really time itself that destroys things in this way, but the changes that do destroy take place concurrently with time.

That there is such a thing as time, therefore, and what it is, and in how many senses we speak of "now," and what "sometime" and "but now" and "already" and "some time ago" and "suddenly" mean, has now been said.

## Chapter XIV

All this being so established, it becomes clear that all changes and everything that moves are conditioned by time. For it is a patent fact that every change may be quicker or slower. And what I mean by one change being quicker than another is that, of two homogeneous change-movements (either both on a periphery, for instance, or both on a straight line, if it be a local movement, and *mutatis mutandis* in other kinds of change), that one is the quicker which reaches a [223ᵃ] certain determined stage or point in its course "before" the other reaches the point at the same distance from the starting-point in its course. Now this "before" means before "in time," for both "before" and "after" are expressions of an interval between the "nows" of arrival; and since the "now" is a boundary between past and future, it follows that the two "nows" (of the former and latter arrival, namely) being both phenomena of time, so must their "before" and "after" be. For, whatever it be that the "now" pertains to, to that must the interval determined by it pertain. (But note that "before" has opposite meanings according to whether it refers to past or future time; for in the past we regard the event that is farther from the present as "before" the other and the nearer event as "after" it, but in the future the nearer as "before" and the farther as "after" the other.) So, inasmuch as "before" pertains to time, and may be a "before" of arrival at a point of any kind of change-movement, it follows that every change or movement occurs "in time."

The relation of time to consciousness deserves examination, and so does the question why we conceive of time as immanent in everything in earth and sea and sky. As to the latter point, it is because time, being the numerator of motion, pertains to such motion wherever it exists, as an affection or disposition of it (namely, that it is either actually counted in units or potentially countable in such); and all things in the material universe are susceptible of motion (for they can all change their positions), and time and movement run in pairs both potentially and actually.

The question remains, then, whether or not time would exist if there were no consciousness; for if it were impossible for there to be the factor that does the counting, it would be impossible that anything should be counted; so that evidently there could be no number, for a number is either that which has actually been counted or that which can be counted. And if nothing can count except consciousness, and consciousness only as intellect (not as sensation merely), it is impossible that time should exist if consciousness did not; unless as the "objective thing" which is subjectively time to us, if we may suppose that movement could thus objectively exist without there being any consciousness. For "before" and "after" are objectively involved in motion, and these, *qua* capable of numeration, constitute time.

It may be asked further to what kind of motion-change time does pertain. We may answer, "It does not matter."

For things being and cease to be, and grow, and change their qualities and their places "in time"; so far, then, as change can be regarded as movement, so far time must be a numerator of every such kind of movement. We conclude, then, that time is the numeration of continuous movement, without any qualification, not only of some particular kind.

But if we take one kind of [223ᵇ] change and say "now" with respect to it, other kinds of change, each of which has a specifically different unit to be counted in, will be at a certain stage of their change at this same "now." Can each of them have a different time, and must there be more than one time running concurrently? No; for it is the same lapse of time that is counted by two "nows," everywhere at once, whatever the units of movement or change; whereas the one-and-sameness of the units is determined by their kind and not by their "at-once-ness"; just as if there were dogs and horses, seven of each, the number would be the same, but the units numbered different. So, too, of all movement-changes determined simultaneously the time is the same; one may be quick and another slow, and one a change of place and the other of quality; the time, however, is the same, if the counting has reached the same number and been made simultaneously, whether of the qualitive modification or of the change of place. So the movements or changes are different and stand apart, but the time is the same everywhere, because the numeration, if made simultaneously and up to the same figure, is one and the same.

And now, keeping locomotion and especially rotation in mind, note that everything is counted by some unit of like nature to itself—monads monad by monad, for instance, and horses horse by horse—and so likewise time by some finite unit of time. But as we have said, motion and time mutually determine each other quantitively; and that because the standard of time established by the motion we select is the quantitive measure both of that motion and of time. If, then, the standard once fixed measures all dimensionality of its own order, a uniform rotation will be the best standard, since it is easiest to count.

Neither qualitative modification nor growth nor genesis had the kind of uniformity that rotation has; and so time as regarded as the rotation of the sphere, inasmuch as all other orders of motion are measured by it, and time itself is standardized by reference to it. And this is the reason of our habitual way of speaking; for we say that human affairs and those of all other things that have natural movement and become and perish seem to be in a way circular, because all these things come to pass in time and have their beginning and end as it were "periodically"; for time itself is conceived as "coming round"; and this again because time and such a standard rotation mutually determine each other. Hence, to call the happenings of a thing a circle is saying that there is a sort of circle of time; and that is because it is measured by a complete revolution, and the whole measurement of a thing is nought else but a de- [224ᵃ] fined number of the units of its measurements.

[It is correct to say that the number of sheep and of dogs is the same number, if that of the sheep and that of the dogs are equal; but it is not the same decad in each case, nor are the units of one the same as the units of the other, any more than a scalene and an isosceles are the same triangle, though they are the same figure, both being triangles; for things bear the same name if they do not differ as to the characteristic in virtue of which that name is borne, in this case the differentia of triangle. They are different as triangles, therefore, but not different as figures, since they belong to one and the same figure denomi-

nation. For, as a figure, this is a circle and that a triangle, but, as a triangle, this isosceles and that scalene. The two, then, have the same figure conformation (for both are triangular), but not the same triangle formation. So with the animals: the number of each ten-groups is the same, for they do not differ in a numerical differentia; but the ten-groups themselves are not the same, for the tenness is predicated of different subjects—dogs in the one case and horses in the other.]

This closes our investigation of time and its properties, in so far as they are germane to our inquiry.

## Book VI
### (Chapter IX : Against Zeno)[1]

**Chapter IX**

The fallacy of Zeno's argument is now obvious; for he says that since a thing is at rest when it has not shifted in any degree out of a place equal to its own dimensions, and since at any given instant during the whole of its supposed motion the supposed moving thing is in the place it occupies at that instant, the arrow is not moving at *any time* during its flight. But this is a false conclusion; for time is not made up of atomic "nows," any more than any other magnitude is made up of atomic elements.

Of Zeno's arguments about motion, there are four which give trouble to those who try to solve the problems they raise. The first is the one which declares movement to be impossible because, however near the mobile is to any given point, it will always have to cover the half, and then the half of that, and so on without limit before it gets there. And this we have already taken to pieces.

The second is what is known as "the

---

1 This translation by P. H. Wicksteed, edited after his death by F. M. Cornford, should be compared with the section on Zeno, above.

Achilles," which purports to show that the slowest will never be overtaken in its course by the swiftest, inasmuch as, reckoning from any given instant, the pursuer, before he can catch the pursued, must reach the point from which the pursued started at that instant, and so the slower will always be some distance in advance of the swifter. But this argument is the same as the former one which depends on bisection, with the difference that the division of the magnitudes we successively take is not a division into halves (but according to any ratio we like to assume between the two speeds). The conclusion of the argument is that the slower cannot be overtaken by the swifter, but it is reached by following the same lines as the "bisection" argument of the first thesis; for the reason why neither supposed process lands us at the limit, is that the method of division is expressly so designed as not to get us there, only in this second thesis a declamatory intensification is introduced by representing the swiftest racer as unable to overtake the slowest. The solution then must be identical in both cases, and the claim that the thing that is ahead is not overtaken is false. It is not overtaken *while* it is ahead, but none the less it *is* overtaken if Zeno will allow it to traverse to the end its finite distance. So much for these two theses.

The third thesis is the one just mentioned, namely that the arrow is stationary while on its flight. The demonstration rests on the assumption that time is made up of "nows," and if this be not granted the inference fails.

The fourth thesis supposes a number of objects all equal with each other in dimensions, forming two equal trains and arranged so that one train stretches from one end of a racecourse to the middle of it, and the other from the middle to the other end. Then if you let the two trains, moving in opposite directions but at the same rate, pass each other, Zeno undertakes to show that half of the time they

occupy in passing each other is equal to the whole of it. The fallacy lies in his assuming that a moving object [240ᵃ] takes an equal time in passing another object equal in dimensions to itself, whether that other object is stationary or in motion; which assumption is false. For this is his demonstration. Let there be a number of objects *AAAA*, equal in number and bulk to those that compose the two trains but stationary in the middle of the stadium. Then let the objects *BBBB*, in number and dimension equal to the *A*'s, form one of the trains stretching from the middle of the *A*'s in one direction; and from the inner end of the B's let *CCCC* stretch in the opposite direction, being the equal in number, dimension, and rate of movement to the *B*'s.

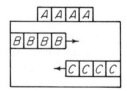

Then when they cross, the first *B* and the first *C* will simultaneously reach the extreme *A*'s in contrary directions.

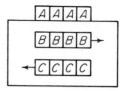

Now during this process the first *C* has passed all the *B*'s, whereas the first *B* has only passed half the *A*'s, and therefore only taken half the time; for it takes an equal time (the minimal time) for the C to pass one B as for the *B* to pass one *A*. But during this same half-time the first *B* has also passed all the

C's (though the first B takes as long, says Zeno, to pass a C as an A) because measured by their progress through the A's the B's and C's have had the same time in which to cross each other. Such is his argument, but the result depends on the fallacy above mentioned.

Nor need we be troubled by any attack on the possibility of change based on the axiom that a thing "must either be or not be" but cannot "both be and not be" this or that at the same time. For, it is argued, if a thing is changing, for instance, from being not-white to being white and is on its way from one to the other, you can truly assert at the same time that it is neither white nor not-white. But this is not true, for we sometimes call a thing "white" even if it is not entirely white, and we sometimes call a thing "not-white" even if there is some trace of white in it; we speak of it according to its prevailing condition or the conditions of its most significant parts or aspects. For to say that a thing is not in a certain condition "at all" and to say that it is not "altogether," in it are two different things.

And so, too, in the case of being or not being or any other pair of contradictory opposites. For during the whole process of changing it must be prevailingly one or the other and can never be exclusively either.

Again it is said that a rotating circle or sphere or anything else that moves within its own dimensions is stationary because in itself and all its parts it will remain in the same place for the given time: so it will be in motion and at rest at the same time. But in the first place its parts are not in the same place during any space of time, and in the second place the whole is also continuously changing to a different (rotational) position; for the circumference measured round from A to A again is [240ᵇ] not identical with the circumference as measured from B to B or from C to C or any other point, except by accidental concomitance, as the cultivated person is a man. Thus one circumference is ever succeeding another and it will never be at rest. So, too, with the sphere, and any other body that moves within fixed dimensions.

# ON THE HEAVENS

## Book I
## (Chapter II-III : The Fifth Element)

### Chapter II

The question of the nature of this Whole, whether it is of infinite magnitude or its total bulk is limited, must be left until later. We have now to speak of its formally distinct parts, and we may start from this, that all natural bodies and magnitudes are capable of moving of themselves in space; for nature we have defined as the principle of motion in them. Now all motion in space (locomotion) is either straight or

circular or a compound of the two, for these are the only simple motions, the reason being that the straight and circular lines are the only simple magnitudes. By "circular motion" I mean motion around the centre, by "straight," motion up the down. "Up" means away from the centre, "down" towards the centre. It follows that all simple locomotion is either away from the centre or towards the centre or around the centre. This appears to follow consistently on what was said at the beginning: body was completed by the number three, and so now is its motion.

Of bodies some are simple, and some are compounds of the simple. By "simple" I mean all bodies which contain a principle of natural motion, like fire and earth and their kinds, and the other bodies of the same order. Hence motions also must be similarly divisible, some simple and others compound in one way or another; simple bodies will have simple motions and com- [269ª] posite bodies composite motions, though the movement may be according to the prevailing element in the compound.

If we take these premises, (a) that there is such a thing as simple motion, (b) that circular motion is simple, (c) that simple motion is the motion of a simple body (for if a composite body moves with a simple motion, it is only by virtue of a simple body prevailing and imparting its direction to the whole), than it follows that there exists a simple body naturally so constituted as to move in a circle in virtue of its own nature. By force it can be brought to move with the motion of another, different body, but not naturally, if it is true that each of the simple bodies has one natural motion only. Moreover, granted that (a) unnatural motion is the contrary of natural, (b) a thing can have only one contrary, then circular motion, seeing it is one of the simple motions, must, if it is not the motion natural to the moved body, be contrary to its nature. Suppose now that the body which is moving in a circle be fire or some other of the four elements, than its natural motion must be contrary to the circular. But a thing can have only one contrary, and the contrary of upward is downward, and *vice versa*. Suppose on the other hand that this body which is moving in a circle contrary to its own nature is something other than the elements, there must be some other motion which is natural to it. But that is impossible: for if the motion were upward, the body would be fire or air, if downward, water or earth.

Furthermore, circular motion must be primary. That which is complete is prior in nature to the incomplete, and the cir-

cle is a complete figure, whereas no straight line can be so. An infinite straight line cannot, for to be complete it would have to have an end or completion, nor yet a finite, for all finite lines have something beyond them: any one of them is capable of being extended. Now if (a) a motion which is prior to another is the motion of a body prior in nature, (b) circular motion is prior to rectilinear, (c) rectilinear motion is the motion of the simple bodies (as *e.g.* fire moves in a straight line upwards and earthy bodies move downward towards the centre), then circular motion also must of necessity be the motion of some simple body. (We have already made the reservation that the motion of composite bodies is determined by whatever simple body predominates in the mixture.) From all these premises therefore it clearly follows that there exists some physical substance besides the four in our sublunary world, and moreover that it is more divine than, and prior to, all these. The same can also be proved on the further assumption that all motion is either natural or unnatural, and that motion which is unnatural to one body is natural to another, as the motions up and down are natural or unnatural to fire and earth respectively; from these it follows that circular motion too, since it is unnatural to these elements, [269ᵇ] is natural to some other. Moreover, if circular motion is natural to anything, it will clearly be one of the simple and primary bodies of such a nature as to move naturally in a circle, as fire moves upward and earth downward. If on the other hand it be maintained that the revolutionary motion of the body which is carried round in a circle is unnatural, it is strange, in fact quite absurd, that being unnatural it should yet be the only continuous and eternal motion, seeing that in the rest of nature what is unnatural is the quickest to fall into decay. And so, if fire be the body carried round, as some say, this motion will be no less unnatural to it than motion downwards;

for we see the natural motion of fire to be in a straight line away from the centre.

Thus the reasoning from all our premises goes to make us believe that there is some other body separate from those around us here, and of a higher nature in proportion as it is removed from the sublunary world.

## Chapter III

After what has been said, whether laid down as hypothesis or demonstrated in the course of the argument, it becomes clear that not every body has either lightness or weight. However, we must first lay down what we mean by heavy and light, at present only so far as it is necessary for the purpose in hand, but later with more precision, when we come to investigate the real nature of the two. Let "the heavy" then be that whose nature it is to move towards the centre, "the light" that whose nature it is to move away from the centre, "heaviest" that which sinks below all other bodies whose motion is downwards, and "lightest" that which rises to the top of the bodies whose motion is upwards. Thus every body which moves downwards or upwards must have either lightness or weight or both. (A body cannot of course be both heavy and light in relation to the same thing, but the elements are so in relation to each other, e.g. air is light in comparison with water, but water in comparison with earth.) Now the body whose motion is circular cannot have either weight or lightness, for neither naturally nor unnaturally can it ever move towards or away from the centre. (a) Naturally it cannot have rectilinear motion, because it was laid down that each simple body has only one natural motion, and therefore it would itself be one of the bodies whose natural motion is rectilinear. (b) But suppose it moves in a straight line contrary to its nature, then if the motion is downwards, upward motion will be its [270ᵃ]

natural one, and *vice versa;* for it was one of our hypotheses that of two contrary motions, if one is unnatural the other is natural. Taking into account then the fact that a whole and its part move naturally in the same direction (as do *e.g.* all earth together and a small clod), we have established (a) that it has neither lightness nor weight, since otherwise it would have been able to move naturally either towards the centre or away from the centre, (b) that it cannot move locally by being violently forced either up or down, for it is impossible for it to move, either naturally or unnaturally, with any other motion but its down, either itself as a whole or any of its parts, seeing that the same argument applies to whole and part.

With equal reason we may regard it as ungenerated and indestructible, and susceptible neither to growth nor alteration. (a) Everything that is generated comes into being out of an opposite and a substrate, and is destroyed only if it has a substrate, and through the agency of an opposite, and passes into its opposite, as has been explained in our first discussions. (b) Opposites have opposite motions. (c) There cannot be an opposite to the body under discussion, because there cannot be an opposite motion to the circular. It looks then as if nature had providently abstracted from the class of opposites that which was to be ungenerated and indestructible, because generation and destruction take place among opposites. Moreover anything which is subject to growth [or diminution] grows [or diminishes] in consequence of substance of the same kind being added to it and dissolving into its matter; but this body has no such matter. And if it is subject neither to growth nor to destruction, the same train of thought leads us to suppose that it is not subject to alteration either. Alteration is movement in respect of quality, and the temporary or permanent states of quality, health and disease for example, do not come into being without changes of affection. But all physical bodies which possess changing affections may be seen to be subject also to growth and diminution. Such are, for example, the bodies of animals and plants and their parts, and also those of the elements. If then the body whose natural motion is circular cannot be subject to growth or diminution, it is a reasonable supposition that it is not subject to alternation either.

From what has been said it is [270ᵇ] clear why, if our hypotheses are to be trusted, the primary body of all is eternal, suffers neither growth nor diminution, but is ageless, unalterable and impassive. I think too that the argument bears out experience and is borne out by it. All men have a conception of gods, and all assign the highest place to the divine, both barbarians and Hellenes, as many as believe in gods, supposing, obviously, that immortal is closely linked with immortal. It could not, they think, be otherwise. If then—and it is true—there is something divine, what we have said about the primary bodily substances is well said. The truth of it is also clear from the evidence of the senses, enough at least to warrant the assent of human faith; for throughout all past time, according to the records handed down from generation to generation, we find no trace of change either in the whole of the outermost heaven or in any one of its proper parts. It seems too that the name of this first body has been passed down to the present time by the ancients, who thought of it in the same way as we do, for we cannot help believing that the same ideas recur to men not once nor twice but over and over again. Thus they, believing that the primary body was something different from earth and fire and air and water, gave the name *aither* to the uppermost region, choosing its title from the fact that it "runs always" (ἀεὶ θεῖν) and eternally. (Anaxagoras badly misapplies the word when he uses *aither* for fire.)

It is also clear from what has been said why the number of the simple bodies, as well call them, cannot be more than we have mentioned. A simple body must have a simple motion, and we hold that these are the only simple motions, circular and rectilinear, the latter of two sorts, away from the centre and towards the centre.

# ON THE SOUL

## Book II
### (Chapters I-III : What Is a Soul?)

I. The theories of the soul [412ᵃ] handed down by our predecessors have been sufficiently discussed; now let us start afresh, as it were, and try to determine what the soul is, and what definition of it will be most comprehensive. We describe one class of existing things as substance; and this we subdivide into three: (1) matter, which· in itself is not an individual thing; (2) shape or form, in virtue of which individuality is directly attributed, and (3) the compound of the two. Matter is potentiality, while form is realization or actuality, and the word actuality is used in two senses, illustrated by the possession of knowledge and the exercise of it.[1] Bodies seem to be pre-eminently

1 If you have the capacity to acquire knowledge of a subject, you may be said to have potential knowledge of it, which will become actual by study. In another sense, if you possess knowledge which you are not using, it may be called potential, actual only when you are using it.

substances, and most particularly those which are of natural origin; for these are the sources from which the rest are derived. But of natural bodies some have life and some have not; by life we mean the capacity for self-sustenance, growth, and decay. Every natural body, then, which possesses life must be substance, and substance of the compound type. But since it is a body of a definite kind, *viz.*, having life, the body cannot be soul, for the body is not something predicated of a subject, but rather is itself to be regarded as a subject, *i.e.*, as matter.[2] So the soul must be substance in the sense of being the form of a natural body, which potentially has life. And substance in this sense is actuality. The soul, then, is the actuality of the kind of body we have described. But actuality has two senses, analogous to the possession of knowledge and the exercise of it. Clearly actuality in our present sense is analogous to the possession of knowledge; for both sleep and waking depend upon the presence of soul, and waking is analogous to the exercise of knowledge, sleep to its possession but not its exercise. Now in one and the same person the possession of knowledge comes first. The soul may therefore be defined as the first actuality of a natural body potentially possessing life; and such will be any body which possesses organs. (The parts of plants are organs too, though very simple [412ᵇ] ones: *e.g.*, the leaf protects the pericarp, and the pericarp protects the seed; the roots are analogous to the mouth, for both these absorb food.) If then one is to find a definition which will apply to every soul, it will be "the first actual-

ity of a natural body possessed by organs." So one need no more ask whether body and soul are one than than whether the wax and the impression it receives are one, or in general whether the matter of each thing is the same as that of which it is the matter; for admitting that the terms unity and being are used in many senses, the paramount sense is that of actuality.

We have, then, given a general definition of what the soul is: it is substance in the sense of formula; *i.e.*, the essence of such-and-such a body. Suppose[3] that an implement, *e.g.* an axe, were a natural body; the substance of the axe would be that which makes it an axe, and this would be its soul; suppose this removed, and it would no longer be an axe, except equivocally. As it is, it remains an axe, because it is not of this kind of body that the soul is the essence or formula, but only of a certain kind of natural body which has in itself a principle of movement and rest. We must, however, investigate our definition in relation to the parts of the body. If the eye were a living creature, its soul would be its vision; for this is the substance in the sense of formula of the eye. But the eye is the matter of vision, and if vision fails there is no eye, except in an equivocal sense, as for instance a stone or painted eye.

---

2 Every "substance" is composed of two factors—matter and form; *e.g.* a billiard ball. Its matter is ivory, its form spherical. An animate body, then, as it is a substance, consists of matter and form. The body must be matter, for it is not itself an attribute, but has attributes. Therefore the soul is form.

---

3 A.'s argument in the rest of this chapter is not quite easy to follow. The introduction of the axe seems at first irrelevant, because, as A. afterwards explains, being inanimate, it is not really parallel to the living creature. But his point is clear, the axe consists of the matter (wood and metal) of which it is composed, and its form (*i.e.* what makes it an axe—cutting edge, weight, and so forth). If you take away (*e.g.*) its edge, what remains? Still an axe, although one that will not cut. But this is not true of the living creature. It has a body which is its matter, and a soul which is its form. Take away the latter and the body perishes, so that the whole is no longer a living creature; by removing the form of a living creature we destroy its identity.

Now we must apply what we have found true of the part to the whole living body. For the same relation must hold good of the whole of sensation to the whole sentient body *qua* sentient as obtains between their respective parts. That which has the capacity to live is not the body which has lost its soul, but that which possesses its soul; so seed and fruit are potentially bodies of this kind. The waking state is actuality in the same sense as the cutting of the axe or the seeing of the eye, while the soul is actuality in the same sense as [413ᵃ] the faculty of the eye for seeing, or of the implement for doing its work. The body is that which exists potentially; but just as the pupil and the faculty of seeing make an eye, so in the other case the soul and body make a living creature. It is quite clear, then, that neither the soul nor certain parts of it, if it has parts, can be separated from the body; for in some cases the actuality belongs to the parts themselves. Not but what there is nothing to prevent some parts being separated, because they are not actualities of any body. It is also uncertain whether the soul as an actuality bears the same relation to the body as the sailor to the ship. This must suffice as an attempt to determine in rough outline the nature of the soul.

II. But since the definite and logically more intelligible conception arises from the vague but more obvious data of sense, we must try to review the question of the soul in this light; for a definitive formula ought not merely to show the fact, as most definitions do, but to contain and exhibit the cause. But in practice the formulae of our definitions are like conclusions; for instance, what is squaring a rectangle? The construction of an equilateral rectangle equal to an oblong rectangle. Such a definition is merely a statement of the conclusion. But if a man says that squaring a rectangle is the finding of a mean pro-

portional, he is giving the underlying cause of the thing to be defined.[4]

We say then, assuming a fresh starting-point for our inquiry, that that which has soul is distinguished from that which has not by living. But the word living is used in many senses, and we say that a thing lives if any one of the following is present in it—mind, sensation, movement or rest in space, besides the movement implied in nutrition and decay or growth. Consequently all plants are considered to live, for they evidently have in themselves a capacity and first principle by means of which they exhibit both growth and decay in opposite directions; for they do not grow up and not down, but equally in both directions, and in every direction, and they are nourished and continue to live, as long as they are able to absorb food. This capacity to absorb food may exist apart from all other powers, but the others cannot exist apart from this in mortal beings. This is evident in the case of plants; for they have no other capacity of the soul.

This, then, is the principle [413ᵇ] through which all living things have life,

---

[4] AB is a straight line divided into two parts at C. On AB a semicircle ADB is described. CD is drawn at right angles to AB to meet the circumference in D. Two conclusions can be proved. (1) The square on CD is equal to the rectangle AC.CB. (2) CD is the mean proportional between AC and CB, or in other words AC:CD::CD:CB. For the proofs of these two propositions *cf.* Euclid ii. 14 and vi. 13.

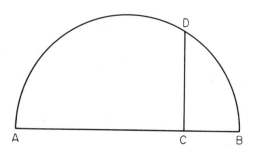

but the first characteristic of an animal is sensation; for even those which do not move or change their place, but have sensation, we call living creatures, and do not merely say that they live. The first essential factor of sensation, which we all share, is a sense of touch. Just as the merely nutritive faculty may exist apart from touch and from all sensation, so touch may exist apart from all other senses. (By "nutritive faculty" I mean that part of the soul which even the plants share; all animals obviously possess the sense of touch.) Why each of these two facts is so, we shall explain later on.

But for the moment let us be satisfied with saying that the soul is the origin of the characteristics we have mentioned, and is defined by them, that is by the faculties of nutrition, sensation, thought and movement. The further questions, whether each of these faculties is a soul, or part of a soul, and, if a part, whether a part in the sense that it is only separable in thought or also in space, are in some cases easy of solution, but others involve difficulty. For just as in the case of plants some parts clearly live when divided and separated from each other, so that the soul in them appears to be one in actuality in each whole plant, but potentially more than one, so we can see that in other varieties of the soul the same thing happens, e.g., in insects which are divided; for each of the parts has sensation and movement in space; and, if it has sensation, it must also have imagination and appetite; for, where sensation is, there is also pain and pleasure, and where these are there must also be desire. But in the case of the mind and the thinking faculty nothing is yet clear; it seems to be a distinct kind of soul, and it alone admits of being separated, as the immortal from the perishable. But it is quite clear from what we have said that the other parts of the soul are

not separable, as some say; though it is obvious that they are theoretically different; for there is a difference between the abstract faculties of sensation and opinion, just as feeling is different from opining. The same is true of all the other faculties we have mentioned. Again, some animals have all these faculties, some only some of them, and others again only one. It is this which constitutes the differences between animals; the reason for it must be [414ᵃ] considered later. It is much the same with the senses; for some animals have all, some only some, and some again one only—the most indispensable— touch.

The phrase "that whereby we live and perceive" has two senses, as has "that whereby we know" (in the one sense we mean knowledge and in the other the soul; for we can say that we know by each of these); similarly we are healthy either by health or by part or the whole of the body. Now of these, knowledge and health are a kind of shape or form, or notion; an actuality, as it were, of the recipient, i.e. of that which is capable of knowledge or health (for the actualization of active processes appears to reside in the patient upon which the effect is produced), and the soul is that whereby we live and perceive and think in the primary sense; so that the soul would be the notion or form, and not the matter or substrate. As we have already said, substance is used in three senses, form, matter, and a compound of the two. Of these matter is potentiality, and form actuality; and since the compound is an animate thing, the body cannot be the actuality of a soul, but the soul is the actuality of some body. For this reason those are right in their view who maintain that the soul cannot exist without the body, but is not itself in any sense a body. It is not a body, it is associated with a body, and therefore resides in a body, and in a body of a particular kind; not at all as our predecessors supposed, who fitted it to any body, without adding any limitations as to what body or what kind of body, although it is unknown for any chance thing to admit any other chance thing. But our view explains the facts quite reasonably;[5] for the actuality of each thing is naturally inherent in its potentiality, that is in its own proper matter. From all this it is clear that the soul is a kind of actuality or notion of that which has the capacity of having a soul.

III. Now of the faculties of the soul which we have mentioned, some living things, as we have said, have all, others only some, and others again only one. Those which we have mentioned are the faculties for nourishment, for appetite, for sensation, for movement in space, and for thought. Plants have the nutritive faculty only, but other living things have the faculty for sensation too. But if for sensation then also for [414ᵇ] appetite; for appetite consists of desire, inclination, and wish, and all animals have at least one of the senses, that of touch; and that which has sensation knows pleasure and pain, the pleasant and the painful, and that which knows these has also desire; for desire is an appetite for what is pleasant. Again, they have a sense which perceives food; for touch is the sense which does this. All animals feed on what is dry or wet, hot or cold, and touch is the sense which apprehends these; the other objects of sense are only indirectly apprehended by touch. Neither sound, nor colour, nor smell contributes anything to nourishment; but flavour is one of the things apprehended by touch. Hunger and thirst are desire, the former for what is dry and hot, the latter for what is cold and wet; flavour is a kind

of seasoning of these. We must be precise about these subjects later, but for the moment let it suffice to say that those animals which have a sense of touch have also appetite. The question of imagination is obscure, and must be considered later. In addition to these senses some also possess the power of movement in space, and others again—viz., man, and any other being similar or superior to him—have the power of thinking and intelligence.

Thus it is clear that there must be a single definition of soul, just as there is of rectilinear figure; for as in the latter case there is no figure besides the triangle and those that follow it (i.e., quadrilateral, pentagon, etc.), so there is no soul besides those we have mentioned. It would be possible in the case of figures to frame a common definition, which would fit them all, but would be descriptive of no particular figure; and similarly in the case of the kinds of soul we have mentioned. Hence it would be ridiculous, in this case as in others, to look for the common definition, which is the particular definition of no existing thing, and has no reference to any special or individual species, while we neglect such a particular definition.[6]

The facts regarding the soul are much the same as those relating to figures; for both in figures and in things which possess soul, the earlier type always exists potentially in that which follows; e.g., the triangle is implied by the quadrilateral, and the nutritive faculty by the sensitive. We must then inquire in each several case, what is the soul of each individual, for instance of the plant, the man, and the beast. But we must also consider why they are thus arranged

---

5 I.e. on general grounds we should expect a particular soul to belong to a particular body.

6 The argument of this paragraph is as follows: Just as figure has a definition applicable to all varieties of figures, so soul has a similar "common" definition; but to understand individual types of soul, e.g., of man, animal, and plant, we must study these types themselves.

in a series. For without the nutri- [415ª] tive faculty the sensitive does not exist, but in plants the nutritive is divorced from the sensitive faculty. Again, without the sense of touch none of the other senses exist, but touch may exist without any others; for many of the animals have neither vision nor hearing nor any sense of smell at all. Again, of those which have sensation, some have the locomotive faculty, and some have not. And lastly, and most rarely, living creatures have power of reasoning and thought. For those perishable creatures which have reasoning power have all the other powers as well, but not all those which have any one of them have reasoning power; some have not even imagination, while others live in virtue of this alone. The consideration of the speculative faculty is another question. It is clear, then, that the account of each of these faculties is also the most relevant account that can be given of the soul.

## Book III
## (Chapters IV-V : Mind and Thinking)

IV. Concerning that part of the soul (whether it is separable in extended space, or only in thought) with which the soul knows and thinks, we have to consider what is its distinguishing characteristic, and how thinking comes about. If it is analogous to perceiving, it must be either a process in which the soul is acted upon by what is thinkable, or something else of a similar kind. This part, then, must (although impassive) be receptive of the form of an object, i.e., must be potentially the same as its object, although not identical with it: as the sensitive is to the sensible, so must mind be to the thinkable. It is necessary then that mind, since it thinks all things, should be uncontaminated, as Anaxagoras says, in order that it may be in control, that is, that it may know; for the intrusion of anything foreign

hinders and obstructs it. Hence the mind, too, can have no characteristic except its capacity to receive. That part of the soul, then, which we call mind (by mind I mean that part by which the soul thinks and forms judgements) has no actual existence until it thinks. So it is unreasonable to suppose that it is mixed with the body; for in that case it would become somehow qualitative, e.g., hot or cold, or would even have some organ, as the sensitive faculty has; but in fact it has none. It has been well said that the soul is the place of forms, except that this does not apply to the soul as a whole, but only in its thinking capacity, and the forms occupy it not actually but only potentially. But that the perceptive and thinking faculties are not alike in their impassivity is obvious if we consider the sense organs and sensation. For the sense loses sensation under the stimulus of a too violent sensible object; e.g., of sound imme- [429ᵇ] diately after loud sounds, and neither seeing nor smelling is possible just after strong colours and scents; but when mind thinks the highly intelligible, it is not less able to think of slighter things, but even more able; for the faculty of sense is not apart from the body, whereas the mind is separable. But when the mind has become the several groups of its objects, as the learned man when active is said to do (and this happens, when he can exercise his function by himself), even then the mind is in a sense potential, though not quite in the same way as before it learned and discovered; moreover the mind is then capable of thinking itself.

Since magnitude is not the same as the essence of magnitude, nor water the same as the essence of water (and so too in many other cases, but not in all, because in some cases there is no difference), we judge flesh and the essence of flesh either by different faculties, or by the same faculty in different relations; for flesh cannot exist without its matter, but like "snub-nosed" implies a definite form in a definite matter. Now it is by the sensitive faculty that we judge hot and cold, and all qualities whose due proportion constitutes flesh; but it is by a different sense, either quite distinct, or related to it in the same way as a bent line to itself when pulled out straight, that we judge the essence of flesh. Again, among abstract objects "straight" is like "snub-nosed," for it is always combined with extension; but its essence, if "straight" and "straightness" are not the same, is something different; let us call it duality. Therefore we judge it by another faculty, or by the same faculty in a different relation. And speaking generally, as objects are separable from their matter so also are the corresponding faculties of the mind.

One might raise the question: if the mind is a simple thing, and not liable to be acted upon, and has nothing in common with anything else, as Anaxagoras says, how will it think, if thinking is a form of being acted upon? For it is when two things have something in common that we regard one as acting and the other as acted upon. And our second problem is whether the mind itself can be an object of thought.[7] For either mind will be present in all other objects (if, that is, mind is an object of thought in itself and not in virtue of something else, and what is thought is always identical in form), or else it will contain some common element, which makes it an object of thought like other things. Or there is the explanation which we have given before of the phrase "being acted upon in virtue of some common element," that mind is potentially identical with the objects of thought but is actually nothing, until it thinks. What the mind

thinks must be in it in the same sense as letters are on a tablet which bears no actual writing; this is just what happens in the case of the mind. It [430ᵃ] is also itself thinkable, just like other objects of thought. For in the case of things without matter that which thinks and that which is thought are the same; for speculative knowledge is the same as its object. (We must consider why mind does not always think.) In things which have matter, each of the objects of thought is only potentially present. Hence while material objects will not have mind in them (for it is apart from their matter that mind is potentially identical with them) mind will still have the capacity of being thought.

V. Since in every class of objects, just as in the whole of nature, there is something which is their matter, *i.e.*, which is potentially all the individuals, and something else which is their cause or agent in that it makes them all—the two being related as an art to its material—these distinct elements must be present in the soul also. Mind in the passive sense is such because it becomes all things, but mind has another aspect in that it makes all things; this is a kind of positive state like light; for in a sense light makes potential into actual colours. Mind in this sense is separable, impassive and unmixed, since it is essentially an activity; for the agent is always superior to the patient, and the originating cause to the matter. Actual knowledge is identical with its object. Potential is prior in time to actual knowledge in the individual, but in general it is not prior in time. Mind does not think intermittently. When isolated it is its true self and nothing more, and this alone is immortal and everlasting (we do not remember[8] because, while mind in this sense cannot be acted upon, mind in the passive sense is perishable), and without this nothing thinks.

---

[7] This and the succeeding sentence are not very satisfactory; but A. is apparently arguing that if mind is *sui generis* it cannot be an object of thought, for this would put it in the same class as other objects of thought.

[8] *Sc.*, its previous activity.

# NICOMACHEAN ETHICS

## Book I

*(Chapters I-VII and XIII: Introduction to Ethics, The Good for Man, Happiness, Intellectual and Moral Virtues)*

I. Every art and every investi- [1094ᵃ] gation, and likewise every practical pursuit or undertaking, seems to aim at some good: hence it has been well said that the Good is That at which all things aim. (It is true that a certain variety is to be observed among the ends at which the arts and sciences aim: in some cases the activity of practising the art it itself the end, whereas in others the end is some product over and above the mere exercise of the art; and in the arts whose ends are certain things beside the practice of the arts themselves, these products are essentially superior in value to the activities.) But as there are numerous pursuits and arts and sciences, it follows that their ends are correspondingly numerous: for instance, the end of the science of medicine is health, that of the art of ship-building a vessel, that of strategy victory, that of domestic economy wealth. Now in cases where several such pursuits are subordinate to some single faculty—as bridle-making and the other trades concerned with horses' harness are subordinate to horsemanship, and this and every other military pursuit to the science of strategy, and similarly other arts to different arts again—in all these cases, I say, the ends of the master arts are things more to be desired than all those of the arts subordinate to them; since the latter ends are only pursued for the sake of the former. (And it makes no difference whether the ends of the pursuits are the activities themselves or some other thing beside these, as in the case of the sciences mentioned.)

II. If therefore among the ends at which our actions aim there be one which we wish for its own sake, while we wish the others only for the sake of this, and if we do not choose everything for the sake of something else (which would obviously result in a process *ad infinitum*, so that all desire would be futile and vain), it is clear that this one ultimate End must be the Good, and indeed the Supreme Good. Will not then a knowledge of this Supreme Good be also of great practical importance for the conduct of life? Will it not better enable us to attain what is fitting, like archers having a target to aim at? If this be so, we ought to make an attempt to determine at all events in outline what exactly this Supreme Good is, and of which of the theoretical or practical sciences it is the object.

Now it would be agreed that it must be the object of the most authoritative of the sciences—some science which is pre-eminently a master-craft. But such is manifestly the science of Politics; for it is this that ordains which of the sciences are to exist in states, and what branches of knowledge the dif- [1094ᵇ] ferent classes of the citizens are to learn, and up to what point; and we observe that even the most highly esteemed of the faculties, such as strategy, domestic economy, oratory, are subordinate to the political science. Inasmuch then as the rest of the sciences are employed by this one, and as it moreover lays down laws as to what people shall do and what things they shall refrain from doing, the end of this science must include the ends of all the others. Therefore, the Good of man must be the end of the science of Politics. For even though it be the case that the Good is the same for the individual and for the state, nevertheless, the good of the state is manifestly a greater and more perfect good, both to attain and to preserve. To secure the good of one person only is better than nothing; but to secure the good of a nation or a state is a nobler and more divine achievement.

This then being its aim, our investigation is in a sense the study of Politics.

III. Now our treatment of this science will be adequate, if it achieves that amount of precision which belongs to its subject matter. The same exactness must not be expected in all departments of philosophy alike, any more than in all the products of the arts and crafts. The subjects studied by political science are Moral Nobility and Justice; but these conceptions involve much difference of opinion and uncertainty, so that they are sometimes believed to be mere conventions and to have no real existence in the nature of things. And a similar uncertainty surrounds the conception of the Good, because it frequently occurs that good things have harmful consequences: people have before now been ruined by wealth, and in other cases courage has cost men their lives. We must therefore be content if, in dealing with subjects and starting from premises thus uncertain, we succeed in presenting a broad outline of the truth: when our subjects and our premises are merely generalities, it is enough if we arrive at generally valid conclusions. Accordingly we may ask the student also to accept the various views we put forward in the same spirit; for it is the mark of an educated mind to expect that amount of exactness in each kind which the nature of the particular subject admits. It is equally unreasonable to accept merely probable conclusions from a mathematician and to demand strict demonstration from an orator.

Again, each man judges correctly those matters with which he is acquainted; it is of these that he is a competent critic. To criticize a particular subject, therefore, a man must have been trained in that subject: to be a good critic generally, he must [1095ᵃ] have had an all-round education. Hence the young are not fit to be students of Political Science. For they have no experience of life and conduct, and it is these that supply the premises and subject matter of this branch of philosophy. And moreover they are led by their feelings; so that they will study the subject to no purpose or advantage, since the end of this science is not knowledge but action. And it makes no difference whether they are young in years or immature in character: the defect is not a question of time, it is because their life and its various aims are guided by feeling; for to such persons their knowledge is of no use, any more than it is to persons of defective self-restraint. But Moral Science may be of great value to those who guide their desires and actions by principle.

Let so much suffice by way of introduction as to the student of the subject, the spirit in which our conclusions are to be received, and the object that we set before us.

IV. To resume, inasmuch as all studies and undertakings are directed to the attainment of some good, let us discuss what it is that we pronounce to be the aim of Politics, that is, what is the highest of all the goods that action can achieve. As far as the name goes, we may almost say that the great majority of mankind are agreed about this; for both multitude and persons of refinement speak of it as Happiness, and conceive "the good life" or "doing well" to be the same thing as "being happy." But what constitutes happiness is a matter of dispute; and the popular account of it is not the same as that given by the philosophers. Ordinary people identify it with some obvious and visible good, such as pleasure or wealth or honour—some say one thing and some another, indeed very often the same man says different things at different times: when he falls sick he thinks health is happiness, when he is poor, wealth. At other times, feeling conscious of their own ignorance, men admire those who propound something grand and above their heads; and it has been held by some thinkers that beside the many good things we have mentioned, there exists another Good, that is good in itself, and stands to all those goods as the cause of their being good.

Now perhaps it would be a somewhat fruitless task to review all the different opinions that are held. It will suffice to examine those that are most widely prevalent, or that seem to have some argument in their favour.

And we must not overlook the distinction between arguments that start from first principles and those that lead to first principles. It was a good practice of Plato to raise this question, and to enquire whether the right procedure was to start from or to lead up to the first principles, as in a race-course one may run from the judges to the far end of the track or reversely. Now no doubt it is proper to start from the [1095b] known. But "the known" has two meanings—"what is known to us," which is one thing, and "what is knowable in itself," which is another. Perhaps then for us at all events it is proper to start from what is known to us. This is why in order to be a competent student of the Right and Just, and in short of the topics of Politics in general, the pupil is bound to have been well trained in his habits. For the starting-point or first principle is the fact that a thing is so; if this be satisfactorily ascertained, there will be no need also to know the reason why it is so. And the man of good moral training knows first principle already, or can easily acquire them. As for the person who neither knows nor can learn, let him hear the words of Hesiod:

Best is the man who can himself advise;
He too is good who hearkens to the wise;
But who, himself being witless, will not heed
Another's wisdom, is worthless indeed.

V. But let us continue from the point where we digressed. To judge from men's lives, the more or less reasoned conceptions of the Good or Happiness that seem to prevail among them are the following. On the one hand the generality of men and the most vulgar identify the Good with pleasure, and accordingly are content with the Life of Enjoyment—for there are three specially prominent Lives, the one just mentioned, the Life of Politics, and thirdly, the Life of Contemplation. The generality of mankind then show themselves to be utterly slavish, by preferring what is only a life for cattle; but they get a hearing for their view as reasonable because many persons of high position share the feelings of Sardanapallus.

Men of refinement, on the other hand, and men of action think that the Good is honour—for this may be said to be the end of the Life of Politics. But honour after all seems too superficial to be the Good for which we are seeking; since it appears to depend on those who confer it more than on him upon whom it is conferred, whereas we instinctively feel that the Good must be something proper to its possessor and not easy to be taken away from him. Moreover men's motive in pursuing honour seems to be to assure themselves of their own merit; at least they seek to be honoured by men of judgement and by people who know them, that is, they desire to be honoured on the ground of virtue. It is clear therefore that in the opinion at all events of men of action, virtue is a greater good than honour; and one might perhaps accordingly suppose that virtue rather than honour is the end of the Political Life. But even virtue proves on examination to be too incomplete to be the End; since it appears possible to possess it while you are asleep, or without putting it into practice throughout the whole of your life; and also for the virtuous man to suffer the greatest misery and misfortune—though no one [1096ᵃ] would pronounce a man living a life of misery to be happy, unless for the sake of maintaining a paradox. But we need not pursue this subject, since it has been sufficiently treated in the ordinary discussions.

The third type of life is the Life of Contemplation, which we shall consider in the sequel.

The Life of Money-making is a constrained kind of life, and clearly wealth is not the Good we are in search of, for it is only good as being useful, a means to something else. On this score indeed one might conceive the ends before mentioned to have a better claim, for they are approved for their own sakes. But even they do not really seem to be the Supreme Good; however, many arguments have been laid down in regard to them, so we may dismiss them.

VI. But perhaps it is desirable that we should examine the notion of a Universal Good, and review the difficulties that it involves, although such an enquiry goes against the grain because of our friendship for the authors of the Theory of Ideas. Still perhaps it would appear desirable, and indeed it would seem to be obligatory, especially for a philosopher, to sacrifice even one's closest personal ties in defence of the truth. Both are dear to us, yet 'tis our duty to prefer the truth.

The originators of this theory, then, used not to postulate Ideas of groups of things in which they posited an order of priority and posteriority (for which reason they did not construct an Idea of numbers in general). But Good is predicated alike in the Categories of Substance, of Quality, and of Relation; yet the Absolute, or Substance, is prior in nature to the Relative, which seems to be a sort of offshoot or "accident" of Substance; so that there cannot be a common Idea corresponding to the absolutely good and the relatively good.

Again, the word "good" is used in as many senses as the word "is"; for we may predicate good in the Category of Substance, for instance of God or intelligence; in that of Quality—the excellences; in that of Quantity—moderate in amount; in that of Relation—useful; in that of Time—a favourable opportunity; in that of Place—a suitable "habitat"; and so on. So clearly good cannot be a single and universal general notion; if it were, it would not be predicable in all the Categories, but only in one.

Again, things that come under a single Idea must be objects of a single science; hence there ought to be a single science dealing with all good things. But as a matter of fact there are a number of sciences even for the goods in one Category: for example, opportunity, for opportunity in war comes under the science of strategy, in disease under that of medicine; and the due amount in diet comes under medicine, in bodily exercise under gymnastics.

One might also raise the question what precisely they mean by their expression "the Ideal so-and-so," seeing that one and the same definition of man applies both to "the Ideal man" [1096ᵇ] and to "man," for in so far as both are man, there will be no difference between them; and if so, no more will there be any difference between "the Ideal Good" and "Good" in so far as both are good. Nor yet will the Ideal Good be any more good because it is eternal, seeing that a white thing that lasts a long time is no whiter than one that lasts only a day.

The Pythagoreans seem to give a more probable doctrine on the subject of the Good when they place Unity in their column of goods; and indeed Speusippus[1] appears to have followed them. But

_____

[1] Speusippus was Plato's nephew, and succeeded him as head of the Academy.

this subject must be left for another discussion.

We can descry an objection that may be raised against our arguments on the ground that the theory in question was not intended to apply to every sort of good, and that only things pursued and accepted for their own sake are pronounced good as belonging to a single species, while things productive or preservative of these in any way, or preventive of their opposites, are said to be good as a means to these, and in a different sense. Clearly then the term "goods" would have two meanings, (1) things good in themselves and (2) things good as a means to these; let us then separate things good in themselves from things useful as means, and consider whether the former are called good because they fall under a single Idea. But what sort of things is one to class as good in themselves? Are they not those things which are sought after even without any accessory advantage, such as wisdom, sight, and certain pleasures and honours? for even if we also pursue these things as means to something else, still one would class them among things good in themselves. Or is there nothing else good in itself except the Idea? If so, the species will be of no use. If on the contrary the class of things good in themselves includes these objects, the same notion of good ought to be manifested in all of them, just as the same notion of white is manifested in snow and in white paint. But as a matter of fact the notions of honour and wisdom and pleasure, as being good, are different and distinct. Therefore, good is not a general term corresponding to a single Idea.

But in what sense then are different things called good? For they do not seem to be a case of things that bear the same name merely by chance. Possibly things are called good in virtue of being derived from one good; or because they all contribute to one good. Or perhaps it is rather by way of a proportion: that is, as sight is good in the body, so intelligence is good in the soul, and similarly another thing in something else.

Perhaps however this question must be dismissed for the present, since a detailed investigation of it belongs more properly to another branch of philosophy. And likewise with the Idea of the Good; for even if the goodness predicated of various things in common really is a unity or something existing separately and absolute, it clearly will not be practicable or attainable by man; but the Good which we are now seeking is a good within human reach.

But possibly someone may think that to know the Ideal Good may be desirable as an aid to achieving those goods which are practicable and attainable: having the Ideal Good as a pattern we [1097ᵃ] shall more easily know what things are good for us, and knowing them, obtain them. Now it is true that this argument has a certain plausibility; but it does not seem to square with the actual procedure of the sciences. For these all aim at some good, and seek to make up their deficiencies, but they do not trouble about a knowledge of the Ideal Good. Yet if it were so potent an aid, it is improbable that all the professors of the arts and sciences should not know it, nor even seek to discover it. Moreover, it is not easy to see *how* knowing that same Ideal Good will help a weaver or carpenter in the practice of his own craft, or how anybody will be a better physician or general for having contemplated the absolute Idea. In fact it does not appear that the physician studies even health in the abstract; he studies the health of the human being—or rather of some particular human being, for it is individuals that he has to cure.

Let us here conclude our discussion of this subject.

VII. We may now return to the Good which is the object of our search, and try to find out what exactly it can be. For good appears to be one thing in one pursuit or art and another in another: it is different in medicine from what it is in strategy, and so on with the rest of the arts. What definition of the Good then will hold true in all the arts? Perhaps we may define it as that for the sake of which everything else is done. This applies to something different in each different art—to health in the case of medicine, to victory in that of strategy, to a house in architecture, and to something else in each of the other arts; but in every pursuit or undertaking it describes the end of that pursuit or undertaking, since in all of them it is for the sake of the end that everything else is done. Hence if there be something which is the end of all the things done by human action, this will be the practicable Good—or if there be several such ends, the sum of these will be the Good. Thus by changing its ground the argument has reached the same result as before. We must attempt however to render this still more precise.

Now there do appear to be several ends at which our actions aim; but as we choose some of them—for instance wealth, or flutes, and instruments generally—as a means to something else, it is clear that not all of them are final ends; whereas the Supreme Good seems to be something final. Consequently if there be some one thing which alone is a final end, this thing—or if there be several final ends, the one among them which is the most final—will be the Good which we are seeking. In speaking of degrees of finality, we mean that a thing pursued as an end in itself is more final than one pursued as a means to something else, and that a thing never chosen as a means to anything else is more final than things chosen both as ends in themselves and as means to that thing; and accordingly a thing chosen always as an end and never as a means we call absolutely final. Now happiness above all else appears to be absolutely final in this sense, since we always choose it for its own sake and never as [1097ᵇ] a means to something else; whereas honour, pleasure, intelligence, and excel-

lence in its various forms, we choose indeed for their own sakes (since we should be glad to have each of them although no extraneous advantage resulted from it), but we also choose them for the sake of happiness, in the belief that they will be a means to our securing it. But no one chooses happiness for the sake of honour, pleasure, etc., nor as a means to anything whatever other than itself.

The same conclusion also appears to follow from a consideration of the self-sufficiency of happiness—for it is felt that the final good must be a thing sufficient in itself. The term self-sufficient, however, we employ with reference not to oneself alone, living a life of isolation, but also to one's parents and children and wife, and one's friends and fellow citizens in general, since man is by nature a social being. On the other hand a limit has to be assumed in these relationships; for if the list be extended to one's ancestors and descendants and to the friends of one's friends, it will go on *ad infinitum*. But this is a point that must be considered later on; we take a self-sufficient thing to mean a thing which merely standing by itself alone renders life desirable and lacking in nothing, and such a thing we deem happiness to be. Moreover, we think happiness the most desirable of all good things without being itself reckoned as one among the rest; for if it were so reckoned, it is clear that we should consider it more desirable when even the smallest of other good things were combined with it, since this addition would result in a larger total of good, and of two goods the greater is always the more desirable.

Happiness, therefore, being found to be something final and self-sufficient, is the End at which all actions aim.

To say however that the Supreme Good is happiness will probably appear a truism; we still require a more explicit account of what constitutes happiness. Perhaps then we may arrive at this by ascertaining what is man's function. For the goodness or efficiency of a flute-player or sculptor or craftsman of any sort, and in general of anybody who has some function or business to perform, is thought to reside in that function; and similarly it may be held that the good of man resides in the function of man, if he has a function.

Are we then to suppose that, while the carpenter and the shoemaker have definite functions or businesses belonging to them, man as such has none, and is not designed by nature to fulfil any function? Must we not rather assume that, just as the eye, the hand, the foot and each of the various members of the body manifestly has a certain function of its own, so a human being also has a certain function over and above all the functions of his particular members? What then precisely can this function be? The mere act of living appears to be shared even by plants, whereas we are looking for the function peculiar to man; we must therefore set aside the vital activity of nutrition and growth. Next in [1098ᵃ] the scale will come some form of sentient life; but this too appears to be shared by horses, oxen, and animals generally. There remains therefore what may be called the practical life of the rational part of man. (This part has two divisions, one rational as obedient to principle, the other as possessing principle and exercising intelligence). Rational life again has two meanings; let us assume that we are here concerned with the active exercise of the rational faculty, since this seems to be the more proper sense of the term. If then the function of man is the active exercise of the soul's faculties[2] in conformity with rational principle, or at all events not in dissociation from rational principle, and if we acknowledge the function of an individual

and of a good individual of the same class (for instance, a harper and a good harper, and so generally with all classes) to be generically the same, the qualification of the latter's superiority in excellence being added to the function in his case (I mean that if the function of a harper is to play the harp, that of a good harper is to play the harp well): if this is so, and if we declare that the function of man is a certain form of life, and define that form of life as the exercise of the soul's faculties and activities in association with rational principle, and say that the function of a good man is to perform these activities well and rightly, and if a function is well performed when it is performed in accordance with its own proper excellence—from these premises it follows that the Good of man is the active exercise of his soul's faculties in conformity with excellence or virtue, or if there be several human excellences or virtues, in conformity with the best and most perfect among them. Moreover this activity must occupy a complete lifetime; for one swallow does not make spring, nor does one fine day; and similarly one day or a brief period of happiness does not make a man supremely blessed and happy.

Let this account then serve to describe the Good in outline—for no doubt the proper procedure is to begin by making a rough sketch, and to fill it in afterwards. If a work has been well laid down in outline, to carry it on and complete it in detail may be supposed to be within the capacity of anybody; and in this working out of details Time seems to be a good inventor or at all events coadjutor. This indeed is how advances in the arts have actually come about, since anyone can fill in the gaps. Also the warning given above must not be forgotten; we must not look for equal exactness in all departments of study, but only such as belongs to the subject matter of each, and in such a degree as is appropriate to the particular line of enquiry. A carpenter and a geometrician both

---

2 Literally "activity of soul"; ψυχή however has a wider connotation than either "soul" or "mind," and includes the whole of the vitality of any living creature.

seek after a right angle, but in different ways; the former is content with that approximation to it which satisfies the purpose of his work; the latter, being a student of truth, looks for its essence or essential attributes. We should therefore proceed in the same manner in other subjects also, and not allow side issues to outweigh the main task in hand.

Nor again must we in all matters alike demand an explanation of the reason why things are what they are; in some cases it is enough if the fact that they are so is satisfactorily established. [1098ᵇ] This is the case with first principles; and the fact is the primary thing—it *is* a first principle. And principles are studied— some by induction, others by perception, others by some form of habituation, and also others otherwise; so we must endeavour to arrive at the principles of each kind in their natural manner, and must also be careful to define them correctly, since they are of great importance for the subsequent course of the enquiry. The beginning is admittedly more than half of the whole, and throws light at once on many of the questions under investigation.

. . .

XIII. Inasmuch as happiness is a certain activity of soul in conformity with perfect goodness, it is necessary to examine the nature of goodness. For this will probably assist us in our investigation of the nature of happiness. Also, the true statesman seems to be one who has made a special study of goodness, since his aim is to make the citizens good and law-abiding men—witness the lawgivers of Crete and Sparta, and the other great legislators of history; but if the study of goodness falls within the province of Political Science, it is clear that in investigating goodness we shall be keeping to the plan which we adopted at the outset.

Now the goodness that we have to consider is clearly human goodness, since

the good or happiness which we set out to seek was human good and human happiness. But human goodness means in our view excellence of soul, not excellence of body; also our definition of happiness is an activity of the soul. Now if this is so, clearly it behoves the statesman to have some acquaintance with psychology, just as the physician who is to heal the eye or the other parts of the body must know their anatomy. Indeed a foundation of science is even more requisite for the statesman, inasmuch as politics is a higher and more honourable art than medicine; but physicians of the better class devote much attention to the study of the human body. The student of politics therefore as well as the psychologist must study the nature of the soul, though he will do so as an aid to politics, and only so far as is requisite for the objects of enquiry that he has in view: to pursue the subject in further detail would doubtless be more laborious than is necessary for his purpose.

Now on the subject of psychology some of the teaching current in extraneous discourses is satisfactory, and may be adopted here: namely that the soul consists of two parts, one irrational and the other capable of reason. (Whether these two parts are really distinct in the sense that the parts of body or of any other divisible whole are distinct, or whether though distinguishable in thought as two they are inseparable in reality, like the convex and concave sides of a curve, is a question of no importance for the matter in hand.) Of the irrational part of the soul again one division appears to be common to all living things, and of a vegetative nature: I refer to the part that causes nutrition and growth; for we must assume that a vital faculty of this nature exists in all things that assimilate nourishment, including embryos—the same [1102ᵇ] faculty being present also in the fully-developed organism (this is more reasonable than to assume a different nutritive faculty in the latter). The excellence of this faculty therefore appears to be common to all animate things and not peculiar to man; for it is believed that this faculty or part of the soul is most active during sleep, but when they are asleep you cannot tell a good man from a bad one (whence the saying that for half their lives there is no difference between the happy and the miserable). This is a natural result of the fact that sleep is a cessation of the soul from the activities on which its goodness or badness depends—except that in some small degree certain of the sense-impressions may reach the soul during sleep, and consequently the dreams of the good are better than those of ordinary men. We need not however pursue this subject further, but may omit from consideration the nutritive part of the soul, since it exhibits no specifically human excellence.

But there also appears to be another element in the soul, which, though irrational, yet in a manner participates in rational principle. In self-restrained and unrestrained people we approve their principle, or the rational part of their souls, because it urges them in the right way and exhorts them to the best course; but their nature seems also to contain another element beside that of rational principle, which combats and resists that principle. Exactly the same thing may take place in the soul as occurs with the body in a case of paralysis: when the patient wills to move his limbs to the right they swerve to the left; and similarly in unrestrained persons their impulses run counter to their principle. But whereas in the body we see the erratic member, in the case of the soul we do not see it; nevertheless it cannot be doubted that in the soul also there is an element beside that of principle, which opposes and runs counter to principle (though in what sense the two are distinct does not concern us here). But this second element also seems, as we said, to participate in rational princi-

ple—and no doubt in the temperate and brave man it is still more amenable, for all parts of his nature are in harmony with principle.

Thus we see that the irrational part, as well as the soul as a whole, is double. One division of it, the vegetative, does not share in rational principle at all; the other, the seat of the appetites and of desire in general, does in a sense participate in principle, as being amenable and obedient to it (in the sense in fact in which we speak of "paying heed" to one's father and friends, not in the sense of the term "rational" in mathematics). And that principle can in a manner appeal to the irrational part, is indicated by our practice of ad- [1103ᵃ] monishing delinquents, and by our employment of rebuke and exhortation generally.

If on the other hand it be more correct to speak of the appetitive part of the soul also as rational, in that case it is the rational part which, as well as the whole soul, is divided into two, the one division having rational principle in the proper sense and in itself, the other obedient to it as a child to its father.

Now virtue also is differentiated in correspondence with this division of the soul. Some forms of virtue are called intellectual virtues, others moral virtues: Wisdom or intelligence and Prudence are intellectual, Liberality and Temperance are moral virtues. When describing a man's moral character we do not say that he is wise or intelligent, but gentle or temperate; but a wise man also is praised for his disposition, and praiseworthy dispositions we term virtues.

### Book II
### (Chapters V-VII : Virtue and the Golden Mean)

V. We have next to consider the formal definition of virtue.

A state of the soul is either (1) an emotion, (2) a capacity, or (3) a disposition; virtue therefore must be one of these three things. By the emotions, I mean desire, anger, fear, confidence, envy, joy, friendship, hatred, longing, jealousy, pity; and generally those states of consciousness which are accompanied by pleasure or pain. The capacities are the faculties in virtue of which we can be said to be liable to the emotions, for example, capable of feeling anger or pain or pity. The dispositions are the formed states of character in virtue of which we are well or ill disposed in respect of the emotions; for instance, we have a bad disposition in regard to anger if we are disposed to get angry too violently or not violently enough, a good disposition if we habitually feel a moderate amount of anger; and similarly in respect of the other emotions.

Now the virtues and vices are not emotions because we are not pronounced good or bad according to our emotions, but we are according to our virtues and vices; nor are we either praised or blamed for our emotions—a man is not praised for being frightened or angry, nor is he blamed for being angry merely, but for being angry in a certain [1106ᵃ] way—but we are praised or blamed for our virtues and vices. Again, we are not angry or afraid from choice, but the virtues are certain modes of choice, or at all events involve choice. Moreover, we are said to be "moved" by the emotions, whereas in respect of the virtues and vices we are not said to be "moved" but to be "disposed" in a certain way.

And the same considerations also prove that the virtues and vices are not capacities; since we are not pronounced good or bad, praised or blamed, merely by reason of our capacity for emotion. Again, we possess certain capacities by nature, but we are not born good or bad by nature: of this however we spoke before.

If then the virtues are neither emotions nor capacities, it remains that they are dispositions.

Thus we have stated what virtue is generically.

VI. But it is not enough merely to define virtue generically as a disposition; we must also say what species of disposition it is. It must then be premised that all excellence has a twofold effect on the thing to which it belongs: it not only renders the thing itself good, but it also causes it to perform its function well. For example, the effect of excellence in the eye is that the eye is good *and* functions well; since having good eyes means having good sight. Similarly excellence in a horse makes it a good horse, and also good at galloping, at carrying its rider, and at facing the enemy. If therefore this is true of all things, excellence or virtue in a man will be the disposition which renders him a good man and also which will cause him to perform his function well. We have already indicated what this means; but it will throw more light on the subject if we consider what constitutes the specific nature of virtue.

Now of everything that is continuous and divisible, it is possible to take the larger part, or the smaller part, or an equal part, and these parts may be larger, smaller, and equal either with respect to the thing itself or relatively to us; the equal part being a mean between excess and deficiency. By the mean of the thing I denote a point equally distant from either extreme, which is one and the same for everybody; by the mean relative to us, that amount which is neither too much nor too little, and this is not one and the same for everybody. For example, let 10 be many and 2 few; then one takes the mean with [1106ᵇ] respect to the thing if one takes 6; $6 - 2 = 10 - 6$, and this is the mean according to arithmetical proportion. But we cannot arrive by this method at the mean relative to us. Suppose that 10 lb. of food is a large ration for anybody and 2 lb. a small one: it does not follow that a trainer will prescribe 6 lb., for perhaps even this will be a large ration, or a small one, for the particular athlete who is to receive it; it is a small ration for a Milo,[3] but a large one for a man just beginning to go in for athletics. And similarly with the amount of running or wrestling exercise to be taken. In the same way then an expert in any art avoids excess and deficiency, and seeks and adopts the mean—the mean, that is, not of the thing but relative to us. If therefore the way in which every art or science performs its work well is by looking to the mean and applying that as a standard to its productions (hence the common remark about a perfect work of art, that you could not take from it nor add to it—meaning that excess and deficiency destroy perfection, while adherence to the mean preserves it)—if then, as we say, good craftsmen look to the mean as they work, and if virtue, like nature, is more accurate and better than any form of art, it will follow that virtue has the quality of hitting the mean. I refer to moral virtue,[4] for this is concerned with emotions and actions, in which one can have excess or deficiency or a due mean. For example, one can be frightened or bold, feel desire or anger or pity, and experience pleasure and pain in general, either too much or too little, and in both cases wrongly; whereas to feel these feelings at the right time, on the right occasion, towards the right people, for the right purpose and in the right manner, is to feel the best amount of them, which is the mean amount—and the best amount is of course the mark of virtue. And similarly there can be excess, deficiency, and the due mean in actions. Now feelings and actions are the objects with which virtue is concerned; and in feelings and actions excess and deficiency are errors, while the mean amount is praised, and constitutes success; and to be praised and to be

successful are both marks of virtue. Virtue therefore, is a mean state in the sense that it is able to hit the mean. Again, error is multiform (for evil is a form of the unlimited, as in the old Pythagorean imagery, and good of the limited), whereas success is possible in one way only (which is why it is easy to fail and difficult to succeed—easy to miss the target and difficult to hit it); so this is another reason why excess and deficiency are a mark of vice, and observance of the mean a mark of virtue:

Goodness is simple, badness manifold.

Virtue then is a settled disposition of the mind determining the choice of actions and emotions, consisting essentially in the observance of the mean relative to us, this being determined by [1107ᵃ] principle, that is, as the prudent man would determine it.

And it is a mean state between two vices, one of excess and one of defect. Furthermore, it is a mean state in that whereas the vices either fall short of or exceed what is right in feelings and in actions, virtue ascertains and adopts the mean. Hence while in respect of its substance and the definition that states what it really is in essence virtue is the observance of the mean, in point of excellence and rightness it is an extreme.

Not every action or emotion however admits of the observance of a due mean. Indeed the very names of some directly imply evil, for instance malice,[5] shamelessness, envy, and, of actions, adultery, theft, murder. All these and similar actions and feelings are blamed as being bad in themselves; it is not the excess or deficiency of them that we blame. It is impossible therefore ever to go right in regard to them—one must always be wrong; nor does right or wrong in their case depend on the circumstances, for instance, whether one commits adultery

---

[3] A famous wrestler.
[4] The formula of the mean does not apply to the intellectual virtues.

[5] The word means "delight at another's misfortune," *Schadenfreude*.

with the right woman, at the right time, and in the right manner: the mere commission of any of them is wrong. One might as well suppose there could be a due mean and excess and deficiency in acts of injustice or cowardice or profligacy, which would imply that one could have a medium amount of excess and of deficiency, an excessive amount of excess and a deficient amount of deficiency. But just as there can be no excess or deficiency in temperance and justice, because the mean is in a sense an extreme, so there can be no observance of the mean nor excess nor deficiency in the corresponding vicious acts mentioned above, but however they are committed, they are wrong; since, to put it in general terms, there is no such thing as observing a mean in excess or deficiency, nor as exceeding or falling short in the observance of a mean.

VII. We must not however rest content with stating this general definition, but must show that it applies to the particular virtues. In practical philosophy, although universal principles have a wider application, those covering a particular part of the field possess a higher degree of truth; because conduct deals with particular facts, and our theories are bound to accord with these.

Let us then take the particular virtues from the diagram. [Here apparently the lecturer displayed a table of virtues, exhibiting each as a mean between two vices of excess and defect in respect of a certain class of action or feeling.] The observance of the mean [1107ᵇ] in fear and confidence is Courage. The man that exceeds in fearlessness is not designated by any special name (and this is the case with many of the virtues and vices); he that exceeds in confidence is Rash; he that exceeds in fear and is deficient in confidence is Cowardly. In respect of pleasures and pains— not all of them, and to a less degree in respect of pains—the observance of the

mean is Temperance, the excess Profligacy. Men deficient in the enjoyment of pleasures scarcely occur, and hence this character also has not been assigned a name, but we may call it Insensible. In regard to giving and getting money, the observance of the mean is Liberality; the excess and deficiency are Prodigality and Meanness, but the prodigal man and the mean man exceed and fall short in opposite ways to one another: the prodigal exeeds in giving and is deficient in getting, whereas the mean man exceeds in getting and is deficient in giving. For the present then we describe these qualities in outline and summarily, which is enough for the purpose in hand; but they will be more accurately defined later.

There are also other dispositions in relation to money, namely, the mode of observing the mean called Magnificence (the magnificent man being different from the liberal, as the former deals with large amounts and the latter with small ones), the excess called Tastelessness or Vulgarity, and the defect called Paltriness. These are not the same as Liberality and the vices corresponding to it; but the way in which they differ will be discussed later.

In respect of honour and dishonour, the observance of the mean is Greatness of Soul, the excess a sort of Vanity, as it may be called, and the deficiency, Smallness of Soul. And just as we said that Liberality is related to Magnificence, differing from it in being concerned with small amounts of money, so there is a certain quality related to Greatness of Soul, which is concerned with great honours, while this quality itself is concerned with small honours; for it is possible to aspire to minor honours in the right way, or more than is right, or less. He who exceeds in these aspirations is called ambitious, he who is deficient, unambitious; but the middle character has no name, and the dispositions of these persons are also un-named, except that that of the ambitious man is called Ambitiousness. Consequently the extreme characters put in a claim to the middle position, and in fact we ourselves sometimes call the middle person ambitious and sometimes un-ambitious: we sometimes praise a man for being ambitious, sometimes for being unambitious. Why we do so shall [1108ᵃ] be discussed later; for the present let us classify the remaining virtues and vices on the lines which we have laid down.

In respect of anger also we have excess, deficiency, and the observance of the mean. These states are virtually without names, but as we call a person of the middle character gentle, let us name the observance of the mean Gentleness, while of the extremes, he that exceeds may be styled irascible and his vice Irascibility, and he that is deficient, spiritless, and the deficiency Spiritlessness.

There are also three other modes of observing a mean which bear some resemblance to each other, and yet are different; all have to do with intercourse in conversation and action, but they differ in that one is concerned with truthfulness of speech and behaviour, and the other with pleasantness, in its two divisions of pleasantness in social amusement and pleasantness in the general affairs of life. We must then discuss these qualities also, in order the better to discern that in all things the observance of the mean is to be praised, while the extremes are neither right nor praiseworthy, but reprehensible. Most of these qualities also are unnamed, but in these as in the other cases we must attempt to coin names for them ourselves, for the sake of clearness and so that our meaning may be easily followed.

In respect of truth then, the middle character may be called truthful, and the observance of the mean Truthfulness; pretense in the form of exaggera-tion is Boastfulness, and its possessor a boaster; in the form of understatement, Self-depreciation, and its possessor the self-depreciator.

In respect of pleasantness in social amusement, the middle character is witty and the middle disposition Wittiness; the excess is Buffoonery and its possessor a buffoon; the deficient man may be called boorish, and his disposition Boorishness. In respect of general pleasantness in life, the man who is pleasant in the proper manner is friendly, and the observance of the mean is Friendliness; he that exceeds, if from no interested motive, is obsequious, if for his own advantage, a flatterer; he that is deficient, and unpleasant in all the affairs of life, may be called quarrelsome and surly.

There are also modes of observing a mean in the sphere of and in relation to the emotions. For in these also one man is spoken of as moderate and another as excessive—for example the bashful man whose modesty takes alarm at everything; while he that is deficient in shame, or abashed at nothing whatsoever, is shameless, and the man of middle character modest. For though Modesty is not a virtue, it is praised, and so is the modest man.

Again, Righteous Indignation is the observance of a mean between Envy and Malice, and these qualities are concerned with pain and pleasure felt at the fortunes of one's neighbours. [1108ᵇ] The righteously indignant man is pained by undeserved good fortune; the jealous man exceeds him and is pained by all the good fortune of others; while the malicious man so far falls short of being pained that he actually feels pleasure.

These qualities however it will be time to discuss in another place. After them we will treat Justice, distinguishing its two kinds—for it has more than one sense—and showing in what way each is a mode of observing the mean.

## Book III
### (Chapters I-III and V: Responsibility)

I. Virtue however is concerned with emotions and actions, and it is only voluntary actions for which praise and blame are given; those that are involuntary are condoned, and sometimes even pitied. Hence it seems to be necessary for the student of ethics to define the difference between the Voluntary and the Involuntary; and this will also be of service to the legislator in assigning rewards and punishments.

It is then generally held that actions are involuntary when done (*a*) under compulsion or (*b*) through ignorance; and that (*a*) an act is compul- [1110ᵃ] sory when its origin is from without, being of such a nature that the agent, who is really passive, contributes nothing to it: for example, when he is carried somewhere by stress of weather, or by people who have him in their power. But there is some doubt about actions done through fear of a worse alternative, or for some noble object— as for instance if a tryant having a man's parents and children in his power commands him to do something base, when if he complies their lives will be spared but if he refuses they will be put to death. It is open to question whether such actions are voluntary or involuntary. A somewhat similar case is when cargo is jettisoned in a storm; apart from circumstances, no one voluntarily throws away his property, but to save his own life and that of his shipmates any sane man would do so. Acts of this kind, then, are "mixed" or composite; but they approximate rather to the voluntary class. For at the actual time when they are done they are chosen or willed; and the end or motive of an act varies with the occasion, so that the terms "voluntary" and "involuntary" should be used with reference to the time of action; now the actual deed in the cases in question is done voluntarily, for the origin of the movement of the parts of the body instrumental to the act lies in the agent; and when the origin of an action is in oneself, it is in one's own power to do it or not. Such acts therefore are voluntary, though perhaps involuntary apart from circumstances— for no one would choose to do any such action in and for itself.

Sometimes indeed men are actually praised for deeds of this "mixed" class, namely when they submit to some disgrace or pain as the price of some great and noble object; though if they do so without any such motive they are blamed, since it is contemptible to submit to a great disgrace with no advantage or only a trifling one in view. In some cases again, such submission though not praised is condoned, when a man does something wrong through fear of penalties that impose too great a strain on human nature, and that no one could endure. Yet there seem to be some acts which a man cannot be compelled to do, and rather than do them he ought to submit to the most terrible death: for instance, we think it ridiculous that Alcmaeon in Euripides' play is compelled by certain threats to murder his mother! But it is sometimes difficult to decide how far we ought to go in choosing to do a given act rather than suffer a given penalty, or in enduring a given penalty rather than commit a given action; and it is still more difficult to abide by our decision when made, since in most of such dilemmas the penalty threatened is painful and the deed forced upon us dishonourable, which is why praise and blame are bestowed according as we do or do not yield to such compulsion.

What kind of actions then are [1110ᵇ] to be called "compulsory"? Used without qualification, perhaps this term applies to any case where the cause of the action lies in things outside the agent, and when the agent contributes nothing. But when actions intrinsically involuntary are yet in given circumstances deliberately chosen in preference to a given alternative, and when their origin lies in the agent, these actions are to be pronounced intrinsically involuntary but voluntary in the circumstances, and in preference to the alternative. They approximate however rather to the voluntary class, since conduct consists of particular things done, and the particular things done in the cases in question are voluntary. But it is not easy to lay down rules for deciding which of two alternatives is to be chosen, for particular cases differ widely.

To apply the term "compulsory" to acts done for the sake of pleasure or for noble objects, on the plea that these exercise constraint on us from without, it to make every action compulsory. For (1) pleasure and nobility between them supply the motives of all actions whatsoever. Also (2) to act under compulsion and unwillingly is painful, but actions done for their pleasantness or nobility are done with pleasure. And (3) it is absurd to blame external things, instead of blaming ourselves for falling an easy prey to their attractions; or to take the credit of our noble deeds to ourselves, while putting the blame for our disgraceful ones upon the temptations of pleasure. It appears therefore that an act is compulsory when its origin is from outside, the person compelled contributing nothing to it.

(b) An act done through ignorance is in every case not voluntary, but it is involuntary only when it causes the agent pain and regret: since a man who has acted through ignorance and feels no compunction at all for what he has done, cannot indeed be said to have acted voluntarily, as he was not aware of his action, yet cannot be said to have acted involuntarily, as he is not sorry

for it. Acts done through ignorance therefore fall into two classes: if the agent regrets the act, we think that he has acted involuntarily; if he does not regret it, to mark the distinction we may call him a "non-voluntary" agent —for as the case is different it is better to give it a special name. Acting *through* ignorance however seems to be different from acting *in* ignorance; for when a man is drunk or in a rage, his actions are not thought to be done through ignorance but owing to one or other of the conditions mentioned, though he does act without knowing, and *in* ignorance. Now it is true that all wicked men are ignorant of what they ought to do and refrain from doing, and that this error is the cause of injustice and of vice in general. But the term "involuntary" does not really apply to an action when the agent is ignorant of his true interests. The ignorance that makes an act blameworthy is not ignorance displayed in moral choice (that sort of ignorance constitutes vice)—that is to say, it is not general ignorance (because that is held to be blameworthy), but particular ignorance, ignorance of the circumstances of the act and of the things affected by it; for in this case the act is pitied and forgiven, because he who acts in ignorance [1111ᵃ] of any of these circumstances is an involuntary agent.

Perhaps then it will be as well to specify the nature and number of these circumstances. They are (1) the agent, (2) the act, (3) the thing that is affected by or is the sphere of the act; and sometimes also (4) the instrument, for instance, a tool with which the act is done, (5) the effect, for instance, saving a man's life, and (6) the manner, for instance, gently or violently.

Now no one, unless mad, could be ignorant of all these circumstances together; nor yet, obviously, of (1) the agent—for a man must know who he is himself. But a man may be ignorant of (2) what he is doing, as for instance when people say "it slipped out while they were speaking," or "they were not aware that the matter was a secret," as Aeschylus said of the Mysteries;[6] or that "they let it off when they only meant to show how it worked" as the prisoner pleaded in the catapult case. Again (3) a person might mistake his son for an enemy, as Merope does;[7] or (4) mistake a sharp spear for one with a button on it, or a heavy stone for a pumice-stone; or (5) one might kill a man by giving him medicine with the intention of saving his life; or (6) in loose wrestling[8] hit him a blow when meaning only to grip his hand. Ignorance therefore being possible in respect of all these circumstances of the act, one who has acted in ignorance of any of them is held to have acted involuntarily, and especially so if ignorant of the most important of them; and the most important of the circumstances seem to be the nature of the act itself and the effect it will produce.

Such then is the nature of the ignorance that justifies our speaking of an act as involuntary, given the further condition that the agent feels sorrow and regret for having committed it.

An involuntary action being one done under compulsion or through ignorance, a voluntary act would seem to be an act of which the origin lies in the agent, who knows the particular circumstances in which he is acting. For it is probably a mistake to say that acts caused by anger or by desire are involuntary. In the first place, (1) this will debar us from speaking of any of the lower animals as acting voluntarily, or children either. Then (2) are none of our actions that are caused by desire or anger voluntary, or are the noble ones voluntary and the base involuntary? Surely this is an absurd distinction when one person is the author of both. Yet perhaps it is strange to speak of acts aiming at things which it is right to aim at as involuntary; and it is right to feel anger at some things, and also to feel desire for some things, for instance health, knowledge. Also (3) we think that involuntary actions are painful and actions that gratify desire pleasant. And again (4) what difference is there in respect of their involuntary character between wrong acts committed deliberately and wrong acts done in anger? Both are to be avoided; and also we [1111ᵇ] think that the irrational feelings are just as much a part of human nature as the reason, so that the actions done from anger or desire also belong to the human being who does them. It is therefore strange to class these actions as involuntary.

II. Having defined voluntary and involuntary action, we next have to examine the nature of Choice. For this appears to be intimately connected with virtue, and to afford a surer test of character than do our actions.

Choice is manifestly a voluntary act. But the two terms are not synonymous, the latter being the wider. Children and the lower animals as well as men are capable of voluntary action, but not of choice. Also sudden acts may be termed voluntary, but they cannot be said to be done by choice.

Some identify Choice with (1) Desire, or (2) Passion, or (3) Wish, or (4) some form of Opinion. These views however appear to be mistaken.

1. The irrational animals do not exercise choice, but they do feel desire, and

---

6 Aeschylus was accused before the Areopagus of having divulged the Mysteries of Demeter in certain of his tragedies, but was acquitted. A phrase of his, "It came to my mouth," became proverbial (Plato, *Rep.* 563 c, etc.), and he may have used it on this occasion.

7 In the lost *Cresphontes* of Euripides.

8 A style of wrestling in which the adversaries only gripped each other's hands without closing.

also passion. Also a man of defective self-restraint acts from desire but not from choice; and on the contrary a self-restrained man acts from choice and not from desire. Again, desire can run counter to choice, but not desire to desire. And desire has regard to an object as pleasant or painful, choice has not.

2. Still less is choice the same as passion. Acts done from passion seem very far from being done of deliberate choice.

3. Again, choice is certainly not a wish, though they appear closely akin. Choice cannot have for its object impossibilities: if a man were to say he chose something impossible he would be thought a fool; but we can wish for things that are impossible, for instance immortality. Also we may wish for what cannot be secured by our own agency, for instance, that a particular actor or athlete may win; but no one chooses what does not rest with himself, but only what he thinks can be attained by his own act. Again, we wish rather for ends than for means, but choose the means to our end; for example, we wish to be healthy, but choose things to make us healthy; we wish to be happy, and that is the word we use in this connexion, but it would not be proper to say that we choose to be happy; since, speaking generally, choice seems to be concerned with things within our own control.

4. Nor yet again can it be opinion. It seems that anything may be matter of opinion—we form opinions about what is eternal, or impossible, just as much as about what is within our power. Also we distinguish opinion by its truth or falsehood, not by its being good or bad, but choice is distinguished rather as being good or bad. Probably therefore nobody actually identifies choice with opinion in general. [1112ᵃ] But neither is it the same as some particular opinion. For it is our choice of good or evil that determines our

character, not our opinion about good or evil. And we choose to take or avoid some good or evil thing, but we opine what a thing is, or for whom it is advantageous, or how it is so: we do not exactly form an opinion to take or avoid a thing. Also we praise a choice rather for choosing the right thing, but an opinion for opining in the right way. And we choose only things that we absolutely know to be good, we opine things we do not quite certainly know to be true. Nor do the same persons appear to excel both at choosing and at forming opinions: some people seem to form opinions better, but yet to choose the wrong things from wickedness. That choice is preceded or accompanied by the formation of an opinion is immaterial, for that is not the point we are considering, but whether choice is the same things as some form of opinion.

What then are the genus and differentia of Choice, inasmuch as it is not any of the things above mentioned? It manifestly belongs to the genus voluntary action; but not every voluntary act is chosen. Perhaps we may define it as voluntary action preceded by deliberation, since choice involves reasoning and some process of thought. Indeed previous deliberation seems to be implied by the very term *proaireton*, which denotes something *chosen before* other things.

III. As for Deliberation, do people deliberate about everything—are all things possible objects of deliberation—, or are there some things about which deliberation is impossible? The term "object of deliberation" presumably must not be taken to include things about which a fool or a madman might deliberate, but to mean what a sensible person would deliberate about.

Well then, nobody deliberates about things eternal, such as the order of the universe, or the incommensurability of the diagonal and the side of a square. Nor yet about things that change but follow a regular process, whether from necessity or by nature or through some other cause: such phenomena for instance as the solstices and the sunrise. Nor about irregular occurrences, such as droughts and rains. Nor about the results of chance, such as finding a hidden treasure. The reason why we do not deliberate about these things is that none of them can be effected by our agency. We deliberate about things that are in our control and are attainable by action (which are in fact the only things that still remain to be considered; for Nature, Necessity, and Chance, with the addition of Intelligence and human agency generally, exhaust the generally accepted list of causes). But we do not deliberate about all human affairs without exception either: for example, no Lacedaemonian deliberates about the best form of government for Scythia; but any particular set of men deliberates about the things attainable by their own actions. Also there is no room for deliberation about matters fully ascertained and completely formulated as sciences; such for instance as orthography, for we have no uncertainty as to [1112ᵇ] how a word ought to be spelt. We deliberate about things in which our agency operates but does not always produce the same results; for instance about questions of medicine and of business; and we deliberate about navigation more than about athletic training, because it has been less completely reduced to a science; and similarly with other pursuits also. And we deliberate more about the arts than about the sciences, because we are more uncertain about them.

Deliberation then is employed in matters which, though subject to rules that generally hold good, are uncertain in their issue; or where the issue is indeterminate, and where, when the matter is important, we take others into our deliberations, distrusting our own capacity to decide.

And we deliberate not about ends, but about means. A doctor does not deliberate whether he is to cure his patient, nor an orator whether he is to convince his audience, nor a statesman whether he is to secure good government, nor does anyone else debate about the end of his profession or calling; they take some end for granted, and consider how and by what means it can be achieved. If they find that there are several means of achieving it, they proceed to consider which of these will attain it most easily and best. If there is only one means by which it can be accomplished, they ask how it is to be accomplished by that means, and by what means that means can itself be achieved, until they reach the first link in the chain of causes, which is the last in the order of discovery. (For when deliberating one seems in the procedure described to be pursuing an investigation or analysis that resembles the analysis of a figure in geometry—indeed it appears that though not all investigation is deliberation, for example, mathematical investigation is not, yet all deliberation is investigation—and the last step in the analysis seems to be the first step in the execution of the design.) Then, if they have come up against an impossibility, they abandon the project—for instance, if it requires money and money cannot be procured; but if on the other hand it proves to be something possible, they begin to act. By possible, I mean able to be performed by our agency—things we do through the agency of our friends counting in a sense as done by ourselves, since the origin of their action is in us.

(In practising an art) the question is at one moment what tools to use, and at another how to use them; and similarly in other spheres, we have to consider sometimes what means to employ, and sometimes how exactly any given means are to be employed.

It appears therefore, as has been said, that a man is the origin of his actions, and that the province of deliberation is to discover actions within one's own power to perform; and all our actions aim at ends other than themselves. It follows that we do not deliberate about ends, but about means. Nor yet do we deliberate about particular facts, [1113ᵃ] for instance, Is this object a loaf? or, Is this loaf properly baked? for these are matters of direct perception. Deliberation must stop at the particular fact, or it will embark on a process *ad infinitum*.

The object of deliberation and the object of choice are the same, except that when a thing is chosen it has already been determined, since it is the thing already selected as the result of our deliberation that is chosen. For a man stops enquiring how he shall act as soon as he has carried back the origin of action to himself, and to the dominant part of himself, for it is this part that chooses. This may be illustrated by the ancient constitutions represented in Homer: the kings used to proclaim to the people the measures they had chosen to adopt.

As then the object of choice is something within our power which after deliberation we desire, Choice will be a deliberate desire of things in our power; for we first deliberate, then select, and finally fix our desire according to the result of our deliberation.

Let this serve as a description in outline of Choice, and of the nature of its objects, and the fact that it deals with means to ends.

∙ ∙ ∙

V. If then whereas we wish for our end, the means to our end are matters of deliberation and choice, it follows that actions dealing with these means are done by choice, and voluntary. But the activities in which the virtues are exercised deal with means. Therefore virtue also depends on ourselves. And so also does vice. For where we are free to act we are also free to refrain from acting, and where we are able to say No we are also able to say Yes; if there-

fore we are responsible for doing a thing when to do it is right, we are also responsible for not doing it when not to do it is wrong, and if we are responsible for rightly not doing a thing, we are also responsible for wrongly doing it. But if it is in our power to do and to refrain from doing right and wrong, and if, as we saw, being good or bad is doing right or wrong, it consequently depends on us whether we are virtuous or vicious. To say that

> None would be vile, and none would not be blest

seems to be half false, though half true: it is true that no one is unwilling to be blessed, but not true that wickedness is involuntary; or else we must contradict what we just now asserted, and say that man is not the originator and begetter of his actions as he is of his children. But if it is manifest that a man is the author of his own actions, and if we are unable to trace our conduct back to any other origins than those within ourselves, then actions of which the origins are within us, themselves depend upon us, and are voluntary.

This conclusion seems to be attested both by men's behaviour in private life and by the practice of lawgivers; for they punish and exact redress from those who do evil (except when it is done under compulsion, or through ignorance for which the agent himself is not responsible), and honour those who do noble deeds, in order to encourage the one sort and to repress the other; but nobody tries to encourage us to do things that do not depend upon ourselves and are not voluntary, since it is no good our being persuaded not to feel heat or pain or hunger or the like, because we shall feel them all the same.

Indeed the fact that an offence was committed in ignorance is itself made a ground for punishment, in cases where the offender is held to be responsible for his ignorance; for instance, the penalty is doubled if the offender was drunk, because the origin of the offence was in the man himself, as he might have avoided getting drunk, which was the cause of his not knowing what he was doing. Also men are punished for offences committed through ignorance of some provision of the law which they ought to have known, and might have known without difficulty; and so [1114ᵃ] in other cases where ignorance is held to be due to negligence, on the ground that the offender need not have been ignorant, as he could have taken the trouble to ascertain the facts.

It may be objected that perhaps he is not the sort of man to take the trouble. Well, but men are themselves responsible for having become careless through living carelessly, as they are for being unjust or profligate if they do wrong or pass their time in drinking and dissipation. They acquire a particular quality by constantly acting in a particular way. This is shown by the way in which men train themselves for some contest or pursuit: they practise continually. Therefore only an utterly senseless person can fail to know that our characters are the result of our conduct; but if a man knowingly acts in a way that will result in his becoming unjust, he must be said to be voluntarily unjust.

Again, though it is unreasonable to say that a man who acts unjustly or dissolutely does not wish to be unjust or dissolute, nevertheless this by no means implies that he can stop being unjust and become just merely by wishing to do so; any more than a sick man can get well by wishing, although it may be the case that his illness is voluntary, in the sense of being due to intemperate living and neglect of the doctors' advice. At the outset then, it is true, he might have avoided the illness, but once he has let himself go he can do so no longer. When you have thrown a stone, you cannot afterwards bring it back again, but nevertheless you are responsible for having taken up the stone and flung it, for the origin of the act was within you. Similarly the unjust and profligate might at the outset have avoided becoming so, and therefore they are so voluntarily, although when they have become unjust and profligate it is no longer open to them not to be so.

And not only are vices of the soul voluntary, but in some cases bodily defects are so as well, and we blame them accordingly. Though no one blames a man for being born ugly, we censure uncomeliness that is due to neglecting exercise and the care of the person. And so with infirmities and mutilations: though nobody would reproach, but rather pity, a person blind from birth, or owing to disease or accident, yet all would blame one who had lost his sight from tippling or debauchery. We see then that bodily defects for which we are ourselves responsible are blamed, while those for which we are not responsible are not. This being so, it follows that we are responsible for blameworthy moral defects also.

But suppose somebody says: "All men seek what seems to them good, but they are not responsible for its seeming good: each man's conception of his end is determined by his character, whatever that may be. Although therefore, [1114ᵇ] on the hypothesis that each man is in a sense responsible for his moral disposition, he will in a sense be responsible for his conception of the good, if on the contrary this hypothesis be untrue, no man is responsible for his own wrongdoing. He does wrong through ignorance of the right end, thinking that wrongdoing will procure him his greatest Good: and his aim at his end is not of his own choosing. A man needs to be born with moral vision, so to speak, whereby to discern correctly and choose what is truly good. A man of good natural disposition is a man well endowed by nature in this respect; for if a thing is the greatest and noblest of gifts, and is something which cannot be acquired or learnt from another, but which a man will possess in such form as it has been bestowed on him at birth, a good and noble natural endowment in this respect will constitute a good disposition in the full and true meaning of the term."

Now if this theory be true, how will virtue be voluntary any more than vice? Both for the good man and the bad man alike, their view of their end is determined in the same manner, by nature or however it may be; and all their actions of whatever sort are guided by reference to their end as thus determined. Whether then a man's view of his end, whatever it may be, is not given by nature but is partly due to himself, or whether, although his end is determined by nature, yet virtue is voluntary because the good man's actions to gain his end are voluntary, in either case vice will be just as much voluntary as virtue; for the bad man equally with the good possesses spontaneity in his actions, even if not in his choice of an end. If then, as is said, our virtues are voluntary (and in fact we are in a sense ourselves partly the cause of our moral dispositions, and it is our having a certain character that makes us set up an end of a certain kind), it follows that our vices are voluntary also; they are voluntary in the same manner as our virtues.

We have then now discussed in outline the virtues in general, having indicated their genus [namely, that it is a mean, and a disposition] and having shown that they render us apt to do the same actions as those by which they are produced, and to do them in the way in which right reason may enjoin; and that they depend on ourselves and are voluntary.

But our dispositions are not voluntary in the same way as are our actions. Our actions we can control from beginning to end, and we are conscious of them at each stage. With our disposi-

tions on the other hand though we can control their beginnings, each separate addition to them is impercep- [1115ᵃ] tible, as is the case with the growth of a disease; though they are voluntary in that we were free to employ our capacities in the one way or the other.

But to resume, let us now discuss the virtues severally, defining the nature of each, the class of objects to which it is related, and the way in which it is related to them. In so doing we shall also make it clear how many virtues there are.

## Book IV
### (Chapter III : Greatness of Soul)

III. Greatness of Soul,⁹ as the word itself implies, seems to be related to great objects; let us first ascertain what sort of objects these are. It will make no difference whether we examine the quality itself of the person that displays the quality.

Now a person is thought to be [1123ᵇ] great-souled if he claims much and deserves much; he who claims much without deserving it is foolish, but no one of moral excellence is foolish or senseless. The great-souled man is then as we have described. He who deserves little and claims little is modest or temperate, but not great-souled, since to be great-souled involves greatness just as handsomeness involves size: small people may be neat and well-made, but not handsome. He that claims much but does not deserve much is vain; though not everybody who claims more than he deserves is vain. He that claims less than he deserves is small-souled, whether his deserts be great or only moderate, or

---

9 μεγαλοψύχια, *magnanimitas*, means lofty pride and self-esteem rather than magnanimity or high-mindedness (in the modern sense of the word).

even though he deserves little, if he claims still less. The most small-souled of all would seem to be the man who claims less than he deserves when his deserts are great; for what would he have done had he not deserved so much?

Though therefore in regard to the greatness of his claim the great-souled man is an extreme, by reason of its rightness he stands at the mean point, for he claims what he deserves; while the vain and the small-souled err by excess and defect respectively.

If then the great-souled man claims and is worthy of great things and most of all the greatest things, Greatness of Soul much be concerned with some one object especially. "Worthy" is a term of relation: it denotes having a claim to goods external to oneself. Now the greatest external good we should assume to be the thing which we offer as a tribute to the gods, and which is most coveted by men of high station, and is the prize awarded for the noblest deeds; and such a thing is honour, for honour is clearly the greatest of external goods. Therefore the great-souled man is he who has the right disposition in relation to honours and disgraces. And even without argument it is evident that honour is the object with which the great-souled are concerned, since it is honour above all else which great men claim and deserve.

The small-souled man falls short both as judged by his own deserts and in comparison with the claim of the great-souled man; the vain man on the other hand exceeds as judged by his own standard, but does not however exceed the great-souled man. 10

And inasmuch as the great-souled

man deserves most, he must be the best of men; for the better a man is the more he deserves, and he that is best deserves most. Therefore the truly great-souled man must be a good man. Indeed greatness in each of the virtues would seem to go with greatness of soul. For instance, one cannot imagine the great-souled man running at full speed when retreating in battle,11 nor acting dishonestly; since what motive for base conduct has a man to whom nothing is great? Considering all the virtues in turn, we shall feel it quite ridiculous to picture the great-souled man as other than a good man. Moreover, if he were bad, he would not be worthy of honour, since honour is the prize of virtue, and the tribute that we pay to the good. Greatness of Soul seems therefore to be as it were a crowning ornament [1124ᵃ] of the virtues: it enhances their greatness, and it cannot exist without them. Hence it is hard to be truly great-souled, for greatness of soul is impossible without moral nobility.

Honour and dishonour then are the objects with which the great-souled man is especially concerned. Great honours accorded by persons of worth will afford him pleasure in a moderate degree: he will feel he is receiving only what belongs to him, or even less, for no honour can be adequate to the merits of perfect virtue, yet all the same he will deign to accept their honours, because they have no greater tribute to offer him. Honour rendered by common people and on trivial grounds he will utterly despise, for this is not what he merits. He will also despise dishonour, for no dishonour can justly attach to him. The great-souled man then, as has been said, is

---

10 That is, the small-souled man claims less than he deserves and less than the great-souled man deserves and claims; the vain man claims more than he deserves, but not more than the great-souled man deserves and claims.

11 Literally "fleeing swinging his arms at his side," i.e. deficient in the virtue of Courage. If this be the meaning, the phrase recalls by contrast the leisurely retirement of Socrates from the stricken field of Delium (Plato, Symposium, 221 A).

especially concerned with honour; but he will also observe due measure in respect to wealth, power, and good and bad fortune in general, as they may befall him; he will not rejoice overmuch in prosperity, nor grieve overmuch at adversity. For he does not care much even about honour, which is the greatest of external goods (since power and wealth are desirable only for the honour they bring, at least their possessors wish to be honoured for their sake); he therefore to whom even honour is a small thing will be indifferent to other things as well. Hence great-souled men are thought to be haughty.

But it is thought that the gifts of fortune also conduce to greatness of soul; for the high-born and those who are powerful or wealthy are esteemed worthy of honour, because they are superior to their fellows, and that which is superior in something good is always held in higher honour; so that even these gifts of fortune make men more great-souled, because their possessors are honoured by some people. But in reality only the good man ought to be honoured, although he that has both virtue and fortune is esteemed still more worthy of honour; whereas those who possess the goods of fortune without virtue are not justified in claiming high worth, and cannot correctly be styled great-souled, since true worth and greatness of soul cannot exist without complete virtue. It is true that even those who merely possess the goods of fortune may be haughty and insolent; because without virtue it is not easy to bear good fortune becomingly, and such men, being unable to carry their prosperity, and thinking themselves superior to the rest of mankind, despise other people, although their own con- [1124ᵇ] duct is no better than another's. The fact is that they try to imitate the great-souled man without being really like him, and only copy him in what they can, reproducing his contempt for others but not his virtuous conduct. For the great-

souled man is justified in despising other people—his estimates are correct; but most proud men have no good ground for their pride.

The great-souled man does not run into danger for trifling reasons, and is not a lover of danger, because there are few things he values; but he will face danger in a great cause, and when so doing will be ready to sacrifice his life, since he holds that life is not worth having at every price.

He is fond of conferring benefits, but ashamed to receive them, because the former is a mark of superiority and the latter of inferiority. He returns a service done to him with interest, since this will put the original benefactor into his debt in turn, and make him the party benefited. The great-souled are thought to have a good memory for any benefit they have conferred, but a bad memory for those which they have received (since the recipient of a benefit is the inferior of his benefactor, whereas they desire to be superior); and to enjoy being reminded of the former but to dislike being reminded of the latter: this is why the poet makes Thetis not specify her services to Zeus; nor did the Spartans treating with the Athenians recall the occasions when Sparta had aided Athens, but those on which Athens had aided Sparta.

It is also characteristic of the great-souled man never to ask help from others, or only with reluctance, but to render aid willingly; and to be haughty towards men of position and fortune, but courteous towards those of moderate station, because it is difficult and distinguished to be superior to the great, but easy to outdo the lowly, and to adopt a high manner with the former is not ill-bred, but it is vulgar to lord it over humble people: it is like putting forth one's strength against the weak. He will not compete for the common objects of ambition, or go where other people take the first place; and he will be idle and slow to act, except when pursuing some high honour or achievement; and will not engage in many undertakings, but only in such as are important and distinguished. He must be open both in love and in hate, since concealment shows timidity; and care more for the truth than for what people will think; and speak and act openly, since as he despises other men he is outspoken and frank, except when speaking with ironical self-depreciation, as he does to common people. He will be incapable of living at the will of another, unless a friend, [1125ᵃ] since to do so is slavish, and hence flatterers are always servile, and humble people flatterers. He is not prone to admiration, since nothing is great to him. He does not bear a grudge, for it is not a mark of greatness of soul to recall things against people, especially the wrongs they have done you, but rather to overlook them. He is no gossip, for he will not talk either about himself or about another, as he neither wants to receive compliments nor to hear other people run down (nor is he lavish of praise either); and so he is not given to speaking evil himself, even of his enemies, except when he deliberately intends to give offence. In troubles that cannot be avoided or trifling mishaps he will never cry out or ask for help, since to do so would imply that he took them to heart. He likes to own beautiful and useless things, rather than useful things that bring in a return, since the former show his independence more.

Other traits generally attributed to the great-souled man are a slow gait, a deep voice, and a deliberate utterance; to speak in shrill tones and walk fast denotes an excitable and nervous temperament, which does not belong to one who cares for few things and thinks nothing great.

Such then being the Great-souled man, the corresponding character on the side of deficiency is the Small-souled man, and on that of excess the Vain man. These also are not thought to be actually vicious, since they do no harm, but rather mistaken. The small-souled man deprives himself of the good things that he deserves; and his failure to claim good things makes it seem that he has something bad about him [and also that he does not know himself],¹² for (people argue), if he deserved any good, he would try to obtain it. Not that such persons are considered foolish, but rather too retiring; yet this estimate of them is thought to make them still worse, for men's ambitions show what they are worth, and if they hold aloof from noble enterprises and pursuits, and forgo the good things of life, presumably they think they are not worthy of them.

The vain on the other hand are foolish persons, who are deficient in self-knowledge and expose their defect: they undertake honourable responsibilities of which they are not worthy, and then are found out. They are ostentatious in dress, manner and so on. They want people to know how well off they are, and talk about it, imagining that this will make them respected.

Smallness of Soul is more opposed than Vanity to Greatness of Soul, being more prevalent and worse.

Greatness of Soul then, as we have said, is concerned with great honours.

## Book VIII
### (Chapter VIII : Giving and Receiving Love)

VIII. Most men however, because they love honour, seem to be more desirous of receiving than of bestowing affection. Hence most men like flattery, for a flatterer is a friend who is your inferior, or pretends to be so, and to love you more than you love him; but to be

---

¹² These words seem to be interpolated. The small-souled man does not claim his deserts, but he may know what they are; he is not charged with ignorance of self, as is the vain man.

loved is felt to be nearly the same as to be honoured, which most people covet. They do not however appear to value honour for its own sake, but for something incidental to it. Most people like receiving honour from men of high station, because they hope for something from them: they think that if they want something, the great man will be able to give it them; so they enjoy being honoured by him as a token of benefits to come. Those on the other hand who covet being honoured by good men, and by persons who know them, do so from a desire to confirm their own opinion of themselves; so these like honour because they are assured of their worth by their confidence in the judgment of those who assert it. Affection on the other hand men like for its own sake; from which we infer that it is more valuable than honour, and that friendship is desirable in itself.

But in its essence friendship seems to consist more in giving than in receiving affection: witness the pleasure that mothers take in loving their children. Some mothers put their infants out to nurse, and though knowing and loving them, do not ask to be loved by them in return, if it be impossible to have this as well, but are content if they see them prospering; they retain their own love for them even though the children, not knowing them, cannot render them any part of what is due to a mother. As then friendship consists more especially in bestowing affection, and as we praise men for loving their friends, affection seems to be the mark of a good friend. Hence it is friends that love each other as each deserves who continue friends and whose friendship is lasting.

Also it is by rendering affection in proportion to desert that friends who are not equals may approach most [1159ᵇ] nearly to true friendship, since this will make them equal. Amity consists in equality and similarity, especially the similarity of those who are alike in virtue; for being true to themselves, these

also remain true to one another, and neither request nor render services that are morally degrading. Indeed they may be said actually to restrain each other from evil: since good men neither err themselves nor permit their friends to err. Bad men on the other hand have no constancy in friendship, for they do not even remain true to their own characters; but they can be friends for a short time, while they take pleasure in each other's wickedness. The friendships of useful and pleasant people last longer, in fact as long as they give each other pleasure or benefit. It is friendship based on utility that seems most frequently to spring from opposites, for instance a friendship between a poor man and a rich one, or between an ignorant man and a learned; for a person desiring something which he happens to lack will give something else in return for it. One may bring under this class the friendship between a lover and the object of his affections, or between a plain person and a handsome one. This is why lovers sometimes appear ridiculous when they claim that their love should be equally reciprocated; no doubt if they are equally lovable this is a reasonable demand, but it is ridiculous if they have nothing attractive about them.

But perhaps there is no real attraction between opposites as such, but only accidentally, and what they actually desire is the mean between them (since this is the Good); the dry for instance striving not to become wet, but to reach an intermediate state, and so with the hot, and everything else. Let us however dismiss this question, as being indeed somewhat foreign to our subject.

## Book IX
### (Chapter IV and VIII : Self-Love)

IV. The forms which friendly [1166ª] feeling for our neighbours take, and the marks by which the different forms of friendship are defined, seem to be derived from the feelings of regard which we entertain for ourselves. A friend is defined as (a) one who wishes, and promotes by action, the real or apparent good of another for that other's sake; or (b) one who wishes the existence and preservation of his friend for the friend's sake. (This is the feeling of mothers towards their children, and of former friends who have quarrelled.) Others say that a friend is (c) one who frequents another's society, and (d) who desires the same things as he does, or (e) one who shares his friend's joys and sorrows. (This too is very characteristic of mothers.) Friendship also is defined by one or other of these marks. But each of them is also found in a good man's feelings towards himself (and in those of all other men as well, in so far as they believe themselves to be good; but, as has been said, virtue and the virtuous man seem to be the standard in everything). For (d) the good man is of one mind with himself, and desires the same things with every part of his nature. Also (a) he wishes his own good, real as well as apparent, and seeks it by action (for it is a mark of a good man to exert himself actively for the good); and he does so for his own sake (for he does it on account of the intellectual part of himself, and this appears to be a man's real self). Also (b) he desires his own life and security, and especially that of his rational part. For existence is good for the virtuous man; and everyone wishes his own good: no one would choose to possess every good in the world on condition of becoming somebody else (for God possesses the good even as it is), but only while remaining himself, whatever he may be; and it would appear that the thinking part is the real self, or is so more than anything else. And (c) the good man desires his own company; for he enjoys being by himself, since he has agreeable memories of the past, and good hopes for the future, which are pleasant too; also his mind is stored with subjects for contemplation. And (e) he

is keenly conscious of his own joys and sorrows; for the same things give him pleasure or pain at all times, and not different things at different times, since he is not apt to change his mind.

It is therefore because the good man has these various feelings towards himself, and because he feels towards his friend in the same way as towards himself (for a friend is another self), that friendship also is thought to consist in one or other of these feelings, and the possession of them is thought to be the test of a friend.

Whether a man can be said actually to feel friendship for himself is a question that may be dismissed for the present; though it may be held that he can do so in so far as he is a dual or [1166ᵇ] composite being, and because very intense friendship resembles self-regard.

As a matter of fact, the feelings of self-regard described appear to be found in most people, even though they are of inferior moral worth. Perhaps men share them in so far as they have their own approval and believe in their own virtue; since the utterly worthless and criminal never possess them, or even have the appearance of doing so. Indeed it may almost be said that no morally inferior persons possess them. For (d) such persons are at variance with themselves, desiring one thing and wishing another: this is the mark of the unrestrained, who choose what is pleasant but harmful instead of what they themselves think to be good. (a) Others again, out of cowardice and idleness, neglect to do what they think best for their own interests. And (b) men who have committed a number of crimes, and are hated for their wickedness, actually flee from life and make away with themselves. Also (c) bad men constantly seek the society of others and shun their own company, because when they are by themselves they recall much that was unpleasant in the past and anticipate the same in the future, whereas with other people they can forget. Moreover they feel no affection for themselves, because they have no lovable qualities. Hence (e) such men do not enter into their own joys and sorrows, as there is civil war in their souls; one part of their nature, owing to depravity, is pained by abstinence from certain indulgences while another part is pleased by it; one part pulls them one way and another the other, as if dragging them asunder. Or if it be impossible to feel pain and pleasure at the same time, at all events after indulging in pleasure they regret it a little later, and wish they had never acquired a taste for such indulgences; since the bad are always changing their minds.

Thus a bad man appears to be devoid even of affection for himself, because he has nothing lovable in his nature. If then such a state of mind is utterly miserable, we should do our utmost to shun wickedness and try to be virtuous. That is the way both to be friends with ourselves and to win the friendship of others.

•  •  •

VIII. The question is also raised whether one ought to love oneself or someone else most. We censure those who put themselves first, and "lover of self" is used as a term of reproach. And it is thought that a bad man considers himself in all he does, and the more so the worse he is—so it is a complaint against him for instance that "he never does a thing unless you make him"— whereas a good man acts from a sense of what is noble, and the better he is the more he so acts, and he considers his friend's interest, disregarding his own.

But the facts do not accord with these theories; nor is this surprising. For we admit that one should love one's [1168ᵇ] best friend most; but the best friend is he that, when he wishes a person's good, wishes it for that person's own sake, even though nobody will ever know of it. Now this condition is most fully realized in a man's regard for himself, as indeed are all the other attributes that make up the definition of a friend; for it has been said already that all the feelings that constitute friendship for others are an extension of regard for self. Moreover, all the proverbs agree with this; for example, "Friends have one soul between them," "Friends' goods are common property," "Amity is equality," "The knee is nearer than the shin." All of these sayings will apply most fully to oneself; for a man is his own best friend. Therefore he ought to love himself most.

So it is naturally debated which of these two views we ought to adopt, since each of them has some plausibility.

Now where there is a conflict of opinion the proper course is doubtless to get the two views clearly distinguished, and to define how far and in what way each of them is true. So probably the matter may become clear if we ascertain what meaning each side attaches to the term "self-love."

Those then who make it a term of reproach call men lovers of self when they assign to themselves the large share of money, honours, or bodily pleasures; since these are the things which most men desire and set their hearts on as being the greatest goods, and which accordingly they compete with each other to obtain. Now those who take more than their share of these things are men who indulge their appetites, and generally their passions and the irrational part of their souls. But most men are of this kind. Accordingly the use of term "lover of self" as a reproach has arisen from the fact that self-love of the ordinary kind is bad. Hence self-love is rightly censured in those who are lovers of self in this sense. And that it is those who take too large a share of things of this sort whom most people usually mean when they speak of lovers of self, is clear enough. For if a man were always bent on outdoing everybody else in acting justly or temperately or in displaying any other of the virtues, and in general were always trying to secure for himself moral nobility, no one will charge him with love of self nor find any fault with him. Yet as a matter of fact such a man might be held to be a lover of self in an exceptional degree. At all events he takes for himself the things that are noblest and most truly good. Also it is the most dominant part of himself that he indulges and obeys in everything. But (*a*) as in the state it is the sovereign that is held in the fullest sense to *be* the state, and in any other composite whole it is the dominant part that is deemed especially to be that whole, so it is with man. He therefore who loves and indulges the dominant part of himself is a lover of self in the fullest degree. Again (*b*), the terms "self-restrained" and "unrestrained" denote being restrained or not by one's intellect, and thus imply that the intellect is the man himself. Also (*c*) it is our reasoned acts that are felt to be in the fullest sense *our* [1169ᵃ] *own* acts, *voluntary* acts. It is therefore clear that man is or is chiefly the dominant part of himself, and that a good man values this part of himself most. Hence the good man will be a lover of self in the fullest degree, though in another sense than the lover of self so-called by way of reproach, from whom he differs as much as living by principle differs from living by passion, and aiming at what is noble from aiming at what seems expedient. Persons therefore who are exceptionally zealous in noble actions are universally approved and commended; and if all men vied with each other in moral nobility and strove to perform the noblest deeds, the common welfare would be fully realized, while individuals also could enjoy the greatest of goods, inasmuch as virtue is the greatest good.

Therefore the good man ought to be a lover of self, since he will then both benefit himself by acting nobly and aid his fellows; but the bad man ought not to be a lover of self, since he will follow his base passions, and so injure both himself and his neighbours. With the bad man therefore, what he does is not in accord with what he ought to do, but the good man does what he ought, since intelligence always chooses for itself that which is best, and the good man obeys his intelligence.

But it is also true that the virtuous man's conduct is often guided by the interests of his friends and of his country, and that he will if necessary lay down his life in their behalf. For he will surrender wealth and power and all the goods that men struggle to win, if he can secure nobility for himself; since he would prefer an hour of rapture to a long period of mild enjoyment, a year of noble life to many years of ordinary existence, one great and glorious exploit to many small successes. And this is doubtless the case with those who give their lives for others; thus they choose great nobility for themselves. Also the virtuous man is ready to forgo money if by that means his friends may gain more money; for thus, though his friend gets money, he himself achieves nobility, and so he assigns the greater good to his own share. And he behaves in the same manner as regards honours and offices also: all these things he will relinquish to his friend, for this is noble and praiseworthy for himself. He is naturally therefore thought to be virtuous, as he chooses moral nobility in preference to all other things. It may even happen that he will surrender to his friend the performance of some achievement, and that it may be nobler for him to be the cause of his friend's performing it than to perform it himself.

Therefore in all spheres of praiseworthy conduct it is manifest that the good man takes the larger share of moral nobility for himself. In this sense then, as we said above, it is right to be [1169ᵇ] a lover of self, though self-love of the ordinary sort is wrong.

## Book X
### (Chapters VI-VIII: The Highest Happiness)

VI. Having now discussed the various kinds of Virtue of Friendship and of Pleasure, it remains for us to treat in outline of Happiness, inasmuch as we count this to be the End of human life. But it will shorten the discussion if we recapitulate what has been said already.

Now we stated that happiness is not a certain disposition of character; since if it were it might be possessed by a man who passed the whole of his life asleep, living the life of a vegetable, or by one who was plunged in the deepest misfortune. If then we reject this as [1176ᵇ] unsatisfactory, and feel bound to class happiness rather as some form of activity, as has been said in the earlier part of this treatise, and if activities are of two kinds, some merely necessary means and desirable only for the sake of something else, others desirable in themselves, it is clear that happiness is to be classed among activities desirable in themselves, and not among those desirable as a means to something else; since happiness lacks nothing, and is self-sufficient.

But those activities are desirable in themselves which do not aim at any result beyond the mere exercise of the activity. Now this is felt to be the nature of actions in conformity with virtue; for to do noble and virtuous deeds is a thing desirable for its own sake.

But agreeable amusements also are desirable for their own sake; we do not pursue them as a means to something else, for as a matter of fact they are more often harmful than beneficial, causing men to neglect their health and their estates. Yet persons whom the world counts happy usually have recourse to such pastimes; and this is why adepts in such pastimes stand in high favour with princes, because they make themselves agreeable in supplying what their patrons desire, and what they want is amusement. So it is supposed that amusements are a component part of happiness, because princes and potentates devote their leisure to them.

But (i) perhaps princes and potentates are not good evidence. Virtue and intelligence, which are the sources of man's higher activities, do not depend on the possession of power; and if these persons, having no taste for pure and liberal pleasure, have recourse to the pleasures of the body, we must not on that account suppose that bodily pleasures are the more desirable. Children imagine that the things they themselves value are actually the best; it is not surprising therefore that, as children and grown men have different standards of value, so also should the worthless and the virtuous. Therefore, as has repeatedly been said, those things are actually valuable and pleasant which appear so to the good man; but each man thinks that activity most desirable which suits his particular disposition, and therefore the good man thinks virtuous activity most desirable. It follows therefore that happiness is not to be found in amusements.

(ii) Indeed it would be strange that amusement should be our End—that we should toil and moil all our life long in order that we may amuse ourselves. For virtually every object we adopt is pursued as a means to something else, excepting happiness, which is an end in itself; to make amusement the object of our serious pursuits and our work seems foolish and childish to excess: Anacharsis's motto, Play in order that you may work, is felt to be the right rule. For amusement is a form of rest; but we need rest because we are not able to go on working without a break, and therefore it is not an end, since we take it as a means to further activity.

(iii) And the life that con- [1177ª] forms with virtue is thought to be a happy life; but virtuous life involves serious purpose, and does not consist in amusement.

(iv) Also we pronounce serious things to be superior to things that are funny and amusing; and the nobler a faculty or a person is, the more serious, we think, are their activities; therefore, the activity of the nobler faculty or person is itself superior, and therefore more productive of happiness.

(v) Also anybody can enjoy the pleasures of the body, a slave no less than the noblest of mankind; but no one allows a slave any measure of happiness, any more than a life of his own. Therefore happiness does not consist in pastimes and amusements, but in activities in accordance with virtue, as has been said already.

VII. But if happiness consists in activity in accordance with virtue, it is reasonable that it should be activity in accordance with the highest virtue; and this will be the virtue of the best part of us. Whether then this be the intellect, or whatever else it be that is thought to rule and lead us by nature, and to have cognizance of what is noble and divine, either as being itself also actually divine, or as being relatively the divinest part of us, it is the activity of this part of us in accordance with the virtue proper to it that will constitute perfect happiness; and it has been stated already that this activity is the activity of contemplation.

And that happiness consists in contemplation may be accepted as agreeing both with the results already reached and with the truth. For contemplation is at once the highest form of activity (since the intellect is the highest thing in us, and the objects with which the intellect deals are the highest things that can be known), and also it is the most continuous, for we can reflect more continuously than we can carry on any form of action. And again we suppose that happiness must contain an element of pleasure; now activity in accordance with wisdom is admittedly the most pleasant of the activities in accordance

with virtue; at all events it is held that philosophy or the pursuit of wisdom contains pleasures of marvellous purity and permanence, and it is reasonable to suppose that the enjoyment of knowledge is a still pleasanter occupation than the pursuit of it. Also the activity of contemplation will be found to possess in the highest degree the quality that is termed self-sufficiency; for while it is true that the wise man equally with the just man and the rest requires the necessaries of life, yet, these being adequately supplied, whereas the just man needs other persons towards whom or with whose aid he may act justly, and so likewise do the temperate man and the brave man and the others, the wise man on the contrary can also contemplate by himself, and the more so the wiser he is; no doubt he will study better with the aid of fellow-workers, but still he is the most self-sufficient of men. Also [1177ᵇ] the activity of contemplation may be held to be the only activity that is loved for its own sake: it produces no result beyond the actual act of contemplation, whereas from practical pursuits we look to secure some advantage, greater or smaller, beyond the action itself. Also happiness is thought to involve leisure for we do business in order that we may have leisure, and carry on war in order that we may have peace. Now the practical virtues are exercised in politics or in warfare; but the pursuits of politics and war seem to be unleisured—those of war indeed entirely so, for no one desires to be at war for the sake of being at war, nor deliberately takes steps to cause a war: a man would be thought an utterly bloodthirsty character if he declared war on a friendly state for the sake of causing battles and massacres. But the activity of the politician also is unleisured, and aims at securing something beyond the mere participation in politics—positions of authority and honour, or, if the happiness of the politician himself and of his fellow-citizens, this happiness conceived as something distinct from political activity (indeed we are clearly investigating it as so distinct).[13] If then among practical pursuits displaying the virtues, politics and war stand out pre-eminent in nobility and grandeur, and yet they are unleisured, and directed to some further end, not chosen for their own sakes: whereas the activity of the intellect is felt to excel in serious worth, consisting as it does in contemplation, and to aim at no end beyond itself, and also to contain a pleasure peculiar to itself, and therefore augmenting its activity: and if accordingly the attributes of this activity are found to be self-sufficiency, leisuredness, such freedom from fatigue as is possible for man, and all the other attributes of blessedness: it follows that it is the activity of the intellect that constitutes complete human happiness—provided it be granted a complete span of life, for nothing that belongs to happiness can be incomplete.

Such a life as this however will be higher than the human level: not in virtue of his humanity will a man achieve it, but in virtue of something within him that is divine; and by as much as this something is superior to his composite nature, by so much is its activity superior to the exercise of the other forms of virtue. If then the intellect is something divine in comparison with man, so is the life of the intellect divine in comparison with human life. Nor ought we to obey those who enjoin that a man should have man's thoughts and a mortal the thoughts of mortality, but we ought so far as possible to achieve immortality, and do all that man may to live in accordance with the highest thing in him; for though this be [1178ᵃ] small in bulk, in power and value it far surpasses all the rest.

It may even be held that this is the true self of each, inasmuch as it is the dominant and better part; and therefore it would be a strange thing if a man should choose to live not his own life but the life of some other than himself.

Moreover what was said before will apply here also: that which is best and most pleasant for each creature is that which is proper to the nature of each; accordingly the life of the intellect is the best and the pleasantest life for man, inasmuch as the intellect more than anything else is man; therefore this life will be the happiest.

VIII. The life of moral virtue, on the other hand, is happy only in a secondary degree. For the moral activities are purely human: Justice, I mean, Courage and the other virtues we display in our intercourse with our fellows, when we observe what is due to each in contracts and services and in our various actions, and in our emotions also; and all of these things seem to be purely human affairs. And some moral actions are thought to be the outcome of the physical constitution, and moral virtue is thought to be the outcome of the physical constitution, and moral virtue is thought to have a close affinity in many respects with the passions. Moreover, Prudence is intimately connected with Moral Virtue, and this with Prudence, inasmuch as the first principles which Prudence employs are determined by the Moral Virtues, and the right standard for the Moral Virtues is determined by Prudence. But these being also connected with the passions are related to our composite nature; now the virtues of our composite nature are purely human; so therefore also is the life that manifests these virtues, and the happiness that belongs to it. Whereas the happiness that belongs to the intellect is separate: so much may be said about it here, for a full discussion of the matter is beyond the scope of our present purpose. And such happiness would appear to need but little external equipment, or less than the happiness based on moral virtue. Both,

---

[13] Probably the sentence should be curtailed to run "or in fact the happiness of himself and his fellow-citizens; and happiness we are clearly investigating as something distinct from the art of politics [whose object it is]."

it may be granted, require the mere necessaries of life, and that in an equal degree (though the politician does as a matter of fact take more trouble about bodily requirements and so forth than the philosopher); for in this respect there may be little difference between them. But for the purpose of their special activities their requirements will differ widely. The liberal man will need wealth in order to do liberal actions, and so indeed will the just man in order to discharge his obligations (since mere intentions are invisible, and even the unjust pretend to wish to act justly); and the brave man will need strength if he is to perform any action displaying his virtue; and the temperate man opportunity for indulgence: otherwise how can he, or the possessor of any other virtue, show that he is virtuous? It is disputed also whether purpose or performance is the more important factor in virtue, as it is alleged to depend on both; now the perfection of virtue will clearly consist in both; but the performance of virtuous ac- [1178ᵇ] tions requires much outward equipment, and the more so the greater and more noble the actions are. But the student, so far as the pursuit of his activity is concerned, needs no external apparatus: on the contrary, worldly goods may almost be said to be a hindrance to contemplation; though it is true that, being a man and living in the society of others, he chooses to engage in virtuous action, and so will need external goods to carry on his life as a human being.

The following considerations also will show that perfect happiness is some form of contemplative activity. The gods, as we conceive them, enjoy supreme felicity and happiness. But what sort of actions can we attribute to them? Just actions? but will it not seem ridiculous to think of them as making contracts, restoring deposits and the like? Then brave actions—enduring terrors and running risks for the nobility of so doing? Or liberal actions? but to whom will they give? Besides, it would be absurd to suppose that they actually have a coinage or currency of some sort! And temperate actions—what will these mean in their case? surely it would be derogatory to praise them for not having evil desires! If we go through the list we shall find that all forms of virtuous conduct seem trifling and unworthy of the gods. Yet nevertheless they have always been conceived as, at all events, living, and therefore living actively, for we cannot suppose they are always asleep like Endymion. But for a living being, if we eliminate action, and a fortiori creative action, what remains save contemplation? It follows that the activity of God, which is transcendent in blessedness, is the activity of contemplation; and therefore among human activities that which is most akin to the divine activity of contemplation will be the greatest source of happiness.

A further confirmation is that the lower animals cannot partake of happiness, because they are completely devoid of the contemplative activity. The whole of the life of the gods is blessed, and that of man is so in so far as it contains some likeness to the divine activity; but none of the other animals possess happiness, because they are entirely incapable of contemplation. Happiness therefore is co-extensive in its range with contemplation: the more a class of beings possesses the faculty of contemplation, the more it enjoys happiness, not as an accidental concomitant of contemplation but as inherent in it, since contemplation is valuable in itself. It follows that happiness is some form of contemplation.

But the philosopher being a man will also need external well-being, since man's nature is not self-sufficient for the activity of contemplation, but he must also have bodily health and a supply of food and other requirements. Yet if supreme blessedness is not pos- [1179ª] sible without external goods, it must not be supposed that happiness will demand many or great possessions; for self-sufficiency does not depend on excessive abundance, nor does moral conduct, and it is possible to perform noble deeds even without being ruler of land and sea: one can do virtuous acts with quite moderate resources. This may be clearly observed in experience: private citizens do not seem to be less but more given to doing virtuous actions than princes and potentates. It is sufficient then if moderate resources are forthcoming; for a life of virtuous activity will be essentially a happy life.

Solon also doubtless gave a good description of happiness, when he said that in his opinion those men were happy who, being moderately equipped with external goods, had performed noble exploits and had lived temperately; for it is possible for a man of but moderate possessions to do what is right. Anaxagoras again does not seem to have conceived the happy man as rich or powerful, since he says that he would not be surprised if he were to appear a strange sort of person in the eyes of the many; for most men judge by externals, which are all that they can perceive. So our theories seem to be in agreement with the opinions of the wise.

Such arguments then carry some degree of conviction; but it is by the practical experience of life and conduct that the truth is really tested, since it is there that the final decision lies. We must therefore examine the conclusions we have advanced by bringing them to the test of the facts of life. If they are in harmony with the facts, we may accept them; if found to disagree, we must deem them mere theories.

And it seems likely that the man who pursues intellectual activity, and who cultivates his intellect and keeps that in the best condition, is also the man most beloved of the gods. For if, as is generally believed, the gods exercise some superintendence over human affairs, then it will be reasonable to suppose that they take pleasure in that part of man which is best and most akin to themselves, namely the intellect, and that they recompense with their favours those men who esteem and honour this most, because these care for the things dear to themselves, and act rightly and nobly. Now it is clear that all these attributes belong most of all to the wise man. He therefore is most beloved by the gods; and if so, he is naturally most happy. Here is another proof that the wise man is the happiest.

## POETICS (Chapters I-XV)

### I

I propose to treat of poetry in [1447a] itself and of its several species, noting the essential quality of each; to inquire into the structure of the plot as requisite to a good poem; into the number and nature of the parts of which each species consists; and similarly into whatever else falls within the same inquiry. Following, then, the order of nature, let us begin with the principles which come first.

Epic poetry and Tragedy, Comedy also and dithyrambic poetry, and the greater part of the music of the flute and of the lyre are all in their general conception modes of imitation. They differ, however, from one another in three respects—the means, the objects, the manner of imitation being in each case distinct.

For as there are persons who, by conscious art or mere habit, imitate and represent various objects through the medium of color and form, or again by the voice; so in the arts above mentioned taken as a whole, the imitation is produced by rhythm, language, and "harmony," either singly or combined.

Thus in the music of the flute and the lyre "harmony" and rhythm alone are employed; also in other arts such as that of the pipe, which are essentially similiar to these; in dancing, rhythm alone is used without "harmony"; for even dancing imitates character, emotion, and action, by rhythmical movement.

The art which imitates by means of language alone, and that either in prose or verse—which verse, again, may either combine different metres or con- [1447ᵇ] sist of but one kind—has hitherto been without a name. For there is no common term we could apply to the mimes of Sophron and Xenarchus and to the Socratic dialogues; or, again, to poetic imitations in iambic, elegiac, or any similar metre. People do, indeed, commonly connect the idea of poetry or "making" with that of verse, and speak of elegiac poets, or of epic (that is, hexameter) poets; implying that it is not imitation that makes them poets, but the metre that entitles them to the common name. Even if a treatise on medicine or natural philosophy be brought out in verse, the name of poet is by custom given to the author; and yet Homer and Empedocles have nothing in common except the metre: the former, therefore, is properly styled poet, the latter, physicist rather than poet.

So too if a writer should, in his poetic imitation, combine every variety of metre, like Chaeremon—whose *Centaur* is a rhapsody in which all metres are mingled—we must, according to usage, call him simply poet. So much then for these distinctions.

There are, again, certain kinds of poetry which employ all the means above mentioned — namely, rhythm, melody and metre. Such are dithyrambic and nomic poetry, and also Tragedy and Comedy; but between them the difference is, that in the first two cases these means are all employed at the same time, in the latter, separately.

Such, then, are the differences of the arts with respect to the means of imitation.

II

Since the objects of imitation [1448ª] are persons acting, and these persons must be either of a higher or a lower type (for moral character mainly answers to these divisions, goodness and badness being the distinguishing marks of moral differences), it follows that we must represent men either as better than in real life, or worse, or as they are. It is the same in painting. Polygnotus depicted men as nobler than they are, Pauson as less noble, Dionysius drew them true to life.

Now it is evident that each of the modes of imitation above mentioned will exhibit these differences, and become a distinct kind in imitating objects that are thus distinct. Such diversities may be found even in dancing, flute-playing, and lyre-playing. So again in prose compositions, and in verse unaccompanied by music. Homer, for example, makes men better than they are; Cleophon as they are; Hegemon the Thasian, the inventor of parodies, and Nicochares, the author of the *Deliad*, worse than they are. The same thing holds good of dithyrambs and nomes; here too one may portray lower types, as Timotheus and Philoxenus represented Cyclopes. The same distinction marks off Tragedy from Comedy; for Comedy aims at representing men as worse, Tragedy as better than in actual life.

III

There is still a third difference—the manner in which each of these objects may be imitated. For the means being the same, and the objects the same, the poet may imitate by narration—in which case he can either take another personality as Homer does, or speak in his own person, unchanged—or he may imitate by making all his actors live and move before us.

These, then, as we said at the beginning, are the three differences which distinguish artistic imitation—the means, the objects, and the manner. So that from one point of view, Sophocles is an imitator of the same kind as Homer—for both imitate higher types of character; from another point of view, of the same kind as Aristophanes—for both imitate persons acting and doing. Hence, some say, the name of "drama" is given to such poems, as representing action. For the same reason the Dorians claim the invention both of Tragedy and Comedy. The claim to Comedy is put forward by the Megarians—not only by those of Greece proper, who allege that it originated under their democracy, but also by the Megarians of Sicily; the poet Epicharmus, who lived not long before Chionides and Magnes, being from their country. Tragedy too is claimed by certain Dorians of the Peloponnese. In each case they appeal to the evidence of language. Villages they say, are by them called χῶμαι, by the Athenians δῆμοι: and they assume that the name Comedians is derived not from χωμάζειν, "to revel," but from the performer wandering about the villages (χῶμαι), when still excluded from the city. They add also that the Dorian word for [1448ᵇ] "doing" is δρᾶν, and the Athenian, πράττειν.

This may suffice as to the number and nature of the various modes of imitation.

## IV

Poetry in general seems to have sprung from two causes, each of them lying deep in our nature. First, the instinct of imitation is implanted in man from childhood, one difference between him and other animals being that he is the most imitative of creatures; and through imitation he acquires his earliest learning. And, indeed, every one feels a natural pleasure in things imitated. There is evidence of this in the effect produced by works of art. Objects which in themselves we view with pain, we delight to contemplate when reproduced with absolute fidelity: such as the forms of the most ignoble beasts and of dead bodies. The cause of this again is, that to learn is a lively pleasure, not only to philosophers but to men in general; whose capacity, however, of learning is more limited. Thus the reason why men enjoy seeing a likeness is, that in contemplating it they are engaged in learning—they reason and infer what each object is: "this," they say, "is the man." For if you happen not to have seen the original, the pleasure will be due not to the imitation as such, but to the execution, the colouring, or some such other cause.

Imitation, then, is one instinct of our nature. Next, there is the instinct for harmony and rhythm, metre being manifestly a species of rhythm. Persons, therefore, with this natural gift little by little improved upon their early efforts, till their rude improvisations gave birth to Poetry.

Poetry now branched off in two directions, according to the individual character of the writers. The more elevated poets imitated noble actions, and the actions of good men. The more trivial sort imitated the actions of meaner persons, at first composing satires, as the former did hymns to the gods and the praises of famous men. A poem of the satirical kind cannot indeed be put down to any author earlier than Homer; though many such writers probably there were. But from Homer onward, instances can be cited—his *Margites*, for example, and other similar compositions. The iambic metre was here introduced, as best fitted to the subject: hence the measure is still called the iambic or lampooning measure, being that in which the lampoons were written.

Thus the older poets were distinguished as writers either or heroic or of iambic verse. As, in the serious style, Homer is preeminent among poets, standing alone not only in the excellence, but also in the dramatic form of his imitations, so he too first sketched out the main lines of Comedy, by dramatising the ludicrous instead of writing personal satire. His *Margites* bears the same relation to Comedy that the [1449$^a$] *Iliad* and *Odyssey* do to Tragedy. But when Tragedy and Comedy had once appeared, writers applied themselves to one or other species of poetry, following their native bent. They composed Comedies in place of lampoons, and Tragedies in place of Epic poems, the newer forms of poetry being higher and more highly esteemed than the old.

Whether Tragedy has as yet perfected its proper types or not; and whether it is to be judged in itself, or in relation also to the stage—this raises another question. Be that as it may, Tragedy— as also Comedy—was at first mere improvisation. The one originated with the leaders of the dithyrambic, the other with those of the phallic songs, which are still in use in many of our cities. Tragedy advanced by slow degrees; each new element that showed itself was in turn developed. Having passed through many changes, it found its natural form, and there it stopped.

Aeschylus first introduced a second actor; he diminished the importance of the Chorus, and assigned the leading part to the dialogue. Sophocles raised the number of actors to three, and added scene-painting. It was not till late that the short plot was discarded for one of greater compass, and the grotesque diction of the earlier satyric form, for the stately manner of Tragedy. The iambic measure then replaced the trochaic tetrameter, which was originally employed when the poetry was of the satyric order, and had greater affinities with dancing. Once dialogue had come in, Nature herself discovered the appropriate measure. For the iambic is, of all measures, the most colloquial: we see it in the fact that conversational speech runs into iambic form more frequently than into any other kind of verse; rarely into hexameters, and only when we drop the colloquial intonation. The number of "episodes" or acts was also increased, and the other embellishments added, of which tradition tells. These we need not here discuss; to enter into them in detail would, probably, be tedious.

<h2 style="text-align:center">v</h2>

Comedy is, as we have said, an imitation of characters of a lower type—not, however, in the full sense of the word bad; for the Ludicrous is merely a subdivision of the ugly. It may be defined as a defect or ugliness which is not painful or destructive. Thus, for example, the comic mask is ugly and distorted, but does not cause pain.

The successive changes through which Tragedy passed, and the authors of these changes are not unknown. It is otherwise with Comedy, which at first was not seriously treated. It was late before the Archon appointed a [1449$^b$] comic chorus; the performers were till then voluntary. From the time, however, when Comedy began to assume certain fixed forms, comic poets, distinctively so called, are recorded. Who introduced masks, or prologues, or increased the number of actors—these and other similar details remain unknown. As for the plot, it came originally from Sicily; but of Athenian writers Crates was the first who, abandoning the "iambic" or lampooning form, generalised his themes and plots.

Epic poetry agrees with Tragedy in

so far as it is an imitation in verse of characters of a higher type. They differ, in that Epic poetry admits but one kind of metre, and is narrative in form. They differ, again, in length: for Tragedy endeavours, as far as possible, to confine itself to a single revolution of the sun, or but slightly to exceed this limit; whereas the Epic action has no limits of time. This, then, is a second point of difference; though at first the same freedom was admitted in Tragedy as in Epic poetry.

Of their constituent parts some are common to both, some peculiar to Tragedy. Whoever, therefore, knows what is good or bad Tragedy, knows also about Epic poetry: for all the parts of an Epic poem are found in Tragedy, but what belongs to Tragedy is not all found in the Epic poem.

## VI

Of the poetry which imitates in hexameter verse, and of Comedy, we will speak hereafter. Let us now discuss Tragedy, resuming its formal definition, as resulting from what has been already said.

Tragedy, then, is an imitation of an action that is serious, complete, and of a certain magnitude; in language embellished with each kind of artistic ornament, the several kinds being found in separate parts of the play; in the form of action, not of narrative; through pity and fear effecting the proper purgation of these emotions.[1] By "language embellished," I mean language into which rhythm, "harmony," and song enter. By "the several kinds in separate parts," I mean, that some parts are rendered through the medium of verse alone, others again with the aid of song.

Now as tragic imitation implies per-

sons acting, it necessarily follows, in the first place, that Scenic equipment will be a part of Tragedy. Next, Song and Diction, for these are the means of imitation. By "Diction" I mean the mere metrical arrangement of the words: or for "Song," it is a term whose full sense is well understood.

Again, Tragedy is the imitation of an action; and an action implies personal agents, who necessarily possess certain qualities both of character and thought. It is these that determine the qualities of actions themselves; these—thought and character—are the two nat- [1450ᵃ] ural causes from which actions spring: on these causes, again, all success or failure depends. Hence, the Plot is the imitation of the action—for by plot I here mean the arrangement of the incidents. By Character I mean that in virtue of which we ascribe certain qualities to the agents. By Thought, that whereby a statement is proved, or a general truth expressed. Every Tragedy, therefore, must have six parts, which parts determine its quality—namely, Plot, Character, Diction, Thought, Scenery, Song. Two of the parts constitute the means of imitation, one the manner, and three the objects of imitation. And these complete the list. These elements have been employed, we may say, by almost all poets; in fact, every play contains Scenic accessories as well as Character, Plot, Diction, Song, and Thought.

But most important of all is the structure of the incidents. For Tragedy is an imitation, not of men, but of an action and of life—of happiness and misery; and happiness and misery consist in action, the end of human life being a mode of action, not a quality. Now the characters of men determine their qualities, but it is by their actions that they are happy or the reverse. Dramatic action, therefore, is not with a view to the representation of character: character comes in as subsidiary to the action.

---

[1] This is Aristotle's vastly influential definition of tragedy. His word for "purgation" is *catharsis*; for "imitation," *mimesis*. W.K.

Hence the incidents and the plot are the end of a tragedy; and the end is the chief thing of all. Again, without action there cannot be a tragedy; there may be without character. The tragedies of most of our modern poets fail in the rendering of character; and of poets in general this is often true. It is the same in painting; and here lies the difference between Zeuxis and Polygnotus. Polygnotus delineates character well: the style of Zeuxis is devoid of ethical quality. Again, if you string together a set of speeches expressive of character, and well finished in point of diction and thought, you will not produce the essential tragic effect nearly so well as with a play, which, however deficient in these respects yet has a plot and artistically constructed incident. Besides which, the most powerful elements of emotional interest in Tragedy—Reversals of Fortune, and Recognition scenes— are parts of the plot. A further proof is, that novices in the art are able to elaborate their diction and ethical portraiture, before they can frame the incidents. It is the same with almost all early poets.

The Plot, then, is the first principle, and, as it were, the soul of the tragedy: Character holds the second place. [1450ᵇ] A similar fact is seen in painting. The most beautiful colours, laid on confusedly, will not give as much pleasure as the chalk outline of a portrait. Thus Tragedy is the imitation of an action, and of the agents, mainly with a view to the action.

Third in order is the Thought—that is, the faculty of saying what is possible and pertinent in given circumstances. In the case of the dramatic dialogue, this is the function of the political or the rhetorical art: for the older poets make their characters speak the language of civic life; the poets of our time, the language of the rhetoricians. Character is that which reveals moral purpose: it shows what kind of things, in cases of doubt, a man chooses or avoids. A dia-logue, therefore, which in no way indicates what the speaker chooses or avoids, is not expressive of character. Thought, on the other hand, is that whereby we prove that something is or is not, or state a general maxim.

Fourth comes the Diction; by which I mean, as has been already said, the expression of our meaning in words; and its essence is the same both in verse and prose.

Of the remaining elements Song holds the chief place among the embellishments.

The Scenery has, indeed, an emotional attraction of its own, but, of all the parts, it is the least artistic, and connected least with poetic theory. For the power of Tragedy, we may be sure, is felt even apart from representation and actors. Besides, the production of scenic effects depends more on the art of the stage manager than on that of the poet.

VII

These principles being established, let us now discuss the proper structure of the Plot, since this is the first, and also the most important part of Tragedy.

Now, according to our definition, Tragedy is an imitation of an action, that is complete, and whole, and of a certain magnitude; for there may be a whole that is wanting in magnitude. A whole is that which has beginning, middle, and end. A beginning is that which does not itself follow anything by causal necessity, but after which something naturally is or comes to be. An end, on the contrary, is that which itself naturally follows some other thing, either by necessity, or in the regular course of events, but has nothing following it. A middle is that which follows something as some other thing follows it. A well constructed plot, therefore, must neither begin nor end at haphazard, but conform to the type here described.

Again, if an object be beautiful— either a living organism or a whole composed of parts—it must not only have its parts in orderly arrangement, it must also be of a certain magnitude. Hence no exceedingly small animal can be beautiful, for the view of it is confused, the object being seen in an almost imperceptible moment of time. Nor, again, can an animal of vast size be beautiful; for as the eye cannot take it all in at once, the unity and sense of the whole is lost for the spectator. So it [1451ᵃ] would be with a creature a thousand miles long. As, therefore, in animate bodies and living organisms, a certain magnitude is necessary, and that such as may be easily embraced in one view; so in the plot, a certain length is necessary and that length one that may be easily embraced by the memory. The limit of length in relation to dramatic competition and sensuous presentment, is no part of artistic theory. For suppose a hundred tragedies had to be played against one another, the performance would be regulated by the hourglass—a method, indeed, that is familiar enough otherwise. But the limit as fixed by the nature of the drama itself is this: —the greater the length, the more beautiful will the piece be in respect of such magnitude, provided that the whole be perspicuous. And as a general rule, the proper magnitude is comprised within such limits, that the sequence of events, according to the law of probability or necessity, will admit of a change from bad fortune to good, or from good fortune to bad.

### VIII

Unity of plot does not, as some persons think, consist in the unity of the hero. For infinitely various are the incidents in one man's life, which cannot be reduced to unity; and so, too, there are many actions of one man out of which we cannot make one action. Hence the error, as it appears, of all poets who have composed a Heracleid, a Theseid, or other poems of the kind.

They imagine that as Heracles was one man, the story of Heracles ought also to be a unity. But Homer, as in all else he is of surpassing merit, here too— whether from art or natural genius— seems to have happily discerned the truth. In composing the *Odyssey* he did not bring in all the adventures of Odysseus—such as his wound on Parnassus, or his feigned madness at the mustering of the host—incidents between which there was no necessary or probable connexion: but he made the *Odyssey,* and likewise the *Iliad,* to centre round an action, that in our sense of the word is one. As therefore in the other imitative arts, the imitation is one, when the object imitated is one, so the plot, being an imitation of an action, must imitate one action and that a whole, the structural union of the parts being such that, if any one of them is displaced or removed, the whole will be disjointed and disturbed. For that which may be present or absent without being perceived, is not an organic part of the whole.

### IX

It is, moreover, evident from what has been said, that it is not the function of the poet to relate what has happened, but what may happen—what is possible according to the law of probability or necessity. The poet and the historian differ not by writing in verse or in prose. The work of Herodotus might be [1451ᵇ] put into verse, and it would still be a species of history, with metre no less than without it. The true difference is that one relates what has happened, the other what may happen. Poetry, therefore, is a more philosophical and a higher thing than history:[2] for poetry tends to express the universal, history the particular. The universal tells us how a person of given character will on occasion speak or act, according to the law of probability or necessity; and

---

2 This dictum is often quoted. W.K.

it is this universality at which Poetry aims in giving expressive names to the characters. The particular is—for example—what Alcibiades did or suffered. In Comedy this is now apparent: for here the poet first constructs the plot on the lines of probability, and then assumes any names he pleases—unlike the lampooners who write about a particular individual. But tragedians still keep to real names, the reason being that what is possible is credible: what has not happened we do not at once feel sure to be possible: but what has happened is manifestly possible; otherwise it would not have happened. Still there are some tragedies in which one or two names only are well known, the rest being fictitious. In others, none are well known —as in Agathon's *Flower*, where incidents and names alike are fictitious, and yet it pleases. We must not, therefore, at all costs keep to the received legends, which are the usual subjects of Tragedy. Indeed, it would be absurd to attempt it; for even familiar subjects are familiar only to a few, and yet give pleasure to all. It clearly follows that the poet or 'maker' should be the maker of plots rather than of verses; since he is a poet because he imitates, and what he imitates are nations. And if he chances to take an historical subject, he is none the less a poet; for there is no reason why some real events should not have that internal probability or possibility which entitles the author to the name of poet.

Of all plots and actions the episodic are the worst. I call a plot episodic in which the episodes or acts succeed one another without probable or necessary sequence. Bad poets compose such pieces by their own fault, good poets, to please the players; for, as they write for competing rivals,, they draw out the plot beyond its capacity, and are often forced to break the natural continuity.

But again, Tragedy is an im- [1452ᵃ] itation not only of a complete action, but of events terrible and pitiful. Such an effect is best produced when the events come on us by surprise; and the effect is heightened when, at the same time, they follow from one another. The tragic wonder will then be greater than if they happened of themselves or by accident; for even accidents are most striking when they have an air of design. We may instance the statue of Mitys at Argos, which fell upon his murderer while he was looking at it, and killed him. Such events seem not to be due to mere chance. Plots, therefore, constructed on these principles are necessarily the best.

X

Plots are either simple or complicated; for such too, in their very nature, are the actions of which the plots are an imitation. An action which is one and continuous in the sense above defined, I call Simple, when the turning point is reached without Reversal of Fortune or Recognition: Complicated, when it is reached with Reversal of Fortune, or Recognition, or both. These last should arise from the internal structure of the plot, so that what follows should be the necessary or probable result of the preceding action. It makes all the difference whether one event is the consequence of another, or merely subsequent to it.

XI

A Reversal of Fortune is, as we have said, a change by which a train of action produces the opposite of the effect intended; and that, according to our rule of probability or necessity. Thus in the *Oedipus*, the messenger, hoping to cheer Oedipus, and to free him from his alarms about his mother, reveals his origin, and so produces the opposite effect. Again in the *Lynceus*, Lynceus is being led out to die, and Danaus goes with him, meaning to slay him; but the outcome of the action is, that Danaus is killed and Lynceus saved.

A Recognition, as the name indicates, is a change from ignorance to knowledge, producing love or hate between the persons destined by the poet for good or bad fortune. The best form of recognition is coincident with a reversal of fortune, as in the *Oedipus*. There are indeed other forms. Even inanimate things of the most trivial kind may sometimes be objects of recognition. Again, the discovery may be made whether a person has or has not done something. But the form which is most intimately connected with the plot and action is, as we have said, the recognition of persons. This, combined with a reversal of fortune, will produce [1452b] either pity or fear; and actions producing these effects are those which, as we have assumed, Tragedy represents. Moreover, fortune or misfortune will depend upon such incidents. Recognition, then, being between persons, it may happen that one person only is recognised by the other—when the latter is already known—or the recognition may need to be on both sides. Thus Iphigenia is revealed to Orestes by the sending of the letter; but another means is required to make Orestes known to Iphigenia.

Two parts, then, of the Plot—Reversal of Fortune and Recognition—turn upon surprises. A third part is the Tragic Incident. The two former have been discussed. The Tragic Incident is a destructive or painful action, such as death on the stage, bodily torments, wounds and the like.

## XII[3]

The parts of Tragedy, which must be treated as elements of the whole, have been already mentioned. We now come to the quantitative parts—the separate parts into which Tragedy is divided—

---

[3] This short chapter is spurious, as Butcher and Else, among others, have pointed out. W.K.

namely, Prologos, Episode, Exodos, Choral element; this last being divided into Parados and Stasimon. These two are sung by the whole Chorus. The songs of the actors on the stage, and the Commoi, are sung by individuals.

The Prologos is that entire part of a tragedy which precedes the Parodos of the Chorus. The Episode is that entire part of a tragedy which is between whole choral songs. The Exodos is that entire part of a tragedy which has no choral song after it. Of the Choral part the Parodos is the first undivided utterance of the Chorus: the Stasimon is a choral ode without anapaests or trochees: the Commos is a joint lamentation of chorus and actors. The parts of Tragedy which must be treated as elements of the whole have been already mentioned. The quantitative parts—the separate parts into which it is divided—are here enumerated.

### XIII

As the sequel to what has already been said, we must proceed to consider what the poet should aim at, and what he should avoid, in constructing his plots; and by what means Tragedy may best fulfil its function.

A perfect tragedy should, as we have seen, be arranged on the complicated not the simple plan. It should, moreover, imitate actions which excite pity and fear, this being the distinctive mark of tragic imitation. It follows plainly, in the first place, that the change of fortune presented must not be the spectacle of a perfectly good man brought from prosperity to adversity: for this moves neither pity nor fear; it simply shocks us. Nor, again, that of a bad man passing from adversity [1453a] to prosperity: for nothing can be more alien to the spirit of Tragedy; it possesses no single tragic quality; it neither satisfies the moral sense, nor calls forth pity or fear. Nor, again, should the downfall of the utter villain be exhibited. A plot of this kind would, doubtless, satisfy the moral sense, but it would inspire neither pity nor fear; for pity is aroused by unmerited misfortune, fear by the misfortune of a man like ourselves. Such an event, therefore, will be neither pitiful nor terrible. There remains, then, the character between these two extremes—that of a man who is not eminently good and just, yet whose misfortune is brought about not by vice or depravity, but by some error or frailty.[4] He must be one who is highly renowned and prosperous—a personage like Oedipus, Thyestes, or other illustrious men of such families.

A well constructed plot should, therefore, be single, rather than double as some maintain. The change of fortune should be not from bad to good, but, reversely, from good to bad.[5] It should come about as the result not of vice, but of some great error or frailty, in a character either such as we have described, or better rather than worse. The practice of the stage bears out our view. At first the poets recounted any legends that came their way. Now, tragedies are founded on the story of a few houses—on the fortunes of Alcmaeon, Oedipus, Orestes, Meleager, Thyestes, Telephus, and those others who have done or suffered something terrible. A tragedy, then, to be perfect according to the rules of art should be of this construction. Hence they are in error who censure Euripides just because he follows this principle in his plays, many of which end unhappily. It is, as we have said, the right ending. The best proof is that on the stage and in dramatic competition, such plays, if they are well represented, are most tragic in their effect; and Euripides, faulty as he is in the general management of his subject,

yet is felt to be the most tragic of poets.

In the second rank comes the kind of tragedy which some place first. Like the *Odyssey*, it has a double thread of plot, and also an opposite catastrophe for the good and for the bad. It is generally thought to be the best owing to the weakness of the spectators; for the poet is guided in what he writes by the wishes of his audience. The pleasure, however, thence derived is not the true tragic pleasure. It is proper rather to Comedy, where those who, in the piece, are the deadliest enemies—like Orestes and Aegisthus—go forth reconciled at last, and no one slays or is slain.

XIV

Fear and pity may be aroused [1453ᵇ] by the spectacle or scenic presentment; but they may also result from the inner structure of the piece, which is the better way, and indicates a superior poet. For the plot ought to be so constructed that, even without the aid of the eye, any one who is told the incidents will thrill with horror and pity at the turn of events. This is precisely the impression we should receive from listening to the story of the *Oedipus*. But to produce this effect by the mere spectacle is a less artistic method, and dependent on extraneous aids. Those who employ spectacular means to create a sense not of the terrible but of the monstrous, are strangers to the purpose of Tragedy; for we must not demand of Tragedy every kind of pleasure, but only that which is proper to it. And since the pleasure which the poet should afford is that which comes from pity and fear through imitation, it is evident that this quality must be stamped upon the incidents.

Let us then determine what are the circumstances which impress us as terrible or pitiful.

Actions capable of this effect must happen between persons who are either friends or enemies or indifferent to one

---

[4] This is the source of the concept of the "tragic flaw." Aristotle's word for "error or frailty" is *hamartia*. W.K.

[5] But see the next chapter. W.K.

another. If an enemy kills an enemy, there is nothing to excite pity either in the act or the intention—except so far as the suffering in itself is pitiful. So again with indifferent persons. But when the tragic incident occurs between those who are near or dear to one another—if, for example, a brother kills, or intends to kill, a brother, a son his father, a mother her son, a son his mother, or any other deed of the kind is done—here we have the situations which should be sought for by the poet. He may not indeed destroy the framework of the received legends—the fact, for instance, that Clytemnestra was slain by Orestes and Eriphyle by Alcmaeon—but he ought to show invention of his own, and skilfully adapt the traditional material. What is meant by skilfully, let us explain more clearly.

The action may be done willingly and with full knowledge on the part of the agents, in the manner of the older poets. It is thus, in fact, that Euripides makes Medea slay her children. Or, again, the deed of horror may be done, but done in ignorance, and the tie of kinship or friendship be discovered afterwards. The *Oedipus* of Sophocles is an example. Here, indeed, the incident is outside the drama proper; but cases occur where it falls within the action of the play: we may cite the *Alcmaeon* of Astydamas, or Telegonus in the *Wounded Odysseus*. Again, there is a third case, where some one is just about to do some irreparable deed through ignorance, and makes the discovery before it it done. These are the only possible ways. For the deed must either be done or not done—and that wittingly or unwittingly. But of all these ways to be about to act knowing the consequences, and then not to act, is the worst. It is shocking without being tragic, for no disaster follows. It is, therefore, never, or very rarely, found in poetry. One instance, however, is in the *Antigone*, where Haemon [1454a]

intends to kill Creon. The next and better way is that the deed should be perpetrated. Still better, that it should be perpetrated in ignorance, and the discovery made afterwards. There is then nothing to shock us, while the discovery produces a startling effect. But the absolutely best way is the last mentioned. Thus in the *Cresphontes*, Merope is in the act of putting her son to death, but, recognising who he is, spares his life. So in the *Iphigenia*, the sister recognises the brother just in time. Again in the *Helle*, the son recognises the mother when on the point of giving her up.[6] This, then, is why a few families only, as has been already observed, furnish the subjects of tragedy. It was not art, but happy chance, that led poets by tentative discovery to impress the tragic quality upon their plots. They are compelled, therefore, to have recourse to those houses in which tragic disasters have occurred.

Enough has now been said concerning the structure of the incidents, and the proper constitution of the plot.

## XV

In respect of character there are four things to be aimed at. First, and most important, it must be good. Now any speech or action that manifests a certain moral purpose will be expressive of character: the character will be good if the purpose is good. This rule applies to persons of every class. Even a woman may be good, and also a slave; though the woman may be said to be an inferior being, and the slave is absolutely bad. The second thing to aim at is propriety. There is a type of manly valour; but for a woman to be valiant in this sense, or terrible, would be inappropriate. Thirdly, character must be true to life:

6 This flatly contradicts the claim in Chapter XIII that the best ending is unhappy. In a book on *Tragedy and Philosophy*, I try to show that Chapter XIV represents Aristotle's considered conclusion. W.K.

for this is a distinct thing from goodness and propriety, as here described. The fourth point is consistency: for even though the original character, who suggested the type, be inconsistent, still he must be consistently inconsistent. As an example of character needlessly bad, we have Menelaus in the *Orestes:* of character incongruous and inappropriate, the lament of Odysseus in the *Scylla,* and the speech of Melanippe: of inconsistency, the *Iphigenia at Aulis*— for the suppliant Iphigenia in no way resembles her later self.

As in the structure of the plot, so too in the portraiture of character, the poet should always aim either at the necessary or the probable. Thus a person of a given character should speak or act in a given way, by the rule either of necessity or of probability; just as this event should follow that by necessary or probable sequence. It is therefore evident that the unravelling of the plot, no less than the complication, must be brought about by the plot itself, and not by Machinery—as in the *Medea,* [1454ᵇ] or in the Return of the Greeks in the *Iliad.* Machinery should be employed only for events external to the drama— either such as are previous to it and outside the sphere of human knowledge, or subsequent to it and which need to be foretold and announced; for to the gods we ascribe the power of seeing all things. Within the action there must be nothing irrational. If the irrational cannot be excluded, it should be outside the scope of the tragedy. Such is the irrational element in the *Oedipus* of Sophocles.

Again, since Tragedy is an imitation of persons who are above the common level, the example of good portrait-painters should be followed. They, while reproducing the distinctive form of the original, make a likeness which is true to life and yet more beautiful. So too the poet, in representing men quick or slow to anger, or with other defects of character, should preserve the type and yet ennoble it. In this way Achilles is portrayed by Agathon and Homer.

These are rules the poet should observe. Nor should he neglect those appeals to the senses, which, though not among the essentials, are the concomitants of poetry: for here too there is much room for error. But of this we have said enough in our published treatises.

### part four

# HELLENISTIC
# PHILOSOPHY

I

For many centuries, Plato and Aristotle were not followed by philosophers of comparable caliber. There was a decline of creative energy, in philosophy as well as in other fields. The great tragedians of the fifth century had no successors either, nor did the Greeks produce another Homer or Thucydides.

Of Socrates' friends and disciples, at least two besides Plato are of some philosophic importance. Antisthenes, a rhetorician with an Athenian father and a Phrygian, non-Greek mother, had been a teacher in his own right before he met Socrates who made the profoundest impression on him. It seems to have been Socrates' character, his perfect self-control and self-sufficiency, his indifference to the cold of the winter (see the *Symposium*) and to the opinions of men (see the *Apology*), his serenely ironic superiority to every fate, that struck Antisthenes with the force of a revelation. What he learned from Socrates, was neither a metaphysic nor even a philosophic method but, as he himself put it, "to live with myself." He disposed of his possessions, keeping only a ragged old coat, whereupon Socrates is said to have taunted him: "I see your vanity through the holes of your coat." Antisthenes also taught the unity of God. He founded a school whose members received the nickname of Cynics, *kynikos* being Greek for doglike. They slept on the ground, neglected their clothes, let their beards grow to unusual lengths, and despised the run of men, insisting that virtue and happiness consist in self-control and independence. Of Antisthenes' disciples none was more famous than Diogenes, who went about during the day carrying a lantern and, asked what he was doing, would reply: "I am looking for an honest man." He made his home in a tub, and his eccentric behavior attracted the attention of Alexander the Great who went to visit him and, greatly impressed, asked whether there was anything at all that he could do to please the Cynic. Diogenes replied: "Yes, get out of my sunlight."

Another so-called Socratic school, that of the Cyrenaics, was founded by another of Socrates' associates and admirers, Aristippus of Cyrene, a city of Libya, in North Africa, about ten miles from the Mediterranean coast. The Greeks had a colony there, and the city is also associated with one of the masterpieces of ancient sculpture, the Aphrodite of Cyrene, a Roman copy of a Greek statue. The Cyrenaics disparaged speculative philosophy and extolled pleasure, but, following Aristippus, they maintained that the purest pleasure attends self-mastery and the philosophic life. Only phiosophy can protect men against passion, which spells suffering. While despising popular opinion, the Cyrenaics did consider custom, law, and altruism justifiable in terms of an appeal to long-range pleasures.

Before long, Cynicism became one of the tributaries of Stoicism, while the Cyrenaics were absorbed by the Epicureans; but it is worth noting to what extent the two dominant Hellenistic philosophies, which remained important and influential through the Roman era, received their inspiration, even if to some extent indirectly, from Socrates.

II

Epicurus was born on the island of Samos, like Pythagoras, approximately seven years after Plato's death, in 342/41 B.C. At the age of eighteen, he went to Athens for a year, then joined his father in Colophon, the city where Xenophanes had been born. He studied the writings of Democritus before returning to Athens in 307, and there he bought a garden that became famous as the place where he taught his disciples. His emphasis on pleasure was distorted by his enemies, and "epicurean" became a synonym for "gourmet." In fact, he and the community that formed around him lived on water and barley bread, and an occasional drink of wine was considered something special. Unlike his critics, he found philosophy more pleasant than fine food.

His philosophy may be gleaned from the two works that follow, both being reprinted complete, without any omissions. His influence was very considerable and was felt for a long time after his death in 270 B.C. A Roman poet, Lucretius (98-55 B.C.), embraced the philosophy of Epicurus and expounded it in a celebrated poem, *De rerum natura* (Of the Nature of Things), which is still extant. Instead of excerpting necessarily inadequate prose translations that cannot hope to do justice to the poetry of the original, the present volume concentrates on Epicurus and Democritus, who were philosophers, not poets, and whose writings have so far been ever so much less accessible.

The last of the major Greek philosophers, like the first, Thales, was probably a Semite: Zeno of Citium, on the island of Cyprus, the founder of the Stoic school. The year of his birth is uncertain: some say 336 B.C., while others hold that he was 98 when he died in 264 B.C., there being agreement on the latter date. It is said that he discovered philosophy by reading Xenophon and that, Socrates being long dead, he attached himself for some time to the Cynics. He read very widely and was greatly respected for his learning and, if possible, even more for his character and the simplicity of his way of life. Like some of the pre-Socratics, he was a sage as well as a philosopher, and an immensely impressive personality besides being a great thinker.

The school received its name from the columned porch (Stoa, in Greek) where he taught. It survived him and proved to have special appeal to the Roman mind: not so much the ample speculative and theoretical contents of Stoicism, which owe much to Heraclitus and a variety of other sources, as the austere moral emphasis, the stress on self-control and superiority to pain. One might even say that in a recognizable sense the pillars of republican Rome all tended to be Stoics, even if they had never heard of Stoicism.

Zeno's first major disciple, Cleanthes, who is said to have starved himself to death at 90 (about 240 B.C.), is remembered chiefly for his "Hymn to Zeus," if for that, while the next major Stoic, Chrysippus, is known to few but specialists in Stoicism. Even Seneca, the tragic poet and philosopher who tutored the young Nero and later was forced by the emperor to commit suicide, in A.D. 65, is much more widely known than the earlier Greek Stoics. But most people associate Stoicism above all with Marcus Aurelius (121-180), who became Roman emperor in 161 and wrote a famous book of *Meditations*, and with Epictetus, an emancipated slave.

Epictetus' precise dates are not known, but he was born in Hierapolis in Phrygia, in Asia Minor, around A.D. 50, and lived most of his life in Rome. He died about A.D. 138. His *Manual* has been much admired as a concise and authentic summary of Stoicism.

The skepticism of Pyrrho, a philosopher from Elis on the Peloponnesus, who lived from about 360 to 270 B.C. but left no writings, is best presented in the *Outlines of Pyrrhonism*, written by Sextus Empiricus, a Greek physician and philosopher who lived in Alexandria and Athens during the first half of the third century A.D. Pyrrho suggested that we confront statements with their contradictories and develop an attitude of suspense of judgment (*epoché*, in Greek) and thus gradually attain to imperturbability (*ataraxia*).

Looking back on the development of Greek philosophy from the pre-Socratics to the Stoics, the Epicureans, and the Skeptics, one is struck by the overwhelming concern of the later schools with peace of mind. There is one quality which the preclassical and classical Greeks possessed pre-eminently and which Skeptics, Stoics, and Epicureans lacked just as signally: enthusiasm. This may help to explain why, for all their intellectual and moral virtues, they could not compete with the growing appeal of Christianity.

The last great school of Greek philosophy was Neoplatonism, and its most famous representative was Plotinus, born in Lycopolis in Egypt of Roman parents in A.D. 204. He certainly did not lack enthusiasm but was, in spite of that, still more remote from classical Greek attitudes than the other

Hellenistic philosophers. He extolled the spirit to the point of saying that he was ashamed to have a body, and his fervor was entirely directed toward mysticism and, to cite his famous words, "the flight of the Alone to the Alone." Thus he perfected the less classical tendencies of Plato's thought, merging them both with Neopythagoreanism and with such Oriental notions as the doctrine of progressive emanations from the One. The ultimate mystical union he sought, he is said to have attained four times before his death in A.D. 270. Porphyry, his pupil, edited his writings in the form of six groups of nine treatises, published as the so-called *Enneads*.

Neoplatonism had a profound influence on Christian thought; for example, but by no means only, on Augustine. Indeed, if St. Thomas is considered an Aristotelian, St. Augustine may be called a Neoplatonist. Of the later non-Christian Neoplatonists, Proclus (410-485) was the most important. He influenced the German philosopher, Hegel; and Neoplatonism generally helped to mold the thought of such other German thinkers as Eckhart, Nicolas of Cusa, Jacob Boehme, and Schelling.

Proclus lived and taught in Athens, where the Academy Plato had founded survived. In 529, it was closed by the Christian emperor Justinian. That date may be said to mark the formal end of Greek philosophy.

III

The original texts of all the selections in Part Four, as in the first three Parts, were written in Greek, while the four men represented in Part Five wrote Latin.

Epicurus' *Letter to Herodotus* was incorporated by Diogenes Laertius in his *Lives of Eminent Philosophers*. The whole of the last book (Book X) of the *Lives* is devoted to Epicurus, and Diogenes Laertius concluded not only "this philosopher's life" but, as he himself emphasized, his "entire work" by also quoting in full Epicurus' *Principal Doctrines*. The whole of the *Lives* is available in The Loeb Classical Library, in two volumes, with the original text and an English translation by R. D. Hicks on facing pages. This is the translation offered here; and the selections concerning Zeno come from the same volume.

The translation of Cleanthes' *Hymn to Zeus* is that of James Adam.

The version of Epictetus' *Encheiridion*, or *Manual*, is that of W. A. Oldfather; the translation of Sextus Empiricus is by R. G. Bury. Both come from the bilingual Loeb editions, which also offer Epictetus' *Discourses*. The *Discourses* are longer than the Manual and consist of lectures recorded by Epictetus' pupil, Arrian.

Finally, Thomas Taylor's translation of *Select Works of Plotinus* has been used.

# EPICURUS

## LETTER TO HERODOTUS (complete)

"Epicurus to Herodotus, greeting.

"For those who are unable to study carefully all my physical writings or to go into the longer treatises at all, I have myself prepared an epitome[1] of the whole system, Herodotus, to preserve in the memory enough of the principal doctrines, to the end that on every occasion they may be able to aid themselves on the most important points, so far as they take up the study of Physics. Those who have made some advance in the survey of the entire system ought to fix in their minds under the principal headings an elementary outline of the whole treatment of the subject. For a comprehensive view is often required, the details but seldom.

"To the former, then—the main heads—we must continually return, and must memorize them so far as to get a

valid conception of the facts, as well as the means of discovering all the details exactly when once the general outlines are rightly understood and remembered; since it is the privilege of the mature student to make a ready use of his conceptions by referring every one of them to elementary facts and simple terms. For it is impossible to gather up the results of continuous diligent study of the entirety of things, unless we can embrace in short formulas and hold in mind all that might have been accurately expressed even to the minutest detail.

"Hence, since such a course is of service to all who take up natural science, I, who devote to the subject my continuous energy and reap the calm enjoyment of a life like this, have prepared for you just such an epitome and manual of the doctrines as a whole.

"In the first place, Herodotus, you must understand what it is that words denote, in order that by reference to this we may be in a position to test opinions, inquiries, or problems, so that our proofs

---

[1] This, as the most authentic summary of Epicurean physics which we possess, serves as a groundwork in modern histories, *e.g.*, Zeller's.

may not run on untested *ad infinitum,* nor the terms we use be empty of meaning. For the primary signification of every term employed must be clearly seen, and ought to need no proving; this being necessary, if we are to have something to which the point at issue or the problem or the opinion before us can be referred.

"Next, we must by all means stick to our sensations, that is, simply to the present impressions whether of the mind or of any criterion whatever, and similarly to our actual feelings, in order that we may have the means of determining that which needs confirmation and that which is obscure.

"When this is clearly understood, it is time to consider generally things which are obscure. To begin with, nothing comes into being out of what is nonexistent. For in that case anything would have arisen out of anything, standing as it would in no need of its proper germs. And if that which disappears had been destroyed and become nonexistent, everything would have perished, that into which the things were dissolved being non-existent. Moreover, the sum total of things was always such as it is now, and such it will ever remain. For there is nothing into which it can change. For outside the sum of things there is nothing which could enter into it and bring about the change.

"Further [*this he says also in the Larger Epitome near the beginning and in his First Book "On Nature"*], the whole of being consists of bodies and space. For the existence of bodies is everywhere attested by sense itself, and it is upon sensation that reason must rely when it attempts to infer the unknown from the known. And if there were no space (which we call also void and place and intangible nature), bodies would have nothing in which to be and through which to move, as they are plainly seen to move. Beyond bodies and space there is nothing which by mental apprehension or on its analogy we can conceive to exist. When we speak of bodies and space, both are regarded as wholes or separate things, not as the properties or accidents of separate things.

"Again [*he repeats this in the First Book and in Books XIV. and XV. of the work "On Nature" and in the Larger Epitome*], of bodies some are composite, others the elements of which these composite bodies are made. These elements are indivisible and unchangeable, and necessarily so, if things are not all to be destroyed and pass into nonexistence, but are to be strong to endure when the composite bodies are broken up, because they possess a solid nature and are incapable of being anywhere or anyhow dissolved. It follows that the first beginnings must be indivisible, corporeal entities.

"Again, the sum of things is infinite. For what is finite has an extremity, and the extremity of anything is discerned only by comparison with something else. <Now the sum of things is not discerned by comparison with anything else:> hence, since it has no extremity, it has no limit; and, since it has no limit, it must be unlimited or infinite.

"Moreover, the sum of things is unlimited both by reason of the multitude of the atoms and the extent of the void. For if the void were infinite and bodies finite, the bodies would not have stayed anywhere but would have been dispersed in their course through the infinite void, not having any supports or counterchecks to send them back on their upward rebound. Again, if the void were finite, the infinity of bodies would not have anywhere to be.

"Furthermore, the atoms, which have no void in them—out of which composite bodies arise and into which they are dissolved—vary indefinitely in their shapes; for so many varieties of things as we see could never have arisen out of a recurrence of a definite number of the the same shapes. The like atoms of each shape are absolutely infinite; but the variety of shapes, though indefinitely large, is not absolutely infinite. [*For neither does the divisibility go on "ad infinitum," he says below; but he adds, since the qualities change, unless one is prepared to keep enlarging their magnitudes also simply "ad infinitum."*]

"The atoms are in continual motion through all eternity. [*Further, he says below, that the atoms move with equal speed, since the void makes way for the lightest and heaviest alike.*] Some of them rebound to a considerable distance from each other, while others merely oscillate in one place when they chance to have got entangled or to be enclosed by a mass of other atoms shaped for entangling.

"This is because each atom is separated from the rest by void, which is incapable of offering any resistance to the rebound; while it is the solidity of the atom which makes it rebound after a collision, however short the distance to which it rebounds, when it finds itself imprisoned in a mass of entangling atoms. Of all this there is no beginning, since both atoms and void exist from everlasting. [*He says below that atoms have no quality at all except shape, size, and weight. But that colour varies with the arrangement of the atoms he states in his "Twelve Rudiments"; further, that they are not of any and every size; at any rate no atom has ever been seen by our sense.*]

"The repetition at such length of all that we are now recalling to mind furnishes an adequate outline for our conception of the nature of things.

"Moreover, there is an infinite number of worlds, some like this world, others unlike it. For the atoms being infinite in number, as has just been proved, are borne ever further in their course. For the atoms out of which a world might arise, or by which a world might be formed, have not all been expended on one world or a finite number of worlds, whether like or unlike this one. Hence there will be nothing to hinder an infinity of worlds.

"Again, there are outlines or films, which are of the same shape as solid bodies, but of a thinness far exceeding that of any object that we see. For it is not impossible that there should be found in the surrounding air combinations of this kind, materials adapted for expressing the hollowness and thinness of surfaces, and effluxes preserving the same relative position and motion which they had in the solid objects from which they come. To these films we give the name of 'images' or 'idols.' Furthermore, so long as nothing comes in the way to offer resistance, motion through the void accomplishes any imaginable distance in an inconceivably short time. For resistance encountered is the equivalent of slowness, its absence the equivalent of speed.

"Not that, if we consider the minute times perceptible by reason alone, the moving body itself arrives at more than one place simultaneously (for this too is inconceivable), although in time perceptible to sense it does arrive simultaneously, however different the point of departure from that conceived by us. For if it changed its direction, that would be equivalent to its meeting with resistance, even if up to that point we allow nothing to impede the rate of its flight. This is an elementary fact which in itself is well worth bearing in mind. In the next place the exceeding thinness of the images is contradicted by none of the facts under our observation. Hence also their velocities are enormous, since they always find a void passage to fit them. Besides, their incessant effluence meets with no resistance, or very little, although many atoms, not to say an unlimited number, do at once encounter resistance.

"Besides this, remember that the production of the images is as quick as thought. For particles are continually streaming off from the surface of bodies, though no diminution of the bodies is observed, because other particles take their place. And those given off for a long time retain the position and arrangement which their atoms had when they formed part of the solid bodies, although occasionally they are thrown into confusion. Sometimes such films are formed very rapidly in the air, because they need not have any solid content; and there are other modes in which they may be formed. For there is nothing in all this which is contradicted by sensation, if we in some sort look at the clear evidence of sense, to which we should also refer the continuity of particles in the objects external to ourselves.

"We must also consider that it is by the entrance of something coming from external objects that we see their shapes and think of them. For external things would not stamp on us their own nature of colour and form through the medium of the air which is between them and us,[2] or by means of rays of light or currents of any sort going from us to them, so well as by the entrance into our eyes or minds, to whichever their size is suitable, of certain films coming from the things themselves, these films or outlines being of the same colour and shape as the external things themselves. They move with rapid motion; and this again explains why they present the appearance of the single continuous object, and retain the mutual interconnexion which they had in the object, when they impinge upon the sense, such impact being due

---

[2] This was the view of Democritus.

to the oscillation of the atoms in the interior of the solid object from which they come. And whatever presentation we derive by direct contact, whether it be with the mind or with the sense-organs, be it shape that is presented or other properties, this shape as presented is the shape of the solid thing, and it is due either to a close coherence of the image as a whole or to a mere remnant of its parts. Falsehood and error always depend upon the intrusion of opinion <when a fact awaits> confirmation or the absence of contradiction, which fact is afterwards frequently not confirmed <or even contradicted> [*following a certain movement in ourselves connected with, but distinct from, the mental picture presented— which is the cause of error.*]

"For the presentations which, *e.g.*, are received in a picture or arise in dreams, or from any other form of apprehension by the mind or by the other criteria of truth, would never have resembled what we call the real and true things, had it not been for certain actual things of the kind with which we come in contact. Error would not have occurred, if we had not experienced some other movement in ourselves, conjoined with, but distinct from, the perception of what is presented. And from this movement, if it be not confirmed or be contradicted, falsehood results; while, if it be confirmed or not contradicted, truth results.

"And to this view we must closely adhere, if we are not to repudiate the criteria founded on the clear evidence of sense, nor again to throw all these things into confusion by maintaining falsehood as if it were truth.

"Again, hearing takes place when a current passes from the object, whether person or thing, which emits voice or sound or noise, or produces the sensation of hearing in any way whatever. This current is broken up into homogeneous particles, which at the same time preserve a certain mutual connexion and a distinctive unity extending to the object which emitted them, and thus, for the most part, cause the perception in that case or, if not, merely indicate the presence of the external object. For without the transmission from the object of a certain interconnexion of the parts no such sensation could arise. Therefore we must not suppose that the air itself is moulded into shape by the voice emitted or something similar; for it is very far from being the case that the air is acted upon by it in this way. The blow which is struck in us when we utter a sound causes such a displacement of the particles as serves to produce a current resembling breath, and this displacement gives rise to the sensation of hearing.

"Again, we must believe that smelling, like hearing, would produce no sensation, were there not particles conveyed from the object which are of the proper sort for exciting the organ of smelling, some of one sort, some of another, some exciting it confusedly and strangely, others quietly and agreeably.

"Moreover, we must hold that the atoms in fact possess none of the qualities belonging to things which come under our observation, except shape, weight, and size, and the properties necessarily conjoined with shape. For every quality changes, but the atoms do not change, since, when the composite bodies are dissolved, there must needs be a permanent something, solid and indissoluble, left behind, which makes change possible: not changes into or from the non-existent, but often through differences of arrangement, and sometimes through additions and subtractions of the atoms. Hence these somethings capable of being diversely arranged must be indestructible, exempt

from change, but possessed each of its own distinctive mass and configuration. This must remain.

"For in the case of changes of configuration within our experience the figure is supposed to be inherent when other qualities are stripped off, but the qualities are not supposed, like the shape which is left behind, to inhere in the subject of change, but to vanish altogether from the body. Thus, then, what is left behind is sufficient to account for the differences in composite bodies, since something at least must necessarily be left remaining and be immune from annihilation.

"Again, you should not suppose that the atoms have any and every size,[3] lest you be contradicted by facts; but differences of size must be admitted; for this addition renders the facts of feeling and sensation easier of explanation. But to attribute any and every magnitude to the atoms does not help to explain the differences of quality in things; moreover, in that case atoms large enough to be seen ought to have reached us, which is never observed to occur; nor can we conceive how its occurrence should be possible, *i.e.* that an atom should become visible.

"Besides, you must not suppose that there are parts unlimited in number, be they ever so small, in any finite body. Hence not only must we reject as impossible subdivision *ad infinitum* into smaller and smaller parts, lest we make all things too weak and, in our conceptions of the aggregates, be driven to pulverize the things that exist, *i.e.* the atoms, and annihilate them; but in dealing with finite things we must also reject as impossible the progression *ad infinitum* by less and less increments.

"For when once we have said that an infinite number of particles, however small, are contained in anything,

---

[3] The opinion of Democritus.

it is not possible to conceive how it could any longer be limited or finite in size. For clearly our infinite number of particles must have some size; and then, of whatever size they were, the aggregate they made would be infinite. And, in the next place, since what is finite has an extremity which is distinguishable, even if it is not by itself observable, it is not possible to avoid thinking of another such extremity next to this. Nor can we help thinking that in this way, by proceeding forward from one to the next in order, it is possible by such a progression to arrive in thought at infinity.

"We must consider the minimum perceptible by sense as not corresponding to that which is capable of being traversed, *i.e.* is extended, nor again as utterly unlike it, but as having something in common with the things capable of being traversed, though it is without distinction of parts. But when from the illusion created by this common property we think we shall distinguish something in the minimum, one part on one side and another part on the other side, it must be another minimum equal to the first which catches our eye. In fact, we see these minima one after another, beginning with the first, and not as occupying the same space; nor do we see them touch one another's part with their parts, but we see that by virtue of their own peculiar character (*i.e.* as being unit indivisibles) they afford a means of measuring magnitudes: there are more of them, if the magnitude measured is greater; fewer of them, if the magnitude measured is less.

"We must recognize that this analogy also holds of the minimum in the atom; it is only in minuteness that it differs from that which is observed by sense, but it follows the same analogy. On the analogy of things within our experience we have declared that the atom has magnitude; and this, small

as it is, we have merely reproduced on a larger scale. And further, the least and simplest things must be regarded as extremities of lengths, furnishing from themselves as units the means of measuring lengths, whether greater or less, the mental vision being employed, since direct observation is impossible. For the community which exists between them and the unchangeable parts (*i.e.* the minimal parts of area or surface) is sufficient to justify the conclusion so far as this goes. But it is not possible that these minima of the atom should group themselves together through the possession of motion.

"Further, we must not assert 'up' or 'down' of that which is unlimited, as if there were a zenith or nadir. As to the space overhead, however, if it be possible to draw a line to infinity from the point where we stand, we know that never will this space—or, for that matter, the space below the supposed standpoint if produced to infinity—appear to us to be at the same time 'up' and 'down' with reference to the same point; for this is inconceivable. Hence it is possible to assume one direction of motion, which we conceive as extending upwards *ad infinitum*, and another downwards, even if it should happen ten thousand times that what moves from us to the spaces above our heads reaches the feet of those above us, or that which moves downwards from us the heads of those below us. None the less is it true that the whole of the motion in the respective cases is conceived as extending in opposite directions *ad infinitum*.

"When they are travelling through the void and meet with no resistance, the atoms must move with equal speed. Neither will heavy atoms travel more quickly than small and light ones, so long as nothing meets them, nor will small atoms travel more quickly than large ones, provided they always find a passage suitable to their size, and provided also that they meet with no obstruction. Nor will their upward or their lateral motion, which is due to collisions, nor again their downward motion, due to weight, affect their velocity. As long as either motion obtains, it must continue, quick as the speed of thought, provided there is no obstruction, whether due to external collision or to the atoms' own weight counteracting the force of the blow.

"Moreover, when we come to deal with composite bodies, one of them will travel faster than another, although their atoms have equal speed. This is because the atoms in the aggregates are travelling in one direction during the shortest continuous time, albeit they move in different directions in times so short as to be appreciable only by the reason, but frequently collide until the continuity of their motion is appreciated by sense. For the assumption that beyond the range of direct observation even the minute times conceivable by reason will present continuity of motion is not true in the case before us. Our canon is that direct observation by sense and direct apprehension by the mind are alone invariably true.

"Next, keeping in view our perceptions and feelings (for so shall we have the surest grounds for belief), we must recognize generally that the soul is a corporeal thing, composed of fine particles, dispersed all over the frame, most nearly resembling wind with an admixture of heat, in some respects like wind, in others like heat. But, again, there is the third part which exceeds the other two in the fineness of its particles and thereby keeps in closer touch with the rest of the frame. And this is shown by the mental faculties and feelings, by the ease with which the mind moves, and by thoughts, and by all those things the loss of which causes death. Further, we must keep in mind that soul has the greatest share in causing sensation. Still, it would not

have had sensation, had it not been somehow confined within the rest of the frame. But the rest of the frame, though it provides this indispensable condition for the soul, itself also has a share, derived from the soul, of the said quality; and yet does not possess all the qualities of soul. Hence on the departure of the soul it loses sentience. For it had not this power in itself; but something else, congenital with the body, supplied it to body: which other thing, through the potentiality actualized in it by means of motion, at once acquired for itself a quality of sentience, and, in virtue of the neighbourhood and interconnexion between them, imparted it (as I said) to the body also.

"Hence, so long as the soul is in the body, it never loses sentience through the removal of some other part. The containing sheath may be dislocated in whole or in part, and portions of the soul may thereby be lost; yet in spite of this the soul, if it manage to survive, will have sentience. But the rest of the frame, whether the whole of it survives or only a part, no longer has sensation, when once those atoms have departed, which, however few in number, are required to constitute the nature of soul. Moreover, when the whole frame is broken up, the soul is scattered and has no longer the same powers as before, nor the same motions; hence it does not possess sentience either.

"For we cannot think of it as sentient, except it be in this composite whole and moving with these movements; nor can we so think of it when the sheaths which enclose and surround it are not the same as those in which the soul is now located and in which it performs these movements. [*He says elsewhere that the soul is composed of the smoothest and roundest of atoms, far superior in both respects to those of fire; that part of it is irrational, this being scattered over the rest of the frame, while the rational part resides in the chest, as is*

*manifest from our fears and our joy;
that sleep occurs when the parts of the
soul which have been scattered all over
the composite organism are held fast in
it or dispersed, and afterwards collide
with one another by their impacts. The
semen is derived from the whole of the
body.*]

"There is the further point to be
considered, what the incorporeal can
be, if, I mean, according to current
usage the term is applied to what can
be conceived as self-existent. But it is
impossible to conceive anything that is
incorporeal as self-existent except
empty space. And empty space cannot
itself either act or be acted upon, but
simply allows body to move through
it. Hence those who call soul incorporeal speak foolishly. For if it were so, it
could neither act nor be acted upon.
But, as it is, both these properties, you
see, plainly belong to soul.

"If, then, we bring all these arguments concerning soul to the criterion
of our feelings and perceptions, and if
we keep in mind the proposition stated
at the outset, we shall see that the subject has been adequately comprehended in outline: which will enable us to
determine the details with accuracy and
confidence.

"Moreover, shapes and colours, magnitudes and weights, and in short all
those qualities which are predicated of
body, in so far as they are perpetual
properties either of all bodies or of
visible bodies, are knowable by sensation
of these very properties: these, I say,
must not be supposed to exist independently by themselves (for that is inconceivable), nor yet to be non-existent,
nor to be some other and incorporeal
entities cleaving to body, nor again to
be parts of body. We must consider the
whole body in a general way to derive
its permanent nature from all of them,
though it is not, as it were, formed by
grouping them together in the same
way as when from the particles themselves a larger aggregate is made up,

whether these particles be primary or
any magnitudes whatsoever less than
the particular whole. All these qualities,
I repeat, merely give the body its own
permanent nature. They all have their
own characteristic modes of being perceived and distinguished, but always
along with the whole body in which
they inhere and never in separation
from it; and it is in virtue of this complete conception of the body as a whole
that it is so designated.

"Again, qualities often attach to
bodies without being permanent concomitants. They are not to be classed
among invisible entities nor are they
incorporeal. Hence, using the term 'accidents' in the commonest sense, we
say plainly that 'accidents' have not
the nature of the whole thing to which
they belong, and to which, conceiving
it as a whole, we give the name of
body, nor that of the permanent properties without which body cannot be
thought of. And in virtue of certain
peculiar modes of apprehension into
which the complete body always enters,
each of them can be called an accident.
But only as often as they are seen actually to belong to it, since such accidents are not perpetual concomitants.
There is no need to banish from reality
this clear evidence that the accident
has not the nature of that whole—by
us called body—to which it belongs,
nor of the permanent properties which
accompany the whole. Nor, on the other
hand, must we suppose the accident to
have independent existence (for this is
just as inconceivable in the case of accidents as in that of the permanent properties); but, as is manifest, they should
all be regarded as accidents, not as permanent concomitants, of bodies, nor
yet as having the rank of independent
existence. Rather they are seen to be
exactly as and what sensation itself
makes them individually claim to be.

"There is another thing which we
must consider carefully. We must not
investigate time as we do the other ac-

cidents which we investigate in a subject, namely, by referring them to the preconceptions envisaged in our minds; but we must take into account the plain fact itself, in virtue of which we speak of time as long or short, linking to it in intimate connexion this attribute of duration. We need not adopt any fresh terms as preferable, but should employ the usual expressions about it. Nor need we predicate anything else of time, as if this something else contained the same essence as is contained in the proper meaning of the word 'time' (for this also is done by some). We must chiefly reflect upon that to which we attach this peculiar character of time, and by which we measure it. No further proof is required: we have only to reflect that we attach the attribute of time to days and nights and their parts, and likewise to feelings of pleasure and pain and to neutral states, to states of movement and states of rest, conceiving a peculiar accident of these to be this very characteristic which we express by the word 'time.' [*He says this both in the second book "On Nature" and in the Larger Epitome.*]

"After the foregoing we have next to consider that the worlds and every finite aggregate which bears a strong resemblance to things we commonly see have arisen out of the infinite. For all these, whether small or great, have been separated off from special conglomerations of atoms; and all things are again dissolved, some faster, some slower, some through the action of one set of causes, others through the action of another. [*It is clear, then, that he also makes the worlds perishable, as their parts are subject to change. Elsewhere he says the earth is supported on the air.*]

"And further, we must not suppose that the worlds have necessarily one and the same shape. [*On the contrary, in the twelfth book "On Nature" he himself says that the shapes of the worlds differ, some being spherical,* some oval, others again of shapes different from these. They do not, however, admit of every shape. Nor are they living beings which have been separated from the infinite.*] For nobody can prove that in one sort of world there might not be contained, whereas in another sort of world there could not possibly be, the seeds out of which animals and plants arise and all the rest of the things we see. [*And the same holds good for their nurture in a world after they have arisen. And so too we must think it happens upon the earth also.*]

"Again, we must suppose that nature too has been taught and forced to learn many various lessons by the facts themselves, that reason subsequently develops what it has thus received and makes fresh discoveries, among some tribes more quickly, among others more slowly, the progress thus made being at certain times and seasons greater, at others less.

"Hence even the names of things were not originally due to convention, but in the several tribes under the impulse of special feelings and special presentations of sense primitive man uttered special cries. The air thus emitted was moulded by their individual feelings or sense-presentations, and differently according to the difference of the regions which the tribes inhabited. Subsequently whole tribes adopted their own special names, in order that their communications might be less ambiguous to each other and more briefly expressed. And as for things not visible, so far as those who were conscious of them tried to introduce any such notion, they put in circulation certain names for them, either sounds which they were instinctively compelled to utter or which they selected by reason on analogy according to the most general cause there can be for expressing oneself in such a way.

"Nay more: we are bound to believe that in the sky revolutions, solstices, eclipses, risings and settings, and the like, take place without the ministration or command, either now or in the future, of any being who at the same time enjoys perfect bliss along with immortality. For troubles and anxieties and feelings of anger and partiality do not accord with bliss, but always imply weakness and fear and dependence upon one's neighbours. Nor, again, must we hold that things which are no more than globular masses of fire, being at the same time endowed with bliss, assume these motions at will. Nay, in every term we use we must hold fast to all the majesty which attaches to such notions as bliss and immortality, lest the terms should generate opinions inconsistent with this majesty. Otherwise such inconsistency will of itself suffice to produce the worst disturbance in our minds. Hence, where we find phenomena invariably recurring, the invariableness of the recurrence must be ascribed to the original interception and conglomeration of atoms whereby the world was formed.

"Further, we must hold that to arrive at accurate knowledge of the cause of things of most moment is the business of natural science, and that happiness depends on this (viz. on the knowledge of celestial and atmospheric phenomena), and upon knowing what the heavenly bodies really are, and any kindred facts contributing to exact knowledge in this respect.

"Further, we must recognize on such points as this no plurality of causes or contingency, but must hold that nothing suggestive of conflict or disquiet is compatible with an immortal and blessed nature. And the mind can grasp the absolute truth of this.

"But when we come to subjects for special inquiry, there is nothing in the knowledge of risings and settings and solstices and eclipses and all kindred subjects that contributes to our happiness; but those who are well-informed about such matters and yet are ignorant what the heavenly bodies really are, and what are the most important causes of phenomena, feel quite as much fear as those who have no such special information—nay, perhaps even greater fear, when the curiosity excited by this additional knowledge cannot find a solution or understand the subordination of these phenomena to the highest causes.

"Hence, if we discover more than one cause that may account for solstices, settings and risings, eclipses and the like, as we did also in particular matters of detail, we must not suppose that our treatment of these matters fails of accuracy, so far as it is needful to ensure our tranquillity and happiness. When, therefore, we investigate the causes of celestial and atmospheric phenomena, as of all that is unknown, we must take into account the variety of ways in which analogous occurrences happen within our experience; while as for those who do not recognize the difference between what is or comes about from a single cause and that which may be the effect of any one of several causes, overlooking the fact that the objects are only seen at a distance, and are moreover ignorant of the conditions that render, or do not render, peace of mind impossible—all such persons we must treat with contempt. If then we think that an event could happen in one or other particular way out of several, we shall be as tranquil when we recognize that it actually comes about in more ways than one as if we knew that it happens in this particular way.

"There is yet one more point to seize, namely, that the greatest anxiety of the human mind arises through the belief that the heavenly bodies are blessed and indestructible, and that at the same time they have volitions and actions and causality inconsistent with his belief; and through expecting or apprehending some everlasting evil, either because of the myths, or because we are in dread of the mere insensibility of death, as if it had to do with us; and through being reduced to this state not by conviction but by a certain irrational perversity, so that, if men do not set bounds to their terror, they endure as much or even more intense anxiety than the man whose views on these matters are quite vague. But mental tranquillity means being released from all these troubles and cherishing a continual remembrance of the highest and most important truths.

"Hence we must attend to present feelings and sense perceptions, whether those of mankind in general or those peculiar to the individual, and also attend to all the clear evidence available, as given by each of the standards of truth. For by studying them we shall rightly trace to its cause and banish the source of disturbance and dread, accounting for celestial phenomena and for all other things which from time to time befall us and cause the utmost alarm to the rest of mankind.

"Here then, Herodotus, you have the chief doctrines of Physics in the form of a summary. So that, if this statement be accurately retained and take effect, a man will, I make no doubt, be incomparably better equipped than his fellows, even if he should never go into all the exact details. For he will clear up for himself many of the points which I have worked out in detail in my complete exposition; and the summary itself, if borne in mind, will be of constant service to him.

"It is of such a sort that those who are already tolerably, or even perfectly, well acquainted with the details can, by analysis of what they know into such elementary perceptions as these, best prosecute their researches in physical science as a whole; while those, on the other hand, who are not altogether entitled to rank as mature students can in silent fashion and as quick as thought run over the doctrines most important for their peace of mind."

## PRINCIPAL DOCTRINES (complete)

Come, then, let me set the seal, so to say, on my entire work as well as on this philosopher's life by citing his Sovran Maxims,[4] therewith bringing the whole work to a close and making the end of

it to coincide with the beginning of happiness.

1. A blessed and eternal being has no trouble himself and brings no trouble upon any other being; hence he is exempt from movements of anger and partiality, for every such movement implies weakness. [*Elsewhere he says that the gods are discernible by reason alone, some being numerically distinct, while others result uniformly from the continuous influx of similar images directed to the same spot and in human form.*]

2. Death is nothing to us; for the body, when it has been resolved into its elements, has no feeling, and that which has no feeling is nothing to us.

---

[4] This collection of forty of the most important articles of faith in the Epicurean creed was famous in antiquity. It consists of extracts from the voluminous writings of Epicurus, and may have been put together by a faithful disciple. On the other hand, Epicurus laid great stress on epitomes of his doctrine being committed to memory; so that his passion for personal direction and supervision of the studies of his pupils may have induced him to furnish them with such an indispensable catechism.

3. The magnitude of pleasure reaches its limit in the removal of all pain. When pleasure is present, so long as it is uninterrupted, there is no pain either of body or of mind or of both together.

4. Continuous pain does not last long in the flesh; on the contrary, pain, if extreme, is present a very short time, and even that degree of pain which barely outweighs pleasure in the flesh does not last for many days together. Illnesses of long duration even permit of an excess of pleasure over pain in the flesh.

5. It is impossible to live a pleasant life without living wisely and well and justly, and it is impossible to live wisely and well and justly without living pleasantly. Whenever any one of these is lacking, when, for instance, the man is not able to live wisely, though he lives well and justly, it is impossible for him to live a pleasant life.

6. In order to obtain security from other men any means whatsoever of procuring this was a natural good.

7. Some men have sought to become famous and renowned, thinking that thus they would make themselves secure against their fellow-men. If, then, the life of such persons really was secure, they attained natural good; if, however, it was insecure, they have not attained the end which by nature's own prompting they originally sought.

8. No pleasure is in itself evil, but the things which produce certain pleasures entail annoyances many times greater than the pleasures themselves.

9. If all pleasure had been capable of accumulation,—if this had gone on not only by recurrence in time, but all over the frame or, at any rate, over the principal parts of man's nature, there would never have been any difference between one pleasure and another, as in fact there is.

10. If the objects which are productive of pleasures to profligate persons really freed them from fears of the mind,

—the fears, I mean, inspired by celestial and atmospheric phenomena, the fear of death, the fear of pain; if, further, they taught them to limit their desires, we should never have any fault to find with such persons, for they would then be filled with pleasures to overflowing on all sides and would be exempt from all pain, whether of body or mind, that is, from all evil.

11. If we had never been molested by alarms at celestial and atmospheric phenomena, nor by the misgiving that death somehow affects us, nor by neglect of the proper limits of pains and desires, we should have had no need to study natural science.

12. It would be impossible to banish fear on matters of the highest importance, if a man did not know the nature of the whole universe, but lived in dread of what the legends tell us. Hence without the study of nature there was no enjoyment of unmixed pleasures.

13. There would be no advantage in providing security against our fellow-men, so long as we were alarmed by occurrences over our heads or beneath the earth or in general by whatever happens in the boundless universe.

14. When tolerable security against our fellow-men is attained, then on a basis of power sufficient to afford support and of material prosperity arises in most genuine form the security of a quiet private life withdrawn from the multitude.

15. Nature's wealth at once has its bounds and is easy to procure; but the wealth of vain fancies recedes to an infinite distance.

16. Fortune but seldom interferes with the wise man; his greatest and highest interests have been, are, and will be, directed by reason throughout the course of his life.

17. The just man enjoys the greatest peace of mind, while the unjust is full of the utmost disquietude.

18. Pleasure in the flesh admits no

increase when once the pain of want has been removed; after that it only admits of variation. The limit of pleasure in the mind, however, is reached when we reflect on the things themselves and their congeners which cause the mind the greatest alarms.

19. Unlimited time and limited time afford an equal amount of pleasure, if we measure the limits of that pleasure by reason.

20. The flesh receives as unlimited the limits of pleasure; and to provide it requires unlimited time. But the mind, grasping in thought what the end and limit of the flesh is, and banishing the terrors of futurity, procures a complete and perfect life, and has no longer any need of unlimited time. Nevertheless it does not shun pleasure, and even in the hour of death, when ushered out of existence by circumstances, the mind does not lack enjoyment of the best life.

21. He who understands the limits of life knows how easy it is to procure enough to remove the pain of want and make the whole of life complete and perfect. Hence he has no longer any need of things which are not to be won save by labour and conflict.

22. We must take into account as the end of all that really exists and all clear evidence of sense to which we refer our opinions; for otherwise everything will be full of uncertainty and confusion.

23. If you fight against all your sensations, you will have no standard to which to refer, and thus no means of judging even those judgements which you pronounce false.

24. If you reject absolutely any single sensation without stopping to discriminate with respect to that which awaits confirmation between matter of opinion and that which is already present, whether in sensation or in feelings or in any presentative perception of the mind, you will throw into confusion even the rest of your sensations by your groundless belief and so you will be rejecting

the standard of truth altogether. If in your ideas based upon opinion you hastily affirm as true all that awaits confirmation as well as that which does not, you will not escape error, as you will be maintaining complete ambiguity whenever it is a case of judging between right and wrong opinion.

25. If you do not on every separate occasion refer each of your actions to the end prescribed by nature, but instead of this in the act of choice or avoidance swerve aside to some other end, your acts will not be consistent with your theories.

26. All such desires as lead to no pain when they remain ungratified are unnecessary, and the longing is easily got rid of, when the thing desired is difficult to procure or when the desires seem likely to produce harm.

27. Of all the means which are procured by wisdom to ensure happiness throughout the whole of life, by far the most important is the acquisition of friends.

28. The same conviction which inspires confidence that nothing we have to fear is eternal or even of long duration, also enables us to see that even in our limited conditions of life nothing enhances our security so much as friendship.

29. Of our desires some are natural and necessary; others are natural, but not necessary; others, again, are neither natural nor necessary, but are due to illusory opinion. [Epicurus regards as natural and necessary desires which bring relief from pain, as e.g. drink when we are thirsty, while by natural and not necessary he means those which merely diversify the pleasure without removing the pain, as e.g. costly viands; by the neither natural nor necessary he means desires for crowns and the erection of statues in one's honour.—SCHOL.]

30. Those natural desires which entail no pain when not gratified, though their objects are vehemently pursued, are also

due to illusory opinion; and when they are not got rid of, it is not because of their own nature, but because of the man's illusory opinion.

31. Natural justice is a symbol or expression of expediency, to prevent one man from harming or being harmed by another.

32. Those animals which are incapable of making covenants with one another, to the end that they may neither inflict nor suffer harm, are without either justice or injustice. And those tribes which either could not or would not form mutual covenants to the same end are in like case.

33. There never was an absolute justice, but only an agreement made in reciprocal intercourse in whatever localities now and again from time to time, providing against the infliction or suffering of harm.

34. Injustice is not in itself an evil, but only in its consequence, viz. the terror which is excited by apprehension that those appointed to punish such offences will discover the injustice.

35. It is impossible for the man who secretly violates any article of the social compact to feel confident that he will remain undiscovered, even if he has already escaped ten thousand times; for right on to the end of his life he is never sure he will not be detected.

36. Taken generally, justice is the same for all, to wit, something found expedient in mutual intercourse; but in its application to particular cases of locality or conditions of whatever kind, it varies under different circumstances.

37. Among the things accounted just by conventional law, whatever in the needs of mutual intercourse is attested to be expedient, is thereby stamped as just, whether or not it be the same for all; and in case any law is made and does not prove suitable to the expediencies of mutual intercourse, then this is no longer just. And should the expediency which is expressed by the law vary and only for a time correspond with the prior conception, nevertheless for the time being it was just, so long as we do not trouble ourselves about empty words, but look simply at the facts.

38. Where without any change in circumstances the conventional laws, when judged by their consequences, were seen not to correspond with the notion of justice, such laws were not really just; but wherever the laws have ceased to be expedient in consequence of a change in circumstances, in that case the laws were for the time being just when they were expedient for the mutual intercourse of the citizens, and subsequently ceased to be just when they ceased to be expedient.

39. He who best knew how to meet fear of external foes made into one family all the creatures he could; and those he could not, he at any rate did not treat as aliens; and where he found even this impossible, he avoided all intercourse, and, so far as was expedient, kept them at a distance.

40. Those who were best able to provide themselves with the means of security against their neighbours, being thus in possession of the surest guarantee, passed the most agreeable life in each other's society; and their enjoyment of the fullest intimacy was such that, if one of them died before his time, the survivors did not lament his death as if it called for commiseration.

# THE STOICS

## ZENO *(from Diogenes Laertius)*

### Ethics

An animal's first impulse, say the [85] Stoics, is to self-preservation, because nature from the outset endears it to itself, as Chrysippus affirms in the first book of his work *On Ends*: his words are, "The dearest thing to every animal is its own constitution and its consciousness thereof"; for it was not likely that nature should estrange the living thing from itself or that she should leave the creature she has made without either estrangement from or affection for its own constitution. We are forced then to conclude that nature in constituting the animal made it near and dear to itself; for so it comes to repel all that is injurious and give free access to all that is serviceable or akin to it.

As for the assertion made by some people that pleasure is the object to which the first impulse of animals is directed, it is shown by the Stoics to be false. For pleasure, if it is really felt, [86] they declare to be a by-product, which never comes until nature by itself has sought and found the means suitable to the animal's existence or constitution; it is an aftermath comparable to the condition of animals thriving and plants in full bloom. And nature, they say, made no difference originally between plants and animals, for she regulates the life of plants too, in their case without impulse and sensation, just as also certain processes go on of a vegetative kind in us. But when in the case of animals impulse has been superadded, whereby they are enabled to go in quest of their proper aliment, for them, say the Stoics, Nature's rule is to follow the direction of impulse. But when reason by way of a more perfect leadership has been bestowed on the beings we call rational, for them life according to reason rightly becomes the natural life. For reason supervenes to shape impulse scientifically.

This is why Zeno was the first (in [87] his treatise *On the Nature of Man*) to designate as the end "life in agreement with nature" (or living agreeably to nature), which is the same as a virtuous life, virtue being the goal towards which nature guides us. So too Cleanthes in his treatise *On Pleasure*, as also Posidonius, and Hecato in his work *On Ends*. Again, living virtuously is equivalent to living in accordance with experience of the actual course of nature, as Chrysippus says in the first book of his *De finibus*; for our individual natures are parts of the nature of the whole [88] universe. And this is why the end may be defined as life in accordance with nature, or, in other words, in accordance with our own human nature as well as that of the universe, a life in which we refrain from every action forbidden by the law common to all things, that is to say, the right reason which pervades all things, and is identical with this Zeus, lord and ruler of all that is. And this very thing constitutes the virtue of the happy man and the smooth current of life, when all actions promote the harmony of the spirit dwelling in the individual man with the will of him who orders the universe. Diogenes then expressly declares the end to be to act with good reason in the selection of what is natural. Archedemus says the end is to live in the performance of all befitting actions.

By the nature with which our life [89] ought to be in accord, Chrysippus understands both universal nature and more particularly the nature of man, whereas Cleanthes takes the nature of the universe alone as that which should be followed, without adding the nature of the individual.

And virtue, he holds, is a harmonious disposition, choice-worthy for its own sake and not from hope or fear or any external motive. Moreover, it is in virtue that happiness consists; for virtue is the state of mind which tends to make the whole of life harmonious. When a rational being is perverted, this is due to the deceptiveness of external pursuits or sometimes to the influence of associates. For the starting-points of nature are never perverse.

•  •  •

They hold the emotions to be [111] judgements, as is stated by Chrysippus in his treatise *On the Passions*: avarice being a supposition that money is a good, while the case is similar with drunkenness and profligacy and all the other emotions.

And grief or pain they hold to be an irrational mental contraction. Its species are pity, envy, jealousy, rivalry, heaviness, annoyance, distress, anguish, distraction. Pity is grief felt at undeserved suffering; envy, grief at others' prosperity; jealousy, grief at the possession by another of that which one desires for oneself; rivalry, pain at the possession by another of what one has oneself. Heaviness or vexation is grief [112] which weighs us down, annoyance that which coops us up and straitens us for want of room, distress a pain brought on by anxious thought that lasts and increases, anguish painful grief, distraction irrational grief, rasping and hindering us from viewing the situation as a whole.

Fear is an expectation of evil. Under fear are ranged the following emotions: terror, nervous shrinking, shame, consternation, panic, mental agony. Terror is a fear which produces fright; shame is fear of disgrace; nervous shrinking is a fear that one will have to act; consternation is fear due to a presentation of some unusual occurrence; panic [113] is fear with pressure exercised by sound; mental agony is fear felt when some issue is still in suspense.

Desire or craving is irrational appetency, and under it are ranged the following states: want, hatred, contentiousness, anger, love, wrath, resentment. Want, then, is a craving when it is baulked and, as it were, cut off from its object, but kept at full stretch and attracted towards it in vain. Hatred is a growing and lasting desire or craving that it should go ill with somebody. Contentiousness is a craving or desire connected with partisanship; anger a craving or desire to punish one who is thought to have done you an undeserved injury. The passion of love is a craving from which good men are free; for it is an effort to win affection due to the visible presence of beauty. [114] Wrath is anger which has long rankled and has become malicious, waiting for its opportunity, as is illustrated by the lines: [1]

> Even though for the one day he swallow his anger, yet doth he still keep his displeasure thereafter in his heart, till he accomplish it.

Resentment is anger in an early stage.

Pleasure is an irrational elation at the accruing of what seems to be choiceworthy; and under it are ranged ravishment, malevolent joy, delight, transport. Ravishment is pleasure which charms the ear. Malevolent joy is pleasure at another's ills. Delight is the mind's propulsion to weakness, its name in Greek (τέρψις) being akin to τρέψις or turning. To be in transports of delight is the melting away of virtue.

And as there are said to be cer- [115] tain infirmities in the body, as for instance gout and arthritic disorders, so too there is in the soul love of fame, love of pleasure, and the like. By infirmity is meant disease accompanied by weakness; and by disease is meant a fond imagining of something that seems desirable. And as in the body there are tendencies to certain maladies such as colds and diarrhoea, so it is with the soul, there are tendencies like enviousness, pitifulness, quarrelsomeness, and the like.

---

[1] *Iliad,* I. 81, 82.

Also they say that there are three [116] emotional states which are good, namely, joy, caution, and wishing. Joy, the counterpart of pleasure, is rational elation; caution, the counterpart of fear, rational avoidance; for though the wise man will never feel fear, he will yet use caution. And they make wishing the counterpart of desire (or craving), inasmuch as it is rational appetency. And accordingly, as under the primary passions are classed certain others subordinate to them, so too is it with the primary eupathies or good emotional states. Thus under wishing they bring well-wishing or benevolence, friendliness, respect, affection; under caution, reverence and modesty; under joy, delight, mirth, cheerfulness.

Now they say that the wise [117] man is passionless, because he is not prone to fall into such infirmity. But they add that in another sense the term apathy is applied to the bad man, when, that is, it means that he is callous and relentless. Further, the wise man is said to be free from vanity; for he is indifferent to good or evil report. However, he is not alone in this, there being another who is also free from vanity, he who is ranged among the rash, and that is the bad man. Again, they tell us that all good men are austere or harsh, because they neither have dealings with pleasure themselves nor tolerate those who have. The term harsh is applied, however, to others as well, and in much the same sense as a wine is said to be harsh when it is employed medicinally and not for drinking at all.

Again, the good are genuinely in [118] earnest and vigilant for their own improvement, using a manner of life which banishes evil out of sight and makes what good there is in things appear. At the same time they are free from pretence; for they have stripped off all pretence or "make-up" whether in voice or in look. Free too are they from all business cares, declining to do anything which conflicts with duty. They will take wine, but not get drunk. Nay more, they will not be liable to madness either; not but what there will at times occur to the good man strange impressions due to melancholy or delirium, ideas not determined by the principle of what is choiceworthy but contrary to nature. Nor indeed will the wise man ever feel grief; seeing that grief is irrational contraction of the soul, as Apollodorus says in his *Ethics*.

•   •   •

It is also their doctrine that [131] amongst the wise there should be a community of wives with free choice of partners, as Zeno says in his *Republic* and Chrysippus in his treatise *On Government* [and not only they, but also Diogenes the Cynic and Plato].² Under such circumstances we shall feel paternal affection for all the children alike, and there will be an end of the jealousies arising from adultery. The best form of government they hold to be a mixture of democracy, kingship, and aristocracy (or the rule of the best).

Such, then, are the statements they make in their ethical doctrines, with much more besides, together with their proper proofs: let this, however, suffice for a statement of them in a summary and elementary form.

## Physics

Their physical doctrine they [132] divide into sections (1) about bodies; (2) about principles; (3) about elements; (4) about the gods; (5) about bounding surfaces and space whether filled or empty. This is a division into species; but the generic division is into three parts, dealing with (i) the universe; (ii) the elements; (iii) the subject of causation.

The part dealing with the universe

admits, they say, of division into two: for with one aspect of it the mathematicians also are concerned, in so far as they treat questions relating to the fixed stars and the planets, *e.g.* whether the sun is not just so large as it appears to be, and the same about the moon, the question of their revolutions, and other inquiries of the same sort. But there [133] is another aspect or field of cosmological inquiry, which belongs to the physicists alone: this includes such questions as what the substance of the universe is, whether the sun and the stars are made up of forms and matter, whether the world has had a beginning in time or not, whether it is animate or inanimate, whether it is destructible or indestructible, whether it is governed by providence, and all the rest. The part concerned with causation, again, is itself subdivided into two. And in one of its aspects medical inquiries have a share in it, in so far as it involves investigation of the ruling principle of the soul and the phenomena of soul, seeds, and the like. Whereas the other part is claimed by the mathematicians also, *e.g.* how vision is to be explained, what causes the image on the mirror, what is the origin of clouds, thunder, rainbows, halos, comets, and the like.

They hold that there are two [134] principles in the universe, the active principle and the passive. The passive principle, then, is a substance without quality, *i.e.* matter, whereas the active is the reason inherent in this substance, that is God. For he is everlasting and is the artificer of each several thing throughout the whole extent of matter. This doctrine is laid down by Zeno of Citium in his treatise *On Existence*, Cleanthes in his work *On Atoms*, Chrysippus in the first book of his *Physics* towards the end, Archedemus in his treatise *On Elements*, and Posidonius in the second book of his *Physical Exposition*. There is a difference, according to them, between principles and elements;

---

² The words in brackets read like a marginal note, afterwards inserted in the text.

the former being without generation or destruction, whereas the elements are destroyed when all things are resolved into fire. Moreover, the principles are incorporeal and destitute of form, while the elements have been endowed with form.

Body is defined by Apollodorus [135] in his *Physics* as that which is extended in three dimensions, length, breadth, and depth. This is also called solid body. But surface is the extremity of a solid body, or that which has length and breadth only without depth. That surface exists not only in our thought but also in reality is maintained by Posidonius in the third book of his *Celestial Phenomena*. A line is the extremity of a surface or length without breadth, or that which has length alone. A point is the extremity of a line, the smallest possible mark or dot.

God is one and the same with Reason, Fate, and Zeus; he is also called by [136] many other names. In the beginning he was by himself; he transformed the whole of substance through air into water, and just as in animal generation the seed has a moist vehicle, so in cosmic moisture God, who is the seminal reason of the universe, remains behind in the moisture as such an agent, adapting matter to himself with a view to the next stage of creation. Thereupon he created first of all the four elements, fire, water, air, earth. They are discussed by Zeno in his treatise *On the Whole*, by Chrysippus in the first book of his *Physics*, and by Archedemus in a work *On Elements*. An element is defined as that from which particular things first come to be at their birth and into which they are finally resolved. The four elements [137] together constitute unqualified substance or matter. Fire is the hot element, water the moist, air the cold, earth the dry. Not but what the quality of dryness is also found in the air. Fire has the uppermost place; it is also called aether, and in it the sphere of the fixed stars is first created; then comes the sphere of the

planets, next to that the air, then the water, and lowest of all the earth, which is at the centre of all things.

The term universe or cosmos is used by them in three senses: (1) of God himself, the individual being whose quality is derived from the whole of substance; he is indestructible and ingenerable, being the artificer of this orderly arrangement, who at stated periods of time absorbs into himself the whole of substance and again creates it from himself. (2) Again, they give the name of cosmos to the orderly arrange- [138] ment of the heavenly bodies in itself as such; and (3) in the third place to that whole of which these two are parts. Again, the cosmos is defined as the individual being qualifying the whole of substance, or, in the words of Posidonius in his elementary treatise on *Celestial Phenomena*, a system made up of heaven and earth and the natures in them, or, again, as a system constituted by gods and men and all things created for their sake. By heaven is meant the extreme circumference or ring in which the deity has his seat.

The world,[3] in their view, is ordered by reason and providence: so says Chrysippus in the fifth book of his treatise *On Providence* and Posidonius in his work *On the Gods*, book iii.—inasmuch as reason pervades every part of it, just as does the soul in us. Only there is a difference of degree; in some parts there is more of it, in others less. For through some parts it passes as a [139] "hold" or containing force, as is the case with our bones and sinews; while through others it passes as intelligence, as in the ruling part of the soul. Thus, then, the whole world is a living being, endowed with soul and reason, and having aether for its ruling principle: so says Antipater of Tyre in the eighth

---

3 "World" is normally the best rendering of κόσμος. "Universe," which some prefer, better suits τὸ ὅλον.

book of his treatise *On the Cosmos*. Chrysippus in the first book of his work *On Providence* and Posidonius in his book *On the Gods* say that the heaven, but Cleanthes that the sun, is the ruling power of the world. Chrysippus, however, in the course of the same work gives a somewhat different account, namely, that it is the purer part of the aether; the same which they declare to be preeminently God and always to have, as it were in sensible fashion, pervaded all that is in the air, all animals and plants, and also the earth itself, as a principle of cohesion.

The world, they say, is one and [140] finite, having a spherical shape, such a shape being the most suitable for motion, as Posidonius says in the fifth book of his *Physical Discourse* and the disciples of Antipater in their works on the Cosmos. Outside of the world is diffused the infinite void, which is incorporeal. By incorporeal is meant that which, though capable of being occupied by body, is not so occupied. The world has no empty space within it, but forms one united whole. This is a necessary result of the sympathy and tension which binds together things in heaven and earth. Chrysippus discusses the void in his work *On Void* and in the first book of his *Physical Sciences*; so too Apollophanes in his *Physics*, Apollodorus, and Posidonius in his *Physical Discourse*, book ii. But these, it is added [*i.e.* sympathy and tension], are likewise bodies.

Time too is incorporeal, being [141] the measure of the world's motion. And time past and time future are infinite, but time present is finite. They hold that the world must come to an end, inasmuch as it had a beginning, on the analogy of those things which are understood by the senses. And that of which the parts are perishable is perishable as a whole. Now the parts of the world are perishable, seeing that they are transformed one into the other. Therefore the world itself is doomed to perish. Moreover, anything is destructible if it admits of deterioration; therefore the world is so, for it is first evaporated and again dissolved into water.

The world, they hold, comes into [142] being when its substance has first been converted from fire through air into moisture and then the coarser part of the moisture has condensed as earth, while that whose particles are fine has been turned into air, and this process of rarefaction goes on increasing till it generates fire. Thereupon out of these elements animals and plants and all other natural kinds are formed by their mixture. The generation and the destruction of the world are discussed by Zeno in his treatise *On the Whole*, by Chrysippus in the first book of his *Physics*, by Posidonius in the first book of his work *On the Cosmos*, by Cleanthes, and by Antipater in his tenth book *On the Cosmos*. Panaetius, however, maintained that the world is indestructible.

The doctrine that the world is a living being, rational, animate and intelligent, is laid down by Chrysippus in the first book of his treatise *On Providence*, by Apollodorus in his *Physics*, and by Posidonius. It is a living thing in the sense of an animate sub- [143] stance endowed with sensation; for animal is better than non-animal, and nothing is better than the world, *ergo* the world is a living being. And it is endowed with soul, as is clear from our several souls being each a fragment of it. Boëthus, however, denies that the world is a living thing. The unity of the world is maintained by Zeno in his treatise *On the Whole*, by Chrysippus, by Apollodorus in his *Physics*, and by Posidonius in the first book of his *Physical Discourse*. By the totality of things, the All, is meant, according to Apollodorus, (1) the world, and in another sense (2) the system composed of the world and the void outside it.

The world then is finite, the void infinite.

Of the stars some are fixed, and [144] are carried round with the whole heaven; others, the wandering stars or planets, have their special motions. The sun travels in an oblique path through the zodiac. Similarly the moon travels in a spiral path. The sun is pure fire: so Posidonius in the seventh book of his *Celestial Phenomena*. And it is larger than the earth, as the same author says in the sixth book of his *Physical Discourse*. Moreover it is spherical in shape like the world itself according to this same author and his school. That it is fire is proved by its producing all the effects of fire; that it is larger than the earth by the fact that all the earth is illuminated by it; nay more, the heaven beside. The fact too that the earth casts a conical shadow proves that the sun is greater than it. And it is because of its great size that it is seen from every part of the earth.

The moon, however, is of a more [145] earthy composition, since it is nearer to the earth. These fiery bodies and the stars generally derive their nutriment, the sun from the wide ocean, being a fiery kindling, though intelligent; the moon from fresh waters, with an admixture of air, close to the earth as it is: thus Posidonius in the sixth book of his Physics; the other heavenly bodies being nourished from the earth. They hold that the stars are spherical in shape and that the earth too is so and is at rest; and that the moon does not shine by her own light, but by the borrowed light of the sun when he shines upon her.

An eclipse of the sun takes place when the moon passes in front of it on the side towards us, as shown by Zeno with a diagram in his treatise *On the Whole*. For the moon is seen approaching at conjunctions and [146] occulting it and then again receding from it. This can best be observed when they are mirrored in a basin of water. The moon is eclipsed when she falls into the earth's shadow: for which reason it is only at the full moon that an eclipse happens [and not always then], although she is in opposition to the sun every month; because the moon moves in an oblique orbit, diverging in latitude relatively to the orbit of the sun, and she accordingly goes farther to the north or to the south. When, however, the moon's motion in latitude has brought her into the sun's path through the zodiac, and she thus comes diametrically opposite to the sun, there is an eclipse. Now the moon is in latitude right on the zodiac, when she is in the constellations of Cancer, Scorpio, Aries and Taurus: so Posidonius and his followers tell us.

The deity, say they, is a living [147] being, immortal, rational, perfect or intelligent in happiness, admitting nothing evil [into him], taking providential care of the world and all that therein is, but he is not of human shape. He is, however, the artificer of the universe and, as it were, the father of all, both in general and in that particular part of him which is all-pervading, and which is called many names according to its various powers. They give the name Dia ($\Delta i\alpha$) because all things are due to ($\delta i\alpha$) him; Zeus ($Z\hat{\eta}\nu\alpha$) in so far as he is the cause of life ($\zeta\hat{\eta}\nu$) or pervades all life; the name Athena is given, because the ruling part of the divinity extends to the aether; the name Hera marks its extension to the air; he is called Hephaestus since it spreads to the creative fire; Poseidon, since it stretches to the sea; Demeter, since it reaches to the earth. Similarly men have given the deity his other titles, fastening, as best they can, on some one or other of his peculiar attributes.

The substance of God is de- [148] clared by Zeno to be the whole world and the heaven, as well as by Chrysippus in his first book *Of the Gods*, and by Posidonius in his first book with the same title. Again, Antipater in the seventh book of his work *On the Cosmos* says that the substance of God is akin to air, while Boëthus in his work *On Nature* speaks of the sphere of the fixed stars as the substance of God. Now the term Nature is used by them to mean sometimes that which holds the world together, sometimes that which causes terrestrial things to spring up. Nature defined as a force moving of itself, producing and preserving in being its offspring in accordance with seminal principles[4] within definite periods, and effecting results homogeneous with their sources. Nature, they hold, aims both at utility and at pleasure, as is clear from the analogy of human craftsmanship. That all things happen by fate or destiny is maintained by Chrysippus in his treatise *De fato*, by Posidonius in his *De fato*, book ii., by Zeno and by Boëthus in his *De fato*, book i. Fate is defined as an endless chain of causation, whereby things are, or as the reason or formula by which the world goes on. What is more, they say that divination in all its forms is a real and substantial fact, if there is really Providence. And they prove it to be actually a science on the evidence of certain results: so Zeno, Chrysippus in the second book of his *De divinatione*, Athenodorus, and Posidonius in the second book of his *Physical Discourse* and the fifth book of his *De divinatione*. But Panaetius denies that divination has any real existence.

The primary matter they make [150] the substratum of all things: so Chrysippus in the first book of his *Physics*, and Zeno. By matter is meant that out of which anything whatsoever is produced. Both substance and matter are

terms used in a twofold sense according as they signify (1) universal or (2) particular substance or matter. The former neither increases nor diminishes, while the matter of particular things both increases and diminishes. Body according to them is substance which is finite: so Antipater in his second book *On Substance*, and Apollodorus in his *Physics*. Matter can also be acted upon, as the same author says, for if it were immutable, the things which are produced would never have been produced out of it. Hence the further doctrine that matter is divisible *ad infinitum*. Chrysippus says that the division is not *ad infinitum*, but itself infinite; for there is nothing infinitely small to which the division can extend. But nevertheless the division goes on without ceasing.

Hence, again, their explanation [151] of the mixture of two substances is, according to Chrysippus in the third book of his *Physics*, that they permeate each other through and through, and that the particles of the one do not merely surround those of the other or lie beside them. Thus, if a little drop of wine be thrown into the sea, it will be equally diffused over the whole sea for a while and then will be blended with it.

Also they hold that there are daemons (δαίμονες) who are in sympathy with mankind and watch over human affairs. They believe too in heroes, that is, the souls of the righteous that have survived their bodies.

Of the changes which go on in the air, they describe winter as the cooling of the air above the earth due to the sun's departure to a distance from the earth; spring as the right temperature of the air consequent upon his approach to us; summer as the heating of the [152] air above the earth when he travels to the north; while autumn they attribute to the receding of the sun from us. As for the winds, they are streams of air, differently named according to the localities from which they blow. And

---

4 Or perhaps "seminal proportions." This obscure expression would seem intended to assimilate all development and evolution to growth, whether of plants or animals, from seed.

the cause of their production is the sun through the evaporation of the clouds. The rainbow is explained as the reflection of the sun's rays from watery clouds or, as Posidonius says in his *Meteorology*, an image of a segment of the sun or moon in a cloud suffused with dew, which is hollow and visible without intermission, the image showing itself as if in a mirror in the from of a circular arch. Comets, bearded stars, and meteors are fires which arise when dense air is carried up to the region of aether. A shooting star is [153] the sudden kindling of a mass of fire in rapid motion through the air, which leaves a trail behind it presenting an appearance of length. Rain is the transformation of cloud into water, when moisture drawn up by the sun from land or sea has been only partially evaporated. If this is cooled down, it is called hoar-frost. Hail is frozen cloud, crumbled by a wind; while snow is moist matter from a cloud which has congealed: so Posidonius in the eighth book of his *Physical Discourse*. Lightning is a kindling of clouds from being rubbed together or being rent by wind, as Zeno says in his treatise *On the Whole*; thunder the noise these clouds make when they rub against each other or burst. Thunderbolt is the term used when the fire is violently kindled [154] and hurled to the ground with great force as the clouds grind against each other or are torn by the wind. Others say that it is a compression of fiery air descending with great force. A typhoon is a great and violent thunderstorm whirlwind-like, or a whirlwind of smoke from a cloud that has burst. A "prester" is a cloud rent all round by the force of fire and wind. Earthquakes, say they, happen when the wind finds its way into, or is imprisoned in, the hollow parts of the earth: so Posidonius in his eighth book; and some of them are tremblings, others openings of the earth, others again lateral displacements, and yet others vertical displacements.

They maintain that the parts of [155] the world are arranged thus. The earth is in the middle answering to a centre; next comes the water, which is shaped like a sphere all round it, concentric with the earth, so that the earth is in water. After the water comes a spherical layer of air. There are five celestial circles: first, the arctic circle, which is always visible; second, the summer tropic; third, the circle of the equinox; fourth, the winter tropic; and fifth, the antarctic, which is invisible to us. They are called parallel, because they do not incline towards one another; yet they are described round the same centre.[5] The zodiac is an oblique circle, as it crosses the parallel circles. And [156] there are five terrestrial zones: first, the northern zone which is beyond the arctic circle, uninhabitable because of the cold; second, a temperate zone; a third, uninhabitable because of great heats, called the torrid zone; fourth, a counter-temperate zone; fifth, the southern zone, uninhabitable because of its cold.

Nature in their view is an artistically working fire, going on its way to create; which is equivalent to a fiery, creative, or fashioning breath. And the soul is a nature capable of perception. And they regard it as the breath of life, congenital with us; from which they infer first that it is a body and secondly that it survives death. Yet it is perishable, though the soul of the universe, of which the individual souls of animals are parts, is indestructible. Zeno of Citium and Antipater, in their [157] treatises *De anima*, and Posidonius define the soul as a warm breath; for by this we become animate and this enables us to move. Cleanthes indeed holds that all souls continue to exist until the

5 The κέντρον is rather an axis (namely, a diameter of the celestial sphere) than a point.

general conflagration; but Chrysippus says that only the souls of the wise do so.

They count eight parts of the soul: the five senses, the generative power in us, our power of speech, and that of reasoning. They hold that we see when the light between the visual organ and the object stretches in the form of a cone: so Chrysippus in the second book of his *Physics* and Apollodorus, The apex of the cone in the air is at the eye, the base at the object seen. Thus the thing seen is reported to us by the medium of the air stretching out towards it, as if by a stick.

We hear when the air between [158] the sonant body and the organ of hearing suffers concussion, a vibration which spreads spherically and then forms waves and strikes upon the ears, just as the water in a reservoir forms wavy circles when a stone is thrown into it. Sleep is caused, they say, by the slackening of the tension in our senses, which affects the ruling part of the soul. They consider that the passions are caused by the variations of the vital breath.

Semen is by them defined as that which is capable of generating offspring like the parent. And the human semen which is emitted by a human parent in a moist vehicle is mingled with parts of the soul, blended in the same ratio in which they are present in the parent. Chrysippus in the second book of [159] his *Physics* declares it to be in substance identical with vital breath or spirit. This, he thinks, can be seen from the seeds cast into the earth, which, if kept till they are old, do not germinate, plainly because their fertility has evaporated. Sphaerus and his followers also maintain that semen derives its origin from the whole of the body; at all events every part of the body can be reproduced from it. That of the female is according to them sterile, being, as Sphaerus says, without tension, scanty, and watery. By ruling part of the soul is meant that which is most truly soul proper, in which arise presentations and impulses and from which issues rational speech. And it has its seat in the heart.

Such is the summary of their [160] Physics which I have deemed adequate.

# CLEANTHES

### Hymn to Zeus (complete)[1]

O God most glorious, called by many a name,
Nature's great King, through endless years the same;
Omnipotence, who by thy just decree
Controllest all, hail, Zeus, for unto thee
Behoves thy creatures in all lands to call.
We are thy children, we alone, of all
On earth's broad ways that wander to and fro,
Bearing thine image whereso'er we go.
Wherefore with songs of praise thy power I will forth show.
Lo! yonder Heaven, that round the earth is wheeled,
Follows thy guidance, still to thee doth yield
Glad homage; thine unconquerable hand

---

1 See also Epictetus, section 53.

Such flaming minister, the levin brand,
Wieldeth, a sword two-edged, whose deathless might
Pulsates through all that Nature brings to light;
Vehicle of the universal Word, that flows
Through all, and in the light celestial glows
Of stars both great and small. A King of Kings
Through ceaseless ages, God, whose purpose brings
To birth, whate'er on land or in the sea
Is wrought, or in high heaven's immensity;
Save what the sinner works infatuate.
Nay, but thou knowest to make crooked straight:
Chaos to thee in order: in thine eyes
The unloved is lovely, who didst harmonize
Things evil with things good, that there should be
One Word through all things everlastingly.
One Word—whose voice alas! the wicked spurn;
Insatiate for the good their spirits yearn:
Yet seeing see not, neither hearing hear
God's universal law, which those revere,
By reason guided, happiness who win.
The rest, unreasoning, diverse shapes of sin
Self-prompted follow: for an idle name
Vainly they wrestle in the lists of fame:
Others inordinately riches woo,
Or dissolute, the joys of flesh pursue.
Now here, now there they wander, fruitless still,
For ever seeking good and finding ill.
Zeus the all-bountiful, whom darkness shrouds,
Whose lightning lightens in the thunder-clouds;
Thy children save from error's deadly away:
Turn thou the darkness from their souls sway:
Vouchsafe that unto knowledge they attain;
For thou by knowledge art made strong to reign
O'er all, and all things rulest righteously.
So by thee honoured, we will honour thee,
Praising thy works continually with songs,
As mortals should; nor higher meed belongs
E'en to the gods, than justly to adore
The universal law for evermore.

# EPICTETUS

## Encheiridion, or Manual (complete)

1. Some things are under our control, while others are not under our control. Under our control are conception, choice, desire, aversion, and in a word, everything that is our own doing; not under our control are our body, our property, reputation, office and, in a word, everything that is not our own doing. Furthermore, the things under our con-

trol are by nature free, unhindered, and unimpeded; while the things not under our control are weak, servile, subject to hindrance, and not our own. Remember, therefore, that if what is naturally slavish you think to be free, and what is not your own to be your own, you will be hampered, will grieve, will be in turmoil, and will blame both gods and men; while if you think only what is your own to be your own, and what is not your own to be, as it really is, not your own, then no one will ever be able to exert compulsion upon you, no one will hinder you, you will blame no one, will find fault with no one, will do absolutely nothing against your will, you will have no personal enemy, no one will harm you, for neither is there any harm that can touch you.

With such high aims, therefore, remember that you must bestir yourself with no slight effort to lay hold of them, but you will have to give up some things entirely, and defer others for the time being. But if you wish for these things also, and at the same time for both office and wealth, it may be that you will not get even these latter, because you aim also at the former, and certainly you will fail to get the former, which alone bring freedom and happiness.

Make it, therefore, your study at the very outset to say to every harsh external impression, "You are an external impression and not at all what you appear to be." After that examine it and test it by these rules which you have, the first and most important of which is this: Whether the impression has to do with the things which are under our control, or with those which are not under our control; and, if it has to do with some one of the things not under our control, have ready to hand the answer, "It is nothing to me."

2. Remember that the promise of desire is the attainment of what you desire, that of aversion is not to fall into what is avoided, and that he who fails in his

desire is unfortunate, while he who falls into what he would avoid experiences misfortune. If, then, you avoid only what is unnatural among those things which are under your control, you will fall into none of the things which you avoid; but if you try to avoid disease, or death, or poverty, you will experience misfortune. Withdraw, therefore, your aversion from all the matters that are not under our control, and transfer it to what is unnatural among those which are under our control. But for the time being[1] remove utterly your desire; for if you desire some one of the things that are not under our control you are bound to be unfortunate; and, at the same time, not one of the things that are under our control, which it would be excellent for you to desire, is within your grasp. But employ only choice and refusal, and these too but lightly, and with reservations,[2] and without straining.

3. With everything which entertains you, is useful, or of which you are fond, remember to say to yourself, beginning with the very least things, "What is its nature?" If you are fond of a jug, say, "I am fond of a jug"; for when it is broken you will not be disturbed. If you kiss your own child or wife, say to yourself that you are kissing a human being; for when it dies you will not be disturbed.

4. When you are on the point of putting your hand to some undertaking, remind yourself what the nature of that undertaking is. If you are going out of the house to bathe, put before your mind what happens at a public bath—those who splash you with water, those who jostle against you, those who vilify

---

[1] The remark, as many others of the admonitions, is addressed to a student or a beginner.

[2] See M. Aurelius, 1, 4, where Mr. Haines (in *L.C.L.*) suggests that the reference is to some such reservations as recommended in James iv. 15: "For that ye ought to say is, If the Lord will, we shall live, and do this, or that."

you and rob you. And thus you will set about your undertaking more securely if at the outset you say to yourself, "I want to take a bath, and, at the same time, to keep my moral purpose in harmony with nature." And so do in every undertaking. For thus, if anything happens to hinder you in your bathing, you will be ready to say, "Oh, well, this was not the only thing that I wanted, but I wanted also to keep your moral purpose in harmony with nature; and I shall not so keep it if I am vexed at what is going on."

5. It is not the things themselves that disturb men, but their judgements about these things. For example, death is nothing dreadful, or else Socrates too would have thought so, but the judgement that death is dreadful, *this* is the dreadful thing. When, therefore, we are hindered, or disturbed, or grieved, let us never blame anyone but ourselves, that means, our own judgements. It is the part of an uneducated person to blame others where he himself fares ill; to blame himself is the part of one whose education has begun; to blame neither another nor his own self is the part of one whose education is already complete.

6. Be not elated at any excellence which is not your own. If the horse in his elation were to say, "I am beautiful," it could be endured; but when you say in your elation, "I have a beautiful horse," rest assured that you are elated at something good which belongs to a horse. What then, is your own? The use of external impressions. Therefore, when you are in harmony with nature in the use of external impressions, then be elated; for then it will be some good of your own at which you will be elated.

7. Just as on a voyage, when your ship has anchored, if you should go on shore to get fresh water, you may pick up a small shell-fish or little bulb[3]

on the way, but you have to keep your attention fixed on the ship, and turn about frequently for fear lest the captain should call; and if he calls, you must give up all these things, if you would escape being thrown on board all tied up like the sheep. So it is also in life: If there be given you, instead of a little bulb and a small shell-fish, a little wife and child, there will be no objection to that; only, if the Captain calls, give up all these things and run to the ship, without even turning around to look back. And if you are an old man, never even get very far away from the ship, for fear that when He calls you may be missing.

8. Do not seek to have everything that happens happen as you wish, but wish for everything to happen as it actually does happen, and your life will be serene.

9. Disease is an impediment to the body, but not to the moral purpose, unless that consents. Lameness is an impediment to the leg, but not to the moral purpose. And say this to yourself at each thing that befalls you; for you will find the thing to be an impediment to something else, but not to yourself.

10. In the case of everything that befalls you, remember to turn to yourself and see what faculty you have to deal with it. If you see a handsome lad or woman, you will find continence the faculty to employ here; if hard labour is laid upon you, you will find endurance; in this fashion, your external impressions will not run away with you.

11. Never say about anything, "I have lost it," but only "I have given it back." Is your child dead? It has been given back. Is your wife dead? She has been given back. "I have had my farm taken away." Very well, this too has been given back. "Yet it was a rascal who took it away." But what concern is it of yours by whose instrumentality the Giver called for its return? So long as He gives it to you, take care of it

---

3 The Greeks ate a good many different bulbous plants, and we use a variety of different plants for "greens."

as of a thing that is not your own, as travellers treat their inn.

12. If you wish to make progress, dismiss all reasoning of this sort: "If I neglect my affairs, I shall have nothing to live on." "If I do not punish my slave-boy he will turn out bad." For it is better to die of hunger, but in a state of freedom from grief and fear, than to live in plenty, but troubled in mind. And it is better for your slave-boy to be bad than for you to be unhappy. Begin, therefore, with the little things. Your paltry oil gets spilled, your miserable wine stolen; say to yourself, "This is the price paid for a calm spirit, this the price for peace of mind." Nothing is got without a price. And when you call your slave-boy, bear in mind that it is possible he may not heed you, and again, that even if he does heed, he may not do what you want done. But he is not in so happy a condition that your peace of mind depends upon him.[4]

13. If you wish to make progress, then be content to appear senseless and foolish in externals, do not make it your wish to give the appearance of knowing anything; and if some people think you to be an important personage, distrust yourself. For be assured that it is no easy matter to keep your moral purpose in a state of conformity with nature, and, at the same time, to keep externals; but the man who devotes his attention to one of these two things must inevitably neglect the other.

14. If you make it your will that your children and your wife and your friends should live forever, you are silly; for you are making it your will that things not under your control should be under your control, and that what is not your own should be your own. In the same way, too, if you make it your will that your slave-boy be free from faults, you are a fool; for you are mak-

ing it your will that vice be not vice, but something else. If, however, it is your will not to fail in what you desire, this is in your power. Wherefore, exercise yourself in that which is in your power. Each man's master is the person who has the authority over what the man wishes or does not wish, so as to secure it, or take it away. Whoever, therefore, wants to be free, let him neither wish for anything, nor avoid anything, that is under the control of others; or else he is necessarily a slave.

15. Remember that you ought to behave in life as you would at a banquet. As something is being passed around it comes to you; stretch out your hand and take a portion of it politely. It passes on; do not detain it. Or it has not come to you yet; do not project your desire to meet it, but wait until it comes in front of you. So act toward children, so toward a wife, so toward office, so toward wealth; and then some day you will be worthy of the banquets of the gods. But if you do not take these things even when they are set before you, but despise them, then you will not only share the banquet of the gods, but share also their rule. For it was by so doing that Diogenes and Heracleitus, and men like them, were deservedly divine and deservedly so called.

16. When you see someone weeping in sorrow, either because a child has gone on a journey, or because he has lost his property, beware that you be not carried away by the impression that the man is in the midst of external ills, but straightway keep before you this thought: "It is not what has happened that distresses this man (for it does not distress another), but his judgement about it." Do not, however, hesitate to sympathize with him so far as words go, and, if occasion offers, even to groan with him; but be careful not to groan also in the centre of your being.

17. Remember that you are an actor in a play, the character of which is

---

4 That is, the slave-boy would be in a remarkable position of advantage if his master's peace of mind depended, not upon the master himself, but upon the actions of his slave-boy.

determined by the Playwright: if He wishes the play to be short; if long, it is long; if He wishes you to play the part of a beggar, remember to act even this rôle adroitly; and so if your rôle be that of a cripple, an official, or a layman. For this is your business, to play admirably the rôle assigned you; but the selection of that rôle is Another's.[5]

18. When a raven croaks inauspiciously, let not the external impression carry you away, but straightway draw a distinction in your own mind, and say, "None of these portents are for me, but either for my paltry body, or my paltry estate, or my paltry opinion, or my children, or my wife. But for me every portent is favourable, if I so wish; for whatever be the outcome, it is within my power to derive benefit from it."

19. You can be invincible if you never enter a contest in which victory is not under your control. Beware lest, when you see some person preferred to you in honour, or possessing great power, or otherwise enjoying high repute, you are ever carried away by the external impression, and deem him happy. For if the true nature of the good is one of the things that are under our control, there is no place for either envy or jealousy; and you yourself will not wish to be a praetor, or a senator, or a consul, but a free man. Now there is but one way that leads to this, and that is to despise the things that are not under our control.

20. Bear in mind that it is not the man who reviles or strikes you that insults you, but it is your judgement that these men are insulting you. Therefore, when someone irritates you, be assured that it is your own opinion which has irritated you. And so make it your first endeavour not to be carried away by the external impression; for if once you gain time and delay, you will more easily become master of yourself.

21. Keep before your eyes day by day death and exile, and everything that seems terrible, but most of all death; and then you will never have any abject thought, nor will you yearn for anything beyond measure.

22. If you yearn for philosophy, prepare at once to be met with ridicule, to have many people jeer at you, and say, "Here he is again, turned philosopher all of a sudden," and "Where do you suppose he got that high brow?" But do you not put on a high brow, and do you so hold fast to the things which to you seem best, as a man who has been assigned by God to this post; and remember that if you abide by the same principles, those who formerly used to laugh at you will later come to admire you, but if you are worsted by them, you will get the laugh on yourself twice.

23. If it should ever happen to you that you turn to externals with a view to pleasing someone, rest assured that you have lost your plan of life. Be content, therefore, in everything to *be* a philosopher, and if you wish also to be taken for one, show to yourself that you are one, and you will be able to accomplish it.

24. Let not these reflections oppress you: "I shall live without honour, and be nobody anywhere." For, if lack of honour is an evil, you cannot be in evil through the instrumentality of some other person, any more than you can be in shame.[6] It is not your business, is it, to get office, or to be invited to a dinner-party? Certainly not. How, then, can this be any longer a lack of honour? And how is it that you will be "nobody anywhere," when you ought to be somebody only in those things which are under your control, wherein

---

5 A reverent designation for God.

6 That is, every man is exclusively responsible for his own good or evil. But honour and the lack of it are things which are obviously not under a man's control, since they depend upon the action of other people. It follows, therefore, that lack of honour cannot be an evil, but must be something indifferent.

you are privileged to be a man of the very greatest honour? But your friends will be without assistance? What do you mean by being "without assistance"? They will not have paltry coin from you, and you will not make them Roman citizens. Well, who told you that these are some of the matters under our control, and not rather things which others do? And who is able to give another what he does not himself have? "Get money, then," says some friend, "in order that we too many have it." If I can get money and at the same time keep myself self-respecting, and faithful, and high-minded, show me the way and I will get it. But if you require me to lose the good things that belong to me, in order that you may acquire the things that are not good, you can see for yourselves how unfair and inconsiderate you are. And which do you really prefer? Money, or a faithful and self-respecting friend? Help me, therefore, rather to this end, and do not require me to do those things which will make me lose these qualities.

"But my country," says he, "so far as lies in me, will be without assistance." Again I ask, what kind of assistance do you mean? It will not have loggias or baths of your providing. And what does that signify? For neither does it have shoes provided by the blacksmith, nor has it arms provided by the cobbler; but it is sufficient if each man fulfil his own proper function. And if you secured for it another faithful and self-respecting citizen, would you not be doing it any good? "Yes." Very well, and then you also would not be useless to it. "What place, then, shall I have in the State?" says he. Whatever place you *can* have, and at the same time maintain the man of fidelity and self-respect that is in you. But if, through your desire to help the State, you lose these qualities, of what good would you become to it, when in the end you turned out to be shameless and unfaithful?

25. Has someone been honoured above you at a dinner-party, or in salutation, or in being called in to give advice? Now if these matters are good, you ought to be happy that he got them; but if evil, be not distressed because you did not get them; and bear in mind that, if you do not act the same way that others do, with a view to getting things which are not under our control, you cannot be considered worthy to receive an equal share with others. Why, how is it possible for a person who does not haunt some man's door, to have equal shares with the man who does? For the man who does not do escort duty, with the man who does? For the man who does not praise, with the man who does? You will be unjust, therefore, and insatiable, if, while refusing to pay the price for which such things are bought, you want to obtain them for nothing. Well, what is the price for heads of lettuce? An obol, perhaps. If, then, somebody gives up his obol and gets his heads of lettuce, while you do not give your obol, and do not get them, do not imagine that you are worse off than the man who gets his lettuce. For as he has his heads of lettuce, so you have your obol which you have not given away.

Now it is the same way also in life. You have not been invited to somebody's dinner-party? Of course not; for you didn't give the host the price at which he sells his dinner. He sells it for praise; he sells it for personal attention. Give him the price, then, for which it is sold, if it is to your interest. But if you wish both not to give up the one and yet to get the other, you are insatiable and a simpleton. Have you, then, nothing in place of the dinner? Indeed you have; you have not had to praise the man you did not want to praise; you have not had to put up with the insolence of his doorkeepers.

26. What the will of nature is may be learned from a consideration of the

points in which we do not differ from one another. For example, when some other person's slave-boy breaks his drinking-cup, you are instantly ready to say. "That's one of the things which happen." Rest assured, then, that when your own drinking-cup gets broken, you ought to behave in the same way that you do when the other man's cup is broken. Apply now the same principle to the matters of greater importance. Some other person's child or wife has died; no one but would say, "Such is the fate of man." Yet when a man's own child dies, immediately the cry is, "Alas! Woe is me!" But we ought to remember how we feel when we hear of the same misfortune befalling others.

27. Just as a mark is not set up in order to be missed, so neither does the nature of evil arise in the universe.[7]

28. If someone handed over your body to any person who met you, you would be vexed; but that you hand over your mind to any person that comes along, so that, if he reviles you, it is disturbed and troubled—are you not ashamed of that?

29.[8] In each separate thing that you do, consider the matters which come first and those which follow after, and only then approach the thing itself. Otherwise, at the start you will come to it enthusiastically, because you have never reflected upon any of the subsequent steps, but later on, when some difficulties appear, you will give up disgracefully. Do you wish to win an Olym-

pic victory? So do I, by the gods! for it is a fine thing. But consider the matters which come before that, and those which follow after, and only when you have done that, put your hand to the task. You have to submit to discipline, follow a strict diet, give up sweet cakes, train under compulsion, at a fixed hour, in heat or in cold; you must not drink cold water,[9] nor wine just whenever you feel like it; you must have turned yourself over to your trainer precisely as you would to a physician. Then when the contest comes on, you have to "dig in" beside your opponent, and sometimes dislocate your wrist, sprain your ankle, swallow quantities of sand, sometimes take a scourging, and along with all that get beaten. After you have considered all these points, go on into the games, if you still wish to do so; otherwise, you will be turning back like children. Sometimes they play wrestlers, again gladiators, again they blow trumpets, and then act a play. So you too are now an athlete, now a gladiator, then a rhetorician, then a philosopher, yet with your whole soul nothing; but like an ape you imitate whatever you see, and one thing after another strikes your fancy. For you have never gone out after anything with circumspection, nor after you had examined it all over, but you act at haphazard and half-heartedly.

In the same way, when some people have seen a philosopher and have heard someone speaking like Euphrates[10] (though, indeed, who can speak like him?), they wish to be philosophers themselves. Man, consider first the nature of the business, and then learn your own natural ability, if you are able to bear it. Do you wish to be a

---

7 That is, it is inconceivable that the universe should exist in order that some things may go wrong; hence, nothing natural is evil, and nothing that is by nature evil can arise. —Thus in effect Simplicius, and correctly, it seems.

8 This chapter is practically word for word identical with Arrian's *Discourses of Epictetus*, III. 15. Since it was omitted in Par., and not commented on by Simplicius, it may have been added in some second edition, whether by Arrian or not.

9 That is, *cold* water not at all; while wine may be drunk, but only at certain times, *i.e.*, probably with one's meals. Such prohibitions are still common in Europe, particularly in popular therapeutics.

10 An eminent Stoic lecturer.

contender in the pentathlon, or a wrestler? Look to your arms, your thighs, see what your loins are like. For one man has a natural talent for one thing, another for another. Do you suppose that you can eat in the same fashion, drink in the same fashion, give way to impulse and to irritation, just as you do now? You must keep vigils, work hard, abandon your own people, be despised by a paltry slave, be laughed to scorn by those who meet you, in everything get the worst of it, in honour, in office, in court, in every paltry affair. Look these drawbacks over carefully, if you are willing at the price of these things to secure tranquillity, freedom and calm. Otherwise, do not approach philosophy; don't act like a child—now a philosopher, later on a tax-gatherer, then a rhetorician, then a procurator of Caesar. These things do not go together. You must be one person, either good or bad; you must labour to improve either your own government principle or externals; you must work hard either on the inner man, or on things outside; that is, play either the rôle of a philosopher or else that of a layman.

30. Our duties are in general measured by our social relationships. He is a father. One is called upon to take care of him, to give way to him in all things, to submit when he reviles or strikes you. "But he is a bad father." Did nature, then, bring you into relationship with a *good* father? No, but simply with a father. "My brother does me wrong." Very well, then, maintain the relation that you have toward him; and do not consider what he is doing, but what you will have to do, if your moral purpose is to be in harmony with nature. For no one will harm you without your consent; you will have been harmed only when you think you are harmed. In this way, therefore, you will discover what duty to expect of your neighbour, your citizen, your commanding officer, if you acquire the habit of looking at your social relations with them.

31. In piety towards the gods, I would have you know, the chief element is this, to have right opinions about them—as existing and as administering the universe well and justly—and to have set yourself to obey them and to submit to everything that happens, and to follow it voluntarily, in the belief that it is being fulfilled by the highest intelligence. For if you act in this way, you will never blame the gods, nor find fault with them for neglecting you. But this result cannot be secured in any other way than by withdrawing your idea of the good and the evil from the things which are not under our control, and placing it in those which are under our control, and in those alone. Because, if you think any of those former things to be good or evil, then, when you fail to get what you want and fall into what you do not want, it is altogether inevitable that you will blame and hate those who are responsible for these results. For this is the nature of every living creature, to flee from and to turn aside from the things that appear harmful, and all that produces them, and to pursue after and to admire the things that are helpful, and all that produces them. Therefore, it is impossible for a man who thinks that he is being hurt to take pleasure in that which he thinks is hurting him, just as it is also impossible for him to take pleasure in the hurt itself. Hence it follows that even a father is reviled by a son when he does not give his child some share in the things that seem to be good; and this it was which made Polyneices and Eteocles enemies of one another, the thought that the royal power was a good thing. That is why the farmer reviles the gods, and so also the sailor, and the merchant, and those

who have lost their wives and their children. For where a man's interest lies, there is also his piety. Wherefore, whoever is careful to exercise desire and aversion as he should, is at the same time careful also about piety. But it is always appropriate to make libations, and sacrifices, and to give of the first-fruits after the manner of our fathers, and to do all this with purity, and not in a slovenly or careless fashion, nor, indeed, in a niggardly way, nor yet beyond our means.

32.[11] When you have recourse to divination, remember that you do not know what the issue is going to be, but that you have come in order to find this out from the diviner; yet if you are indeed a philosopher, you know, when you arrive, what the nature of it is. For if it is one of the things which are not under our control, it is altogether necessary that what is going to take place is neither good nor evil. Do not, therefore, bring to the diviner desire or aversion, and do not approach him with trembling, but having first made up your mind that every issue is indifferent and nothing to you, but that, whatever it may be, it will be possible for you to turn it to good use, and that no one will prevent this. Go, then, with confidence to the gods as to counsellors; and after that, when some counsel has been given you, remember whom you have taken as counsellors, and whom you will be disregarding if you disobey. But go to divination as Socrates thought that men should go, that is, in cases where the whole inquiry has reference to the outcome, and where neither from reason nor from any other technical art are means vouchsafed for discovering the matter in question. Hence, when it is your duty to share the danger

of a friend or of your country, do not ask of the diviner whether you ought to share that danger. For if the diviner forewarns you that the omens of sacrifice have been unfavourable, it is clear that death is portended, or the injury of some member of your body, or exile; yet reason requires that even at this risk you are to stand by your friend, and share the danger with your country. Wherefore, give heed to the greater diviner, the Pythian Apollo, who cast out of his temple the man who had not helped his friend when he was being murdered.[12]

33. Lay down for yourself, at the outset, a certain stamp and type of character for yourself, which you are to maintain whether you are by yourself or are meeting with people. And be silent for the most part, or else make only the most necessary remarks, and express these in few words. But rarely, and when occasion requires you to talk, talk, indeed, but about no ordinary topics. Do not talk about gladiators, or horse-races, or athletes, or things to eat or drink—topics that arise on all occasions; but above all, do not talk about people, either blaming, or praising, or comparing them. If, then, you can, by your own conversation bring over that of your companions to what is seemly. But if you happen to be left alone in the presence of aliens, keep silence.

Do not laugh much, nor at many things, nor boisterously.

---

11 See *Discourses*, II. 7 where the principal points made here are illustrated at greater length.

12 A few more unimportant details are given by Aelian, *Varia Historia*, 3, 44; and Simplicius in his commentary on this passage, p. 258 c ff. (Heinsius), or p. 411 (Schweighäuser). The point of the story is that a man does not need to go to a diviner in order to learn whether he should defend his country or his friends. That question was long ago settled by the greatest of diviners, Apollo at Delphi, who ordered to be cast out of his temple an inquirer that had once failed to defend his own friend.

Refuse, if you can, to take an oath at all, but if that is impossible, refuse as far as circumstances allow.

Avoid entertainments given by outsiders and by persons ignorant of philosophy; but if an appropriate occasion arises for you to attend, be on the alert to avoid lapsing into the behaviour of such laymen. For you may rest assured, that, if a man's companion be dirty, the person who keeps close company with him must of necessity get a share of his dirt, even though he himself happens to be clean.

In things that pertain to the body take only as much as your bare need requires, I mean such things as food, drink, clothing, shelter, and household slaves; but cut down everything which is for outward show or luxury.

In your sex-life preserve purity, as far as you can, before marriage, and, if you indulge, take only those privileges which are lawful. However, do not make yourself offensive, or censorious, to those who do indulge, and do not make frequent mention of the fact that you do not yourself indulge.

If someone brings you word that So-and-so is speaking ill of you, do not defend yourself against what has been said, but answer, "Yes, indeed, for he did not know the rest of the faults that attach to me; if he had, these would not have been the only ones he mentioned."

It is not necessary, for the most part, to go to the public shows. If, however, a suitable occasion ever arises, show that your principal concern is for none other than yourself, which means, wish only for that to happen which does happen, and for him only to win who does win; for so you will suffer no hindrance. But refrain utterly from shouting, or laughter at anyone, or great excitement. And after you have left, do not talk a great deal about what took place, except in so far as it contributes to your own improvement; for such behaviour indicates that the spectacle has aroused your admiration.

Do not go rashly or readily to people's public reading,[13] but when you do go, maintain your own dignity and gravity, and at the same time be careful not to make yourself disagreeable.

When you are about to meet somebody, in particular when it is one of those men who are held in very high esteem, propose to yourself the question, "What would Socrates or Zeno have done under these circumstances?" and then you will not be at a loss to make proper use of the occasion. When you go to see one of those men who have great power, propose to yourself the thought, that you will not find him at home, that you will be shut out, that the door will be slammed in your face, that he will pay no attention to you. And if, despite all this, it is your duty to go, go and take what comes, and never say to yourself, "It was not worth all the trouble." For this is characteristic of the layman, that is, a man who is vexed at externals.

In your conversation avoid making mention at great length and excessively of your own deeds or dangers, because it is not as pleasant for others to hear about your adventures, as it is for you to call to mind your own dangers.

Avoid also raising a laugh, for this is a kind of behaviour that slips easily into vulgarity, and at the same time is calculated to lessen the respect which your neighbours have of you. It is dangerous also to lapse into foul language. When, therefore, anything of the sort occurs, if the occasion be suitable, go even so far as to reprove the person who has made such a lapse; if, however, the occasion does not arise, at all events show by keeping silence, and blushing,

---

[13] A favourite way of introducing a new work of literature to the reading public, somewhat like our modern musical recitals, or artists' exhibitions. See also III. 23 for similar public lectures given by a philosopher.

and frowning, that you are displeased by what has been said.

34. When you get an external impression of some pleasure, guard yourself, as with impressions in general, against being carried away by it; nay, let the matter wait upon *your* leisure, and give yourself a little delay. Next think of the two periods of time, first, that in which you will enjoy your pleasure, and second, that in which, after the enjoyment is over, you will later repent and revile your own self; and set over against these two periods of time how much joy and self-satisfaction you will get if you refrain. However, if you feel that a suitable occasion has arisen to do the deed, be careful not to allow its enticement, and sweetness, and attractiveness to overcome you; but set over against all this the thought, how much better is the consciousness of having won a victory over it.

35. When you do a thing which you have made up your mind ought to be done, never try not to be seen doing it, even though most people are likely to think unfavourably about it. If, however, what you are doing is not right, avoid the deed itself altogether; but if it is right, why fear those who are going to rebuke you wrongly?

36. Just as the propositions, "It is day," and "it is night," are full of meaning when separated, but meaningless if united; so also, granted that for you to take the larger share at a dinner is good for your body, still, it is bad for the maintenance of the proper kind of social feeling. When, therefore, you are eating with another person, remember to regard, not merely the value for your body of what lies before you, but also to maintain your respect for your host.

37. If you undertake a rôle which is beyond your powers, you both disgrace yourself in that one, and at the same time neglect the rôle which you might have filled with success.

38. Just as you are careful, in walking about, not to step on a nail or to sprain your ankle, so be careful also not to hurt your governing principle. And if we observe this rule in every action, we shall be more secure in setting about it.

39. Each man's body is a measure for his property,[14] just as the foot is a measure for his shoe. If, then, you abide by this principle, you will maintain the proper measure, but if you go beyond it, you cannot help but fall headlong over a precipice, as it were, in the end. So also in the case of your shoe; if once you go beyond the foot, you get first a gilded shoe, then a purple one, then an embroidered one. For once you go beyond the measure there is no limit.

40. Immediately after they are fourteen, women are called "ladies" by men. And so when they see that they have nothing else but only to be the bedfellows of men, they begin to beautify themselves, and put all their hopes in that. It is worth while for us to take pains, therefore, to make them understand that they are honoured for nothing else but only for appearing modest and self-respecting.

41. It is a mark of an ungifted man to spend a great deal of time in what concerns his body, as in much exercise, much eating, much drinking, much evacuating of the bowels, much copulating. But these things are to be done in passing; and let your whole attention be devoted to the mind.

42. When someone treats you ill or speaks ill of you, remember that he acts or speaks thus because he thinks it is

---

14 That is, property, which is of use only for the body, should be adjusted to a man's actual bodily needs, just as a shoe is (or at least should be) adjusted to the actual needs of a man's foot. The comparison seems to have been a commonplace; see Demophilus, *Similitudines*, 20 (Mullach); Horace, *Epist.* I. 7, 98 and 10, 42 f.

incumbent upon him. That being the case, it is impossible for him to follow what appears good to you, but what appears good to himself; whence it follows that, if he gets a wrong view of things, the man that suffers is the man that has been deceived. For if a person thinks a true composite judgement to be false, the composite judgement does not suffer, but the person who has been deceived. If, therefore, you start from this point of view, you will be gentle with the man who reviles you. For you should say on each occasion, "He thought that way about it."

43. Everything has two handles, by one of which it ought to be carried and by the other not. If your brother wrongs you, do not lay hold of the matter by the handle of the wrong that he is doing, because this is the handle by which the matter ought not to be carried; but rather by the other handle —that he is your brother, that you were brought up together, and then you will be laying hold of the matter by the handle by which it ought to be carried.

44. The following statements constitute a *non sequitur*: "I am richer than you are, therefore I am superior to you"; or, "I am more eloquent than you are, therefore I am superior to you." But the following conclusions are better: "I am richer than you are, therefore my property is superior to yours"; or, "I am more eloquent than you are, therefore my elocution is superior to yours." But *you* are neither property nor elocution.

45. Somebody is hasty about bathing; do not say that he bathes badly, but that he is hasty about bathing. Somebody drinks a good deal of wine; do not say that he drinks badly, but that he drinks a good deal. For until you have decided what judgement prompts him, how do you know that what he is doing is bad? And thus the final result will not be that you receive convincing sense-impressions of some things, but give your assent to others.

46. On no occasion call yourself a philosopher, and do not, for the most part, talk among laymen about your philosophic principles, but do what follows from your principles. For example, at a banquet do not say how people ought to eat, but eat as a man ought. For remember how Socrates had so completely eliminated the thought of ostentation, that people came to him when they wanted him to introduce them to philosophers, and he used to bring them along. So well did he submit to being overlooked. And if talk about some philosophic principle arises among laymen, keep silence for the most part for there is great danger that you will spew up immediately what you have not digested. So when a man tells you that you know nothing, and you, like Socrates, are not hurt, then rest assured that you are making a beginning with the business you have undertaken. For sheep, too, do not bring their fodder to the shepherds and show how much they have eaten, but they digest their food within them, and on the outside produce wool and milk. And so do you, therefore, make no display to the laymen of your philosophical principles, but let them see the results which come from these principles when digested.

47. When you have become adjusted to simple living in regard to your bodily wants, do not preen yourself about the accomplishment; and so likewise, if you are a water-drinker, do not on every occasion say that you are a water-drinker. And if ever you want to train to develop physical endurance, do it by yourself and not for outsiders to behold; do not throw your arms around statues,[15] but on occasion, when you are very thirsty, take cold water into your

---

[15] Diogenes the Cynic was said to have done that nude in cold weather, so as to harden himself. Diog. Laert. 6, 23.

mouth, and then spit it out, without telling anybody.

48. This is the position and character of a layman: He never looks for either help or harm from himself, but only from externals. This is the position and character of the philosopher: He looks for all his help or harm from himself.

Signs of one who is making progress are: He censures no one, praises no one, blames no one, finds fault with no one, says nothing about himself as though he were somebody or knew something. When he is hampered or prevented, he blames himself. And if anyone compliments him, he smiles to himself at the person complimenting; while if anyone censures him, he makes no defence. He goes about like an invalid, being careful not to disturb, before it has grown firm, any part which is getting well. He has put away from himself his every desire, and has transferred his aversion to those things only, of what is under our control, which are contrary to nature. He exercises no pronounced choice in regard to anything. If he gives the appearance of being foolish or ignorant he does not care. In a word, he keeps guard against himself as though he were his own enemy lying in wait.

49. When a person gives himself airs because he can understand and interpret the books of Chrysippus, say to yourself, "If Chrysippus had not written obscurely, this man would have nothing about which to give himself airs."

But what is it I want? To learn nature and to follow her. I seek, therefore, someone to interpret her; and having heard that Chrysippus does so, I go to him. But I do not understand what he has written; I seek, therefore, the person who interprets Chrysippus. And down to this point there is nothing to justify pride. But when I find the interpreter, what remains is to put his precepts into practice; this is the only thing to be proud about. If, however, I admire the mere act of interpretation, what have I done but turned into a grammarian instead of a philosopher? The only difference, indeed, is that I interpret Chrysippus instead of Homer. Far from being proud, therefore, when somebody says to me, "Read me Chrysippus," I blush the rather, when I am unable to show him such deeds as match and harmonize with his words.

50. Whatever principles are set before you, stand fast by these like laws, feeling that it would be impiety for you to transgress them. But pay no attention to what somebody says about you, for this is, at length, not under your control.

51. How long will you still wait to think yourself worthy of the best things, and in nothing to transgress against the distinctions set up by the reason? You have received the philosophical principles which you ought to accept, and you have accepted them. What sort of a teacher, then, do you still wait for, that you should put off reforming yourself until he arrives? You are no longer a lad, but already a full-grown man. If you are now neglectful and easy-going, and always making one delay after another, and fixing first one day and then another, after which you will pay attention to yourself, then without realizing it you will make no progress, but, living and dying, will continue to be a layman throughout. Make up your mind, therefore, before it is too late, that the fitting thing for you to do is to live as a mature man who is making progress, and let everything which seems to you to be best be for you a law that must not be transgressed. And if you meet anything that is laborious, or sweet, or held in high repute, or in no repute, remember that *now* is the contest, and here before you are the Olympic games, and that it is impossible to delay any longer, and that it depends on a single day and a single action, whether progress is lost or saved. This is the way Socrates became what he was, by pay-

ing attention to nothing but his reason in everything that he encountered. And even if you are not yet a Socrates, still you ought to live as one who wishes to be a Socrates.

52. The first and most necessary division in philosophy is that which has to do with the application of the principles, as, for example, Do not lie. The second deals with the demonstrations, as, for example, How comes it that we ought not to lie? The third confirms and discriminates between these processes, as, for example, How does it come that this is a proof? For what is a proof, what is logical consequence, what contradiction, what truth, what falsehood? Therefore, the third division is necessary because of the second, and the second because of the first; while the most necessary of all, and the one in which we ought to rest, is the first. But we do the opposite; for we spend our time in the third division, and all our zeal is devoted to it, while we utterly neglect the first. Wherefore, we lie, indeed, but

are ready with the arguments which prove that one ought not to lie.

53. Upon every occasion we ought to have the following thoughts at our command:

Lead thou me on, O Zeus, and Destiny,
To that goal long ago to me assigned.
I'll follow and not falter; if my will
Prove weak and craven, still I'll follow on.[16]

"Whoso has rightly with necessity complied,
We count him wise, and skilled in things divine."[17]

"Well, O Crito, if so it is pleasing to the gods, so let it be."[18]

"Anytus and Meletus can kill me, but they cannot hurt me."[19]

---

[16] From Cleanthes. Seneca, who translated these lines into Latin (*Epist.* 107. 11), has a fifth line: *Ducunt volentem fata, nolentem trahunt.* (The fates lead the willing and drag the unwilling.)

[17] Euripides, frag. 965 Nauck.

[18] Plato, *Crito*, 43 D (slightly modified).

[19] Plato, *Apology*, 30 C-4 (somewhat modified).

# SEXTUS EMPIRICUS

## OUTLINES OF PYRRHONISM

### Book I

#### Chapter I. Of the Main Difference Between Philosophic Systems

The natural result of any investigation is that the investigators either discover the object of search or deny that it is discoverable and confess it to be inapprehensible or persist in their search. So, too, with regard to the objects investigated by philosophy, this is probably why some have claimed to have discovered the truth, others have asserted that it cannot be apprehended, while others again go on inquiring. Those who believe they have discovered it are the "'Dogmatists," specially so called— Aristotle, for example, and Epicurus and the Stoics and certain others; Cleitomachus and Carneades and other Academics treat it as inapprehensible: the Sceptics keep on searching. Hence it seems reasonable to hold that the

main types of philosophy are three— the Dogmatic, the Academic, and the Sceptic. Of the other systems it will best become others to speak: our task at present is to describe in outline the Sceptic doctrine, first premising that of none of our future statements do we positively affirm that the fact is exactly as we state it, but we simply record each fact, like a chronicler, as it appears to us at the moment.

• • •

#### Chapter IV. What Scepticism Is

Scepticism is an ability, or mental attitude, which opposes appearances to judgements in any way whatsoever, with the result that, owing to the equipollence of the objects and reasons thus opposed, we are brought firstly to a state of mental suspense and next to a state of "unperturbedness" or quietude. Now we call it an "ability" not in

491

any subtle sense, but simply in respect of its "being able." By "appearances" we now mean the objects of sense-perception, whence we contrast them with the objects of thought or "judgements." The phrase "in any way whatsoever" can be connected either with the word "ability," to make us take the world "ability," as we said, in its simple sense, or with the phrase "opposing appearances to judgements"; for inasmuch as we oppose these in a variety of ways—appearances to appearances, or judgements to judgements, or *alternando* appearances to judgements,—in order to ensure the inclusion of all these antitheses we employ the phrase "in any way whatsoever." Or, again, we join "in any way whatsoever" to "appearances and judgements" in order that we may not have to inquire how the appearances appear or how the thought-objects are judged, but may take these terms in the simple sense. The phrase "opposed judgements" we do not employ in the sense of negations and affirmations only but simply as equivalent to "conflicting judgements." "Equipollence" we use of equality in respect of probability and improbability, to indicate that no one of the conflicting judgements takes precedence of any other as being more probable. "Suspense" is a state of mental rest owing to which we neither deny nor affirm anything. "Quietude" is an untroubled and tranquil condition of soul. And how quietude enters the soul along with suspension of judgement we shall explain in our chapter (XII.) "Concerning the End."

• • •

## Chapter VI.  Of the Principles of Scepticism

The originating cause of Scepticism is, we say, the hope of attaining quietude. Men of talent, who were perturbed by the contradictions in things and in doubt as to which of the alternatives they ought to accept, were led on to inquire what is true in things and what false, hoping by the settlement of the question to attain quietude. The main basic principle of the Sceptic system is that of opposing to every proposition an equal proposition; for we believe that as a consequence of this we end by ceasing to dogmatize.

## Chapter VII.  Does the Sceptic Dogmatize?

When we say that the Sceptic refrains from dogmatizing we do not use the term "dogma," as some do, in the broader sense of "approval of a thing" (for the Sceptic gives assent to the feelings which are the necessary results of sense-impressions, and he would not, for example, say when feeling hot or cold "I believe that I am not hot or cold"); but we say that "he does not dogmatize" using "dogma" in the sense, which some give it, of "assent to one of the non-evident objects of scientific inquiry"; for the Pyrrhonean philosopher assents to nothing that is non-evident. Moreover, even in the act of enunciating the Sceptic formulae concerning things non-evident—such as the formula "No more (one thing than another)," or the formula "I determine nothing," or any of the others which we shall presently mention,—he does not dogmatize. For whereas the dogmatizer posits the things about which he is said to be dogmatizing as really existent, the Sceptic does not posit these formulae in any absolute sense; for he conceives that, just as the formula "All things are false" asserts the falsity of itself as well as of everything else, as does the formula "Nothing is true," so also the formula "No more" asserts that itself, like all the rest, is "No more (this than that," and thus cancels itself along with the rest. And of the other formulae we say the same. If then, while the dogmatizer posits the matter of his dogma as substantial truth, the Sceptic enunciates his formulae so that they are virtually cancelled by themselves, he should not be said to dogmatize in his enunciation of them. And, most important of all, in his enunciation of these formulae he states what appears to himself and announces his own impression in an undogmatic way, without making any positive assertion regarding the external realties.

• • •

## Chapter XII. What Is the End of Scepticism?

Our next subject will be the End of the Sceptic system. Now an "End" is "that for which all actions or reasonings are undertaken, while it exists for the sake of none"; or, otherwise, "the ultimate object of appetency." We assert still that the Sceptic's End is quietude in respect of matters of opinion and moderate feeling in respect of things unavoidable. For the Sceptic, having set out to philosophize with the object of passing judgement on the sense-impressions and ascertaining which of them are true and which false, so as to attain quietude thereby, found himself involved in contradictions of equal weight, and being unable to decide between them suspended judgement; and as he was thus in suspense there followed, as it happened, the state of quietude in respect of matters of opinion. For the man who opines that anything is by nature good or bad is for ever being disquieted: when he is without the things which he deems good he believes himself to be tormented by things naturally bad and he pursues after the things which are, as he thinks, good; which when he has obtained he keeps falling into still more perturbations because of his irrational and immoderate elation, and in his dread of a change of fortune he uses every endeavour to avoid losing the things which he deems good. On the other hand, the man who determines nothing as to what is naturally good or bad neither shuns nor pursues anything eagerly; and, in consequence, he is unperturbed.

The Sceptic, in fact, had the same experience which is said to have befallen the painter Apelles. Once, they say, when he was painting a horse and wished to represent in the painting the horse's foam, he was so unsuccessful that he gave up the attempt and flung at the picture the sponge on which he used to wipe the paints off his brush, and the mark of the sponge produced the effect of a horse's foam. So, too, the Sceptics were in hopes of gaining quietude by means of a decision regarding the disparity of the objects of sense and of thought, and being unable to effect this they suspended judgement; and they found that quietude, as if by chance, followed upon their suspense, even as a shadow follows its substance. We do not, however, suppose that the Sceptic is wholly untroubled; but we say that he is troubled by things unavoidable; for we grant that he is old at times and thirsty, and suffers various affections of that kind. But even in these cases, whereas ordinary people are afflicted by two circumstances,—namely, by the affections themselves and in no less a degree, by the belief that these conditions are evil by nature,—the Sceptic, by his rejection of the added belief in the natural badness of all these conditions, escapes here too with less discomfort. Hence we say that, while in regard to matters of opinion the Sceptic's End is quietude, in regard to things unavoidable it is "moderate affection." But some notable Sceptics have added the further definition "suspension of judgement in investigations."

## Chapter XIII.   Of the General Modes Leading to Suspension of Judgment

Now that we have been saying that tranquillity follows on suspension of judgement, it will be our next task to explain how we arrive at this suspension. Speaking generally, one may say that it is the result of setting things in opposition. We oppose either appearances to appearances or objects of thought to objects of thought or *alternando*. For instance, we oppose appearances when we say "The same tower appears round from a distance, but square from close at hand"; and thoughts to thoughts, when in answer to him who argues the existence of Providence from the order of the heavenly bodies we oppose the fact that often the good fare ill and the bad fare well, and draw from this the inference that Providence does not exist. And thoughts we oppose to appearances, as when Anaxagoras countered the notion that snow is white with the argument, "Snow is frozen water, and water is black; therefore snow also is black." With a different idea we oppose things present sometimes to things present, as in the foregoing examples, and sometimes to things past or future, as, for instance, when someone propounds to us a theory which we are unable to refute, we say to him in reply, "Just as, before the birth of the founder of the School to which you belong, the theory it holds was not as yet apparent as a sound theory, although it was really in existence, so likewise it is possible that the opposite theory to that which you now propound is already really existent, though not yet apparent to us, so that we ought not as yet to yield assent to this theory which at the moment seems to be valid."

But in order that we may have a more exact understanding of these antitheses I will describe the Modes by which suspension of judgement is brought about, but without making any positive assertion regarding either their number or their validity; for it is possible that they may be unsound or there may be more of them than I shall enumerate.

## Chapter XIV.   Concerning the Ten Modes

The usual tradition amongst the older Sceptics is that the "modes" by which "suspension" is supposed to be brought about are ten in number; and they also give them the synonymous names of "arguments" and "positions." They are these: the first, based on the variety in animals; the second, on the differences in human beings; the third, on the different structures of the organs of sense; the fourth, on the circumstantial conditions; the fifth, on positions and intervals and locations; the sixth, on intermixtures; the seventh, on the quantities and formations of the underlying objects; the eighth, on the fact of relativity; the ninth, on the frequency or rarity of occurrence; the tenth, on the disciplines and customs and laws, the legendary beliefs and the dogmatic convictions. This order, however, we adopt without prejudice.

•  •  •

## Chapter XV.   Of the Five Modes

The later Sceptics hand down Five Modes leading to suspension, namely these: the first based on discrepancy, the second on regress *ad infinitum*, the third on relativity, the fourth on hypothesis, the fifth on circular reasoning. That based on discrepancy leads us to find that with regard to the object presented there has arisen both amongst ordinary people and amongst the philosophers an interminable conflict because of which we are unable either to choose a thing or reject it, and so fall back on suspension. The Mode based upon regress *ad infinitum* is that whereby we assert that the thing adduced as a proof of the matter proposed needs a further proof, and this again another, and so on *ad infinitum,* so that the consequence is suspension, as we possess no starting-point for our argument. The Mode based upon relativity, as we have already said, is that whereby the object has such or such an appearance in relation to the subject judging and to the concomitant percepts, but as to its real nature we suspend judgement. We have the Mode based on hypothesis when the Dogmatists, being forced to recede *ad infinitum,* take as their starting-point something which they do not establish by argument but claim to assume as granted simply and without demonstration. The Mode of circular reasoning is the form used when the proof itself which ought to establish the matter of inquiry requires confirmation derived from that matter; in this case, being unable to assume either in order to establish the other, we suspend judgement about both.

That every matter of inquiry admits of being brought under these Modes we shall show briefly in this way. The matter proposed is either a sense-object or a thought-object, but whichever it is, it is an object of controversy; for some say that only sensibles are true, others only intelligibles, others that some sensible and some intelligible objects are true. Will they then assert that the controversy can or cannot be decided? If they say it cannot, we have it granted that we must suspend judgement; for concerning matters of dispute which admit of no decision it is impossible to make an assertion. But if they say that it can be decided, we ask by what is it to be decided. For example, in the case of the sense-object (for we shall base our argument on it first), is it to be decided by a sense-object or a thought-object? For if they say by a sense-object, since we are inquiring about sensibles that object itself also will require another to confirm it; and if that too is to be a sense-object, it likewise will require another for its confirmation, and so on *ad infinitum.* And if the sense-object shall have to be decided by a thought-object, then, since thought-objects also are controverted, this being an object of thought will need examination and confirmation. Whence then will it gain confirmation? If from an intelligible object, it will suffer a similar regress *ad infinitum;* and if from a sensible object, since an intelligible was adduced to establish the sensible and a sensible to establish the intelligible, the Mode of circular reasoning is brought in.

If, however, our disputant, by way of escape from this conclusion, should claim to assume as granted and without demonstration some postulate for the demonstration of the next steps of his argument, then the Mode of hypothesis will be brought in, which allows no escape. For if the author of the hypothesis is worthy of credence, we shall be no less worthy of credence every time that we make the opposite hypothesis. Moreover, if the author of the hypothesis assumes what is true he causes it to be suspected by assuming it by hypothesis rather than after proof; while if it is false, the foundation of his argument will be rotten. Further, if hypothesis conduces at all to proof, let the subject of inquiry itself be assumed and not some other thing which is merely a means to establish the actual subject of the argument; but if it is absurd to assume the subject of inquiry, it will also be absurd to assume that upon which it depends.

It is also plain that all sensibles are relative; for they are relative to those who have the sensations. Therefore it is apparent that whatever sensible object is presented can easily be referred to one of the Five Modes. And concerning the intelligible object we argue similarly. For if it should be said that it is a matter of unsettled controversy, the necessity of our suspending judgement will be granted. And if, on the other hand, the controversy admits of decision, then if the decision rests on an intelligible object we shall be driven to the regress *ad infinitum*, and to circular reasoning if it rests on a sensible; for since the sensible again is controverted and cannot be decided by means of itself because of the regress *ad infinitum*, it will require the intelligible object, just as also the intelligible will require the sensible. For these reasons, again, he who assumes anything by hypothesis will be acting illogically. Moreover, objects of thought, or intelligibles, are relative; for they are so named on account of their relation to the person thinking, and if they had really possessed the nature they are said to possess, there would have been no controversy about them. Thus the intelligible also is referred to the Five Modes, so that in all cases we are compelled to suspend judgement concerning the object presented.

Such then are the Five Modes handed down amongst the later Sceptics; but they propound these not by way of superseding the Ten Modes, but in order to expose the rashness of the Dogmatists with more variety and completeness by means of the Five in conjunction with the Ten.

•　•　•

# PLOTINUS

## ENNEADS

### v. ii.

I. The one is all things, and yet no one of all. For the principle of all is not all things; but *the one* is all, because all things run as it were into it, or rather do not as yet exist, but will be. How, therefore, [does multitude proceed] from *the one* which is simple, and in which no variety, nor any duplicity present themselves to the view? Is it because there was nothing in it, on this account all things are from it? Hence, in order that being might exist, *the one* is not being, but being is the progeny of it, and as it were its firstborn. For *the one* being perfect, in consequence of not seeking after, or possessing, or being in want of any thing, it becomes as it were overflowing, and the superplenitude of it produces something else. That, however, which is generated from it is converted to it, and is filled, and was generated looking to it. But this is intellect. And the per-

manency indeed of it about *the one*, produced being; but its vision of *the one*, intellect. When, therefore, it is established about *the one*, in order that it may see it, then it becomes at once intellect and being. Hence, being in the same manner as *the one* produces things similar to itself, through an effusion of abundant power. Its offspring also has the form of it, in the same manner as prior to this it likewise flowed forth from *the one*. And this energy from essence is soul, which was generated from intellect permanently abiding. For intellect also was generated, that which is prior to it abiding. Soul, however, does not produce abiding, but being moved generates an image of itself. Soul, therefore, looking thither whence it was generated, is filled. But proceeding into another and contrary motion, it generates an image of itself, viz., sense, and the nature which is in plants. Nothing, however, is separated or cut off from that which is prior to itself. Hence, also, the soul of man is seen to proceed as far as to plants. For after *a certain* manner it proceeds into them, because that which is in plants is derived from it. Nevertheless, the whole of the human soul is not in plants, but it is thus ingenerated in plants, because it so far proceeds into an inferior nature, having made another hypostasis by its progression into and propensity to that which is subordinate; since the soul which is prior to this, being suspended from intellect, permits intellect to abide in itself.

### VI. ix.

VI. How, therefore, can we speak of *the one*, and how can we adapt it to intellectual conception? Shall we say that this may be accomplished, by admitting that it is more transcendently one than the monad and a point? For in these, indeed, the soul taking away magnitude and the multitude of number, ends in that which is smallest, and fixes itself in a certain thing which is indeed impartible, but which was in a partible nature, and is in something different from itself. But *the one* is neither in another thing, nor in that which is partible. Nor is it impartible in the same way as that which is smallest. For it is the greatest of all things, not in magnitude, but in power. So that it is without magnitude in power. For the natures also which are [immediately] posterior to it, are impartible in powers, and not in bulk. The principle of all things likewise must be admitted to be infinite, not because he is magnitude or number which cannot be passed over, but because the power of him is incomprehensible. For when you conceive him to be intellect or God, he is more [excellent] than these. And again, when by the dianoetic power you equalize him with *the one*, or conceive him to be God, by recurring to that which is most united in your intellectual perception, he even transcends these appella-

tions. For he is in himself, nor is any thing accidental to him. By that which is sufficient to itself also the unity of his nature may be demonstrated. For it is necessary that the principle of all things should be most sufficient both to other things, and to itself, and that it should also be most un-indigent. But every thing which is multitudinous and not one, is indigent; since consisting of many things it is not one. Hence the essence of it requires to be one. But *the one* is not in want of itself. For it is *the one*. Moreover, that which is many, is in want of as many things as it is. And each of the things that are in it, as it subsists in conjunction with others, and is not in itself, is indigent of other things; and thus a thing of this kind exhibits indigence, both according to parts and according to the whole. If, therefore, it is necessary there should be something which is most sufficient to itself, it is necessary there should be *the one*, which alone is a thing of such a kind, as neither to be indigent with reference to itself, nor with reference to another thing. For it does not seek after any thing in order that it may be, nor in order that it may be in an excellent condition, nor that it may be there established. For being the cause of existence to other things, and not deriving that which it is from others, nor its happiness, what addition can be made to it external to itself? Hence its happiness, or the excellency of its condition, is not accidental to it. For it is itself [all that is sufficient to itself.] There is not likewise any place for it. For it is not in want of a foundation, as if it were not able to sustain itself. For that which is established in another thing is inanimate, and a falling mass, if it is without a foundation. But other things are established on account of *the one*, through which also they at the same time subsist, and have the place in which they are arranged. That, however, which seeks after place is indigent.

But the principle is not indigent of things posterior to itself. The principle, therefore, of all things is unindigent of all things. For that which is indigent, is indigent in consequence of aspiring after its principle. But if *the one* was indigent of any thing it would certainly seek not to be *the one;* so that it would be indigent of its destroyer. Every thing, however, which is said to be indigent, is indigent of a good condition, and of that which preserves it. Hence to *the one* nothing is good, and, therefore, neither is the wish for any thing good to it. But it is *super-good*. And it is not good to itself, but to other things, which are able to participate of it. Nor does *the one* possess intelligence, lest it should also possess difference; nor motion. For it is prior to motion, and prior to intelligence. For what is there which it will intellectually perceive? Shall we say itself? Prior to intellection, therefore, it will be ignorant, and will be in want of intelligence in order that it may know itself, though it is sufficient to itself. It does not follow, however, that because *the one* does not know itself, and does not intellectually perceive itself, there will be ignorance in it. For ignorance takes place where there is diversity, and when one thing is ignorant of another. That, however, which is *alone* neither knows any thing, nor has any thing of which it is ignorant. But being one, and associating with itself, it does not require the intellectual perception of itself; since neither is it necessary, in order that you may preserve *the one*, to adapt to it an association with itself. But it is requisite to take away intellectual perception, an association with itself, and the knowledge of itself, and of other things. For it is not proper to arrange it according to the act of perceiving intellectually, but rather according to intelligence. For intelligence does not perceive intellectually, but is the cause of intellectual perception to another thing. Cause, however, is not the same with the thing caused. But the cause of all things is not any one of them. Hence neither must it be denominated that good which it imparts to others; but it is after another manner *the good*, in a way transcending other goods.

· · ·

XI. This, therefore, is manifested by the mandate of the mysteries, which orders that they shall not be divulged to those who are uninitiated. For as that which is divine cannot be unfolded to the multitude, this mandate forbids the attempt to elucidate it to any one but him who is fortunately able to perceive it. Since, therefore, [in this conjunction with deity] there were not two things, but the perceiver was one with the thing perceived, as not being [properly speaking] vision but union; whoever becomes one by mingling with deity, and afterwards recollects this union, will have with himself an image of it. But he was also himself one, having with respect to himself no difference, nor with respect to other things. For then there was not any thing excited with him who had ascended thither; neither anger, nor the desire of any thing else nor reason, nor a certain intellectual perception, nor, in short, was even he himself moved, if it be requisite also to assert this; but being as it were in an ecstasy, or energizing enthusiastically, he became established in quiet and solitary union, not at all deviating from his own essence, nor revolving about himself, but being entirely stable, and becoming as it were stability itself. Neither was he then excited by any thing beautiful; but running above the beautiful, he passed beyond even the choir of the virtues. Just as if some one having entered into the interior of the adytum should leave behind all the statues in the temple which on his departure from the adytum will first present themselves to his view, after the inward spectacle, and the association that was there, which was not with a statue or an image, but with the thing itself [which the images represent], and which necessarily become the second objects of his perception. Perhaps, however, this was not a spectacle, but there was another mode of vision, viz. ecstasy, and an expansion and accession of himself, a desire of contact, rest, and a striving after conjunction, in order to behold what the adytum contains. But nothing will be present with him who beholds in any other way. The wise prophets, therefore, obscurely signified by these imitations how this [highest] God is seen. But the wise priest understanding the enigma, and having entered into the adytum, obtains a true vision of what is there. If, however, he has not entered, he will conceive this adytum to be a certain invisible thing, and will have a *knowledge* of the fountain and principle, as the principle of things. But when situated there, he will *see* the principle, and will be conjoined with it, by a union of like with like, neglecting nothing divine which the soul is able to possess. Prior to the vision also it requires that which remains from the vision. But that which remains to him who passes beyond all things, is that which is prior to all things. For the nature of the soul will never accede to that which is entirely non-being. But proceeding indeed downwards it will fall into evil; and thus into non-being, yet not into that which is perfect nonentity. Running, however, in a contrary direction, it will arrive not at another thing, but at itself. And thus not being in another thing, it is not on that account in nothing, but is in itself. *To be in itself alone, however, and not in being, is to be in God.* For God also is something which is not essence, but beyond essence. Hence the soul when in this condition, associates with him. He, therefore, who perceives himself to associate with God, will have himself the similitude of him. And if he passes from himself as an image to the archetype, he will then have the end of his progression. But when he falls from the vision of God, if he again excites the virtue which is in himself, and perceives himself to be perfectly adorned; he will again be elevated through virtue, proceeding to intellect and wisdom, and afterwards to the principle of all things. *This, therefore, is the life of the Gods, and of divine and happy men, a liberation from all terrene concerns, a life unaccompanied with human pleasures, and a flight of the alone to the alone.*

### part five

# MEDIEVAL PHILOSOPHY

I

In their evaluations of medieval philosophy, interpreters are far apart, and religious attitudes become relevant. Many Catholic scholars and a minority of non-Catholics consider scholastic philosophy, and especially the system of Saint Thomas Aquinas, the culmination and fulfilment of Greek philosophy, while the great majority of non-Catholic philosophers take far less interest in medieval philosophy.

One striking discontinuity between ancient and medieval philosophy meets the eye: ancient philosophy was pagan, while the philosophies of Saint Augustine, Saint Anselm, and Saint Thomas Aquinas are Christian. To be sure, not all medieval philosophers were Christians: Moses Maimonides, for example, was a Jew. But he, too, like the Christians, appealed to God's revelation in Scripture.

References to God are encountered in Greek philosophy, too, though much more rarely than in medieval philosophy. But when Heraclitus, Plato, and Aristotle speak of God, they are not appealing to any Scripture, to any traditional revelation, or to any acknowledged authorities. They are not quoting earlier writers to establish doctrines: on the contrary, when they refer to earlier thinkers, it is almost always to find fault.

The pre-Socratics broke with the exegetic mode of thought. Some openly derided Homer and the widely revered poems of the past, while others simply ignored previous writers. Each of these early Greek philosophers confronts us as a human being who insists on thinking for himself and who invites us to do likewise.

In the Middle Ages this is changed. The great Christian scholastics may be compared to the rabbis of the Talmud, as well as to Plato and Aristotle; unlike the Greeks, they are in the possession of sacred Scriptures and a great tradition that they accept with humility and pride. A large part of their elected task is to interpret this great heritage; but there is still ample room for acumen, originality, and ingenuity. After all, on the face of it, Scripture does not take up every problem; it treats many questions more than once, and it even seems to contain contradictions. Passages that to the lay mind are quite void of philosophical significance and possibly seem of no particular importance whatsoever are seen in a different light by the devout, who are quite certain that God's word is richly significant at every point. While some of the problems that confronted the religious thinkers of the Middle Ages were quite unlike any of the questions treated by the Greek philosophers—some of the problems about Christ, the Trinity, and angels, for example—most of the topics of ancient philosophy had to be reconsidered, too, in the light of revelation.

II

Saint Augustine (354-430) is as highly esteemed by many Protestants as he is by most Catholics. The story of his life is fairly well known and easily accessible because he himself recorded it in his celebrated *Confessions.* Originally written in Latin, like his many other works, the *Confessions* have been translated into all the major tongues. The book is of great interest for at least three reasons.

First, it may be considered the first great autobiography of world literature. The historical perspective of the Old Testament is here applied to an individual. The Jews, like the Greeks, had considered themselves different from all the other nations. But while the Greeks had believed that they were different by *nature* (according to Julius Jüthner's amply documented monograph on *Hellenen und Barbaren,* 1923, "the average Greek was convinced that he was even physically different from the barbarians," as different, in fact, as from the animals, and comparison of barbarians, i.e., non-Greeks, with animals was a "current commonplace"), the ancient Hebrews thought they were differentiated from other nations by their *history.* In large part, the Old Testament is the record of this history, but it also contains accounts of the growth of several individuals: Jacob and David are outstanding examples of this developmental approach to the human personality. Still lacking, however, was autobiography until Augustine, steeped in the Bible, founded this new genre.

Second, the *Confessions* is the autobiography of a particularly interesting person. His mother was a Christian, but he was brought up a pagan and relished a life that, as he grew older, seemed to him more and more a life of sin. Eventually, he became a Christian, after having first absorbed Manicheanism and Neoplatonism. The Manicheans were the heirs of Zoroaster's (or Zarathustra's) ancient Persian teaching that there are two great forces in the world, one good and one evil. (See the Preface to the selections from Heraclitus, above.)

Finally, there are some things of considerable philosophic interest in the *Confessions*, most notably the long discussion of time, which is widely admired as the most striking sample of Augustine's philosophic acumen. This is reprinted here, translated by J. G. Pilkington.

Of his many other works, *The City of God* is by far the most famous. During the fourth century, Christianity had become the state religion of the Roman Empire; in 410 Rome fell to the Visigoths, and the eternal city was sacked for the first time. Naturally, there were many who considered the sack of Rome a punishment for the betrayal of the old Roman religion. Augustine wrote *The City of God* to answer this charge; but the book is no single-track tract. Rather, it is an encyclopedic work that purports to inform the reader not only about earthly matters but also about heaven and hell. One may thus compare it with Plato's *City* (known as *The Republic* in the English-speaking world). The two books differ, however, in that Plato's book is predominantly philosophical and contains only a little theology whereas Augustine's is for the most part theological and contains relatively little philosophy. In the following pages, only two short chapters from *The City of God*, translated by Marcus Dods, are offered: Book XI, Chapter 26, because it is one of several passages in Augustine's writings that more or less anticipate Descartes' celebrated *cogito ergo sum* (I think, therefore I am); and Book XXI, Chapter 12, which suggests at least a little of the over-all theological setting of Augustine's thought. Although this final sample of Augustine's theology comes to little more than one-thirtieth of our total selections from his writings, it has probably been thirty times as influential as his philosophical reflections.

### III

Saint Anselm of Canterbury (1033-1109) is chiefly remembered for an ingenious proof of God's existence that is usually called the ontological argument. Saint Thomas Aquinas did not accept this argument, but it was later taken up in various forms by Descartes, Spinoza, and Leibniz. Eventually, in 1781, Immanuel Kant tried to show in his *Critique of Pure Reason* that all arguments for God's existence are reducible to three, of which the ontological argument is one—and that the other two (to which he would reduce Saint Thomas' five) can be shown to fall back at a crucial point upon the ontological argument (which Thomas rejected). Kant's discussion is included in the companion volume, *Philosophic Classics: Bacon to Kant*.

In spite of Kant, a few later thinkers have returned to Anselm's argument. It has even been claimed that one's response to this proof shows whether one has any flair for metaphysics. Nor is appreciation of Anselm's argument confined to any one school. Philosophers of widely different outlooks have referred to it with great respect and have attempted to defend it.

The selections from *Proslogium* are translated by Sidney Norton Deane.

### IV

Saint Thomas Aquinas (1225-1274) has come to be generally considered the greatest of all the scholastics. An Italian, he studied with Albertus

Magnus, an outstanding German theologian who outlived him. In those days, the philosophy of Aristotle had been newly rediscovered. For centuries, Aristotle had been known chiefly as a logician. Beginning a few years before Aquinas' birth, Aristotle's other works were translated into Latin, some from the original Greek, others from Arabic versions. There was an enormous excitement: a non-Christian world had come into view—an alternative to Christianity. Ten years before the saint's birth, Aristotle's works on metaphysics and on natural philosophy were banned at the University of Paris, where Thomas was to teach later. When Thomas was a little boy, in 1229, the faculty of the University of Toulouse announced lectures on Aristotle, hoping to attract students. In 1245, an attempt was made to extend the prohibition to Toulouse, but, as Father Frederick Copleston, S.J., puts it in his little book on *Aquinas*, "by that date it had become impossible to check the spread of Aristotelianism."

Thomas lived in an age of lively controversy, and though he enjoyed great prestige in his lifetime, he found, being a Dominican, that his arguments met with stubborn resistance among Franciscans, for example. And three years after his death, Robert Kilwardby, the archbishop of Canterbury, himself a Dominican, "followed the example of the bishop of Paris in censuring a number of propositions, which included a few that had been held by Aquinas." In 1323, Aquinas was canonized, and then "the Parisian censures of 1277 were withdrawn, as far as they affected Aquinas" (Copleston).

In 1879, Pope Leo XII commended the study of Aquinas' philosophy in an encyclical, *Aeterni Patris*. This papal proclamation did not *launch* the revival of Thomism, as is often said, but it did lend an enormous impetus to the study of Thomas' writings. The encyclical praises the saint in the highest terms: "as far as man is concerned, reason can now hardly rise higher than she rose, borne up in the flight of Thomas; and Faith can hardly gain more helps from reason than those which Thomas gave her." Leo XIII also cited many previous popes who had spoken of Thomas in a similar vein. "Pius V acknowledges that heresies are confounded and exposed and scattered by his doctrine, and that by it the whole world is daily freed from pestilent errors. . . . The words of Blessed Urban V to the University of Toulouse seem to be most worthy of mention: 'It is our will, and by the authority of these letters we enjoin on you, that you follow the doctrine of Blessed Thomas as true and Catholic, and strive to unfold it with your whole strength.' This example of Urban was followed by Innocent XII . . . and by Benedict XIV. . . ." Leo XIII cites, "as a crown, the testimony of Innocent VI: 'His doctrine above all other doctrine, with the one exception of the Holy Scriptures, has such a propriety of words, such a method of explanation, such a truth of opinions, that no one who holds it will ever be found to have strayed from the path of truth. . . .'" Still, Leo XIII took care not to suggest that all of Thomas' teachings have to be accepted: "We, therefore, while We declare that everything wisely said should be received with willing and glad mind, . . . exhort all of you, Venerable Brothers, with the greatest earnestness to restore the golden wisdom of St. Thomas, and to spread it as far as you can.... We say the wisdom of St. Thomas; for it is not by any means in our mind to set before this age, as a standard, those things which have been inquired into by Scholastic Doctors with too great subtlety; or anything taught by them with too little consideration, not agreeing with the investigations of a later age; or, lastly, anything that is not probable."

In much the same spirit, Etienne Gilson, as respected and renowned a Thomist as the twentieth century has produced, says in the Foreword to *The Christian Philosophy of St. Thomas Aquinas:* "Personally, I do not say of Thomas the he *was* right, but that he *is* right." Gilson does not mean that Thomas was right about everything. Although Thomas wrote detailed commentaries on the works of Aristotle, he read Aristotle in Latin translations, and Gilson admits that, in his *Summa*, Thomas made "Aristotle say so many things he never said," and that he altogether metamorphosed Aristotle's doctrines by ascribing "a new meaning to Aristotle's principles." Gilson also concedes that Thomas used quotations from Augustine to buttress claims that are at variance with Augustine's real views. And it is a commonplace of modern scholarship that Dionysius, whom Aquinas very often cites to prove his point, was not a contemporary of the Blessed Virgin and St. Paul, as Thomas thought, but a Neoplatonist of the fifth century who wrote under the name of the first-century Dionysius. In sum, even Aquinas' greatest devotees do not claim that he was infallible. And large numbers of Catholic philosophers, by no means all of them Franciscans, have no wish whatever to be identified as Thomists.

On the other hand, large numbers of non-Catholics would cheerfully concede that Aquinas was one of the most remarkable thinkers of all time, and that he created a staggering synthesis of the Christian heritage he had received with the philosophy of Aristotle. Two more quotations from Gilson's great *History of Christian Philosophy in the Middle Ages* not only sum up the views of one outstanding historian, but may be safely accepted:

"The doctrine of Thomas Aquinas surprised his contemporaries. He was not a promoter of scientific learning like Albert the Great or Robert Grosseteste. To him the scientific knowledge of nature was in Aristotle, whose doctrine he had learned, commented upon and accepted, on the whole, in logic, physics, astronomy, biology, psychology, metaphysics and ethics" (p. 381). "Thomism was not the upshot of a better understanding of Aristotle. ... Thomas uses the language of Aristotle everywhere to make the Philosopher say that there is only one God the pure Act of Being, Creator of the World, infinite and omnipotent.... Thomas changed the water of philosophy to the wine of theology. Thomas always considered himself a theologian.... In his own view, he was not only a theologian, but a monk who had no right to indulge in philosophical activities except in the spirit of his religious vocation" (p. 365).

His greatest work is, by common consent, the vast *Summa Theologica*. Among his many other writings, his *Summa Contra Gentiles* is probably best known. His complete works in Latin comprise twenty-five volumes; a superior edition, not completed yet, is expected to fill thirty-four. Under these circumstances it is difficult to give a clear idea of his thought in a few pages.

v

The Summa Theologica is divided into so-called Questions. Every question is broached in the same way: first it is posed; then an answer is offered which Thomas considers false; then this answer is buttressed with a few quotations that appear to support it; and next, we are confronted with a quotation that seems to contradict the stand defended so far. A dramatic tension is created, reminiscent of the disputatious climate of opinion in which Thomas wrote. It is resolved by the author's concise and straightforward *Respondeo*, or "I reply," which introduces his own view. He agrees with the immediately preceding quotation, gives his reasons, and then replies, one by one, to the objections raised before he stated his position. In this manner, every question is answered—no matter what its nature; for example, there are a vast number of questions about angels, including such fine points as whether an inferior angel can address a superior one, or, in the book on *Truth*, which is generally regarded as exceptionally important, "Whether one angel can speak to another in such a way that others will not know what he is saying?" In the *Summa* itself, the proverbial question, how many angels can dance on the head of a needle, is asked in this form: "Whether several angels can be at the same time in the same place?" Other questions, treated in the same manner, may strike twentieth-century readers as even stranger; for example, whether the semen in man is produced from surplus food?

Although it is well to keep in mind that comparable passages are found in Plato, there are also two differences. In Plato we find mostly philosophy, but also some material of this kind; in Thomas, the proportion is almost reversed, and one has to look for philosophic passages. Second, Plato generally offers matter of this sort in the form of frankly avowed myths, or says outright that the ideas presented are only probable; he neither cites nor claims authority, but offers, at most, his own view and often not even that. He writes dialogues, leaving the reader to decide what Plato's own conclusions might be. Plato is unsystematic and invites us to join a process of reflection and inquiry. In the *Summa* and the book on *Truth*, which is organized in the same way, the air is altogether different: the avowed purpose is to answer every question.

The following selections concentrate on matters of philosophic interest. From *Summa*, I, the second question, on "The Existence of God," is offered in its entirety. It contains the celebrated "five ways" of demonstrating God's existence. From Question 16, "On Truth," two Articles are offered. Concerning God and his relation to man, few questions are asked as frequently, and genuinely bother so many people as persistently, as the three from which selections are offered next: "Predestination," and quite especially "Whether God reprobates any man?" "The Power of God," and particularly "Whether

God can do what he does not?" and "Whether God can do better than what he does?" "The Cause of Evil," and above all, "Whether the Supreme Good, God, is the cause of evil?"

From *Summa*, I-II, five Articles are offered from four Questions. The first concerns the old Socratic quandary "Whether ignorance causes involuntariness?" The second has a distinctly modern ring, as if it came from Oxford around the middle of the twentieth century: "Whether one can intend two things at the same time?" The third harks back to Aristotle and to Plato: "Whether there are four cardinal virtues?" And the last two deal with the natural law, which is once again the focal point of much modern discussion.

Our selections from Aquinas conclude with the complete text of his treatise *On the Principles of Nature*, translated by Vernon J. Bourke. The bulk of his writings is theological or exegetical; *De principiis naturae* is a philosophical essay and was written in Paris between 1252 and 1256, like the better known treatise *On Being and Essence* (*De ente et essentia*). It proved to be impossible to get permission to reprint a good translation of that essay; I am doubly grateful to the publishers of *On the Principles of Nature*.

VI

William of Ockham was born in Ockham, in Surrey, near London, between 1280 and 1290, and died in 1349, probably of the Black Plague. He studied at Oxford, where Duns Scotus had taught around 1300; but in 1302 Scotus had gone to Paris, and in 1307 to Cologne, where he had died in 1308; and Ockham came to Oxford only in 1309 or 1310. Even so, Ockham studied Scotus very closely and was far closer to him, philosophically, than he was to Aquinas.

Accused of having upheld dangerous and heretical doctrines, Ockham was summoned to Avignon in 1324 by Pope John XXII. The affair dragged on; in 1326 a commission of theologians submitted two lists of suspect doctrines from his writings; but apparently no final action was ever taken. Meanwhile Ockham kept writing and gradually became involved in a dispute about apostolic poverty in which he sided with the general of the Franciscan order to which he belonged, against the pope.

In 1328 Ockham fled from Avignon as it became clear that the pope was about to condemn the rival position officially, and he found refuge in Munich under the protection of emperor Louis IV, who had just engineered the election of an antipope, Nicholas V, who after separating from his wife had joined the Franciscans and gained a name as a preacher. Pope John had refused to recognize Louis' title to the empire; the antipope had crowned him; and the pope excommunicated the antipope in 1329. Assured of pardon, Nicholas confessed his sins to the pope at Avignon, and died in honorable imprisonment in the papal palace there in 1333.

Ockham, too, was excommunicated along with the companions of his flight from Avignon. Until the death of the emperor in 1347, Ockham was one of the intellectual leaders of the fight against the Avignon popes (John died in 1334, and his successor in 1342), and in *An Encyclopaedia of World History* (1940, edited by Professor William Langer of Harvard) it is said that Ockham, "defending the imperial position, gave wide currency to pre-Reformation ideas." But with Louis' death the antipapal position collapsed, and in the words of Father Philotheus Boehner, whose translations of Ockham have been used in the following pages, "Ockham's situation became hopeless. There is good evidence that he sought a reconciliation with the Pope. . . ." He sent back the seal of the Franciscan order, of which he had taken possession when the general of the order had died in 1342, and a document of submission was drawn up.

Father Boehner emphasizes that the document "does not mention any errors of Ockham in his teachings on theology and philosophy during his first period in Oxford. Thus ended the career of one who was a brilliant philosopher, a great theologian, and too modern a politician. Ockham died soon after the formula of submission was drawn up. Whether he signed it or not, we do not know."

Philosophically, Ockham is best known for a statement he never appears to have made: *entia non sunt multiplicanda sine necessitate*, entities are not to be multiplied without necessity. This principle is widely referred to as "Ockham's Razor." In fact he said much the same thing in different words: *pluralitas non est ponenda sine necessitate*, plurality is not to be posited without necessity. And he also said, less often: *frustra fit per plura quod potest fieri per pauciora*, which Father Boehner translates, "What can be explained by the assumption of fewer things is vainly explained by the assumption of more things," while Ernest A. Moody renders it, "What can be done with fewer [assumptions] is done in vain with more" (article on Ockham in *Encyclopaedia of Philosophy*). Applying the principle to its own formulation, I should prefer a version that captured something of its terseness: "Why use many if few will do?"

Alas—and this sort of discovery is typical in the history of ideas—Ockham was not the first to enunciate this principle. Not only is the same idea to be found in the writings of Duns Scotus, but a still earlier Franciscan scholastic, Odo Rigaldus, who died about 1275, had said, *frustra fit per plura quod potest fieri per unum*, or "Why use many if one will do?" (See Boehner's edition, p. xx.) It does not follow, of course, that his predecessors wielded this razor with the skill that earned Ockham his fame as a brilliant philosopher; nor should Ockham be remembered only for his razor.

Ernest A. Moody calls him "the most influential philosopher of the fourteenth century," and Gilson explains that "Ockham denies that theology is a science. . . . Of the rational understanding of faith attempted by Bonaventure, Albert the Great, Thomas Aquinas and their contemporaries, very little, if anything, was left after Ockham. This is the reason why we described Ockhamism as marking the end of the golden age of scholasticism . . . In theology his doctrine was paving the way to the 'positive theology' of the moderns. In philosophy, it was paving the way to modern empiricism." (*History of Christian Philosophy in the Middle Ages*, 1954, 498 f.)

One might add that his denial of the existence of universals led to the spread of so-called nominalism. But it is time to let Ockham himself speak. Our selections come from Philotheus Boehner's translation of Ockham's *Philosophical Writings*. The first three pieces on the problem of universals come from Ockham's *Summa totius logicae*, I, C. xiv, xv, and xvi; the next two from *Ordinatio*, D. II, Q. viii, *prima redactio* and from *Expositio super librum Perihermenias*; and the last one from *Summa totius logicae*, II. C. ii. The two pieces on being, essence, and existence, are taken from *Summa totius logicae*, I, C. xxxviii, and III, II, C. xxvii. The final item, about God, is from *Quodlibeta*, I, Q. i.

This volume begins and ends with snippets rather than classics. But the pre-Socratics are represented in this manner because no complete works by them have survived, and all we have are brief quotations in later writers. The scholastic philosophers, on the other hand, wrote large works that have come down to us intact, but only short passages here and there are of considerable philosophical interest and have been translated.

In his "Bibliographical Note," Father Boehner distinguishes writings on logic, physics, and theology. Of the seven items in the first category, the *Summa totius logicae* from which most of our selections are taken, is much the most important, four of the others being exegeses—three of them, including the *Expositio* from which our fifth piece comes, of Aristotle, and the fourth an explanation of Porphyry's *Introduction* to Aristotle's *Categories*. The three works on physics are characterized by Father Boehner as, respectively, "An explanation of Aristotle's *Physics*," "A summary of Aristotelian physics," and "Questions on Aristotle's *Physics*."

Two of our pieces come from two of the "works on theology." The *Ordinatio* is "the first book of Ockham's commentary on the first book of the *Sentences* of Peter Lombard," and the *Quodlibeta* "contain discussions 'on anything and everything' (*quodlibet*)." Such discussions were held twice a year, and "on those occasions there was little restriction on the nature of the questions which could be asked, though it was required that they should be discussed in the form of the scholastic disputation."

I have made no omissions in the pieces selected by Father Boehner, except for the first few lines of the first piece. Otherwise, each item is taken unabridged from his edition of Ockham's *Philosophical Writings*.

# AUGUSTINE

## A. CONFESSIONS

### Book XI. The Discussion of Time

#### Chapter XII. What God Did Before the Creation of the World

Behold, I answer to him who asks, "What was God doing before He made heaven and earth?" I answer not, as a certain person is reported to have done facetiously (avoiding the pressure of the question), "He was preparing hell," said he, "for those who pry into mysteries." It is one thing to perceive, another to laugh—these things I answer not. For more willingly would I have answered, "I know not what I know not," than that I should make him a laughing-stock who asks deep things, and gain praise as one who answers false things. But I say that Thou, our God, art the Creator of every creature; and if by the term "heaven and earth" every creature is understood. I boldly say that before God made heaven and earth, He made not anything. For if He did, what did He make unless the creature? And would that I knew whatever I desire to know to my advantage, as I know that no creature was made before any creature was made.

#### Chapter XIII. Before the Times Created by God, Times Were Not

But if the roving thought of any one should wander through the images of bygone time, and wonder that Thou, the God Almighty, and All-creating, and All-sustaining, the Architect of heaven and earth, didst for innumerable ages refrain from so great a work before Thou wouldst make it, let him awake and consider that he wonders at false things. For whence could innumerable ages pass by which Thou didst not make, since Thou art the Author and Creator of all ages? Or what times should those be which were not made by Thee? Or how should they pass by if they had not been? Since, therefore, Thou art the Creator of all times, if any time was before Thou madest heaven and earth, why is it said Thou didst refrain from working? For that very time Thou madest, nor could times pass by before Thou madest times. But if before heaven and earth there was no time, why is it asked, What didst Thou then? For there was no "then" when time was not.

Nor dost Thou by time precede time; else wouldest not Thou precede all times. But in the excellency of an ever-present eternity, Thou precedest all times past, and survivest all future times, because they are future, and when they have come they will be past; but Thou art the same, and Thy years shall have no end. Thy years neither go nor come; but ours both go and come, that all may come. All Thy years stand at once since they do stand; nor were they when departing excluded by coming years, because they pass not away; but all these of ours shall be when all shall cease to be. Thy years are one day, and Thy day is not daily, but to-day; because Thy to-day yields not with to-morrow, for neither doth it follow yesterday. Thy to-day is eternity; therefore didst Thou beget the Coeternal, to whom Thou saidst, "This day have I begotten Thee." Thou hast made all time; and before all times Thou art, nor in any time was there not time.

## Chapter XIV.  Neither Time Past nor Future, but the Present Only, Really Is

At no time, therefore, hadst Thou not made anything, because Thou hadst made time itself. And no times are co-eternal with Thee, because Thou remainest for ever; but should these continue, they would not be times. For what is time? Who can easily and briefly explain it? Who even in thought can comprehend it, even to the pronouncing of a word concerning it? But what

in speaking do we refer to more familiarly and knowingly than time? And certainly we understand when we speak of it; we understand also when we hear it spoken of by another. What, then, is time? If no one ask of me, I know; if I wish to explain to him who asks, I know not. Yet I say with confidence, that I know that if nothing passed away, there would not be past time; and if nothing were coming, there would not be future time; and if nothing were, there would not be present time. Those two times, therefore, past and future how are they, when even the past now is not, and the future is not as yet? But should the present be always present, and should it not pass into time past, truly it could not be time, but eternity. If, then, time present—if it be time— only comes into existence because it passes into time past, how do we say that even this is, whose cause of being is that it shall not be—namely, so that we cannot truly say that time is, unless because it tends not to be?

## Chapter XV.  There Is Only a Moment of Present Time

And yet we say that time is long and time is short; nor do we speak of this save of time past and future. A long time past, for example, we call a hundred years ago; in like manner a long time to come, a hundred years hence. But a short time past we call, say, ten days ago: and a short time to come, ten days hence. But in what sense is that long or short which is not? For the past is not now, and the future is not yet. Therefore let us not say, "It is long"; but let us say of the past, "It has been long," and of the future, "It will be long." O my Lord, my light, shall not even here Thy truth deride man? For that past time which was long, was it long when it was already past, or when it was as yet present? For then it might be long when there was that which could be long, but when past it no longer was; wherefore that could not be long which was not at all. Let us not, therefore, say, "Time past has been long"; for we shall not find what may have been long, seeing that since it was past it is not; but let us say that present time was long, because when it was present it was long. For it had not as yet passed away so as not to be, and therefore there was that which could be long. But after it passed, that ceased also to be long which ceased to be.

Let us therefore see, O human soul, whether present time can be long; for to thee is it given to perceive and to measure periods of time. What wilt thou reply to me? Is a hundred years when present a long time? See, first, whether a hundred years can be present. For if the first year of these is current, that is present, but the other ninety and nine are future, and therefore they are not as yet. But if the second year is current, one is already past, the other present, the rest future. And thus, if we fix on any middle year of this hundred as present, those before it are past, those after it are future; wherefore a hundred years cannot be present. See at least whether that year itself which is current can be present. For if its first month be current, the rest are future; if the second, the first has already passed, and the remainder are not yet. Therefore neither is the year which is current as a whole present; and if it is not present as a whole, then the year is not present. For twelve months make the year, of which each individual month which is current is itself present, but the rest are either past or future. Although neither is that month which is current present, but one day only: if the first, the rest being to come, if the last, the rest being past; if any of the middle, then between past and future.

Behold, the present time, which alone we found could be called long, is abridged to the space scarcely of one day. But let us discuss even that, for there is not one day present as a whole.

For it is made up of four-and-twenty hours of night and day, of which the first has the rest future, the last has them past, but any one of the intervening has those before it past, those after it future. And that one hour passes away in fleeting particles. Whatever of it has flown away is past, whatever remains is future. If any portion of time be conceived which cannot now be divided into even the minutest particles of moments, this only is that which may be called present; which, however, flies so rapidly from future to past, that it cannot be extended by any delay. For if it be extended, it is divided into the past and future; but the present has no space. Where, therefore, is the time which we may call long? Is it future? Indeed we do not say, "It is long," because it is not yet, so as to be long; but we say, "It will be long." When, then, will it be? For if even then, since as yet it is future, it will not be long, because what may be long is not as yet; but it shall be long, when from the future, which as yet is not, it shall already have begun to be, and will have become present, so that there could be that which may be long; then does the present time cry out in the words above that it cannot be long.

## Chapter XVI.  Time Can Only Be Perceived or Measured While It Is Passing

And yet, O Lord, we perceive intervals of times, and we compare them with themselves, and we say some are longer, others shorter. We even measure by how much shorter or longer this time may be than that; and we answer That this is double or treble, while that is but once, or only as much as that. But we measure times passing when we measure them by perceiving them; but past times, which now are not, or future times, which as yet are not, who can measure them? Unless, perchance, any one will dare to say, that that can be measured which is not. When, therefore, time is passing, it can be perceived and measured; but when it has passed, it cannot, since it is not.

## Chapter XVII.  Nevertheless There Is Time Past and Future

I ask, Father, I do not affirm. O my God, rule and guide me. Who is there who can say to me that there are not three times (as we learned when boys, and as we have taught boys), the past, present, and future, but only present, because these two are not? Or are they also; but when from future it becomes present, comes it forth from some secret place, and when from the present it becomes past, does it retire into anything secret? For where have they, who have foretold future things, seen these things, if as yet they are not? For that which is not cannot be seen. And they who relate things past could not relate them as true, did they not perceive them in their mind. Which things, if they were not, they could in no wise be discerned. There are therefore things both future and past.

## Chapter XVIII.  Past and Future Times Cannot Be Thought of but as Present

Suffer me, O Lord, to seek further; O my Hope, let not my purpose be confounded. For if there are times past and future, I desire to know where they are. But if as yet I do not succeed, I still know, wherever they are, that they are not there as future or past, but as present. For if there also they be future, they are not as yet there; if even there they be past, they are no longer there. Wheresoever, therefore, they are, whatsoever they are, they are only so as present. Although past things are related as true, they are drawn out from the memory—not the things themselves, which have passed, but the words conceived from the images of the things which they have formed in the mind as footprints in their passage through the senses. My childhood, indeed, which no

longer is, is in the time past, which now is not; but when I call to mind its image, and speak of it, I behold it in the present, because it is as yet in my memory. Whether there be a like cause of foretelling future things, that of things which as yet are not the images may be perceived as already existing, I confess, my God, I know not. This certainly I know, that we generally think before on our future actions, and that this premeditation is present; but that the action on which we premeditate is not yet, because it is future; which when we shall have entered upon, and have begun to do that which we were premeditating, then shall that action be, because then it is not future, but present.

In whatever manner, therefore, this secret preconception of future things may be, nothing can be seen, save what is. But what now is is not future, but present. When, therefore, they say that things future are seen, it is not themselves, which as yet are not (that is, which are future); but their causes or their signs perhaps are seen, which already are. Therefore, to those already beholding them, they are not future, but present, from which future things conceived in the mind are foretold. These conceptions again now are, and they who foretell those things behold these conceptions present before them. Let now so multitudinous a variety of things afford me some example. I behold daybreak; I foretell that the sun is about to rise. That which I behold is present; what I foretell is future—not that the sun is future, which already is; but his rising, which is not yet. Yet even its rising I could not predict unless I had an image of it in my mind, as now I have while I speak. But that dawn which I see in the sky is not the rising of the sun, although it may go before it, nor that imagination in my mind; which two are seen as present, that the other which is future may be foretold. Future things, therefore, are not as yet; and if they are not as yet, they are not. And if they are not, they cannot be seen at all; but they can be foretold from things present which now are, and are seen.

## Chapter XIX. We Are Ignorant in What Manner God Teaches Future Things

Thou, therefore, Ruler of Thy creatures, what is the method by which Thou teachest souls those things which are future? For Thou hast taught Thy prophets. What is that way by which Thou, to whom nothing is future, dost teach future things; or rather of future things dost teach present? For what is not, of a certainty cannot be taught. Too far is this way from my view; it is too mighty for me, I cannot attain unto it; but by Thee I shall be enabled, when Thou shalt have granted it, sweet light of my hidden eyes.

## Chapter XX. In What Manner Time May Properly Be Designated

But what now is manifest and clear is, that neither are there future nor past things. Nor is it fitly said, "There are three times, past, present and future"; but perchance it might be fitly said, "There are three times; a present of things past, a present of things present, and a present of things future." For these three do somehow exist in the soul, and otherwise I see them not: present of things past, memory; present of things present, sight; present of things future, expectation. If of these things we are permitted to speak, I see three times, and I grant there are three. It may also be said, "'There are three times, past, present and future," as usage falsely has it. See, I trouble not, nor gainsay, nor reprove; provided always that which is said may be understood, that neither the future, nor that which is past, now is. For there are but few things which we speak properly, many things improperly; but what we may wish to say is understood.

## Chapter XXI. How Time May Be Measured

I have just now said, then, that we measure times as they pass, that we may be able to say that this time is twice as much as that one, or that this is only as much as that, and so of any other of the parts of time which we are able to tell by measuring. Wherefore, as I said, we measure times as they pass. And if any one should ask me, "Whence dost thou know?" I can answer, "I know, because we measure; nor can we measure things that are not; and things past and future are not." But how do we measure present time, since it has not space? It is measured while it passes; but when it shall have passed, it is not measured; for there will not be aught that can be measured. But whence, in what way, and whither does it pass while it is being measured? Whence, but from the future? Which way, save through the present? Whither, but into the past? From that, therefore, which as yet is not, though that which has no space, into that which now is not. But what do we measure, unless time in some space? For we say not single, and double, and triple, and equal, or in any other way in which we speak of time, unless with respect to the spaces of times. In what space, then, do we measure passing time? Is it in the future, whence it passes over? But what yet we measure not, is not. Or is it in the present, by which it passes? But no space we do not measure. Or in the past, whither it passes? But that which is not now, we measure not.

## Chapter XXII. He Prays God That He Would Explain This Most Entangled Enigma

My soul yearns to know this most entangled enigma. Forbear to shut up, O Lord my God, good Father—through Christ I beseech Thee—forbear to shut up these things, both usual and hidden, from my desire, that it may be hindered from penetrating them; but let them dawn through Thy enlightening mercy, O Lord. Of whom shall I inquire concerning these things? And to whom shall I with more advantage confess my ignorance than to Thee to whom these my studies, so vehemently kindled towards Thy Scriptures, are not troublesome? Give that which I love; for I do love, and this hast Thou given me. Give, Father, who truly knowest to give good gifts unto Thy children. Give, since I have undertaken to know, and trouble is before me until Thou dost open it. Through Christ, I beseech Thee, in His name, Holy of Holies, let no man interrupt me. For I believed, and therefore do I speak. This is my hope; for this do I live, that I may contemplate the delights of the Lord. Behold, Thou hast made my days old, and they pass away, and in what manner I know not. And we speak as to time and time, times and times—"How long is the time since he said this?" "How long the time since he did this?" and, "How long the time since I saw that?" and, "This syllable has double the time of that single short syllable." These words we speak, and these we hear; and we are understood, and we understand. They are most manifest and most usual, and the same things again lie hid too deeply, and the discovery of them is new.

## Chapter XXIII.  That Time Is a Certain Extension

I have heard from a learned man that the motions of the sun, moon, and stars constituted time, and I assented not. For why should not rather the motions of all bodies be time? What if the lights of heaven should cease, and a potter's wheel run round, would there be no time by which we might measure those revolutions, and say either that it turned with equal pauses, or, if it were moved,

at one time more slowly, at another more quickly, that some revolutions were longer, others less so? Or while we were saying this, should we not also be speaking in time? Or should there in our words be some syllables long, others short, but because those sounded in a longer time, these in a shorter? God grant to men to see in a small thing ideas common to things great and small. Both the stars and luminaries of heaven are for signs and for seasons, and for days and years. No doubt they are; but neither should I say that the circuit of that wooden wheel was a day, nor yet should he say that therefore there was no time.

I desire to know the power and nature of time, by which we measure the motions of bodies, and say (for example) that this motion is twice as long as that. For, I ask, since "day" declares not the stay only of the sun upon the earth, according to which day is one thing, night another, but also its entire circuit from east even to east—according to which we say, "So many days have passed" the nights being included when we say "so many days," and their spaces not counted apart)—since, then, the day is finished by the motion of the sun, and by his circuit from east to east, I ask, whether the motion itself is the day, or the period in which that motion is completed, or both? For if the first be the day, then would there be a day although the sun should finish that course in so small a space of time as an hour. If the second, then that would not be a day if from one sunrise to another there were but so short a period as an hour, but the sun must go round four-and-twenty times to complete a day. If both, neither could that be called a day if the sun should run his entire round in the space of an hour; nor that, if, while the sun stood still, so much time should pass as the sun is accustomed to accomplish his whole course in from morning to morning. I shall not therefore now ask, what that is which is called day, but what time is, by which we, measuring the circuit of the sun, should say that it was accomplished in half the space of time it was wont, if it had been completed in so small a space as twelve hours; and comparing both times, we should call that single, this double time, although the sun should run his course from east to east sometimes in that single, sometimes in that double time. Let no man then tell me that the motions of the heavenly bodies are times, because, when at the prayer of one the sun stood still in order that he might achieve his victorious battle, the sun stood still, but time went on. For in such space of time as was sufficient was that battle fought and ended. I see that time, then, is a certain extension. But I do see it, or do I seem to see it? Thou, O Light and Truth, wilt show me.

## Chapter XXIV.  That Time Is Not a Motion of a Body Which We Measure by Time

Dost Thou command that I should assent, if any one should say that time is the motion of a body? Thou dost not command me. For I hear that no body is moved but in time. This Thou sayest; but that the very motion of a body is time, I hear not; Thou sayest it not. For when a body is moved, I by time measure how long it may be moving from the time in which it began to be moved till it left off. And if I saw not whence it began, and it continued to be moved, so that I see not when it leaves off, I cannot measure unless, perchance, from the time I began until I cease to see. But if I look long enough, I only proclaim that the time is long, but not how long it may be; because when we say, "How long," we speak by comparison, as, "This is as long as that," or, "This is double as long as that," or any other thing of the kind. But if we were able to note

down the distances of places whence and whither comes the body which is moved, or its parts, if it moved as in a wheel, we can say in how much time the motion of the body or its part, from this place to that, was performed. Since, then, the motion of a body is one thing, that by which we measure how long it is another, who cannot see which of these is rather to be called time? For, although a body be sometimes moved, sometimes stand still, we measure not its motion only, but also its standing still, by time; and we say, "It stood still as much as it moved"; or, "It stood still twice or thrice as long as it moved"; and if any other space which our measuring has either determined or imagined, more or less, as we are accustomed to say. Time, therefore, is not the motion of a body.

## Chapter XXV. He Calls on God to Enlighten His Mind

And I confess unto Thee, O Lord, that I am as yet ignorant as to what time is, and again I confess unto Thee, O Lord, that I know that I speak these things in time, and that I have already long spoken of time, and that very "long" is not long save by the stay of time. How, then, know I this, when I know not what time is? Or is it, perchance, that I know not in what wise I may express what I know? Alas for me, that I do not at least know the extent of my own ignorance! Behold, O my God, before Thee I lie not. As I speak, so is my heart. Thou shalt light my candle; Thou, O Lord my God, wilt enlighten my darkness.

## Chapter XXVI. We Measure Longer Events by Shorter in Time

Doth not my soul pour out unto Thee truly in confession that I do measure times? But do I thus measure, O my God, and know not what I measure? I measure the motion of a body by time; and the time itself do I not measure? But, in truth, could I measure the motion of a body, how long it is, and how long it is in coming from this place to that, unless I should measure the time in which it is moved? How, therefore, do I measure this very time itself? Or do we by a shorter time measure a longer, as by the space of a cubit the space of a crossbeam? For thus, indeed, we seem by the space of a short syllable to measure the space of a long syllable, and to say that this is double. Thus we measure the space of stanzas by the spaces of the verse, and the spaces of the verses by the spaces of the feet, and the spaces of the feet by the spaces of the syllables, and the spaces of long by the spaces of short syllables; not measuring by pages (for in that manner we measure spaces, not times), but when in uttering the words they pass by, and we say, "It is a long stanza because it is made up of so many verses; long verses, because they consist of so many feet; long feet, because they are prolonged by so many syllables; a long syllable, because double a short one." But neither thus is any certain measure of time obtained; since it is possible that a shorter verse, if it be pronounced more fully, may take up more time than a longer one, if pronounced more hurriedly. Thus for a stanza, thus for a foot, thus for a syllable. Whence it appeared to me that time is nothing else than extension; but of what I know not. It is wonderful to me, if it be not of the mind itself. For what do I measure, I beseech Thee, O my God, even when I say either indefinitely, "This time is longer than that"; or even definitely, "This is double that"? That I measure time, I know. But I measure not the future, for it is not yet; nor do I measure the present, because it is extended by no space; nor do I measure the past, because it no longer is. What, therefore, do I measure? Is it times passing, not past? For thus had I said.

## Chapter XXVII. Times Are Measured in Proportion as They Pass By

Persevere, O my mind, and give earnest heed. God is our helper; He made us, and not we ourselves. Give heed, where truth dawns. Lo, suppose the voice of a body begins to sound, and does sound, and sounds on, and lo! it ceases —it is now silence, and that voice is past and is no longer a voice. It was future before it sounded, and could not be measured, because as yet it was not; and now it cannot, because it no longer is. Then, therefore, while it was sounding, it might, because there was then that which might be measured. But even then it did not stand still, for it was going and passing away. Could it, then, on that account be measured the more? For, while passing, it was being extended into some space of time, in which it might be measured, since the present has no space. If, therefore, then it might be measured, lo! suppose another voice has begun to sound, and still sounds, in a continued tenor without any interruption, we can measure it while it is sounding; for when it shall have ceased to sound, it will be already past, and there will not be that which can be measured. Let us measure it truly, and let us say how much it is. But as yet is sounds, nor can it be measured, save from that instant in which it began to sound, even to the end in which it left off. For the interval itself we measure from some beginning to some end. On which account, a voice which is not yet ended cannot be measured, so that it may be said how long or how short it may be; nor can it be said to be equal to another, or single or double in respect of it, or the like. But when it is ended, it no longer is. In what manner, therefore, may it be measured? And yet we measure times; still not those which as yet are not, nor those which no longer are, nor those which are protracted by some delay, nor those which have no limits. We, therefore, measure neither future times, nor past, nor present, nor those passing by; and yet we do measure times.

*Deus Creator omnium*; this verse of eight syllables alternates between short and long syllables. The four short, then, the first, third, fifth and seventh, are single in respect of the four long, the second, fourth, sixth, and eighth. Each of these has a double time to every one of those. I pronounce them, report on them, and thus it is, as is perceived by common sense. By common sense, then, I measure a long by a short syllable, and I find that it has twice as much. But when one sounds after another, if the former be short the latter long, how shall I hold the short one, and how measuring shall I apply it to the long, so that I may find out that this has twice as much, when indeed the long does not begin to sound unless the short leaves off sounding? That very long one I measure not as present, since I measure it not save when ended. But its ending is its passing away. What, then, is it that I can measure? Where is the short syllable by which I measure? Where is the long one which I measure? Both have sounded, have flown, have passed away, and are no longer; and still I measure, and I confidently answer (so far as is trusted to a practised sense), that as to space of time this syllable is single, that double. Nor could I do this, unless because they have past, and are ended. Therefore do I not measure themselves, which now are not, but something in my memory, which remains fixed.

In Thee, O my mind, I measure times. Do not overwhelm me with thy clamor. That is, do not overwhelm thyself with the multitude of thy impressions. In thee, I say, I measure times; the impression which things as they pass by make on Thee, and which, when they have passed by, remains, that I measure as time present, not those things which have passed by, that the impression should be made. This I measure when I measure times. Either, then, these are times, or I do not measure times. What when we measure silence, and say that this silence has lasted as long as that voice lasts? Do we not extend our thought to the measure of a voice, as if it sounded, so that we may be able to declare something concerning the intervals of silence in a given space of time? For when both the voice and tongue are still, we go over in thought poems and verses, and any discourse, or dimensions of motions; and declare concerning the spaces of times, how much this may be in respect of that, not otherwise than if uttering them we should pronounce them. Should any one wish to utter a lengthened sound, and had with forethought determined how long it should be, that man has in silence surely gone through a space of time, and, committing it to memory, he begins to utter that speech, which sounds until it be extended to the end proposed; truly it has sounded, and will sound. For what of it is already finished has surely sounded, but what remains will sound; and thus does it pass on, until the present intention carry over the future into the past; the past increasing by the diminution of the future, until, by the consumption of the future, all be past.

## Chapter XXVIII. Time in the Human Mind, Which Expects, Considers, and Remembers

But how is that future diminished or consumed which as yet is not? Or how does the past, which is no longer, increase, unless in the mind which enacts this there are three things done? For it both expects, and considers, and remembers, that that which it expects, through that which it considers may pass into that which it remembers. Who, therefore, denies that future things as yet are not? But yet there is already in the mind the expectation of things future. And who denies that past things are now no longer? But, however, there is still in the mind the memory of things past. And who denies that time present wants space, because it passes away in a moment? But yet our consideration endures, through which that which may be present may proceed to become absent. Future time, which is not, is not therefore long; but a "long future" is "a long expectation of the future." Nor is time past, which is now no longer, long; but a long past is "a long memory of the past."

I am about to repeat a psalm that I know. Before I begin, my attention is extended to the whole; but when I have begun, as much of it as becomes past by my saying it is extended in my memory; and the life of this action of mine is extended both ways between my memory, on account of what I have repeated, and my expectation, on account of what I am about to repeat; yet my consideration is present with me, through which that which was future may be carried over so that it may become past. The more this is done and repeated, by so much (expectation being shortened) the memory is enlarged, until the whole expectation be exhausted, when that whole action being ended shall have passed into memory. And what takes place in the entire psalm, takes place also in each individual part of it, and in each individual syllable: this holds in the longer action, of which that psalm is perchance a portion; the same holds in the whole life of man, of which all the actions of man are parts; the same holds in the whole age of the sons of men, of which all the lives of men are parts.

## Chapter XXIX. That Human Life Is a Distraction, but that Through the Mercy of God He Was Intent on the Prize of His Heavenly Calling

But because Thy loving-kindness is better than life, behold, my life is but a distraction, and Thy right hand upheld me in my Lord, the Son of man, the Mediator between Thee, The One, and us the many—in many distractions amid many things—that through Him I may apprehend in whom I have been apprehended, and may be re-collected from my old days, following The One, forgetting the things that are past; and not distracted, but drawn on, not to those things which shall be and shall pass away, but to those things which are before, not distractedly, but intently, I follow on for the prize of my heavenly calling, where I may hear the voice of Thy praise, and contemplate Thy delights, neither coming nor passing away. But now are my years spent in mourning. And Thou, O Lord, art my comfort, my Father everlasting. But I have been divided amid times, the order of which I know not; and my thoughts, even the inmost bowels of my soul, are mangled with tumultuous varieties, until I flow together unto Thee, purged and molten in the fire of Thy love.

## Chapter XXX. Again He Refutes the Empty Question, "What Did God Before the Creation of the World?"

And I will be immovable, and fixed in Thee, in my mould, Thy truth; nor will I endure the questions of men, who by a penal disease thirst for more than they can hold, and say, "What did God make before He made heaven and earth?" Or, "How came it into His mind to make anything when He never before made anything?" Grant to them, O Lord, to think well what they say, and to see that where there is no time, they cannot say "never." What, therefore, He is said "never to have made," what else is it but to say, that in no time was it made? Let them therefore see that there could be no time without a created being, and let them cease to speak that vanity. Let them also be extended unto those things which are before, and understand that thou, the eternal Creator of all times, art before all times, and that no times are co-eternal with Thee, nor any creature, even if there be any creature beyond all times.

## Chapter XXXI. How the Knowledge of God Differs from That of Man

O Lord my God, what is that secret place of Thy mystery, and how far thence have the consequence of my transgressions cast me? Heal my eyes, that I may enjoy Thy light. Surely, if there be a mind, so greatly abounding in knowledge and foreknowledge, to which all things past and future are so known as one psalm is well known to me, that mind is exceedingly wonderful, and very astonishing; because whatever is so past, and whatever is to come of after ages, is no more concealed from Him than was it hidden from me when singing that psalm, what and how much of it had been sung from the beginning, what and how much remained unto the end. But far be it that Thou, the Creator of the universe, the Creator of souls and bodies —far be it that Thou shouldest know all things future and past. Far, far more wonderfully, and far more mysteriously, Thou knowest them. For it is not as the feelings of one singing known things, or hearing a known song, are—through expectation of future words, and in remembrance of those that are past— varied, and his senses divided, that anything happeneth unto Thee, unchangeably eternal, that is, the truly eternal Creator of minds. As, then, Thou in the Beginning knewest the heaven and the earth without any change of Thy knowledge, so in the Beginning didst Thou make heaven and earth without any distraction of Thy action. Let him who understandeth confess unto Thee; and let him who understandeth not, confess unto Thee. Oh, how exalted art Thou, and yet the humble in heart are Thy dwelling-place; for Thou raisest up those that are bowed down, and they whose exaltation Thou art fall not.

# B. THE CITY OF GOD

## Book XI

### Chapter XXVI. Of the Image of the Supreme Trinity, Which We Find in Some Sort in Human Nature Even in Its Present State

And we indeed recognize in ourselves the image of God, that is, of the supreme Trinity, an image which, though it be not equal to God, or rather, though it be very far removed from Him—being neither co-eternal, nor, to say all in a word, consubstantial with Him—is yet nearer to Him in nature than any other of His works, and is destined to be yet restored, that it may bear a still closer resemblance. For we both are, and know that we are, and delight in our being, and our knowledge of it. Moreover, in these three things no true-seeming illusion disturbs us; for we do not come into contact with these by some bodily sense, as we perceive the things outside of us—colors, e.g., by seeing, sounds by hearing, smells by smelling, tastes by tasting, hard and soft objects by touching—of all which sensible objects it is the images resembling them, but not themselves which we perceive in the mind and hold in the memory, and which excite us to desire the objects. But, without any delusive representation of images or phantasms, I am most certain that I am, and that I know and delight in this. In respect of these truths, I am not at all afraid of the arguments of the Academicians, who say, What if you are deceived? For if I am deceived, I am. For he who is not, cannot be deceived; and if I am deceived, by this same token I am. And since I am if I am deceived, how am I deceived in believing that I am? for it is certain that I am if I am deceived. Since, therefore, I, the person deceived, should be, even if I were deceived, certainly I am not deceived in this knowledge that I am. And, consequently, neither am I deceived in knowing that I know. For, as I know that I am, so I know this also, that I know. And when I love these two things, I add to them a certain third thing, namely, my love, which is of equal moment. For neither am I deceived in this, that I love, since in those things which I love I am not deceived; though even if these were false, it would still be true that I *loved* false things. For how could I justly be blamed and prohibited from loving false things, if it were false that I loved them? But, since they are true and real, who doubts that when they are loved, the love of them is itself true and real? Further, as there is no one who does not wish to be happy, so there is no one who does not wish to be. For how can he be happy, if he is nothing?

## Book XXI

### Chapter XII. Of the Greatness of the First Transgression, on Account of Which Eternal Punishment Is Due to All Who Are Not Within the Pale of the Saviour's Grace

But eternal punishment seems hard and unjust to human perceptions, because in the weakness of our mortal condition there is wanting that highest and purest wisdom by which it can be perceived how great a wickedness was committed in that first transgression. The more enjoyment man found in God, the greater was his wickedness in abandoning Him; and he who destroyed in himself a good which might have been eternal, became worthy of eternal evil. Hence the whole mass of the human race is condemned; for he who at first gave entrance to sin has been punished with all his posterity who were in him as in a root, so that no one is exempt from this just and due punishment, unless delivered by mercy and undeserved grace; and the human race is so apportioned that in some is displayed the efficacy of merciful grace, in the rest the efficacy of just retribution. For both could not be displayed in all; for if all had remained under the punishment of just condemnation, there would have been seen in no one the mercy of redeeming grace. And, on the other hand, if all had been transferred from darkness to light, the severity of retribution would have been manifested in none. But many more are left under punishment than are delivered from it, in order that it may thus be shown what was due to all. And had it been inflicted on all, no one could justly have found fault with the justice of Him who taketh vengeance; whereas, in the deliverance of so many from that just award, there is cause to render the most cordial thanks to the gratuitous bounty of Him who delivers.

# ANSELM

## PROSLOGIUM

### Chapter II. Truly There Is a God, Although the Fool Hath Said in His Heart, There Is No God

And so, Lord, do thou, who dost give understanding to faith, give me, so far as thou knowest it to be profitable, to understand that thou art as we believe; and that thou art that which we believe. And, indeed, we believe that thou art a being than which nothing greater can be conceived. Or is there no such nature, since the fool hath said in his heart, there is no God? (Psalms xiv. 1). But, at any rate, this very fool, when he hears of this being of which I speak—a being than which nothing greater can be conceived—understands what he hears, and what he understands is in his understanding; although he does not understand it to exist.

For, it is one thing for an object to be in the understanding, and another to understand that the object exists. When a painter first conceives of what he will afterwards perform, he has it in his understanding, but he does not yet understand it to be, because he has not yet performed it. But after he has made the painting, he both has it in his understanding, and he understands that it exists, because he has made it.

Hence, even the fool is convinced that something exists in the understanding, at least, than which nothing greater can be conceived. For, when he hears of this, he understands it. And whatever is understood, exists in the understanding. And assuredly that, than which nothing greater can be conceived, cannot exist in the understanding alone. For, suppose it exists in the understanding alone: then it can be conceived to exist in reality; which is greater.

Therefore, if that, than which nothing greater can be conceived, exists in the understanding alone, the very being, than which nothing greater can be conceived, is one, than which a greater can be conceived. But obviously this is impossible. Hence, there is no doubt that there exists a being, than which nothing greater can be conceived, and it exists both in the understanding and in reality.

## Chapter III. God Cannot Be Conceived Not to Exist.—God Is That, than Which Nothing Greater Can Be Conceived.—That Which Can Be Conceived Not to Exist Is Not God

And it asssuredly exists so truly, that it cannot be conceived not to exist. For, it is possible to conceive of a being which cannot be conceived not to exist; and this is greater than one which can be conceived not to exist. Hence, if that, than which nothing greater can be conceived, can be conceived not to exist, it is not that, than which nothing greater can be conceived. But this is an irreconcilable contradiction. There is, then, so truly a being than which nothing greater can be conceived to exist, that it cannot even be conceived not to exist; and this being thou art, O Lord, our God.

So truly, therefore, dost thou exist, O Lord, my God, that thou canst not be conceived not to exist; and rightly. For, if a mind could conceive of a being better than thee, the creature would rise above the Creator; and this is most absurd. And, indeed, whatever else there is, except thee alone, can be conceived not to exist. To thee alone, therefore, it belongs to exist more truly than all other beings, and hence in a higher degree than all others. For, whatever else exists does not exist so truly, and hence in a less degree it belongs to it to exist. Why, then, has the fool said in his heart, there is no God (Psalms xiv. 1), since it is so evident, to a rational mind, that thou dost exist in the highest degree of all? Why, except that he is dull and a fool?

# THOMAS AQUINAS

## SUMMA THEOLOGICA

### Part One

**Question II. The Existence of God (complete)**

Because the chief aim of sacred doctrine is to teach the knowledge of God not only as He is Himself, but also as He is the beginning of things and their last end, and especially of rational creatures, as is clear from what has been already said, therefore, in our endeavor to expound this science, we shall treat: (1) of God; (2) of the rational creature's movement towards God; (3) of Christ, Who as man is our way to God.

In treating of God there will be a threefold division:—

For we shall consider (1) whatever concerns the divine essence. (2) Whatever concerns the distinctions of Persons. (3) Whatever concerns the procession of creatures from Him.

Concerning the divine essence, we must consider:—

(1) Whether God exists? (2) The manner of His existence, or, rather, what is *not* the manner of His existence. (3) Whatever concerns His operations—namely, His knowledge, will, power.

Concerning the first, there are three points of injury:—

(1) Whether the proposition *God exists* is self-evident? (2) Whether it is demonstrable? (3) Whether God exists?

FIRST ARTICLE. WHETHER THE EXISTENCE OF GOD IS SELF-EVIDENT?

*We proceed thus to the First Article:—*

*Objection 1.* It seems that the existence of God is self-evident. For those things are said to be self-evident to us the knowledge of which exists naturally in us, as we can see in regard to first principles. But as Damascene says, *the knowledge of God is naturally implanted in all.* Therefore the existence of God is self-evident.

*Obj. 2.* Further, those things are said to be self-evident which are known as soon as the terms are known, which the Philosopher says is true of the first principles of demonstration. Thus, when the nature of a whole and of a part is known, it is at once recognized that every whole is greater than its part. But as soon as the signification of the name *God* is understood, it is at once seen that God exists. For by this name is signified that thing than which nothing greater can be conceived. But that which exists actually and mentally is greater than that which exists only mentally. Therefore, since as soon as the name *God* is understood it exists mentally, it also follows that it exists actually. Therefore the proposition *God exists* is self-evident.

*Obj. 3.* Further, the existence of truth is self-evident. For whoever denies the existence of truth grants that truth does not exist: and, if truth does not exist, then the proposition *Truth does not exist* is true: and if there is anything true, there must be truth. But God is truth itself: *I am the way, the truth, and the life* (Jo. xiv. 6). Therefore *God exists* is self-evident.

*On the contrary,* No one can mentally admit the opposite of what is self-evident, as the Philosopher states concerning the first principles of demonstration. But the opposite of the proposition *God is* can be mentally admitted: *The fool said in his heart, There is no God* (Ps. lii. 1). Therefore, that God exists is not self-evident.

*I answer that,* A thing can be self-evident in either of two ways: on the one hand, self-evident in itself, though not to us; on the other, self-evident in itself, and to us. A proposition is self-evident because the predicate is included in the essence of the subject: *e.g., Man is an animal,* for animal is contained in the essence of man. If, therefore, the essence of the predicate and subject be known to all, the proposition will be self-evident to all; as is clear with regard to the first principles of demonstration, the terms of which are certain common notions that no one is ignorant of, such as being and non-being, whole and part, and the like. If, however, there are some to whom the essence of the predicate and subject is unknown, the proposition will be self-evident in itself, but not to those who do not know the meaning of the predicate and subject of the proposition. Therefore, it happens, as Boethius says, that there are some notions of the mind which are common and self-evident only to the learned as that incorporeal substances are not in space. Therefore I say that this proposition, *God exists,* of itself is self-evident, for the predicate is the same as the subject, because God is His own existence as will be hereafter shown. Now because we do not know the essence of God, the proposition is not self-evident to us, but needs to be demonstrated by things that are more known to us, though less known in their nature—namely, by His effects.

*Reply Obj. 1.* To know that God exists in a general and confused way is implanted in us by nature, inasmuch as God is man's beatitude. For man naturally desires happiness, and what is naturally desired by man is naturally known by him. This, however, is not to know absolutely that God exists; just as to know that someone is approaching is not the same as to know that Peter is approaching, even though it is Peter who is approaching; for there are many who imagine that man's perfect good, which is happiness, consists in riches, and others in pleasures, and others in something else.

*Reply Obj. 2.* Perhaps not everyone who hears this name *God* understands it to signify something than which nothing greater can be thought, seeing that some have believed God to be a body. Yet, granted that everyone understands that by this name *God* is signified something than which nothing greater can be thought, nevertheless, it does not therefore follow that he understands that what the name signifies exists actually, but only that it exists mentally. Nor can it be argued that it actually exists, unless it be admitted that there actually exists something than which nothing greater can be thought; and this precisely is not admitted by those who hold that God does not exist.

*Reply Obj. 3.* The existence of truth in general is self-evident, but the existence of a Primal Truth is not self-evident to us.

### SECOND ARTICLE. WHETHER IT CAN BE DEMONSTRATED THAT GOD EXISTS?

*We proceed thus to the Second Article:—*

*Objection 1.* It seems that the existence of God cannot be demonstrated. For it is an article of faith that God exists. But what is of faith cannot be demonstrated, because a demonstration produces scientific knowledge, whereas faith is of the unseen, as is clear from the Apostle (Heb. xi. 1). Therefore it cannot be demonstrated that God exists.

*Obj. 2.* Further, essence is the middle term of demonstration. But we cannot know in what God's essence consists, but solely in what it does not consist, as Damascene says. Therefore we cannot demonstrate that God exists.

*Obj. 3.* Further, if the existence of God were demonstrated, this could only be from His effects. But His effects are not proportioned to Him, since He is infinite and His effects are finite, and between the finite and infinite there is no proportion. Therefore, since a cause cannot be demonstrated by an effect not proportioned to it, is seems that the existence of God cannot be demonstrated.

*On the contrary,* The Apostle says: *The invisible things of Him are clearly seen, being understood by the things that are made* (Rom. i. 20). But this would

not be unless the existence of God could be demonstrated through the things that are made; for the first thing we must know of anything is, whether it exists.

*I answer that,* Demonstration can be made in two ways: One is through the cause, and is called *propter quid,* and this is to argue from what is prior absolutely. The other is through the effect, and is called a demonstration *quia;* this is to argue from what is prior relatively only to us. When an effect is better known to us than its cause, from the effect we proceed to the knowledge of the cause. And from every effect the existence of its proper cause can be demonstrated, so long as its effects are better known to us; because, since every effect depends upon its cause, if the effect exists, the cause must pre-exist. Hence the existence of God, in so far as it is not self-evident to us, can be demonstrated from those of His effects which are known to us.

*Reply Obj. 1.* The existence of God and other like truths about God, which can be known by natural reason, are not articles of faith, but are preambles to the articles; for faith presupposes natural knowledge, even as grace presupposes nature and perfection the perfectible. Nevertheless, there is nothing to prevent a man, who cannot grasp a proof, from accepting, as a matter of faith, something which in itself is capable of being scientifically known and demonstrated.

*Reply Obj. 2.* When the existence of a cause is demonstrated from an effect, this effect takes the place of the definition of the cause in proving the cause's existence. This is especially the case in regard to God, because, in order to prove the existence of anything, it is necessary to accept as a middle term the meaning of the name, and not its essence, for the question of its essence follows on the question of its existence. Now the names given to God are derived from His effects, as will be later shown. Consequently, in demonstrating the existence of God from His effects, we may take for the middle term the meaning of the name *God*.

*Reply Obj. 3*. From effects not proportioned to the cause no perfect knowledge of that cause can be obtained. Yet from every effect the existence of the cause can be clearly demonstrated, and so we can demonstrate the existence of God from His effects; though from them we cannot know God perfectly as He is in His essence.

### THIRD ARTICLE. WHETHER GOD EXISTS?

*We proceed thus to the Third Article:—*

*Objection 1*. It seems that God does not exist; because if one of two contraries be infinite, the other would be altogether destroyed. But the name *God* means that He is infinite goodness. If, therefore, God existed, there would be no evil discoverable; but there is evil in the world. Therefore God does not exist.

*Obj. 2*. Further, it is superfluous to suppose that what can be accounted for by a few principles has been produced by many. But it seems that everything we see in the world can be accounted for by other principles, supposing God did not exist. For all natural things can be reduced to one principle, which is nature; and all voluntary things can be reduced to one principle, which is human reason, or will. Therefore there is no need to suppose God's existence.

*On the contrary*, It is said in the person of God: *I am Who am* (Exod. iii. 14).

*I answer that*, The existence of God can be proved in five ways.

The first and more manifest way is the argument from motion. It is certain, and evident to our senses, that in the world some things are in motion. Now whatever is moved is moved by another, for nothing can be moved except it is in potentiality to that towards which it is moved; whereas a thing moves inas-

much as it is in act. For motion is nothing else than the reduction of something from potentiality to actuality. But nothing can be reduced from potentiality to actuality, except by something in a state of actuality. Thus that which is actually hot, as fire, makes wood, which is potentially hot, to be actually hot, and thereby moves and changes it. Now it is not possible that the same thing should be at once in actuality and potentiality in the same respect, but only in different respects. For what is actually hot cannot simultaneously be potentially hot; but it is simultaneously potentially cold. It is therefore impossible that in the same respect and in the same way a thing should be both mover and moved, *i.e.*, that it should move itself. Therefore, whatever is moved must be moved by another. If that by which it is moved be itself moved, then this also must needs be moved by another, and that by another again. But this cannot go on to infinity, because then there would be no first mover, and, consequently, no other mover, seeing that subsequent movers move only inasmuch as they are moved by the first mover; as the staff moves only because it is moved by the hand. Therefore it is necessary to arrive at a first mover, moved by no other; and this everyone understands to be God.

The second way is from the nature of efficient cause. In the world of sensible things we find there is an order of efficient causes. There is no case known (neither is it, indeed, possible) in which a thing is found to be the efficient cause of itself; for so it would be prior to itself, which is impossible. Now in efficient causes it is not possible to go on to infinity, because in all efficient causes following in order, the first is the cause of the intermediate cause, and the intermediate is the cause of the ultimate cause, whether the intermediate cause be several, or one only. Now to take away the cause is to take away the effect. Therefore, if there be no first cause among efficient causes, there will be no ultimate, nor any intermediate, cause. But if in efficient causes it is possible to go on to infinity, there will be no first efficient cause, neither will there be an ultimate effect, nor any intermediate efficient causes; all of which is plainly false. Therefore it is necessary to admit a first efficient cause, to which everyone gives the name of God.

The third way is taken from possibility and necessity, and runs thus. We find in nature things that are possible to be and not to be, since they are found to be generated, and to be corrupted, and consequently, it is possible for them to be and not to be. But it is impossible for these always to exist, for that which can not-be at some time is not. Therefore, if everything can not-be, then at one time there was nothing in existence. Now if this were true, even now there would be nothing in existence, because that which does not exist begins to exist only through something already existing. Therefore, if at one time nothing was in existence, it would have been impossible for anything to have begun to exist; and thus even now nothing would be in existence—which is absurd. Therefore, not all beings are merely possible, but there must exist something the existence of which is necessary. But every necessary thing either has its necessity caused by another, or not. Now it is impossible to go on to infinity in necessary things which have their necessity caused by another, as has been already proved in regard to efficient causes. Therefore we cannot but admit the existence of some being having of itself its own necessity, and not receiving it from another, but rather causing in others their necessity. This all men speak of as God.

The fourth way is taken from the gradation to be found in things. Among beings there are some more and some loss good, true, noble, and the like. But more and less are predicated of different things according as they resemble in their different ways something which is the maximum, as a thing is said to be hotter according as it more nearly resembles that which is hottest; so that there is something which is truest, something best, something noblest, and, consequently, something which is most being, for those things that are greatest in truth are greatest in being, as it is written in *Metaph.* ii. Now the maximum in any genus is the cause of all in that genus, as fire, which is the maximum of heat, is the cause of all hot things, as is said in the same book. Therefore there must also be something which is to all beings the cause of their being, goodness, and every other perfection; and this we call God.

The fifth way is taken from the governance of the world. We see that things which lack knowledge, such as natural bodies, act for an end, and this is evident from their acting always, or nearly always, in the same way, so as to obtain the best result. Hence it is plain that they achieve their end, not fortuitously, but designedly. Now whatever lacks knowledge cannot move towards an end, unless it be directed by some being endowed with knowledge and intelligence; as the arrow is directed by the archer. Therefore some intelligent being exists by whom all natural things are directed to their end; and this being we call God.

*Reply Obj. 1.* As Augustine says: *Since God is the highest good, He would not allow any evil to exist in His works, unless His omnipotence and goodness were such as to bring good even out of evil.* This is part of the infinite goodness of God, that He should allow evil to exist, and out of it produce good.

*Reply Obj. 2.* Since nature works for a determinate end under the direction of a higher agent, whatever is done by nature must be traced back to God as to its first cause. So likewise whatever is done voluntarily must be traced back to some higher cause other than human reason and will, since these can change and fail; for all things that are changeable and capable of defect must be traced back to an immovable and self-necessary first principle, as has been shown.

## Question XVI.   On Truth

### FIRST ARTICLE.   WHETHER TRUTH RESIDES ONLY IN THE INTELLECT?

*We proceed thus to the First Article:—*

*Objection 1.* It seems that truth does not reside only in the intellect, but rather in things. For Augustine condemns this definition of truth, *That is true which is seen,* since it would follow that stones hidden in the bosom of the earth would not be true stones, as they are not seen. He also condemns the following, *That is true which is as it appears to the knower, who is willing and able to know;* for hence it would follow that nothing would be true, unless someone could know it. Therefore he defines truth thus: *The true is which is.* It seems, then, that truth resides in things, and not in the intellect.

*Obj. 2.* Further, whatever is true, is true by reason of truth. If, then, truth is only in the intellect, nothing will be true except in so far as it is understood. But this is the error of the ancient philosophers, who said that whatever seems to be true is so. Consequently contradictories can be true at the same time, since contradictories seem to be true as seen by different persons at the same time.

*Obj. 3.* Further, *that because of which a thing is so, is itself more so,* as is evident from the Philosopher. But *it is from the fact that a thing is or is not, that our thought or word is true or false,* as the Philosopher teaches. Therefore truth resides rather in things than in the intellect.

*On the contrary,* The Philosopher says, *The true and the false reside not in things, but in the intellect.*

*I answer that,* As *good* names that towards which the appetite tends, so *the true* names that towards which the intellect tends. Now there is this difference between the appetite and the intellect, or any knowledge whatsoever, that knowledge is according as the thing known is in the knower, while appetite is according as the desirer tends towards the thing desired. Thus the term of the appetite, namely good, is in the desirable thing, and the term of the intellect, namely the true, is in the intellect itself. Now as good exists in a thing so far as that thing is related to the appetite— and hence the aspect of goodness passes on from the desirable thing to the appetite, in so far as the appetite is called good if its object is good; so, since the true is in the intellect in so far as the intellect is conformed to the thing understood, the aspect of the true must needs pass from the intellect to the thing understood, so that also the thing understood is said to be true in so far as it has some relation to the intellect.

Now a thing understood may be in relation to an intellect either essentially or accidentally. It is related essentially to an intellect on which it depends as regards its being, but accidentally to an intellect by which it is knowable; even as we may say that a house is related essentially to the intellect of the architect, but accidentally to the intellect upon which it does not depend. Now we do not judge of a thing by what is in it accidentally, but by what is in it essentially. Hence, everything is said to be true absolutely, in so far as it is related to the intellect on which it depends; and thus it is that artificial things are said to be true as being related to our intellect. For a house is said to be true that fulfills the likeness of the form in the architect's mind; and words are said to be true so far as they are the signs of truth in the intellect. In the same way, natural things are said to be true in so far as they express the likeness of the species that are in the divine mind. For a stone is called true, which possesses the nature proper to a stone, according to the preconception in the divine intellect. Thus, then, truth resides primarily in the intellect, and secondarily in things according as they are related to the intellect as their source.

Consequently, there are various definitions of truth. Augustine says, *Truth is that whereby is made manifest that which is;* and Hilary says that *Truth makes being clear and evident:* and this pertains to truth according as it is in the intellect. As to the truth of things in so far as they are related to the intellect, we have Augustine's definition, *Truth is a supreme likeness, without any unlikeness, to its source;* also Anselm's definition, *Truth is rightness, perceptible by the mind alone;* for that is right which is in accordance with its source; also Avicenna's definition, *The truth of each thing is a property of the being which has been given to it.* The definition that *Truth is the equation of thought and thing* is applicable to it under either aspect.

*Reply Obj. 1.* Augustine is speaking about the truth of things, and from the notion of this truth excludes relation to our intellect; for what is accidental is excluded from every definition.

*Reply Obj. 2.* The ancient philosophers held that the species of natural things did not proceed from any intellect, but came about by chance. But as they saw that truth implies relation to intellect, they were compelled to base the truth of things on their relation to our intellect. From this fact there followed the various awkward consequences that the Philosopher attacks. Such consequences, however, do not follow, if we say that the truth of things consists in their relation to the divine intellect.

*Reply Obj. 3.* Although the truth of our intellect is caused by the thing, yet it is not necessary that the essence of truth should be there primarily, any more than that the essence of health should be primarily in medicine, rather than in the animal: for it is the power of medicine, and not its health, that is the cause of health, since the agent is no univocal. In the same way, the being of the thing, not its truth, is the cause of truth in the intellect. Hence the Philosopher says that an opinion or a statement is true *from the fact that a thing is, not from the fact that a thing is true.*

### FIFTH ARTICLE. WHETHER GOD IS TRUTH?

*We proceed thus to the Fifth Article:—*

*Objection 1.* It seems that God is not truth. For truth consists in the intellect composing and dividing. But in God there is no composition and division. Therefore in God there is no truth.

*Obj. 2.* Further, truth, according to Augustine, is a *likeness to the source.* But in God there is no likeness to a source. Therefore in God there is no truth.

*Obj. 3.* Further, whatever is said of God, is said of Him as of the first cause of all things. Thus the being of God is the cause of all being, and His goodness the cause of all good. If therefore there is truth in God, all truth will be from Him. But it is true that someone sins. Therefore this will be from God; which is evidently false.

*On the contrary,* Our Lord says, *I am the Way, the Truth and the Life* (Jo. xiv. 6).

*I answer that,* As was said above, truth is found in the intellect according as it apprehends a thing as it is; and in things according as they have being conformable to an intellect. This is to the greatest degree found in God. For His being is not only conformed to His intellect, but it is the very act of His intellect; and His act of understanding is the measure and cause of every other being and of every other intellect; and He Himself is His own being and act of understanding. Whence it follows not only that truth is in Him, but that He is the highest and first truth itself.

*Reply Obj. 1.* Although in the divine intellect there is neither composition nor division, yet in His simple act of intelligence He judges of all things and knows all propositions; and thus there is truth in His intellect.

*Reply Obj. 2.* The truth of our intellect is according to its conformity with its source, that is to say, the things from which it receives knowledge. The truth also of things is according to their conformity with their source, namely, the divine intellect. Now this cannot be said, properly speaking, of divine truth; unless perhaps in so far as truth is appropriated to the Son, Who has a source. But if we speak of divine truth in its essence, we cannot understand what Augustine has said unless the affirmative proposition be resolved into the negative one, as when one says: *the Father is of Himself, because He is not from another.* Similarly, the divine truth can be called *a likeness of its source,* inasmuch as His being is not unlike His intellect.

*Reply Obj. 3.* Non-being and privation have no truth of themselves, but only in the apprehension of the intellect. Now all apprehension of the intellect is from God. Hence all the truth that exists in the statement,—*that this person commits fornication is true,* is entirely from God. But to argue, *Therefore that this person fornicates is from God,* is a fallacy of accident.

## Question XXIII. Predestination

### THIRD ARTICLE. WHETHER GOD REPROBATES ANY MAN?

*We proceed thus to the Third Article:—*

*Objection 1.* It seems that God reprobates no man. For nobody reprobates what he loves. But God loves every man, according to the words (Wis. xi. 25): *Thou lovest all things that are,* *and Thou hatest none of the things Thou hast made.* Therefore God reprobates no man.

*Obj. 2.* Further, if God reprobates any man, it would be necessary for reprobation to have the same relation to the reprobate as predestination has to the predestined. But predestination is the cause of the salvation of the predestined. Therefore reprobation will likewise be the cause of the loss of the reprobate. But this is false. For it is said (Osee xiii. 9): *Destruction is thy own, O Israel; Thy help is only in Me.* God does not, then, reprobate any man.

*Obj. 3.* Further, to no one ought anything to be imputed which he cannot avoid. But if God reprobates anyone, that one must perish. For it is said (Eccles. vii. 14): *Consider the works of God, that no man can correct whom He hath despised.* Therefore it could not be imputed to any man, were he to perish. But this is false. Therefore God does not reprobate anyone.

*On the contrary,* It is said (Malach. i. 2, 3): *I have loved Jacob, but have hated Esau.*

*I answer that,* God does reprobate some persons. For it was said above that predestination is a part of providence. To providence, however, it belongs to permit certain defects in those things which are subject to providence, as was said above. Thus, as men are ordained to eternal life through the providence of God, it likewise is part of that providence to permit some to fall away from that end; this is called *reprobation.* Thus, as predestination is a part of providence, in regard to those divinely ordained to eternal salvation, so reprobation is a part of providence in regard to those who turn aside from that end. Hence reprobation implies not only foreknowledge, but also something more, as does providence, as was said above. Therefore, as predestination includes the will to confer grace and glory, so also reprobation includes the will to permit a person to fall into sin, and to impose the punishment of damnation because of that sin.

*Reply Obj. 1.* God loves all men and all creatures, inasmuch as He wishes them all some good; but He does not wish every good to them all. So far, therefore, as He does not wish for some this particular good—namely, eternal life—He is said to hate or reprobate them.

*Reply Obj. 2.* Reprobation differs in its causality from predestination. This latter is the cause both of what is expected in the future life by the predestined—namely, glory—and of what is received in this life—namely, grace. Reprobation, however, is not the cause of what is in the present—namely, sin; but it is the cause of abandonment by God. It is the cause, however, of what is assigned in the future—namely, eternal punishment. But guilt proceeds from the free choice of the person who is reprobated and deserted by grace. In this way the word of the prophet is true—namely, *Destruction is thy own, O Israel.*

*Reply Obj. 3.* Reprobation by God does not take anything away from the power of the person reprobated. Hence, when it is said that the reprobated cannot obtain grace, this must not be understood as implying absolute impossibility, but only conditional impossibility; just as it was said above that the predestined must necessarily be saved, yet by a conditional necessity, which does not do away with the liberty of choice. Whence, although anyone reprobated by God cannot acquire grace, nevertheless, that he falls into this or that particular sin comes from the use of his free desire. Hence it is rightly imputed to him as guilt.

## Question XXV. The Power of God

### FIFTH ARTICLE. WHETHER GOD CAN DO WHAT HE DOES NOT?

*We proceed thus to the Fifth Article:—*

*Objection 1.* It seems that God can do only what He does. For God cannot do what He has not foreknown and pre-ordained that He would do. But He neither foreknew nor pre-ordained that He would do anything except what He does. Therefore He can do only what He does.

*Obj. 2.* Further, God can do only what ought to be done and what is just. But God is not bound to do what He does not; nor is it just that He should do what He does not. Therefore He can do only what He does.

*Obj. 3.* Further, God cannot do anything that is not good and befitting creation. But it is not good for creatures nor befitting them to be otherwise than as they are. Therefore God can do only what He does.

*On the contrary,* It is said: *Thinkest thou that I cannot ask My Father, and He will give Me presently more than twelve legions of angels?* (Matt. xxvi. 53). But He neither asked for them, nor did His Father show them to refute the Jews. Therefore God can do what He does not.

*I answer that,* In this matter certain persons erred in two ways. Some laid it down that God acts from natural necessity in such way that, just as from the action of natural things nothing else can happen beyond what actually takes place—as, for instance, from the seed of man, a man must come, and from that of an olive, an olive; so from the divine operation there could not come forth other things, nor another order of things, than that which now is. But we showed above that God does not act from natural necessity, but that His will is the cause of all things; we showed also that the divine will is not naturally and from any necessity determined to these creatures. Whence in no way is the present scheme of things produced by God with such necessity that other things could not come to be.

Others, however, said that the divine power is restricted to this present scheme of things because of the order of the divine wisdom and justice, without which God does nothing. But since the power of God, which is His essence, is nothing else but His wisdom, it can indeed be fittingly said that there is nothing in the divine power which is not in the order conceived by the divine wisdom; for the divine wisdom comprehends the power of God in its entirety. However, the order established in creation by divine wisdom (in which the notion of His justice consists, as was said above), is not so equal to the divine wisdom that the divine wisdom should be restricted to it. For it is clear that the whole nature of the order which a wise man puts into the things made by him is taken from their end. So, when the end is proportionate to the things made for that end, the wisdom of the maker is restricted to a definite order. But the divine goodness is an end exceeding created things beyond all proportion. Therefore, the divine wisdom is not so restricted to any particular order that no other scheme of things could proceed from it. Hence we must say absolutely that God can do other things than those He has done.

*Reply Obj. 1.* In ourselves, in whom power and essence are distinct from will and intellect, and in whom intellect is distinct from wisdom, and will from justice, something can reside in our power which cannot reside in a just will or in a wise intellect. But in God, power, essence, will, intellect, wisdom and justice are one and the same. Whence, there can be found nothing in the divine power which cannot also be found in His just will or in His wise intellect. Now, because His will cannot be determined from necessity to this or that order of things, except upon supposition, as was said above; and because the wisdom and justice of God are likewise restricted not to this present order, as was shown above; for this reason, nothing prevents there being something in the divine power which He does not

will, and which is not included in the order that He has established in things. Furthermore, because power is considered as *executing,* will as *commanding,* and intellect and wisdom as *directing,* what is attributed to His power considered in itself God is said to be able to do in accordance with His *absolute power.* Of such a kind is everything which verifies the nature of being, as was said above. On the other hand, what is attributed to the divine power, according as it carries into execution the command of a just will, God is said to be able to do by His *ordained power.* In this manner, we must say that by His absolute power God can do other things than those He has foreknown and pre-ordained to do. But it could not happen that He should do anything which He has not foreknown and not pre-ordained that He would do. For His doing is subject to His foreknowledge and preordination, though His power, which is His nature, is not. For God does things because He so wills; yet He is able to do so, not because He so wills, but because He is such in His nature.

*Reply Obj. 2.* God is bound to nobody but Himself. Hence, when it is said that God can do only what He ought, nothing else is meant by this than that God can do nothing but what is for Him fitting and just. But these words *fitting* and *just* may be understood in two ways: one, in direct connection with the verb *is;* and thus they would be restricted to signifying the present order of things. They would therefore refer to His power under this restriction. In that case, what is said in the objection is false, for its meaning is that God can do nothing except what is now fitting and just. If, however, *fitting* and *just* are joined directly with the verb *can* (which has the effect of extending their application), and then secondly with *is,* the result will be a present signified in a confused and general way. The proposition would then be true, and its meaning would be: *God cannot do anything except that which, if He did it, would be suitable and just.*

*Reply Obj. 3.* Although the present order of things is restricted to what now exists, the divine power and wisdom are not thus restricted. Whence, although no other order would be suitable and good for the things which now exist, yet God can make other things and impose upon them another order.

### SIXTH ARTICLE. WHETHER GOD CAN DO BETTER THAN WHAT HE DOES?

*We proceed thus to the Sixth Article:—*

*Objection 1.* It seems that God cannot do better than He does. For whatever God does, He does in a most powerful and wise way. But a thing is so much the better done as it is more powerfully and wisely done. Therefore God cannot do anything better than He does.

*Obj. 2.* Further, Augustine argues thus: If *God could, but would not, beget a Son His equal, He would have been envious.* For the same reason, if God could have made better things than He has done, but was not willing so to do, He would have been envious. But envy is far removed from God. Therefore God has made everything perfect. He cannot therefore make anything better than He has done.

*Obj. 3.* Further, what is very good and the best of all cannot be bettered; because nothing is better than the best. But as Augustine says, *each thing that God has made is good, and, taken all together they are very good; because in them all consists the wondrous beauty of the universe.* Therefore the good in the universe could not be made better by God.

*Obj. 4.* Further, Christ as man is full of grace and truth, and possesses the Spirit without measure; and so He cannot be better. Again, created happiness is described as the highest good, and thus could not be better. And the Blessed Virgin Mary is raised above all the choirs of angels, and so cannot be better than she is. God cannot therefore make all things better than He has made them.

*On the contrary,* It is said (Ephes. iii. 20): *God is able to do all things more abundantly than we desire or understand.*

*I answer that,* The goodness of anything is twofold. One belongs to its essence:—thus, for instance, to be rational belongs to the essence of man. As regards this good, God cannot make a thing better than it is itself, although He can make another thing better than it. In the same way, He cannot make the number four greater than it is, because if it were greater it would not longer be four, but another number. For the addition of a substantial difference in definitions is after the manner of the addition of unity in numbers. Another kind of goodness is that which is over and above the essence; thus, the good of a man is to be virtuous or wise. As regards this kind of goodness, God can make better the things He has made. Absolutely speaking, however, God can make something else better than each thing made by Him.

*Reply Obj. 1.* When it is said that God can make better things than He does, if *better* is taken substantively, this proposition is true. For He can always make something else better than any individual thing: and He can make the same thing in one way better than it is, and in another way not; as was explained above. If, however, *better* is taken as an adverb, referring to the mode of God's activity, then God cannot make anything better than He makes it, because He cannot make it from greater wisdom and goodness. Finally, if it implies the mode of being in the things that God has made, then He can make something better; because He can give to things made by Him a better manner of being as regards accidents, although not as regards the substance.

*Reply Obj. 2.* It is of the nature of a son that he should be equal to his father, when he comes to maturity. But it is not of the nature of anything created that it should be better than it was made by God. Hence the comparison fails.

*Reply Obj. 3.* Given the things which actually exist, the universe cannot be better, for the order which God has established in things, and in which the good of the universe consists, most befits things. For if any one thing were bettered, the proportion of order would be destroyed; just as if one string were stretched more than it ought to be, the melody of the harp would be destroyed. Yet God could make other things, or add something to the present creation; and then there would be another and a better universe.

*Reply Obj. 4.* An infinite dignity, resulting from the infinite good which is God, is in a way possessed by the humanity of Christ because it is united to God; by created beatitude because it is the enjoyment of God; and by the Blessed Virgin because she is the mother of God. From this point of view, nothing better than these can be made; just as there cannot be anything better than God.

## Question XLIX. The Cause of Evil

### SECOND ARTICLE. WHETHER THE HIGHEST GOOD, GOD, IS THE CAUSE OF EVIL?

*We proceed thus to the Second Article:—*

*Objection 1.* It would seem that the highest good, God, is the cause of evil. For it is said (Isa. xlv. 5, 7) : *I am the Lord, and there is no other God, forming the light, and creating darkness, making peace, and creating evil.* It is also said (Amos iii. 6), *Shall there be evil in a city, which the Lord hath not done?*

*Obj. 2.* Further, the effect of the secondary cause is reduced to the first cause. But good is the cause of evil, as was said above. Therefore, since God is the cause of every good, as was shown above, it follows that also every evil is from God.

*Obj. 3.* Further, as is said by the Philosopher, the cause of both *the safety and danger of the ship* is the same. But God is the cause of the safety of all things. Therefore He is the cause of all perdition and of all evil.

*On the contrary,* Augustine says that, *God is not the author of evil, because He is not the cause of tending to non-being.*

*I answer that,* As appears from what was said, the evil which consists in the defect of action is always caused by the defect of the agent. But in God there is no defect, but the highest perfection, as was shown above. Hence, the evil which consists in defect of action, or which is caused by defect of the agent, is not reduced to God as to its cause.

But the evil which consists in the corruption of some things is reduced to God as the cause. And this appears as regards both natural things and voluntary things. For it was said that some agent, inasmuch as it produces by its power a form which is followed by corruption and defect, causes by its power that corruption and defect. But it is manifest that the form which God chiefly intends in created things is the good of the order of the universe. Now, the order of the universe requires, as was said above, that there should be some things that can, and sometimes do, fail. And thus God, by causing in things the good of the order of the universe, consequently and, as it were by accident, causes the corruptions of things, according to I Kings ii. 6: *The Lord killeth and maketh alive.* But when we read that *God hath not made death* (Wis. i. 13), the sense is that God does not will death for its own sake. Nevertheless, the order of justice belongs to the order of the universe; and this requires that penalty should be dealt out to sinners. And so God is the author of the evil which is penalty, but not of the evil which is fault, by reason of what is said above.

*Reply Obj. 1.* These passages refer to the evil of penalty, and not to the evil of fault.

*Reply Obj. 2.* The effect of the deficient secondary cause is reduced to the first non-deficient cause as regards what it has of being and perfection, but not as regards what it has of defect; just as whatever there is of motion in the act of limping is caused by the motive power, whereas what is unbalanced in it does not come from the motive power, but from the curvature of the leg. So, too, whatever there is of being and action in a bad action is reduced to God as the cause; whereas whatever defect is in it is not caused by God, but by the deficient secondary cause.

*Reply Obj. 3.* The sinking of a ship is attributed to the sailor as the cause, from the fact that he does not fulfill what the safety of the ship requires; but God does not fail in doing what is necessary for safety. Hence there is no parity.

## First Part of the Second Part

### Question VI.   On the Voluntary and the Involuntary

#### EIGHTH ARTICLE.   WHETHER IGNORANCE CAUSES INVOLUNTARINESS?

*We proceed thus to the Eighth Article:—*

*Objection. 1.* It would seem that ignorance does not cause involuntariness. For *the involuntary act deserves pardon,* as Damascene says. But sometimes that which is done through ignorance does not deserve pardon, according to 1 Cor. xiv. 38: *If any man know not, he shall not be known.* Therefore ignorance does not cause involuntariness.

*Obj. 2.* Further, every sin implies ignorance, according to Prov. xiv. 22: *They err, that work evil.* If, therefore, ignorance causes involuntariness, it would follow that every sin is involuntary; which is opposed to the saying of Augustine, that *every sin is voluntary.*

*Obj. 3.* Further, *involuntariness is not without sadness,* as Damascene says. But some things are done out of ignorance, but without sadness. For instance, a man may kill a foe, whom he wishes to kill, thinking at the time that he is killing a stag. Therefore ignorance does not cause involuntariness.

*On the contrary,* Damascene and the Philosopher say that *what is done through ignorance is involuntary.*

*I answer that,* If ignorance cause involuntariness, it is in so far as it deprives one of knowledge, which is a necessary condition of voluntariness, as was declared above. But it is not every ignorance that deprives one of this knowledge. Accordingly, we must take note that ignorance has a threefold relationship to the act of the will: in one way, *concomitantly;* in another, *consequently;* in a third way, *antecedently.* Concomitantly, when there is ignorance of what is done, but so that even if it were known, it would be done. For then ignorance does not induce one to will this to be done, but it just happens that a thing is at the same time done and not known. Thus, in the example given, a man did indeed will to kill his foe, but killed him in ignorance, thinking to kill a stag. And ignorance of this kind, as the Philosopher states, does not cause involuntariness, since it is not the cause of anything that is repugnant to the will; but it causes *non-voluntariness,* since that which is unknown cannot be actually willed.

Ignorance is *consequent* to the act of the will, in so far as ignorance itself is voluntary; and this happens in two ways in accordance with the two aforesaid modes of the voluntary. First, because the act of the will is brought to bear on the ignorance, as when a man wills not to know, that he may have an excuse for sin, or that he may not be withheld from sin, according to Job xxi. 14: *We desire not the knowledge of Thy ways.* And this is called *affected ignorance.*— Secondly, ignorance is said to be voluntary, when it regards that which one can and ought to know, for in this sense *not to act* and *not to will* are said to be voluntary, as was stated above. And ignorance of this kind happens either when one does not actually consider what one can and ought to consider (this is called *ignorance of evil choice,* and arises from some passion or habit), or when one does not take the trouble to acquire the knowledge which one ought to have; in which sense, ignorance of the general principles of law, which one ought to know, is voluntary, as being due to negligence.

Accordingly, if in either of these ways ignorance is voluntary, it cannot cause what is involuntary absolutely. Nevertheless it causes involuntariness in a certain respect, inasmuch as it precedes the movement of the will towards the act, which movement would not be, if there were knowledge.

Ignorance is *antecedent* to the act of the will when it is not voluntary, and yet is the cause of man's willing what he would not will otherwise. Thus a man may be ignorant of some circumstance of his act, which he was not bound to know, with the result that he does that which he would not do if he knew of that circumstance. For instance, a man, after taking proper precaution, may not know that someone is coming along the road, so that he shoots an arrow and slays a passer-by. Such ignorance causes what is involuntary absolutely.

From this may be gathered the solution of the objections. For the first objection deals with ignorance of what a man is bound to know. The second, with ignorance of choice, which is voluntary to a certain extent, as was stated above. The third, with that ignorance which is concomitant with the act of the will.

## Question XII. On Intention

### THIRD ARTICLE. WHETHER ONE CAN INTEND TWO THINGS AT THE SAME TIME?

*We proceed thus to the Third Article:*—

*Objection 1.* It would seem that one cannot intend several things at the same time. For Augustine says that man's intention cannot be directed at the same time to God and to bodily benefits. Therefore, for the same reason, neither to any other two things.

*Obj. 2.* Further, intention designates a movement of the will towards a terminus. Now there cannot be several termini in the same direction of one movement. Therefore the will cannot intend several things at the same time.

*Obj. 3.* Further, intention presupposes an act of the reason or of the intellect. But *it is not possible to understand several things at the same time,* according to the Philosopher. Therefore, neither is it possible to intend several things at the same time.

*On the contrary,* Art imitates nature. Now nature intends two purposes by means of one instrument. Thus *the tongue is for the purpose of taste and speech.* Therefore, for the same reason, art or reason can at the same time direct one thing to two ends; so that one can intend several ends at the same time.

*I answer that,* Two things may be taken in two ways, namely, as related to one another, or as unrelated. And if they be related to one another, it is evident, from what has been said, that a man can intend several things at the same time. For intention is not only of the last end, as was stated above, but also of an intermediary end. Now a man intends, at the same time, both the proximate and the last end: *e.g.,* the mixing of a medicine and the giving of health.

But if we take two things that are not related to one another, thus also a man can intend several things at the same time. This is evident from the fact that a man prefers one thing to another because it is the better of the two. Now one of the reasons for which one thing is better than another is that it is available for more purposes; and so one thing can be chosen in preference to another because of the greater number of purposes for which it is available; so that evidently a man can intend several things at the same time.

*Reply Obj. 1.* Augustine means to say that man cannot at the same time direct his intention to God and to bodily benefits, as to two last ends; for, as was stated above, one man cannot have several last ends.

*Reply Obj. 2.* There can be several termini of the same movement and in the same direction, if one is related to the other; but there cannot be two unrelated termini of the same movement and in the same direction. At the same time, it must be observed that what is not one in reality may be taken as one by the reason. Now intention is a movement of the will to something already ordained by the reason, as was stated above. Therefore, where we have many things in reality, we may take them as one term of intention, in so far as the reason takes them as one; and this either because two things concur in the integrity of one whole, as a proper measure of heat and cold conduce to health, or because two things are included in one which may be intended. For instance, the acquiring of wine and clothing is included in wealth, as in something common to both; and so nothing hinders the man who intends to acquire wealth from intending both the others.

*Reply Obj. 3.* As was stated in the First Part, it is possible to understand several things at the same time in so far as, in some way, they are one.

## Question LXI.    The Cardinal Virtues

### SECOND ARTICLE.    WHETHER THERE ARE FOUR CARDINAL VIRTUES?

*We proceed thus to the Second Article:—*

*Objection 1.* It would seem that there are not four cardinal virtues. For prudence is the directing principle of the other moral virtues, as is clear from what has been said above. But that which directs others ranks before them. Therefore prudence alone is a principal virtue.

*Obj. 2.* Further, the principal virtues are, in a way, moral virtues. Now we are directed to moral works both by the practical reason and by a right appetite, as is stated in *Ethics* vi. Therefore there are only two cardinal virtues.

*Obj. 3.* Further, even among the other virtues one ranks higher than another. But in order that a virtue be principal, it need not rank above all the others, but above some. Therefore it seems that there are many more principal virtues.

*On the contrary,* Gregory says: *The entire structure of good works is built on four virtues.*

*I answer that,* Things may be numbered either in respect of their formal principles, or according to the subjects in which they are; and in either way we find that there are four cardinal virtues.

For the formal principle of the virtue of which we speak now is the good as defined by reason. This good can be considered in two ways. First, as existing in the consideration itself of reason, and thus we have one principal virtue called *prudence.*—Secondly, according as the reason puts its order into something else, and this either into operations, and then we have *justice*, or into passions, and then we need two virtues. For the need of putting the order of reason into the passions is due to their thwarting reason; and this occurs in two ways. First, when the passions incite to something against reason, and then they need a curb, which we thus call *temperance;* secondly, when the passions withdraw us from following the dictate of reason, *e.g.,* through fear of danger or toil, and then man needs to be strengthened for that which reason dictates, lest he turn back, and to this end there is *fortitude.*

In like manner, we find the same number if we consider the subjects of virtue. For there are four subjects of the virtue of which we now speak, viz., the power which is rational in its essence, and this is perfected by *prudence;* and that which is rational by participation, and is threefold, the will, subject of *justice,* the concupiscible power, subject of *temperance,* and the irascible power, subject of *fortitude.*

*Reply Obj. 1.* Prudence is absolutely the principal of all the virtues. The others are principal, each in its own genus.

*Reply Obj. 2.* That part of the soul which is rational by participation is threefold, as was stated above.

*Reply Obj. 3.* All the other virtues, among which one ranks before another, are reducible to the above four, both as to the subject and as to the formal principles.

### Question XCIV. The Natural Law

#### FOURTH ARTICLE. WHETHER THE NATURAL LAW IS THE SAME IN ALL MEN?

*We proceed thus to the Fourth Article:—*

*Objection 1.* It would seem that the natural law is not the same in all. For it is stated in the *Decretals* that *the natural law is that which is contained in the Law and the Gospel.* But this is not common to all men, because, as it is written (Rom. x. 16), *all do not obey the gospel.* Therefore the natural law is not the same in all men.

*Obj. 2.* Further, *Things which are according to the law are said to be just,* as is stated in *Ethics* v. But it is stated in the same book that nothing is so just for all as not to be subject to change in regard to some men. Therefore even the natural law is not the same in all men.

*Obj. 3.* Further, as was stated above, to the natural law belongs everything to which a man is inclined according to his nature. Now different men are naturally inclined to different things,— some to the desire of pleasures, others to the desire of honors, and other men to other things. Therefore, there is not one natural law for all.

*On the contrary,* Isidore says: *The natural law is common to all nations.*

*I answer that,* As we have stated above, to the natural law belong those things to which a man is inclined naturally; and among these it is proper to man to be inclined to act according to reason. Now it belongs to the reason to proceed from what is common to what is proper, as is stated in *Physics* i. The speculative reason, however, is differently situated, in this matter, from the practical reason. For, since the speculative reason is concerned chiefly with necessary things, which cannot be otherwise than they are, its proper conclusions, like the universal principles, contain the truth without fail. The practical reason, on the other hand, is concerned with contingent matters, which is the domain of human actions; and, consequently, although there is necessity in the common principles, the more we descend towards the particular, the more frequently we encounter defects. Accordingly, then, in speculative matters truth is the same in all men, both as to principles and as to conclusions; although the truth is not known to all as regards the conclusions, but only as regards the principles which are called *common notions*. But in matters of action, truth or practical rectitude is not the same for all as to what is particular, but only as to the common principles; and where there is the same rectitude in relation to particulars, it is not equally known to all.

It is therefore evident that, as regards the common principles whether of speculative or of practical reason, truth or rectitude is the same for all, and is equally known by all. But as to the proper conclusions of the speculative reason, the truth is the same for all, but it is not equally known to all. Thus, it is true for all that the three angles of a triangle are together equal to two right angles, although it is not known to all. But as to the proper conclusions of the practical reason, neither is the truth or rectitude the same for all, nor, where it is the same, is it equally known by all. Thus, it is right and true for all to act according to reason, and from this principle it follows, as a proper conclusion, that goods entrusted to another should be restored to their owner. Now this is true for the majority of cases. But it may happen in a particular case that it would be injurious, and therefore unreasonable, to restore goods held in trust; for instance, if they are claimed for the purpose of fighting against one's country. And this principle will be found to fail the more, according as we descend further towards the particular, *e.g.*, if one were to say that goods held in trust should be restored with such and such a guarantee, or in such and such a way; because the greater the number of conditions added, the greater the number of ways in which the principle may fail, so that it be not right to restore or not to restore.

Consequently, we must say that the natural law, as to the first common principles, is the same for all, both as to rectitude and as to knowledge. But as to certain more particular aspects, which are conclusions, as it were, of those common principles, it is the same for all in the majority of cases, both as to rectitude and as to knowledge; and yet in some few cases it may fail, both as to rectitude, by reason of certain obstacles (just as natures subject to generation and corruption fail in some few cases because of some obstacle), and as to knowledge, since in some the reason is perverted by passion, or evil habit, or an evil disposition of nature. Thus at one time theft, although it is expressly contrary to the natural law, was not considered wrong among the Germans, as Julius Cæsar relates.

*Reply Obj. 1.* The meaning of the sentence quoted is not that whatever is contained in the Law and the Gospel belongs to the natural law, since they contain many things that are above nature; but that whatever belongs to the natural law is fully contained in them. Therefore Gratian, after saying that *the natural law is what is contained in the Law and the Gospel*, adds at once, by way of example, by *which everyone is commanded to do to others as he would be done by*.

*Reply Obj. 2.* The saying of the Philosopher is to be understood of things that are naturally just, not as common principles, but as conclusions drawn from them, having rectitude in the majority of cases, but failing in a few.

*Reply Obj. 3.* Just as in man reason rules and commands the other powers, so all the natural inclinations belonging to the other powers must needs be directed according to reason. Therefore it is universally right for all men that all their inclinations should be directed according to reason.

### FIFTH ARTICLE. WHETHER THE NATURAL LAW CAN BE CHANGED?

*We proceed thus to the Fifth Article:—*

*Objection 1.* It would seem that the natural law can be changed. For on Ecclus. xvii. 9. (*He gave them instructions, and the law of life*),[1] the *Gloss* says: *He wished the law of the letter to be written, in order to correct the law of nature.* But that which is corrected is changed. Therefore the natural law can be changed.

*Obj. 2.* Further, the slaying of the innocent, adultery and theft are against the natural law. But we find these things changed by God: as when God commanded Abraham to slay his innocent son (Gen. xxii. 2); and when He ordered the Jews to borrow and purloin the vessels of the Egyptians (Exod. xii. 35); and when He commanded Osee to take to himself *a wife of fornications* (Osee i. 2). Therefore the natural law can be changed.

*Obj. 3.* Further, Isidore says *that the possession of all things in common, and universal freedom, are matters of natural law.* But these things are seen to be changed by human laws. Therefore it seems that the natural law is subject to change.

*On the contrary,* It is said in the *Decretals: The natural law dates from the creation of the rational creature. It does not vary according to time, but remains unchangeable.*

*I answer that,* A change in the natural law may be understood in two ways. First, by way of addition. In this sense, nothing hinders the natural law from being changed, since many things for the benefit of human life have been added over and above the natural law, both by the divine law and by human laws.

Secondly, a change in the natural law may be understood by way of subtraction, so that what previously was according to the natural law, ceases to be so. In this sense, the natural law is altogether unchangeable in its first principles. But in its secondary principles, which, as we have said, are certain detailed proximate conclusions drawn from the first principles, the natural law is not changed so that what it prescribes be not right in most cases. But it may be changed in some particular cases of rare occurrence, through some special causes hindering the observance of such precepts, as was stated above.

*Reply Obj. 1.* The written law is said to be given for the correction of the natural law, either because it supplies what was wanting to the natural law, or because the natural law was so perverted in the hearts of some men, as to certain matters, that they esteemed those things good which are naturally evil; which perversion stood in need of correction.

*Reply Obj. 2.* All men alike, both guilty and innocent, die the death of nature; which death of nature is inflicted by the power of God because of original sin, according to 1 Kings ii. 6: *The Lord killeth and maketh alive.* Consequently, by the command of God, death can be inflicted on any man, guilty or innocent, without any injustice whatever.—In like manner, adultery is intercourse with another's wife; who is allotted to him by the law emanating from God. Consequently intercourse with any woman, by the command of God, is neither adultery nor fornication. —The same applies to theft, which is the taking of another's property. For whatever is taken by the command of God, to Whom all things belong, is not taken against the will of its owner, whereas it is in this that theft consists.—

---

[1] The reference is to Ecclesiasticus, or The Wisdom of Jesus, the Son of Sirach, which does not form part of the Hebrew or Protestant Bible but is one of the Apocrypha. In the Revised Standard Version, moreover, this verse is omitted as not well attested, although a footnote says: "Other authorities add *and he gave them to boast of his marvels for ever.*" W.K.

Nor is it only in human things that whatever is commanded by God is right; but also in natural things, whatever is done by God is, in some way, natural, as was stated in the First Part.

*Reply Obj. 3.* A thing is said to belong to the natural law in two ways. First, because nature inclines thereto: *e.g.*, that one should not do harm to another. Secondly, because nature did not bring with it the contrary. Thus, we might say that for man to be naked is of the natural law, because nature did not give him clothes, but art invented them. In this sense, *the possession of all things in common and universal freedom* are said to be of the natural law, because, namely, the distinction of possessions and slavery were not brought in by nature, but devised by human reason for the benefit of human life. Accordingly, the law of nature was not changed in this respect, except by addition.

# ON THE PRINCIPLES OF NATURE

Observe that some things can exist though they do not exist, while other things do exist. That which can be is said to exist in potency; that which already exists is said to be in act. But there are two sorts of existence: the essential or substantial existence of a thing, for example, a man is, and this is to be in the unqualified sense; and the other is accidental existence, for example, a man is white, and this is to be in some qualified way.

Now, something may be in potency to either sort of existence. For it may be in potency to be a man, as is the case with male seed or the menstrual blood; or it may be in potency to be white, as is the case with a man. Both that which is in potency to substantial existence and that which is in potency to accidental existence may be called matter; as the seed in regard to man, and the man in regard to whiteness. But there is this difference: the matter that is in potency to substantial existence is called the matter *out-of-which;* while that which is in potency to be accidentally is called the matter *in-which.*

Again, properly speaking, that which is in potency to be substantially is called prime matter; but what is in potency to be accidentally is called the subject. So, we say that accidents are in a subject but not that the substantial form is in a subject. This is the difference between matter and a subject: the subject does not get its existence from that which comes to it; of itself it has complete existence. For example, a man does not get his existence from his whiteness. But matter does get existence from that which comes to it, for by itself it possesses incomplete existence. So, to speak without qualification, form gives existence to matter but an accident does not give existence to a subject, rather a subject gives existence to an accident. However, at times one is used for the other, that is, matter for subject, and the reverse.

Just as everything that is in potency can be called matter, so everything from which a thing gets existence, either substantial or accidental, may be called form. Thus a man, when potentially white, becomes actually white through whiteness; and the seed [sperma], when potentially man, becomes an actual man through the soul. Because the form makes something to be actually, the form is said to be an act. Now, that which makes substantial existence actual is called substantial form, and that which produces actual accidental existence is called accidental form.

Moreover, since generation is a movement toward a form, there are two kinds of generation corresponding to the two sorts of form. Generation terminating in accidental form is the qualified sense. In fact, when a substantial form is introduced, something is said to come into being without any qualification; thus, we say that a man comes to exist or is generated. However, when an accidental form is introduced, we do not say that a thing simply comes into existence but that it becomes this sort of thing; thus, when a man becomes white, we do not say that he comes into being or is generated in the unqualified sense, but that he becomes or is generated as a white man.

Again, two kinds of corruption stand in opposition to these two meanings of generation. Of course, generation and corruption in the unqualified sense occur only in the genus of substance. Yet, in the qualified sense generation and corruption occur in all the other genera, and since generation is a change from nonbeing to being, while conversely corruption moves from being to nonbeing, generation does not come about from merely any instance of nonbeing but from that nonbeing which is being in potency. Thus, a statue comes from the copper which is potentially, but not actually, a statue.

So, three items are needed in order that generation may occur: potential being, that is, matter; the fact that the product does not actually exist, and this is privation; and that through which it comes to be actually, namely the form. For example, when a statue is made from copper, the copper which is in potency to the form of the statue is the matter; the fact that it is shapeless or not structured is the privation; and the shape by which it is called a statue is the form—not the substantial form, of course, for the copper actually existed before the advent of this form, and its existence does not depend on this shape which is an accidental form. Indeed, all artificial forms are acciden-

tal. As a matter of fact, art operates only on that which is already established in existence by virtue of nature.

There are, then, three principles of nature, namely matter, form, and privation. One of these, form, is that toward which generation is directed; the other two are on the side of that from which generation begins. Consequently, matter and privation are identical in their subject but differ in meaning. Thus, the same thing which is bronze is also an unshaped thing prior to the incoming of the form; but it is called bronze for one reason, and shapeless for a different reason. Hence, privation is called a principle not essentially but accidentally, for it coincides with matter. In the same way, we say that a physician builds a house accidentally. For the fact that a physician builds is not because he is a doctor but rather because he is a builder and this coincides in one subject with the physician.

However, there are two sorts of accident: the necessary, which is inseparable from the thing, as the risible in man, and that which is not necessary but is separable, as whiteness is from man. Consequently, though privation is an accidental principle, it does not follow that it is unnecessary for generation, since matter is never stripped from privation. In fact, inasmuch as it exists under one form, it has privation for another, and conversely. For example, in fire there is a privation of air and in air a privation of fire.

We should note, further, that though generation starts from nonexistence, we do not say that negation is a principle, but rather privation, for negation does not determine its subject. The inability to see may be predicated even of nonbeings, as in the phrase "a chimera does not see"; and it can be predicated of beings not equipped by their origin to have sight, as in the case of a stone. But privation is predicated only of a subject that is determined, that is, one born to become so endowed, as blindness is attributed only to those that are born to see. Moreover, since generation does not come about from nonbeing in the unqualified sense but from the nonbeing which is in some subject—not just any subject but one of a determinate kind (for fire does not come about from just anything but from that kind of nonfire that is by origin disposed to the form of fire)—therefore, we say that privation is a principle.

Yet, it differs from the other principles by the fact that the others are principles both in the act of being and in that of becoming. In order that a statue may come into being, there must be bronze and that which finally is the shape of the statue; and then, when the statue is already existing, these two principles must be present. Privation, on the other hand, is a principle in the act of becoming but not in that of being; because, while a statue is being made, it cannot as yet be a statue. If it were, then it could not come into being, since that which is becoming has no existence, except for items whose existence is successive, as are time and motion. But as soon as the statue is in existence there is no longer a privation of statue there, for affirmation and negation are not capable of coexistence, and likewise privation and possession. Privation is also an accidental principle, as explained above, while the other two are essential principles.

From what has been said, it is obvious that matter differs in meaning from form and privation. For matter is that in which form and privation are understood; thus, it is in regard to copper that shape and the shapeless are understood. Indeed, sometimes matter is denominated along with privation, and sometimes without privation. In the case of bronze, when it is the matter of a statue, then it does not imply a privation, for, from the fact that I say, "bronze," there is no suggestion that it is without structure or shape. On the

other hand, flour, taken as matter in relation to bread, implies essentially a privation of the form of bread, for, from the fact that I say, "flour," there is signified a lack of disposition or an inordination opposed to the form of bread. And since matter or the subject endures throughout the process of generation, while privation does not, nor does the combination of matter and privation, therefore the matter that does not imply privation is enduring, but that which does imply it is transient.

Yet, we should note that in some cases, matter includes form in its composition; for instance, though bronze is matter in relation to a statue, nevertheless this very bronze is composed of matter and form. Thus, bronze is not called first matter, for it possesses a matter already. On the other hand, that matter which is understood without any form and privation but which is the subject of form and privation is called prime matter because there is no other matter prior to it. This is also called "hyle."

Now, since every definition and act of knowing depends on form, prime matter cannot be known or defined in itself but only in terms of the composite, as it may be said that prime matter is that which is related to all forms and privations as bronze is to the statue and to the shapeless. In this sense, it is called prime without qualification. Of course, it is possible for something to be called prime with respect to some definite genus, as water is prime matter in the genus of wet things. Yet, it is not prime in the simple sense, for it is composed of matter and form and consequently has a prior matter.

It should be noted, also, that prime matter, and form, too, are not generated or corrupted, because every generation is from something to something. Now, that from which generation takes place is matter, and that to which it is directed is form. So, if matter or form were generated, there would be matter for matter, and form for form, on to infinity. Hence, to speak strictly, there is generation of the composite only.

Observe, also, that prime matter is said to be numerically one in all things. Numerically one, of course, has two meanings: it may mean that which possesses one form which is numerically determined, as in the case of Socrates. Now, this is not the way in which prime matter is said to be numerically one, since it does not have in itself any form. Another meaning of numerically one is that which exists without dispositions making it numerically different. It is in this way that matter is said to be numerically one, for it is understood without any dispositions by which it is numerically differentiated.

Again, we should note that although prime matter includes no form or privation in its rational character, yet it is never stripped away from form and privation. Sometimes it exists under one form, sometimes under another. But it can never exist by itself because, since it has no form within its own rational character, it possesses no actual existence, for to be in act is impossible without a form; it is in potency only. So, whatever is in act cannot be called prime matter.

It is clear from the foregoing that there are three principles of nature, namely, matter, form, and privation. Yet, these are not enough for generation. In fact, that which is in potency cannot reduce itself to act. Thus, the copper which is potentially a statue does not make itself into a statue; it needs an operating agent to draw the form of the statue from potency into act. Now, the form cannot draw itself from potency into act—I am talking about the form of the product of generation, what we call the terminus of the process of generation. As a matter of fact, the form is not present except in that which actually exists: that which

is being worked on is in the process of becoming, that is, while the thing is being made. So, beside the matter and form there must be some principle that acts and this is called a producer, a mover, or an agent, or that from which change takes its beginning.

Again, because everything that acts does so only by tending toward something, as Aristotle explains in the second book of the *Metaphysics* (II, text 8-9), there must be a fourth principle, namely, that which is intended by the agent. This is called the end. It should also be noted that although every agent both natural and voluntary intends an end, it does not follow that every agent knows its end or deliberates about its end. To know their end is necessary in the case of those agents whose actions are not determined but are open to opposite possibilities, as is true of voluntary agents. So, they must know their end, whereby they may determine their own actions. On the other hand, in the case of physical agents, their actions are determined; consequently, they do not have to choose the means to their end. Avicenna gives the example of a harpist (*Physics*, II, 10) who does not have to deliberate over each plucking of the strings, because the pluckings have become determinate in his case; otherwise, there would be a delay between the pluckings and that would not sound right.

Now, it is more obvious that the voluntary agent deliberates than that the physical agent does. So, there is greater force to the conclusion that if even the voluntary agent (in whose case deliberation is more evident) sometimes does not deliberate, therefore the physical agent does not. It is possible for the physical agent to tend towards its end without deliberation; and this intending is nothing but having a natural inclination toward something.

From the previous explanations, then, it is clear that there are four causes: material, efficient, formal, and final. Now, although "principle" and "cause" may be employed interchangeably (as is stated in the *Metaphysics*, V, 1, 1013a17), still, Aristotle in the *Physics* (I, 7, 191a20; II, 3, 195a15) gives four causes and three principles. He takes causes as extrinsic as well as intrinsic. Matter and form are said to be intrinsic to a thing, in the sense that they are constitutive parts of the thing. The efficient and final causes are called extrinsic because they are outside the thing. But he is taking principles as intrinsic causes only. Now, privation is not named among the causes because it is an incidental principle, as they say. So, when we speak of four causes, we mean essential [*per se*] causes, to which the incidental causes may be reduced; for everything that is incidental may be reduced to what is essential.

However, although in the first book of the *Physics* Aristotle speaks of principles as intrinsic causes, still (as is stated in the *Metaphysics*, XII, 4, 1070b22), "principle" is properly used of extrinsic causes and "element" of causes that are parts of the thing, that is, of intrinsic causes. However, "cause" is used for both; sometimes one of these terms is used for the other, since every cause may be called a principle and every principle a cause. Nevertheless, "cause" seems to add something to the usual way of speaking about a principle; for, whatever is first, whether the being of the consequent follows from it or not, can be called a principle. Thus, a metalworker is called the principle of a knife, because the existence of the knife is due to his work; but when something is changed from black to white, we also say that black is the principle of this change (and generally, everything from which a change takes its start is called a principle), yet black is not that from which the existence of the white flows as a consequent. Rather, we only use "cause" for that sort of first item from which the existence of the consequent

follows. Hence, the statement is made that a cause is that from whose being another being follows. So, that first item from which motion takes its start cannot be called an essential cause, though it may be called a principle. For this reason, privation is placed among the principles and not among the causes; for privation is that from which generation takes its start. Of course, it can also be called an incidental cause, in the sense that it is coincident with matter, as has been explained above.

In the proper sense, "element" is used only in reference to the causes out of which the thing is composed, and these are properly the material ones. Again, this will not apply to every material cause but to that from which the primary composition takes place. Thus, we do not say that bodily members are elements of a man, because his members are also composed of other items. But we do say that earth and water are elements, for they are not composed of other bodies. Rather, the primary composition of natural bodies is made out of them.

As a result, Aristotle in the *Metaphysics* (V, 3, 1014a26) says that "element" means the primary component of a thing, immanent in it, and indivisible into other kinds of stuff. The meaning of the first phrase, "the primary component of a thing," is clear from what we have just said. The second phrase, "immanent in it," is included to differentiate "element" from matter that is wholly corrupted by generation. For example, food is the matter for blood, but blood is not produced unless the food is used up; hence, the food does not remain in the blood, and so, food cannot be called an element of blood. Of course, elements must remain in some way, for they are not completely corrupted, as is explained in the book *On Generation* (I, 10, 327b30). The third phrase, "and indivisible into other kinds of stuff," is included to differentiate "element" from things that have parts that are formally or specifically different; for instance, the hand, whose parts are flesh and bones which do differ in kind. But an element is not divisible into parts that differ in kind; water, for example, each part of which is water. It is not required that an element be indivisible quantitatively; it is enough if it be indivisible into different kinds of stuff. Of course, if it is also indivisible in all ways, it is called an element; thus, letters are called the elements of words. It is obvious, then, from what has been said that principle is as it were a more extensive term than cause, and cause more extensive than element. This is what the Commentator says in explaining Book V of the *Metaphysics* [Averroes, *Metaphysica*, Venice, 1552, fol. 50].

Having seen that there are four kinds of causes, we should next observe that it is not impossible for the same thing to have several causes. Thus, the cause of a statue is the copper and the sculptor, but the sculptor as efficient, the copper as matter. Nor is it impossible for the same thing to be the cause of contrary effects. For instance, a pilot may be the cause of saving or sinking a ship: of the former by his presence, of the latter by his absence.

It is even possible for one thing to be both cause and effect with regard to another item, but in a different fashion. Thus, walking, taken as efficient, is the cause of health; but health, as an end, is the cause of walking, for walking is sometimes done for the sake of health. So, too, the body is as matter to the soul; while the soul is as form to the body. In fact, the efficient is called a cause in relation to the end, since the end does not actually function without the activity of the agent. On the other hand, the end is called the cause of the agent, since the latter will not work unless it tend toward the end. Hence, the efficient is the cause of the fact that a certain item stands as an end, for instance, walking in order that there may be health; however, it does not cause

the end to be an end, so it is not the cause of the causality of the end; it does not make the end a final cause. For example, a physician may make health to be present actually but he does not cause health to be an end. On the other hand, the end is not the cause of the fact that a given being is efficient but it is the cause of the fact that the agent is acting. Health does not make a physician exist as a physician (I am talking about the health that is produced by the physician's activity) but it does result in the fact that the physician is acting. Hence, the end is the cause of the causality of the agent, because it makes the agent to be an agent; likewise, it makes matter function as matter, and form as form. For matter will not take on form except for the sake of an end; and form will not perfect matter except for the sake of an end. That is the reason for the statement: the end is the cause of causes, for it is the cause of the causality in all the causes.

Matter is also called the cause of the form, in the sense that the form does not exist except in the matter. Likewise, the form is the cause of the matter, because the matter has no actual being except by virtue of the form. In fact, matter and form are correlatives, as is stated in the *Physics* (II, 2, 194b10). They are predicated of the composite as parts of the whole, and as the simple in relation to the complex.

Moreover, since every cause as cause is naturally prior to its effect, we should note that "prior" has two meanings, as Aristotle says in the treatise *On Animals* (XVI, 743a19-22). As a result of these different meanings, a thing can be called both prior and posterior in the same relationship, and the cause can be called the effect. Indeed, something is said to be prior to another, (1) in generation and time, and (2) in substance and perfection. So, since a natural activity proceeds from the imperfect to the perfect, and from the incomplete to the complete, the imperfect is prior to the perfect according to generation and time; however, the perfect is prior to the imperfect in substance. Thus, one can say that the man is before the boy in substance and perfection, but the boy is before the man in generation and time. However, although the imperfect is prior to the perfect, and potency is prior to act, in the order of generable things (considering the fact that in any one thing the imperfect is prior to the perfect and it is in potency before it is in act), yet, absolutely speaking, act and the perfect must be prior. For that which reduces potency to act exists actually; and that which perfects the imperfect is something perfect. Matter, then, is prior to form in generation and time, for that to which something happens is prior to the fact that it happens. But form is prior to matter in substance and complete being, for matter has no complete being without form. Likewise, the agent is prior to the end in generation and time, since motion toward the end comes from the agent. However, the end is prior to the agent, as agent in substance and perfection, since the action of the agent is only completed by virtue of the end. And so, these two causes, material and efficient, are prior in the way of generation; but the form and the end are prior in the way of perfection.

Note, next, that necessity is twofold: namely, absolute and conditional. Absolute necessity is that which proceeds from causes that are prior in the way of generation, and these are the matter and the end. Such is the necessity of death; it results from matter, that is, from the disposition of its constituent contraries. This is called absolute because nothing impedes it. It is also called the necessity of matter. On the other hand, conditional necessity proceeds from causes that are posterior in the process of generation, that is, from the form and the end. Thus, we say that if a man is to be generated, there must be an act of conception. This kind is called conditional

because in the absolute sense there is no necessity that this certain woman conceive, but only under this condition, namely, if a human being is to be generated. This is also called the necessity of the end.

It is to be noted, too, that three of the causes can coincide: namely, form, end, and agent. This is illustrated in the production of fire. Indeed, fire generates fire, and thus fire is an efficient cause, inasmuch as it generates. Then, fire is a form, since it makes something that was previously in potency to be actually. Again, it is an end, in that the agent's activity terminates in it. Of course, the end is twofold: namely, the end of the process of generation and the end of the thing that is generated. This is evident in the production of a knife: the form of the knife is the end of the process of production, but cutting (which is the work of a knife) is the end of the thing itself that is produced, of the knife. Now, the end of the process of generation sometimes coincides with the two causes under discussion—that is to say, when generation takes place from a specifically similar being. For instance, when a man generates a man, or an olive produces an olive. But this does not apply to the end of the thing that is generated. Still, we should note that the end coincides with the form numerically; for numerically the same item that is the form of the thing generated is the end of the process of generation. However, this end does not coincide with the agent numerically but only specifically. It is impossible for the maker and his product to be numerically identical but they can be of the same species. For instance, when a man generates a man, the man generating and the one that is generated are numerically different but specifically the same. Matter, however, does not coincide with the other causes, for matter has the character of something imperfect because it is being in potency; while the other causes, since they are in act, have the character of something perfect. Now, the perfect and the imperfect do not coincide in the same subject.

Now that we have seen that there are four causes, the efficient, material, formal, and final, we should observe that each of these causes can be analyzed in many ways. We speak of something as a prior cause and of something else as a posterior cause. For instance, we say that art and the physician are the cause of health: art being the prior cause and the physician the posterior one. The same distinction applies to the formal and the other causes. Observe that we should always reduce a question to the primary cause. For example, if the question is: *Why is this man healthy?*, the answer should be: *Because a physician has cured him*; and again: *Why did the physician cure him? Because of the art of healing which he possesses.*

Note also that the so-called proximate cause is the same as the posterior cause; and the remote cause is the same as the prior cause. Hence, these two analyses of the causes—sometimes as prior and posterior, sometimes as remote and proximate causes—mean the same thing. Moreover, it is to be observed that, in all cases, that which is more general is called the remote cause, while that which is more special is the proximate cause. Thus, we say that man's proximate form is his definition, rational mortal animal, but "animal" is a more remote form, and "substance" is still more remote. Indeed, all higher things are as forms to lower things. Likewise, the proximate matter of a statue is bronze, the remote is metal, and still more remote is body.

Next, one kind of cause is essential [*per se*] and another incidental [*per accidens*]. A cause is called essential when it is the cause of a certain thing as such. Thus, a builder is the cause of a house and wood is the material cause of a bench. An incidental cause means that which happens incidentally to an essential cause; for instance, when we speak of a grammarian who is building. In fact, the grammarian is called the cause of the building incidentally, not because he is a grammarian but because it is incidental to the builder that he is a grammarian. The same thing holds in the case of the other causes.

Again, some causes are simple and some are composite. A cause is called simple when it alone is assigned as cause to that of which it is the essential cause, or also when it alone is the incidental cause. Thus, we say that the builder is the cause of the house, and we may also say that the physician is the cause of the house. It is called composite when both are assigned as cause; thus we might say the physician-builder is the cause of the house. It is also possible to talk about simple cause in the way that Avicenna explains it (*Physics*, II, 8), as that which is a cause without the addition of anything else; thus is bronze for the statue (for the statue is made from bronze without the addition of any other matter). Similarly, we may say that the physician causes health, or that fire causes heating. Then, the composite cause means that several items must combine in order that there be a cause. For example, one man is not the cause of the motion of a ship but many are; and one stone is not the material cause of a house but many are.

Furthermore, some causes are in act and some in potency. A cause in act is one that is actually causing something; for example, the builder when he is building. Note that in speaking of causes in act, it is necessary for cause and effect to be simultaneous, in the sense that if one is, then the other is, too. In fact, if there is a builder in act, then be must be building; if the building process is in act, then there must be a builder in act. However, this is not required in the case of causes that are only in potency. Observe, too, that the universal cause is correlative with the universal effect, while a singular cause corresponds to a singular effect. Thus, we say that a builder is the cause of a house, and this builder of this house.

We should also note that in speaking about intrinsic principles, that is, matter and form, the points of resemblance or difference in the principles depend on the resemblance and difference of the consequents. Some are numerically the same, as Socrates and this man is, when we are pointing at Socrates. Others are numerically different but the same in species: for instance, Socrates and Plato, though alike in their human species, are nevertheless different in number. Still others differ specifically but are the same in their genus: thus, man and donkey agree in their animal genus. Of course, others are different generically and are the same only according to analogy: thus are substance and quantity, which do not agree in any genus but agree only according to analogy. Indeed, they agree only in the fact that each is a being; but being is not a genus, because it is not predicated univocally but analogically.

To understand this, we should observe that an item is predicable of several things in three ways: univocally, equivocally, and analogically. It is predicated univocally when the predication uses the same name and the same meaning or definition; thus is animal predicated of man and donkey. Both mean animal, and both mean an animate substance capable of sensing, since this is the definition of an animal. Predication is equivocal when the predication applies the same name to several things but with different meanings; thus we use "dog" to speak of a thing that barks and of a constellation in the heavens. They agree in name only and not in definition or signification. In fact, that which is signified by a name is the definition, as is stated in the *Metaphysics* (IV, 7, 1012a24). It is said to be predicated analogically when the predication applies to several items whose meanings are different but are at-

tributed to some one meaning that is the same. For example, "healthy" is predicated of the animal body, of urine, and of a drink, but the meaning is not entirely the same in all the cases. It is predicated of urine as a sign of health, of a body as of its subject, of a drink as of its cause; nevertheless, all these meanings are attributed to one end, namely, health. Sometimes, items that agree analogically (that is, proportionally, comparatively, or by way of adaptation) are attributed to one end, as appears in the preceding example; and sometimes to one agent, as when "physician" is predicated of a person who practices by means of the art of medicine, and of one who practices without the art, like a midwife. And it may even be predicated of instruments, but by way of attribution to one basic item, as being is predicated of substance and of quantity, quality, and the other categories. For, the meaning whereby substance is being is not entirely the same as that for quantity and the others; but all are called being from the fact that they are attributed to substance, which is, indeed, the subject of the others. So, being is predicated primarily of substance and secondarily of the others. Thus, being is not the genus of substance and quantity, because no genus is predicated primarily and secondarily of its species, but being is predicated analogically. This is why we say that substance and quantity differ generically but are similar by way of analogy.

Of those items that are numerically the same, both form and matter are the same in a numerical unit, as in the example of Tully and Cicero [two names for the same man]. On the other hand, in things that are the same specifically but different numerically, the matter and form are also not the same in number but only in species: as in the case of Socrates and Plato. Similarly, for those things that are generically the same, the principles are also the same in their genus: thus the soul and body of a donkey and of a horse are different in species but the same in genus. Likewise, in those things that are in agreement by analogy only, the principles are the same by analogy only, or by proportion. For matter, form, and privation, or potency and act, are principles of substance and also of the other genera. Yet, the matter of substance and of quantity, and similarly their form and privation, differ generically but agree only by way of proportion—in the sense that just as the matter of substance is related to the substance according to the characteristic meaning of matter, so, too, is the matter of quantity related to quantity. However, as substance is the cause of the rest of the genera, so are the principles of substance principles for all the others.

# OCKHAM

## THE PROBLEM OF UNIVERSALS

First we must realise that "singular" is taken in two senses. In one sense the name "singular" signifies whatever is one thing and not several. If it is so understood, then those who hold that a universal is a certain quality of the mind predicable of many things (but standing for these many things, not for itself) have to say that every universal is truly and really a singular. For just as every word, no matter how common it may be by convention, is truly and really singular and numerically one, since it is one thing and not many, so likewise the mental content that signifies several things outside is truly and really singular and numerically one, since it is one thing and not many things, though it signifies several things.

In another sense the name "singular" is taken for that which is one and not several things and is not of such a nature as to be the sign of several things. If "singular" is understood in this sense,

then no universal is singular, since every universal is of such a nature as to be a sign of, and to be predicated of, several things. Hence, if a universal is that which is not numerically one—a meaning attributed by many to "universal"— then I say that nothing is a universal, unless perhaps you wish to abuse this word by saying that a population is a universal, since it is not one but many. But that would be childish.

Hence we have to say that every universal is one singular thing. Therefore nothing is universal except by signification, by being a sign of several things. This is what Avicenna says in the fifth book of the *Metaphysics*: "One form in the intellect has reference to a multitude, and in this sense it is a universal, since the universal is a content in the intellect which is equally related to anything you take." And later on: "This form, though universal in reference to individuals, is nevertheless individual in reference to the particular mind in which it is impressed, for it is one of the forms in the intellect." He wishes to say here that the universal is one particular content of the mind itself, of such a nature as to be predicated of several things; therefore, it is by the very fact that it is of such a nature as to be predicated of several things (standing not for itself, but for those many things), that it is called a "universal." By the fact, however, that it is one form really existing in the intellect, it is called a "singular." Hence "singular" in the first sense is predicated of the universal, but not "singular" in the second sense. In like manner, we say that the sun is a universal cause, and nevertheless it is in truth a particular and singular thing, and consequently a singular and particular cause. For the sun is called "universal cause," because it is the cause of many things, namely of all that can be generated and corrupted here below. It is, on the other hand, called "particular cause," because it is one cause and not several causes. Likewise the content of the soul is called "universal," because it is a sign predicable of many; on the other hand, it is called "singular," because it is one thing and not many things.

It must, however, be understood that there are two sorts of universal. There is one sort which is naturally universal; in other words, is a sign naturally predicable of many things, in much the same way as smoke naturally signifies fire, or a groan the pain of a sick man, or laughter an inner joy. Such a universal is nothing other than a content of the mind; and therefore no substance outside the mind and no accident outside the mind is such a universal. It is only of such a universal that I shall speak in the chapters that follow.

The other sort of universal is so by convention. In this way, an uttered word, which is really a single quality, is universal; for it is a conventional sign meant to signify many things. Therefore, just as the word is said to be common, so it can be said to be universal. But it is not so by nature, only by convention.

## A Universal Is Not a Thing Outside the Mind

Since it is not sufficient merely to assert this without proving it by manifest reasoning, I shall advance a few reasons for what has been said above and I shall confirm by arguments from authority.

That a universal is not a substance existing outside the mind can in the first place be evidently proved as follows: No universal is a substance that is single and numerically one. For if that were supposed, it would follow that Socrates is a universal, since there is no stronger reason for one singular substance to be a universal than for another; therefore no singular substance is a universal, but every substance is numerically one and singular. For everything is either one thing and not many, or it is many things. If it is one and not many, it is numerically one. If, however, a substance is many things, it is either many singular things or many universal things. On the first supposition it follows that a substance would be several singular substances; for the same reason, then, some substance would be several men; and thus, although a universal would be distinguished from one particular thing, it would yet not be distinguished from particular things. If, however, a substance were several universal things, let us take one of these universal things and ask "Is this one thing and not many, or is it many things?" If the first alternative is granted, then it follows that it is singular; if the second is granted, we have to ask again "Is it many singular or many universal things?" And thus either this will go on *in infinitum,* or we must take the stand that no substance is universal in such a way that it is not singular. Hence, the only remaining alternative is that no substance is universal.

Furthermore, if a universal were one substance existing in singular things and distinct from them, it would follow that it could exist apart from them; for every thing naturally prior to another thing can exist apart from it by the power of God. But this consequence is absurd.

Furthermore, if that opinion were true, no individual could be created, but something of the individual would pre-exist; for it would not get its entire being from nothing, if the universal in it has existed before in another individual. For the same reason it would follow that God could not annihilate one individual of a substance, if He did not destroy the other individuals. For if He annihilated one individual, He would destroy the whole of the essence of the individual, and consequently he would destroy that universal which is in it and in others; consequently, the other individuals do not remain, since they cannot remain without a part of themselves, such as the universal is held to be.

Furthermore, we could not assume such a universal to be something entirely extrinsic to the essence of an individual; therefore, it would be of the essence of the individual, and consequently the individual would be composed of universals; and thus the individual would not be more singular than universal.

Furthermore, it follows that something of the essence of Christ would be miserable and damned; since that common nature which really exists in Christ, really exists in Judas also and is damned. Therefore, something is both in Christ and in one who is damned, namely in Judas. That, however, is absurd.

Still other reasons could be advanced which I pass over for the sake of brevity.

The same conclusion I will now confirm by authorities. . . .

From these and many other texts it is clear that a universal is a mental content of such nature as to be predicated of many things. This can also be confirmed by reason. All agree that every universal is predicable of things. But only a mental content or conventional sign, not a substance, is of such nature as to be predicated. Consequently, only a mental content or a conventional sign is a universal. However, at present I am not using "universal" for a conventional sign, but for that which is naturally a universal. Moreover, it is clear that no substance is of such nature as to be predicated; for if that were true, it would follow that a proposition would be composed of particular substances, and consequently that the subject could be in Rome and the predicate in England. That is absurd.

Furthermore, a proposition is either in the mind or in spoken or written words. Consequently, its parts are either in the mind or in speech or in writing. Such things, however, are not particular substances. Therefore, it is established that no proposition can be composed of substances; but a proposition is composed of universals; hence universals are in no way substances.

## Scotus' Opinion on Universals and Its Refutation

Although it is clear to many that a universal is not a substance existing outside the mind in individuals and really distinct from them, still some are of the opinion that a universal does in some manner exist outside the mind in individuals, although not really but only formally distinct from them. Hence they say that in Socrates there is human nature, which is "contracted to" Socrates by an individual difference which is not really but only formally distinct from this nature. Hence the nature and the individual difference are not two things, although the one is not formally the other.

However, this opinion appears to me wholly untenable. Proof: In creatures no extra-mental distinction of any kind is possible except where distinct things exist. If, therefore, some kind of distinction exists between this nature and this difference, it is necessary that they be really distinct things. I prove the minor premise in syllogistic form as follows: This nature is not formally distinct from itself; this individual difference is formally distinct from this nature; therefore this individual difference is not this nature.

Furthermore, the same thing is not common and proper; however, according to them, the individual is proper, but the universal is common; therefore the individual difference is not common; consequently no universal is the same thing as the individual difference.

Furthermore, opposites cannot belong to the same created thing; "common" and "proper" are opposites; therefore the same thing is not common and proper, as would follow if individual difference and common nature were the same thing.

Furthermore, if common nature were really the same as the individual difference, then there would be in reality as many common natures as there are individual differences, and hence none of them would be common, but each one would be proper to the difference with which it is really identical.

Furthermore, everything which is distinguished from something else is distinguished either of itself or by some thing intrinsic to itself; but the humanity of Plato is one thing and the humanity of Socrates another; therefore they are distinguished of themselves; therefore *not* by having differences added to them.

Furthermore, according to Aristotle, things specifically different are also numerically different;; but the nature of a man and the nature of a donkey are of themselves specifically different; therefore, of themselves, they are numerically different; consequently, each of these natures is on its own account numerically one.

Furthermore, what no power can

cause to belong to several things no power can make predicable of several things; now on power can make such a nature, if it is really the same as the individual difference, belong to several things, because in no manner can [something really identified with one individual] belong to another individual; therefore, no power can make it predicable of several things, and consequently no power can make it universal.

Furthermore, I take this individual difference and the nature that it "contracts" and ask "Is the distinction greater or less than between two individuals?" It is not greater, since they do not differ really; whereas individuals do differ really. Nor is it less, for then the two things said to be distinct would fall under the same concept, just as two individuals fall under the same concept. Consequently, if the one is numerically one on its own account, the other will also be so on its own account.

Furthermore, I ask "Is the nature the individual difference, or is it not?" If it is, then I shall argue in syllogistic form as follows: This individual difference is proper and not common, this individual difference is the nature; consequently the nature is proper and not common, which is what we intended to prove. Likewise I argue in syllogistic form as follows: This individual difference is not formally distinct from this individual difference; this individual difference is the nature; therefore, this nature is not formally distinct from the individual difference. If, however, the other alternative is granted, namely "This individual difference is not the nature," our thesis is admitted, since this therefore follows: The individual difference is not the nature, therefore the individual difference is not really the nature. For from the opposite of the consequent the opposite of the antecedent follows, by this argument: The individual difference is really the nature, therefore the individual difference is the nature. The inference is clear, since it is a valid inference to argue from a determinable as qualified by a determination which does not cancel or diminish it,[1] to the determinable without the qualification. "Really," however, is not a cancelling or diminishing determination, hence this follows: The individual difference is really the nature, therefore the individual difference is the nature.

Therefore it must be said that in creatures there is no such formal distinction; but whatever in creatures is distinct, is really distinct, and constitutes a distinct thing, if each of the two things distinguished is truly a thing. Just as in creatures we must never deny the validity of such modes of arguing as "This is *A*, this is *B*, consequently a *B* is *A*," or "This is not *A*, this is *B*, consequently a *B* is not *A*," so also as regards creatures whenever contradictory predicates are true of certain things, we must not deny that the things are distinct; unless of course some determination or some syncategorematic term should be what causes this to be true, as should not be assumed in our present case.

Therefore we must say with the Philosopher that in a particular substance nothing whatsoever is substantial except the particular form and the particular matter or a compound of matter and form. Hence we must not imagine that in Socrates we have human nature or humanity distinct in any way from Socrates, to which is added an individual difference that "contracts" this nature. But any imaginable substantial reality that exists in Socrates is either the particular matter or the particular form or a compound of the two. Therefore every essence and quiddity and everything substantial, if it really exists outside the mind, is either simply and absolutely matter or form, or a compound of them, or it is a separate immaterial substance, according to the teachings of the Peripatetics.

## A Universal Is a Thought-object[2]

Another theory [different from those opinions concerning the nature of universals previously criticised by Ockham] could be advanced. I maintain that a universal is not something real that exists in a subject [of inherence], either inside or outside the mind, but that it has being only as a thought-object in the mind. It is a kind of mental picture which as a thought-object has a being similar to that which the thing outside the mind has in its real existence. What I mean is this: The intellect, seeing a thing outside the mind, forms in the mind a picture resembling it, in such a way that if the mind had the power to produce as it has the power to picture, it would produce by this act a real outside thing which would be only numerically distinct from the former real thing. The case would be similar, analogously speaking, to the activity of an artist. For just as the artist who sees a house or building outside the mind first pictures in the mind a similar house and later produces a similar house in reality which is only numerically distinct from the first, so in our case the picture in the mind that we get from seeing something outside would act as a pattern. For just as the imagined house would be a pattern for the architect, if he who imagines it had the power to produce it in reality, so likewise the other picture would be a pattern for him who forms it. And this can be called a universal, because it is a pattern and relates indifferently to all the singular things outside the mind. Because of the similarity between its being as a thought-object and the being of like things outside the mind, it can stand for such things. And in this way a universal is not the result of generation, but of

---

1 This saving clause means that e.g., we cannot infer validly: A dead man is inanimate, *ergo* some man is inanimate.

2 Ockham's first opinion, later abandoned.

abstraction, which is only a kind of mental picturing.

I shall first show that something exists in the mind whose being is that of an object of thought only, without inhering in the mind as an independent subject.

This is clear from the following: According to the philosophers, existence is primarily divided into existence in the mind and existence outside the mind, the latter being subdivided into the ten categories. If this is admitted, then I ask "What is understood here by "existence in the mind?" It means either existence as a thought-object, and then we have our intended thesis, or it means existence as in a subject. The latter, however, is not possible; for, whatever exists truly in the mind as a subject, is contained under existence that is divided into the ten categories, since it falls under quality. For an act of intellect, and indeed in general every accident or form of the mind, is a true quality, like heat or whiteness, and hence does not fall under the division of existence that is set over against existence in the ten categories. [Consequently the main distinction of the philosophers would be futile.]

Furthermore, fictions have being in the mind, but they do not exist independently, because in that case they would be real things and so a chimera and a goat-stag and so on would be real things. So some things exist only as thought-objects.

Likewise, propositions, syllogisms, and other similar objects of logic do not exist independently; therefore they exist only as thought-objects, so that their being consists in being known. Consequently, there are beings which exist only as thought-objects.

Again, works of art do not seem to inhere in the mind of the craftsman as independent subjects any more than the creatures did in the divine mind before creation.

Likewise, conceptual relations are commonly admitted by the [scholastic] doctors. If this is conceded, then I ask "Do they exist only in a subject?" In that case they will be genuine things and real relations. Or do they exist only as thought-objects? In that case we have our intended thesis.

Again, according to those who think differently, the term "being" means a univocal concept, and nevertheless does not mean a distinct reality.

Likewise, practically all men distinguish second intentions from first intentions, and they do not call the second intentions real qualities of the mind. Since they are not in reality outside the mind, they can only exist as thought-objects in the mind.

Secondly, I maintain that this mental picture is what is primarily and immediately meant by the concept "universal," and has the nature of a thought-object, and is that which is the immediate term of an act of intellection having no singular object. This mental picture, in the manner of being that a thought-object has, is just whatever the corresponding singular is, in the manner of being proper to a subject; and so by its very nature it can stand for the singulars of which it is in a way a likeness. . . .

I maintain, therefore, that just as a spoken word is universal and is a genus or a species, but only by convention, in the same way the concept thus mentally fashioned and abstracted from singular things previously known is universal by its nature. . . .

### A Universal Is an Act of the Intellect[3]

There could be another opinion, according to which a concept is the same as the act of knowing. This opinion appears to me to be the more probable one among all the opinions which assume that these concepts really exist in the soul as a subject, like true qualities of

---

3 Second opinion, finally held by Ockham.

the soul; I shall first explain this opinion in its more probable form.

I maintain, then, that somebody wishing to hold this opinion may assume that the intellect apprehending a singular thing performs within itself a cognition of this singular only. This cognition is called a state of mind, and it is capable of standing for this singular thing by its very nature. Hence, just as the spoken word "Socrates" stands by convention for the thing it signifies, so that one who hears this utterance, "Socrates is running," does not conceive that this word, "Socrates," which he hears, is running, but rather that the thing signified by this word is running; so likewise one who knew or understood that something was affirmatively predicated of this cognition of a singular thing would not think that the cognition was such and such, but would conceive that the thing to which the cognition refers is such and such. Hence, just as the spoken word stands by convention for a thing, so the act of intellect, by its very nature, and without any convention, stands for the thing to which it refers.

Beside this intellectual grasp of a singular thing the intellect also forms other acts which do not refer more to one thing than to another. For instance, just as the spoken word "man" does not signify Socrates more than Plato, and hence does not stand more for Socrates than Plato, so it would be with an act of intellect which does not relate to Socrates any more than to Plato or any other man. And in like manner there would be also a knowledge whereby this animal is not more known than that animal; and so with other notions.

To sum up: The mind's own intellectual acts are called states of mind. By their nature they stand for the actual things outside the mind or for other things in the mind, just as the spoken words stand for them by convention. . . .

. . . By such a common or confused intellection, singular things outside the mind are known. For instance, to say that we have a confused intellection of man, means that we have a cognition by which we do not understand one man rather than another, but that by such a cognition we have cognition of a man rather than a donkey. And this amounts to saying that such a cognition, by some kind of assimilation, bears a greater resemblance to a man than to a donkey, but does not resemble one man rather than another. In consequence of the aforesaid, it seems necessary to say that an infinity of objects can be known by such a confused cognition. Still this seems no more untenable than that an infinity of objects can be liked or desired by the same act of liking or desiring. Yet the latter does not seem to be untenable. For a man may like all the parts of a continuous thing, which are infinite in number, or he may desire that all these parts remain in existence. Now in such a case, what was desired would simply be a part of the continuous thing, but not one part rather than another; therefore all parts must be desired; these parts, however, are infinite in number. Likewise, somebody can desire the existence of all men who can exist. Now these are infinite in number, since an infinity of men can be generated.

And so it could be said that one and the same cognition refers to an infinite number of singulars without being a cognition proper to any one of them, and this is so because of osme specific likeness between these individuals that does not exist between others. However, no singular thing can be distinguished from another by such a cognition.

• • •

## What Is Requisite to the Truth of a Singular Proposition?

. . . Let us first speak of singular propositions of inherence in the present tense [and not determined by a modality], which have both the predicate and the subject in the nominative case, and are not equivalent to a hypothetical proposition. For the truth of such a singular proposition, which is not equivalent to many propositions, it is not required that the subject and the predicate be really the same, nor that the predicate be really in the subject, or really inhere in the subject, nor that it be really united with the subject outside the mind. For instance, for the truth of the proposition "This is an angel" it is not required that this common term "angel" be really the same with that which has the position of subject in this proposition, or that it be really in it, or anything of the sort; but it is sufficient and necessary that subject and predicate should stand for the same thing. If, therefore, in the proposition "This is an angel" subject and predicate stand for the same thing, the proposition is true. Hence it is not denoted, by this proposition, that this [individual] has "angelity," or that "angelity" is in him, or something of that kind, but it is denoted that this [individual] is truly an angel. Not indeed that he is this predicate ["angel"], but that he is that for which the predicate stands. In like manner also the propositions "Socrates is a man," "Socrates is an animal," do not denote that Socrates has humanity or animality, nor that humanity or animality is in Socrates, nor that man or animal is in Socrates, nor that man or animal belongs to the essence or quiddity of Socrates or to the quidditative concept of Socrates. They rather denote that Socrates is truly a man and that he is truly an animal; not that Socrates is the predicate "man" or the predicate "animal," but that he is something that the predicate "man" and the predicate "animal" stand for or represent; for each of these predicates stands for Socrates.

From this is becomes clear that all the following propositions are false in their literal meaning: "Man belongs to the quiddity of Socrates,' "Man is of the es-sence of Socrates," "Humanity is in Socrates," "Socrates has humanity," "Socrates is a man by his humanity," and many such propositions, which almost everyone concedes. The falsity of such propositions is clear; I take one of them, viz. "Humanity is in Socrates," and I ask: For what does "humanity" stand? Either for a thing, or for a mental content; that is, such a proposition denotes either that a real thing outside the mind is in Socrates, or that a mental content is in Socrates. If "humanity" stands for a thing, then I ask, For which thing? Either for Socrates, or for a part of Socrates, or for a thing that is neither Socrates nor a part of Socrates. If it stands for Socrates, then the proposition is false. For no thing that is Socrates is in Socrates, because Socrates is not in Socrates, although Socrates is Socrates. And likewise humanity is not in Socrates, but *is* Socrates, if "humanity" stands for a thing that is Socrates. If, however, "humanity" stands for a thing that is part of Socrates, then, again, the proposition is false, because every thing which is part of Socrates is either matter, or form, or a composite of matter and form (only one human substantial form, not any other such form, is in question), or else an integral part of Socrates. But none of these parts is humanity, as can be shown case by case. For the intellective soul is not humanity; because then true humanity would have remained in Christ during the three days after his death, and consequently humanity would have been truly united with the divine Word during this time, and therefore the World would then have been truly a man, which is false. Likewise, matter is not humanity, nor is the body of Socrates humanity, nor the foot nor the head, nor any of the other parts of Socrates, because no part of Socrates is humanity, but only a part of humanity. Consequently, "humanity" cannot stand for a part of Socrates. If, however, it stands for a thing which is neither

Socrates nor a part of Socrates, such a thing is only an accident or some other thing which is not Socrates; and therefore "humanity" in this case would stand for an accident or for some other thing which is neither Socrates nor a part of Socrates. This is manifestly false.

If, however, "humanity" stands for a content of the mind, then also our proposition is manifestly false, since a content of the mind is not Socrates. It is clear then that the proposition "Humanity is in Socrates" is utterly false.

•  •  •

# BEING, ESSENCE, AND EXISTENCE

## The Notion of Being

The first thing to know about "being" (*ens*) is that "being" can assume two meanings. In the first sense, the noun "being" is associated with a concept which is common to all things and can be predicated of all things in the manner of a quiddtiy,[1] in the way that a transcendental term can be predicated in the manner of a quiddity. In favour of the statement that there is a concept common to and predicable of all things, the following persuasive argument can be adduced. If there is no such common concept, then diverse concepts—let us call them *A* and *B*—are common to diverse things. However, I can show that there is a concept, more common than *A* and *B*, and predicable of any given subject, let us say *C*. For example: just as the three spoken propositions "*C* is *B*," "*C* is *A*," "*C* is something," can be formulated, so likewise three such mental propositions can be formed. Of these mental propositions two are doubtful and the third is known to be true. For it is possible that someone should doubt both propositions "*C* is *B*" and "*C* is *A*," and nevertheless know that *C* is something. If this is granted, then I argue in the following manner: Two of the aforesaid propositions are doubtful and one is known; but all three propositions have the same subject, consequently they must have distinct predicates. For if they did not, then the same proposition would be known and would be dubious, since we assumed that the two are doubtful. If, however, they have distinct predicates, then there is another predicate in this proposition, "*C* is something," which is not the predicate in one of the other two propositions, viz. "*C* is *B*," "*C* is *A*." Therefore this predicate "something" is distinct from the other predicates. Yet it is manifest that this predicate is not less common than either, and with at least one of them it is not coextensive; consequently, it is more common than at least one of them. This is what was to be proved, namely that some concept of the mind other than these less extensive concepts is common to every being. And this must be conceded. For of every being, or of the pronoun pointing to any being, the same mental concept can be truly predicated, just as the same word can be predicated of every thing.

Notwithstanding there is a concept thus common to every being, the name "being" is equivocal. For it is not in accordance with one concept that it is predicated of all its possible subjects taken in their significative function. Rather, to the name "being" there cor-

---

[1] I.e., so that it answers the question "What is it?"

respond diverse concepts, as I have explained in my exposition of Porphyry.

Furthermore, it is known that according to the Philosopher in the fourth book of the *Metaphysics*, "is" is applied both to what *is* incidentally and to what *is* intrinsically. This distinction does not mean that some being exists intrinsically and another exists incidentally. Aristotle is rather pointing out the different ways of predicating one term of another by means of the verb "is." This is sufficiently clear from the examples used by the Philosopher. He says: "We say that the musician is incidentally just, and also that the musician is incidentally a man, and we say that the musician is incidentally building." From this it is clear that he is speaking only about the diverse modes of predicating one term of another. For something is asserted of something intrinsically, and something is asserted of something incidentally. For it is manifest that there is not one thing which is intrinsically existent and another that is incidentally existent, for this reason: there is nothing besides substance or accident; but both substance and accident exist intrinsically; therefore, etc. However, notwithstanding this, something is predicated of another thing intrinsically, and something else of something else incidentally

The distinction between potential existence and actual existence is similar. It does not mean that something which is not in the universe, but can exist in the universe, is truly a being, or that something else which is in the universe is also a being. Rather, when Aristotle divides "being" into potentiality and actuality in the fifth book of the *Metaphysics*, he has in mind that the name "being" is predicated of some thing by means of the verb "is," in a proposition which merely states a fact concerning a thing and is not equivalent to a proposition containing the mode of possibility. For instance, "Socrates is a being," "Whiteness is a being." About some-thing, however, "being" is predicated only in a proposition containing the mode of possibility or equivalent to one containing this mode. For instance, "The Antichrist can be a being," or "The Antichrist is potentially a being," and so also with other propositions. Hence, Aristotle declares in the same place that "being is divisible into potential and actual, as knowledge and rest are"; but nothing is knowing or resting unless it is actually knowing or resting.

## The Distinction Between Existence and Essence

Since we have touched upon "existence" (*esse existere*), we shall make a digression for a while and consider how the existence of a thing is related to the thing, i.e. whether the existence of a thing and its essence are two entities extra-mentally distinct from each other. It appears to me that they are not two such entities, nor does "existence" signify anything different from the thing itself. For if there were something distinct, then it would be either a substance or an accident. But it is not an accident, because in that case the existence of a man would be a quality or a quantity, which is manifestly false, as can be shown by considering cases. Nor can it be a substance, because every substance is either matter or form, or a composition of matter and form, or a separated substance. But it is manifest that none of these can be called the existence of a thing, if existence is a thing distinct from the essence (*entitas*) of the thing itself.

Furthermore, if essence and existence were two things, then either they would constitute something that is intrinsically one, or they would not. If they did, then the one must be actuality and the other potentiality; hence the one would be matter and the other form; but that is absurd. If, however, they did not constitute something that is intrinsically one, then they would be one as an aggregate is one, i.e. they could constitute some one thing only incidentally. From this, however, it would follow that the one is an accident of the other.

Furthermore, if they were two things, then no contradiction would be involved if God preserved the essence of a thing in the world without its existence, or vice versa, its existence without its essence; both of which are impossible.

We have to say, therefore, that essence (*entitas*) and existence (*existentia*) are not two things. On the contrary, the words "thing' 'and "to be" (*esse*) signify one and the same thing, but the one in the manner of a noun and the other in the manner of a verb. For that reason, the one cannot be suitably substituted for the other, because they do not have the same function. Hence the verb "to be" can be put between two terms by saying "Man is (*est*) an animal," but the same cannot be done with the noun "thing" or "essence" (*entitas*). Hence "existence" (*esse*) signifies the thing itself. Now, it signifies the first simple cause, when it is predicated of this cause without signifying that it depends on something else. However, when it is predicated of other things, it signifies them in their dependence on, and subordination to, the first cause. And this is so, because these things are things only in as much as they are dependent on and ordered towards the first cause, just as it is only thus that they exist. Hence, just as a man does not exist when he is not depending on God, so likewise he is not, in that case, a man.

Therefore there is no more reason to imagine that essence (*essentia*) is indifferent in regard to being (*esse*) and non-being, than that it is indifferent in regard to being an essence and not being an essence. For as an essence may exist and may not exist, so an essence may be an essence and may not be an essence. For this reason the following arguments are invalid: "Essence may exist and may not exist, therefore existence is distinct from essence"; "Essence can come under the opposite of existence, therefore essence differs from existence." Just as the following ones are not valid: "Essence may be or may not be an essence, therefore essence differs from essence"; "Essence can come under the opposite of essence, therefore essence differs from essence." Hence, there is no more reason for essence and existence to be two things, than for essence and essence to be two things. Therefore existence is not a thing different from the essence of a thing.

This is the teaching of the Lincolnian [Robert Grosseteste], when he says on the second book of the *Posterior Analytics*: "When 'it exists' is said of the first cause, what is predicated is just the absolutely simple essence of the first cause; but when 'it exists' is said of other things, what is predicated only is just their order and dependence on the first being, which exists of itself. And this ordering or dependence does not add anything to the dependent essence. For that reason, the question whether or not a thing exists does not figure among the demonstrative questions, whether it be raised about the first being or about a being dependent on the first being."

The reason why the saints and others say that God is His very existence is this. God exists in such a manner that He cannot not exist; in fact, He exists necessarily; and He is not from something else. A creature, on the other hand, exists in such a manner that it does not necessarily exist, just as it is not necessarily a thing; and it is from something else, just as it is a thing on account of something else as its efficient cause. For that reason, there is no distinction in God between "that which is" and "that in virtue of which it is," because there is not anything different from God in virtue of which God is. But in a creature there is a distinction, because that which a creature is and that in virtue of which a creature is are simply distinct, just as God and a creature are distinct.

. . .

# GOD

## Can It Be Proved by Natural Reason that There Is Only One God

*It can be proved*: For one world has only one ruler, as is stated in the 12th book of the *Metaphysics*; but it can be proved by natural reason that there is only one world, according to Aristotle in the first book of the *De Caelo*; therefore by natural reason it can be proved that there is only one ruler; but this ruler of the world is God, therefore, etc.

*To the contrary*: An article of faith cannot be evidently proved; but that there is only one God is an article of faith; therefore, etc.

*As regards this question,* I shall first explain what is meant by the name "God"; secondly I shall answer the question.

Concerning the first point I say that the name "God" can have various descriptions. One of them is: "God is something more noble and more perfect than anything else besides Him." Another is: "God is that than which nothing is more noble and more perfect."

Concerning the second point, I maintain that if we understand "God" according to the first description, then it cannot be demonstratively proved that there is only one God. The reason for this is that it cannot be evidently known that God, understood in this sense, exists. Therefore it cannot be evidently known that there is only one God. The inference is plain. The antecedent is proved in this way. The proposition "God exists" is not known by itself, since many doubt it; nor can it be proved from propositions known by themselves, since in every argument something doubtful or derived from faith will be assumed; nor is it known by experience, as is manifest.

Secondly I maintain: If it could be evidently proved that God exists— "God" being understood in the present sense—then the unicity of God could be evidently proved. The reason for this is the following: If there were two Gods, let us call them *A* and *B*, then in virtue of our description God *A* would be more perfect than anything else, therefore God *A* would be more perfect than God *B*, and God *B* would be more imperfect than God *A*. But God *B* would also be more perfect than God *A*, because according to our assumption God *B* would be God. Consequently God *B* would be more perfect and more imperfect than God *A*, and God *A* than God *B*, which is a manifest contradiction. If, therefore, it could be evidently proved that God exists —"God" being understood in the present sense—then the unicity of God could be evidently proved.

Thirdly I maintain that the unicity of God cannot be evidently proved if we understand "God" according to the second description. Yet this negative proposition, "The unicity of God cannot be evidently proved," cannot be proved demonstratively either. For it cannot be demonstrated that the unicity of God cannot be evidently proved, except by rebutting the arguments to the contrary. For instance, it cannot be demonstratively proved that the stars make up an even number, nor can the Trinity of Persons be demonstrated. Nevertheless, these negative propositions, "It cannot be demonstrated that the stars make up an even number," "The Trinity of Persons cannot be demonstrated," cannot be evidently proved.

We must understand, however, that it can be proved that God exists, if we understand "God" according to the second description. For otherwise we could go on *ad infinitum*, if there were not some one among beings to which nothing is prior or superior in perfection. But from this it does not follow that it can be demonstrated that there is only one such being. This we hold only by faith.

The answer to the main objection is clear from the aforesaid.